Is It

God's Word?

An Exposition of the Fables and Mythology
of the Bible and the Fallacies of Theology

"Behold, the false pen of the Scribes hath wrought falsely."
—Jeremiah VIII, 8 (R.V.)

Joseph Wheless

ISBN 1-56459-226-X

PREFACE

THE MENACE OF RELIGIOUS INTOLERANCE

"In the experience of a year in the White House"—so spoke the great-hearted President Harding—"there has come to me no other such unwelcome impression as the manifest *religious intolerance* which exists among many of our citizens. There is no relationship here between Church and State. Religious liberty has its unalterable place, along with civil and human liberty, in the very foundation of the Republic. I hold it (religious intolerance) to be a *menace* to the very liberties which we boast and cherish." [1]

This was as a voice crying unheeded in the wilderness; the evil spirit was not laid but marched on intensified in force and malignity. The tocsin of warning was again sounded by the Ex-Secretary of State, Hon. Charles E. Hughes, before the convention of the American Bar Association, at Detroit, September 2, 1925, when he said:

"The most ominous sign of our times, as it seems to me, is the indication of the growth of an intolerant spirit. It is the more dangerous when armed, as it usually is, with sincere conviction. It is a spirit whose wrath must be turned away by the soft answers of a sweet reasonableness. . . . We may justly prize our safeguards against abuses, but they will not last long if intolerance gets under way." [2]

The fatal influence of religious intolerance was raised to the dignity and importance of a national issue by the earnest words of President Coolidge, before the convention of the American Legion, at Omaha, October 5, 1925, where the subject was the main burden of his thought and speech:

"Among some of the varying racial, religious, and social groups of our people, there have been manifestations of an intolerance of opinion, a narrowness of outlook, a fixity of judgment against which we may well be warned. . . .

"It is not easy to conceive of anything that would be more unfortunate in a community based upon the ideals of which Americans boast than any considerable development of intolerance as regards religion." [3]

[1] Address before the Bible Class of Calvary Baptist Church, Washington, March 24, 1922; *N. Y. Times*, March 25th, p. 1, col. 7.
[2] *American Bar Ass'n. Journal*, Sept., 1925, p. 564.
[3] *N. Y. Times*, Oct. 6th.

Coming thus publicly and solemnly from three of the most serious and potent spokesmen of public opinion in this Republic, such assertions are not idle talk; such warnings of menace and danger are not lightly to be disregarded. Evidences of the funest truth of the fact thus announced, of the timeliness of the warnings thus solemnly sounded, abound in the land and in the world, in kind if not in degree, in this twentieth century after Christ as in the Dark Ages of faith long ago. Since President Harding sounded his monition, many demonstrations of the evil spirit which he sought to conjure have been manifested, which give added weight to the repeated warnings above quoted.

A brilliant, capable, and unprecedentedly popular public man, thrice chief magistrate of the Empire State, aspired to the high magistracy to which the loved and lamented Harding had just laid down his life a sacrifice to its heavy burdens and grave cares. By reason alone of the "Romish" religion of the highly qualified aspirant, the national convention of his party, before which his name was placed, broke into a fury, and raged for weeks an unseeming and seething caldron of religious intolerance and hates; and that historic party is to-day rent and all but wrecked into hostile camps of the partisans of two historically enemistic brands of religious belief. The strife yet wages and threatens to be repeated.

Portentous of evil and sinister menace is the nation-wide ferment of the spirit of hostility and strife of races and religious factions existent between the masked and hooded sectaries of the Klan whose lurid ensign is the Fiery Cross and the sacrament-bound votaries of a Foreign Ecclesia whose emblem they call the Cross of Christ. Between the two lies the menace of a crucifixion of our dearest American ideals. The fearful tocsin of armed religious conflict in America was none too covertly sounded in the following *defi* hurled just after the embittered political convention referred to:

"URGES CATHOLIC ACTION AGAINST THE KLAN. MAYOR OF BUFFALO WANTS KNIGHTS OF ST. JOHN TO STRENGTHEN MILITARY DEPARTMENT.

(Special to the New York Times.)

"Rochester, N. Y., July 15 (1924). Frank X. Schwab, Mayor of Buffalo and Supreme General of the Catholic Knights of St. John, delivered an impressive address at the first business session of the Convention to-day. . . .

"The Ku Klux Klan came in for fierce denunciation at the hands of Buffalo's militant Mayor. In urging that the Knights strengthen their military organization, he said:

" 'I want to ask you with all sincerity to advance with all your power the *military* department of our Order. This department, I believe, is more essential now than ever. God only knows if the time is not coming when our country, as well as our *Church*, will have to be *protected* against the un-American organization which is now becoming so strong in this country.' " [4]

This flagrant incitation to civil war for armed "protection" of a minority religious sect and Church under foreign supreme control —its confession that a sectarian military organization exists in this country ready to be used for such "protection," and this appeal to prepare it for such use—in any other country might be high treason; under the Constitution of the country which protects this ill-conceived organization it falls short of that crime and may be immune save to aroused public resentment. But the point is not now that, but to illustrate the acute menace of religious bigotry and intolerance in our country to-day.

Other instances there are galore. Two American States, since Harding spoke, have enacted laws, from medieval precedents, to stop the mouth of Science when its teachings cast doubt or discredit on the primitive cosmological concepts of Theology; and in a third a like Bill failed by the very narrow margin of one vote. Other States have passed laws seeking to bar theological interference with primary lay instruction in the schools; others to force or to forbid the reading or teaching in the public schools of the Book wherein all religious controversy and intolerance find their fruitful source and inspiration. In a New York city to-day an unlawful practice is enforced of compelling time to be taken from the public school-time to herd the pupils to sectarian "religious instruction" under priest, rabbi, or parson, at the expense of public taxation, contrary to the precepts and prohibitions of the Constitution. The Churches seethe with dissent and controversy; primitive "Fundamentalism" cries "heresy" at more rational "Modernism," while the latter tauntingly retorts "bunk" at the medieval theology of the former. A "Christian" Bishop, nightly broadcasting Macedonian cries for help financial to raise fifteen millions of dollars to be sunk mortmain in a luxurious "House of God," sneeringly refuses $500 sent in by a Divine of his own cloth who is under the taint of heretical Modernism, and will not be curbed by episcopal authority. This Bishop appeals

[4] *N. Y. Times*, July 16, 1924, p. 6, col. 3.

for money from all sects and from non-sectarians, broadcasting the plea that this is to be "a house of worship for all the people." The distinguished Dean of St. Paul's, London, arriving in New York, thus commented on this pious pretense: "The people of such a Church would not get on because they would fight like they did in Jerusalem." He added, that he "did not believe there ever would be church unity, because the difficulties are too great." [5] The storm still rages, and the godly Churchmen and clergy are at daggers' points of holy enmity. Thus doth religious intolerance have free intercourse and abound in the land of boasted religious liberty, which it menaces to subvert.

Not America only, but all "Christian" Europe, most of the "civilized" world, is in a ferment of religious and bitter sectarian hostility. Nearly every European country has its strong and reactionary "Catholic" or Church party, bent upon maintaining the "rights" of the Church as against the civil State and its sovereign rights. Italy is embroiled with "Rome" these fifty years since patriot arms canceled with the bayonet the forged "Donation of Constantine" and united the Italian State by the forced restoration of its territories. In France virtual threats of violence are hurled by the heads of the Church to force the State to maintain the obsolete Concordat and diplomatic relations with the "Vatican" as a temporal sovereign. The Church is stirring up furious hatreds over questions of "religious education" in Alsace-Lorraine. Ireland, ever-faithful Isle, after centuries of bitter and deadly religious strife between the faithful and the heretic Orangemen, perpetuates its religious discord by the erection of two half-starved petty "States" divided and hostile over religious differences. Greece and Turkey are strident before the League of Nations and the world over questions of religious politics, which perpetuate the historic *filioque* schism between the Churches Roman and Greek. Islam is in eternal conflict with its Christian neighbors; India, Egypt, and other Moslem countries are forever contriving against the "Infidel Dogs" of Christian faith and very un-Christian works; threats of the Jehad or "Holy War," of Crescent against Cross, are heard at every turn and strain in Near East relations. Even in the reputed Sepulcher of the Christ at Jerusalem, (as alluded to by Dean Inge), for ages until the late post-War Mandate ended it, has the "Infidel" Turk had to maintain armed soldiers on constant guard, and especially on the sacred festivals, to restrain the bitter strife of hostile sects

---

[5] *N. Y. Times*, April 19, 1925, p. 7, col. 1.

of devout Christian pilgrims coming to visit the holiest shrine of their discordant faith.

And coming back to our own America, on every hand we see and hear the evidences of discord and strife, of distrust, prejudice and malevolence, mutually between Christian and Jew, between Catholic and Protestant Christians, between the multiplied inharmonious sects within each of these great divided religious clans— all due simply and alone to differences of dogmatic theological opinion and of intolerant religious belief. With profound and disheartening truth did President Harding declare: "I hold religious intolerance to be a menace to the very liberties which we boast and cherish."

Why this fratricidal and destructive religious intolerance? the sober-minded seeker after Truth and the public weal is in civic duty bound to ask. Why such funest and fatal differences, hatreds, strifes, all about questions simply of theological belief? Yea, as the Poet so acutely queries of Belief:

> "Why meanly bargain to *believe*,
> Which only means thou *ne'er canst know?*"   (The Kasidah.)

It is the presumption of human ignorance of the Unknowable, fondly vaunted as Divinely "revealed" unto faith as the immaterial "substance of things hoped for," as the creditable "evidence of things not seen" and not knowable, which lies at the root of all bigoted religious intolerance. It is the honest purpose of the chapters which follow to "search the Scriptures," if haply may be found and revealed to the human understanding the evidences of the truth or of the fallacy of the claim voiced in the same hymnal words by so variant and discordant Sects of Believers:

> "How firm a foundation, ye Saints of the Lord,
> Is laid for your Faith in his wonderful Word"!

The key-note of the whole Hymn of Hate of religious discord and intolerance may be picked out of two equally assured and presumptuous outgivings of the spirit of sectarian rivalry, each of the highest authority in the respective hostile camps; these out of innumerable others are cited as fairly representative of the conflicting beliefs but unanimous intolerance of both.

The most absolute of ecclesiastical authorities thus formulates and fulminates its Creed of Intolerance: "The gravest *obligation requires* the *acceptance* and *practice*, not of the religion which one may *choose*, but that which *God prescribes*, and which is *known* by *certain and indubitable* marks to be *the only true one*." (Pope Leo XIII, in Encyclical "*Immortali Dei*," of November 1, 1885.) This excerpt is truth itself to one sect of Christianism; all the other sects are branded by it as false and heretical. All the other Christian sects subscribe fervently to the, for them, truism of the XXXIX Articles: "The Romish Doctrine . . . is a fond thing, vainly invented, grounded on no warrant of Scripture, but rather repugnant to the Word of God."

Religion, in its popular and all but universal acceptance as a system of belief in theological dogma and Church creeds, is all but exclusively a matter of birth and early teaching, of environment: this cannot be gainsaid. A man takes and holds, though often most indifferently, the religion or brand of belief, of his fathers, of his family. Born a pagan, a Jew, a Buddhist, a Mohammedan, a Mormon, that he remains, except one time in many thousands, through life; though if taken in infancy and brought up in the most contrary faith, this will he as naturally fall heir to and believe: Witness the famous Janizaries, Christian children trained in the Moslem faith, and Islam's most fanatic soldiers. If born into a Christian family, Catholic or Protestant, or of one of the many sects of either, of its faith he usually remains till death, at least nominally Catholic or Protestant, as he was born and taught. That is the prime reason why the great cults so strive to gain and mold, and so to hold, the childish mind. In New York City the poor waifs and foundlings gathered up by the police and charities are evenly distributed, in numerical rote, among the Institutions, Catholic, Protestant, and Jewish, that each may have an equal chance to make proselytes to their respective creeds or brands of belief. One of the great cults imposes as a condition precedent to its reluctant consent for the faithful of its sect to marry what it stigmatizes as "heretics" of any other Christian Sect, that all children of the marriage shall be taught and brought up in the faith of its own communicant.

Children believe anything they are taught: Santa Claus, fairies, goblins, and witches, are as real, as veritably true, to a child, as Jesus the Christ to a cleric—much more so often. It is a maxim of the Master of the new Faith: "Except ye become as little Children ye cannot enter the Kingdom of Heaven—for of such is the Kingdom" (Matt. xviii, 3; xix, 14). Religious belief or faith is thus avowed to be essentially of the childish mind. Hence the reason of the churchly maxim: "*Disce primum quod credendum est*—Learn first of all what is to be believed."

Since man emerged from the earliest dawn of recorded time and left the crudest records, and in later times the most enduring monuments, of himself, he has had, first rude notions, then elaborate systems, of religious cult and theological belief. All men at all times, from the infancy of the race, saw and contemplated with wonder and awe the mysterious wonders of nature about them; they sought to account for and explain these wonders and mysteries by attributing them to the work of supernatural powers whom they personified as spirits or gods, beneficent and maleficent, which they worshiped and offered sacrifices to, to propitiate their favor or to appease their disfavor and wrath. This is in a word the origin and end of religions all. This is seen in its primitive forms and significance to-day among the aboriginal peoples of Africa, Australia, America, and among the Esquimos of the Arctic. These are all admittedly childish superstitions and false religions.

The Father of History, Herodotus of Halicarnassus, greatest traveler of ancient times, who visited every known country and recorded imperishably their history, traditions, and customs, has left it written, as evidence of the universality of religious cults and superstitions, that he had visited all lands, had seen many strange and wondrous things unheard of to his own cultured Greeks; cities even without walls, nations without any form of money or tokens for barter; but never a people, however low or high in culture, that had not gods and some form of religion.

Great in their times and very splendid and powerful were the greater religions of the ancient world—those false and superstitious beliefs of the pagans. Europe, Asia, northern Africa, primitive America, too, are filled with the massive and amazing remains of temples and monuments attesting the greatness and splendor of the Gods and the unsurpassed wealth and power of their cults and priests and worshipers. The Temple of Diana of Ephesus was a wonder of the ancient world; so the Parthenon or Temple to the Virgin, (Minerva), at Athens, the Temples of the Gods at Baalbek, at Luxor, at Nippur, at "Ur of the Chaldees,"—at a thousand holy sites, in Assyria, Babylonia, Carthage, Chaldea, Egypt, Greece, India, Rome, were wonders of magnificence and might; the religions which they attest and served divided and held the then world in the thrall of their holy awe and divine power.

Great gods in veritable Galaxies—Ammon, Asshur, Ashtoreth, Bel, Baal, Brahma, Buddha, Chemosh, Dagon, Isis, Jove, Marduk, Osiris, Ra, Sin, Zeus—held sovereign sway in heaven and on earth, powerful and compelling in the minds and hearts and lives of countless millions of human beings through thousands of years before Jesus Christ and for centuries since, some of them even yet. Religion was the one great, devout, consuming passion and occupation of all the ancient world, from the cradle to the grave, to an extent far beyond the paler ardors of the faith to-day. And their wonderful forms of sepulture of the dead, extant through the centuries and disclosed by the excavators of to-day, betray their deep religious life and their abiding faith in the immortality of the soul and in the resurrection of the dead: the Pyramids and the Tomb of Tut-ankh-Amen are everlasting monuments to ancient false faith.

Every nation of antiquity had its national supreme God, Maker of heaven and earth and Creator of Man, Ruler of the national destinies and Divine Providence in the human life, of whom it was the specially "Chosen People," to whom fervent prayer and praise were rendered and hecatombs of sacrifices made; great and rich temples abounded, maintained by Kings and people, and served by armies of powerful priests, who elaborated sacred mysteries and vast systems of theology. The Hebrew Scriptures abound with references to these Gods and religions of their pagan neighbors, and even the Hebrew God Yahveh recognizes and admits the reality of existence and power of these "strange" Gods, as we shall abundantly see in the course of our review of those Sacred Writings. Every nation, too, had its own "Sacred Writings," given and inspired by its Gods through their priests and prophets. Most notable of these were the Egyptian "Book of the Dead," and the "Zend-Avesta" of the Persians, for their lofty pious fervor and elaborate theology. The Koran and the Book of Mormon are later but living truths to those who believe them.

Yahveh, Tribal God of the Hebrews, only attained his position as national deity, and a national recognition as a One and Only God of the whole world, very late in Hebrew national life: after the Captivity and the restoration under Ezra; previously he had been only a "God above all Gods"—a Jealous local God, declaring "thou shalt have no other Gods before (i.e. above, superior to) me." But he recognized the actual existence and activities of the "other Gods," and he commanded respect to them: "Thou shalt not revile the Gods" (Ex. xxii, 28). He said, "I am Yahveh thy God; fear not the Gods of the Amorites" (Jud. vi, 10). Throughout the Hebrew Scriptures these "other Gods" are recognized by the inspired writers, and by Yahveh, as actual beings, and are worshiped by the Chosen People: "Chemosh thy God and Yahveh our God" (Jud. xi, 24); "Dagon our God" (1 Sam. v, 7); "Ashtoreth, Goddess of the Zidonians, and Chemosh, God of Moab, and Milcom, God of the Children of Ammon" (1 Kings xi, 33); "Baal-zebub, God of Ekron" (2 Kings i, 2); "the Gods of Sepharvaim" (2 Kings xvii, 31); "the star of your God Moloch" (Amos v, 26).

These false pagan Gods were creator, father and friend to their zealous votaries; kings gave laws and waged wars in their name and by their command, exactly as with Yahveh and his Chosen People. To illustrate the intense religion of the pagan neighbors of the Hebrews, and show their exact parallel with the genius of the "revealed" Hebrew religion, as well as to give some spread to popular knowledge of such highly important and interesting records of the past, I think it not amiss in this connection to quote, almost at random, from some of the great archeological recoveries of the historical and literary treasures of the mighty past, discovered and translated in recent years by the scholars.

Moses gave the Law by command of the Hebrew God Yahveh. Long centuries before, the Babylonian God Bel, through the Sun-God Shamash, revealed the Law to Hammurabí, King of Abraham's City of Ur of the Chaldees; in that great Code, the religious oath was to be accepted in the Courts: "that man shall swear by the name of God" (Art. 20). In the famous Tell-el-Amarna Tablets is an Egyptian Proclamation using a very familiar form of invocation—"I make God my witness—God is my witness" (92-B). Solomon in a Proverb says, "The fear of Yahveh is the beginning of wisdom"; in an Egyptian hymn to Amen the pagan Psalmist sings: "I cry, the beginning of wisdom is the way of Amen. . . . Thou art he that giveth bread to him who has none, that sustaineth the servant in his house. . . . My Lord is my defender; . . . there is none mighty except him alone. Strong is Amen, knowing how to answer; fulfilling the desires of him who cries to him."

From the Book of the Dead is a beautiful Hymn to Ra, of a fervor and diction quite equal to a Psalm of David: "Homage to thee, O Ra. . . . Thou art adored; thy beauties are before mine eyes . . . O thou Lord who livest and art established. . . . O thou Divine Substance, from whom all forms of life come into being. Thou sendest forth the Word . . . O thou Holy One, who didst dwell in Heaven before ever the earth and the mountains came into existence. . . . O Osiris, make thou to be divine my Soul . . . O Lord of the Gods, thou art exalted by reason of thy wondrous works."

The celebrated Moabite Stone, of date about 890 B.C., refers to —and thus "confirms" in part (for the result of the war is reversed) —some records of Hebrew Scriptures, as related in 2 Kings III, 4–27: it reads very much as if it were taken bodily from Holy Writ:

"I, Mesha, erected this stone to Chemosh at Korcha, a Stone of Salvation, for he saved me from all despoilers, and let me see my desire upon all my enemies. Now Omri, King of Israel, he oppressed Moab many days, and *Chemosh was angry* with his land. . . . And *Chemosh had mercy* on it in my days. . . . The King of Israel fortified Ataroth, and I assaulted the wall and captured it, and killed all the warriors of the wall, for the well-pleasing of Chemosh and Moab; and I removed from it all the spoil, and offered it before Chemosh in Kirjath. . . . And *Chemosh said* to me, Go, take Nebo against Israel. And I went in the night, and took it, and slew in all 7000 men, but I did not kill the women and maidens, for I devoted them to Ashtar-Chemosh; and I took the vessels of Yahveh and offered them before Chemosh. . . . And *Chemosh drove* out the King of Israel before me. . . . And *Chemosh said to* me, Go down, make war against Horonaim and take it."

The Birs-Nimrud inscription of the great King Nebuchadnezzar, in the British Museum, contains this record of pious temple building as a work deserving reward by the God: "When Marduk the Great Lord had created me King he commanded me to complete his holy buildings. Nebo who bestows the thrones of heaven and earth, placed the scepter of justice in my hand. The Temple of Saggathu, the great Temple of heaven and earth, the dwelling of Marduk Lord of the Gods, (and other Temples named), with shining gold I splendidly adorned. . . . The great Lord Marduk incited my heart . . . my noble works of piety behold joyfully. A long life, abundant offspring, a firm throne, a prolonged reign, the subjection of all rebels, the conquest of my enemies, grant to me as a recompense. By thy noble favor, O Founder of the fabric of heaven and earth, may my days be blessed. In the presence of Marduk, King of heaven and earth, present these my works, and may my fortunate name of Nebuchadnezzar, or 'Heaven-adoring King,' dwell continually in thy mouth."

From among the thousands of these remarkable records of the past, these few are cited as bearing witness to the universality and power of false religions and faith in false Gods, among the peoples of the earth through all the centuries of the past. All the prayers, and hymns, and sacrifices were vain: "all the Gods of the Nations are Devils" (Ps. xcvi, 5, Vulgate). But great and sublime was the false faith of the nations in them and in their powers to help and to save.

DELUSION OR CONSCIOUS IMPOSTURE?

When Hammurabí, to give greater sanctity and sanction to his Code of Law, engraved upon the stele that it was decreed by the Supreme God Bel and "revealed" to him by the Sun God Shamash, the King well knew that he and not the gods was the author of the Law; his pious pretense was none the less false; he consciously deceived the superstitious people. If the priests of Josiah wrote instead of "found" the Law of Yahveh, and to give it great sanctity and ready acceptance by the people, pretended that Yahveh had "revealed" it to Moses on Sinai, is this too not false pretense and conscious pious fraud? The priests of every ancient religion avowed the presence and power of the pagan gods, and their oracles spoke in their name, "thus and so saith our god"; the great kings just named and all others avowed their acts and deeds to have been by the command of the respective gods: it was all consciously false and intended to deceive the superstitious subjects and believers. The priests knew that their gods spoke not with or through them; the oracles were duplicious liars. It has passed into a proverb, that the Roman Augurs, on meeting one another, used to "wink the eye" at each other, conscious of the gross deception with which they "gulled" the superstitious votaries. Is it just possible that the priests and prophets of Yahveh were the only honest and truthful oracles of the only true God, and that when they raved "thus saith Yahveh," and by their dreams, dice and ephods proclaimed "it is Yahveh's will," they only of all their kindred of priestcraft spoke God's truth? The following chapters will throw an interesting light on this question.

The greatest and noblest minds of antiquity—Aristotle, Socrates, Plato, Alexander, Demosthenes, Cicero, Caesar, Cato, the Plinys, Marcus Aurelius, Epictetus, the Antonines, the Philosophers, the Poets—faithfully believed, fervently worshiped, these false religions, these false Gods, long since dead and gone. So firm did they hold the foundations of their errant faith, their superstitious fables, the old pagans, that throughout the ancient world they sacrificed inestimable treasure, and their dearest treasures, their tender children, to their false faith in their false Gods. Countless hecatombs of tender baby children, the idols of their loving parents' hearts, were made to "pass through the fire to Moloch"—living burnt sacrifices to gratify, and to appease the superstitiously fancied wrath of their mythical idol Gods. The newspapers of to-day carry long reports and photographic pictures of the countless little funerary urns brought to light in the excavations by the Comte de Prorok, of ancient Carthage, in the ruins of the Temple of Tanit-Baal, holding the ashes of the little children of the pagans burnt alive in sacrifice on the altars of the Gods of these true believers in false religion.

And such faith was found and flourished in Israel, too. Throughout their Bible history the pagan Hebrews, in their origin pagan Chaldeans, and closest neighbors and cousins of the pagan Phenicians, whose colony Carthage was, religiously held and practiced the same cult of human sacrifices of their children to their idol Gods, as scores of times attested by their Bible Scriptures. In the Mosaic Law it is time and time decreed: "Thou shalt not let any of thy seed pass through the fire unto Molech" (Lev. xviii, 21 and xx, 2; Deut. xii, 31 and xviii, 10). But the faith in and practice of child burnt sacrifice prevailed in their orthodox religious cult to the end, as numberless texts testify: "They (Israel) caused to pass through the fire all that opened the womb" (Ezek. xx, 26); "Ye make your sons to pass through the fire . . . even unto this day" (Ezek. xx, 31); "Thou hast taken thy sons and thy daughters . . . and these thou hast sacrificed unto them [their idols]. Thou hast slain thy children and delivered them to cause them to pass through the fire for them" (Ezek. xvi, 20, 21; xxiii, 37). "They [Israel] had slain their children to their idols" (Ezek. xxiii, 39; xxvi, 36). "They have built the high places of Tophet—[of Baal], to burn their sons and daughters in the fire unto Moloch" (Jer. vii, 31; xix, 5; xxxii, 35; Is. lvii, 5; 2 Kings xvi, 3; xvii, 17, 31; xxiii, 10; xxviii, 3; xxxiii, 6; 2 Chron. xi, 15). "Our fathers (v. 7) . . . sacrificed their sons and their daughters unto Devils" (Ps. cvi, 37–38). The thorough pagan idol religion of the pagan Hebrews will appear in many remarkable instances from their sacred Scriptures noted in the chapters to follow.

All religions and systems of religious belief which have ever held sway among the greater races of Peoples have been Oriental in origin and imagination; all—saving for the nonce the Hebrew and Christian faiths—were wholly and admittedly mythical, however ethical, in character and fact: their Gods were figments of the pious fervent, but errant, imaginations of their priests and worshipers. This all will admit.

Dead and gone are all the "Immortal Gods" loved and worshiped by the ancients: the great God of ancient Israel, the Hebrew Yahveh, adopted and worshiped to-day as also the Christian God Jehovah, alone is self-"revealed" and is immortal, true and living God. All the great Religions of the ancient world—of Assyria, Egypt, Greece,

Palestine, Rome—were pagan mythologies all, and long since are perished off the face of the earth. All Christians assert and admit them all to have been wholly mythical, fabulous, false: "all the Gods of the peoples are Devils," they and their Bible say, are "false Gods"; all these great religions, they admit and aver, were false religions and darkened childish superstitions. Admitted. So also of the great systems of religious belief which divide the world to-day—Brahmanism, Buddhism, Confucianism, Hebraism, Mohammedanism, Mormonism, Shintoism, Taoism—believed and lived unto death by untold millions more of people than in all Christendom—all these and many and all others, say the Christians, are false and fabulous superstitions: Hebreo-Christianism remains and is "*known, by certain and indubitable marks, to be the only true one*," of all the religious "isms" of the World, past and of to-day.

Yet Christians, through all the centuries of their Christ, of their faith, have martyred and murdered one another in fierce dispute as to just what are these "certain and indubitable marks" whereby the "only true" brand of belief is so certainly known. Each Christian sect pretends to the certain hall-mark of truth for its peculiar brand of belief: all the other brands are maverick and heretic. Bigotry and intolerance each of the other sect and brand mark and mar them all, and its malign influence oppresses the world to-day, the same in kind and moderated little in degree, in this twentieth century after the promulgation of the disputed doctrines of the Christ. Each Christian sect and faction lays claim to the Bible as the inspired and inerrantly true fount of its diverse brand of faith. This Bible is indeed the fount of all the woes unnumbered inflicted by bigotry and intolerance of belief in its manifestly inharmonious presentation of facts, dogma and theology.

The Christian religion depends for the sanction and validity of its beliefs upon the Bible as does the earth upon the sun for its light and heat and life. The Bible is the pregnant source—the only source—of the Christian faith; it is the unique fount of faith in its own truth—of the accepted belief in the truth of its own revelations. But of the whole body of Christians who accept it and believe in it, who found their faith upon it, no two sects believe it alike; all the schisms, and heresies, and persecutions, and religious wars, and religious intolerances and bigotries which past history has recorded and current history chronicles, are due alone to the differences of belief engendered by the indubitable inconsistencies and contradictions of the texts of inspired truth of this "Holy Bible, Book Divine." Of this remarkable "confusion of tongues" of inspirations and revela-

tions throughout the Book we shall have the amplest instances in
the chapters which follow.

The Master Himself laid the injunction, "Search the Scriptures,"
for, he added, "in them ye *think* ye have eternal life, and they are
they which testify of me" (John v, 39). Obeying this Divine precept, the Jews and pagan Greeks who were the early proselyting
subjects of the new Gospel, "searched the Scriptures daily, *whether
these things were so*" (Acts xvii, 11); and it is added, "Therefore
many of them believed" (v, 12). But it is notorious that most of
them, Jews and Gentiles alike, did *not* believe—though they all had
the same inspired Scriptures before them for their faith. For those
who, after searching, believed not, certainly these things of Scripture
were *not so* and were not to be believed. Even the Disciples, when
told by the women that their Crucified Christ was risen from the
dead, "their words seemed to them as idle tales, and they believed
them not" (Luke xxiv, 11).

How "Conversion" Works

The Gentile pagans who, for one reason or another, or upon
no *reason* at all, "believed" the propaganda of the Apostles, and
became Christians, the moment before their "conversion" were, and
all their lives had been, heathen who "believed" false religions and
false Gods. When at a given moment, they changed their belief,
by what token, by what "certain and indubitable mark," satisfying
to their reason, did they all of a sudden *know* that their old belief
was false, that their new belief was indubitably and only true? The
new proselytes, like the Apostles, were mostly "unlearned and
ignorant men": their change of belief could not mean that they had
suddenly come to sure knowledge of the unknowable. Proof that
their "conversion" was without knowledge, and left them totally
ignorant of the most essential novelty of their new faith, is given
by an amusing episode. Paul, at Ephesus, met a squad of about
a dozen new proselytes, and catechized them: "Have ye received the
Holy Ghost since ye believed"? To which the new true believers
with naïve surprise replied: "We have not so much as heard whether
there be any Holy Ghost"! (Acts xix, 2). Though "the Gift of
the Holy Ghost" was the very first insignia, as it were, promised to
be bestowed on the neophytes in token of their acceptance into the
Order of Christ, by Grand Master Peter himself: "Repent, and be
baptized every one of you, . . . and ye shall receive the gift of the
Holy Ghost. For the promise is unto you, and to your children,

and to all" (Acts ii, 38–39). When then told in effect, "Sure, there is a Holy Ghost," they no doubt at once believed it unto their soul's satisfaction and salvation; but wholly without proof or knowledge that it was so, beyond the bare statement that so it was.

For a thousand years "conversion"—change of belief—proceeded slowly before all the principal pagan peoples became Christians,—and in just such an ignorant way as at Ephesus. Many fought for, were "martyrs" to, their admittedly false faith: but faith only means one does not know. Mohammedans, Mormons, certainly, the Christians say, have false faith, errant belief; yet they too make "converts"—they are actively "proselyting religions." Christians, those of the only true faith—while they held it—have become "converts" to Islam, to Mormon—all Mormons were originally Christians; and immediately, for these converts, their just previously true faith became false, and the previously admittedly false faith becomes powerfully true. But truth is one and unchangeable. The fault must be with the religious belief; the faith-faculty is faulty.

Mature and honest Christian men and women "believe" the Christian religion because from their tender youth they have been taught it to be true; have been taught that "he that believeth not shall be damned" (Mark xvi, 16); that "he that doubteth is damned" Rom. xiv, 23). They have either had no occasion to think and doubt, or have not dared to doubt—and incur *ipso facto*, eternal damnation, besides, too, the bitter and hostile intolerance of all good Christians and the fearful voodoo of Church excommunication. Since the Church foisted itself firmly into the saddle of the State, about the year A.D. 386, these have been no idle threats through the long centuries of the ages of faith: the Holy Inquisition, the rack and the stake, and the terrors of outlawry from Church and State alike, made disbelief and doubt a damned reality on God's earth, whatever might be the feared result in some other world hereafter. Men were ignorant during the Dark Ages of Faith, and did not think and dared not doubt. Although the Inquisition of Faith was abolished (less than a century ago), and the rack is only now a ghastly relic, and the *autos da fé* are extinguished by law—even yet the malignant same spirit of presumptious bigotry of belief and of religious intolerance of dissent, still flames throughout Christendom and Islam. Its blight and its menace give pause for anxious thought to all who cherish the principles of civil and religious liberty. To remove the cause would be to find a sovereign remedy for the existence and the ills of religious intolerance.

All know the apt old story of the two knights who quarreled

and challenged each other to mortal combat to settle their differences of opinion or belief as to the color of the Shield: one declaring that it was white, the other that it was red. Each had seen the Shield from a different position and on but one face. A sensible friend who had seen the subject of dispute from both sides, intervened and induced them before fighting to take another view, and led them to the Shield. Lo, it was white on one side and red on the other, as each had seen it from his partial viewpoint. They shook hands, remained friends, and lived to combat the common enemy in friendly alliance, for the honor of chivalry.

THE "NO CONFLICT" MANIFESTO

Recently a group of some forty distinguished theologians and men of Science, in the United States, put forth a published manifesto purporting to convey the assurance that there is "no conflict between science and religion." [6] It was, I think, the same number of equally eminent theologians and scientists who, in Germany, in 1914, emitted another manifesto to the effect that the World War was wickedly begun against Germany by its Allied enemies, and that Germany's going to war was forced, defensive, and righteous altogether. Both manifestos create a mis-impression.

The misleading impression carried abroad by the "No Conflict" manifesto lies in its failure to define terms,—which confuses and misleads as to what is meant, and involves in a very unscientific, but highly theological, begging of the very question at issue.

The whole difficulty lies simply in the failure to define the terms used. Science is simply "orderly and exact knowledge on any subject, gained by accurate observation or experiment, and correct thinking" (Standard Dictionary). The validity of the manifesto depends upon what is meant by its term "religion."

If, by religion, is meant the system of supernatural dogma and beliefs culled from the Bible, and distorted into so many hundreds of gross and grotesque creeds by some hundreds of conflicting sects, then the manifesto is grievously misleading, and is harmful in the extreme to the cause of truth. If, however, as a proper reading of the manifesto shows, is meant simply a belief in an infinitely great and wise Creator, who has made the "revelation" of his power and greatness and goodness alone in his works, in nature,—in the works of God rather than in the word of God, and in the soul of man, then all can agree. The manifesto so clearly reads and distinguishes the right from the wrong understanding, when rightly read.

[6] Issued at Washington, D. C., May 26, 1923; *N. Y. Times*, May 27th.

In an accompanying explanation, it is avowed that the purpose of this pronunciamiento was "to assist in correcting two erroneous impressions which seem to be current among certain groups of persons —the first, that religion stands to-day for medieval theology; the second, that science is materialistic and irreligious."

The manifesto, which in truth is a crushing arraignment of Bible theology—(which is and can only be medieval theology, which is *in toto* Biblical) and is a demolishing blow to the Bible as the foundation of supernatural faith, which it repudiates, reads as follows:

"We, the undersigned, deeply regret that in recent controversies there has been a tendency to present science and religion as irreconcilable and antagonistic domains of thought, for in fact they meet distinct human needs, and in the rounding out of human life they supplement rather than displace or oppose each other.

"The purpose of science is to develop, without prejudice or preconception of any kind, a knowledge of the facts, the laws, and the processes of nature. The even more important task of religion, on the other hand, is to develop the consciences, the ideals, the aspirations of mankind. Each of these two activities represents a deep and vital function of the soul of man, and both are necessary for the life, the progress, and the happiness of the human race.

"It is a sublime conception of God which is furnished by science, and one wholly consonant with the *ideals* of religion, when it represents Him as *revealing Himself through countless ages* in the development of the earth as an abode for man, and in the *age-long* inbreathing of life into its constituent matter, *culminating in man* with his spiritual nature and all his God-like powers."

The Manifesto thus plainly exalts the true religion of the spirit in spiritual ideals, not the gross belief in miraculous facts of theology. It avers God as revealing Himself through countless ages in the work of creation to fit the earth as an abode for its culminating creation, Man; it totally repudiates the fabled six-day work of Creation of the world, the out-of-hand-made Adam, and the rib-carved Eve, and thus destroys at a breath the whole Christian "Plan of Salvation," built upon the Garden of Eden, the apple and the talking snake, the "fall" and the "curse," and the far-off divine "Redemption from the Curse," by the Crucifixion and the Resurrection, which is the whole of theological Christianity.

No more admirable Golden Text than this same manifesto, could be framed as the statement of the purpose and ideal of this Book, which is to speed the destruction of Bible and theological fables and superstition as religion, and to exalt into the true, universal religion the high concepts of Micah, "to do justly, and to love mercy, and to walk humbly with thy God" (Micah vi, 8), and of James, to do deeds of kindness and to keep one's self unspotted from the world (James i, 27), and of the Institutes, "to live honestly, to injure no one, to render to every man his due" (Inst. i, 1, 3); and of the Kasidah: "Do good for good is good to do; spurn bribe of heaven and threat of hell" (Kasidah, ix, 27).

Science proves that the true and only revelation of God is written large and luminous in His Book of Nature. This searching of the Hebreo-Christian Scriptures demonstrates that the true Architect God of the far-flung universe is not the man-made Deity, Yahveh, therein depicted, and that those Scriptures, far from being the "Word of God," are a sorry libel upon the wisdom, power, goodness, and common sense of the True Creator God.

"A Christian Country"?

It has long been vogue to speak of these United States as a Christian country," and to prate of the "Christian religion is part of the law of the land." This latter is an idle *dictum* without the least legal basis; the former is as a matter of fact very far from being true. One of the earliest public treaties made by the just-created Federal Government, ratified by the United States Senate and promulgated by the President, makes this formal declaration: "The Government of the United States of America is not in any sense founded on the Christian Religion." [7]

On April 1, 1923, was published throughout the country the Statistical Report of the Federal Council of Churches in the United States. According to this Report: "The present membership of all religious bodies, according to the latest available figures, is 47,461,553." This total is made up of the following main groupings: Protestants, 27,454,080; Roman Catholics, 18,104,804; Jews, 1,600,000 out of a Jewish population of 3,300,000, Mormons, 604,-082; various minor sects making up the balance. But with a population of the United States, at that time, of over 110,000,000 souls, there is significance in Mr. Wm. J. Bryan's grief over this report, that only about 41 per cent of the population is Christian at all; he says: "More than half of the adult men of the United States are not members of any religious organization, and a large number of women are not members of any religious organization." [8] The Jews

[7] Treaty of Peace and Friendship, U. S. and Tripoli, 1796; Art. XI, Vol. 2 U. S. Treaties, p. 1786.

[8] *N. Y. Times*, May 17, 1923, p. 21; Statement at 135th General Assembly of the Presbyterian Church, at Indianapolis.

and Mormons are not Christians at all; and as Mark Twain remarks, the Christian Scientists are "neither Christian nor Science," but all are as good citizens as any.

From these figures of Christian population and percentages, two signal facts appear in relief. First, that while of all countries on earth, our country, whatever its popular faults, is the most moral, righteous, orderly, peaceful, and just, it is all this despite a large un-Christian majority: which proves that creeds and dogmas of religion are non-essential to good morals, personal and national honor, good government, to the highly successful administration of justice, or to the effective pursuit of peace and happiness. The other signal fact is, that a small and ever-decreasing minority continues to impose its will on the whole country by laws unjust, oppressive and repressive, as witness the multitude of "blue" laws and "Sunday" laws upon the statute books, ever sought to be increased; and more grievously yet, that this minority enjoys from the secular State which indulgently protects its pretensions, a total and perpetual exemption of religious property from all taxation for the support of that State; to such extent, that in the single State of New York, over $3,000,000,000 (three billions of dollars), or about one-fifth of the total assessed taxable valuation of the property in the State,[9] is dead-head and dead-handed property, mostly held mortmain and tax-free by a favored and faithful minority, and escapes the common burden of taxation—thus greatly and unduly increasing that borne by the tax-paying citizens, saint and sinner alike; and the Church is thus supported by the State, its Constitution and the spirit of its laws to the contrary notwithstanding.

It is this minority of Christian sectarians who have the country and the world by the ears through their incessant and bitter disputes over dogmas and creeds, and who, by their embittered religious intolerance constitute a menace to the civil and religious peace and liberties of the country and of the world. Are their dogmas and creeds and Bible theology even in minim part valid and worth fighting for? or is the whole a vain credulity and superstition without foundation in actual truth and reason, and useless to true religion?

THE BIBLE THE TEST OF TRUTH

"Truth and Reason," says Montaigne, "are common to every one, and are no more his who spoke them first than his who spoke

---

[9] Report, State Association of Real Estate Boards, *N. Y. Herald*, Dec. 3, 1922.

them after." By what token of truth, and on what basis of reason, is it, can it honestly be claimed, that this intricate system of Christian creeds and dogmas is "indubitably known to be the only true" religion, or true, or is religion, at all? All these conflicting· and controverted creeds and dogmas are found in the Bible, there have their only source and claim for faith and credit. Their truth or want of credibility must be tested and proven by the Bible itself, for obviously other test or proof there is none.

Confessedly, all that we know or can know of God, in a theological sense, and of his accredited Son Jesus Christ, is what we are told as facts in the Bible itself. The only possible source of human knowledge of and belief in the supernatural data of the Christian religion is the Bible, in a few brief monographs written, the first of them some half a century, a whole generation and more after the crucified death of their Divine Subject, by Jewish converts to the new beliefs. These Hebreo-Christian Scriptures of the so-called New Testament, are founded wholly, for their facts and for their faith and credit, on the ancient Hebrew Scriptures known as the Old Testament—for "they are they which testify of Me," averred the Divine Founder of the new Faith. Thus the all of formal Christianity as a system of theological dogma and religious creed, is reared altogether upon the ancient Hebrew Bible theology—or as we shall see, mythology.

The God of the Bible, Old and New alike, is the God Yahveh, or Jehovah, of the Hebrew Old Testament. His reputed son, Jesus Christ, is a Jewish figure exclusively of the Jewish-Christian New Testament; except that these latter writings make claim that the Old Testament, through numerous so-called "Prophecies," foretells the coming and mission of Jesus Christ—who is certainly nowhere *named* or even clearly identified in them—as the "Promised Messiah." All of these so-called "Prophecies of the Messiah" will in due course be candidly examined, and the aptness of their application to Jesus, the son of Joseph the Carpenter, will be appreciated.

The Hebrew word "Mashiach" (Eng. Messiah), means simply "Anointed"; it is exactly the same as the Greek word "Christos," or Christ, used in the New Testament, which was written by Jews in the Greek language. Both words mean, exactly, "The Anointed One"; just as all Kings in the Bible, and in all profane history up to date, are "anointed," and as are all the species of priests in and out of the Bible. Saul was the first King in Israel whose anointing is recorded: "Samuel took the vial of oil, and poured it upon his (Saul's) head, and said, Is it not that Yahveh hath anointed—

(Mashiach-ed)—thee to be a prince over his inheritance"? (I Sam. x, 1). Time and again King David calls himself "the Mashiach of Yahveh"—the "Lord's Anointed." At one time Yahveh took a great liking to Cyrus, the pagan King of the Medes and Persians; and Isaiah quotes: "Thus saith Yahveh to his Messiah (Anointed), to Cyrus, whose right hand I have holden" (Is. xlv, 1).

The only basis of claim of Jesus, Carpenter of Nazareth, to be the Christ (Mashiach—Christos—Anointed), and the only anointment he ever got, was when the friendly prostitute broke the "alabaster box of ointment" on his head (Matt. xxvi, 7; Mark xiv, 3), or on his feet (Luke vii, 37; Jno. xii, 3), whichever it was, and wiped the excess of it off with her disheveled hair; and on the strength of this he was hailed by the street rabble as Yahveh's "Mashiach" and as "King of the Jews."

As Paul said, "With the *heart* man believeth" (Rom. x, 10). This excludes the mind and the intelligence from the act of faith. But neither with heart nor mind would or could any man consciously believe what he knew was not real and true. Man is entitled of Divine right to know the truth; and once known, "the truth shall make man free" from all false beliefs or superstitions. Thereupon religious differences and intolerance will cease to be, for they will have naught left to feed upon.

Surely a God of truth could not "send a strong delusion that man should believe a lie" (2 Thess. ii, 11), as Paul wonderfully avers his God to have done. No honest man in this day and age can sympathize with or tolerate this same Paul's Jesuistic plea and confession, that "the truth of God hath more abounded through my lie unto his glory" (Rom. iii, 7). We shall fearlessly inquire whence came this strong delusion to believe religious lies, and search out the lies amazingly confessed to have been told aboundingly in Holy Writ to the pretended "glory of God."

Thus I take up the challenge of the Christ, to "search the Scriptures," haply thus to demonstrate to the seeker after truth "whether these things were so," as in this Bible related for belief, under the threat "he that doubteth is damned: . . . suffering the vengeance of eternal fire" (Rom. xiv, 23; Jude 7).

No man, priest, parson, or zealot for his inherited faith, can say with truth that this book "attacks the Bible," or seeks to defame the Bible God or to ridicule the Christian Religion. If such results follow, the Bible itself is to blame, if this book of mine speaks truly. This Book is based wholly on the Bible; its all but every reference and citation is to the texts of the Bible, faithfully quoted in exact words of inspiration. The Hebreo-Christian God is depicted in the plain words of revelation for his every word and deed attributed to him by the inspired writers. This book is simply the Bible taken as a whole, and thus viewed in a light not shed upon it by pulpit expoundings of golden texts or private casual readings of isolated choice fragments.

If the Bible and its derived dogmas suffer from this simple process of "searching the Scriptures whether these things were so," the fault, dear reader, is not in the candid writer of this book, but in The Book, which utters the things which are simply and truly quoted and compared, in simple juxtaposition of contradictory texts, and not in the usual isolated and scattered passages as is the custom of sermons and pious tracts. Here is my book; there lies the open Bible: any man who will read, and is curious or interested for the truth, may judge wherein is the truth.

The earnest hope is cherished, for this book, that the simple and sincere search here made of the Scriptures for truth's sake, will serve to make only religious intolerance vain and ridiculous, and to shame contending Christians from an unfounded faith in the untrue, and encourage them and all men into the brotherhood of the only possible true and pure religion—to

> "Do good for good is good to do;
> Spurn bribe of heaven and threat of hell."

Then will indeed be realized the burden of the Herald Angel's Song:

> "Peace on earth to men of good will."

CONTENTS

IS IT GOD'S WORD?

CHAPTER I

THE GENESIS OF CHRISTIANITY

"WHAT IS TRUTH?" asked the mystified Pilate of Jesus the Christ, as he stood before the Roman Governor, accused by the Priests of the Jews of having proclaimed himself king of the Jews, and Messiah, thus "perverting the nation, and forbidding to give tribute to Caesar, and stirring up the People, saying, That he himself is Christ a King" (Luke xxiii, 2). Pilate asked Jesus, "Art thou the king of the Jews?" and a second time he queried, "Art thou a king then?" After standing some time mute, Jesus finally, and equivocally, answered: "Thou sayest that I am a king"; and he added: "To this end was I born, and for this cause came I into the world, that I should bear witness unto the truth"; but, he averred, "My Kingdom is not of this world" (Jno. xviii, 37).

Then Pilate's challenging Question, which has rung down the nearly twenty centuries since, and yet challenges answer concerning "this just person": Was he Christ? Was he the Son of God, Virgin-born? Was he the heralded King of the Jews, to be? Was he King of a Kingdom not of this world? Whether these things recorded of him were so?

The system of Christian theology grown up around this unique Subject, and inseparable in current acceptance from the concept of a real and true religion of the spirit, is wrought upon the basis of an implicit belief in a composite of two miraculous "revelations of God to Man." Of these the one is known as the Old Testament or will of God, revealed in olden times to the Hebrew people; the other, of the century of Jesus Christ, and revealed through himself and his Jewish propagandists, known as the New Testament or will of God. These two revelations of God to man are committed to mankind through a compilation of sixty-six small separate brochures of "Scriptures" or Writings, together called The Bible— from the Greek "Ta Biblia" or "The Books." This Bible constitutes all that we have or know of the "revealed Word of God."

Truth, pure and without alloy of possible error, lies in the inspired and sacred pages of this wonderful Word of God—if full faith and credit be given to its claims for itself, and to the claims made for it by the theologians who champion and defend it.

As for its own claims of inspired and inerrant truth, they abound: "All Scripture is given by inspiration of God" (2 Tim. iii, 16); "For the prophecy came not in old time by the will of man: but holy men of God spake as they were moved by the Holy Ghost" (2 Peter i, 21); though the Hebrew Deity himself, as quoted by Jeremiah, avers: "the prophets prophesy lies in my name" (Jer. xxiii, 25); and this prophet adds, "The false pen of the Scribes hath wrought falsely" (Jer. viii, 8, R. V.). John the Evangelist avows, "He that saw it bare record, and his record is true; and he knoweth that he saith true, that ye might believe" (Jno. xix, 35). And his Divine Subject declares: "I have greater witness than John. . . . Though I bear record of myself, yet my record *is* true" (Jno. v, 36, viii, 14)—though he had just previously avowed, "If I bear witness of myself, my witness is *not* true" (Jno. v, 31). Paul the chief of the propagandists, assures, "I speak the truth in Christ; I lie not" (Rom. ix, 1)—though with amazing naïveté he has just admitted that he does "lie unto the glory of God" (Rom. iii, 7), that His truth may the more abound! The credit of truth usually is attached to a confession.

The Scriptures, Old and New, thus vouched for their verity, we well know to be a collection of many separate pieces of writing by many different inspired Hebrew writers, through many ages of their history. The Bible has not thus the advantage of unity of authorship, as have the Sacred Scriptures of some other widespread faiths of the present day.

The justly celebrated Koran of Mohammed was brought down to this Prophet from heaven by the Archangel Gabriel, full-written on the parchment skin of the ram which was miraculously provided in the nick of time just as Father Abraham was about to cut the throat of his son Isaac as a sacrifice to Yahveh on Mt. Moriah; while the later but renowned Book of Mormon was specially revealed to the late Prophet J. Smith, here in New York State, in the year 1823, by the Angel Moroni, miraculously written on golden plates, and hidden in a câche on Cumorah Hill, near Palmyra. As these sacred texts were written in an unknown hieroglyph, the angel loaned to Prophet Smith a pair of patent heavenly spectacles called Urim and Thummim, with the miraculous faculty of rendering the strange script into rather faulty English words to the eye of the seer, and so enabling him, hidden from curious prying behind a screen, to translate the mystic manuscript, upon the completion of which pious work the golden plates and spectacles were taken by the angel back to heaven.

Over 600,000 people in the United States live and die in the faith of this "revelation," and have been considerably persecuted and martyred for their faith by other Americans who believed other and more ancient Hebrew revelations, though they hate and persecute the Jews; while more millions of human beings have for 1200 years believed the "revelations" of Mohammed than ever did believe the Hebreo-Christian revelations. So much for revealed faiths. Before forgetting Prophet J. Smith, it may be recalled, as a bit of American history, that in the year 1829, less than one hundred years ago, John the Baptist himself, he who baptised the Jewish Jesus, came down from heaven to New York State, and publicly "ordained" Prophet Smith and his confrère Oliver Cowdery, into "the Priest-hood of Aaron"; and the immortal Saints Peter, James the Brother of Jesus, and John (which one not specified), then and there conferred upon the two Prophets "the Order of the Priesthood of Melchizedek" of which same Order Jesus Christ was himself a perpetual member (Heb. vi, 20).

We will seek the truth of the Christian theology, searching the Scriptures whether the miraculous things therein recounted for faith can possibly be so. Incidentally we will catch an occasional sidelight from sacred or secular history, but chiefly will keep closely to our search of Holy Writ. First we will take a brief retrospect at some of the secular and historic phases of Christianity as it has prevailed unto the Christian civilization of past and present times of its era.

The Rise of Christianity

Judea, the birthplace of the Christ, was a small, outlying province of the far-flung Pagan Roman Empire, its turbulent Jewish fanaticism curbed by Roman law and legions.

The new religion rose there, but met with little acceptance in its native place, where the Jews could not recognize in the humble Carpenter of Nazareth the tokens of the kingly "Messiah" of their older prophecy. It spread with readier acceptance among the neighboring pagans, who believed all Gods and had no objection to taking on another; they were familiar with Virgin-births and with Gods coming to earth in human form. At Lystra the pagan populace even acclaimed Paul and Barnabas as pagan deities, crying, "The Gods are come down to us in the likeness of men," Barnabas being called Jupiter himself, and Paul the lesser divinity, Mercury, "because he was the chief speaker" (Acts xiv, 11–12). This greater pagan honor to Barnabas seems to have offended Paul's sense of dignity and importance; for shortly afterward they quarreled, "and the contention was so sharp between them, that they departed asunder one from the other" (Acts xv, 39).

But the proselyting campaigns continued, pushed with much zeal among the pagans now almost exclusively; naturally the new faith drifted toward imperial Rome, the head and heart of the ancient pagan world. There, too, it took root and slowly spread, among the lowly and the slaves, hidden away in the slums and in the catacombs.

This new religion, besides being purer and simpler—at first—than some of the older cults, was coupled with some very effective inducements and persuasions to acceptance. Its Founder proclaimed himself as very God; that he had come to establish a kingdom on earth and in heaven. To those who would abandon their families and their poor possessions, he made the positive promise of immense and immediate reward: "There is no man that hath left house . . . or lands for my sake, but he shall receive a hundredfold now in this time, houses . . . and lands; and in the world to come eternal life" (Mark x, 29–30; Matt. xix, 29; Luke xviii, 30). He proclaimed again and again, that in a very short time the existing world should end, that he would come in glory to establish his kingdom and a new earth where he would reign forever; so soon, indeed, would this great reward be realized, the prospective king assured, that there be some "standing here, who shall not taste of death, till they see the Son of Man coming in his Kingdom" (Matt. xvi, 28). The new religion assured everlasting felicity in its heaven to all who would just believe; it threatened eternal torment in the fires of its hell, for all who would not believe and accept it.

Under the spell of these promises and these threats, and of the assurance of a quick end of the then earth, the propagandists of the new Cult promptly established a strange new scheme of which they were the administrators—a scheme of pure communism. As the world would quickly come to an end, there was no reason and no need to take heed of temporal affairs; they must all watch and pray: and pool all their poor belongings in their leaders' hands for the common benefit. This the trembling and zealous proselytes did, under the sanction of greatest fear: "Neither was any among them that lacked: for as many as were possessors of lands or houses sold them, and brought the price of the things that were sold, and they laid them down at the Apostles' feet; and distribution was made unto every man according as he had need" (Acts iv, 34–35). And the story of what befell Ananias and Sapphira for holding out a part of their substance from the common pool was wholesome warning to any who, with a cautious eye to a possible hitch in the "second coming," might be inclined to "lie to the Holy Ghost," who kept the score of the contributions. The history of Dowie and his New Zion, and of "Moses II, younger brother of Jesus Christ," here in twentieth century United States, illustrates that certain human traits are not yet extinct.

Such was the degree of intellectual enlightenment of the classes among whom the new faith was propagated, and for whom the inspired Gospel biographies of the Christ were composed and put into circulation. The chief of the Disciples and his associate propagandists were admittedly "unlearned and ignorant men" (Acts iv, 13); the new cult was that of fishermen and peasants, of the ignorant, the disinherited, the slave, as the New Testament and all early Church history—as well as many of their acts and sayings—prove.

Naturally thus the new religion gained adherents and slowly spread—as have done all other religions: Mithraism, its closest and all but successful rival; Mohammedanism, which far outspread it; Mormonism, Spiritualism, Mother-Eddyism; what-not of religious cults or even superstitions that have ever been promulgated: just as did the thousand religious "heresies" broken away from and combatted and persecuted by the new faith from the very first, and several of which—as well as some entirely "pagan" religions—all but overthrew and supplanted the struggling new "orthodox" creed of the Christ. But by virtue of its superior moral merits, its exceptional system of rewards and punishments, and by the great zeal of its propagandists, it slowly grew and strengthened and finally gained the upperhold in the centuries-long struggle with paganism.

The New and the Older Religions

The new religion, Christianity, was not so new or novel as we are very generally disposed to think it. Practically, in all its essentials, it was not new at all, and had hardly a new thought in it—except hell fire and the oft-repeated and never realized "the end of all things is at hand" (1 Pet. iv, 7). Instead of the plurality of Gods of the pagan religions, it adopted the One God Yahveh as finally evolved from old Hebrew mythology, into Three-in-One Christian Godhead. The other Pagan Gods became, in effect, the "saints" of the new cult; or, as quoted in the Catholic Encyclopedia: "the saints are the successors to the Gods" (Vol. xv, 710). Though maybe more accurately the theory of the Psalmist became that of the new Theology: "All the gods of the heathen are Devils" (Ps. xcvi, 5, Vulgate). The incarnation of Gods in human form by Virgin-birth was commonplace myth; their death, resurrection, transition to and fro from heaven to earth, etc., were articles of faith of many pagan creeds and of all mythologies. Practically, Monotheism, without idol-worship, is the only single essential of the Christian religion wherein it differs from the pagans; and when one recalls the Trinity, and the icons and sacred images of saints, even this difference seems attenuated. Its intolerances and bloody cruelties are other signal differences.

The death and resurrection of pagan Gods is alluded to specifically by Ezekiel. Yahveh had brought him in his Vision to the north door of the Temple at Jerusalem; "and, behold, there sat women weeping for Tammuz" (Ezek. viii, 14). Tammuz was a so-called God of Vegetation, who is fabled to have died and to have been resurrected with the returning seasons. One month of the Hebrew calendar is named Tammuz. It is simply a myth of the death of vegetation in the winter and its rebirth or resurrection in the spring. It was a very prevalent superstition in ancient times, in Assyria, in Egypt with the myths of Isis and Osiris, in Palestine, Greece, and other pagan countries; and the Tammuz myth was one of the heathenish cults followed by the pagan Hebrews. The women referred to by Ezekiel were celebrating the annual death of their God Tammuz by weeping for him. Now they weep annually over the death of Jesus Christ, and rejoice each year on the Easter of his resurrection. This so-called Tammuz-cult was native to Babylonia; and, says the Catholic Encyclopedia, "it was unmistakably allied with the worship of Adonis and Attis, and even of Dionysius. Much might have been hoped for these religions with their yearly festival of the dying and rising Gods" (Vol. xi, 388). But they were otherwise corrupt and moribund, and gave way slowly and finally to the newer purer religion, but identical cult, of the Christ.

It would be intensely interesting to develop the records of the adoption by the new Christianity of the pagan myths and ceremonies. It is a very large subject; and we cannot here go into it at length, where our object is limited to a study of the sacred texts for the proofs or disproofs which themselves so abundantly afford. But some brief extracts from a couple of authoritative works may be made, for their own significance, and to point the way for further inquiry to the interested reader.

True, it will be found that practically every single tenet and ceremonial of the Christian religion has practically its exact counterpart in—and was derived and adapted from—the beliefs and ceremonies of the pagan religions which preceded it and for centuries lived along side of it. We have just noticed the "yearly festival of the dying and rising God" in the ceremonials of paganism. This is very like the Death and Resurrection of the Christian God, Jesus Christ; and it is the Resurrection of Jesus which is the cornerstone of the Christian religion: "If Christ be not risen, then is our preaching vain, and your faith is also vain" (1 Cor. xv, 14). To be as brief as may be in outlining this very suggestive subject, I will quote a paragraph from a well known recent work on Comparative Religion, by Sellars; supplemented by extracts from the Catholic Encyclopedia, as the best brief outlines of Christian adoptions and adaptations of paganism. Says Mr. Sellars:

"The Orphic cults in Greece, the Osiris and Isis cult in Egypt, the worship of Attis and Adonis in Syria (of which Palestine is part), the Purification and Communion ceremonies of Mithraism, all turned about the idea of a secret means of salvation. The God dies and is resurrected; the Virgin Goddess gives birth to a Son; the members of the religious community eat of their God and gain strength from the Sacred Meal. The Church Fathers were aware of these similarities, and sought to explain away their resemblances by means of the theory that the Devil had blasphemously imitated Christian rites and doctrines."—(I may pause to point out that these pagan rites long antedated the Christian analogies, and therefore the Theory loses force).—"The Death and Resurrection of a Savior-God was very prevalent in Tarsus, Paul's own city. The Attis Mysteries were celebrated in a season which corresponded to the end of our Lenten season and the beginning of Easter. They were preceded by fasting and began with lamentations; the votaries gathered in sorrow around the bier of the dead Divinity; then followed the Resurrection; and the Risen God gave hope of salvation to the Mystic Brotherhood; and the whole service closed with the feast of rejoicing, the Hilaria." (Sellars, pp. 23–24.)

Much more comprehensive, and constituting a very notable admission, are the following passages from the Catholic Encyclopedia. By way of introductory, it well says: "Speaking from the standpoint of pure history, no one will deny that much in the antecedent and environing aspirations and ideals of paganism formed, to use the Church phrase, a *praeparatio evangelica* of high value. '*Christo jam tum venienti, crede, parata via est,*' sings the Hymn of Prudentius. The pagan world 'saw the road,' Augustine could say, 'from its hill-top.' '*Et ipse Pilaetus Christianus est,*' said the Priest of Attis; while, of Heraclitus and the old Philosophers, Justin avers that 'there were Christians before Christ.' Indeed, the earlier apologists for Christianity go far beyond anything we should wish to say, and indeed made difficulties for their successors" (Vol. xi, 393). And again: "It has indeed been said that the 'Saints are the successors to the Gods.' Instances have been cited of pagan feasts becoming Christian; of pagan temples consecrated to the worship of the true God; of statues of pagan Gods baptised and transformed into Christian Saints" (Vol. XV, 710).

A few instances out of the great number of these "analogies" between pagan and Christian rites, are here quoted from the Catholic Encyclopedia:

"The Christian ritual developed when, in the third century, the Church left the Catacombs. Many forms of self-expression must needs be identical, in varying times, places, cults, as long as human nature is the same. Water, oil, light, incense, singing, procession, prostration, decoration of altars, vestments of priests, are naturally at the service of universal religious instinct. Little enough, however, was directly borrowed by the Church—nothing, without being 'baptised,' as was the Pantheon. In all these things the spirit is the essential: the Church assimilates to herself what she takes, or, if she cannot adapt, she rejects it.

"Even pagan feasts may be "baptised': certainly our processions of April 25th are the Robigalia; the Rogation Days may replace the Ambarualia; the date of Christmas Day may be due to the same instinct which placed on December 25th the *Natalis Invictis* of the Solar Cult (Vol. XI, 390).

"The Roman Virtues, Fides, Castitas, Virtus (manliness) were canonized (p. 391). The Mysteries had already fostered, though not created, the conviction of immortality. It was thought that 'initiation' insured a happy after life, and atoned for sins that else had been punished, if not in this life, in some place of expiation (Plato, Rep. 366; cf. Pindar, Sophocles, Plutarch). These Mysteries usually began with the selection of *Initiandi*, their preliminary baptism, fasting, and confession. After many sacrifices, the Mysteries proper were celebrated, including tableaux showing heaven, hell, purgatory, the soul's destiny, the gods. Appuleius (in *Metamorphoses*) tells us his thrilling and profoundly religious experiences.

"There was often seen the 'Passion' of the god Osiris; the rape and return of Kore and the sorrows of Demeter (Eleusis)—the sacred marriage and divine births (Zeus, Brimos). Finally, there was usually the Meal of mystic foods; grains of all sorts at Eleusis, bread and water in the cult of Mithra, wine (Dionysius), milk and honey (Attis), raw bull's flesh in the Orphic Dionysius-zagreus cult. Sacred formulae were certainly imparted, of magical value (Vol. XI, 391–2). In the Taurobolium, the *Initiandi* were baptised by dipping in the bull's blood, whence the dipped emerged *renatus in aeternum* ('reborn into Eternity'). In the sacred Meal (which was not a sacrifice), the worshipers communicated in the God and with one another.

"The sacred Fish of Atargatis have nothing to do with the origin of the Eucharist, nor with the Ichthys Anagram of the Catacombs. The Anagram—(Ichthys, the Greek word for Fish), does indeed represent *'Iesous Christos Theou Uios Soter'*—(Jesus Christ, Son of God, Saviour); the propagation of the symbol was often facilitated owing to the popular Syrian Fish-cult (from Dagon, Syrian Fish-god). That the terminology of the Mysteries was largely transported into Christian use is certain (Paul, Ignatius, Origen, Clement, etc.); that the liturgy, especially of baptism, organization of the Catechumenate, Disciplina Arcana, etc., were affected by them, is highly probable. Always the Church has forcefully molded words, and even concepts (as Savior, Epiphany, Baptism, Illumination (*photismos*), Mysteries (*teletes*), *Logos*, to suit her own Dogma and its expression. Thus it was that John could take the expression 'Logos,' mold it to his Dogma, cut short all perilous speculation among Christians, and assert once for all that the 'Word was made Flesh' and was Jesus Christ" (Cath. Encyclopedia, XI, 392).

The foregoing is as comprehensive a statement of the admitted "borrowings" or "adaptations" by Christianity from paganism as can well be made in brief quotations. They are authoritative, and completely prove that there is nothing new in the Christian religion except Hebrew Monotheism, and threats of hell and damnation, and temporal torture and punishments for the unbeliever.

It may surprise and maybe grieve many good and zealous Christians to know that all their pious observances, prayers, hymns, baptism, communion at the altar, redemption, salvation, the celebration of Christmas as the birth of their God in mid-winter, and of Easter, his resurrection as spring breaks, all, all, are pagan practices and myths, thousands of years antedating what they fondly think is their wonderful Jesus-religion.

The simple truth is, that paganism was outworn; its myths were too childish to be believed, by the enlightened minds of those days. Four centuries before Christ, Socrates was put to death for disbelief

in the Gods of Greece. Paganism, too, had become corrupt in many
of its practices; the time was ripe for a reform in religion, and
for a purer system, based on a belief in a One God. One of the
many pretended "Messiahs" of Israel served as the occasion for
this reform. His own people did not largely accept him; his propaganda found readier acceptance among the pagans who had a freer
form of worship, and who were very prone to believe in any gods
and in every fable. So the new cult made its way slowly through
the pagan Roman world.

The new religion was tolerated throughout the Empire, and at
Rome, at first. As it grew and spread, it interfered with the business
of many "Demetrius silversmiths," who violently opposed it as
destroying their idol-trade (Acts xix, 24). By their evil reports,
maybe, its votaries became suspected of criminal practices and con-
spiracies against the Empire; so it suffered intermittent persecutions, but it persisted. It was persecuted, or sought to be suppressed,
—not as a religion, but as opposed to State policy. After three
hundred years, during which paganism flourished decadently, and
paganism was yet the religion of "the best peoples and best portions
of the earth," the new religion gained the adherence of the pagan
Emperor Constantine, who became sole Emperor of the pagan world
through a victory due, as he was falsely made by Christian priests
superstitiously to believe, to a miraculous Sign of the Cross, with
the legend: "In Hoc Signo Vinces," hung out in heaven for him during
the battle by the Christians' God himself. The Emperor, in gratitude,
or as a shrewd policy of State, adopted the new God and creed;
and at the instigation of the priests set it up as the State religion
and enthroned its priests in place and power in the State. In the
spirit of pagan tolerance, which one would think should be the spirit
of Christianity, Constantine decreed religious liberty throughout the
Empire. The terms of his Edict of Milan, in 313, are worthy to
be recalled, and are shaming to the very sect which was its intended
beneficiary.

Pagan Tolerance and Christian Intolerance

The proselyted Emperor decreed: "It seems to us proper that the
Christians and all others should have liberty to follow that mode of
religion which to each of them appears best; for it befits the well-
ordered State and the tranquillity of our times, that each individual
be allowed, according to his own choice, to worship the Divinity."

But no sooner had the priests of the new religion foisted themselves securely into power, and by their threats of hell fire dominated the superstitious minds of the Emperors, than the old decrees of persecution under which they themselves had previously suffered were revamped and turned into engines of torture and destruction of both pagans and "heretic" Christians alike; and religious intolerance became the corner-stone of the Church Apostolic. Without mentioning earlier laws, in which they cautiously felt their way, it was enacted, at priestly instigation, in the famous Codex Theodosianus, about 384: "We desire that all the people under the rule of our clemency should live by that religion which Divine Peter the Apostle is said to have given the Romans. . . . We desire that heretics and schismatists be subjected to various fines. . . . We decree also that we shall cease from making sacrifices to the gods. And if any one has committed such a *crime*, let him be stricken with the avenging sword (Cod. Theod. XVI, 1, 2; 5, 1; 10, 4). What a contrast to the Edict of Milan, granting tolerance to the Christians and to all! In these laws of the now "Christian" Empire is priestly intolerance made the law of the land; and the accursed words "Inquisition" and "Inquisitors" first appear in this Code.

The Deadly Sanctions of Religion

But the priests should not bear alone the infamy of these laws of persecution and death, instigated by them. To the Devil his due! The "Holy Ghost" itself, it is claimed by the Bible and Church, inspired and decreed by positive command all the bloody murders and tortures by the priests from Moses to the last one committed; and the spirit of them lives and is but hibernating to-day. The Holy God of Israel, whose name is Merciful, thus decreed on Sinai: "He that sacrificeth to any gods (*Elohim*), save unto the Lord (Yahveh) alone, he shall be utterly destroyed" (Ex. xxii, 20). And hear this, which the ancient priests attribute to their God:

"If thy brother, the son of thy mother, or thy son, or thy daughter, *or the wife of thy bosom,* or thy friend, which is as thine own soul, entice thee, saying, Let us go serve other gods; Thou shalt not consent unto him, nor hearken unto him; neither shall thine eye pity him, neither shalt thou spare, neither shalt thou conceal him: But thou shalt surely kill him; thy hand shall be the first upon him to put him to death, and afterward the hand of all the people. And thou shalt stone him with stones that he die" (Deut. xiii, 6–9).

Words are inadequate to comment this decree of a barbarian God! And not only must all under penalty of a fiendish death worship the Holy Yahveh of Israel, but, listen to this other fatal, infamous decree of the Priests in the name of this God:

"The man that will do presumptuously, and will not hearken unto the priest, even that man shall die" (Deut. xvii, 18).

And the tergiversant slaughter-breathing persecutor for pay of the early Christians, now turned for profit their chief Apostle of Persecution, pronounces time and again the anathema of the New Dispensation against all dissenters from his superstitious, tortuous doctrines and dogmas, all such "whom I have delivered unto Satan" (I Tim. i, 20), as he writes to advise his adjutant Timothy. He flings at the scoffing Hebrews: "He that despised Moses' Law died without mercy: Of how much sorer punishment, suppose ye, shall he be thought worthy who hath trodden under foot the Son of God" (Heb. x, 28–29). All such "are set forth for an example, suffering the vengeance of eternal fire" (Jude 7); "that they might all be damned who believed not the truth" (2 Thess. ii, 12); and even "he that doubteth is damned" (Rom. xiv, 23). This Paul, who with such presumption of bigotry "deals damnation 'round the land on all he deems the foe" of his dogmas, is first seen "consenting to the death" of the first Martyr Stephen (Acts viii, 1); then he blusters through the country "breathing out threatenings and slaughter against the disciples of the Lord" (Acts ix, 1), the new converts to the new faith. Then of a sudden professing miraculous "conversion" himself, his old masters turned on him and sought to kill him, and he fled to these same disciples for safety, to their great alarm (vv. 23–26); and straightway begins to bully and threaten all who will not now believe his new preachments. To Elymas, who "withstood them," the doughty new dogmatist, "set his eyes on him," and thus blasted him with inflated vituperation: "O full of all subtilty and all mischief, thou child of the Devil, thou enemy of all righteousness, wilt thou not cease to pervert the right ways of the Lord"? (Acts xiii, 8–10). Even the "meek and loving Jesus" is quoted as giving the fateful admonition: "Fear him who is able to destroy both soul and body in hell" (Matt. x, 28)—here first invented and threatened by Jesus the Christ himself, for added terror unto belief. Paul climaxes the terror: "It is a fearful thing to fall into the hands of the living God" (Heb. x, 31).

Thus "breathing out threatenings and slaughter" against all who would believe not their Gospel of miracles and damnation, the founders of the new faith forged and fastened the fetters of the new faith upon the already superstitious pagans about them, and gradually throughout the Roman world. By fear of hell, pagan individuals, and in later times, by the choice proffered by "Christian" conquerors, between the Cross and the sword, whole pagan peoples fell under the sway and domination of the new militant faith. Whole tribes and nations were given the choice between Christianity and death, as the early history abounds in instances. The Hungarians adopted Christianity as the alternative to extermination in A.D. 1000; so the pagan Wends when conquered in 1144; the same is true of most of the pagan Teutonic tribes. Charlemagne required every male subject of the Holy Roman Empire above the age of twelve to renew his oath of allegiance and swear to be not only a good subject but also a good Christian. To refuse baptism and to retract after baptism were crimes punishable with death. It was indeed fearful danger and death, by torture, rack, and fire, to show faintest symptoms of doubt of the faith of the Christian religion and of the Holy Church. To speak the truth in a whisper even was rack and stake and death.

"LIKE KING LIKE PEOPLE"

Following the truism of Isaiah, "like king like people," very great sections of the people throughout the Empire, especially the official and subservient classes, hastened to adopt the name and outward indicia of Christianity, now become official and therefore popular. But so "joined to their idols" were the masses of pagan "converts" for convenience, and so addicted to its showy forms and ceremonies, that the now officially recognized Church of Christ was not slow to popularize itself with the pagan-Christian masses by taking over bodily and "baptizing" to itself the Temples, idols, rituals, ceremonials, the whole pomp and glorious circumstance of paganism, as we have just seen admitted by the paragraphs of Church history quoted from the work of Sellars and the authoritative Catholic Encyclopedia. Christianity became thus scarcely more than a refined veneer of paganism; a devout pagan becoming, either from convenience or conviction, a Christian, no doubt felt quite comfortable and at home in a "baptized" pagan-Christian Temple, aglow with all the trappings and ceremonials and resonant with all the old familiar rituals and litanies of his just recanted paganism, with just the names of Zeus or Jupiter substituted by Jehovah and of Adonis or Tammuz by that of Jesus. As the missionaries of Rome carried the new cult into yet other countries, and various kings and rulers fell to the appeal and pomp of the priests, whole tribes and nations of heathens, followed their leaders into the Church, veneering their paganism with the name, forms and ceremonials of Roman Christianity. This is the testimony of early ecclesiastical and secular history.

Later instances more generally known, but the significance of which is as generally overlooked, further confirm Isaiah's maxim. For a millennium all Europe was more or less Roman Christian; the Greek Church had its own Patriarch, but, with considerable vicissitudes of constancy, recognized the supremacy of Papal Rome, and the formulas of faith and creed were the same, with the exception of the age-long controversy over the "*filioque*" clause of the Nicene Creed, and the bitter feuds over image-worship known as iconoclasm. The rancors engendered from these differences of belief, together with the respective bigoted pretensions of Patriarch and Pope, led to the final rupture between Greek and Roman Churches in the year 1053. All the West followed their leader the Pope, the East clung with equal tenacity to the tenets of the Patriarch. So bitter were the hatreds thus perpetuated, that the Western popes and emperors refused all aid to the beleagured emperors and Church of the East in the fatal conflicts with the Turks, till in 1453 Constantinople and the whole Eastern empire fell before the Crescent, and Europe became Turkish and Mohammedan right up to the gates of Vienna.

But Western and Northern Europe remained of one and Roman Faith until the Reformation begun by Luther in 1517. Here a most signal vindication of "like king like people" is witnessed. The Christian kings and rulers who had political grievances against the Pope quickly took up the quarrel of Luther with the Roman Church; those who were politically friendly to the Pope seized arms to defend him and the Church; their respective peoples flocked to their standards and followed them in their rival faiths, and Europe was a welter of blood and strife during the ensuing fierce wars between Catholic and Protestant Christians. The strife of hostile Christian faiths yet endures, the same in kind, abated somewhat in degree.

England was wholly Romish before the Reformation; so staunch a supporter was the lecherous Henry VIII of the True Faith, that the Pope bestowed on him the title *Fidei Defensor*, Defender of the Faith. Papal sanction being refused to his scandalous project of divorce from Catharine, in order to marry Anne Boleyn, Henry broke with the Pope and became Protestant; carried England with him into the Protestant ranks; founded the Church of England and became its supreme spiritual head. The old Romish practice of burning Dissenters at the stake was turned upon the English

Catholics to suppress that sect entirely. His Romish daughter "Bloody Mary" succeeded him, and she was in turn succeeded by her Protestant bar-sinister sister Elizabeth: each in turn kept the fires of Smithfield blazing with the burning of the "heretics" of the opposite faith. Finally Protestantism won with the Revolution against the Catholic Stuarts, and England became what she is to-day, the staunch bulwark of the Reformed Faith and the Established Church.

On such chances and caprices of vanity and spite, in Providence, doth the religious complexion of whole nations of loyal Christians turn and depend. It is curious to remember that the Protestant sovereigns of England yet bear the Popish title "*Fidei Defensor*," which is blazoned on the national escutcheon and stamped on the coin of the realm to-day.

And so, through the long Dark Ages of Faith, and so long as the priest-prostituted State would prostitute its civil power in superstitious aid of the Holy Church, the Holy Church has zealously fulfilled its Bible's murderous commands and has murdered and tortured men, women, and tender children by fire and sword through its special agency of faith, the Holy Inquisition. This priest-ordained institution was only abolished by the Infidel Napoleon in Italy in 1808; but the moment his dreaded power fell, the "Scourge of God" was eagerly re-established in the Papal States by God's Vicar Pope Pius VII in 1814, and in Tuscany and Sardinia in 1835. It was only finally abolished, along with the usurped "Temporal Power" of God's vicars on earth, as one of the first glorious acts of the new Kingdom of Italy, in 1870,—just at the time when the Holy Ghost came to the "Vatican Prisoner" to reassert that the torture and murder of Dissenters from theological dogma was a God-imposed duty and divine right of his Holy Church. We shall see how this is.

"Not Dead but Sleepeth"

It would appear, from what is quoted below, that Holy Church accepts not complaisantly this deprivation of power to execute this bloody feature of the Divine commands committed to it. It recognizes perforce its temporal impotence, and seems, like the Modern Hun, to bide if not to toast "The Day," as it often suggests: "To-day the temporal penalties formerly inflicted on apostates and heretics cannot be enforced, and have fallen into abeyance";— abeyance, temporary suspension, reluctant disuse, if you please, and as may be read in Vol. I, p. 625 of the Catholic Encyclopedia, published under the "Imprimatur" of Holy Church but a few years ago (1907), in New York City, and several times repeated in its volumes. Its whole system for suppression even to extermination yet exists intact, ready for instant recourse when and should "changed conditions" again permit. From Vol. XIV, p. 761, *et seq.*, commended to very thoughtful perusal, are quoted several precious pregnant paragraphs:

"Nearly all ecclesiastical legislation in regard to the repression of heresy proceeds upon the assumption that Heretics *are in wilful revolt against lawful authority;* that they are, in fact, *Apostates* who by their own *culpable act* have renounced the True Faith. . . . It is easy to see that in the Middle Ages this was *not an unreasonable assumption.* . . .

"No one could be ignorant of the *claims* of the Church; and if certain people repudiated her *authority* it was by an *act of rebellion* inevitably carrying with it a menace to the sovereignty which the rest of the world accepted. . . .

"The Canon Law deals very largely with the enunciation of principles of *right* and *wrong* which are in their own nature *irreformable;* the direct repeal of its provisions has never or very rarely been resorted to; but there remain upon the statute book a number of enactments which owing to *changed conditions* are to all practical intents and purposes obsolete. . . .

"*The custom of burning heretics is really not a question of justice, but a question of civilization* (p. 769). . . .

"The gravest obligation," says Pope Leo XIII in his Encyclical "*Immortale Dei*" of Nov. 1, 1885, "*requires the acceptance and practice, not of the religion which one may choose, but of that which God prescribes and which is known by certain and indubitable marks to be the only true one*"! (p. 764).

There we have the incubating germs of potential hell on earth again in the name of God and the Christian religion. It is not the Roman Church alone which is guilty; now, and throughout this book, I make no imputations against it as Catholic, but only as Christian; and its greater guilt lies only in its being the father of all these priestly dogmas which have been and are the blight of civilization. The Dissenters were, and well might be again, their Providence permitting, all that this same Article above quoted imputes to them; for in a typical *tu quoque* conclusion (which admits its own guilt), Holy Church thus recites history: "On the other hand, the ferocity of the leading Reformers more than equaled that of the most fiercely denounced Inquisitors. Even the 'gentle' Melanchthon wrote to Calvin to congratulate him on the burning of Servetus: 'The Church, both now and in all generations, owes and will owe you a debt of gratitude.' And, says Luther, 'Let there be no pity; it is a time of wrath, not of mercy. Therefore, dear Lords, let him who can slay, smite, destroy.' John Knox 'thought that every Catholic in Scotland ought to be put to death.' "—And the authorized and authoritative Encyclopedic article just quoted, solemnly assures that the inspired Canon Laws, including those prescribing the torture and burning to death of "heretics," are in their divine nature "irreformable," have accordingly never been repealed and merely lie "in abeyance" or are "for *practical* purposes obsolete," because only of "changed conditions"; and that the infernal "custom of burning heretics is really not a question of justice" (i.e. of right or wrong), "but a question of civilization"—which has gradually brought about these "changed conditions," so that "burning heretics," while yet a divinely sanctioned and unrepealed law of God and Church, cannot in these days be enforced because of this "civilization" which renders the burning laws of God and Church unpopular and impotent.

Revolting and truly significant as this is, it is also a confession which suggests the truth of the assertion often made, that "Christian civilization" is a misnomer, and that such civilization as the world to-day enjoys, exists not because of the Christian religion, but despite and in defiance of that religion and its ministers. Only so far as the world has broken away from the superstitition and thrall of the theological dogmas of this religion, and caught something of its better spirit, making "obsolete" the fires of the Church on earth and in hell, has civilization slowly and painfully progressed, and human liberty of thought and conscience, and political and civil liberty, become possible and been slowly and painfully realized in some parts of the "Christian" world.

FAITH FLOURISHED ON IGNORANCE

With the decline and fall of the Roman Empire the Christian religion spread and grew, among the Barbarian destroyers of Rome. The Dark Ages cotemporaneously spread their intellectual pall over Europe. Scarcely any but priests and monks could read. Charlemagne learned to wield the pen only to the extent of scrawling his signature. The Barons who wrested Magna Carta from John Lackland signed with their marks and seals. The worst criminals, provided they were endowed with the rare and magic virtue of knowing to read even badly enough, enjoyed the "benefit of clergy," i.e., of clerical, or clerkly, learning, and went immune or with greatly mitigated punishment. There were no books, save painfully-written and very costly manuscripts, worth the ransom of princes, and utterly unattainable except by the very wealthy and by the Church; not till about 1450 was the first printed book known in Europe. The Bible existed only in Hebrew, Greek, and Latin, and the ignorant masses were totally ignorant of it other than what they heard from the priests, who told them that they must believe it or be tortured and killed in life and damned forever in the fires of hell after death. It is no wonder that faith flourished under conditions so exceptionally favorable.

During the long Dark Ages of Faith, the Holy Church and benightedness were at their apogee and holy heyday. Miracles of superstition happened every day by the conjuration of unwashed Saints and the exorcisms of motley priests, just as they do to-day in the jungles of Africa and the Arctic regions of America, through the conjure of Hottentot medicine-men and Esquimo Shamans; but never a single true miracle such as the modern ones of medicine, of surgery, of sanitation, of the physical sciences!

Any who may question the accuracy—or desire astonishing details—of this reference to the miracles and superstitions of Saints and Holy Church, is cheerfully recommended to the exhaustless fount of authentic lore and accredited vouchers for it all, in the 16-volume Catholic Encyclopedia, under the Titles of Miracles, Magic, Exorcism, Necromancy, Sorcery, Witchcraft, and scores of other precious such, all vouched for and triumphantly vindicated of truth under the *Imprimatur* and sanction of authority. And none of this, with such sanction, can possibly be impeached of error; for the same high Source defines: "Error is in one way or another the product of ignorance." The priestly maxim of those Dark Ages of Faith is found in the accredited axiom of Hugo of St. Victor: "*Disce primum quod credendum est*"—"Learn first what is to be believed"! Though amongst the Churchmen it is said to have been a privileged maxim for themselves, that they might "hold anything so long as they hold their tongues."

Under the sway and dominion of such "sacred science," genius was dead; the human intellect atrophied; credulity rampant. All this followed swiftly upon the grafting of the Christian religion upon the wonderful though decadent civilization of the Roman Empire in East and West. These all are simple facts of history.

"Christian Civilization"

Dickens' History of England, in speaking of the early pagan inhabitants of that island at the time of the Roman invasion, 55 years before the era of the so-called "Prince of Peace," says: "The ancient Britons, being divided into as many as thirty or forty tribes, each commanded by its own little king, were constantly fighting with each other, as savage people usually do."

That single sentence epitomizes the whole history of "Christian-civilized" Europe from that day to this: the Christian has been no whit different from the savage as regards the savage pastime of "constantly fighting with one another, as savage people usually do." Read any history of Europe, as a whole, or of any particular people of Europe: its pages are replete with next to nothing absolutely but fighting and wars, internecine and international, in every single year almost of its bloody annals. And wars about what?

Without an exception they have been all of one of three inveterate classes: wars instigated by lust of conquest and power on the part of "Divine Right" Kings or even more popular rulers, seeking to rob and steal each other's territories or to force their will upon others; wars, and the most terrible and brutal of all, incited by this Holy Christian religion: before the Reformation, with the holy purpose of exterminating unbelievers, as in the Crusades and the Spanish butcheries of the Moors; or with the pious object of exterminating, at Popish instigation, dissenting "heretics," as the Albigenses, Waldenses, Netherlanders, Cathari, Huguenots, the Jews, and scores of other murderous instances; and after the Reformation, furious exterminating Wars of one fanatical faction of Christians against the other, all blasphemously in the name of God! A third, and redeeming, class of European wars have been those glorious and righteous struggles for liberty by oppressed and debased peoples, ground to misery and desperation by Holy Church and Divine Right Kings—both which institutions are thoroughly Biblical and Christian—to throw off their galling yokes and to win political freedom and liberty of conscience for themselves and their posterity. But the Christian religion, while instigating and waging many of the most cruel of wars, has never once prevented a single accursed war, of which over fifty have plunged "civilized Christian Europe" into a welter of blood and misery in the past century alone; while the world to-day yet staggers under the devastation of the greatest and most destructive War of all history, which desolated humanity and all but overthrew civilization.

And no war has been in which the name of God is not inscribed upon the bloody banners of the aggressor; while assailants and defenders alike swamp high heaven with frantic and fatuous prayers to God to give victory to each against the other—prayers which

God has never heard or attended; for God, as cynically and truly said by Napoleon, "is always on the side of the heaviest guns,"—or of the deadliest poison-gas and most ruthless butchery of man.

Until wicked, brutal, damned war is ended on earth, there is and can be no true civilization; for all war—unless defensive—is uncivilized, brutish barbarism. And to this holy consummation the Christian religion, as such, will never lead or even contribute. He whom the Christians fondly call "The Prince of Peace"—for what reason and with what reason God only knows—is not to be counted on to aid; for himself explicitly avers: "I am not come to bring Peace, but the Sword: For I am come to set men at variance" (Matt. x, 34–35)! Far from preventing war, truly has his theology, or creedal religion, throughout his era been the prolific cause and miserable pretext of wars and woes unnumbered: of human misery, degradation, ignorance, intolerance, persecution, pogroms, murders by fire and sword—in a word, of most of the ills and sorrows and blights which humanity, subject to its sway, has suffered from the days of Constantine's league with the Church, A.D. 312, to this very year of Christ and his religion. Gainsay this no man who knows history can.

The Christian religion has been the fearful sanction of human slavery, of "Divine Right" rulers, of "God-anointed" priestly domination of the mind and soul of man, of the subjection and imposed inferiority of woman. The deadly dogma of Divine Right of Kings, and of the sin of just resistance to the oppression of humanity, is positively ordained: "The powers that be are ordained of God. Whosoever therefore resisteth the power resisteth the ordinance of God: and they that resist shall receive to themselves damnation" (Romans xiii, 1). But the Declaration of Independence asserts otherwise. As for the priestly dominance, we will take ancient Scripture for authority—more modern instances may occur to some: "The prophets prophesy falsely, and the priests bear rule by their means; and the people love to have it so" (Jer. v, 31).

THE "CHRISTIAN" PEOPLES

The best and most highly civilized portion of the human race is within the pale of Christendom; but are these peoples so because they profess the Christian religion? Just as well and truly say that they are the most intelligent of mind, the fairest of complexion, the most comely of form and face, because they are Christian.

But as pagans, before ever they heard of Christianity, they were the same: because they were of the Caucasian race, Aryan—which means "noble." All know the story of St. Augustine and his seeing a group of "barbarian" captives exposed for sale in the Christian slave-market of a Roman city; struck with their personal beauty, he asked of what country they were. Being told "They are Angles," he exclaimed, "No, they are angels," and was thus moved to go to their Teutonic homeland to "convert" their nation from paganism to the True faith. Deathless in history, in song and story, are "the glory that was Greece, the power that was Rome"—the two highest civilizations of antiquity as well as of the early Christian Era: they were of pagan Greece, of pagan Rome, long before and long after the Christian religion came, and that glory, that high civilization were eclipsed, swamped, by the night of the Christian Dark Ages—which were the Ages of Faith.

Not only these greatest civilizations, but the greatest minds of the ages, the best of men, were pagans: Aristotle, Plato, Socrates, Epictetus, Demosthenes, Cicero, Seneca, the Plinys, the Antonines, Marcus Aurelius, the Philosophers, the Poets, Pilate himself—the catalogue is long and illustrious: Justin had to explain it thus—"there were Christians before Christ." The Augustan Age, just at the time of the Advent of the Man of Sorrows, was the glorious Golden Age of the ancient world—and purely pagan. And for centuries after Christ the greater part of Europe remained pagan, and but slowly, and bloodily, gave way to Christianity after the league of State with Church under Constantine, as we may again notice in this sketch.

Having given a rapid retrospect of some of the phases of Christian history, and sought to clear away some popular misconceptions, I shall proceed, in the following chapters, in all conscience and truth of statement, easily verifiable by all, to "search the Scriptures," Hebrew and Hebreo-Christian, whether these things which they contain for our faith are worthy of faith and credit. This search will truly "reveal" the Bible and its God in the very words of inspiration. If they be found inspired of truth, the first and highest duty of man is to reverently cherish and obey them—"for therein ye think ye have eternal life." If inspiration and truth, divine and human, are found none of, let us cease wrangling and being intolerant about them, and let us have peace over "idle tales" and fables.

CHAPTER II

A SKETCH OF HEBREW SCRIPTURES

THE BIBLE, as all must admit, is the only earthly source of human knowledge which we have, or possibly can have, of the great questions of miracle and of "revealed religion" which come to us through its pages. The authenticity and verity of its remarkable contents, as the asserted word and will of God, Yahveh, can only be tested and ascertained by itself; by the "internal evidences" of its own words and texts must its divine origin and inspired truth be vindicated, or its possible mere human origin and want of inspired truth be demonstrated. On a matter of such *prima facie* high importance to man and to the soul and its destiny, no candid and honest mind can offer reasonable objection to a candid and honest inquiry, made by a frank and faithful examination of its own words and texts. To this capital end, therefore, we will follow the injunction of the Man of Galilee, and "search the Scriptures"; haply to find the answer to the eternal question posed by Pilate, "What is truth?"

THE "BIBLE" A COLLECTION OF "LITTLE BOOKS"

What, first, is this Bible? It is *not* one single and homogeneous Book, in the form we see it printed; indeed, it was first printed in the year A.D. 1452, by Gutenberg, in Mainz. And what we have and know—and fondly cherish—as the Bible, is *not* the Bible at all—but a translation, or version, more or less faulty and incorrect—and often intentionally very misleading, of ancient manuscripts of Hebrew and Greek writings, themselves very faulty and conflicting, forming together the so-called Bible. The very name, Bible, indicates its nature as a collection of writings. The name Bible is the Latin *Biblia*, from the Greek diminutive plural, *ta biblia*, or "the little books," a term first used, as referring to the Hebrew Scriptures, in 1 Maccabees, xii, 9. The Greek word *biblos*, from which comes the diminutive *biblia*, is from the Greek *bublus*, for papyrus, the name of the famous material, from Egypt, on which ancient books were written in manuscript. The title *Ta Biblia*, for the whole

Scriptures, Hebrew and Christian, was first used in the 2nd Epistle of Clement (xiv, 2), written in A.D. 170.

The Bible, thus so-called, is a compilation, or gathering into one volume, of sixty-six separate and different "little books," or fragmentary "sacred" writings, which compose it, from Genesis to Revelation. These sixty-six little books, or manuscripts, were written, or edited and compiled, in very different ages of the world, over the space of some centuries, by wholly different, and mostly unknown, persons, in different countries and languages, Hebrew and Greek principally; but, except maybe one Book, by Jews invariably. Together they form the "sacred writings" of the later Hebrews and of the early Jewish and Pagan Christians—the name given, first at Antioch (Acts xi, 26), to the followers of the Jewish Jesus Christ.

THE LANGUAGE OF THE BOOKS

The Hebrew "little books," thirty-nine in number according to the accepted Hebrew and Protestant "Canon," forty-six according to the Catholic acceptance, were written of course, mainly in the Hebrew language, though Aramaic elements enter into some of the later compositions. This Hebrew language, like several others of the allied Semitic languages, was written entirely with consonants, they having no vowels, and no means of expressing vowel sounds; their words consist mostly of words of only three consonantal letters. The whole Hebrew Scriptures is a solid mass of words in consonants only, with not a single vowel among them. This consonantal mass of words was written from right to left, letter after letter unbrokenly, without separation or spacing between words, and without a single mark of punctuation from end to end. There were of course no divisions, as at present, into Chapters and verses, these divisions having been invented only some three or four hundred years ago to facilitate quotations and references; even now the chapter and verse divisions differ considerably between the Hebrew text and the English translations in frequent instances. The Hebrew Rabbis and scholars, somewhere between the fifth and eighth centuries A.D., devised and put into use in their manuscripts of the Bible, a system of so-called "vowel points"—dots and dashes like in modern shorthand—to express and preserve what they considered to be the probable ancient pronunciation of the Hebrew words. No wonder there are infinite doubts and difficulties as to the original words and their pronunciation.

The Bible Language—Hebrew

Such a thing as the "Hebrew" language, as a separate and distinctive speech of the ancient Israelites, in which they held familiar converse with Yahveh, and which Yahveh spoke with Adam and Eve and with the Patriarchs and Moses, never existed; no more than an "American" language now exists as distinct from the mother speech of England, or than the "Latin" languages of South America differ from the Spanish and Portuguese of the Iberian Peninsula. As to the language of Yahveh and Adam and Eve, says the Catholic Encyclopedia: "The contention that Hebrew was the original language bestowed upon mankind may be left out of discussion, being based merely on *pietistic a priori* considerations" (VII, p. 176).

Abraham was a native of "Ur of the Chaldees," and hence naturally, with all his family and people, spoke the Chaldean or Babylonian language, which was very much akin to that of Canaan, where Abraham migrated, and was spoken by him and his descendants until the "70" migrated to Egypt, 215 years later. Indeed, even as late as Isaiah, the language of the Chosen People is expressly said to be the "language of Canaan" (Is. xix, 18). The scholarly Encyclopedia further says: "The name Hebrew (as applied to the language spoken by the ancient Israelites, and in which are composed nearly all the Books of the Old Testament), is quite recent in Biblical usage, occurring for the first time in the Greek prologue of Ecclesiasticus, about 130 B.C." (Cath. Encyc. VII, 176). And further, as to the language of Abraham and the Patriarchs: "That it was simply a dialect belonging to the Canaanitish group of Semitic languages is plain from its many recognized affinities with the Phoenician and Moabitic dialects. Its beginnings are consequently bound up with the origin of this group of dialects. . . . The language spoken by the clan of Abraham was a dialect closely akin to those of Moab, Tyre, and Sidon, and it bore a greater resemblance to Assyrian and Arabic than to Aramaic" (Id.). Indeed, the Dictionary of the Hebrew language which lies before me is called "The Analytical Hebrew and Chaldee Lexicon"—so nearly one and the same are the two dialects.

So, if Yahveh, God of Abraham and of Israel, spoke all these wonderful things to his Chosen People, he spoke them in the common language of the peoples and gods of Canaan and Assyria, and not in some choice and peculiar "Hebrew language" as a special idiom of his Chosen People and of his divine revelations to his People and through them, as claimed, to mankind. Very highly important sidelights on inspiration and the verity of sundry characteristic Scripture histories, flow from this fact; so that its importance and interest justify this brief paragraph.

The Name of the Hebrew Tribal God

So obsolete and "dead" had the "Hebrew" language become, following the world-conquests of Alexander the Great and the almost universal spread of the Greek language and culture throughout the Orient, that several centuries before the time of Christ even the form and proper pronunciation of the name YHVH of the Hebrew tribal deity were lost and unknown; though a few Jews, as Philo of Alexandria and Josephus, about the time of Christ, professed to know it, but held it unlawful to pronounce or divulge it (Josephus, *Antiq.*, II, xii, 4; see Cath. Encyc., tit. Jehovah, vol. VIII).

Again the authoritative Catholic Encyclopedia speaks on this very significant point: "The modern Jews are as uncertain of the proper pronunciation of the sacred Name as their Christian contemporaries. . . . The name was not pronounced after the destruction of the Temple" (VIII, p. 329). On page 330 it gives a list of the forms of the name as found in ancient writers named, and lists: Jao, Jaoth, Jaou, Jeuo, Ja, Jabe, Jaho, Jehjeh. It then comments: "The judicious reader will perceive that the Samaritan pronunciation *Jabe* probably approaches the real sound of the Divine Name closest. Inserting the vowels of Jabe into the original Hebrew consonantal text, we obtain the form Jahweh (Yahweh), which has been generally accepted by modern scholars as the true pronunciation of the Divine Name" (p. 330).

Very remarkably, for an Orthodox Christian authority, this very scholarly thesaurus of Theology—which so often seems to forget orthodox theology when engaged in questions of pure scholarship—reviews at some length inquiries of scholars to discover the origin of the old Hebrew tribal Yahveh—that is, whence the Chosen People got or "borrowed" their tribal god. The colloquy between the God and Moses at the Burning Bush, demonstrates that neither Moses nor the Chosen People knew or ever had heard of Yahveh, or of any other "God of their fathers"; for Moses says to the God: "Behold, when I come unto the children of Israel, and shall say unto them, The God of your fathers hath sent me unto you; and they shall say to me, *What is his name?* what shall I say unto them?" (Ex. iii, 13). The matter of the traditional "revelation" of the name of the God to Moses we will duly consider a few pages later.

The Encyclopedic article referred to reviews amply the suggested origins of Yahveh and his adoption by the Chosen People, of which but one or two—but very significant ones, may be here noticed. Under the sub-caption, "Origin of the Name Jahveh (Yahweh)," this high authority says: "The opinion that the name Jahveh was adopted by the Jews from the Chanaanites, has been defended by (naming a number of eminent scholars), but has been rejected by (others named). It is antecedently *improbable* that Jahveh, the irreconcilable enemy of the Chanaanites, should be originally a Chanaanite god" (VIII, p. 331). Passing other suggested origins, it says: "The theory that Jahveh is of Egyptian origin *may have a certain amount of* a priori *probability*, as Moses was educated in Egypt. Still, the *proofs* are *not convincing*. . . . Plutarch (*De Iside*, 9) tells us that a statue of Athene (Neith) in Saïs bore the inscription, 'I am all that has been, is, and will be.' . . . the common Egyptian formula, *Nuk pu Nuk*, but though its literal signification is 'I am I,' its real meaning is 'It is I who'" (Id.). Again: "As to the theory that Jahveh has a Chaldean or Accadian origin, its foundation is not very solid," citing the familiar Assyrian forms Yahu or Yah and Yau; and adding "Jahveh is said to be merely an artificial form introduced to put a meaning into the name of the *national god*" (Id.).

The immense significance of this scholarly confession, that the theory of Egyptian origin of Yahveh may have "a certain amount of *a priori probability*," and that this name is said to have been adopted "to put meaning into the name of the *national god*" Yahveh, or that the Hebrews may have adopted or adapted their tribal or "national god" from Egypt, Chaldea, or some other of their heathen neighbors, is that such concessions, or the bare possibility of such fact, destroy at once utterly the Bible assurances and the pietistic Hebreo-Christian assertions that YHVH is eternal and "self revealed" God since from before the foundations of the world. It totally explodes the pretended "revelation" to Moses at the Burning Bush, soon to be noticed. In a word, such fact or the admission of it wholly destroys Yahveh, except as a Pagan Hebrew Myth and a Christian "strong delusion" to believe ancient primitive myths for revealed truth of God.

The name of the God, too, is often and variously abbreviated in the Hebrew texts. Dozens of times in Genesis it is written simply "yy," the first time in Gen. ii, 4, the first mention of Yahveh. Elsewhere it occurs as "Yah," or Yehu, Yeho, and as "Yah-Yahveh," often as Yahveh-Elohim. It is always, as we shall see, falsely rendered in the translations as "Lord" and "Lord God," for reasons which will duly appear.

The Bible All Copies of Copies

There is not preserved nor is there existent in the world a single original book or manuscript of Hebrew or Christian Scriptures, containing the inspired word of Yahveh. The most ancient manuscripts of the Hebrew texts date only from the Eighth Century of the Era of Christ; while of the Christian Books, said to have been written by the direct inspiration of the Holy Ghost within the first century of the Era, all, all are lost, and the oldest "copies" bear the marks of the Fourth Century. And even in this Fourth Century, so gross was the corruption of text, so numberless the errors and conflicting readings, that the great St. Jerome, author of the celebrated Latin Vulgate Version of the Scriptures, has left it recorded, as his reason for his great work, that the sacred texts "varied so much that there were almost as many readings as Codices," or MSS. copies of the text. And just now and for years past, the Papal authorities are collating all known extant versions and bits of Scriptures for the purpose of trying to edit them into one approved Version of the inspired Word of Yahveh.

Curious indeed it seems, that in this inspired revelation of Yahveh, the Hebrew God to Man, wherein the awful destinies of the human soul are said to be revealed to eternal salvation or damnation, some ten thousand different, conflicting, and disputed readings, and verbal slips of inspiration, and textual corruptions, admittedly, and improvidently, exist in the inspired texts, with the obvious knowledge and sufferance of the God whose awful will it all is; while the Providence of that same God, Yahveh, by special miraculous intervention in that behalf, has preserved wholly "incorrupt" through all the Ages of Faith, the cadavers and ghastly scraps and relics of holy Saints and Martyrs galore, from the very Year One on, and which are yet today (or at last reports were—Cath. Encyc., *passim*)—as fresh, fragrant, and wholly "incorrupt" of flesh as when alive— which, in very truth, in the case of many Saints—as their "Lives" are recorded by the Monks—is not saying very much for either freshness or fragrance. An instance—*e pluribus unum*—is that of the pioneer Saint Pachomius, who, ambitious to outdo in bodily mortification his companions in filth, left the pig-sty in which he dwelt, and sat himself on the ground at the entrance of a cave full of hyenas, in the pious desire of entering Glory via their bestial maws; but the hyenas, rushing out upon the holy Saint, stopped short of a sudden, sniffed him all over the body, turned tail and left him in disgust uneaten.

WHEN THE BOOKS WERE WRITTEN

It will be of signal value to inquire, for a moment, concerning the times and periods of time indicated by the Bible, and the times when the principal Books of it were written and by whom they were written—or rather, as that is the only course possible, to show, negatively, by whom, and when, they were *not* written. This inquiry will be confined to the "internal evidences" of the Bible texts themselves, with just a bit of reference to its marginal editorial annotations. The force of such "internal proofs" is self-evident, and is very easily understood, and its effect appreciated.

To assist to an easier understanding, take this illustration: If one picks up a book, a newspaper, a letter, or any piece of written or printed matter, which bears no date-mark or name of some known writer, one may not be able to ascertain just when or by whom it was written or printed. But one can, in many instances, very readily determine, by the very nature of its contents, that it was *not* written or published until *after* such or such a time, which *is* known; and hence that it *could not* have been written by or of some person already dead or not yet born.

If such a document, for instance, contains the name of Julius Caesar or of Jesus Christ, this proves at once that it was written sometime within the past 1900-odd years, and not possibly before the advent and events of these two personages. If it mentions President Washington or some incident of his administration, it is evident that it could not have been written before Washington became President in 1789; if it mentions Presidents Washington, Lincoln and Coolidge, proof it is that it was written as late as the date the latter became President. So of every factual or fanciful allusion—it can go no higher than its source. If the document speaks of the World War, or of some battle or event of it, or subsequent to it, this is "internal proof" that it was written since August, 1914, or *after* the event mentioned; if it relates something known to have happened yesterday, we know at once that it was written, and could only have been written, since that happening of yesterday. In a word, we know that no writing can speak as of a matter of fact of any event, person or thing, until *after* such event has become an accomplished fact, or such person or thing exists or has existed. No one can today write even the name of the President of the United States in the year A.D. 1929.

With this simple thumb-rule of ascertaining or approximating the time of production of written documents, by what is known as their "internal evidences," or the certain indications which they bear on their face, we may gather some astonishing proofs as to when, and by whom, sundry inspired records of Holy Writ were *not* written—contrary to some currently accepted theories.

Some Lights on Bible Chronology

According to the Chronology, or Time-computations, worked out of the Bible narratives (principally by Bishop Ussher), and printed in the margins of all well-edited Bibles, Catholic and Protestant alike, the world and Man were created, by the fiat of the Hebrew God Yahveh just about 4004 years before the present so-called Christian Era, not yet 2000 years old; so that the reputed first man, "Adam," inhabited the new-made earth just less than 6000 years before the present time.

The revealed record of this interesting event—which by every token of human knowledge outside the Bible is known *not* to have occurred just when and how there related—together with many equally accredited events, are recorded (for wonder of mankind) in the first five books of the Bible—Genesis to Deuteronomy, called the Pentateuch or Five Books, or as entitled in the Bible, "The Five Books of Moses," who is reputed to have written them at the inspiration or by the revelation of Yahveh, the God of Israel.

According to the Bible chronology, Moses lived some 1500 years before Christ; the date of his Exodus out of Egypt with the Israelites is laid down as the year 1491 Before Christ, or some 2500 years after the Biblical creation of the world. So, if Moses wrote the account of the creation, the fall of man, the flood, and other notable historical events recorded in Genesis, he wrote of things happening, if ever they happened, 2500 years more or less before his earthly time, and some of them before even man was created on earth; things which Moses of course could not personally have known.

But it is explained, that while this is true, yet Yahveh inspired Moses with a true knowledge or "revelation" of all those to him unknown things, and so what he wrote was revealed historical fact. This is a matter which will be noticed a little later.

But the Book of Genesis, and all the "five Books of Moses," contain many matters of "revealed" fact which occurred, if ever at all, many hundreds of years *after the death* of Moses. Moses is not technically "numbered among the Prophets," and he does not claim for himself to have been inspired both backwards and forwards, so as to write both past history and future history. It is evident therefore, by every internal and human criterion, that these "five Books of Moses," containing not only the past events referred to, but many future events narrated—not in form of prophecy of what would be, but as actual occurrences and *faits accomplis*—could not have been written by Moses, the principal character of the alleged Exodus and of the forty years' wandering in the Wilderness of Sin, at the end of which he died. The cardinal significance of this fact, and of others connected with it, as bearing upon the historicity of Mosaic narrative and revelation, will appear in due course of this review.

Some Sidelights on Moses

Moses, as the traditional great leader and Law-giver of Israel, is worthy of very interested attention; the results can but be of interest. In no accurate sense was Moses, if he ever lived, a Hebrew at all; indeed, he is expressly called "an Egyptian man" (Ex. ii, 19). Certainly he did not speak the Hebrew language, as it was non-existent as such, as noticed in another place; for after 400 years in Egyptian slavery, evidently the slave descendants of Jacob the Syrian, of Chaldea, had ceased to have any knowledge of their old Chaldean tongue, and could speak only an Egyptian dialect. As well should the descendants of the African slaves brought to America 300 years ago speak today the strange dialects of their native jungles. In another place we shall see that neither they nor Moses knew or had ever heard of Yahveh, God of Israel; and that during the "sojourn" in Egypt and for a millennium afterwards, they continued to worship the Gods of Chaldea and of Egypt.

All know the story of "Moses and the Bulrushes"; how the unnamed Pharaoh sought to destroy all the new-born male children of the Israelites, commanding the Hebrew midwives to slay them at birth; how the yet unnamed infant son of Amram was put into an "ark of bulrushes" and hidden on the bosom of the sacred Nile, watched over by his sister Miriam, found by Pharoah's daughter, drawn from the water by her, raised by his own mother, and adopted by the daughter of the Pharaoh. All this is very romantic, but not novel.

Sargon, King of Accad about 3800 B.C., as shown by his monuments yet existing, was also secretly born, was placed by his mother in an Ark of Bulrushes, just like Baby Moses, and turned adrift on the bosom of the Euphrates, where he was found by a kindly gardener (as were also Romulus and Remus, born of the God Mars and the Vestal Virgin, Rhea Silvia)—who nurtured him, until his royal birth was discovered; he became beloved of the Goddess Ishtar, and was raised by his valorous deeds to the throne of his country. Sargon then conquered all Western Asia, including the land of Canaan, and set up his monuments of victory even on the shores of the Mediterranean Sea, where they remained, undisturbed by the Floods of Noah, Xisuthros, and Deucalion, until discovered in recent years, and their records confronted with those of Holy Writ, in the British Museum in London, and in others elsewhere, where they may be seen today. The stele of Hammurabi's Code, we may also recall, stands today an eloquent and unimpeachable witness of the mighty Past, in the Louvre at Paris; while Moses' Tables of Stone, writ by the finger of the Hebrew God Yahveh, are even as the sepulchre of Moses, whereof no man knoweth unto this day.

To return from the digression. As the story is recorded in Exodus ii, the princess of Pharaoh spied the Ark in the Nile, took a fancy to the babe and rescued it, afterwards, when it grew, "he became her son." Now the remarkable incident: "And she called his name Moses: and she said, Because I *drew* him out of the water" (v. 10). What has "Moses" to do with "drew" out of the water? In English speech nothing discernible; but in the original Hebrew it is a plain play on words or pun: "and she called his name *Mosheh*, . . . Because *meshethi* (I drew) him out of the waters" (Heb. *mashad*, to draw). The curious thing about it all is, that the Egyptian Princess is represented as speaking *in Hebrew*, or Chaldee, and making a pun-name for her protegé in that evidently unknown tongue. That it hardly happened that way is obvious. The birth, rescue and "christening" of Moses have every indicia of myth. This evidently fabled beginning must raise grave doubts as to the historicity of Moses himself and of all his reputed career. Other indications of the legendary will not be wanting as we proceed to review the life and times of Moses, and his "Five Books."

The "Five Books of Moses"

The first and most obvious proof regarding the authorship of the so-called "Five Books of Moses," and the fact that they were not written by Moses, but date from a time many centuries after his reputed life and death, is very simple and indisputable. This proof consists of very numerous instances of what are called "Post-Mosaica," or "after-Moses" events, related in those Books under the name of Moses as their inspired author; events of which Moses of course could not have known or written, as they occurred long after his death.

It may be remarked, parenthetically, that Moses nowhere claims to have written the "Five Books," nor does the Bible elsewhere impute their authorship to Moses. It is only "the Law" which is attributed to Moses. Indeed, the Books are written throughout in the third person—Moses did or said this or that; never, in all the relations of the doings and sayings of Moses, said to have been written by himself, does "I did" or "I said," once occur, except when Moses is recorded as making a speech.

A very singular passage in Exodus VI illustrates this point, and is striking evidence that Moses did not and could not have written the Books. In verse 13 it is related: "And Yahveh spake unto Moses and unto Aaron, and gave them a charge unto the children of Israel, and unto Pharaoh king of Egypt, to bring the children of Israel out of the land of Egypt." Immediately, verses 14 to 27, follows a strange interruption of the narrative and the insertion of a series of family genealogies, beginning "These be the heads of their fathers' houses," with many names, including the pedigrees of Moses and Aaron and the marriage of Aaron and names of his offspring; then this careful explanation: "*These are that Aaron and Moses*, to whom Yahveh said, Bring out the children of Israel from the land of Egypt. *These are they* which spake to Pharaoh king of Egypt, to bring out the children of Israel from Egypt: *these are that Moses and Aaron*" (vv. 26–27). Moses could never have written in this form and manner, right there among his contemporaries who knew him and all about the "bringing out of Egypt." A thousand years afterwards the thing was written, and the sacred Scribe took these pains, thrice reiterated, to identify the Aaron and Moses mentioned in the genealogies with the traditional Moses and Aaron of the traditional Exodus.

It is recognized by scholars that all these elaborate genealogies, inserted in the "Five Books," are post-exilic compositions. Their exact duplicates are found in the post-exilic Books of Chronicles, and some in Ezra. This too is the origin of the use of "Adam" as a proper name instead of the common noun that it is. Again, if Moses had written the Books, surely he would have at least once written the *name* of the Pharaoh of his intimate dealings of the

Exodus. But in the verses cited several times is it said, as often elsewhere in the Five Books, "Pharaoh king of Egypt," as if Pharaoh were the name of the king instead of simply the official title of the ruler. The writer did not know the name of the Pharaoh, and thought that Pharaoh was his personal name. In later and more historical Books, several Pharaohs are mentioned by their proper names.

Some "Post-Mosaica"

The instance is well known of the graphic account in the last Chapter, XXXIV, of Deuteronomy, of the death and burial of Moses: this he could hardly have written himself. Even if he were inspired, as some people explain, to write of his own coming death and funeral, it would be odd for him to add (v. 6), when he was not yet dead or buried, "but no man knoweth of his sepulchre unto this day"—which was evidently very long afterwards, and proves an authorship much later than Moses.

In the same Chapter is another similar proof of much later authorship by some other than Moses; for it is written: "And there hath not arisen a prophet since in Israel like unto Moses" (v. 10)— a statement which could only have been made long afterwards, when many later and great prophets had arisen with whom Moses could be compared. Moses could not himself have written that no prophet had arisen "since" himself, when he was yet alive and when no prophet was or could as yet be his successor.

In Exodus XI, 3 it is stated "the man Moses was very great"; and in Numbers XII, is the information, "Now the man Moses was very meek, above all the men which were upon the face of the earth" (v. 3). So meek a man would not likely have made so immodest boasts of himself. It must have been some later chronicler sounding his praises. This conclusion is strengthened by the use of "was" and "were," in the historical past tense. And Moses no doubt well knew the name of his own Pagan father-in-law; but the latter is variously named in the "Five Books" by four different names: Jethro (Ex. iii, 1); Reuel (Ex. ii, 18); Raguel (Num. x, 29); Jether (Ex. iv, 18), while in Judges he is given a fifth name, Hobab (Jud. iv, 11), all which indicates several different authors, or one very careless one, but not Moses.

Moses is reputed to have written the "Five Books" in the same chronological order as the inspired events occurred, and of course he must have written it all, before he died, which was months before the Israelites entered the Promised Land. The events of the forty years in the wilderness must have been written there in the wilderness where they occurred. Yet in Numbers xv it is recorded: "And while the children of Israel *were* in the wilderness, they found a man that gathered sticks upon the Sabbath day" (v. 32); and he was brought to Moses, and "they put him in ward, because it was not declared what should be done to him. And Yahveh said to Moses, The man shall surely be put to death" (vv. 33–36). This shows that the writer was not "in the Wilderness" when this was written, or he would never have added that phrase to it, as everything that occurred at all was "in the Wilderness." Moreover, the "Law" had already (as is alleged) been declared at Sinai, "whoever doeth any work on the Sabbath day, he shall surely be put to death" (Ex. xxxi, 15)—so this narrative is just another "mistake of Moses."

In Genesis XL Joseph tells Pharaoh, "I was stolen away out of the land of the Hebrews" (v. 15). There was no "land of the Hebrews" in the days of Joseph, nor of Moses, nor until some years later when the Hebrews more or less possessed the land of Canaan or the "Promised Land" under Joshua after the death of Moses. The famous Song of Moses in Exodus xv, in exultation over the destruction of the Pharaoh and his army in the Red Sea, declaims upon the effects of that catastrophe, occurred that very day, upon the nations for hundreds of miles around about, to wit: of Palestina, of Edom, of Moab, of Canaan (vv. 14–15). Moses sings: "The peoples *have* heard, they tremble" (v. 14, R.V.); which was impossible, as they could not so soon have heard the wonderful news, and their reactions to it be known again so soon to Moses. But the significant proof of long post-Mosaic authorship is in these anachronic strophes of the Song: "Thou shalt bring them in, and plant them in the Mountain of thine inheritance, in the place, O Yahveh, which thou *hast made* for thee to dwell in, in the Sanctuary, O Yahveh, which thy hands *have established*" (v. 17). This mountain was Zion, at Jerusalem, and the sanctuary was Solomon's Temple; and Jerusalem did not come into the hands of the Chosen until partly captured by David; and the Temple was built by his son Solomon, some 500 years after the so-called Song of Moses at the Red Sea, wherein these things are spoken of as already existing, made and established. So this reputed Song of Moses was written centuries after the death of Moses.

In Genesis XIV is the account of the capture of Lot, nephew of Abram, in a battle; Abram took a posse of 318 of his armed retainers and went to his rescue; and "pursued as far as Dan" (v. 14).

Now, "Dan" clearly did not exist in those times, nor in the time of Moses. This name of one of the tribes of Israel, descended from Abraham through his grandson Jacob, was given to the town (then named Laish) of the Promised Land which was captured by the Tribe of Dan during the Conquest (Jud. xviii, 27–29) some 700 years after Abraham and long after the death of Moses.

In Deuteronomy III, Moses is supposed to tell of a war which he had with the giant Og, King of Bashan, whom he conquered and killed. It is related (v. 11), that Og had an iron bedstead 16½ feet long and 7⅓ feet wide; and for proof of the whole story, it says: "Is it not in Rabbath of the children of Ammon?"—preserved as a relic unto those days. But Moses never saw or heard of Rabbath, and could not have known what was in its local Museum; for the town was first captured and entered by the Hebrews under David (2 Sam. xii, 26), some 500 years after Moses died.

A significant incident may be mentioned. During the forty years in the Wilderness the Hebrews were provided each day, it is recorded, with Manna to eat. In Exodus it is said, "the taste of it *was* like wafers made with honey" (xvi, 31); while in Numbers it is averred, "the taste of it *was* as the taste of fresh oil" (xi, 8). If Moses had eaten it as a steady diet for forty years, he would have known just what it did taste like, and he would have said, "the taste *is* like" oil or honey, if it were so diversely tasteful.

But the strangest feature of this inspired story is this—in Exodus it is averred that the People ate manna for forty years "until they came unto the borders of the land of Canaan" (Ex. xvi, 35). It was Joshua who led them across Jordan into Canaan, some time after the death of Moses, and Joshua relates for a fact, that when they got across the Jordan, they "did eat of the old corn of the land in the salfsame day, and the Manna ceased on the morrow, after they had eaten of the corn" (Josh. v, 11–12). Moses could not possibly have known when the manna ceased or have written of this incident happening some time after his death.

In Genesis XXXVI a list of Edomite kings is given and it is recited: "And these are the kings that reigned in the land of Edom, before there reigned any king over the Children of Israel" (v. 31). It was some 500 years after the death of Moses before Saul became the first King (B.C. 1095); hence Genesis could not have been written by Moses, or by any one until after the time when there were kings over Israel so that such a comparison could be possible. Again, in Judges xvii, it is stated: "In those days there was no king in Israel, every man did that which was right in his own eyes" (v. 6); which shows two things: that the Book of Judges was not written until during or after the time when there were kings in Israel; and that the "five Books of Moses," containing the Laws of Yahveh, were not written by Moses, and that the "Law" claimed to have been "given" at Sinai was not existent; for that "Law" specially forbade and fearfully denounced idolatry and minutely governed the whole lives of the Chosen People.

Several of the "Five Books" abound with the provisions of the priestly code of sacrifices attributed to Moses in the Wilderness, and are full of accounts of the manifold kinds of sacrifices made all during the forty years in the Wilderness. But all this is denied by the later Prophets; "Thus saith Yahveh Saboath, Elohe of Israel: I spake not unto your fathers, nor commanded them in the day that I brought them out of the land of Egypt, concerning burnt offerings and sacrifices" (Jer. vii, 21–22); and a chorus of them join in this refrain: "I hate, I despise your feast days; though ye offer me burnt sacrifices and meat offerings, I will not accept them" (Amos v, 21–26; Hosea viii, 13; Micah vi, 6–7; Is. i, 11, et seq.).

All this shows that Moses never received or wrote the Laws attributed to him and did not write the Five Books which relate all these things; and it confirms that this elaborate and intricate Code of sacrificial and ceremonial Law was a late priestly invention, unheard of by Moses, impossible in the wilderness, and unknown in all the intervening history of Israel, as we shall see in other places.

OTHER LATE-WRITTEN BOOKS

This same sort of simple but conclusive proofs produces the same result with the succeeding Books—Joshua, Judges, Samuel, Kings, Chronicles, etc., showing that they likewise are of a date many centuries later than their supposed times and authors, as they relate matters occurring all the way from David to the Exile about 500 B.C. To mention but an instance or two.

The Book of Joshua relates the death and burial of Joshua (Josh. xxiv, 29–30), and records that "Israel served Yahveh all the days of Joshua, and all the days of the elders that overlived Joshua" (v. 31), thus showing that the Book was written many years after Joshua's death by some one else.

In the Book of Judges it is recorded: "Now the Children of Judah had fought against Jerusalem and had taken it" (i, 8); whereas it was not until King David had reigned seven years and six months in Hebron, that "the King and his men went to Jerusalem unto the Jebusites, the inhabitants of the land," and tried to take the city and failed; "Nevertheless, David took the stronghold of Zion, and called it the City of David" (2 Sam. v, 5–9). So Judges and Samuel must have been written long after David was King and after Samuel was long since dead.

A most conclusive proof of Post-exilic composition or editing of these Books now appears. In Judges XVII is the account of Micah and the elaborate Idol-worship which he established, and of the silver phallic ephod which he set up in his house; how he hired a Levite to be his idol-master and priest; then these sacred trophies were captured by the Danites; and this remarkable historical recital is made: "And the children of Dan set up for themselves the graven image (Micah's ephod); and Jonathan, the son of Gershom, the son of Moses, he and his sons were priests to the Tribe of Dan *until the captivity of the land*" (Jud. xviii, 30). Here we have the grandson of Moses himself, and his descendants for generations, acting as heathen priests of idol-worship in Israel, so fearfully forbidden by Moses in his Law. This "until the captivity of the land" proves that Judges was not written for nearly a thousand years after the events related, and *after* the Captivity.

In 1 Chronicles reference is made to "the kings of Israel and Judah, who were carried away to Babylon for their transgressions" (ix, 1); which shows that these Books, too, were not contemporary chronicles of passing current events, but were compiled after the carrying away into Babylon.

As the Hebrew God and religion are principally to be found in the "Five Books of Moses," these instances of the late authorship of the other Books cited are sufficient for present purposes; other instances will be noted here and there as they may be pertinent. The purpose of thus pointing out the internal proofs that the Five Books of Moses, and the others, are of a date and authorship ages after Moses, is to show by the Bible itself that the records of the origins and development of the Hebrew legends, history, and religion, were not written by Moses, who is accounted to have been the medium through whom the Hebrew God Yahveh revealed these events and this religion; hence, that these revelations are not authentic emanations from Yahveh, God of Israel, but are mere tribal traditions reduced to their present form of writing many centuries after their misty and mythical origin; and that much of it all and particularly the Law, as we shall more fully see, was the creation of the Priests in the late and declining days of the nation, and after the captivity. These facts also illuminate the question of the inspiration of the

"Holy Scriptures," on which depends their claim to full faith and credit.

The "Yahveh" and "Elohim" Phases

In connection with the question of authorship of the Hebrew "Scriptures," there is another feature which is eloquent and conclusive proof of the human workmanship, and not divine "revelation" of the Holy Writ. This is very apparent in the Books written in the Hebrew language, and is of course known to all scholars. It is also evident in our English translations, where it can be readily traced through large portions of the Books by the use of the English words "God," "Lord" and "Lord God," as the original Hebrew words are therein translated falsely.

In a word, by these proofs it is manifest: that there were at least two older, independent, and contradictory sources of the present "Scriptures," that have been used, and very uncritically and carelessly patched together by later compilers who have worked them into more or less their present form. This is very apparent and very easily followed through the Books. One of the older writers or schools of writers, of the Scripture records, *always*, in speaking of the Hebrew deity, makes use of the generic words "El," "Elohe," or "Elohim" (God, Gods), to designate their tribal divinity; the other or second school *invariably* uses the *personal name* "Yahveh," or Jehovah.

The first writer, or school is thus designated as Elohist, or by the initial "E"; the latter is called "Jahvist," and designated by the letter "J": these two original sources are together designated as "EJ." As even a cursory perusal of the Books will prove, these two original "Elohim" and "Yahveh" records were at some later time combined into one record, in more or less its present form, evidently by reckless and "priestly" editors, adding much material of their own; this composite product is designated by the initial "P," for priestly. Other minor sources and combinations are also to be discovered; but "E" and "J" tell the remarkable tale—the "twice-told tale"—of revelation and inspiration, beyond all contradiction—but *contradictorily, always.*

A Parenthesis of Explanation

A critical study of the Hebrew Scriptures by competent scholars reveals that their present form results from much and very uncritical editing and patching together of ancient traditions, folk lore tales, and older written records, long after the times usually attributed to the several Books; and indicates that the "Hexateuch," or "five Books of Moses" plus the Book of Joshua, took its present form around 620 B.C. The older parts of the composite, by the "Yahveh" writer, or "J," thus roughly date from about 800 B.C.; the "Elohist" or "E" document about 750 B.C.; one is considered to have been composed in Israel, the other in Judah, after the division of the Kingdom upon the death of Solomon. Each hostile faction of the Hebrews had common traditions, but each gave partisan interpretation and color to them; this resulted in the signal discrepancies and contradictions which are apparent when the two records are worked up into one without careful pruning.

Later, during and after the Captivity, to about 450 B.C., when national longings and aspirations were very strong, and the earlier tribal Yahveh was being evolved into a "one God of all the world," the Priestly editors, or "P," worked the Yahveh and Elohim documents into one whole, with fine dramatic skill, and much original editing, but total want of critical sense. Yet other editors, designated from their traces as "J2," "E2," "JE," and "R," worked the composite "JEP" over from time to time, to suit their own views, policies and tastes, and very freely making editorial additions and changes. All this can be followed by the Critic's eye through the Hebrew texts almost as distinctly as the blue water of the Gulf Stream can be distinguished by the traveler winding its way through the green waters of the ocean. And so the interested English reader can readily distinguish and follow the main sources of composition by the use of the different terms for the Deity, "God" for "El," "Elohe" or "Elohim," "Lord" for "Yahveh," and "Lord God" for the Hebrew "Yahveh Elohim."

It may not be without interest to mention that the personal God-name "Yahveh" occurs some 6000 times in the Hebrew Scriptures; the noun "El," meaning God or Spirit, occurs but two hundred and sixteen times, while "Elohim," which is the plural and means Spirits or gods, is found some 2570 times; and the "dual plural" form "Elohe" is used many times, in "composition," as "Yahveh, Elohe Yishrael." Further on we shall note another highly significant fact connected with this plural usage.

Other "Sources" of Scripture

The fact is very obvious throughout the Hebrew Books that the later compilers or editors of the "Scriptures" in their present form, often made use of older written materials, rather than always "spake as they were moved by the Holy Ghost"—who is not in those Scriptures revealed as having been known or to have existed in their days. This fact is proven by the fact that these "inspired" writers frequently refer to and quote copiously from older, uninspired, and now lost Books as the source of information as to the matters which they relate. The instances of this editorial use of wholly profane sources are numerous.

Thus in Numbers XXI, 14, it is stated, "Wherefore it is said in the Book of the Wars of Yahveh," followed by the quotation. The famous account of the sun and moon standing still for Joshua is related not as original "inspired" matter, but the story is told, and the writer makes his citation, "Is not this written in the Book of Jashar?" (Josh. x, 13); and this shows that the Joshua record was compiled long afterwards. David's Lament over Jonathan and Saul, in 2 Samuel (i, 17–27), is quoted in full, with the reference, "Behold, it is written in the Book of Jashar." This Book of Jashar is several other times quoted, as is the "Book of the Wars of Yahveh."

After relating all that is told of Solomon down to the time of his death, it is stated, "Now the rest of the acts of Solomon, and all that he did, and his wisdom, are they not written in the Book of the Acts of Solomon?" (1 Kings xi, 41). There are repeated references to, and quotations from the "Book of the Chronicles of the Kings of Judah" (e.g., 1 Kings xv, 7, 23); and the "Book of the Chronicles of the Kings of Israel" (e.g., 2 Kings, xiv, 15, 28). Other lost Books of sources, of uninspired secular records, are referred to, three in a single verse: "The History of Samuel the Seer, the History of Nathan the Prophet, the History of Gad the Seer" (1 Chron. xxix, 29). In another verse we have references showing matter taken from "the Book of Nathan the Prophet, and in the Prophecy of Ahijah, and the Visions of Iddo the Seer" (2 Chron. ix, 29). Again we are referred to "the Histories of Shemaiah the Prophet and of Iddo the Seer, concerning Genealogies" (2 Chron. xii, 15). And we are told that "the rest of the acts of Abijah, and his ways, and his sayings, are written in the Commentary of the Prophet Iddo" (2 Chron. xiii, 22).

Again, "Now the rest of the acts of Jehoshaphat, first and last, behold, they are written in the Book of Jehu, who is mentioned (which is inserted) in the Book of the Kings of Israel" (2 Chron. xx, 34). And so, as to the other acts of Hezekiah, "they are written in the Vision of Isaiah, the Prophet, and in the Book of the

Kings of Judah and Israel" (2 Chron. xxxii, 32). At the close of
the Scripture sketch of each of the several Kings of Judah and of
Israel occurs the editorial reference to the source of the chronicled
events in the formula, "Now the rest of his acts are written in the
Book" the name of which is given in each instance.

That the whole of Chronicles, 1 and 2, was written after the
"return from Captivity," is apparent from the plain statement of
the text, following the first eight chapters of "genealogies," "So all
Israel were reckoned by genealogies; and behold, they were written
in the Book of the Kings of Israel and Judah, who were carried away
to Babylon for their transgression" (1 Chron. ix, 1). This is true,
too, of the Books of Kings, which together with Chronicles, form
each one single Book in the Hebrew sacred Writings.

The "Vision of Isaiah the Prophet, in the Book of the Kings
of Judah and Israel" (2 Chron. xxxii, 32), and also "The Acts of
the Kings of Israel" (2 Chron. xxxiii, 18), are other cited works
lost to posterity; as is also the quaint and curious volume of forgotten lore entitled "The Sayings of the Seers" (2 Chron. xxxiii,
19). A purely Pagan source of some of the apochryphal material
of the Book of Esther is said to be found in "The Book of the
Chronicles of the Kings of Media and Persia" (Esther x, 2). There
is no claim at all that any of these many Books of "sources" of
Hebrew Scripture was inspired or was in any sense the "Word of
God"; they were commonplace lay chronicles and books of history
or literature. So that very large and material portions of "inspired" Hebrew Scriptures are from entirely uninspired and human
sources. We shall see and judge of the other portions in due order.

DUPLICATIONS OF INSPIRATION

There are, moreover, numerous passages and even whole Chapters of the Hebrew Bible which are in identical words, showing that
the one was copied bodily from the other, or from a common older
source, as is mostly the case, and without giving the customary
editorial credit to the original authors. A God would hardly "repeat
himself" thus. Instances of these duplications of text may be multiplied: they very materially discount the theory of original inspiration of the copyists.

A notable instance, because the duplications immediately follow one another in the English versions (but not in the Hebrew
Scriptures), are the last two verses of the last Chapter of 2 Chronicles (xxxvi, 22–23), which are identical with the first two and a

half verses of Ezra (i, 1–3). The Hebrew writer puts into the mouth of the Pagan King Cyrus the avowal, "The Lord God (Heb. Yahveh Elohim) of heaven hath given me all the kingdoms of the earth; and he (Yahveh) hath charged me to build him an house at Jerusalem" (Ezra i, 2). Cyrus could hardly, as a good Persian Pagan, have thus discredited his own gods in favor of the tribal god of the captive Jews. The latter half of verse 3 affords a signal instance of conscious mis-translation on the part of the Clergymen of King James who did the work. It is recited that Yahveh "stirred up the spirit of Cyrus, King of Persia," to build a house for Yahveh in Jerusalem; and Cyrus issued a proclamation in writing to the Captive Hebrews, which is quoted in the English Versions thus deceptively: "Whosoever there is among you of all his people, his God be with him, and let him go up to Jerusalem, which is in Judah, and build the house of Yahveh, the God of Israel, (*he is the God,*) which is in Jerusalem" (Ezra i, 3). Thus the Pagan King Cyrus is made to appear to make the wonderful public admission (though in parentheses) that "Yahveh he is *the* God." But the original Hebrew text reads: "Yahveh, Elohe Israel, he is the *God which is in Jerusalem*"; as may be read in the original Hebrew without the parentheses, and as is shown in small type in the margin of the Revised Version; but the Authorized or King James Version wholly distorts the truth.

Several other instances of duplication of long passages or Chapters may be cited out of many others. The "Song of David" in 2 Samuel XXII and Psalm XVIII; the battle between the Philistines and Israelites, in which Saul was killed, in 1 Samuel XXXI and 1 Chronicles X. The latter account adds two verses extra (13–14), giving as the reason why Saul was killed in the battle, because he went and inquired of the Witch of En-Dor, "and enquired not of Yahveh"; though it is expressly stated, in the account of his visit to the Witch, and as the reason why Saul had recourse to her: "Saul enquired of Yahveh, and Yahveh answered him not" (1 Sam. xxviii, 6); and "then said Saul unto his servants, Seek me a woman that hath a familiar spirit" (v. 7)—after Yahveh had been enquired of and refused response. The Priest applied to was evidently not friendly to Saul.

Other whole Chapters practically identical, are the accounts of the buildings of Solomon's Temple, in 1 Kings v–vii and 2 Chronicles ii–iv; though in 1 Kings it is stated that the two pillars Jachin and Boaz were each 18 cubits high (vii, 15, and 2 Kings xxv, 17), while in 2 Chronicles it is affirmed that they were each 35 cubits high (iii, 15). The making of David King and his taking of Sion, part of Jerusalem, in 2 Samuel v, 1–10 and 1 Chron. xi, 1–9; the removal of the Ark to Jerusalem, in 2 Samuel vi, 1–11 and 1 Chron. xiii; the "Finding of the Law" by Josiah, in 2 Kings XXII–XXIII, and 2 Chronicles xxxiv–xxxv. Other striking instances of such duplications of inspiration may be found, in 2 Kings xix and Isaiah XXXVII; 1 Samuel XXXI and 1 Chronicles X (see verse 10 of each for a contradiction); 1 Chronicles XVI, 8–36 and Psalm cv. All these and many other like duplications, with their many variations and contradictions, clearly show that the writers used older sources, which they copied and changed to suit their own notions or purposes, and were not worried with "inspiration" at all.

Inspiration and Contradictions

The composite origin and character of these Hebrew Scriptures, and the fact of distinct and contradictory sources worked up into a sort of composite hodge-podge with utter lack of literary or historical criticism and total disregard of self-contradiction, is further very evident from the many double and contradictory accounts of the same alleged event. Some minor instances of this we have just noticed.

These contradictions are indeed too many to be even cited here—they infest every Book and almost every chapter of Holy Writ from Genesis to Revelation, wherever the same event becomes a twice-told tale. At this place we shall notice particularly only the major early instances: the double and contradictory accounts of the Creation and of Adam and Eve; of Noah's Flood; or the Tower of Babel, and other lesser legends of Genesis. In other chapters we give special attention to the notable contradictions of the Exodus, of the Ten Commandments and the Law, of the conquest and possession of the Promised Land; of the Prophecies, of the Life and career of Jesus Christ; together here and there with such others as may be incident to the matter at the time in hand. But first of a highly important consideration to be borne in mind throughout.

The Laws and Test of Truth

In connection with the numerous examples of flagrant conflicts and contradictions in the inspired revelations of the "word of God" as recorded in the Hebreo-Christian Scriptures, I wish at the outset to call particularly to attention and constant remembrance, two very simple principles of correct judgment, which must govern at all times in determining what is truth. One is an eternal principle of human thought, the other an ancient and valid maxim of the law of evidence.

At the base of all human knowledge and judgment there are three simple rules known as the "Three Primary Laws of Thought." Of these the third in order is this simple proposition, on which all valid judgment depends: "Of two contradictories, one *must be false.*" Both of the contradictories may indeed be false; but one must be false inevitably. If an object is spoken of, and one person says "it is white," and another says "it is black," one or the other such statement must of necessity be false. Of course both may be false, as the object may be red or blue or vari-colored; but in any event, one or the other statement, that it is white or black, must be false, for it cannot be both. This is a fundamental law of thought or correct judgment, or of truth.

The other principle is somewhat complementary. Every judge declares it to his juries as the law of every jury case on trial,—for this ancient maxim is the law in every court to-day. As a Latin maxim it is: "*Falsus in uno, falsus in omnibus*"—that is, "false in one thing, false in all things." Not necessarily so as to the whole; for one part of the testimony of a witness, or of the contents of a document or book, or of anything said or written, may be false or mistaken while the remainder may be quite true and correct. The maxim merely means, as the court always explains to the jury, that if the jury believe that a witness "knowingly or wilfully has testified falsely as to any material fact" in his testimony, they are at liberty to disbelieve him entirely and to reject all of his testimony as false. The reason is evident; for if a person orally or in his document or book says one thing which is detected as false, everything else which he says or writes is at once discredited and thrown into doubt, and unless otherwise corroborated or shown to be true, may well be considered to be all erroneous or false. Often it is impossible to know with certainty what things, if any, apart from the provenly false ones, may possibly be true; all are tainted and discredited for belief by the parts shown to be false. This is peculiarly true with respect to the Scriptures, said to be in totality inspired and true: if some parts are proven false, the whole is discredited beyond possibility of faith and credit for any part.

Upon these two simple and fundamental principles of reason and of law, I shall proceed to "search the Scriptures, whether these things were so," to the end that all may judge of their inspiration and their truth.

If we find that the "Word of God" tells the same story in two or more totally different and contradictory ways, or that one inspired writer is "moved by the Holy Ghost" of Yahveh to tell his tale one way, and another inspired writer is so moved to tell it altogether another way, totally different and contradictory in the essence of the alleged facts of the same recorded event, we are forced to know and confess that one or the other record at least is wanting in God's inspiration of truth and is inevitably false. This being so, and there being no possible way or manner of determining which version is the false and which may not be, both must be rejected as equally false, or equally uninspired and incredible; and in either event, the theory of inerrant inspiration and of revealed truth of the "Word of God" is irreparably damaged and destroyed.

FATAL CONTRADICTIONS OF REVELATION

THE CREATION

The first Chapter of Genesis declares by inspiration that creation took place in six days, in this exact order: 1. On the first day light and day and night were created,—(though the sun and moon were not created until the fourth day); 2. on the second day, the "firmament of heaven," a solid something "dividing the waters which were under the firmament from the waters which were above the firmament"; 3. on the third day, the dry land, the seas, and all manner of plants and trees were created; 4. on the fourth day, the sun, moon and stars were created; 5. on the fifth day, every living creature that moveth in the waters, and every winged fowl; 6. on the sixth day, all manner of beasts, and cattle and creeping thing: then, afterwards, on the same sixth day, "God (Elohim) created man in his own image; *male and female* created he *them.*" And then (v. 28), "God (Elohim) blessed *them;* and God (Elohim) said unto *them,* Be fruitful, and multiply, and replenish the earth, and subdue it." And, running over into the second Chapter, this "Elohim" account concludes: "(v. 1) And the heaven and the earth were finished; and all the host of them. (v. 2) And on the seventh day God (Elohim) finished his work which he had made, and he rested on the seventh day." Thus all creation, *including man and woman,* was fully made and finished, in six days: no mention is made of any Adam and Eve, or Eden. This is the "Elohist" version of the creation.

Then, beginning with the fourth verse of the second Chapter, a totally different "Yahveh" account of creation of the world and of man, and without woman, all in one day, is related: "(v. 4) These are the generations of the heaven and earth when they were created, in *the day* that the Lord God (Yahveh Elohim) made earth and heaven." Then follows this description of the processes after the earth was thus already created: "(5) And no plant or herb of the field was yet in the earth; and there was no man to till the ground. (7) And Yahveh Elohim formed man out of the dust of the ground, and breathed into his nostrils the breath of life, and man became a living soul. (8) And Yahveh Elohim planted a garden eastward in Eden; and there he put *the man* whom he had formed. And he planted all kinds of trees in the Garden, and put the man in the Garden to till it (15). Then (v. 18) Yahveh Elohim said, "It is not good that the man should be alone, I will make an help meet (i.e., fit, appropriate) for him." Then (v. 19) "out of the ground Yahveh Elohim formed every beast of the field, and every fowl of the air, and brought them unto the man."

Before proceeding further, to the creation of the woman, we will note the glaring contradictions already apparent in these two accounts so far. First we see a creation of everything by *Elohim* (Gods) in six days; then a creation of the heaven and naked earth by *Yahveh* in one day. In the first or Elohim account, on the *third* day, after creating the dry land, Elohim (Gods) commanded, "(v. 12) and the earth brought forth grass, herb yielding seed, and tree bearing fruit," etc. But in the second or "Yahveh" account, after the earth was *all rough-finished* and ready, on the one day, it is declared: "(v. 5) no plant of the field was yet in the earth, and no herb of the field had yet sprung up." Then immediately follows the declaration (v. 7) "And Yahveh Elohim (Eng. Lord God) formed man out of the dust of the ground"; then planted the Garden of Eden, and all its trees, and put the man into the Garden. Nothing could be more contradictory than this.

There is another very notable contradiction: In I, 20–21, on the *fifth* day, the "living creatures" (Heb. nephesh hayyah), and the "winged fowl" were brought forth *out of the waters*—"Let the *waters* bring forth abundantly the *living creatures* (nephesh hayyah) and the *winged fowl*"; and this, of course, *before* the creation of man and woman on the sixth day; whereas, in ii, 19, *after* the creation of the man, and when Yahveh was trying to find a "help mate" for him among the animals not yet created, "out of the *ground* Yahveh formed every *beast* of the field and every *fowl* of the air, and brought them to the man."

Another notorious contradiction: In the Elohim version (i, 24–25), Elohim made every beast, and animal, and cattle on the *sixth* day *before* man was created. In the Yahveh account, as we have just seen, *after* the man was created and put into the Garden of Eden, Yahveh, "out of the ground formed every beast of the field, and brought them to the man" (ii, 19).

Most notorious of these creation contradictions, is that of the creation of the Woman. In the Elohim account, as we have seen, on the *sixth* day—after all else was created and done—"Elohim created man in his own image, *male and female* created he *them* (i.e. *man and woman*); and Elohim said, Be fruitful, and multiply, and replenish the earth" (i, 27–28): thus both man and woman were created on the sixth day, and were sexually equipped and commanded to multiply and reproduce. But in the second or Yahveh account, we have man created all alone, put into the Garden of Eden alone, afterwards Yahveh considers "it is not well for the man to be alone, I will make a help meet for him" (ii, 18). Then we have the very remarkable, not to say ridiculous, episode of Yahveh making all kinds of animals and parading them before the man, for him to choose a female animal help-mate or wife, but none was "meet," or fit, or satisfactory to him,—"but for the man there was not found an help meet (fit) for him" (v. 20). Then follows the Rib story, of woman being made from the rib of the man, and brought to him to be his wife (v. 22).

These are two totally contradictory stories of the creation of the earth, and of living creatures, and of man and woman. So, one is false. Hence, the notion of the inspired truth of God in one or the other of them must be abandoned as impossible. Of course, we know that both are mere fables and equally false, as wholly disproved by every fact of the sciences of geology, and anthropology, and astronomy, which prove that the earth, and sun and stars were countless ages in formation, and that human and animal life has existed for maybe hundreds of thousands of years, far beyond the lately discovered Neanderthal and Crô-Magnon men, who outdated the Biblical Adam by tens of thousands of years. But we will stick to our Bible "facts," and appeal not to the discoveries of Science, nor to the common elements of modern human knowledge, to gainsay divine inspiration of the Bible. The Book and its truth must be tried by itself. It is also evident on the face of these two conflicting accounts, that two different writers, "E" and "J" wrote them, and not Moses; and also that the third man, "P," who patched them together, did it in a very apprentice-like manner, and without any inspiration or critical knack at all.

The "Days" and Matter of Creation

A word of comment may be made in passing on a couple of points which have given occasion to much concern and controversy, in the attempt of some to "accommodate" revelation to the everyday facts of science. It is argued that the "days" of creation may be used allegorically or figuratively; that as "a day with Yahveh is as a thousand years," these Genesis "days" may well denote the indefinite eons assigned by science to the vast work of universal creation. (Catholic Enc., Tit. Creation, Vol. IV, p. 473.) But that the old Hebrew writers of these primitive myths had no such figurative notions, and by "*yom*," day, meant exactly the solar day of 24 hours, is very clear: six times, at the close of each day's recorded work, it is declared, "and the evening and the morning were the first day," or second, third, day, etc.

Why evening and morning marking the "day," instead of the morning and the evening, as is more natural and of all but universal usage in speech? Why, simply because the Jewish day began, and yet begins, in the evening, at sunset, and their "day" is from one sunset to another; so in writing up these myths it was conformable with Jewish customs to put the evening as the beginning of the day. Moreover, all the *eight* works of creation were stuffed into six days, so that Yahveh could "rest" on the seventh day, the Jewish Sabbath, or day of rest. In order to accomplish this, two distinct works, the creation of the seas and the dry land, and the creation of trees and plants, are assigned to one, the third, day; and two other works, the creation of the animals, and the creation of man and woman, are crowded into another, the sixth day, eight distinct works in all; so that all the work might be finished in the six secular days of Jewish ceremonial, and Yahveh thus be made to appear to institute and sanction the Sabbath by resting on the tabooed seventh day.

This obvious conclusion it is pleasing to find confirmed by the Catholic Encyclopedia—which makes many wonderful admissions without seeming to see their logically fatal effects. This scholarly authority thus admits: "The third day and the sixth day are distinguished by a *double work*, while each of the other four days has only one production assigned to it"; and it adds, curiously for it, but acutely and correctly: "Hence the *suspicion* arises that the division of God's creative acts into *six days* is really a schemation employed to inculcate the importance and the sanctity of the *seventh* day" (Vol. VII, p. 311)! From this it is palpably evident that the seven days of the ordinary calendar week were in the inspired mind and thought of the old Jewish chronicler who worked up the Hebrew Creation Myth.

All these material works of creation, the earth and the seas, the sun, moon and stars, were not created by the "fiat" or by the architectural skill of Yahveh out of just nothing,—for "*ex nihil nihil fit.*" From before the "beginning" of creation, or its constructive works, the material earth itself existed, but simply was "without form and void," or as the Hebrew words are, "*thohu,* desolation" and "*bohu,* waste" (Gen. i, 2). And the material waters existed, for "the spirit (wind) of Elohim moved upon the face of the waters" (v. 2); the waters not being collected together into seas until the third day (vv. 9–10). It is curious how the otherwise intelligent human mind can so struggle through centuries to "accommodate" sense and science to "what are patently early myths and naïve, childish, primitive folklore," as Dr. Fagnani, D.D., frankly calls these tales of Genesis, where these works are ascribed to "the gods" (*ha-Elohim*) by the express words of the Hebrew texts, as we shall see.

Some Significant Mis-Translations

Before passing further to consider variently recorded and contradictory phases of inspiration in the Book of Genesis and other sections of the sacred history, it is pertinent to call particular attention to some very peculiar mis-translations, rather than errors of translation, which with painful frequency occur just in those passages where they are most significant. As the translators were theologians, as well as indifferent Hebrew scholars, their scholarship may subconsciously have been tinged with theological preconceptions in choosing just the word in English to meet the needs of theological translation from the uncritical Hebrew. This practice began early and is persistent.

It is some very simple instances which I shall give, such as are apparent to one of very limited knowledge of the Hebrew text of the sacred Books. Any one merely knowing the Hebrew alphabet, and comparing a few Hebrew words in the original with the words used by the theolgians to translate them, possesses the whole secret.

"Adam" Means Only "Man"

The word "Adam," as the proper name of a man, is pure fiction and deception of the theologian translators of Genesis. The original Hebrew text, which a school-boy can follow in the excellent Beginner's

Text Book, "Magil's Lineal School Bible," says not "Adam" as a proper name, but "ha-adam—the-man," a common noun. There are no capital letters in Hebrew. We will notice some instances of this.

In Genesis I, 26, occurs the first mention of man, the first use of "*adam:* "And Elohim (gods) said, Let *us* make man (*adam*) in *our* image"; and (v. 27), "and Elohim created *ha-adam* (the-man) in his image"—male and female both together.

In Chapter II, it is said in the translations, that Yahveh formed the beasts of the field out of the ground (*adamah*), "and brought them unto Adam" (v. 19); "and Adam gave names, etc., but for Adam there was not found an help meet for him" (v. 20). But the Hebrew text says not so, mentions no "Adam"; it simply reads that Yahveh brought the animals "unto *ha-adam*" (the-man), and "*ha-adam* (the-man) gave names," etc.

In Genesis II, 7, "Yahveh formed *ha-adam* (the-man) out of the dust of ha-adamah" (the ground). And so, throughout the Book and throughout the Hebrew Bible, "man" is "*adam*" (not Adam), and ground is "*adamah*." Man is called in Hebrew "*adam*" because he was formed out of "*adamah*," the ground: just as in Latin man is called "*homo*" because formed from (Latin) "*humus*," the ground, —"*homo ex humo*," in the epigram of Lactantius. It may be instanced, that the Prophet Ezekiel many times represents Yahveh as addressing him as "*ben adam*" (son of man)—the identical term Jesus so often uses of himself in long after ages.

As the whole of the "sacred Science of Christianity" is built upon and dependent upon the factual existence of a "first man" *named Adam*, the now attenuated ghost of this mythical "Adam" must be laid beyond the peradventure of resurrection. The texts of the Hebrew Books will themselves effectively lay the ghost.

In Hebrew "*adam*" is a common noun, used to signify "man" or "mankind" in a general or generic sense; the noun for an individual man is "*ish*": and so the sacred texts make manifest. The distinction is exactly that of "*mann*" and "*mensch*" in the Teutonic languages. A few out of thousands of instances must suffice.

Chapters I and II of Genesis afford a number of these instances, as above seen, but these may be repeated along with the others, to get a fair view. Elohim said, "let us make *adam*" (v. 26), and "Elohim created *ha-adam*," male and female (v. 27). In Chapter ii: "and there was not *adam* to till the *adamah*" (v. 5); "and Yahveh-Elohim formed *ha-adam* (the-man), . . . and *ha-adam* became a living soul" (v. 3); and Yahveh-Elohim placed in the Garden "*ha-adam* whom he had formed" (v. 8); and "Yahveh-Elohim took *ha-adam*" (v. 15), and "commanded *ha-adam*" (v. 16); and said "it is not good for *ha-adam* to be alone" (v. 18); and made the animals and "brought them to *ha-adam*, . . . and whatsoever *ha-adam* should call them" (v. 19); and "*ha-adam* called names; but for *ha-adam* he did not find a help meet" (v. 20); and "Yahveh-Elohim caused a deep sleep upon *ha-adam*" (v. 21); and from his rib made the woman, and he "brought her unto *ha-adam*" (v. 22); and "*ha-adam* said, . . . and called her woman (Heb. *isshah*), because out of man (Heb. *ish*) was she taken" (v. 23); "therefore shall a man (*ish*) leave his father, etc., and cleave unto his *isshah* (v. 24); "and they were both naked, *ha-adam* and his *isshah*" (v. 25).

Chapter III: "And Yahveh-Elohim called unto *ha-adam* (v. 9); "and *ha-adam* said, *ha-isshah* whom thou gavest me" (v. 12); and Yahveh-Elohim said to *ha-isshah*, thy longing shall be unto thy *ish*" (v. 16); "and to *adam* he said" (v. 17); and "*ha-adam* called the name of his *isshah Havvah* (life), because she was the mother of all living" (v. 20); and "Yahveh-Elohim made for *adam* and for his *isshah* coats of skins" (v. 21). And Yahveh-Elohim said, "Because *ha-adam* has become like one of *us*" (v. 22); therefore "he drove out *ha-adam*" (v. 24).

Thereupon, "*ha-adam* knew his wife *Havvah*, and she conceived, and bore *Kain;* and she said: I-have-acquired (Heb. *kanithi*) a man (*ish*) with Yahveh" (Gen. iv, 1). Lamech said to his wives, "I have killed a man -*ish*" (v. 23). Chapter V is "the book of the generations of *adam:* in the day that Elohim created *adam;* male and female created he them, and blessed them, and called their name *adam*". (vv. 1–2); "and *adam* lived; and the days of *adam* were; and all the days of *adam* were" (vv. 3–5). In these latter verses "adam" is used (indifferently) without the article, and the Translators write it Adam, as a proper name; but all the previous and subsequent usage shows it is the same common noun for mankind. In the next Chapter, vi, "*ha-adam* began to multiply upon the face of *ha-adamah*" (v. 1); and "the sons of the Gods saw the daughters of *ha-adam*" (v. 2); and Yahveh said, My spirit shall not strive with *adam* ("Adam" was dead) forever (v. 3). And Yahveh "saw the wickedness of *ha-adam*" (v. 5), and he repented that he "had made *ha-adam*" (v. 6); "And Yahveh said, I will destroy *ha-adam*, both *adam* and beast" (v. 7); "and all adam perished" (Gen. vii, 21). And Noah was "a just man *ish*" (v. 9). Yahveh said to Noah: "And surely your blood I will require it; at the hand of *ha-adam;* at the hand of *ish* will I require the soul of *ha-adam*" (Gen. ix, 5).

The "Egyptians are men (*adam*) and not God—*El*" (Is. xxxi, 3); "El is not a man (*ish*) . . . neither the son of man—*ben adam*" (Num. xxiv, 19); prophets are "*ish ha-elohim*—men of the gods" (Jud. xiii, 6); "put not your trust in the son of man—ben adam" (Ps. cxlvi, 3).

All through the Hebrew Bible *adam, ha-adam,* is for generic man, *ish* for individual man; never Adam as a proper name.

"LIVING CREATURES" AND "LIVING SOUL"

Another signal instance of the pious practice of mis-translation at critical points for Dogma, occurs in these first two Chapters of Genesis. The Hebrew word for "soul" is "*nephesh*" always, and it means nothing else but soul wherever used. *Ha-adam* called his wife's name "*Havvah*"-life, "for she was the mother of all living."

In Chapter I we are given the account of how the gods (Elohim), on the fifth day, created "the moving creature that hath life" and "every living creature," out of the *waters* (vv. 20–21); and on the sixth day "the living creature" out of the *ground* (v. 24); and he gave to *ha-adam* dominion over "everything . . . wherein there is life" (v. 30). All these renditions are untrue: in each of the four instances the Hebrew is plainly "*nephesh hayyah*"—"*living soul,*"—as is stuck into the margin of the King James Version. The significance of this appears below.

In Chapter II Yahveh-Elohim (v. 7) formed *ha-adam* out of the dust of *ha-adamah,* and—in wonderful contrast to these lowly "living creatures," "breathed into his nostrils *nishmath hayyim* (living breaths), and *ha-adam* became a living soul (*nephesh hayyah*)." So here we have the humble "living creatures" (*nephesh hayyah*) of the dumb animal world, while "Creation's microcosmical masterpiece, Man," is endowed out-of-hand by Yahveh-Elohim with a "living soul" (but the self-same *nephesh hayyah*), and is thus the crowning work of creation, but "little lower than the angels" (Ps. viii, 5)! And then right afterwards, Yahveh-Elohim, wanting to provide a "help meet" for his wonderful "living soul"—man, out of *ha-adamah* formed and brought to *ha-adam* "every living creature" (again *nephesh hayyah*), for the-Man to choose a she-animal for his wedded wife! But the "living soul" man refused to be satisfied with a female "living soul" animal; so Yahveh resorted to the Rib expedient to provide a real human "help meet" for his masterpiece Man! So reads in good Hebrew the truth-inspired revelation of Yahveh, spake by "holy men of old as they were moved by the Holy Ghost"! So we see, that all "living creatures," animals, fishes, fowls, had or were "*nephesh hayyah*" (living soul), just exactly as the-man: or, the-man, with Yahveh's breath of life in his nostrils, became a simple "living creature"—(*nephesh hayyah*")—like all the other animals.

It is perfectly evident, that the "*nephesh hayyah*" or man, was regarded by the inspired writer as no higher in the order of creation than any other "*nephesh hayyah*" or animalistic "living creature." For he represents Yahveh as creating all the beasts of the field for the express purpose of providing the-man with a "help meet" from among them, a female animal consort by which to fulfill the Divine command, "Be fruitful, and multiply, and replenish the earth!"

So much for the peculiar "nephesh," which every where is the Hebrew word for "soul" throughout the Bible. No Theologian who is a Hebrew scholar will gainsay the two foregoing instances of purposeful mis-translation. Others will be noted as the occasion occurs.

THE "FLOOD" CONTRADICTIONS

To return to the contradictions of inspiration. The History of Noah's Flood shows the same conflicting compound of Elohist and Jahvist stories, and notable contradictions. Only one will here be noted. In Genesis vi, "Elohim" commanded Noah, and told him, "of every living thing of all flesh *two* of every sort shalt thou bring into the Ark, to keep them alive with thee; and they shall be male and female" (v. 19); and in v. 22 the Elohist assures us, "Thus did Noah, according to all that Elohim commanded him, so did he": that is, he took in two of every kind into the Ark.

But in Chapter vii, it is Yahveh who speaks, and it is recorded: "And Yahveh said unto Noah, . . . Of every *clean* beast thou shalt take to thee by *sevens*, the male and his female; and of beasts that are *not clean* by *two*, the male and his female" (vv. 2–3); and in v. 5 the Jahvist avows, "And Noah did according to all that Yahveh commanded him"—that is, Noah took into the Ark seven (or maybe fourteen, 7 male and 7 female) of all kinds of clean beasts and of fowls, and two of all the others.

Though it is curious to note, that the distinction between "clean" and "unclean" animals was never heard of until the Levitical Law of "Kosher" was prescribed and described by Moses, as is alleged, about 1000 years later (Lev. xi).

A remarkable circumstance, illustrating the great piety, if reckless improvidence, of Noah, may be noted in this connection. The very first thing the pious Noah did, after he and his family and

his animals landed in the neck-deep mud and slime of the year's
Deluge, was to build an altar and offer up a Thanksgiving sacrifice
to the loving God who in his Providence had destroyed all His Creation except the little Noah family ménage. It is recorded that Noah
took one each "of every clean beast and of every clean fowl, and
offered burnt offerings on the altar" to Yahveh there in the mud
(Gen. viii, 20). We have noted that it is curious how Noah knew
anything about "kosher" animals first defined by Moses. But the
prime wonder is, that as there were only two of all these different
kinds of animals and fowls ("the male and his female") in the Ark,
and Noah killed and burnt in sacrifice one (whether male or female)
of each kind, how the species was ever afterwards replenished on
the earth. Revelation—as so often at crucial points—is silent on
this wonder.

The Tower of Bab-el

The historical sketch given in Genesis X–XI of the gathering of
the Nations in the Plain of Shinar, their ambitious project of building Bab-el—"a Gate of God" to reach to heaven (xi, 4), and the
consequent "confusion of tongues" by Yahveh, is quite as confusing
as the resulting babel of their strange new tongues.

Vainly, it may be remarked, may one seek to understand why a
Fatherly God, who would not let a sparrow fall to the ground without pitying concern, should have wrought this grievous affliction
upon the new population of his earth, just at the time when they
would seem to need all the aid and comfort they could render each
other, in order to repair the devastating damage wrought by the yet
recent Flood, only about 144 years previously. But speculation
aside, we will carefully note the recorded facts of sacred History.

Chapter X tells of the families and descendants of the triplet
sons of Noah, Shem, Ham and Japhet; and how their prolific offspring, in only about 144 years since the Flood, had grown into
many different nations; and how these nations, of whom about a
score are particularly named, with their lands and great cities, were
"divided in their lands, every one after his tongue"—which would
lead one to the inference that each nation already spoke a different
language of its own; that there were, indeed, as many "tongues"
as there were "nations," sprung so suddenly from the three sons
of Noah.

This inference, that there were already as many different
languages as there were nations (it is probably true), would seem
to be strengthened by the repetition of that positive statement three

times, after the account of the offspring of each of the three sons of Noah. For the sacred record, after each catalogue of off-sprung nations, asserts, that thus the several nations "were divided in their lands; every one after his tongue, after their families, in their nations" (Gen. x, 5, 20, 31). And for a final seal of inspired assurance, it is in the closing verse averred: "These are the families of the sons of Noah, after their generations, in their nations; and by these were the nations divided in the earth after the Flood" (v. 32). And all these Nations from three sons of Noah, in only 144 years; while it took the seed of Abraham 215 years to attain to only 70 souls.

And in the same inspired Chapter x we read of the founding by these numerous nations of extensive kingdoms and of their building of great cities—including Babel itself already (v. 10), and mighty Nineveh (v. 11), and a dozen others named by their names in the inspired record. And it is recorded that these several large kingdoms extended from Assyria on the East unto Gaza, by the Mediterranean Sea on the West (v. 19), many hundreds of miles; and all these wonders of nations, and kingdoms, and cities, in 144 years of Bible time since the Flood. But, then, when one thinks of what the Yankees did in France in just one year, Faith is encouraged.

Had one read this in some less inspired and sacred chronicle, some more human record, less would be the surprise when one reads the Bible record, the first verse of the very next Chapter xi, that: "And the whole earth was of *one language*, and of *one speech*." Next follows a truly remarkable migration; that "they," i. e., all the people of the whole earth, all these widely scattered Nations in their great kingdoms and cities scattered from Euphrates to the Sea, of a sudden, abandoned home, and city, and kingdom, and strangely journeyed from the east,—(though many must come from the West from towards the Sea)—and they found a plain in the Land of Shinah; and they dwelt there" (v. 2),—certainly camped in the open plain, without house or home, for all this they had left and abandoned in their great Hegira. In proof of this, "And they said one to another, Go to, let us make brick; . . . and let us build us a City, and a Tower, whose top may reach unto Heaven; lest we be scattered abroad upon the face of the whole earth" (vv. 3–4). We need not stop to wonder why all these nations had left all their kingdoms and cities just to come out here in the Plain and build one City for them all; nor how, speaking each a different language, they could talk understandingly together to concert such ambitious projects.

Yahveh heard of this project, and, with natural curiosity, he *"came down* to see the City and the Tower" (v. 5), which were abuilding. And Yahveh said, to some one not named, "Behold, the people is *one*, and they have all *one language*"—(instead of the many Nations and many tongues of the just previous records)— "Go to, let *us* (who else not specified) go down, (though he was already come down), and there confound their language, that they may not understand one another's speech" (vv. 6–7). And this Yahveh is said to have straightway done, and he "scattered them abroad from thence upon the face of all the earth; and they left off to build the city" (v. 8); and it is further recorded: "Therefore is the name of it called Babel: because Yahveh did there confound the language of all the earth" (v. 9). This attempt at pun or play on words, and the meaning assigned to "Babel" as "confusion" is fanciful and erroneous; as below explained, Bab-el means "gate of God," and was the Chaldee-Hebrew name for Babylon. The Hebrew word for "confusion" is "*balel*." But as Moses,—if he lived at all— was "an Egyptian man," and probably spoke only the Egyptian language, it may be excused that he should mistake the philology of Hebrew words.

It may be wondered who of them called it Bab-el, for all their languages now at least were different, and what would be Babel in one of them might be a foreign word that meant the Bowery, or Hoboken, or Hell in some of the others. And it is a little curious that "Bab-el" should mean "confusion"; for already there was a City, built by Nimrod the mighty hunter, named Bab-el (Gen. x, 10); and we know that in Assyrian, Hebrew, Arabian, and other Semitic languages, "Bab-el" means "Gate of God," just as "Beth-el" is "house of God"; and "Bab-el" is exactly the native and Hebrew Bible name of what we know as Babylon, the City or Gateway of the God El, or Bel, certainly there an entirely Pagan Deity. What great sin all these new inhabitants of the earth had been guilty of, to bring on them this new great vengeance, is not revealed: mayhap by trying to build a Tower to reach to Heaven, they may have provoked a "Jealous God" by an effort to reach Him in such a direct and unorthodox fashion; though as yet the world had not received the revelation of the only possible route to enter Heaven, Belief.

JACOB'S LADDER, AND BETH-EL

Notably taller than the abortive Tower of Bab-el had yet reached toward Heaven, is the justly famous Ladder of Jacob, which actually reached from earth right up into Heaven, so that Yahveh and the wingèd Angels could and did pass back and forth upon it. True, Jacob dreamed all this; but then, "Life is a Dream," and very many of the most historical facts of the Bible, are they not also admitted therein to be dreams? Such was Abram's, of the Promise and the Covenant; and Joseph's, he of the coat of many colors, about the sun, and the moon, and the eleven stars: such also was that of the other Joseph, the Carpenter, about the paternity of the Virgin-born Child of Yahveh. And Jacob's wonderful Ladder was at least 5,883,928,333,800,000,000 miles in length to reach from earth to Heaven, as is elsewhere approximately shown.

Shortly after Jacob had hoaxed the blessing and the inheritance from his blind father Isaac, thus robbing his elder brother Esau of his dearest rights, Jacob started off to look for a wife, and was on his way toward Haran. Being overtaken of night, he slept on the wayside, a stone for his pillow. In his dream he saw the Ladder which reached to heaven, with the Angels; and Yahveh appeared to him and renewed the Promise. On awakening, Jacob recalled his dream, set up the stone pillow for a "pillar" (mazzebah); "and he called the name of that place Beth-el; but the name of that *City* was called Luz at first" (Gen. xxviii, 10–19).

The event is quite otherwise related in Genesis XXXII. Here Jacob had just tricked his heathen father-in-law Laban by the famous device whereby all the cattle were born "ringstreaked, speckled, and grizzled" (Gen. xxxi, 8–12), had stolen away in the night with his wives and the cattle; and after sundry incidents, Jacob was on his way somewhere (xxxii, 1), and he passed over the ford Jabbok (v. 22). Here stopping alone overnight, "there wrestled a man with him until the breaking of the day" (v. 24); and the stranger, who appeared to be Yahveh, changed Jacob's name to Isra-el, which means "Soldier of God"—though Jacob was fighting with God. And all this happened there by the ford Jabbok, which name Jacob changed to Peni-el (Gen. xxxii, 24–30). It is a bit mystifying to read a little later, that Yahveh met Jacob somewhere near a place called Padan-Aram, and without any fight at all, and without any apparent reason at all, Yahveh changed Jacob's name to Israel; and Jacob, on his part, set up a stone which he had not slept on, for his wives were along and he slept with them, and called the name of the place Beth-el (Gen. xxxv, 9–15). But the name of the place was already Beth-el, for in verse 1 Yahveh said to Jacob, "Arise, go up to Beth-el, and dwell there"; "so Jacob came to Luz, that is Beth-el" (v. 6); and such had been the name of the place when Abraham camped there 200 years before (Gen. xii, 8, xiii, 3).

JACOB'S BARGAINING VOW

A very instructive feature of this Biography of Jacob is the curious instance of his well-known commercial instinct, here recorded in connection with the last mentioned bit of sacred history. For Jacob vowed a vow to Yahveh, which in the Bible is a very solemn thing—but coupled here with a bargaining condition precedent, saying: "If Elohim will be with me, and will keep me in this way that I go, and will give me bread to eat, and raiment to put on, so that I come again to my father's house, then shall Yahveh be my God" (Gen. xxviii, 20–21); which seems to prove that Jacob had not yet adopted Yahveh. And Jacob makes a peculiar offer of bribe of Yahveh, saying: "and of all that *thou shalt give me* I will surely *give the tenth* unto thee" (v. 22),—which no one can deny was quite a liberal commission in return for wealth bestowed, even to a God.

In this proposition Jacob anticipated both the rule and the reason of the "Law," laid down some 500 (or 1000) years later: "Remember Yahveh thy God, for it is he that giveth thee *power to get wealth*" (Deut. viii, 18),—a reason often suggested for loving Yahveh. By some it has been thought that this exemplary bargain of Jacob served later as the approved precedent for the Priestly system of tithes, decreed by Moses (Lev. xxvii, 30–32), and every where and always since commanded and cajoled of all the Faithful. In any event, the constant Ecclesiastical refrain has ever been the same as that of something represented in Scripture as the Horse Leech: "Give, Give"; and the preferred measure has been that of Jacob's offered bribe to Yahveh of the Tithe.

SUNDRY OTHER CONTRADICTIONS

In addition to these larger contradictions pointed out in a small part of Scripture—and many others remain yet to examine, there are numbers of minor flat contradictions, of which a few may be cited.

It is recorded, "And Yahveh spake unto Moses face to face, as a man speaketh unto his friend" (Ex. xxxiii, 11); but just below, Moses is reported as asking Yahveh to show himself to him, but Yahveh replied: "Thou canst not see my face; for there shall no man see me and live" (v. 20). But Yahveh evidently desired to be reasonably accommodating; so he had Moses hide in a cleft of the rock, and Yahveh covered Moses with his hand; then Yahveh "passed by," and took away his hand, and let Moses see his "back parts," for, he said, "my face shall not be seen" (vv. 22–23). How Yahveh could "pass by," and still keep Moses covered with his hand, is not explained; but it seems to confirm Yahveh's repeated description of himself as being of "a mighty hand and an outstretched arm."

However, there must be some mistake in regard to the fatal consequences of seeing Yahveh. Holy Writ is full of recorded instances of "seeing Yahveh face to face." In Exodus XXIV, Yahveh celebrated the making of the "Covenant" by a Banquet on Sinai to Moses, Aaron, Nadab, Abihu, and the Seventy Elders, "and they saw the Gods (ha-Elohim) of Israel," and "they beheld the Gods, and did eat and drink" (vv. 9–11).

When Joshua crossed over Jordan between the parted waters, whether with the original Hosts of Yahveh or with their offspring "increase of sinful men" (Num. xxxii, 14), Yahveh commanded him to take twelve stones out of the middle of the river, "out of the place where the priests' feet stood firm" (v. 2), and to set them up "in the lodging place where ye shall lodge this night" (Josh. iv, 3) for a memorial; and it is stated, that Joshua had the twelve stones taken "and carried them over with them unto the place where they lodged, and laid them down there" (v. 8), which was "in Gilgal, in the east border of Jericho" (v. 20). But in the very next verse it is averred: "And Joshua set up twelve stones in the midst of Jordan, in the place where the feet of the priests which bare the Ark of the Covenant stood: and they are there unto this day" (v. 9), sticking up out of the waters in the middle of the river. But this is curious, that the stones were piled up in the middle of the river at the place where the priests had stood; for that is the very place where the stones were to be taken from, as commanded by Yahveh in v. 3.

In 2 Sam. XXIV, it is recorded, "Yahveh moved David to number Israel and Judah" (v. 1); while of the same incident it is recorded in I Chronicles XXI, that "Satan provoked David to number Israel" (v. 1)—a strange confusion of personages.

In 1 Samuel XVI, the first meeting of Saul and David is related, to the effect: that "an evil spirit from Yahveh troubled Saul" quite often; and music was recommended to him as having "power to soothe the savage breast," and that "a son of Jesse" was a good musician, "cunning in playing, and a mighty man of valor, and a man of war." So Saul sent messengers to Jesse, saying "Send me David thy son, which is with the sheep"; and Jesse sent David to Saul, who saw him now for the first time, and David became Saul's armor-bearer.

But in the next Chapter XVII, David is introduced to Saul as if
never heard of before, as the youngest of eight sons of Jesse.
Three older sons of Jesse were in Saul's army, while the "mighty
man of war," David, stayed home tending his father's sheep; his
father sent him to the camp to carry food to his soldier brothers.
Here David saw Goliath and heard his braggart defiance of the
"living gods" of Israel, and David wanted to fight him; this was
reported to Saul, and "Saul sent for David" (v. 31), thus for the
first time meeting David. Saul expostulated with David, saying,
"Thou art not able to go against this Philistine to fight with him;
for thou art but a youth, and he is a man of war from his youth"
(v. 33)—which seems to discount the just previous description of
David as "a mighty man of valor, a man of war" himself.

But greater surprises follow. Every child in Sunday School
knows the heroic encounter between David and Goliath; how the
stripling David went out unarmed save with a sling and some pebbles
against the full-panoplied Giant; how David put a pebble in his
sling as he ran forward, "and slang it, and smote the Philistine in
his forehead, that the stone sunk into his forehead; and he fell upon
his face to the earth" (1 Sam. xvii, 49); and David took Goliath's
sword and cut off the dead giant's head (v. 51); and David took
the head "and brought it to Jerusalem; and he put his armor in
his tent" (v. 54). David, a country shepherd, just come to camp
to bring dinner, would hardly have had a tent; and surely he did
not take Goliath's head to Jerusalem; for Jerusalem was the stronghold of the Jebusites, and not till David was seven and a half years
King, many years after, did he even take and enter a small corner
of Jerusalem, Sion.

But all the romance and heroism of the Tale are entirely robbed
away by the flat contradiction of the whole episode; David did not
kill Goliath at all. Some forty years later, when Saul was long since
dead, and when David was King and was at war with the Philistines,
"there was again a battle in Gob with the Philistines, where Elhanan
the son of Jaareoregim, a Bethlehemite, slew Goliath the Gittite, the
staff of whose spear was like a weaver's beam" (2 Sam. xxi, 19)!
Here the Translators slip in another "pious fraud": the verse is
made to read "slew *the brother of* Goliath"—the words "the brother
of" being in italics, to indicate to the knowing that such italicized
words are not in the original; nor are they in the Hebrew, as any
honest scholar will admit. The Revised Version fairly omits "the
brother of," but puts these words in the margin, with a reference
to 1 Chronicles xx, 5. Here it is quite differently related, that

"Elhanan the son of *Jair* slew *Lahmi* the brother of Goliath the Gittite, whose spear staff was like a weaver's beam." Further confusion of both phases of the narrative is furnished by the duplicated verses about the giant in Gath, with six fingers and six toes on each hand and foot, who like Goliath, "defied Israel," and Jonathan, the son of Shimeah the *brother* of David slew him" (2 Sam. xxi, 20–21, and 1 Chron. xx, 6–7).

As for Saul's death, in 1 Samuel xxxi, it is related that in a battle with the Philistines, Saul's army was defeated, and Saul was wounded and in danger of capture; so Saul ordered his armorbearer (but clearly not David), to kill him, but the latter refused; "therefore Saul took a sword and fell upon it" (v. 4); he killed himself, and "so Saul died" (v. 5). But in 2 Samuel i, the story is quite otherwise: Saul made this request to a young Amalekite (v. 8), who "happened by chance" (v. 6) upon the scene of battle at Mt. Gilboa,—(therefore *not* Saul's armorbearer)—and this stranger complied with Saul's request and killed Saul (v. 10), and took his crown and bracelet to David, who rewarded him by murdering him on the spot (v. 15).

This must suffice for the nonce; many, many other contradictions abound in the inspired records. But these instances of patent contradictions between these recorded "revelations" and "inspired" truths, suffice to illustrate the constant violation of the two rules of reason and of law which I have quoted, and to demonstrate that at least one of each version of these inspired conflicting records is wholly wanting in truth. Besides, we have seen some high lights of Scripture inspiration.

CHAPTER III

THE PATRIARCHS AND THE COVENANTS OF YAHVEH

In the year 1996 b.c. according to the chronology of Bishop Ussher printed in the margins of well-edited Bibles, or just 352 years after Noah's Flood which destroyed the world and all that therein was, except the Noah ménage and menagerie, was born a heathen Chaldee who was christened Abram—(Abu-ramu, an ancient and ordinary Babylonian name, meaning a high father). Abram's father Terah was at that time 70 years old (Gen. xi, 26); although born, according to the Bishop, in 2126, which would make him 130 years old; and the sacred text (Gen. xi, 32) tells us that he died at the age of 205 years, just as Abram was celebrating his 75th, or 130th, anniversary, according as the Bible or the Bishop is followed,—this being his age when, upon the death of Terah, Abram started on his memorable Trek for the Land of Canaan, below related.

The Terah-Abram family were Chaldean nomads and lived in tents, and had some cattle and sheep, which Abram helped tend. On their own initiative, the family had started West—"to go into the Land of Canaan" (Gen. xi, 31); but stopped on the way and dwelt, until Terah's death, at Haran. Up to this time the Terah-Abram family, like their Chaldean neighbors, were of course heathens, who had never heard of Yahveh—"they served other gods" (Josh. xxiv, 2), wandering about and herding cattle, with nothing unusual in their lives, except that Sarai, Abram's wife, was barren, and gave him no hopes of a posterity to preserve his name and to worship his ancestral numen.

The Splendid Civilization of Abram's Time

At this time, despite Noah's then recent Flood, which "destroyed everything from upon the earth" (Gen. vii, 23), the Chaldean, Assyrian and Egyptian Kingdoms all about him were and for centuries had been mighty and highly civilized nations, with a culture and a literature preeminent in the cultured East. Books and

62

Libraries abounded, in which were graven tablets and monuments preserving their most ancient records and sacred legends, all of which long antedated the much later Hebrew lore, and many of which sound suspiciously like the actual prototype and source of the inspired Bible records of the descendants of Father Abram, as a cursory glance at some of them will reveal.

The Assyrian Libraries, of Abram's own country, contained wonderful riches of the most primitive literature of the ancient world, occurring from prehistoric, and ante-Deluvian, times, or about 7000 years B.C. Among the ruins of its ancient cities some 300,000 writings and inscriptions have been discovered, of which only about one-fifth has as yet been published; but even this contains more than eight times as much literature as the bulk of the Hebrew Old Testament. One of the famous Assyrian Books, the Babylonian "Epic of Creation," may be noticed; it begins, very like Genesis:

> "When the heavens above were not yet named,
> Or the earth beneath had recorded a name,
> In the beginning the Deep was their generator,
> The Chaos of the Sea was the mother of them all."

Out of this primeval Chaos the great God Bel brought forth Ansar and Kisar, the upper and lower firmaments; in a death-struggle between Bel-Merodach, the Supreme Creator God, and the Chaos-Dragon Tiamât, the latter was slain, and out of its divided body the earth and the seas were created by the victorious Bel, who established their fixed laws and orderly government; the heavenly bodies were next set up to rule the day and night and to determine the seasons; plants and animals were next created; and finally, in innocence and purity, the first parents, Adamu and his wife; then followed their temptation by the Dragon Tiamât, their Fall and Curse; the subsequent sinfulness of the people of the earth, and the ensuing Deluge, which destroyed all except the pious Khasisadra or Xisuthros and his household, who escaped in an Ark which he was warned by the friendly God Ea to build, and into which he took with him, by Divine command, "the seed of all life," to preserve it for future regeneration; the waters overwhelmed mankind; the Ark stranded on Mt. Nizir in Armenia; the Chaldean Noah sent out, one after the other, a dove, a swallow, and a raven, the latter of which returned not, having found dry land; whereupon the pious Xisuthros went forth from the Ark, and made a thanksgiving sacrifice of some of his animals, but not so improvidently as did Noah; the repopulation

of the earth proceeded; the presumptious people began the building
of a great Tower of Bab-el to reach to Heaven, to the wrath of
the great God Anu, the Father, who,

> "In his anger also the secret counsel he poured out,
> To scatter abroad his face he set;
> He gave command to make strange their speech,
> Their progress he impeded."

All which has a very familiar and "inspired" sound to pupils of a
modern Christian Sunday School, whom it is quite unnecessary to
warn that all this is nothing but crude mythological fables of the
heathen God Bel. It is, of course, only the merest casual coincidence
that it sounds very much like the really true and inspired history
which, a millennium or more afterwards, "holy men (of the Hebrew
God El) spake as they were moved by the Holy Ghost," by way of
revelation from their God Yahveh, as we are assured it really
happened.

Among these venerable and wonderful records of the past, too,
is the most perfect of the Chaldean monuments yet unearthed from
the débris of the ages, the beautiful black diorite stele of Hammurabí, King of Abram's own native country about 2350 B.C., or
some 300 or 400 years before the advent of that Pagan Patriarch.
On this pillar of stone is engraved this monarch's now celebrated
Code of Laws, a thousand years before Moses got his famous Tables
of Stone on Sinai, writ by the finger of the Jealous God Yahveh
of the Hebrews; whereas, on Hammurabí's Stele it is the Babylonian
God Bel, from whom, through the Sun-God Shamash, Hammurabí
receives this code of Divine laws. In the preamble of his code he
styles himself "King of Righteousness," the self-same title as that
of Abram's Bible friend Melchizedek, the heathen Jebusite King of
Salem,—"priest of El-Elyon, God Most High" (Gen. xiv, 18); and
the Code ends with a series of blessings for those who will obey the
Laws, and a long crescendo series of curses against him who will
give no heed to the Laws or interferes with the words of the Code.
All which again savors of Biblical Sunday School lore, and is maybe
another singular coincidence.

The noblest of the Sciences, Astronomy, was a favorite of
Chaldean research, at the time and long before the time of Abram;
their libraries contained records, chiseled on enduring stone or
stamped on burnt tablets of clay, dating from the time of Sargon
of Accad, about 3800 B.C., some 1500 years before Noah's Bible

Flood, showing expert knowledge of the skies; the stars were numbered and known by name, and the Constellations were set in their glorious array; eclipses of the sun and moon were accurately predicted; the mysterious Zodiac was invented by the Chaldeans and had assumed its present order, a millennium before good old Father Abram roamed the Chaldean plains so uncivilized and superstitious as to make ready to murder his Heaven-sent child at the instigation of an idle dream or an inspired nightmare.

Such in a glimpse was the high state of civilization which, at the time our review opens, prevailed in the Chaldean country, and which then or a little later pervaded the land of Canaan, as is shown by its monuments and by the celebrated Tell-el-Amarna Tablets. While in Egypt, where the descendants of Abram migrated several hundred (215) years after, civilization was in glorious splendor: as far back as the 1st Dynasty, the Calendar had been astronomically calculated and established, in the year 4241 B.C., about 240 years before Father Adam's advent; and no break in its wonderful history, monuments and records occurs since that remote time. (See Cath. Enc., vol. v, p. 336). But the nomad Abram is not known to have had any schooling or to have been able to read and write; while some of his actions show him to have been far behind the culture of his times and country.

THE "PROMISE" TO ABRAHAM

In the year 1921 B.C. Yahveh, who seems to have been a total stranger to the Pagan Chaldean Abram up to that time, and had not been even mentioned since the Tower of Babel some hundreds of years previously, of a sudden appears to Abram, and told him, for some reason not recorded, "Get thee out of thy country, and from thy kindred, and from thy father's house, unto a land that I will shew thee" (Gen. xii, 1),—which is the very thing that Abram and his family had already done and had started to go to the very same place, of his own motion some years previously; for the whole family several years before "went forth from Ur of the Chaldees, to go into the Land of Canaan; and they came unto Haran, and dwelt there" (Gen. xi, 31).

Another mistranslation occurs in this connection. The English text of Gen. XII, 1, reads, "Now Yahveh (the Lord) *had* said unto Abram" to get up and leave his country, etc., as if this command had been given before the Terah-Abram family had left Ur "to go into the land of Canaan," and as if they had set out in consequence of such Divine command. But the Hebrew text simply reads, "And Yahveh *said* unto Abram" (*v-yomer Yhvh*), exactly as in every other instance where the English correctly reads (as to the verb) "And Yahveh said."

The Promise is here at Haran first made, and it is thus stated:

"And I will make thee a great nation, and I will bless thee, and make thy name great; and thou shalt be a blessing; . . . and in thee shall all the nations of the earth be blessed" (Gen. xii, 2–3).

So Abram again picked up, and disregarding Yahveh's command to leave his family and kindred, he took them all along (Gen. xii, 5), and they took the trail for Canaan, where they duly arrived at Sichem (v. 6). Here at Sichem Yahveh again appeared to Abram and renewed the Promise: "Unto thy seed will I give *this* land" (Gen. xii, 7), this being the first identification of the "land which I will shew you,"—after Abram was already there. Abram then moved on and "pitched his tent near Beth-el" (v. 8; xiii, 3),—though this place is said to have first been so named by his grandson Jacob, its name having been changed from Luz (Gen. xxviii, 19 and xxxv, 6, 15), as the incident is variously related.

A famine soon happening, as so frequently did in this "land flowing with milk and honey," Abram took his wife Sarai, who was about 90 but evidently attractive, and went to Egypt. The only thing which divine revelation vouchsafes us of this trip is the amorous passages between Sarai and the Pharoah of the land (Gen. xii, 14–16), which is omitted here as bearing a scent of scandal in Patriarchal high life. The same kind of incident occurred afterwards, with Abimelech (Gen. xx), with the connivance and even instigation of Abram; which does not speak well for his concern for the morals of his wife or for his own sense of decency and dignity, but it was well paid (Gen. xii, 16, and xx, 16). Isaac likewise, with his wife Rebekah, some 75 years later visited the same good King Abimelech, where a like sportive incident occurred with great pecuniary profit to Isaac (Gen. xxvi).

The Egyptian Slavery Proviso

After Abram's return from Egypt, quite enriched with the reward of Sarai's sporting with Pharaoh (Gen. xii, 16), Yahveh came to Abram again, and indulged in a bit of pleasant hyperbole, saying: "Look now toward heaven, and tell the stars, if thou shalt be able to number them: so shall thy seed be; I give thee this land to inherit it." The inspired historian then tells us: "And he (Abram) believed in Yahveh, and he counted it to him for righteousness" (Gen. xv, 6). But in the next breath (v. 8), Abram negatives this assurance, for he expresses his doubts and requires proofs, asking: "O Lord Yahveh, whereby shall I *know* that I shall inherit it?"—thus seeming to be not quite so believing without some proof. So, while Abram was in a deep sleep, Yahveh gave him a sign, or Abram dreamed that Yahveh gave him the sign (v. 17), which might have proved anything else or nothing at all just as well, but is pleasantly related, with accompaniments of the horror of a great darkness. Then and there Yahveh radically qualified his former direct and simple promises of inheritance, by a *proviso* (v. 13), promising servitude and affliction in a strange land for 400 years, but that after the 400 years, and "in the fourth generation" (v. 16), they should come into the Promised Land with great substance, the booty of the "spoiling of the Egyptians."

The territorial features of the Promise were amplified this time, the boundaries of the Promised Land being defined with the precision almost of a modern Treaty: "Unto thy seed have I given this land, from the River of Egypt unto the great River, the River Euphrates"; and Yahveh names ten nations over which they should rule (Gen. xv, 18–21), including the Canaanites and the Jebusites.

We may pass over Abram's barbarous treatment of Hagar and his illegitimate Ishmael, in sending them into the wilderness to die of starvation, because of the barren-wifely jealousy of Sarai and by the personal command of his God; though we may pause a moment to dry the tear we are wont to shed at the inspired picture of Hagar, with the loaf of bread, and bottle of water, and her little bastard Ishmael, all on her shoulder, wandering in the wilderness of Beer-sheba; which tears swell into sobs of pity as we see Hagar, when the water is spent, "cast the child under one of the shrubs," and go aside and weep, saying, "Let me not see the death of the chee-ild." It is very affecting; but when we look more closely at the inspired text of Genesis, we see (xvi, 16), that Ishmael was born in 1911 B.C., when Abram was 86 years old; that both were circumcised when Abram was 99 years old and Ishmael 13 (Gen. xvii, 24–25), the year before Isaac was born, when Abram was 100 and Ishmael 14 (Gen. xxi, 5); that it was at the "great feast" which Abram made when Isaac "was weaned" (Gen. xxi, 8–9), several years later (in 1892 B.C.), that Ishmael was caught "mocking Sarah," and was cast out into the desert with Hagar;" and thus the "child," which Hagar carried "on her shoulder" and held in her hand, along with the other·

impedimenta, was quite 16 or 19 years old, when the angel interposed and provided a well of water for them, saying, "Arise, lift up the lad, and hold him in thine hand"; and shortly afterwards Hagar "took him (Ishmael) a wife out of the land of Egypt." Thus even an inspired scribe may sometimes get his dates confused.

THE PROMISE OF ISAAC

In the meanwhile, Yahveh was pleased to visit Abram and repeat his Promise of "all the land of Canaan for an everlasting possession," but the Promise was burdened this time with what lawyers call a "condition precedent," and which Yahveh termed an "Everlasting Covenant," but of the kind that evidently does not "run with the land," towit: "Every man child among you shall be circumcised, when he is eight days old; and the uncircumcised man child shall be cut off from his people; he hath broken my Covenant" (Gen. xvii, 9–14). And Yahveh changed Abram's name to Abraham, "For a father of many nations have I made thee." When Abraham supposed that this meant through Ishmael, Yahveh told him, No, but Sarah thy wife shall bear thee a son, to be named Isaac; at which statement Abraham fell down in a fit of laughter, taking it all for a Jahvistic joke; but Yahveh confirmed his assurance and declared that Sarah should bear that child "at this set time in the next year" (Gen. xvii, 17–21).

This promise was later confirmed by three Angels; and when Sarah, who was behind the tent-door listening in, heard it, she laughed outright, saying, "After I am waxed old shall I have pleasure, my lord (Heb. *Adonai*) being old also?" for it had ceased to be with Sarah "after the manner of women." And when the Angels heard her laugh behind the door, they,—No, it is Yahveh who unexpectedly becomes interlocutor, he not having been as yet identified among the three men-angels;—Yahveh asks, "Wherefore did Sarah laugh?" and Sarah denied it and said, "I laughed not"; and Yahveh said, "Nay, but thou didst"; and we know not where this "passing the lie" between the Lord and the Lady would have led, had not the angel-men suddenly left and Yahveh abruptly changed the subject (Gen. xviii, 10–16).

ISAAC'S DUBIOUS PATERNITY

In this connection a subtle suspicion as to the paternity of Isaac intrudes itself. Yahveh had promised Abraham (v. 10) "and Sarah thy wife shall have a son." But the inspired record is silent as to any performance or attempt thereat on the part of the aged Patriarch; and Yahveh himself, when Sarah laughed behind the tent door that her "lord is old also," reassured her, "Is anything too hard for Yahveh?" (v. 14). And it is afterwards recorded (Gen. xxi, 1–2) that "Yahveh visited Sarah as he had said, and *Yahveh did unto Sarah as he had spoken, for Sarah conceived* and bare Abraham a son in his old age." So the record is somewhat ambiguous as to whether Abraham or Yahveh is to be credited with the paternity of the young Isaac, though the more positive indications favor the latter. And many ancient mythologies credit their gods with like visitations to fair human women. But, in any event, Sarah had her "pleasure," and she died happy "in Kirjath-arba: the same is Hebron in the land of Canaan" (Gen. xxiii, 2); another bit of geographic data which proves that Moses did not write the story; for the name Hebron for this place did not exist until Caleb captured Kirjath-arba (Josh. xiv, 13–15) in 1444 B.C., and changed its name to Hebron, several years after the death of Moses.

THE PROMISE RENEWED TO ISAAC

To Isaac Yahveh renewed the Promise, saying, "Unto thee, and unto thy seed, will I give all these countries, and I will perform the oath which I sware unto Abraham thy father" (Gen. xxvi, 3). Isaac and his people dwelt for a long time in the country of the Philistines, enjoying the hospitality and bounty of its King Abimelech; so great and many, indeed, are they said to have been, that Abimelech and the Chief of his army went to Isaac and complained, and said, "Go from us; for thou art much mightier than we" (Gen. xxvi, 16). This curiosity may be borne in mind when we notice the migration of the Jacob family, but 70 strong, including women and children, to Egypt; and remember how, after the Exodus of the millions of Chosen out of Egypt, they were time and again conquered and oppressed by these same Philistines.

THE PROMISE RENEWED TO JACOB

The Promise was repeated by Yahveh to Jacob, according to his dream there at the Ladder, with the same glittering assurances. Yahveh said, or Jacob dreamed that he said: "The land whereon thou liest, to thee will I give it, and to thy seed; and thy seed shall be as the dust of the earth" (Gen. xxviii, 13–14).

A striking peculiarity of the Promise is that it was given in-

variably in a dream, or dreamed; we shall see, in the event, that it
was in effect largely of such stuff as dreams are made of.

At Peniel (Gen. xxxii, 28–30), or at Padan-Aram (Gen. xxxv,
9), as the case may be, Yahveh changed Jacob's name to Israel, and
repeated his Promise, "To thee and to thy seed will I give the land"
—which was at the time owned and occupied by "seven nations more
and mightier" than all Israel, as often the inspired record avers.

THE MIGRATION TO EGYPT

In Bishop Ussher's year 1706, or 215 years after the Original
Promise to Father Abraham, the Jacob Family migrated into Egypt,
having multiplied to only 70 persons in all the 215 years since
Abraham; though we have just seen that Abimelech had complained
to Isaac many years before that his Israelites were "much mightier"
than the whole Philistine nation (Gen. xxvi, 16). It is important
to get this and its sequences straight, if the inspired texts can be
coaxed into intelligent semblance of accuracy.

Let us examine the inspired record. Jacob had twelve sons,
each of whom married or "took" women and had children. The
record and genealogies are set forth in Genesis xlvi, where they are
stated under the caption: "And these are the names of the Children
of Israel, which came into Egypt" (v. 8)—"Jacob and all his seed
with him" (v. 6); and after naming them all by name (vv. 9–25),
the record avers: "All the souls that came with Jacob into Egypt,
which came out of his loins, besides Jacob's sons' wives, all the souls
were three score and six (66); and the sons of Joseph, which were
born him in Egypt, were two souls: all the souls of the house of
Jacob, which came into Egypt, were three score and ten," or 70
(vv. 26–27). Nothing in the Bible is more positively stated than
this 70 into Egypt. Some very curious family data are revealed
respecting some of these 70, particularly as to Judah and Benjamin,
which reluctantly we omit in this cursory review.

AMAZING MULTIPLYING

The Jacob Family, 70 strong after 215 years since Abraham,
went down in the year 1706 B.C. to sojourn in Egypt. Here they
settled and dwelt in the "land of Goshen" (Gen. xlvii, 6), a sort
of original Ghetto of about the size of a small American county,
assigned to them because they were shepherds and cattle-rustlers,
"for every shepherd is an abomination unto the Egyptians"
(xlvi, 34).

In Egypt the Chosen soon became a race of slaves, under circumstances truly remarkable, and utterly incredible anywhere outside the Bible. In due course of Nature—"Joseph died, and all his brethren, and all that (first) generation" (Ex. i, 6), which was the 70 persons of the Migration; "and the Children of Israel were fruitful, and increased abundantly, and multiplied, and waxed exceeding mighty; and the land was filled with them (v. 7). Now there arose up a new King over Egypt, which knew not Joseph (v. 8); and he said unto his people, Behold, the Children of Israel are more and mightier than we" (v. 9); so he proposed making slaves of them, and proceeded at once to carry this plan into effect (vv. 10–11), without opposition.

How 70 persons, after one generation, could fill all Egypt and be "more and mightier" than the population of the greatest Empire of those times, is passing strange. And all this in only 30 years after the arrival of the 70; for we know through inspiration that the Chosen "sojourned in Egypt 430 years" (Ex. xii, 40); and Yahveh, whose word is sure, said "Of a surety they shall afflict them 400 years" (Gen. xv, 13), which 400 years is vouched for by the High Priest in Acts vii, 6. The "Oppression" naturally began only when the Chosen were made slaves by this Pharaoh "which knew not Joseph" (v. 8, *supra*), and it lasted 400 years; this necessarily makes the beginning of the "bondage" to date from only 30 years after the arrival of the Jacob Family of 70; so that in these only 30 years the 70 had become "more and mightier" than all the Empire of Egypt. Passing strange indeed. And stranger still, that without a word of protest nor a blow of resistance, this "more and mightier" Chosen People should submit to be made a race of slaves by a confessedly weaker and inferior Nation, passeth all but inspired understanding.

The "Sojourn" in Egypt

There in Egypt the Chosen People were totally forgotten by their Yahveh for 215 years, or 350 years, or 430 years, or whatever other length of time they were there, for here again the inspired record reads several and diverse ways.

In Genesis xv, as we have seen, when Abram was in his deep sleep and in the "horror of great darkness" (v. 12), Yahveh said to him, or he dreamed that Yahveh said: "Know for a surety that thy seed . . . shall serve them; and they shall afflict them 400 years" (v. 13); and Yahveh added, "But in the fourth generation they shall come hither again" (v. 16),—Yahveh giving the unique and seemingly inconsequent reason for this four-century "affliction" of his Chosen, "for the iniquity of the Amorites is not yet full" (v. 16).

The "Original Promise" is dated in the margin, according to Bishop Ussher, B.C. 1921, and the date of the Migration into Egypt as B.C. 1706, a lapse of 215 years; while the date of the Exodus out of Egypt is given as B.C. 1491, this indicating a "sojourn" in Egypt of only 215 years. This must be a mistake of the good Bishop, for the inspired text (Ex. xii, 40) expressly says: "Now the sojourning of the Children of Israel, who dwelt in Egypt, was 430 years"; while the same verse, in the Revised Version, even more explicitly reads: "Now the sojourning of the Children of Israel, which they sojourned in Egypt, was 430 years,"—which proves that they must have passed the full tale of 430 years in Egypt from the Migration of the 70 under Jacob to the Exodus under Moses. But the check-up of the "four generations" gives us only a total "sojourn" of 350 years, as we will now examine.

The "Four Generations"

The Chosen were, in any event, to "come hither again" into Canaan, said Yahveh, "in the fourth generation" (Gen. xv, 16);—which however they did not, if the fourth generation, which left Egypt, all perished during the Forty Years in the Wilderness, as we shall inquire later.

These "four generations" are set out with minute genealogical detail of name and family, birth and ages, in the inspired record (Exodus vi, 16–20), running down the line of Levi, one of the sons of Jacob who migrated into Egypt with the 70, in the year 1706 B.C., by Bishop Ussher's chronology. We will examine this genealogy, as recorded in Exodus vi, 16–20.

Levi was one year older than Judah, and therefore, maybe, 43 years old, when the Jacob Family went down into Egypt. According to the recorded genealogy, which I will only briefly summarize, Levi was 137 years old when he died (Ex. vi, 16); his son Kohath, through whom the descent runs, was 133 years old when he died (v. 18); his son Amram, father of Aaron and Moses, was 137 years of age also when he died (v. 20); his son Moses was 80 years old when he led the Exodus from Egypt, in the Bishop's year 1491 B.C. (Ex. vii, 7).

With the greatest liberality of allowance in order to "accommodate" the inspired record: if Kohath had been a yearling infant

when his father Levi brought him into Egypt (Gen. xlvi, 11), and
if Kohath had begotten his son Amram in the last of his 133 years,
and if Amram had begotten his son Moses in the last of his 137
years,—which things are of course possible in the Bible, although it
would have been more remarkable than the 100-year-old paternity
feat of Abraham, which required a "special dispensation of
Providence" to procreate Isaac; yet these extreme numbers, plus
the 80 years of Moses at the time of the Exodus, total only 350
years instead of the 430 years of the inspired record of Exodus
xii, 40.

Moreover, Amram's wife, the mother of Moses, was his (Amram's) Aunt Jochebed, his father's sister (Ex. vi, 20), and hence
"the daughter of Levi, whom her mother bare to Levi in Egypt"
(Num. xxvi, 59). Levi, as we have seen, was at least 43 years old
when he went into Egypt, and he died there at the age of 137 years
(Ex. vi, 16), so that he lived in Egypt 94 years. If therefore his
daughter Jochebed had been born only in the last year of the 137 of
Levi's life, which was 94 years after his arrival in Egypt, and if
the "sojourn in Egypt" were 430 years, Moses, who was 80 years
of age at the Exodus (Ex. vii, 7), must necessarily have been born
—(430 minus 80)—in the 350th year of the "sojourn"; and his
mother Jochebed, would at that time—(deducting the assumed 94
years of "sojourn" before her birth)—have been at least—(350
minus 94)—256 years old;—which is somewhat liberally over the
allotted ages of the Patriarchs in those degenerate days; and even
with Sarai at 90 years of age, some 600 years previously, "it had
ceased to be after the manner of women," in the matter of child-
bearing. If the inspired Historian leads us into such mazes, the
present uninspired commentator will not presume to try to rewrite
sacred Scripture to improve upon it.

A Forgetful God and People

However, whether the "Sojourn in Egypt" were 430 years, as
the Scripture time and again says, or 215 years as the apologists
for this tangle say, or 350 years, as the inspired figures work out,—
it is true, as the inspired Record says, that their Yahveh had entirely
forgotten his Chosen People there for all this time; until, perchance,
at last, he "heard their groanings, and Yahveh *remembered* his
Covenant with Abraham, with Isaac, and with Jacob" (Ex. ii, 24).

And, reciprocally, for all these centuries, the Chosen People of
Israel were heathens utterly ignorant of the Yahveh of their heathen

Father Abraham: for Abraham and all the Patriarchs (as we shall most clearly see), all the time "served other gods" (Josh. xxiv, 2), and they all, while in Egypt and for ages after the Exodus, worshipped and continued to "worship the gods of the Egyptians" (Josh. xxiv, 14).

This total and mutual ignorance of Yahveh and his "Chosen," is proven by the inspiredly recorded fact, that when Yahveh after 430 years finally "remembered" his People and came down in the Burning Bush to see Moses about the Exodus business, and introduced himself as "the God (Elohe) of Abraham, the God of Isaac, and the God of Jacob" (Ex. iii, 6), Moses did not at all know or recognize him, nor had he or his People ever heard of him, for Moses had to ask, "What is thy name?" (v. 13); for, said Moses; "Behold, when I come unto the Children of Israel, and shall say unto them, The God of thy fathers hath sent me unto you; and they shall say unto me, *What is his name?* What shall I say unto them?" (Ex. iii, 13). A more complete ignorance of an "Unknown God" could not be imagined than this of the Chosen People of Yahveh the God who had forgotten them; though it seems strange for a God to forget, and particularly his own Peculiar and Chosen People for over four centuries.

The "Ineffable Name" Revealed

To Moses' very agnostic query, "What is thy name?" the stranger God replied: "And Elohim said unto Moses, *I am that I am:* and he said, thus shalt thou say unto the children of Israel, *I am* hath sent me unto you" (Ex. iii, 14). If Moses had been born and brought up in Egypt, and were indeed "learned in all the wisdom of the Egyptians," as Stephen assures (Acts vii, 22), and if he could have understood Yahveh speaking Chaldean-Hebrew, this name, or designation, or definition, or what not it is, should have sounded very familiar and homelike to Moses as well as to the Pharaoh, for it is exactly the current "ineffable name" of Supreme Deity in Egypt—"*Nuk Pu Nuk,*" as found explained under the title "Jehovah" in the Catholic Encyclopedia and in the New International Encyclopedia, among other learned works.

But this vague cognomen was evidently not at all informative to Moses, nor later to the elders, and was quite puzzling to the Pharaoh (Ex. v, 2); indeed Moses did not obey Yahveh and report this name to them, but oddly enough another, as we shall soon be surprised to see. Moses fared ill on this first trip to the elders and to the Pharaoh; and when he returned to report to the God, he addressed him simply as "Adonani—my Lord—the same exactly as Adonis of the Pagans); and Moses accused him to his face of "evil entreating the People," and that he had not delivered the People at all (Ex. v, 22–23).

Thereupon the God said, "Now thou shalt see what I will do to Pharaoh"; and he volunteered to Moses that his real name was Yahveh; and he explained that he had always appeared to the good old Patriarchs by the name of "El Shaddai (Heb. God my Daemon, rendered in the English translations as "God Almighty"), but that he had *not* been known to them by his real name of Yahveh (Ex. vi, 2–3).

A "PIOUS FRAUD" OF TRANSLATION

Let us quote this highly important declaration of Yahveh in the exact words in which he made it—as it involves an other truly remarkable instance of Jahvistic *lapsus memorie*, as well as one of the most notorious "mistakes of Moses" in all Holy Writ, and the most flagrant and persistent of the intentional falsifications of the ecclesiastical translators and editors of the Bible,—the deceptive motive for which will be made clear very shortly:

"And God (Heb. Elohim) spake unto Moses, and said unto him, I am the Lord (Heb. anoki YHVH = I am Yahveh):

"And I appeared unto Abraham, unto Isaac, and unto Jacob, by the name of God Almighty (Heb. El-Shaddai = God my Daemon), but by my name JEHOVAH (Heb. YHVH) was I not known to them". (Ex. vi, 2–3).

This explicit positive assertion from the mouth of the Hebrew God is belied by scores of contradictory instances, of which a sufficient number will be cited from the Hebrew texts, concealed as they purposefully are by the English and other translations, made to hide the patent contradictions of the Hebrew originals.

Here we have the positive averment of the Hebrew God himself, to the effect that here, for the first time since the world began, is "revealed" to mankind his "ineffable name" of YHVH, here printed as JEHOVAH in capital letters in every Bible translation. And in every Bible translation, from "In the beginning" of Genesis 1 to these vv. 2 and 3 of Exodus, and thence to the end of Malachi, the *name* Jehovah or Yahveh never once (or but half a dozen times) appears: always and only we read the *title* "the Lord" or "the Lord God" (for Yahveh Elohim), falsely for the actual and 6000-times reiterated *name* of the Hebrew deity. This usage conceals the fact that the *personal name YHVH* of the God thousands of times is used in the Hebrew texts, and thus apparently "harmonizes" the whole Hebrew Bible with v. 3 of Exodus VI, that "by my name YHVH was I *not known*" to Abraham, Isaac and Jacob.

To one who can but spell out words by the Hebrew letters, this "pious fraud" is apparent. "The sacred name," says the Catholic Encyclopedia, "occurs in Genesis about 156 times; this frequent occurrence can hardly be a mere prolepsis" (VIII, p. 331); and it adds, "in round numbers it is found in the Old Testament 6000 times, either alone or in conjunction with another Divine name" (Id. p. 329). Beginning in Genesis II, 4, where it is first abbreviated "YY," the *name* Yahveh runs throughout the Hebrew Scriptures. Scores of times the three Patriarchs named use the name Yahveh, and speak to and of their tribal deity by his *name* Yahveh, as well as by the designations of El, Elohim, Elohe, and by the title of address Adonai—"my Lord"; the same form in which superiors or masters are always addressed.

A very few specific instances among many, out of the Chaldee mouths of Abraham, Isaac, and Jacob, will serve to expose the falsity of the translation—and then the motive therefor.

As for Abraham: The very first appearance of the strange deity to Abram is thus recorded: "Now Yahveh had said unto Abram, Get thee out of thy country," etc. (Gen. xii, 1);—though the translators make it read, "Now the Lord had said." And so, every one of 6000 times, "the Lord" is used throughout, where the Hebrew original uses the *proper name* "Yahveh." Again: "And Abram said, O Adonai *Yahveh* (my Lord Yahveh), what wilt thou give give me?" (Gen. xv, 2, 8). And in verse 7 Yahveh says to Abram, "I am *Yahveh* that brought thee out of Ur of the Chaldees" (Gen. xv, 7). And again: "And Abraham said unto his servant, I will make thee swear by *Yahveh*, the Elohe of the heaven and the Elohe of the earth" (Gen. xxiv, 3).

As for Isaac: "And *Yahveh* appeared unto him and said, Go down into Egypt" (Gen. xxvi, 2). Again: "And Isaac said, Truly now *Yahveh* has made room for us" (Gen. xxvi, 22). And again he builded an altar there, "and called upon the name of *Yahveh*" (Gen. xxvi, 25).

As for Jacob: At the Ladder the God appeared and said to Jacob: "I am *Yahveh*, the Elohe of Abraham, the Elohe of Isaac" (Gen. xxviii, 13). Again: "And Jacob awaked out of his sleep, and he said, Surely *Yahveh* has been in this place" (Gen. xxviii, 16). And again: "And Jacob vowed a vow and said, if Elohim (the Gods) will be with me . . . then shall *Yahveh* be my God" (Gen. xxviii, 20–21).

Some 6000 times the personal name *Yahveh*, as the special name of the Pagan tribal deity of Israel, is used throughout the Hebrew Scriptures, and is every time falsely rendered "Lord"—which is not a name at all, but a form of address—as Abraham himself says, "Adonai Yahveh—"my Lord Yahveh." But some half dozen times is the name correctly rendered "Jehovah," and mostly where this rendering is forced by the compounding of the name "Yahveh" with another word or name, as "Yahveh-nissi" (Ex. xvii, 5); "Yahveh-jireh" (Gen. xxii, 14); "Yahveh-shalom" (Jud. vi, 24), passages where it cannot be well rendered "Lord-nissi," etc., and the translators are obliged for any sense at all to render it truly as "Jehovah-nissi," etc. And in Psalms and Isaiah, in a few instances: as where David sings, "That they may know that thou alone, whose *name* is Jehovah (Yahveh) art most high (*elyon*) over all the earth" (Ps. lxxxiii, 18); and where Isaiah says, "For the Lord Jehovah (Yah Yahveh) is my strength" (Is. xii, 2); and even here "Yah" has no business to be rendered "Lord."

However, as some 430 years had elapsed up to the incident of the Burning Bush, since anybody had used the name at all, or had even mentioned the God, it is not to be blamed that one's memory, even Yahveh's, may have been a bit rusty in the matter of names. The real blame, and shame, is on the deceptive translators: "The false pen of the scribes hath wrought falsely" (Jer. viii, 8, R.V.). But it didn't matter to Moses anyhow, for he was a Heathen who had never heard the name either way, and a fugitive murderer, his first recorded act being the murder of an Egyptian, for which crime he fled from justice into the Midian desert (Ex. ii, 12), where he married the daughter of the Heathen Priest of Midian, by whom he had one (Ex. ii, 22), or two (Ex. xviii, 3) sons, as later we shall notice with curious interest. But it is either an error about Moses marrying the Midianite, or he became a polygamist; for there at Sinai we are told that Moses "had married an Ethiopian woman" (Num. xii, 1), a Negress, to the great scandal of his family, and in flagrant violation of his own prohibitory Law against marrying heathen and strangers.

A CURIOUS MUDDLING

The most curious feature of this fable of the Burning Bush, betraying the utter childish-mindedness of the inspired historian, is the muddled use he makes of the "divine name" of his new-found deity. It is in Exodus iii, 13, that Moses asks the strange new God "What is thy name?" and in reply "Elohim said unto Moses: I Am that I Am"; and he said, "Thus shalt thou say to the children of Israel: I Am has sent me unto you" (v. 14). It is not until Moses returns from his first trip to the elders and the Pharaoh, that the God is made to make the wonderful "revelation" of his "ineffable name" Yahveh (Ex. vi, 2–3).

In Exodus I and II, and up to III, 6, the deity is spoken of as Elohim, ha-Elohim (gods, the-gods); but in verse 7, "And Yahveh said" to Moses, and told him all about his Patriarchal Covenant, and to Go, bring my People out of Egypt. Then, after telling Moses that he is "I Am" (v. 14), straightway "Elohim said unto Moses: Thus shalt thou say unto the children of Israel: *Yahveh,* the God of your fathers, etc., has sent me unto you: this (*Yahveh*) *is my name* forever" (v. 15)—thus anticipating by three chapters the unique first revelation of his *name* Yahveh (Ex. vi, 3). And the God again says, "Go, and assemble the elders of Israel, and say unto them: Yahveh, elohe of your fathers, has appeared unto me, the elohe of Abraham, Isaac, and Jacob" (v. 16). Also that "thou and the elders of Israel shall come unto the king of Egypt, and you shall say unto him, Yahveh, the God of the Hebrews, has met with us; and now, let us go, we pray thee, a journey of three days in the wilderness, and let us sacrifice to Yahveh our God" (v. 18). But Yahveh did not say "the God of the Hebrews"; for there were no "Hebrews" at that epoch.

Moses replied that they would not believe or hearken unto him, "for they will say, Yahveh has not appeared unto thee" (Ex. iv, 1); a rather remarkable telepathic knowledge of a name they had never heard of. Some ten or a dozen times the *name* Yahveh is again used in this chapter; and in verse 10 Moses uses both his name and the title of address, "my Lord," saying, "And Moses said unto Yahveh, Adonai—my Lord"; and Yahveh replied, "Am I not Yahveh?" (v. 12); "and he (Moses) said, Adonai—O Lord" (v. 13)—"and the anger of Yahveh glowed against Moses" (v. 14). So Moses and Aaron went to the Pharaoh and said, "Thus hath said Yahveh, elohe Yishrael, Send away my People," etc.; "And Pharaoh said, Who is Yahveh; I know not Yahveh" (Ex. v. 1–2); and so several times in Chapter v, always the name Yahveh—but always falsely, as everywhere, translated "the Lord." Then in vi, "And Yahveh said unto Moses" (v. 1); then comes "And Elohim said unto Moses, I am Yahveh" (v. 2), and in verse 3 the novel revelation of the supernal name Yahveh—as if never heard of, in Hebrew, before; and as never heard of—in the false translations, before or after, in all the translated Bible.

WHY THIS "PIOUS" FRAUD?

Why this persistent falsification in the Holy Word of God? First, as pointed out, and as must be very apparent, with purpose to conceal the contradiction of Yahveh's "revelation" in Exodus vi, 3. But there are other very signal motives for falsification. These I submit, not in my own words, but as capital, fatal, admissions of two high Theological authorities.

The distinguished Hebrew scholar, a Doctor of Divinity and Professor of Scripture in Union Theological Seminary, thus admits away the Christian Godhood of Yahveh:

"The god who is the hero of these (Genesis) stories is not the Supreme Cosmic God, the Father of the Lord Jesus Christ, in whom we live, and move, and have our being, but the tribal god of the Hebrews, according to their earliest and crudest conception of his character.

"He is known by two names: Elohim, meaning god, in general, and Yaho. The latter is a proper name, like Asshur, Moloch, Baal, etc. He is only one god out of many. Every nation and people had one or more gods. The Hebrews were forbidden to worship any other god but Yaho.

"Yaho is generally but less correctly given as Yahveh and Jehovah (better Yehovah).

"To use the word God or Lord God instead of Elohim or Yaho is misleading and disastrous. It conceals from the unsuspecting reader that the un-Godlike sayings and doings recorded are those of an imagined, primitive deity, not those of the God of the New Testament." (Fagnani, "The Beginnings of History according to the Jews," pp. 18–19; 1925).

This bodily takes the *Deus ex machina*, and leaves Yahveh and his pretended "Holy Word" a myth and fables.

The learned Doctor, after a number of other highly significant admissions of revealed Genesis tales as "patently early myths and naïve, childish, primitive folklore" (Id., p. 23), then with evident gusto quotes the Shavian aphoristic epigram, that "Fundamentalism is Infantilism," and comments: "Whatever we call it, it means complete paralysis of the intelligence, resulting from irrational surrender to *the blight of theological dogma*" (Id. p. 24). But it may be in turn commented, that "Modernism" is measurably worse as a display of arrested development of once-awakened mentality, than ever Fundamentalism. The Fundamentalists are victims of their own perfect and correct logic from, however, false premises; their theology is unimpeachably true if Genesis and the Bible be true. The Modernists, who repudiate Genesis, Adam, Eve, the Fall, the Curse, the Virgin-birth and Hell, are either wholly wanting in the logical faculty, or have not the courage of their convictions of the fundamental fallacies of their Bible. This is made so evident throughout, and particularly in Chapter XVII, that the proofs may be left to further perusal without repetition here.

Writing in the classic Encyclopedia, another scholarly Divine says of this habitual concealment of the name Yahveh in the Bible translations: "Various motives may have concurred to bring about the suppression of the name. . . . An instinctive feeling that a *proper name for God implicitly recognizes the existence of other gods* may have had some influence" (Encyc. Brit., vol. XV, p. 311–d). But as Yahveh himself and all his Book explicitly and a thousand times recognize the existence, power and effects of other gods, this apologetic reason loses force, and cannot excuse the pious fraud. A more frank admission of the reason for falsely rendering Yahveh as "Lord" is given as "the preference (by the Jewish translators of the Septuagint) for a term that should not bring to mind the old tribal deity after a more transcendental conception had been gained" (New Int. Encyc., vol. XII, p. 625).

This frankly admits Yahveh, with all the inspired revelations of him—to have been naught but an imaginative and local pagan divinity, and no true God at all. Yahveh is thus admittedly, by consensus of scholarly opinion, relegated to the pale shades of Mythology. Many Bible proofs confirming the modern scholars we shall duly pass in review, returning now to Moses and Yahveh and the Exodus.

A Peculiar Test of Prophecy

There at the Burning Bush, Yahveh told Moses, Go, bring the Chosen out of Egypt. But Moses was dubious of the Commission of the new-found Deity, and also feared to return to the jurisdiction where he had committed the murder. So Yahveh reassured him: "Go, return into Egypt; for all the men are dead who sought thy life" (Ex. iv, 19).

And Yahveh gave Moses a very peculiar *ex post facto* kind of proof of the validity of his present commission, assuring him: "Certainly I will be with thee; and this will be a token unto thee, that *I have sent thee*: When thou *hast brought forth* the people out of

Egypt, ye shall serve God upon this mountain" (Ex. iii, 12) ; which mountain was Horeb, or Sinai, the shrine of the Pagan Moon God Sin, somewhere in the Arabian wilderness, where Moses then was, tending the sheep of his heathen father-in-law (Ex. iii, 1).

And Yahveh thereupon told Moses of his Promise to the Fathers, and told him to report it to the elders of Israel—proving that neither Moses nor the elders of Israel had ever before heard of Yahveh and his Everlasting Covenant of 645 years ago to Abraham: "And I have said, I will bring you up out of the affliction of Egypt, unto the land of the Canaanites, and the Hittites, and the Amorites, and the Perizites, and the Hivites, and the Jebusites" (Ex. iii, 17) ; which peoples, as Yahveh himself and Moses several times assert, were "seven nations greater and mightier" than all Israel (Deut. iv, 38) ; and the Pharaoh is quoted as complaining 400 years before: "Behold, the people of the Children of Israel are more and mightier than we" (Ex. i, 9) ; while Yahveh, again to the contrary, expressly says that his Chosen of Israel "were the fewest of all people (Deut. vii, 7).

Some Assurances of Success

Yahveh God of Israel further told Moses to gather together the elders of Israel, and to go to Pharaoh and give him a false reason: "Let us go three days' journey into the wilderness, that we may sacrifice unto Yahveh our God" (Ex. iii, 18) ; and added, that he knew that Pharaoh would not let them go; and that he, Yahveh, would then smite Egypt with all his wonders—the Plagues—after which the Pharaoh would let them go. And the same God of Israel told Moses that he, God, would help the Chosen to cheat the Egyptians and enable them to steal all their jewelry and clothes—"and ye shall spoil the Egyptians" (Ex. iii, 22). This would be wicked enough on the part of Ali Baba and his 40 Thieves, or of Barbary Pirates, and under any ordinary Code of human law would be common crime, and the instigator would be criminal "accessory before the fact"; but this is the Holy Bible, and Yahveh is called holy and just.

But this advice did not at once appeal to Moses, who had been well brought up in the Court of Egypt, although now a fugitive murderer; and he objected that the elders would not believe him or that Yahveh had appeared to him and told him these things. So the mighty Yahveh resorted to conjure, and turned a stick into a snake and turned the snake back into the stick—a trick that the conjurors of Egypt afterwards quite outdid (Ex. vii, 10–11).

So Moses was persuaded, and he took his heathen wife and two sons (Ex. iv, 20, xviii, 3), or one son (Ex. ii, 22, iv, 25), or left them all at home (Ex. xviii, 2–3)—according to the inspired text preferred—and started on the trek across the desert to Egypt, carrying the conjure rod with him. And the parting word of the God to Moses was: "Tell Pharaoh to let my People, my first born, go; and if thou refuse to let them go, behold, I will slay thy son, even thy first born" (Ex. iv, 23). And maybe for practice in slaying, for no other reason appears, the God soon sought Moses himself for his first victim: for as Moses, with his wife and one child passed by a certain inn on the way, Yahveh the God waylaid Moses "and sought to kill him"! (Ex. iv, 24). But he was saved apparently by a bloody exorcism of his wife Zipporah (v. 25). This episode further proves that Moses was a heathen ignorant of Yahveh and his "Everlasting Covenant" of circumcision, without which, "that soul shall be cut off from his People; he hath broken my covenant" (Gen. xvii, 14).

Conjure Contests

Having escaped this frustrated assassination, Moses went on to the Elders and told them what Yahveh had said; and he performed all the wonder works which Yahveh had taught him so that the People should believe, and they believed. Then Moses, and his spokesman or Publicity Man, Aaron, went to the Pharaoh, and told to him Yahveh's ingenuous plea about taking a three days' holiday in the wilderness to worship the new-found Yahveh. But the Pharaoh had never heard of Yahveh; and he said, "Who is Yahveh, that I should obey his voice and let Israel go? I know not Yahveh" (Ex. v, 2); and he drove Moses and Aaron out, and redoubled the tasks of the Israelite slaves.

The elders and the people thereupon complained to Moses of the evil case which had befallen them on his account, and said to Moses, "Yahveh judge you!" (Ex. v, 21)—which is maybe Hebrew for another way of saying it in English. And Moses went back to Yahveh, and accused him roundly of doing evil to the people, and outright of lying, saying, "Neither hast thou delivered thy People at all" (Ex. v, 23). But the God said, "I am Yahveh" (Ex. vi, 2); Go, tell Pharaoh that he let the Children of Israel go out of his land; and the God assured Moses that he would "harden Pharaoh's heart" so that he would *not* let them go, until he, Yahveh, had performed against Egypt all the wonderful works of desolation, destruction and death which the sacred pages now relate *ad horrendum*.

THE FEARFUL AND WONDERFUL "PLAGUES OF EGYPT"

Almost skeptical wonder is caused, in these modern times, by the series of inspired narratives of the famous Plagues of Egypt. One is greatly astonished at the preliminary miracle which Yahveh wrought in order to prove to Pharaoh that he, Yahveh, was indeed the Lord, and knew what he was about when he sent Moses to him: by turning Aaron's rod into a snake and then turning the snake back into Aaron's rod again. But this did not feaze the Pharaoh at all, for at his call his sorcerers and magicians turned all their rods into snakes (Ex. vii, 10–12), and honors thus far were even; although it is true that Aaron's rod swallowed up all the rods of the other conjurers. It is difficult at this distance of time and altered faith to quite understand the feat of Aaron's rod swallowing the other rods after they were turned back from snakes to rods again, it being more natural and reasonable that the swallowing act should have occurred while they were all snakes.

The next wonder recorded is when Aaron stretched out his rod that had been the snake but was now a rod full of other rods that had been snakes, and caused every drop of water in all Egypt to turn into actual blood. But the conjure of Pharaoh's heathen enchanters was equal to the miracle of the Hebrew Yahveh again, and they did the very same miracle with their enchantments (Ex. vii, 19–22), and turned all the waters of Egypt into blood. The principal feature of this conjurer's-miracle, as it would seem to a detached observer, is, how they could perform this second miracle at all, as all the water in the Kingdom, including that of the River Nile, and in every pool and vessel in the land, was already pure blood by the miracle of Aaron. The sacred text does not pause to explain this.

The same curious phenomenon occurs with respect to the third Plague, when Aaron conjured up frogs out of the waters, which were not waters but blood, and the frogs came "and covered the land of Egypt." And being so recorded in Scripture, so it must be in ample measure: the whole land was covered and filled the river, the land and the houses of Egypt. So when it is straightway recorded that "the magicians did so with their enchantments" (Ex. viii, 5–7), one can only wonder where those enchanters' frogs came from and what they covered, and how, seeing that all Egypt was already full of frogs as was Aaron's rod with swallowed rods, or even more so. At any event, honors were again even between Aaron

and the enchanters. And the smell that they produced between them
was something awful (v. 14).

Like miracles on the part of Yahveh and Aaron, with counter-
valent conjure tricks on the part of the Pharaoh's magicians, were
repeated in the Plagues of the Lice (vv. 17–18), and of the Flies
(v. 24), to the most utter annoyance and suffering of the Egyptian
people, but all the glory this time was Yahveh's and Aaron's, as this
was more "conjure" than the Egyptian magicians had at their command on such short notice. So the enchanters and magicians all
dropped out of the contest from then on and left the field undisputed
to Yahveh's and Aaron's plagueful miracles; which was just as well,
for a few days afterwards they all got the boils and blains (Ex.
ix, 11), whatever that is, and could not have worked their magic to
advantage.

A Plague of very remarkable, truly wonderful consequences is
next recorded in the inspired Story, just as it occurred in the Providence of Yahveh. The Lord God of the Hebrews turned his attention now to afflicting the dumb animal kingdom, which seemingly had
little or nothing to do with the controversy between the King of
Heaven and the Pharaoh of Egypt. The God sent a "very grievous
murrain" on the cattle of every kind of the Egyptians, "and all the
cattle of Egypt died" (Ex. ix, 3–6). Think of it! every single one
in all Egypt, horses, asses, cows, oxen, sheep, and camels, except
those of the holy Israelites, all wholly killed. Then, Lo! no sooner
had all the animals in the Kingdom died, than the Lord Yahveh sent
a Plague of boils and blains "upon man and upon beast," including
the Egyptian magicians (vv. 10–11), whose conjure had been out-
conjured by the miracles of Aaron. As the beasts were already all
dead of the murrain (v. 6), it may be wondered what was the point
in sending boils and blains upon dead animals.

But the very next Plague miracle showed that an unrecorded
miracle must undoubtedly have intervened overnight, for all the
dead animals are recorded as come to life. The proof of this
unrecorded miracle is very clear and logical: for Moses announced
one day, after all the animals and cattle had been killed and had
died of the murrain (Ex. ix, 6), and then had been infested with
boils and blains (v. 9), that on the next day he would bring on a
"very grievous hail" (v. 18); and he considerately, this time, gave
ample notice and chance of escape, and warned the Egyptians to
gather up their cattle at once and get them under cover; for upon
every man and beast which was left out in the open the hail should
come down, and they should die; and some of the cattle were herded

in, and some were left out in the fields (vv. 19–21). So, those cattle killed of the murrain must have resurrected overnight, or there would have been none alive to be herded in or left out to be killed again. The hail came as scheduled, mingled with fire, and smote man and beast, and smote every herb of the field and brake every tree of the field, and destroyed Egypt (vv. 24–25). Some may think this a good deal like poaching on the Covenant of the Rainbow, whereby Yahveh had promised no general destruction again by rain; but then hail is after the rain is frozen hard, and Egypt was not all the world, so there was a reasonable degree of difference. And when the Pharaoh saw the wrack and ruin of the hail, he said "Yahveh is righteous" (v. 27), which same he might not have said if he had seen the Flood; so this is another difference.

The Plague of the Locusts comes next in the sacred text, and rightly interests a curious mind greatly, showing the terrible swarms of these scourges, which blew up on the evil-laden east wind, so vastly "that one cannot be able to see the earth" (Ex. x, 5), and which "covered the face of the whole earth, so that the land was darkened" (v. 15); and "they did eat every herb of the land, and all the fruit of the trees which the hail had left" (v. 15). Although, as every herb and tree in all Egypt had been already destroyed by the hail (ix, 25), the Locusts must have had pretty poor picking this trip.

One is immensely puzzled over the famous Plague of Egyptian Darkness which Yahveh next in his Providence sent upon the doomed land—"even Darkness which may be felt" (Ex. x, 21–23). So dark it was for three whole days that it was all the same as if they were nights, only much more so, for so thick was the darkness that lights could not be seen; though the Chosen had lights in their dwellings and could see as well as ever. To all human reasoning, this would seem to have been an excellent opportunity for the Chosen to have taken French leave and left the country under cover of the Darkness; and this would have rendered unnecessary the fearful Massacre of the First Born to soften Pharaoh's heart so often hardened by Yahveh to prevent him from letting the People go.

The fatal Climax of Plagues, the Massacre of the First Born, is next recorded by Inspiration, and is indeed terrible to contemplate. The Angel of Yahveh God of Heaven swept through the land of Egypt with a flaming sword dripping human and animal blood, and slaughtered the first-born of every family of Egypt, from that of the Pharaoh upon his throne to the very prisons (Ex. xii, 29). And what is more curious, and somewhat less brutal, the Angel slaughtered also the first-born of all cattle; although all the cattle were already dead of the murrain (ix, 6), of the boils and blains (v. 10), and of the hail (vv. 19–25). But as wonders were plenty as blackberries in those days, there is either some unrevealed way to explain it all, or it needs no explanation to those who would believe it anyhow.

One may well wonder, in a human way of wondering, why it was that every time, after each terrible Plague, the God of the Hebrews "hardened Pharaoh's heart," even when he was very eager to let the People go; and why this God, "long-suffering and plenteous in mercy," did not use his influence to soften Pharaoh's heart to let the Children go in peace and a hurry; for several times, after a peculiarly harrowing Plague, the Pharaoh urged upon Moses and Aaron, "Go, and serve your God"; but every time the God said, "I have hardened his heart, that I might shew these my signs before him."

After the Plague of Darkness, and a stormy passage between Pharaoh and Moses and Aaron (Ex. x, 24–29), the latter doughty Plague-invokers left the presence of the Pharaoh with a direful threat of what was to come (Ex. xi); and went forth to prepare for the great Massacre of the First Born, and for the final scene of the Exodus of the People from blood-stricken Egypt. A chapter apart is worthy to be devoted to this notable triumph of the Plagues, the Exodus.

CHAPTER IV

THE WONDERS OF THE EXODUS

THIS Exodus is so really wonderful, and so humanly impossible, that its accomplishment in Providence deserves our especial attention. We will therefore attentively review its superlative wonders, if so be it that one Bible wonder may excel another; they differ rather in wonder as one star differeth from another star in glory.

IN THE "FOURTH GENERATION"

It was in the "fourth generation" from the time of the original Migration into Egypt; we have seen the four degrees down from Jacob: Levi, Kohath, Amram, Moses. Making extreme allowance for length of life and progeneration of each, we have been able to sum up only 350 years for the "sojourn in Egypt," though the inspired text says 430 years positively: in any event, the Exodus was "in the fourth generation" (Gen. xv, 16).

Watch the Chosen People grow and multiply: "Thy fathers went down into Egypt with three score and ten (70) persons; and now Yahveh thy God hath made thee as the stars of the heaven for multitude" (Deut. x, 22). The 70 Jacobites who migrated into Egypt were the slow increase of the 215 years since Abraham. Although it is a bit confusing, according to the schedule in the text (Gen. xlvi, 8–27), of these 70 there were 68 males and two females named, to-wit, Jacob and his twelve sons; their 51 sons, grandsons of Jacob; four sons of two of the grandsons, thus great-grandsons of Jacob; and two females, Dinah daughter of Jacob, and Serah, daughter of Asher and grand-daughter of Jacob. Joseph and his two sons by his Egyptian heathen wife were already in Egypt, but are included in the seventy; two of the sons of Judah, Er and Onan, were killed by Yahveh in Canaan before the Migration (v. 12; Gen. xxxviii, 3, 7, 10). These 51 living sons of the twelve sons of Jacob who came into Egypt, give an average of $4\frac{1}{4}$ male children to each of the sons of Jacob; none of the Twelve is recorded to have had any children, sons or daughters, after the arrival in Egypt, except the one daughter to Levi, Jochebed, who married her nephew Amram, father of Moses (Ex. vi, 20), and was thus the mother of Moses and his great-aunt. Adding the four great-grandsons of Jacob to the 51 grandsons, makes 55 male descendants of Jacob who formed the Migration; these, together with Jacob and his twelve sons and the two women make up the total of the seventy; though this does not include the wives of the Twelve. But it is recited, "all the souls that came with Jacob into Egypt . . . besides Jacob's sons' wives . . . all the souls of the house of Jacob, which came into Egypt, were threescore and ten (Gen. xlvi, 26–27).

Assuming that all the 55 male descendants of Jacob who came into Egypt married and had only sons for children, or sons to the average number of 4¼, and that this score held through the four generations, the Hebrew population in Egypt would naturally augment in just about the following human manner: The first generation (offspring of the Twelve) that came into Egypt was 55 males; liberally allowing five male children each, the second generation, sprung from these, would number 275; the third generation, offspring of the second, would number 1375; the fateful "fourth generation," that of Moses and the Exodus, would reach the sum total of 6875 male persons. This liberally estimated natural increase is obviously exaggerated; it allows five male children to each male of the four generations, all marrying and producing his quota of five sons each, and takes no account of females who would naturally be quite half of each generation, to furnish wives for the then generation and mothers for the next succeeding. Moreover, it errs in discounting mortality and assuming that each male of each generation would live at least until he was married and had his five male children. Thus the actual total of males must needs be even less than the 6875 above allowed. Even on the impossible hypothesis that not one died throughout the four generations, of 215, or 350 or 430 years, so that all would be living at the time of the Exodus, the grand total would be but 8580 persons. But we know, of course, that this assumed immunity from death is not true: for "Joseph died, and all his brethren, and all that (first) generation" (Ex. i, 6); and it is a safe assumption that most of the first three generations died before the Exodus.

Any rational rearrangement of these obvious vital statistics, allowing anything short of fabulous, and therefore not natural, increase could make no appreciable augment over the totals stated. Even if we begin the count of the "four generations" with that

succeeding the original 51 sons and four grandsons of the 12 sons
of Jacob (themselves of different generations), and count their 275
assumed offspring as the first generation, we would then have: first,
275; second, 1375; third, 6875; fourth, 34,375 altogether.   But
this would be a fifth generation to "sojourn in Egypt," and therefore unscriptural.

The Hosts of the Lord of Hosts

Hear now what "holy men of old spake as they were moved by
the Holy Ghost" to tell us about the numbers of this Exodus.   The
inspired record, after recording the "spoiling of the Egyptians"
by the Chosen in preparation for the God-guided Exodus, avers:
"And the Children of Israel journeyed from Rameses to Succoth,
about 600,000 on foot that were men, besides children.   And a mixed
multitude went up also with them; and flocks, and herds, even very
much cattle" (Ex. xii, 37–38)!

Only about a year later (Num. i, 1), there at Sinai, the formal
census of this warrior host was taken, of every male "from 20
years old and upwards, all that were able to go forth to war in
Israel; even all that were numbered were 603,550"! (Num. i, 45–46).
Even in this host the Levites were not numbered (v. 45); when
afterwards they were separately numbered, "all the males from a
month old and upward, were 22,000" (Num. iii, 39).   On the very
conservative, and quite inadequate, basis of estimating these warrior-
males to be but one out of every four only of old men, women, and
young children, we would have a Hebrew population of Goshen,
or of all Egypt, who went out in the Exodus, of 2,414,200 souls, not
counting in the 22,000 Levites and the great "mixed multitude" of
slaves, camp-followers, etc., who accompanied the Hosts of Yahveh.
Indeed, the Jewish Encyclopedia, and most accepted "authorities"
estimate the total numbers of the Exodus to be about 3,000,000!

Some Pregnant Figures

If the sacred historian had taken his stylus and a scrap of
papyrus, and calculated a bit, he would have figured out that in
order to accomplish this prodigy, each of the 55 males of the first
generation in Egypt must have had 40-odd children each, about
equally divided between males and females; each of these 40-odd
males must have had again 40-odd children, male and female, and
so on to the fourth generation, in order to have produced 603,550
soldier-men 20 years of age and over, or the total of 2,414,200

(plus) Children of Israel who set out upon that famous Exodus from Egypt.

But the inspired history nowhere indicates any such prodigious proliferation on the part of the Chosen People in Egyptian slavery. The highest number of children to one family, anywhere noted during the "sojourn," is the five daughters of Zelophehad; Amram had only three children, Moses, Aaron, and Miriam; Aaron had four sons (two of them killed by Yahveh), and no daughter.

The mothers of Israel were also evidently of the Hebrew race: it is hardly probable that the Hebrew slaves were permitted to marry the free native women; if this had been customary, the Syrian "seed of Abraham" would have been sadly mixed in 430 years. Indeed, the fact is indicated otherwise by the inspired statement (Ex. i, 19), "the Hebrew women are not as the Egyptian women" in child-birth, which clearly indicates that the wives of the Chosen were also of the Chosen. So that it is out of the 70 only that the 2,414,200—plus of the Exodus could have sprung, and it is evident that they could not. At best, 8000 is a liberal calculation, if not one of them had died in the 430 years; and Yahveh himself, just after the Exodus, avers that his Chosen were "the fewest of all people" (Deut. vii, 7).

But we will not discount the inspired arithmetic, and will take its figures at their face value; which leads to some truly wonderful and highly interesting considerations. Where and how did these children live, and move, and have their being in Egypt—at that time (1491) the mightiest and most splendid Empire of the ancient world? This is the first puzzle. Already, shortly after the death of Joseph, the "new King which knew not Joseph" is found complaining to his people, "Behold, the Children of Israel are more and mightier than we" (Ex. i, 9); and he therefore made slaves of this more numerous and more mighty race, and set them to building his treasure cities and other construction jobs, for which Egypt had long been justly famous, as witness the Great Pyramid, built but a few years (3933 B.C.) after the celebrated Garden of Eden was closed down in the Fall. All this host of Israel could hardly have lived in the cities along with their masters, as there were likely no cities so large as to contain them. They were needs scattered in the country, and for the reason, curious enough, that these poor slaves, at the time of the Exodus, owned several millions of sheep, horses and cattle, "even very much cattle," and it would require great areas of land to pasture all these herds.

Let us look the sheep in the face, as seen in the institution of the Passover, on the eve of the Exodus. Moses told the Children on that day, "Take you a lamb according to your families, and kill the Passover"; these lambs were to be "without blemish, a male of the first year," and were to be taken, "every man a lamb, according to the house of their fathers, a lamb for an house" (Ex. xii, 3); though if a household were too little to eat a whole lamb, the next door neighbors might be invited to share it. Very liberally allowing ten persons, including neighbors of small families, to "an house," 2,414,200 persons would require 241,420 male lambs of the first year for this one day's Passover sacrifice. There would probably be as many female lambs of the same first year, which would make 482,840 first year lambs, to say nothing of the sheep and goats. Sheep-raising statistics show that, in average flocks of all ages, the total number is about five times that of the increase of one season's births: this would give us exactly the same number of sheep as of Hebrews, 2,414,200. Modern sheep-raisers seldom have grazing lands which will support more than two sheep to the acre; but we will allow five to the acre for Biblical Egypt. This would require 482,840 acres of land, or 754 square miles, nearly two-thirds as large as the State of Rhode Island, merely for pasturing the sheep of the slave Israelites, not to allow for their other cattle and horses, none of which had been killed in the Plagues, and of which the Children had large "flocks and herds, even very much cattle." So the Children must have been considerably scattered through the land, and have quite overflowed the bounds of their original Ghetto of Goshen, in order to tend their herds,—if slaves could be so rich and be allowed to attend to their own affairs to such extent.

THE AMAZING PASSOVER

All Scripture, besides being "given by inspiration of God," is said to be "profitable for instruction"; so we find other curiously instructive features of this Exodus Passover. In Exodus xii we have the tangled and marvelous story. Yahveh tells Moses that "in the *tenth* day of this month," the people should "take every man a lamb, . . . and ye shall keep it until the *fourteenth* day of the same month; and the whole congregation of Israel shall kill it in the evening"—of the fourteenth day; and "of the blood, strike it on the two side posts and on the upper door post of the houses wherein they shall eat it"; for which ceremony he gives particular directions: "And thus shall ye eat it: with your loins girded, your shoes on your feet, and your staff in your hand; and ye shall eat it in haste"

(v. 11). It is here ordered that there should be a four-day interval between the "taking" on the *tenth* day of the month, and the killing on the *fourteenth* day; but Yahveh overlooks this, evidently, or changes his mind, for (v. 12) he says: "For I will pass through the land of Egypt *this night,* and will smite all the first-born in the land of Egypt. . . . (v. 14). And *this day* shall be unto you for a memorial. . . . (v. 21). Then Moses called for all the elders of Israel," and told them all about it, and to "take you a lamb according to your families, and kill the Passover," and strike the blood on the door posts, etc. . . . (v. 28). "And it came to pass that at midnight Yahveh smote all the first-born in the land of Egypt." This clearly proves that the entire Passover transaction, from the first commands of Yahveh about the lambs to the massacre of the first-born at midnight, took place all on one and the selfsame day, and at latest on the "tenth day":—the four-day interval is forgotten and eliminated.

But how was such a thing possible? We see the two and a half millions of people scattered over an indefinitely large territory; Yahveh appears sometime during the day (the *tenth*), and tells Moses and Aaron, "Speak ye unto all the congregation of Israel," giving them life-and-death orders and minute Passover cooking instructions, which they must perform that same day "in the evening," in order to escape the massacre of the first-born. Then Moses called for all the elders of Israel and repeated the instructions to them. There were no telephones or radio broadcasting plants in those days to help disseminate this order in all its details to the head of every family of Israel, scattered throughout Egypt, or Goshen, or the Delta, or wherever they were, so that they might pick out 241,420 first-year male lambs without blemish, kill and cook them, according to entirely new recipes (vv. 8–10), and strike the blood, in this novel way, on the door posts, so that, says Yahveh, "when I see the blood, I will pass over you, and the plague shall not be upon you to destroy you, when I smite the land of Egypt." So, how these fateful orders and directions were ever delivered "unto all the congregation of Israel" in that fatal fraction of a day, Yahveh only knows, as it is not revealed unto us in his Holy Word.

THE MARCHING ORDERS

But this is not all of this bit of Scripture, given for the profit of our instruction, as is wonderful to observe. That same night, "at midnight Yahveh smote all the first-born in the land of Egypt, and the firstborn of cattle," of the Egyptians (Ex. xii, 29),—though all these same cattle had already been killed by each of several prior Plagues: "all the cattle of Egypt died" of the murrain (Ex. ix, 6); then these dead cattle had the boils (v. 9); then they were all killed over again by the hail (v. 25). So, as soon as this fatal decree of Yahveh was executed, that midnight, "Pharaoh rose up in the night [that same night] . . . and he called for Moses and Aaron by night [that same night, after midnight], and said, Rise up, and get you forth from among my people, both ye and the Children of Israel; and go, serve Yahveh as ye have said; and be gone" (xii, 31)—"and bless me also", (v. 32), he added, maybe ironically. So, as "the Egyptians were urgent upon the people, that they might send them out of the land in haste; for they said, We be all dead men" (v. 33), haste became the order of the day, or rather of that same night.

As soon as the royal leave was thus granted to Moses, after midnight it was, he must at once get the marching orders to the scattered millions of Israel. These were in their respective homes throughout the land, dressed and ready, in "watchful waiting" for what, they knew not as yet, for it could not be known what effect the massacre of the firstborn would have upon Pharaoh; and the people were under strict command, "And none of you shall go out of the door of his house until morning." But in some strange and unrevealed way, whether by angels, miracle or telepathy, the divine command through Moses to all the millions of Israel went broadcast (the second time in one day), first to "borrow" all the clothes and jewelry they could, and to "spoil the Egyptians" (v. 36); after which feat they should all mobilize immediately at the great city Rameses. So that self-same day, somehow, all the hosts of Israel, 2,414,200 of them, with "their dough before it was leavened, their kneading-troughs being bound up in their clothes upon their shoulders" (v. 34), their "spoiled" plunder how hidden and carried is not revealed, their old and decrepit, their babes and sucklings, their sick and infirm, their women in confinement and childbirth—(for in such a population there are scores of births every mortal hour, and inspiration tells us that "the Hebrew women are lively" in this);—all these and the whole "mixed multitude," driving with them their "flocks and herds, even very much cattle, there was not an hoof left behind";—all this and these, at the divine command, began their wonderful and world's greatest one-day feat.

First, from all Egypt, east, west, north, south, "the hosts of Yahveh" rendezvoused at Rameses. Such a mobilization is without a single parallel in history, sacred or profane, since Noah's animals flocked from the four corners of the earth into his famous Ark, for which feat they had a whole week; while the millions of Israel and their millions of animals and cattle, in one single day-light mobilized from the four corners of Egypt to Rameses. Arrived there, some-how, somewhen, during the day, behold, "even the selfsame day it came to pass, that all the hosts of Yahveh *went out from* the land of Egypt" (v. 41). That there may be no sceptical doubting about it, the divine assurance is vouchsafed a second time in the same chapter: "And it came to pass the selfsame day, that Yahveh did bring the Children *out of the land of Egypt* by their armies" (v. 51); and they marched from Rameses across the desert sands to Succoth; which, according to the Bible maps, is just about thirty miles. But, apparently, this was not "out of the land of Egypt"; it was evidently yet in Egypt, on the western or Egyptian border of the Red Sea. For when Pharaoh and his army "pursued after the children of Israel" (Ex. xiv, 8), the children were still on the Egyptian side, and the miracle of the "parting of the waters" of the Red Sea had to be performed to enable the hosts of Yahveh to cross to the eastern or Arabian side of the Red Sea.

THE HOSTS ON THE MARCH

They went not as a straggling rabble of fugitive slaves, hasten-ing to escape, but proudly in formal marching array, as armies march. Let us watch this wonderful parade of the armied hosts of Yahveh. If they marched in close order, as many as fifty abreast, with only one yard interval between their serried ranks, there would have been 48,284 ranks, which would form a column just 28 miles long! But the truth is even worse than this, if the Bible is accurate on the point: for the original Hebrew text says: "And the children of Israel went up *by five in a rank* out of the land of Egypt" (Ex. xiii, 18; see Marginal note),—which would make the column 280 miles long! As such a "mixed multitude," with all its encumbrances, could not possibly march through the desert sands very many miles a day, say ten, fifteen, or twenty for an extreme,—(the American army of chosen foot-troop marches but 12 to 15 miles a day under average conditions). Moreover, the front ranks must march the whole 28 (or 280) miles before the rearward ranks could even start. So hardly more than half, or a much smaller fraction of the "hosts of Yahveh" could even get away that first day, even if they had started early. But they had first to rendezvous to Rameses from all over Egypt,—several hundreds of miles in length—and we know not how much of that wonderful day they occupied in the rendezvous; and the whole host could not possibly reach Succoth, wherever that was, but somewhere, according to the text, "out of the land of Egypt," till the second or third day, or next week, or next month, even if they could all have mobilized at Rameses on that "selfsame day," as we have seen that it is said to have come to pass. And as for those millions of sheep and cattle, not marching of course, unless divinely inspired, in close battle array, but in much more "open order" scattered, how many interminable miles they stretched out the column we have no revelation, nor adequate data to compute.

And what the millions of cattle fed upon in the prolonged hike to the Red Sea, across the desert sands, with whatever scant vegetation tramped extinct, divine revelation does not vouchsafe, possibly as in no wise profitable for our instruction. Nor were the children much better provided for such a journey; they had only a little unleavened dough on their shoulders, "because they were thrust out of Egypt, and could not tarry, neither had they prepared for themselves any victual" (Ex. xii, 39). How they ever "got there" at all seems like a second edition of "all these wonders" which Yahveh did before Pharaoh.

A truly remarkable circumstance may be noted here: this "mixed multitude" of fugitive slaves are represented as having slaves of their own which they carried away with them; and their truly provident Yahveh, in his ordinance of the Passover, the very first Law he ever gave them, just as they fled from slavery in Egypt, made provision for the observance of that pious ceremony by "every man's servant that is bought for money," after the bloody violence of circumcision had been perpetrated upon him (Ex. xii, 44).

THE HOSTS AFRAID OF WAR

Wonders, such as these, never cease, in the Providence of Yahveh to his Chosen People Israel; or, the relation of such wonders by the sacred writers, for our wonder, is incessant. When the armied "hosts of Yahveh" and their army of camp-followers and cattle got to Succoth, whenever they did, Yahveh was afraid for them, and "led them not through the way of the Philistines, although that was near; for Elohim said, Lest peradventure, the people repent when they see war, and return to Egypt" (Ex. xiii, 17); although they were 603,550 armed warriors bold, and were being led expressly to the armed conquest and extermination of "seven nations greater and mightier" than all Israel! So "Elohim led the people about, through the way of the wilderness of the Red Sea: and the Children of Israel went up harnessed (armed) out of the land of Egypt" (v. 18).

This is truly remarkable. Where did these fleeing slaves get their arms,—swords, spears, shields, bows and arrows, armor, for 603,550 soldiers? Slaves are not usually allowed to keep arms, nor to be so trained, that on one day's sudden notice, they can, presto! change from a horde of slaves to soldiers who march out "by their armies" full panoplied for war. And if armed soldiers going forth to conquest, under the personal command of their God, a notable "Man of War," why should they "repent if they see war," between *other* peoples, too, and wish to return in fright to slavery? Revelation is silent to solve these mysteries. And despite all of Yahveh's concern for his Warriors "lest they see war," they had not been three months out of Egypt before they had war with the Amalekites there at Rephidim, when Aaron and Hur had to hold up the hands of Moses all day before the Children could finally win the battle (Ex. xvii, 8–13).

THE RED SEA MASSACRE

Yahveh was not yet satisfied with "plagueing" the Egyptians and with showing off his terrible and holy wonders upon them. He had bloodily baited Pharaoh into letting his slaves go; a dozen times Pharaoh in terror had "inclined to let the people go," but Yahveh had interefered and "hardened Pharaoh's heart that he should not let them go." And now when the Children finally got away and Pharaoh was happily rid of them, Yahveh devises another wholesale destruction, to his own honor; and says, "I will harden Pharaoh's heart that he shall follow after them, and I will be honored upon Pharaoh, and upon all his host, that the Egyptians may know that I am Yahveh" (Ex. xvi, 4);—as if they didn't know it already to their infinite sorrow and disgust! The tragedy of the Red Sea and the death by drowning of the hosts of Pharaoh do not concern us now; but it is interesting to note that as soon as the valiant warriors, 603,550 strong, saw the hosts of Pharaoh, also very suddenly mustered, appear in pursuit, "they were sore afraid; and the Children of Israel cried out unto Yahveh," and they cravenly said, "Let us alone that we may serve the Egyptians; for it had been better for us to serve the Egyptians, than that we should die in the wilderness"

(Ex. xiv, 10–12) ;—which has a different thrill, this cry of 603,550 armed warriors of Yahveh, than that of one later patriot who fired his country's heart with the cry, "I know not what course others may take, but as for me, Give me Liberty or give me death!" And through their whole sacred history the People of Yahveh blubbered and wailed at every trial and in every time of danger, real or fancied, as from some instances we shall see.

The Children Wail for Water

Only three days after this wonderful Red Sea massacre in the Providence of Yahveh, his Chosen People got further into the wilderness of Shur, and "found no water" (Ex. xv, 22) ; whereupon they wailed again and started an insurrection; then moved on to Marah, the waters of which were bitter so they could not drink, and they wailed again, and cried, "What shall we drink?" (v. 24). So Yahveh made the bitter waters sweet for his crying Children; then brought them on to Elim, where there were twelve wells of water, and 70 palm trees; and the whole 2,414,200 Children, all their "mixed multitude" of camp-followers, and their millions of cattle, encamped there by the twelve wells under the 70 palm trees (v. 27). This is the last natural water supply they ever saw for 38 years; though in the last year they did happily encounter a whole Well of Beer! (Num. xxi, 16). They were supplied miraculously with water only twice, or once told two ways, which phenomenon we may here pause to notice. It is no metaphor about the want of water in that "desert land," in that "waste howling wilderness," as it is so often described; and again, "that great and terrible wilderness, wherein were fiery serpents, and scorpions, and drought, where there was no water"; and again the Children wail and cry, "Why have ye brought the congregation of Yahveh into this wilderness, that we and our cattle should die in this evil place; neither is there any water to drink."

Smiting the Rock for Water

After leaving the twelve wells of Elim, the Children came into the wilderness of Sin, in the middle of the second month out, and started a bread riot, which was quieted by the miracle of a mess of quails and the daily manna (Ex. xvi) ; then they marched on to Rephidim, and at once rioted because "there was no water for the people to drink," and they were about to stone Moses to death. Yahveh here came to the rescue, and told Moses to take his wonder rod and "smite the rock in Horeb" and bring water from it; and Yahveh stood upon the rock to watch the performance. Moses smote the rock, the waters gushed out and the people drank; and Moses "called the name of the place Meribah, because of the chiding of the Children of Israel." This is related in Exodus xvii, and is said to have occurred in or near the wilderness of Sin, and some three months (Ex. xvi, 1) after leaving Egypt, in 1491.

But in Numbers XX, under the marginal date 1453, that is, 38 years later, the same or very similar story is told again, but differently. For "then came the Children of Israel into the desert of Zin [instead of Sin], in the first month," and stopped at Kadesh; and "there was no water for the congregation"; so they wailed and rioted again, because they and their cattle were like to die. This time Yahveh told Moses to take his rod and go with Aaron to a certain rock, and "speak ye to the rock,"—instead of using the rod to smite it. But Moses was peeved this time, and he meekly yelled at the Children, "Hear now, ye rebels" (v. 10), and instead of gently speaking to the rock, as Yahveh had commanded, he "lifted up his hand, and with his rod he smote the rock twice," and the waters gushed forth abundantly.

But now Yahveh was real angry with Moses and Aaron, and he said to them: "Because ye have not believed me, therefore ye shall not bring this congregation into the land which I have given them"; and the sacred writer informs us, "This is the water of Meribah; because the Children of Israel strove with Yahveh" (v. 13). Here we have the desert of Sin and the desert of Zin, and two waters Meribah, but 38 years apart, and each with entirely different "trimmings"; but which was which let him unravel who is curious over such histories. In either event, so far as revealed, this is about all the water that the millions of Chosen and their millions of cattle had to drink in that terrible wilderness for quite forty years.

Food Riots.—Heavenly Manna and Quails

As for food, both human food and cattle-feed, this mystery of the ages had never been satisfactorily solved by revelation or speculation. The Children started out, as we have seen, with a little unleavened dough, but "neither had they prepared for themselves any victual" (Ex. xii, 39); and of course they carried no cattle-feed. So one naturally wonders what they, and their cattle, had to eat until "on the fifteenth day of the second month after their departing out of Egypt," they struck the wilderness of Sin (Ex.

xvi). Here was their first recorded food riot; the whole congregation rebelled, crying, "Would to God we had died by the hand of
Yahveh in Egypt, when we did sit by the flesh pots, and when we
did eat bread to the full! For ye have brought us forth into this
wilderness, to kill this whole assembly with hunger" (v. 3). It is
curious that they should die with hunger, when they had at least
2,414,200 sheep and "very much cattle" along with them, which
same sheep alone, with nothing at all to eat or drink, throve and
produced at least 241,420 male lambs every year of the forty years
in the wilderness—for the annual Passover feasts; which is another
divine mystery, as we shall see. And it is truly to marvel, that
while the Chosen started out with only a little dough on their
shoulders, quickly consumed raw, and then for forty years were
complaining and rioting because they had no bread to eat, where
they ever got the tons of "fine flour" with which to make the famous
"shew bread" for the altar of Yahveh, and the untold amounts of
"unleavened bread" which they must eat in their feasts, and the
"fine flour" they were required to offer with their countless sacrifices;
to say nothing of the great quantities of oil accompanying them,
nor of the millions of animals and birds for the manifold and interminable sacrifices which they are said to have made all through the
forty years in the wilderness. Though Amos questions (v, 25), and
Jeremiah (vii, 22 seq.) denies flesh sacrifices in the wilderness. And
as we shall soon see, the Aaron family were simply gorged with
meat from these sacrifices, which they were under dire obligation to
eat at all hazards.

However, when the Children started their food riot, Yahveh was
merciful, and said he would "rain bread from heaven" (v. 4) for his
Children; but Moses misinterpreted or exaggerated the message, and
reported to them that "Yahveh shall give you in the evening flesh
to eat, and in the morning bread to the full" (v. 8); so Yahveh
graciously accepted the amendment, and amended his promise to conform to the version which Moses had reported. And this is the way
that Yahveh fulfilled his bounteous promises: that evening "quails
came up, and covered the camp" (Ex. xvi, 13), and in the morning
that wonderful heavenly manna, which had some very peculiar qualities, and tasted (Ex. xvi, 31) "like wafers made with honey," or
(Num. xi, 8) "the taste thereof was like the taste of fresh oil,"
according to which inspired text one prefers; but whether olive oil,
castor oil, kerosene oil, hair oil, or Oil of Saints is not revealed
unto us. Anyhow, the Children didn't like it at all as a steady
diet. But this is all they had to eat for those forty years, as the

quails were a special treat for that one day only; for we hear them complaining at their next food riot, longing for the leeks and onions and garlic of Egypt, and saying, "Who shall give us flesh to eat; there is nothing at all, beside this manna" (Num. xi, 6); and again they said, "Our souls do loathe this light bread" (id. xxi, 5); and, odd as it is, "they wept in the ears of Yahveh, saying, Who shall give us flesh to eat?" (Num. xi, 4).

Passing strange was this danger of starvation, again, in the face of several million sheep and cattle right there with them,— unless, indeed, the poor beasts were so starved themselves as to be not fit to eat. And Moses explicitly had this fact of cattle in mind; for when Yahveh promised him flesh for the Children to eat, he reasoned thus with Yahveh, saying: "The people among whom I am are 600,000 footmen; and thou hast said, I will give them flesh, that they may eat a whole month. Shall the flocks and herds be slain for them? or shall all the fish of the sea be gathered together for them, to suffice them?" (Num. xi, 21–22). To starve to death under such circumstances! And "the anger of Yahveh was kindled greatly"; and he graciously promised—note this: "Ye shall not eat one day, nor two days, nor five days, nor twenty days; but even a whole month, until it come out at your nostrils, and it be loathsome unto you!" (Num. xi, 19–20). Anyhow, here was the Divine Promise of meat to eat for a whole month.

So, in his lovingkindness and bounteous Providence, Yahveh provided a new quail feast on truly prodigious scale; for "there went forth a wind from Yahveh, and brought quails from the sea,"— (maybe it was flying-fishes, for sea-quail are not known on the market, at least these days); and, please give profound attention: Those quails fell and stacked upon the face of the earth "as it were a day's journey round about the camp, and as it were two cubits high upon the face of the earth!" (v. 31). This simple inspired narrative, related in one Bible verse, and about which I never heard a single sermon or even mention in my life, is the most stupendous miracle of Divine bounty in all sacred history; and peremptorily challenges our admiring attention for a moment.

Miracle and Mathematics

Let us figure a bit on this astonishing hail of quails, and see how far figures, which lie not, may be an aid, or handicap, to faith. Those amazing quails were stacked up two cubits high for a distance of a day's journey round about the camp, i.e. on every side. A

Bible cubit is 22 good American inches; two cubits are therefore 44 inches that the quails lay stacked high upon the face of the earth. A Biblical "day's journey," according to the "Jewish Encyclopedia," is 44,815 meters (1 meter is 39.37 inches, or 1.1 yards); which equals 49,010 yards, equal to 27.8 miles. Now, the Camp of Israel (laid out as indicated in Numbers ii, and glowingly described by Balaam in Numbers xxiv), was, according to accepted calculations, twelve miles square in extent. It would even then be terribly crowded, with about 168,000 persons to the square mile; the densest population in the worst slums of any modern city is only some 2500 to the square mile!—and that in many-storied Tenement Houses. And this doesn't allow a square foot for the millions of cattle.

Well, around and about this 12-mile square camp on all its four sides lay heaped these miraculous quails, piled 44 inches high. Assuming, for the sake of a minimum of miracle, and therefore of strain on faith, that this stack of quails began close up to the four sides of the camp, and extended for 27.8 miles in every direction, we have a great solid square of quails, measuring from one outer edge to another 67.6 miles, deducting of course the 12-mile square center occupied by the camp. The solid mass therefore covered 4569.76 square miles, from which deducting the 144 square miles of the central camp, leaves us 4425.76 square miles of solid quails, 44 inches in height of pile. This stack of quails thus covered an area by 500 square miles larger than the whole States of Delaware and Rhode Island, plus the City of Greater New York, by way of comparison! Such is the wondrous bounty of Yahveh, or such the boundlessness of inspiration. As to the space occupied by each quail, packed tight by the weight of the mass, one quail might by liberal allowance occupy about 3 inches of space each way, which would be 27 cubic inches of space per quail, or 64 quails to the cubic foot of space throughout the mass. Now, a surface of 4425.76 square miles, heaped 44 inches high, with objects each occupying 27 cubic inches, would make a considerable mass which we must, reduce to terms.

One linear mile contains 5280 feet; one square mile therefore contains 27,478,480 square feet. The whole area of 4425.76 square miles would aggregate the sum of 121,613,157,644.80 square feet. Each square foot of all these being covered 44 inches, or 3.66 feet high with quails, this would give us, in cubic content, a total of 445,104,156,980 cubic feet of quails; each quail occupying 27 cubic inches of space, or 64 quails to the cubic foot. A bit of ready reckoning, on this conservative basis, gives us just 29,612,991,260,-160 quails in this divine prodigy of a pot-hunt! Every soul of the 2,414,200 of the "Hosts of Yahveh" therefore had a liberal per capita allowance of 12,266,171 quails. No wonder, if the Children had to eat so many quails, even in "a whole month," as Yahveh promised, or threatened, that they should "come out at your nostrils and be loathsome to you"! We can well believe this phase of the inspired Word.

It was a prodigious task to harvest all those quails; indeed, inspiration (v. 32) tells us, "the people stood up all that day, and all that night, and all the next day, and they gathered the quails; and they spread them all abroad for themselves round about the camp." This must mean all around within the camp; for the quails were already spread abroad for 67.6 miles "round about the camp" on the outside. Indeed, as these wonderful quails stretched for nearly 28 miles, a whole day's journey away, on every hand around the camp, an ordinary uninspired mind cannot grasp the process by which the millions of Chosen ever accomplished the incessant going back and forth, out and in, the hundreds of thousands of times necessary to harvest their marvelous crop of quails. And how quails covering compactly an area of 4425 square miles could be "spread abroad," when gathered in, in the 144 square miles of the camp, already crowded full of tents and people, or where they ever put the feathers and "cleanings," is another holy wonder,—if the whole affair were not simply a matter of simple faith. And it is curious where the 2,414,200 Children stood to be able to all get at the quail-picking; and how each person could gather up 12,266,171 quails in 36 hours, which would require them to gather up, each one, 340,727 quails per hour, or 5768 quails every mortal minute, or nearly 97 quails per second of uninterrupted time, leaving them no time to carry the quails on the average 28 miles into camp to spread them abroad, and no time to eat, or sleep, or sacrifice, or die, which over 1700 a day did, or to bury their dead, or to be born, which also happened at the rate of 1700 per diem, as the comparison of the two censuses shows, nor for any other of the daily necessities of camp-life, for which, as we shall see, there would indeed be no space left.

But devoutly conjuring away all these trifling speculations, let us behold the climax of tragedy which capped this miracle of Divine bounty. Yahveh had promised his flesh-famishing Children flesh to eat for "even a whole month," and that they should be so gorged with eating quail that it should come out loathesomely at their

nostrils; and Yahveh's Divine Word would seem to be inviolable.
But, when the Children had each gathered up his twelve-million
ration of quails, and started with great joy and hunger, as we may
imagine, after 36 hours' hungry wait, to eat them, Lo! "while the
flesh was yet between their teeth, ere it was chewed, the wrath of
Yahveh was kindled against the people, and Yahveh smote the people
with a very great plague" (v. 33), and untold numbers of the
Children were slain by their bounteous loving heavenly Father! And
this simply because they "lusted" for something to eat besides that
soul-loathed impossible oily-honey manna. Whether the miraculous
quails were divinely instilled with miraculous venom and gave
Yahveh's Chosen wholesale ptomaine poisoning, or whether it was
simply another case of Jahvistic slaying, so abounding in his sacred
record, the Divine revelation leaves us unadvised. In either event,
Yahveh seems to have violated his sacred Word, or at best "Kept the
word of promise to the ear, but broke it to the hope"; as his Children
did not get their promised "flesh to eat for even a whole month,"
nor at all. There are other sacred curiosities of this inspired tale
of woe in the wilderness, which we will note in their proper sequence.

THE MOSES FAMILY

While still here at Rephidim, we may note two little incidents
of inspired narrative. But a few months previously, when Moses
started on his divine mission extraordinary from Jethro's sheep
herd to the Pharaoh of Egypt, and of course before the famous
Exodus, he took along "his wife and sons" (Ex. iv, 20), whose names
are not there given. A very few months later, when Moses had
led the Children into camp at Rephidim (Ex. xviii), his father-in-
law, Jethro (or however named), who lived somewhere in those parts
near Rephidim, "took Zipporah and her two sons" and went to pay
a visit to Moses at the camp. The two sons are now named, according to the Hebrew—(American Indian and other savage)—usage
of naming children in commemoration of some notable event: "the
name of the one was Gershom; for, he said, I have been an alien in
a strange land; and the name of the other was Eliezer; for the God
of my father, he said, was mine help, and delivered me from the
sword of Pharaoh." The name of the first son thus commemorated
the sojourn of Moses in the land of Midian, whither he fled when
he murdered the Egyptian, and married Zipporah, daughter of
Jethro, heathen priest of Midian; the name of the second son, in
likewise, commemorated the Exodus from Egypt and deliverance

"from the sword of Pharaoh." But as the Exodus had occurred only a couple of months previously, it is a bit curious how this son of Moses, born and we know not how long before Moses ever left Midian "to go unto Pharaoh," could have a name commemorative of an event which had just, in the Providence of Yahveh, come to pass to his People.

Who Proposed the Judges of Israel?

The other incident is also connected with this visit of Jethro, as related in Exodus XVIII. Moses was very much overworked with the strenuous task of trying to run the whole encampment alone and to hold in the "stiff-necked and rebellious people," and he "sat to judge the people from the morning unto the evening"; for Moses said, "I judge between one and the other, and I do make them know the statutes of Yahveh and his laws." But this was at Rephedim, before the "hosts of Yahveh" ever came to Sinai, where the "statutes and laws of Yahveh" are said to have originated; so Moses is errant in talking about making known such statutes and laws before even he ever knew them himself, which, as we shall see, he never did. Moreover, he admits that he was very unsuccessful in his teachings, for 40 years later he complains to them, "Yet in this thing ye did not believe Yahveh your God" (Deut. i, 32).

However, his good pagan father-in-law felt sorry for Moses, and said to him: "The thing that thou doest is not good. Thou wilt surely wear away, for this thing is too heavy for thee; thou art not able to perform it thyself alone." And Jethro further said: "Hearken now to my voice, and I will give thee counsel"; and this was his advice to Moses: "Provide out of all the people, able men, and place such over them, to be rulers" over different sections, "and let them judge all the people at all seasons." So "Moses hearkened to the voice of his father-in-law, and did all that he said. And Moses chose able men, and they judged the people" (Ex. xviii, 13–26). Certainly Jethro is entitled to the credit for this plan, which he originated. We might therefore be quite surprised, but that all sense of surprise has been paralyzed in this search of the Scripture, to find Moses in his harangue to the people by Jordan (Deut. i, 9–19) bragging about this institution of Judges as a device all his own and framed up at Horeb, at a later date, if it ever happened at all. Moses there says, as he is quoted: "I spake unto you at that time, saying, I am not able to bear you myself alone. How can I myself alone bear your cumbrance, and your burden, and your strife? Take you wise men, and I will make them rulers over you. And ye answered me, and said, The thing which thou hast spoken is good for us to do. So I took the chiefs of your tribes, wise men, and known, and made them heads over you," etc. Both of these inspired stories cannot be accurate, whatever one may think as to the historicity of either.

THE TENTS OF ISRAEL

While the Chosen are resting up in their camp at Rephidim, we may notice several other peculiar remarkable points of sacred history. In Egypt the Chosen, though slaves, lived in houses: they escaped the Passover massacre by smearing blood on the "door posts of their houses"; the Egyptians, being highly civilized, with great and wonderful cities, lived also in houses, not in tents. Yet we find the 2,414,200 Chosen, from Succoth on through the forty years' hike, encamped in tents; scores of times these tents are mentioned in the sacred texts. We will inspect these tents with the eyes of faith.

The encampment of spreading tents must have presented a beautiful and impressive spectacle; for, when he saw it, "Balaam lifted up his eyes, and he saw Israel abiding in his tents, according to their Tribes; and the spirit of (Elohim) God (Balaam was a pagan) came upon him"; and he took up his parable and said: "How goodly are thy tents, O Jacob! And thy tabernacles, O Israel! As the valleys are they spread forth, as gardens by the river's side, as the trees of lign aloes, and as cedar trees beside the waters" (Num. xxiv, 2–6). But, this glowing record of the encampment of tents flatly contradicts another inspired text, which is the foundation of one of the great sacred festivals of the Chosen even to this day, the "Feast of Tabernacles," a little later instituted (Lev. xxiii, 40–43) by Yahveh himself. Here Moses commands the Chosen to take, every year at harvest time, "boughs of goodly trees, branches of palm trees, and the boughs of thick trees, and willows of the brooks," wherewith to construct "booths"; and, says Yahveh, "ye shall dwell in booths seven days; all that are Israelites shall dwell in booths: That your generations may know that I made the Children of Israel *to dwell in booths* when I brought them out of the land of Egypt: I am Yahveh your God." It needs no comment that the waste howling wilderness "where no water is," could not afford trees such as these "goodly" ones, nor any trees at all, and certainly not trees enough to build "booths" for forty years for 2,414,200

Chosen People. However this may be, they never did it—never till after the "discovery" of the "Book of the Law," and the return from the Captivity,—for, "since the days of Joshua unto that day had not the Children of Israel done so" (Neh. viii, 17), to observe the dwelling in booths; which is an indication that the "Law of Moses" had never existed through all those ages.

If the Children were in the Wilderness at all, and lived in anything, it was in tents. So for a moment we will consider these tents, and the holy camp, and several truly curious features connected with their encampments. Where did the Chosen get their tents, and how did they manage to lug them along on their flight out of Egypt? The inspired history tells us that the Children fled in such haste that they carried only some unleavened dough and their kneading troughs bound up in their clothes on their shoulders, without even any victuals (Ex. xii, 39); not a word about heavy and cumbersome tents. Tents are heavy, with canvas or hair-cloth, ropes, poles and pegs; in the U. S. Army a little "dog-tent" merely to shelter two soldiers lying down, is divided between its two occupants as luggage. But these tents of the Israelites must have been big family affairs, for men, women and children to live in decency and some degree of comfort, and must have been very heavy: how did they carry them? But first, how did they get them? As they lived in houses in Egypt, it would be remarkable indeed if each family should have a well-equipped tent in the garret, awaiting marching orders for the Promised Land, which until a single day previously they had no premonition of.

And how many tents must they have had? To crowd indecently ten persons, male and female, old and young, and sick and dying, into each tent, would have required at least 241,420 quite large and heavy tents, to be lugged in their first flight, and for forty years wandering in the waste howling wilderness. We are nowhere told that the Children had any horses, or knew even how to ride horseback; indeed, it seems that even 750 years later the Chosen could not ride horses even if they had had them; for Rab-shakeh offered them, on behalf of the King of Assyria,—"I will deliver thee 2000 horses, if thou be able on thy part to set riders upon them" (2 Kings xix, 23). And while it is true, or said to be true (Deut. xxix, 5) that in the whole forty years "your clothes are not waxen old upon you, and thy shoe is not waxen old upon thy foot," yet we are not told that those tents were thus providentially preserved. As for the clothes and shoes, it is an old joke, as to how the clothes and shoes of the little children and young persons who started on the forty-year tramp sufficed for them as they grew older and larger, unless the clothes and shoes expanded along with their skins, from year to year. But no such Providence is recorded as to the Tents of Israel.

THE GREAT ENCAMPMENTS

As for their encampments, who shall justly estimate their size and extent, for a host of two and a half million people, with all their "mixed multitude" of slaves and camp-followers, and with more than that number of sheep and cattle? The question would be of no concern, if it did not involve some further strains on faith, as we will now notice. Every time the camp was pitched, forty-one times (Num. xxxiii), there must be suitable space found for some 250,000 tents, laid out (Num. ii) regularly four-square around the Holy Tabernacle, after that was constructed, and with the necessary streets and passages, and proper spaces between the tents. A man in a coffin, dead, occupies about six feet by two, or twelve square feet; of course living people would not be so packed, like corpses or sardines, within their tents; they must have at least say three times that space, or 36 square feet or 4 square yards, each. A tent, to house ten persons, with minimum decency, must occupy therefore an average of 40 square yards.

If the 241,420 such tents were set one against another, with no intervening space or separating streets, they would occupy 9,656,800 square yards, or over 1995 acres of ground; a little more than 3 square miles. But the desert was vast, there was no need for such impossible crowding; ample room was available for seemly spacing of tents, for streets and areas, for the great central Tabernacle and its Court, and for the 22,000 Levites, not counted in the soldier-census, who must "pitch round about the Tabernacle," as well as space for the rounding up of the millions of cattle. These allowances for order, decency and comfort would much extend the circuit of the camp, and make more reasonable the accepted estimate that "this encampment is computed to have formed a movable city of twelve miles square," or an area of 144 square miles, which is certainly modest for a population equal to that of Chicago, which covers 198 square miles. The Tabernacle stood in the center, thus six miles from the outskirts of the camp in either direction.

Some Features of Camp-Life

So much for the lay-out of the sacred encampment. What is the point of faith involved? Whenever a sacrifice of sin-offering was made by the priest, a daily and constant service, "the skin of the bullock, and all his flesh and his inwards (etc.), even the whole bullock shall he carry forth without the camp unto a clean place, where the ashes are poured out, and burn him on the wood with fire" (Lev. iv, 11–12). This was the personal chore of the priest himself, of whom there were only three, Aaron and his sons Eleazar and Ithamar. And there were thousands upon thousands of sacrifices, for every imaginable thing and occasion; and the carcasses and offal of the slaughtered cattle must always be taken "without the camp" and burned, by these three poor priests, and Father Aaron was over 80 years old. So these chores would keep them going, time after time, six miles out and six miles back, lugging heavy and bloody carcasses and offal through the main streets of the camp, incessantly, and leave them no time for their holy, bloody, sacrifices of myriads of animals, as described to raise your gorge in Exodus xxix, and all through Leviticus. Moreover, the entire garbage, refuse, ashes, rubbish and filth of every kind of two and a half millions of people, and millions of cattle, must be constantly and with extreme care carried without the camp, and all their sewage, under the awful sanction of practical annihilation; for "Yahveh thy God walketh in the midst of thy camp, to deliver thee, and to give up thine enemies before thee; therefore shall thy camp be holy: that he see no unclean thing in thee, and turn away from thee" (Deut. xxiii, 12–14); and everybody who reads the Bible knows what the Chosen's enemies used to do to them whenever their Yahveh wasn't looking closely after them.

These inspired verses enshrine, too, for our admiration, the material details of the command: even the ordinary personal necessities of nature must be relieved "without the camp," and covered up by digging with a paddle (v. 13); the 603,500-odd valiant soldiers of Yahveh were oddly commanded by Yahveh: "thou shalt have a paddle upon thy weapon" for this digging operation! Unless there was a special revelation in advance as to this peculiar pattern of paddle-spears, it is curious how the Chosen could have gotten these funny weapons, manufactured to special order by the armorers of Egypt, with a spear-point on one end and a scavenger-paddle on the other. And it is to wonder how the non-combatants, women-folk and little children, did their digging on these personal occasions, unless, indeed, they borrowed some warrior-paddle not then in use, or had a paddle-armed soldier for an escort when they went perforce "without the camp." Just think for a moment, and then admire the strange Providences of Yahveh: two and a half millions of his Chosen People, old and young, sick and infirm, men, women and children, treking and trotting at all hours and every mortal minute of day and night, hundreds of thousands of them from the more central parts of the encampment, some twelve miles there and back, to find a suitable spot "without the camp" to respond to their several calls; and often, by or even before the time they got back home, having to turn and trek all over again! And every mother's son and daughter of the "hosts of Yahveh" must make an average of six miles, both ways, many times daily.

Moreover, as Yahveh got angry with his Chosen, whom he had so repeatedly promised to bring into the Promised Land, and refused to bring them, but caused every one of them to die, except Joshua and Caleb, there in the wilderness, there were on the average 1700 deaths and funerals per day for forty years, at the rate of 72 per hour, more than one for every minute of every day: all which remains must also be carried "without the camp" for burial, an average of six miles going and returning; which must have kept the Children pretty busy all day long. And as the census taken at the end of the forty years shows but a slight decrease under the census at the beginning, the entire host was renewed by a birth-rate of over one a minute for forty years; and all the débris of this operation must be lugged without the camp and disposed of. Verily, the Chosen had their troubles.

THE "BURNING QUESTION" OF FUEL

Moreover, there is the question of fires and fuel. The myriads of sacrifices and burnt offerings at the Tabernacle, besides the terribly wasteful burning "without the camp" of practically the entire animals, and that too when the Children were starving and rioting for "flesh to eat," required many fires and hence very much firewood. Where, there in the "waste howling wilderness," did they get the wood for so much fuel?—a burning question nowhere answered by Revelation. And there in the Arabian wilderness, at certain seasons, and always at nights, when the fiery sun had set, the cold was fearfully intense; the Chosen must have been grievously beset to find firewood to keep themselves from freezing: and it is never once recorded that stove-wood was miraculously provided either to keep them warm or to cook that wonderful honey-oily manna, to say nothing of the big quail feast. The inspired Word tells us much of the fires and of the ashes, but vouchsafes not a word about the immense forests of goodly trees which must have quite covered that "waste howling wilderness" in order to supply a population like that of modern Chicago with firewood for heating, cooking, and burning hecatombs of sacrifices, every day for forty years.

CHAPTER V

THE FORTY YEARS IN THE WILDERNESS

In the third month after the Hegira from Egypt the Hosts of Yahveh came to the "desert of Sinai, and pitched in the wilderness, and encamped before the Mount" (Ex. xix, 1-2). This was Mt. Sinai—(named for the Pagan Moon-God, Sin), also confusedly called Horeb, and sacred as the "Mount of God,"—though in Hebrew it is called "Har-Elohim," the "Mount of the Gods."

Mt. Sinai is said by the Bible Dictionary, with a marvelously developed bump of locality, to be "156 miles southeast of Cairo, Egypt"; but the Encyclopedia Britannica says that the sacred writers locate the place "only by aid of the imagination" (Vol. XXV, p. 138), and that the "Mount of Yahveh" has never been identified—though Olympus, Mount of Jove, is there to-day and is well known, though it does not necessarily prove all of the storied feats of its deified dwellers.

· But if anywhere, Mt. Sinai was in the "great and terrible wilderness," at a choice locality where the 3,000,000 Chosen People could spread their 12-mile-square Camp and corral their vast herds of sheep and cattle; and a mountain of such special and peculiar shape that the Chosen could build a fence around it (if they had the timber there in the waste howling wilderness), or some otherhow "set bounds about the Mount" to keep the People and the cattle away from its fatal sides,—lest Yahveh "break forth upon them, and many of them perish." Indeed, it was also fearfully fenced off with a taboo of terror from the curious: "whosoever toucheth the mount shall surely be put to death," stoned or shot through, even beasts, declared Yahveh (Ex. xix, 12, 21-24).

After these remarkable precautions for mystery and secrecy, the Chosen were required to be "sanctified," an operation consisting of washing their clothes, (v. 10)—though where they got the water there in the wilderness for laundering, when they were rioting for water to drink, is not revealed,—and of three days' mortification of the flesh by abstaining from their one and only recorded pleasurable pastime in the Wilderness—the carnal knowledge of their wives and women (v. 15). These mystic directions were given by Yahveh to Moses on the day of arrival at Sinai, when Moses, without being invited, and apparently without knowing that Yahveh was up there, made an informal call up the mountain on Yahveh, or two calls (vv. 3, 8); on the second of which Yahveh said that he would "come down in sight of all the People" on the third day thereafter. But it was not Yahveh alone whom Moses visited on these occasions; the Hebrew text distinctly says: "And Moses went up *to the Gods* (ha-Elohim), and Yahveh called unto him from the mountain" (v. 3).

Just how these things did pass at that mysterious place, all these different appearances of Yahveh, and the numerous errand-boy trips of 80-year-old Moses up and down the steep mountain during a year's time, is a veritable Chinese Puzzle, which we need not try to work out. In any event, Moses went down and "sanctified the People" in the manner and form indicated, and built the big fence. On the third day, Yahveh, amid thunders and lightnings, descended in fire upon the mountain, which was altogether on a smoke; and Moses went up for the third visit (v. 20).

Curiously enough, Moses had hardly gotten to the top of the mountain, than Yahveh, without so much as "Good Morning, Moses," told him, "Go down, charge the People" about washing up and sanctifying and making the fence around the mountain (vv. 21–22). Moses expostulated that all this had already been done (v. 23); but Yahveh cut him short, saying, "Away, get thee down" (v. 24); so, meekly enough, "Moses went down unto the People, and spake unto them" (v. 25); though apparently he did not tell them of Yahveh's peculiar command to do what had already been done three days previously, as Moses had reported to him (v. 23).

The Mistake About the Priests

Before seeking to unravel what next is related, we may note another big mistake that Yahveh made, as to which one might think a God should have known better. In sending Moses back this last time to do what had already been done, Yahveh expressly commanded: "And let the priests also, which come near to Yahveh, sanctify themselves" (v. 22); and he told Moses that Brother Aaron might come up with him next trip; but, said Yahveh, "let not the priests and the people" try to come up (v. 24). This is a remarkable slip on the part of Yahveh: for there were no Priests at that time; the Priests were not instituted until some time later in the

Siniatic proceedings, when Brother Aaron and his four sons were first designated to be the first priests (Ex. xxviii, 1); and it was made death for any one else to presume to act as priest. As further proof of there being no priests as yet, we find Moses, after delivering the first batch of "Law" (Ex. xxiv, 4–5), himself building an altar under the hill, and twelve phallic mazzeboth, and sending "young men of the Children of Israel" to do the priestly job of making some burnt offerings and to sacrifice peace-offerings unto Yahveh; for all the Chosen were at that time "a kingdom of Priests" (Ex. xix, 6),—every man his own priest. And Brother Aaron, as a Priest, during Moses' next forty-day sojourn up on the Mountain, made gods of the Golden Calves, and sacrificed to them: thus again proving that there was no "Law" as to "priests of Yahveh," and that "thou shalt have no other gods before me" was not yet Law.

The remarkable Puzzles of the Giving of the Law, and the Ten Commandments, here at Sinai, we will reserve for consideration in another Chapter, and will proceed with the wonders of the wanderings in the Wilderness.

THE TWO CENSUSES IN THE WILDERNESS

Before leaving Sinai, in the beginning of the second year of the Exodus (Num. i, 1), Yahveh ordered a Census to be taken of "every male from twenty years old and upward, all that are able to go forth to war in Israel" (vv. 2–3); and they were so numbered by Moses and Aaron. If the all-knowing Yahveh, who is reputed to number even all the hairs of the head, had just stated the number himself, it would have saved his inspired recorder much trouble besides some suspicions of padded returns. Indeed, this is exactly what we are surprised to find is revealed as having happened, in very curious anticipation of the formal and tedious census enumeration. For, there at Sinai, some months before the taking of the first Census, Yahveh ordered assessments to be laid on the People for the expenses of making and outfitting the holy Ark and Tabernacle; and he commanded: "When there thou takest the sum of the children of Israel after their number, then shall they give every man a ransom for his soul unto Yahveh, that there may be no plague among them when thou numberest them" (Ex. xxx, 11–12);—a very persuasive argument to pay up. So there was levied upon every soldier-man of Israel "a bekah for every man, that is, half a shekel for every one that went to be numbered, from twenty years old and upward, for 603,550 men" (Ex. xxxviii, 26),—the exact tally disclosed by the first Census when it was later taken. So the whole labor was unnecessary.

The Census was taken by Tribes, and curiously enough, every single tribe polled even numbers of hundreds, except one, Gad, which had an odd fifty in its tally.

Again, at the end of the celebrated Forty Years' wandering in the wilderness, and just after the massacre of the Plague of Fiery Serpents, another like Census was taken there in the Plains of Moab, near Jordan; and here the inspired total is rightly given as 601,730 (Num. xxvi, 51). Evidently the birth-rate had not quite kept pace with the natural mortality and the frequent large massacres by Yahveh of his Chosen. In neither Census were the Levites numbered in these totals, as we shall presently notice.

Some Census Oddities

Several curiosities of these two Censuses may be briefly noticed. We have seen how extraordinary are the inspired vital statistics which serve as the basis of the accepted figures showing that 70 persons had expanded in only four generations into quite two and a half millions, or more. Indeed, the pious editor of the "Self-Interpreting Bible" appends a solemn note to the first tabulation of returns, saying: "If to this number (603,550) we add the Levites, and all the women and children below 20 years of age, it will make about three millions of Israelites, besides the 'mixed multitude' "! But in order not to overcrowd Providence, we will be content with our more modest figures.

One of the sons of Jacob migrating into Egypt was Dan. For him, the first generation was one son, Hushim (Gen. xlvi, 23), and he had no other, for in the second Census lists (Num. xxvi, 42), the "sons of Dan" constitute but one family, here called Shuhamites. In the returns of the first Census, however, the number of Danites, males of military age, was 62,700 (Num. i, 39); in the second Census their number is recorded as 64,400 (xxvi, 43): all these offspring (males fit for war over 20 only), of one single son in three generations! To accomplish this prodigy, Hushim or Shuham, and each of his sons and grandsons must each have had over 80 children of both sexes. And it is curious that the offspring of the one son of Dan should be nearly twice as many as those of the ten sons of Benjamin, who numbered only 35,400 warriors in the first Census (i, 37), and 45,600 in the second (xxvi, 41).

The Levites

As the sons of Levi, or the Levites, came early into prominence, we may briefly follow their family genealogy with interest. In Genesis, "the sons of Levi: Gershon, Kohath, and Merari" (xlvi, 11), are among the 70 Jacobites who migrate to Egypt; these three were the first generation, named again in Exodus (vi, 16). The second generation is enumerated again by names in Exodus vi, 17–19: "The sons of Gershon, 2; the sons of Kohath, 4; and the sons of Merari, 2"; a total second generation of eight persons. The third generation is partially accounted for in verses 20–23—Three of the four sons of Kohath (v. 18) increased to eight, to wit: the sons of Amram, 2, Aaron and Moses; the sons of Izhar, 3; of Uzziel, 3; the fourth, Hebron, is credited with no sons: thus the third generation so far as named is only eight persons. The same names of these generations are recorded in Numbers iii. Assuming that the two sons of both Gershon and Merari showed the same increase, four each, then all the male Levites of the third generation would be 16 persons. For the fourth generation, we have only the record of the two sons of Amram, Moses and Aaron, the first of whom had two sons, the latter four: at the same rate of increase, the sixteen males of the third generation would amount, in the fourth, that is, at the first Census of the Exodus, to 48 persons (male and female),—rather, to 44, as the four sons of Aaron were numbered, not with the Levites, but as Priests. Yet the inspired word of Yahveh, avers that the number of Levites, of "service age," from 30 unto 50 years, amounted to 8580 (Num. iv, 47–48); while "all the males (Levites) from a month old and upward, were 22,000" (Num. iii, 40); while at the second Census they numbered 23,000 (xxvi, 62). And this was only the males; there would naturally be about the same number of females, or some 45,000 Levites. We have seen that the total number of male "sons of Levi" of this fourth generation was approximately 44 souls.

The Mothers of Israel

We have noted already the returns of the first Census, at Sinai, giving 603,550 warriors over 20 years of age, 22,000 male Levites, and an estimated nearly 2,500,000 total of the Hosts of Yahveh. Now the credit of this whole story is impeached by another inspired contradiction. Yahveh had first (Ex. xiii, 2) claimed to himself, as sanctified, or devoted, "all the first-born, whatsoever openeth the womb among the Children of Israel, both of man and of beast: it is mine," in commemoration of his massacre of the first-born of Egypt on the night of the celebrated Exodus (v. 15). But later Yahveh changed his mind (Num. iii, 41, 45), and said, "Take the Levites for me, instead of all the first-born among the Children of Israel"; and he ordered Moses, "Number all the first-born of the males of the Children of Israel from a month old and upward, and take the number of their names" (v. 40). Moses did so, and reported the number of male first-born to be 22,273 (v. 43). These first-born were not simply the first-born sons of their fathers, who might polygamously have many other sons by different mothers; they were the first-born of the mothers as well,—"the first-born that openeth the womb"; hence the mothers' first-born, too. Thus there could have been, at the very most, 22,273 mothers of Israel in the Host who had sons, and naturally, a like number—22,273—of fathers.

Now, the male sons of all order of birth, "from 20 years of age and upward, able to bear arms in Israel," (and which number of course included many first-born sons), are averred to have been 603,550: the other males, under 20 years of age and those over military age, and the unfit for service, would bring the total males to approximately one-half of the total Host of 2,414,200, or about 1,207,100 males; all which Hebrew males must of course have had Hebrew mothers. For 22,273 mothers to have 1,207,100 sons would require every mother in Israel to have an average of fifty-five sons; and, of course, about as many daughters! But as the average mother of Israel has been seen to have averaged 3 or 4 sons,—but the whole thing is too preposterous to be worth more figuring: and with only 22,273 child-bearing women to 1,207,100 men, only about one man in some scores could have a wife and children! We change the subject.

The Puzzle of "Same" or "Not Same"

When Yahveh first came down to Moses in regard to the Chosen People, he said: "I am come down to deliver them and to bring them" to the Land of Promise (Ex. iii, 8); and he told Moses to lead them thither, and assured him, "Certainly I will be with thee" (v. 12). At Sinai, just after the Golden Calf incident, Yahveh said to Moses: "Depart, and go up hence, thou, and the People, unto the Land which I sware I will give thee" (Ex. xxxiii, 7); but, said Yahveh, "I will *not* go up in the midst of thee, for thou art a stiff-necked People,"—but I will send my Angel, and *some hornets* (!)

along with you, and drive out the inhabitants" (xxiii, 23, 28)—the "seven nations more and mightier" than Israel. Thus, in the very year of the Exodus 1491 B.C., the Promised Land was promised distinctly and positively to this identical same "Host of Yahveh" which had just exodused from Egypt, and Yahveh promised to Moses that he, Moses, should lead the Hosts into the Promised Land. These are promises.

Now for the performances. Thereupon—(we pass now to the Book of Numbers)—the Hosts left Sinai, and marched forward promptly and without much incident, to very near the borders of the Promised Land, quite ready to enter it, and camped at Kadesh (Num. xiii, 26). This was a little more than a year after leaving Egypt. From Kadesh, Moses, as a prudent leader, sent the twelve spies "to spy out the Land of Canaan." The majority report of the spies was of an alarming nature, they reporting, "We saw giants there, in whose sight we were as grasshoppers" (xiii, 33). Thereupon, all the People "lifted up their voice and cried, and wept that night," crying, "Would to God we had died in Egypt, or in the wilderness" (xiv, 1–2), and they wanted to elect a captain and go back home to Egypt.

Yahveh had now one of his frequent mad spells, and said, "I will smite them with the pestilence," and kill them all; but Moses again cajoled Yahveh out of his fatal purpose by an argument to his divine vanity, saying: "Now, if thou shalt kill all the People as one man, then the nations which have heard of the fame of thee will speak, saying, Because Yahveh was not able to bring this People into the Land which he sware unto them, therefore hath he slain them in the wilderness" (v. 16). So Yahveh, seeing the force of this, compromised by swearing, "As I live, surely they shall not see the Land which I sware unto their fathers, save Caleb and Joshua; but your little ones, them will I bring in; but as for you, your carcasses they shall fall in this wilderness. And your children shall wander in the wilderness forty years" (vv. 21–23). So Yahveh commanded Moses, "To-morrow turn you, and get you into the wilderness by the way of the Red Sea" (v. 25).

We need not here follow their unhappy rambles of nearly forty years, until "in the fortieth year, in the eleventh month, on the first day of the month" (Deut. i, 3), we find the "Hosts of Yahveh,"— Yahveh only knows where. According to verse 1, "These be the words which Moses spake (at the time *supra*) unto all Israel on this side Jordan in the wilderness, in the plain over against the *Red Sea*"; that is, west and south of Jordan, and yet a long way from the Promised Land. But in verses 3 and 5, it is averred that all the following words, chapter after chapter long, and the same words referred to in verse 1,—"Moses spake unto the Children of Israel, on this side Jordan, *in the land of Moab*,"—which is up by and to the east of the *Dead Sea*, therefore very near their promised goal; so near, indeed, that Moses says (ix, 1) in that same speech: "Hear, O Israel, Thou art to *pass over Jordan this day*, to go in to possess" the land; although Moses guessed wrong about this, as it was not till some six months and more later, after his death, that the Children crossed over, under Joshua. Nothing short of Infinite Wisdom can, it is believed, unravel all these inspired tangles of revelation. Wherever it was, there it was that Moses delivered his famous Harangue, reviewing first the forty years' wanderings, and falling into inextricable contradictions of statement. On the point before us, the identity of the "Hosts of the Lord" now assembled, with those who exodused from Egypt, the inspired record reads much like the maiden's game, plucking daisy petals and reciting— "He loves me, he loves me not, he loves me,"—different with every sacred page we turn, and frequently different several ways on the same inspired page.

Moses begins (i, 6), as if he were speaking to the identical Host which left Egypt forty years before with him and encamped under Sinai: "Yahveh our God spake to *us* in Horeb (i.e. Sinai)"; and (v. 9), "And I spake unto *you* at that time"; and (v. 18). "And I commanded *you* at that time all the things which *ye* should do"; and (v. 19), "And when *we* departed from Horeb" *we* did this and that, and *ye* suggested and I sent spies to spy out the land; and (v. 26) "*ye* murmured in your tents"; and (v. 34), "Yahveh heard the voice of *your* words, and was wroth, and sware, saying: Surely there shall not one of this evil generation see that good Land"; and (v. 39) "Moreover, *your* little ones, they shall go thither, and unto them will I give it"; and so on through this and the next chapter, "we" and "ye" and "you" did this and that, until (ii, 14), "And the space in which *we* came from Kadesh-Barnea, until *we* were come over the Brook Zered, was thirty-eight years; until *all* the generation of men-of-war were wasted out from among the Host, as Yahveh sware unto *them*." First, "ye" and "we" are the same Host that left Egypt; then that Host is all dead, and "ye" and "we" are a different Host altogether: *id est*, the now-grown-up "little ones" of the original Exodus-Host and the after-born of the Chosen. Later (v, 2–3) in the same Harangue, it is *positively averred* that the Host to whom Moses was then and there speaking was the *identical Host* whom he had led out of Egypt, and hadn't died off at all: "Yahveh our God made a Covenant with *us* in Horeb —(there at Sinai, 38 years ago)—Yahveh made *not* this Covenant with *our fathers*, but with *us*, even *us*, who are *all of us here alive this day*"! Either these are bald contradictions, or there was an unrecorded resurrection of all the dead "Hosts of Yahveh," whose "carcasses fell in the wilderness," here on the borders of the Promised Land, so as to hear this swan-song of Moses, and his review of their manifold sins and shortcomings in life.

Again (viii, 2–4), in the same Harangue, the inspired historian contradicts his former story of the death and destruction of the original Hosts, during the forty years, and explicitly admits that they are alive: "And thou shalt remember all the way which Yahveh thy God led *thee* these forty years in the wilderness, etc., etc.; Thy raiment waxed not old upon thee, neither did thy feet swell, these forty years,"—certainly proving the entire survival of the original Hosts. This must have been so—for the clothes and shoes of the original children, which were miraculously preserved, and enlarged with the growth of the wearers, would hardly have comfortably fitted, as hand-me-downs, the bodies and feet of the deceased original wearers' children. The fathers' outfit would not have answered for their younger or smaller offspring. And again (xi), the positive assertion of identity is made in unequivocal terms: "(2) And know ye this day: for I speak *not* with your children which have not known, and which have not seen Yahveh your God's (3) miracles, and his acts, which he did *in the midst of Egypt unto Pharaoh;* (5) And what he did unto *you* in the wilderness, until *ye* came into this place; (7) But *your* eyes have seen all the great acts of Yahveh which he did. (10) For the Land, whither thou goest in to possess it, is not as the land of Egypt, *from whence ye came out.*" So Inspiration has here got its stories mixed again; Yahveh evidently kept not his oath about destroying all his Children and scattering their carcasses in the wilderness, for he didn't do it: so the record of the second Census cannot be true when it recites: "Among these there was not a man of them whom Moses and Aaron numbered, when they numbered the Children of Israel in the wilderness of Sinai. For Yahveh had said of them, They shall surely die in the wilderness. And there was not left a man of them, save Caleb and Joshua" (Num. xxvi, 64–65). A more remarkable "confusion of tongues" is hard to find in all the inspired History, since Babel.

The Tabernacle and its Activities

While at Sinai, or Horeb, the whole "Law of God," with a few minor exceptions, is recorded as having been delivered by Yahveh to Moses, and by Moses written in his book: an inspired record which we reserve for another place. Let us now inspect several curios of inspired impossibilities.

Yahveh and Moses spent a good part of forty days on Sinai, again without eating or drinking (Ex. xxxiv, 28), engaged in framing up plans and specifications for a big portable Tent called the Tabernacle or Sanctuary, in which were kept the holy altar and the wonder-working Ark, and in devising the whole system of priests and priestly services. This Tabernacle, as described in Exodus xxvi, was a portable Tent about 18 feet broad by 54 feet in length, with a door in one end: it and the Ark, with their furnishings, must have been marvels of luxurious beauty (or the product of remarkable imagination)—gold, and silver, and brass, and blue and purple and scarlet fine linen cloths, and precious stones galore. One may wonder where all this finery—the property of slaves—came from, there in the howling wilderness, unless a part of the spoils "borrowed" from the Egyptians, after midnight of the Passover Massacre—only that we are told that the Children hurried off with nothing except their bundles of clothes and kneading-troughs and a little dough (Ex. xii, 34).

This famous Tabernacle was to stand in the center of a court, or yard, about 180 feet long by 90 feet broad (100 × 50 cubits (22 inches)—Ex. xxvii, 11–12), surrounded by silver-filleted pillars about 7½ feet high. It was known as the Tabernacle of the Congregation, and was the central point of the Camp. The area of the Court-yard was thus 1800 square yards, and that of the Tabernacle 108 square yards: deducting the area of the Tabernacle from that of the Court-yard, leaves a free space within the Court-yard of 1692 square yards. Why all these details? Why, all Scripture is important, and several inspired wondrous tales hang thereby.

In Leviticus viii, 3–5, as in many similar instances, Yahveh said unto Moses: "Gather thou all the Congregation together unto the door of the Tabernacle of the Congregation. And Moses did as Yahveh commanded him; and the assembly was gathered unto the door of the Tabernacle of the Congregation. And Moses said unto the Congregation," etc. This Congregation, or Assembly, as appears scores of places, was the whole People, the entire "Hosts of Yahveh," 2,414,200—plus strong, as is also proven by the verses to be cited below. Needless to calculate: the millions of the Chosen, packed their tightest, would have extended for miles all around and about the Tabernacle, even if the hundreds of thousands of surrounding tents were not there to prevent such a massing. So it cannot be perceived, as the inspired Word relates, how that "the Assembly was gathered unto the door of the Tabernacle."

Again, here as often elsewhere, it is said, "And Moses said unto the Congregation": in Deut. I, 1, it is more explicitly stated "These be the words which Moses spake unto all Israel"; and in v, 1, "And Moses called all Israel and said unto them"; and, most explicitly, in Joshua VIII, 35: "There was not a word of all that Moses commanded, which Joshua read not before all the Congregation of Israel, with the women, and the little ones, and the strangers that were conversant among them." Now, a wayfaring man though a fool, need not be told that Moses could not speak nor Joshua read so that the fifty-thousandth part of "all Israel" could hear them, or get anywhere near the door of the Tabernacle: unless, indeed, the truth is, as it surely was, that the total horde of fugitive slaves, if it ever existed at all, was no more than the three to five thousand to which Nature would have increased the original 70 in four generations, as we have already figured it out.

SACRIFICES

The Book of Leviticus is almost wholly a Priestly Code of most elaborate and intricate and burdensome regulations of priestcraft and bloody sacrifices. One grows dizzy and nauseated in simply scanning the insanguinated catalogue of burnt-offerings, meat-offerings, peace-offerings, sin-offerings, trespass-offerings, *et id omne genus* of superstitious and blood-reeking butchery which fills these pages *ad nauseum*. Nearly every act of life and of death involved some pious propitiatory sacrifice, thousands of them every day, on the part of nearly every one of these more than two millions of poor victims of their Yahveh. It would seem that whole regiments of priests would be required for these holy services. How many priests then does divine revelation afford us for these millions? Three! "Thou shalt appoint Aaron and his sons, and they shall wait on their priest's office: and the stranger that cometh nigh shall be put to death" (Num. iii, 10); a murderous priestly monopoly in the Moses family, limited to Brother Aaron and his sons in perpetuity, under penalty of death.

Skipping over all the other multitudinous kinds of sacrifices which kept this holy trinity busy (if they ever got time to do them at all), let us take just one species, which we can calculate with some probability from our inspired data. That is, if Yahveh kept his awful Word of wrath and killed off the entire original millions who set out with Moses from Egypt, with the exception of the "little ones, your children, which in that day had no knowledge between good and evil," as divine inspiration assures us in Deut. i, 39, and if the balance of the whole millions which reached the Promised Land was from new births during the forty years in the wilderness, then, as we have seen, these births must have averaged some 1700 for every day of the forty years.

Now, according to the Holy Law of God, child-bearing was the worse defilement which could come upon the holy Children of Yahveh: the mother of a child was "unclean," for forty or eighty days according as her child was a boy or a girl baby; for 40 or 80 days, on the same basis, she must undergo a humiliating "purification"; she must "touch no hallowed thing, nor come into the sanctuary, until the days of her purifying be fulfilled"! Then, at the end of that God-imposed penance, "she shall bring a lamb of the first year for a burnt-offering, and a young pigeon or a turtle-dove for a sin-offering, unto the door of the Tabernacle of the Congregation, unto the priest, who shall offer it before Yahveh, and make an atonement for her, and she shall be cleaned from her issue of blood" (Lev. xii). A sin-atonement and purification for obedience to Yahveh's very first command: "Be fruitful, and multiply, and replenish the earth"!

Of course these lambs and turtle-doves must be slain (Lev. i, 10–17), cleaned, washed, burnt, the blood smeared on the bloody holy altar, and the offal and feathers "carried without the Camp," twelve miles there and back. If Aaron and his two sons team-worked like Trojans every second of their time, day and night, and only took five minutes for each of these elaborate bloody ceremonies, three going on unceremoniously at the same time, they could perform only 36 sacrifices in an hour, or 864 in all the 24 hours of the day, without even stopping to eat or sleep; while for 1700 births 3400 sacrifices would be required, 1700 burnt-offerings and 1700 sin-offerings per diem. And where these 1700 spring lambs and 1700 pigeons or turtle-doves per day, and the water to wash them, in the howling waste desert came from, is also a divine mystery,—and the children always crying and rebelling for "meat to eat," and wailing for water to drink. The Children did not carry bird-cages containing turtle-doves in their hasty flight from Egypt, and no miracle of grace, blowing pigeons into Camp, like the quails, is recorded in Sacred Scripture. We needn't go into the details: indeed, we cannot, for the poor priests need have worked so fast and furious, killing, skinning, cleaning, cutting up, sprinkling blood, etc., that the motions of their hands and arms, like the spokes of a mighty fly-wheel, could not be followed with the naked eye; only the eye of faith can follow such performance. They far broke the record of Samantha skinning eels—one eel in the air all the time. And, all this butcher-work must be performed "in the court of the Tabernacle," and "at the door of the Tabernacle of the Congregation," in the very center of the great Camp. We have seen that the court of the Tabernacle would accommodate very few scores of People, and probably much fewer lambs being led bleating to the slaughter.

But, the divine Law of Compensation was strikingly exemplified here: the laborer was indeed worthy of his hire. These three poor overworked bloody drudges of priests were bounteously rewarded, in the matter of eating, if they ever really got time to eat, amid their overwhelming tasks. Out of many super-bounteous provisions of Yahveh's Law for his monopoly of priests, this one (Num. xviii, 9–11) may be cited to show the munificence of Yahveh to his holy servants the priests: "This shall be thine of the most holy things, reserved from the fire: every oblation, every meat-offering, etc., etc., which they shall render unto me, shall be most holy for thee and thy sons. In the most holy place *shalt thou eat it;* every male shall eat it"; all this, and very very much and many more "I have given them unto Aaron the Priest, and unto his sons, by a statute forever," decrees Yahveh. Aaron at first had four sons, but two of them, Nadab and Abihu, were early slain by Yahveh because they put "strange fire" into their censers (Lev. x, 1–2); so this left but Aaron and two sons, and their families, to enjoy the daily offerings of the 2,414,200 Children. And as Yahveh had commanded, he must be obeyed: these countless thousands of offerings daily must be eaten, by the three and family, and "in the most holy place of the Sanctuary."

One time Moses must have suspected that they were hedging on this divine edict and not eating all they ought to: the remains of a goat sin-offering were missing from the Sanctuary larder, with no signs that Aaron's sons had done their duty by it. So "Moses diligently sought the goat of the sin-offering, and, behold, it was burnt: and he was angry with Eleazar and Ithamar, the sons of Aaron which were left alive, saying, Wherefore have ye not eaten the sin-offering? ye should indeed have eaten it in the holy place, as I commanded" (Lev. x, 16–19). And all this time, with the Priests in danger of dyspepsic overgorging, the millions of Chosen were rioting for "meat to eat" and sighing for the flesh pots of Egypt, while they were being rationed for forty years on that oily Manna "which our soul loatheth." Such is again the Providence of Yahveh, or the abundant perquisites of Priestcraft—or, more likely, the vivid imagination or fluent exuberance of Inspiration.

MORE OF THE PRIESTS AND LEVITES

A like largess of munificence towards his holy priests is shown by the allotment to them at little later (Josh. xxi, 19) of "all the cities of the children of Aaron, the priests, thirteen cities, with their suburbs"; whereas, there were but two sons of Aaron, who was now himself dead, and one of them only had a son, Phineas. The priests were thus as bountifully supplied with residences as with victuals.

The Levites, too, received their full share of the bounties of Yahveh. They were the Chosen of the Chosen, as a reward for their holy zeal there at Sinai, when Moses was angered about the Golden Calf: he "stood in the gate of the Camp, and said, Who is on the Lord's side? Let him come unto me. And all the sons of Levi gathered themselves together unto him"; and at his command, they proceeded to "consecrate themselves to Yahveh" by slaying "every man his brother, and every man his companion, and every man his neighbor," and massacring 3000 of Yahveh's Chosen Children (Ex. xxxii, 26–28). Now, if there were 8580 "operative" Levites (Num. iv, 48), every man of them evidently did not "consecrate himself" in murdering only 3000 of the Children; while, if there were only 44, the 3000 assassinated would seem to have deserved their fate for submitting to it. It may be noted, that Aaron, who made the golden calf, was not among the massacred, nor was he ever punished; and the Levites, who did the bloody work, were of his own family.

However, for this pious service, these Levites were not numbered among the common hosts of the Chosen, but separately; they were then appointed "over the Tabernacle of Testimony, and over all the vessels thereof, and over all things that belong to it: and they shall bear the Tabernacle, and all the vessels thereof; and they shall minister unto it: and the stranger that cometh nigh shall be put to death" (Num. i, 47–51). At the first Census, as we have seen, these Levites, "from 30 years old and upward even unto 50 years, every one that came to do the service of the ministry in the Tabernacle of the Congregation," numbered 8580; and all this Army Brigade to do the kitchen-police work and 'tend the pots and kettles of this little 18-by-54-foot Tent in the Wilderness, and to lug it and its holy Ark from place to place, while only three priests were provided to do all the bloody heavy work of the service of Yahveh. And the Levites were made perpetual pensioners on the bounty of all Israel, and were assigned 48 cities and their suburbs for their residence (Num. xxxv, 7). These 44 or 8580, or 22,000 "sons of Levi" in the fourth generation, must have been rather lonesome scattered in their 48 cities. Here we will leave them to their own devices, wondering simply how, scattered in 48 cities, they could be "pitched about the Tabernacle," as they were commanded by Yahveh (Num. i, 53), so as to be handy with their daily chores of blood-washing and kettle-scraping. And we may reflect with interest on the providence of Moses in getting Yahveh to settle these rich per-quisites in perpetuity and exclusive monopoly upon his own kith and kin: for the priests were his sons and the Levites were his nephews by family relation. Here is an inspired precedent for the "nepotism" of modern politics.

Some Jahvistic Murderings

All the miseries, and rebellions, and abominations of the Chosen People of Yahveh during these forty years in the wilderness, nor all the murderings inflicted upon them by their merciful Yahveh, cannot be recounted for number and contradictions. Their Yahveh himself denounced his Chosen as a "stiff-necked and rebellious People"; and on the theory, maybe, that "whom Yahveh loveth he chasteneth," he made their whole life a miserable failure, and time and again they wept and wailed and wanted to die. Yahveh liberally answered this prayer; and several Special Providences to the People of Yahveh assisted in this work of death and destruction.

Two sons of Aaron, Nadab and Abihu, just consecrated priests, and may be not yet skilled in their new functions, put the wrong kind of fire in their sacred incense-burners, and there came forth fire from Yahveh and devoured them; and the Compassionate God commanded their bereaved Father Aaron not to mourn for his murdered sons, "lest ye die, and lest wrath come upon all the People" (Lev. x, 1–6). The son of a widow swore, and Yahveh ordered the Congregation to stone him to death (Lev. xxiv, 11–14); and then wholly *ex post facto*, for the first time decreed a law against such offense (vv. 15–16). The People murmured, saying, "Who shall give us flesh to eat?"; and when Yahveh heard of it, "his anger was kindled, and the fire of Yahveh burnt among them throughout the Camp" (Num. xi, 1); and later, for a like offense, he smote his People with a very great Plague. How many were massacred by the fire and the plague Yahveh, who committed it, only knows. A man gathered some sticks on the tabooed Sabbath; Yahveh was speedily consulted as to his fate, and he commanded all the People to stone the guilty culprit to death.

Again, Korah, Dathan and Abiram, and 250 "Princes of the Assembly" among this "Kingdom of Priests and an holy nation," wished to act as priests against the monopoly of Aaron and Sons, saying to Moses and Aaron, "Ye take too much upon you, seeing all the Congregation are holy." Moses retorted that Yahveh would show them "who is holy." So the "Jealous God" caused them all to stand aside "in the door of their tents, and their wives, and their sons, and their little children"; and at the potent word of Yahveh the Merciful God, "the earth opened her mouth, and swallowed them up, and their *houses* (but it was only *tents*), and all the men that appertained unto Korah, and all their goods. They went down alive into Sheol, and the earth closed upon them; and they perished from among the Congregation. And there came out a fire from Yahveh, and consumed the 250 men that offered incense" (Num. xvi). This is a truly signal vindication of the God of All Mercy who "visiteth the iniquity of the fathers upon the children unto the third and the fourth generation." But our faith in it is somewhat affected by the flat contradiction, a few chapters later, where the inspired history is repeated, with the explicit saving, "notwithstanding, the children of Korah died not" (Num. xxvi, 11), with not a blush for the flagrant contradiction of the previous inspired assertion that they "all perished," wives, sons and little children included. The next day, because "the People murmured" about this massacre, saying "Ye have killed the People of Yahveh," the good God said "consume them as in a moment," and he sent a Plague and murdered 14,700 of them (Num. xvi, 49). Because Moses smote the Rock instead of simply speaking to it, he was prohibited from entering the Promised Land, despite Yahveh's oft-repeated promises. The Chosen People got tired of their steady diet of Manna, and said, "our soul loatheth this light-bread"; so "Yahveh sent fiery serpents among the People, and they bit the People, and much People of Israel died," (Num. xxi, 6)—the statistics of this massacre not being preserved.

Just before starting across into the Land of Promise, some of the Chosen took to loving some of the daughters of Moab, "and the anger of Yahveh was kindled against Israel, and Yahveh said unto Moses, Take all the heads of the People, and hang them up before Yahveh against the sun, that the fierce anger of Yahveh may be turned away from Israel" (Num. xxv, 4–7); and 24,000 of Yahveh's Chosen Children were murdered and their heads strung up, to appease the angry God.

THE RAPE OF MIDIAN

The most revolting villiany in history, sacred or profane, if it were not attributed to so Merciful a God, and one of the biggest Fables extant, but for being related in the Holy Word of Yahveh, which is alleged to be inextricably true, is recorded in Numbers XXXI, when Yahveh's valiant warriors warred with Midian; the land, be it remembered, of one of Moses's wives, and of his father-in-law, and where Moses had lived many years as a fugitive murderer. Midian, as shown on the Bible Maps, was way down behind and beyond Sinai, in the Arabian desert; the Hosts of Yahveh were at this very time, immediately before the death of Moses (v. 2), in "the Camp at the plains of Moab, which are by Jordan near Jericho," —therefore several hundred miles from Midian, with all the great and terrible wilderness of their forty years' misery stretching between their Camp and the land of Midian. Of a sudden Yahveh says to Moses, "Avenge the Children of Israel of the Midianites" (v. 2), though only Yahveh knows what the Midianites had done to Israel or to Yahveh to merit the monstrous barbarities which the Holy Word of Yahveh says were now inflicted upon them. So Moses told off 12,000 of his warriors, 1000 for each Tribe, and "sent them to the war" (v. 6).

These are the wonderful accomplishments of the 12,000, which quite pale the exploits of the celebrated 10,000 of Xenophon. They marched across the hundreds of miles of wilderness, "warred with Midian," slew all the male Midianites, slew the Five Kings of Midian (a rather numerous Royalty for a small Desert Tribe), and they slew poor old Balaam, him of the Talking Ass,—(though he lived hundreds of miles away at Pethor in Mesopotamia); they took all the women of Midian captives, with all their little ones, and took the spoil of all their cattle, and all their flocks, and all their goods; they burnt all their cities, and all their goodly castles, with fire (it is a wonder how many "cities" and how many "goodly castles" a Tribe of Bedouin Arabs living in a corner of the Desert would have); and they took all the spoil, and prey, both of men (but they had already "slew all the males" (v. 7), and of beasts; and they brought the captives, and the cattle, and the spoils back hundreds of miles across the wilderness into the Camp near Jericho, and delivered all to Moses. And, if anything could be more wonderful, all this was achieved without the loss of one single Soldier of Yahveh.

These 12,000 wonderful Soldiers of Yahveh took, according to the inspired account, about 100,000 human captives, women and children, over 675,000 sheep, more than 72,000 beeves, and over 61,000 asses (vv. 32–34), a total of over 808,000 head of live animals, and brought them all across the wild terrible deserts "where there was no water," for some 300 miles to the sacred Camp. Yet, with all this addition of live-stock to their already great flocks and herds, "even very much cattle," the poor beef-famished Children had nothing to eat but that "loathsome Manna"—"until they came unto the borders of the land of Canaan" (Ex. xvi, 35)—"we have nought save this Manna" (Num. xi, 6). Which is a wonder.

And when the meek and holy Man of God saw all the multitude of female captives alive, "Moses was wroth with the officers of the Host," and in his holy wrath he demanded, "Have ye saved all the women alive?" (Num. xxxi, 14–15). Then, in the name of his God, the Merciful, he gave this bloody order,—an order which if given by an Apache War-Chief crazed by Christian Fire-water, would have damned him and his Tribe and the "Great Spirit" of his Tribe to execration forever;—in the name of Yahveh Moses commanded: "Now, therefore, kill every male among the little ones, and kill every woman that hath known man by lying with him. But all the women children, that have not known man by lying with him, keep alive for yourselves" (v. 17)! So records the Holy Word of Yahveh, writ by "holy men of old as they were moved by the Holy Ghost." So the Chosen of Yahveh, at Yahveh's holy command, to the eternal glory of God, straightway put into pious execution this holy command of their God, and in holy zeal butchered some 68,000 women and young children; then these "peculiar treasures unto Yahveh" took the remaining 32,000 tender young virgins to glut their hallowed lusts upon in God-ordained rape!" Verily, as the Psalmist sings, "the commandment of Yahveh is pure, enlightening the eyes" (Ps. xix, 8). And Yahveh got his fair share of the-accursed booty, human and animal alike (vv. 36–42).

THE WONDERFUL LAST DAYS OF MOSES

Let us pause here a moment, while we recover best we may from this inspiring revelation of Yahveh's Holy Word, and cast a rapid glance at the rush of divinely appointed events to their great Consummation, the triumphal entry of Yahveh's Chosen—this "kingdom of priests and an holy nation"—into the Promised Land. Surely, after keeping his Chosen People for forty long years in miserable watchful waiting, Yahveh wonderfully expedited events for the bungling finish. It is truly interesting to follow this climax of wonders of unrealized accomplishment.

On the "first day of the fifth month of the fortieth year" after the memorable Exodus from Egypt, Aaron died in Mt. Hor (Num. xx, 28; xxxiii, 38);—though Moses himself, in amazing contradiction, avers that Brother Aaron died in Mosera, just after leaving Sinai, 39 years previously (Deut. x, 6). Moses uttered his swan-song Harangue "in the fortieth year, in the eleventh month, on the first day of the month" (Deut. i, 3), and died promptly thereafter, "on Nebo's lonely mountain, this side of Jordan's wave" (Deut. xxxiv). Thus, peculiarly just six months to the day elapsed between the deaths of Aaron and Moses. Let us now see what a miracle or muddle of impossibilities happened, in Yahveh's inspired History, in these short and eventful six months.

MOURNING FOR AARON

1. Upon the death of Aaron, "all Israel mourned for Aaron thirty days" (Num. xx, 29). This leaves five months.

WAR WITH CANAAN

2. Then, Arad, King of the Canaanites, made a foray against Israel, and took some prisoners (Num. xxi, 1). Israel made a vow to Yahveh, that if he would deliver the Canaanites into their hand, "then I will utterly destroy their cities" (v. 2); Yahveh accepted the bloody bargain, and Israel warred against the Canaanites, "and utterly destroyed them and their cities" (v. 3). This, in passing, as we shall soon see, is not true; for all through their sacred history we find Israel at war with the Canaanites: in Judges iii, after the "Conquest," it is expressly averred: "Now these are the nations which Yahveh left, to prove Israel by them (although he had expressly and repeatedly declared he would destroy them all), . . . namely, . . . *all* the Canaanites; . . . and the Children of Israel

dwelt among the Canaanites" (vv. 1, 3, 5). But, for the sake of "proving" the rapid march of the events of our inspired history of the last five months, we will assume the "Gospel truth" of the inspired record. This attack by Arad and the retaliatory war of utter extermination of the Canaanites and all their cities must have reasonably taken a month's time, by ordinary human military campaign standards. This leaves us four months.

Ten Encampments

3. Then, the Children "journeyed from Mt. Hor by the way of the Red Sea, to compass the land of Edom" (v. 4). It may be remarked that according to the Bible Maps, the land of Edom lies just east of the Canaanites, and Mt. Hor is about between the two countries, and both are some 150 miles or more from the Red Sea, across the trackless deserts to the west; so that to go from the territory of Canaan by way of the Red Sea to reach Edom, would be much like going from New York City to Albany in order to get to Brooklyn. So on this hike the People "were much discouraged because of the way," and rioted because there was no water nor bread, and declared their loathing of the Heavenly Manna: Yahveh retaliated by sending Fiery Serpents, which murdered many of them, until Moses made his famous Brazen Serpent, which conjured the Plague (vv. 4–9). They then set forward on the march, and made nine several encampments, including that at the celebrated Well of Beer (v. 16), which greatly rejoiced the thirsty Children, and which they celebrated by a rather spiritless drinking-song. Ten encampments, allowing but three days for each and the intervening marches, would easily occupy another month. This leaves us three months.

War with Amorites

4. From the last encampment, at Pisgah, in the land of Moab (v. 20), and therefore further north of Edom and more distant from the Red Sea, the Children sent messengers to Sihon, King of the Amorites, to negotiate passage through his lands, which was refused. The two Peoples thereupon went to war; Israel smote the Amorites with the sword, took all their cities, and conquered their whole country; and "Israel dwelt in the land of the Amorites" (vv. 21–31). One would reasonably allow a month for these diplomatic negotiations and the ensuing exterminating war, to allow nothing for the "dwelling" in the land. Thus two months remain.

War with Jaazer

5. Then Moses sent spies to Jaazer, fought against it, took all its villages and drove the inhabitants out (v. 32). This conquering expedition may well have taken a couple of weeks. We have then a month and a half remaining.

War with Bashan

6. Then the Hosts of Yahveh "turned and went up by the way of Bashan," engaged in a war with the redoubtable giant King Og, "smote him, and all his sons, and all his people, until there was none left him alive: and they possessed his land" (vv. 33–35). As this episode is recorded more in inspired detail in Deuteronomy iii: "We took all his cities, three score (60) cities; all these cities were fenced with high walls, gates, and bars; besides unwalled towns a great many; and we utterly destroyed them, utterly destroying the men, women, and children, of every city" (vv. 3–6). As Og was a great Giant who had a bed 16½ feet long (preserved as proof in the Municipal Museum of Rabbath: v. 11), we may suppose that he and his people, a considerable nation occupying 60 great walled cities, put up a sturdy fight against this wonderful conquest of utter destruction; so that this war of extermination may not unreasonably have cost the Hosts of Yahveh six weeks: this would complete the entire tale of six months between the death of Aaron and the great Harangue just preceding the death of Moses. And the whole time would appear to have been pretty well filled with these divinely chronicled historical events, all crowded into one chapter of the historical Word of Yahveh (Num. xxi).

But we are surprised to find several more chapters of this inspired History of Numbers filled with exploits recorded to have taken place after the conquest of Bashan and before the swan-song of Moses,—events which must have occupied many weary months or years of any history but that of the "inspired Word of Yahveh." Let us cast a wondering eye at the panorama of supplementary proceedings of the valiant Hosts of Yahveh, in this well crowded 5 months.

The Episode of Balaam

1. In the very next Chapter, XXII, the Hosts "set forward, and pitched in the plains of Moab on this side Jordan by Jericho" (Num. xxii, 1). We may observe that the writer, here as so often

elsewhere, was hazy about his sacred geography; for, according to all the Bible Maps, Moab lay along the lower half of the Dead Sea, East of the Dead Sea, and to the south of the Brook Arnon, the northern boundary of Moab; as says Scripture: "For Arnon is the border of Moab, between Moab and the Amorites" (xxi, 13), and is thus about midway the length of the Dead Sea; while Jericho is some distance north and west of the northern end of the Dead Sea, and opposite the land of the Ammonites, north of Arnon; and not the border between Moab and the Amorites, who were far to the south and west, near the wilderness of Paran. However, we are told that Balak, King of Moab, being greatly frightened at the approach of the devastating hordes of Yahveh, bethought him of the superstitious expedient of securing the services of the celebrated Prophet of Baal, Balaam, to "come curse Israel," which, the truth to tell, it seems to have richly deserved. But the story involves several very curious and tangled considerations of high improbability.

Balaam was (maybe) a Midianite, which people, as we have seen, inhabited the extreme southeast of the Siniatic or Arabian Peninsular,—hence some 300 miles across trackless deserts from Moab. It appears from the Sacred History, that by some odd chance, some "elders of Midian" were visiting some "elders of Moab" (possibly a Pagan Church Conference of Baalites); so King Balak arranged with these two companies of elders, and he sent them "with the rewards of divination in their hands," as messengers to solicit the religious services of Balaam, who was a pagan heathen Prophet of Baal, to "come, curse me this People" (Num. xxii, 6–7). And the elders came unto Balaam, "to Pethor, which is by the river of the land of the children of his people" (v. 5); hence, one would suppose from these texts, at his home town in Midian,—though no river is known in the deserts of Midian, for there is "the waste howling wilderness, where no water is." But the inspired geographer tells us, to our further surprise, in Deuteronomy xxiii, in a reference to this incident, that Balaam was "of Pethor of Mesopotamia" (v. 4), —therefore some hundreds of miles eastward, and beyond the River Euphrates. However, where and in what direction soever, it was several hundred miles either way from where Balak was in Moab by the Dead Sea. At the very least, it must have taken the messengers some ten (or forty) days to make the trip, on their slow asses, across the deserts.

When they arrived and delivered their message, "God (Elohim, gods) came unto Balaam" (v. 9), and had a dream-talk with him, and asked, "What men are these with thee?"—as if an all-knowing God oughtn't to know without asking; and God commanded Balaam *not* to go (v. 12). So Balaam "rose up in the morning" (showing it was all a dream), and refused to accompany the ambassadors, "princes of Balak," (v. 13) whereas they were plain Pagan "Elders" (v. 7) when they set out. So the embassy returned to Moab to Balak, and reported the refusal (v. 14): maybe another ten-day journey. But Balak was in sore straits, and sent another embassy of Princes, "more, and more honorable" than the first; and they made the ten-day trip again to Balaam, and repeated the invitation and offer of reward. But Balaam, Prophet of Baal, loyally replied, "I cannot go beyond the word of Yahveh my God" (v. 18); the "Yahveh Elohim" of Balaam being none other than the Midianitish God Baal, the rival and abomination of Yahveh, or El, the Hebrew Deity, although the inspired historian makes no distinction between them. However, again "God (Elohim) came unto Balaam at night," and told him in a dream, "If the men (who were spending the night in town before returning) come to call thee, rise up, and *go* with them" (v. 20). So Balaam, taking God at his word, rose up in the morning, and saddled his ass, and went with the Princes of Moab" (v. 21); "and Elohim's anger was kindled *because he went*" (v. 22),—a very strange caprice for a just God "in whom there is neither variableness nor shadow of turning," and whose commands should be obeyed. This makes the fourth ten-day trip back and forth,—forty days for travel alone, at the minimum reckoning. And when Balaam arrived at last, the long, tedious, and fruitless proceedings of blessing and cursing—both equally ineffective for anything —must have taken up several days additional time (Num. xxii-xxiv). So at least a month or six weeks must have been consumed with this Balaam episode, for which we have no available room in the five months under consideration to sandwich it in. The "active" period was only five months, for the first month was spent idly mourning for Aaron (Num. xx, 29).

SPORTING WITH MOAB

2. After this failure of strategy, King Balak and Balaam went their respective ways; the Hosts of Yahveh entered Moab, "and Israel abode in Shittim, and the People began to commit whoredom with the daughters of Moab" (Num. xxv, 1). To "abide" in a place would seem to indicate a considerable permanence of residence, an indication strengthened by the fact recorded of the amatory

relations of the Chosen with the "daughters of Moab"; as it must have taken some space of time for these strangers and newcomers to become acquainted and to get into the good graces of the fair daughters of the land, as well as to adopt the worship of the land and become "joined to Baal-Peor," so as to "kindle the wrath of Yahveh" (v. 3), who was notoriously "slow to anger." So that Yahveh ordered a great and bloody massacre of his Children, and he said to Moses, "Slay ye every one his men that were joined unto Baal-Peor," and "Take all the heads of the People, and hang them up before Yahveh against the sun"; and 24,000 of the Chosen were massacred, but it seems not by cutting off their heads, but by a Plague which Yahveh sent (v. 9). So here we have an indefinitely long space of time saddled upon the already overcrowded six months between the deaths of Aaron and Moses.

CENSUS TAKING

3. Then "it came to pass after the Plague,"—how long after is not revealed, that Yahveh commanded Moses (Num. xxvi, 2), to take a second Census of the Hosts of Yahveh, "all that are able to go to war in Israel, from 20 years old and upward." How long it required to take the Census of 601,730 Soldiers of Yahveh is not stated, so we will not count it in this score.

EXPEDITION TO MIDIAN

4. Then, after several chapters of new Laws said to have been handed down by Yahveh through Moses, we have the inspired history (Num. xxxi), of that fearful and wonderful expedition, already described, of the 12,000, against Midian, 300 miles away across the great and terrible wilderness, and the utter destruction of the Midianites, including the luckless Balaam, who was now evidently in Midian instead of at Pethor of Mesopotamia. Surely such a great military achievement as this, marching 600 miles through scorching deserts, the return trip with thousands of women and children and nearly a million cattle, and the destruction of a whole nation, must have taken a month or six weeks, at a minimum allowance of time for wonderful Biblical historical events.

"MOPPING UP"

5. After all this, time was found for the very elaborate parcelling out and settling of the whole East Palestine country—"the kingdom

of Sihon, king of the Amorites, and the kingdom of Og, king of Bashan, the land, with the cities thereof in the coasts, even the cities of the country round about," all to the east of the River Jordan, upon the Tribes of Reuben, of Gad, and of the half-Tribe of Manasseh, who did not want to go West over the River (Num. xxxii, 16–42). So Moses entered into stipulations with them for their military aid in the further Conquest, and gave them the land; and they "built" (probably rebuilt, as all the cities of these two kingdoms are said in the sacred history to have been "utterly destroyed") fifteen cities, "fenced cities," named in the text (Num. xxxii, 34–38), and a number of "sheep-folds" for their "very great multitude of cattle." Moreover, what is more remarkable (for, again, every city had been utterly destroyed when they captured the kingdoms), they made military campaigns against Gilead, "and took it, and dispossessed the Amorite which was in it" (v. 39)—(though every inhabitant had already been massacred); and they captured a number of villages and small towns; and they settled their families in all these places throughout the eastern borders of the Jordan, before making ready, as they had agreed with Moses, to "go armed before the Children of Israel" to help conquer the Promised Land west of Jordan (v. 32). Such operations of allotment, city-building, family-settling, and further fighting and conquest, must have consumed considerable time, a month, six months, a year, how can one tell, when "the ways of Yahveh are past finding out"? and we have no revelation on the point, except that it was all within the six months already so replete with such notable divinely appointed events as we have just reviewed in brief detail, and which must have necessarily more than completely occupied the five months at their disposal.

Moreover, either the inspired writer has told us another "story," or the warlike and city-building operations just mentioned must have required several years instead of a fraction of these five months. We recall that the inspired historian has told us, that upon the conquest of Bashan, the Chosen warriors "smote Og, the King of Bashan, and his sons, and all his people, until there was none left of him alive, and they possessed his land" (Num. xxi, 35); and for our greater assurance this is repeated and the important details added: "And we took all his cities at that time, there was not a city which we took not from them, three score (60) cities; all these cities were fenced with high walls, gates and bars; beside unwalled towns a great many" (Deut. iii, 3–5). Yet here we have this long delay in order to "build cities," and not only cities, but walled, armed cities, although they had just captured sixty of them; and

such defended cities were necessary for defense against the inhabitants of the land,—of whom "none was left him alive"; for the
warriors of the Tribes who were going to settle in these eastern
districts asked time, before crossing Jordan to the Conquest, to
build these walled cities to leave their families in, so that "our little
ones shall dwell in the fenced cities because of the inhabitants of the
land" (Num. xxxii, 17).

The closing Cantos of Numbers are largely devoted to detailed
plans for the allotment and settlement of the cis-Jordan territories
of the Promised Land, among the remaining warrior tribes and the
kitchen-police Levites—when the Hosts of Yahveh, captained by
Joshua, and convoyed by an angel and the Hornets, should have
triumphantly possessed the Land which Yahveh had so often
promised to go before and prepare it for them. Just how all these
promises and covenants were performed by the Divine Promisor, we
shall soon admiringly see. First we pause to consider briefly but
wonderingly the puzzling problem of the giving of the Law there
at Sinai, in the first year of the Exodus.

CHAPTER VI

THE "TEN COMMANDMENTS" AND THE "LAW"

EVERYBODY in Christian communities knows, supposedly, and many can even quote the (supposed) celebrated "Ten Commandments," given by God to Moses on Sinai, and hung neatly framed in all well conducted Sunday Schools, Christian and Jewish alike: for here the two Faiths are at one.

But to discover the genuine "Ten Commandments" in the Hebrew Scriptures is an exercise for the ingenuity of Aristotle, as it will appear when we undertake the task. Even more intricate and hopeless is the task of unraveling the mysteries of the "Law of God by the hand of Moses," as said to have been delivered amid the clouds and thunders and lightnings of Sinai. An examination of the texts of the "Five Books of Moses" demonstrates that Moses did not promulgate these Commandments and Laws; and even cursory review of the religious history of Israel confirms that they were quite unknown for a thousand years nearly after Moses. If any solid ground for judgment can be at all arrived at from the study, it is that some elementary precepts of "Law" of course existed from earliest times in Israel, as everywhere; and were not unnaturally attributed to the traditional "Law Giver" Moses. Later the Priests framed up the very elaborate and cumbrous priestly system of ritual and offerings, and to give it currency and sanction, averred it to be Law given by Yahveh on Sinai through Moses; just as the Laws of Hammurabí were represented as given by the great God Bel through the sun-god Shamash: and as were God-given the Koran of Mohammed, the Book of Mormon, if not the Baker-Eddy "revelations" of Science and Truth.

DIVERGENT DECALOGUES

There are generally recognized two, but as we will see, there are actually three, versions of the well-known "Ten Commandments"; and the giving of the "Law" is quite variously reported, by the Elohist and Jahvist scribes. As the Decalogue is for the

137

most part reported in the same language in the two usually recognized versions, I will only call attention to the points of material difference in their texts, and then consider the third.

It is first set out in Exodus XX, 2 to 17 inclusive; and repeated in Deuteronomy V, 6 to 21 inclusive. The first verse of the Elohist version recites: "And Elohim spake all these words, saying"; then follow the reputed "Ten Words"; and this is the first Law recorded in the Book of Exodus,—except as to the Passover and slavery, in Chapter XII. The Fourth Commandment, regarding the Sabbath Day, contains several important differences in the two versions. In the Elohist version (v. 8) it begins: "Remember the Sabbath day, to keep it holy." The Yahvist version (v. 12), reads: "Observe the Sabbath day, to keep it holy, as Yahveh thy God commanded thee."

The Elohist continues (v. 10):

"in it thou shalt not do any work, thou, nor thy son, nor thy daughter, thy manservant, nor thy maidservant, nor thy cattle, nor thy stranger that is within thy gates."

But the second version, instead of simply "nor thy cattle," adds (v. 14),

"nor thine ox, nor thine ass, nor any of thy cattle";

and after the words, "thy stranger that is within thy gates," further adds:

"that thy manservant and thy maidservant may rest as well as thou."

This is not all. In the Exodus version, after the words "within thy gates," the reporter adds, as the "reason for the rule" (v. 11):

"For in six days Yahveh made heaven and earth, etc., and rested the seventh day: *wherefore* Yahveh blessed the Sabbath day, and hallowed it."

But the second version, after having added the words "may rest as well as thou," gives an entirely different statement of the "reason" (v. 15) thus:

"And thou shalt remember that thou wast a servant in the land of Egypt, and Yahveh thy God brought thee out thence by a mighty hand and an outstretched arm: *therefore* Yahveh thy God commanded thee to keep the Sabbath day."

There are several other noticeable differences between these two versions. In the first (v. 12) it is commanded: "Honor thy father and thy mother: that thy days may be long upon the land which

Yahveh thy God giveth thee." In the second version this is amplified, thus: "Honor thy father and thy mother, *as Yahveh thy God
commanded thee:* that thy days may be long, *and that it may go
well with thee,* upon the land which Yahveh thy God giveth thee"
(v. 16).

In Exodus the four commandments, "Thou shalt not kill, commit
adultery, steal, and bear false witness," are stated in four separate
verses (13–16) both in the English and Hebrew texts; and each
begins, "Thou shalt not," while in Deuteronomy, English version,
the four commandments are stated in separate verses (17–20),
though they are all in one verse (17) of the Hebrew text, and each,
after the first, reads "neither shalt thou." The Commandment,
"Thou shalt not covet" (v. 17), begins in Exodus, "Thou shalt not
covet thy neighbor's house, thou shalt not covet thy neighbor's
wife"; while in Deuteronomy (v. 21, Heb. v. 18) it begins, "Neither
shalt thou covet thy neighbor's wife; neither shalt thou desire thy
neighbor's house," and adds "his field," which is not in the Exodus
version. These may seem small differences, but they are differences.
Yahveh is not reported as having given two sets of "Ten Words";
and what he only said once, he could not have said two ways; and
Yahveh himself assured that he did "write upon these (second) tables
the words which were in the first tables, which thou breakest" (Ex.
xxxiv, 1). Revelation should at least be consistent and accurate.
But now to the origins and substance of the "Ten Commandments,"
if haply we may discover them.

Yahveh, as we have seen in Exodus XIX, sent Moses immediately
back down the mountain from his third trip up, after a few curt
words about sanctifying the non-existent priests and building the
already built and existent fence: not a word as to any Law or
Commandments or Tables of Stone: "So Moses went down unto the
People, and *spake* unto them" (v. 25), ending the Chapter XIX.

Then immediately follows Chapter XX, headed by the Bible
Editors "The Ten Commandments," and beginning with the words:
"And *Elohim spake* all these words, saying" (v. 1); and this is what
the Gods *spake*—the celebrated Ten Commandments, first or Elohist
edition! And Moses was not on the "Mountain of the Gods" at
that time at all—but had just come down from his third trip to
report about the priests and fence (Ex. xix, 25).

And "all these words" which Elohim "spake," were not only the
so-called "Ten Words" of the Decalogue (Ex. xx, 3–17), but four
whole Chapters (Ex. xx–xxiii) of "Law," on many subjects, much
of it very puerile and barbarous. And, as Elohim "spake all these

words, saying" (Ex. xx, 1), then and there to Moses, clearly they were not *written*, by the finger of Yahveh, on those two celebrated Tables of Stone at all, not on this trip anyhow.

These four Chapters of other "Law" immediately following the Elohist version of the "Ten Commandments," begin in Exodus XX, 22, with the words: "And Yahveh *said* unto Moses, thus shalt thou *say* unto the children of Israel"; and in verse 1, chapter XXI, "Now these are the judgments (laws) which thou shalt set before them." And it is explicitly recorded, that "Moses came and *told* the people all the words of Yahveh"—the whole four chapters of Law *told* to the entire 2,414,000 of them; "and all the people answered with one voice, and said, All the words which Yahveh hath *said* will we do" (Ex. xxiv, 3); which they never did at all, in all their idol-worshiping Bible history.

And Divine revelation then tells us, that, after thus *telling* them to all the people, "*Moses wrote all* the words of Yahveh,"—evidently during that night, for he then "rose up early in the morning" (xxiv, 4), and he "took the *Book of the Covenant* (which he had just then written), and read in the audience of the people," and the people again promised to perform it all and be obedient (v. 7), which they never did or were. And Moses immediately, after receiving orally, repeating orally, writing into a Book of Covenant, and promulgating the Law terribly forbidding the making of "any likeness of anything" in heaven, earth or hell, and to bow down to the gods of the heathen,—"but thou shalt utterly overthrow them, and quite break down their images" (mazzeboth, Ex. xxiii, 24)— rose up and builded his altar under the hill, "and twelve pillars" (mazzeboth; Ex. xxiv, 4). Which again proves that the "Law" denouncing this very thing was not given through Moses the very day before, and did not yet exist.

The Tables of Stone

Evidently, now, the whole thing had been done and finished—the so-called "Ten Commandments," followed by four whole chapters of "Law" (Ex. XX-XXIII), had been duly "spake" by Yahveh, while apparently Moses was down in the camp, following his abrupt send-off from his third trip. And not yet a word about any Tables of Stone.

Here occurs a very odd episode, a dinner-party or banquet given by the Gods to celebrate, apparently, the giving of the Divine Law. For as soon as the last words were spake, Yahveh extends this invitation: "And unto Moses he said: Come up unto Yahveh, thou, and Aaron, Nadab, and Abihu, and seventy of the elders of Israel"; but he adds this curious limitation: "and prostrate yourselves afar off. And Moses shall come near unto Yahveh, but they shall not come near" (Ex. xxiv, 1–2). So Moses reported the invitation; after which, as above related, he *told* the people all the words of the new Laws; then *wrote* them in a Book; then *read* the Book to all the people. Then Moses and the other invited guests, all 74 of them, went together up the Mount (this being the fourth trip for Moses), quite disregarding the orders for all but Moses to stay afar off. And then and there, it is related, "they saw the Gods (ha-Elohim) of Israel, and they ate and they drank" (v. 11).

And here it was, during this fourth-trip celebration of the "giving of the Law," that Yahveh very unexpectedly turns to Moses and summons him for a fifth trip, saying: "Come up to me in the Mount, and be there," and, said Yahveh, here for the first time referring to this matter, "I will give thee Tables of Stone, and a Law, and commandments which *I have written;* that thou mayest teach them" (v. 12); though all these commandments are already on record as having been *dictated* by Yahveh and written in a Book by Moses and taught to the people several chapters previously, following his third mountain-climb and return to camp, as we have seen.

THE FIFTH MOUNTAIN TRIP

So Moses went up again, for the fifth trip, into the Mount of the Gods, and Yahveh kept himself hidden from Moses for six days in a cloud (Ex. xxiv, 15–16), while Moses had to pass the time as best he could up there in the dark; and on the seventh day Yahveh called Moses into the cloud, "and Moses was in the Mount forty days and forty nights," without anything to eat or drink (Ex. xxiv, 15–18). The entire time, and seven chapters (XXV–XXXI) are then taken up by the Almighty Architect of the Universe in dictating minutest details of drafting plans, of carpentry, upholstering, tailoring and general handicraft instructions in regard to making a most holy Tabernacle and Ark, gaudily adorned with (evidently, for that is all they had), stolen Egyptian finery; and all its sacred ceremonials, such as killing a ram and putting some of its blood upon the tip of the right ear of Brother Aaron, and upon the tips of the right ears of his four sons, and upon their right thumbs and right big toes, and then sprinkling the blood on the Holy Altar of Yahveh (Ex. xxix, 19–20), and such like holy mysteries. And the

Mighty God concocted a special kind of patent perfumery which should by "holy unto Yahveh," and laid the fatal penalty: "Whoever shall make like unto that, to smell thereto, shall even be cut off from his people" (Ex. xxx, 84–38),—murdered to the glory of the God.

All this was the work of Infinite Wisdom for forty days,—instead of teaching these Holy Ones civilization and humanity, and common decency and honesty, and most of all, to tell the truth, instead of the atrocious things they say about God in their wondrous Holy Scriptures which they presumptuously call the Holy Word of God. But instead, four times amid the awful fires and thunders of Sinai the fateful injunction was reiterated by the God: "Thou shalt not seethe a kid in its mother's milk"; and reams of stone tablets, or whatever other writing material it was that they used, were covered with childish Medicine-Man hocus-pocus for telling whether a poor victim had the leprosy, or some other loathsome infection, and with maudlin incantations for his "purification," if by chance he recovered from it, all alone and unattended, in the filthy lazzaretto outside the holy camp: but never a single word from the All-Wise God, the "Great Physician," who calls himself "the Lord who healeth thee," about how to *cure* the leprosy and other diseases, or how to prevent them; nor a word anywhere of hygiene, sanitation, useful sciences, or any of the common humanities. If a few of these things had been laid down for the Chosen, they might have been, to their lasting advantage, somewhat less of a "peculiar people," and have escaped the ravages of some of the plagues and epidemics which devastated their Promised Land then and to the present time.

THE FIRST TABLES OF STONE

At the end of these forty days of the fifth trip, Yahveh, we are told, "gave unto Moses two Tables of Testimony, Tables of Stone, written with the finger of Elohim" (Ex. xxxi, 18); and presumably containing all the "Law and commandments which I have written" (Ex. xxiv, 12), about which Yahveh *spake* when he invited Moses up for this fifth trip, and which Moses had already written in his Book of the Covenant (Ex. xxiv, 4), following his third mountain trip.

It is perfectly evident, if anything can be evident from these muddled records, that these first Tables of Stone did *not* contain the "Ten Commandments" of Chapter xx; but contained only, if anything, the building plans and specifications for the Tabernacle and Ark (Ex. xxv, 40), and the other matters set out, drawn up during the forty days of the fifth trip up the "Mountain of the Gods" and detailed in Chapters xxv–xxxi, as we have seen.

The Golden Calf Incident

While Moses dallied the forty-six days on the "Mount of the Gods" this fifth trip, conning all those precious revelations of Yahveh's holy will, the Chosen got restless, and "wot not what has become" of Moses, and they demanded of Brother Aaron that he "make us Gods, which shall go before us" (Ex. xxxii, 1). Aaron took their jewelry, probably that stolen from the Egyptians several months previously with their Yahveh's help, and melted it up and made the celebrated Golden Calf, designed no doubt after the sacred Bull Apis of the Egyptians. And Aaron, High Priest of Yahveh, proclaimed, "These be thy Gods (Elohim), O Israel, which brought thee up out of the land of Egypt" (v. 4); and said, "To-morrow is a feast to Yahveh" (v. 5)—proving that the Calf represented Yahveh, and celebrated by naked Baal-Orgies to Yahveh (v. 25).

Yahveh, looking down from the Mount of the Gods, saw this and got very angry, and said to Moses: "Now let me alone, that my wrath may wax hot against them and that I may consume them." But Moses cajoled the Lord Yahveh, saying that the Egyptians would mock him (Yahveh) about it; and reminded Yahveh of his promise, and asked him to "repent of this evil against thy people" (v. 12). So Yahveh, who "is not a man that he should repent," thereupon "repented of the evil which he thought to do unto his people" (v. 14).

Moses thereupon rushed down the mountain into the camp, and in his own righteous wrath willfully threw down and broke his two famous Tables of Stone (first edition), and smashed up the Golden Calf, ground it to powder, mixed the gold dust with water (where he got the water there in the wilderness not being revealed), and he made the 2,414,000 Chosen to drink the very diluted mixture (vv. 15–20). And Yahveh commanded the sons of Levi to "consecrate yourselves this day to Yahveh, that he may bestow upon you a blessing this day" (v. 29), and to take their swords, and "slay every man his brother, his companion, and his neighbor" (v. 27), throughout the camp and 3000 of the naked (v. 25) Chosen were murdered. This is the second wholesale massacre attributed to the God "whose name is Jealous" (Ex. xxxiv, 14).

This fearful punishment was inflicted for the pretended offense of making a "graven image" of Yahveh himself, as to which there was as yet no law—if we accept the Tables of Stone as containing the "Ten Commandments"; for Moses, according to that theory, was yet on Sinai receiving the Law, "Thou shalt not make unto thee any graven image," when the Golden Calf was set up; and he rushed down from the Mount and broke his Tables of Stone containing that very Law, before he had promulgated it as Law. This was a case, therefore, not only of *ignorantia juris* on the part of the people, but of *lex post facto* on the part of the God. And, as we have seen, this was not a case of idolatry to "other gods before me," for the Golden Calf expressly represented the great Yahveh, whom the whole people, naked as in the Baal worship, proclaimed, "These be thy Elohim, O Israel, which brought thee up out of the land of Egypt" (v. 4); and "Aaron made a proclamation and said, To-morrow is a feast to Yahveh" (v. 5), proving their belief that they were worshiping their Rescuer from Egypt, and that they had no idea that Yahveh was any diffrent from any other God, either in identity or in his form of worship.

But these first Tables, broken by Moses, assuredly were not the "Ten Commandments" of Exodus xx and of the Sunday Schools. The Ten Commandments are quite short; while these first Tables of Stone broken by Moses, and which Yahveh declared contained "two Tables of Testimony" (Ex. xxxi, 18), whatever that was, were evidently quite lengthy, as described. For when Moses rushed from the mount down into the camp to destroy the Golden Calf, "The two Tables of Testimony were in his hand: the Tables were written on both their sides; on the one side and on the other were they written" (Ex. xxxii, 15). As the Hebrew writing is very abbreviated, consisting entirely of consonants in words mostly of only three letters each, two Stone Tables written on both sides would not have been required to contain the brief "Ten Commandments," but maybe rather the extensive "Testimony."

THE SECOND TABLES OF STONE

Chapter XXXIII of Exodus forgets all about the broken first Tables; and in it Yahveh breaks his Promise and tells Moses that he, Yahveh, will *not* go with his Chosen into the Promised Land, but will send an angel along instead, together with other matters immaterial to the subject in review.

Chapter XXXIV returns to the Tables, and opens with the command of Yahveh to Moses: "Hew thee two Tables of Stone like unto the first: and I will write upon the Tables *the words that were in the first Tables,* which thou breakest" (v. 1), and to bring them up into the mountain the next day (v. 2), for the sixth trip. So Moses went up, for the sixth trip, and took along the two new Stone Tablets that he, Moses, had made; and Yahveh talked at length, giving the substance of previous "Law"—but not a single word of "Ten Commandments" as reported in Exodus xx or Deuteronomy v, and which are popularly known and called "The Ten Commandments," and hung on the walls of modern Sunday Schools. And these Tables wind up with the awful and wonderful command of the God: "Thou shalt not seethe (boil) a kid in his mother's milk" (v. 26)!

And even these Commandments *Yahveh* did not write on the famous second set of Stone Tables, but Moses did the work. The "Commandments" begin with the words (v. 10), "And he (Yahveh) *said,* Behold, I make a Covenant." Yahveh then states it by word of mouth orally (vv. 12 to 26 inclusive); and then: "And Yahveh *said* unto Moses, *Write thou these words* (commandments), for after the tenor of *these words* have I made a *Covenant* with thee and with Israel (v. 27). . . . And *he (Moses) wrote upon the Tables* the words of the *Covenant,* the *Ten Commandments*" (vv. 28). Then Moses, after having spent another forty days and forty nights there with Yahveh without anything to eat or drink (v. 28), brought the "two Tables of the Testimony" down, and "gave the people in commandment all that Yahveh had *spoken* with him in Mt. Sinai" (v. 32).

The Actual "Ten Words"

Now, if there were ever any "Commandments" written on Tables of Stone, these 15 verses of Exodus XXXIV (12–26), contain them: it is expressly declared by Yahveh, "*I will write* upon these (second) Tables the words which were in the first Tables, which thou breakest" (v. 1); and when Yahveh finished the dictation, and told Moses to "*write thou* these words," he verified their identity with the first Tables by averring, "for after the tenor of *these words* have I made a *Covenant* with thee and with Israel" (v. 27). The so-called "Ten Commandments" in Exodus XX and Deuteronomy V are therefore, *not* the genuine Ten Commandments written on the first and second Tables of Stone, nor was either set "written by the finger of God"; but they were both, first and last edition, dictated to and written down by Moses. They were strikingly different from the popularly so-called "Ten Commandments" of much later date. The original

"Tables" will be seen to contain only a ceremonial Ritual, with but *two commandments*, to wit, the prohibition of "other gods," and the observance of the Sabbath, which are contained, among other things, in the versions of Exodus XX and Deuteronomy V, and in entirely different form and words. It is curious to note how nearly all the "Laws of Moses," like many other ancient laws, run in series of tens—the number being evidently derived from counting the fingers of the two hands,—as may be verified by checking them up in the Books of Exodus and Leviticus. The "Ten Commandments" most nearly resemble the "Ten highest Laws of Buddha"; the "Ten Virtues of Brahma" are also enumerated by Manu.

We need not puzzle ourselves further with these inextricable tangles of inspiration. It suffices to show that the "Ten Commandments," as we are taught them in the Sunday Schools, are not the "Ten Words" of the two fabled Tables of Stone; and to demonstrate that the whole muddle of the "giving of the Law" to and by Moses is a thing apochryphal and impossible, and never happened that way at all, as we shall presently further see.

The Law of the Decalogue

The very first avowal of the popular "Ten Commandments," reveals what in any other and "false" religion would be no doubt a terrible and iniquitous Deity: "I Yahveh thy God am a Jealous God, visiting the iniquity of the fathers upon the children unto the third and fourth generation of them that hate me" (Ex. xx, 5). A more hateful and diabolic character could not be drawn even by an inspired pen: the same implacable Deity who, according to the inspired Eden Fable, damned all humanity through the ages of time because an inexperienced woman, seduced by a talking snake, ate an apple in disregard of a whimsical prohibition; and then drowned nearly all creation in a fit of wrath over the misconduct of his own progeny, "the sons of the gods" (Gen. vi, 4); now writes in stone his stony-hearted decree that the unborn innocent shall pay the penalty of those guilty of not loving such a God! Thus Yahveh "repayeth them that hate him to their face, to destroy them" (Deut. vii, 10).

The other enactments of the Decalogue are mainly such as existed for ages in the Codes of all the nations of antiquity and ever since—and needed no God to enact them; prohibitions simply against murder, adultery, theft, false testimony—precepts common to all systems of even primitive law. The Babylonian Code of Hammurabí, of date about 2350 B.C., nearly a thousand years before Moses, might be and maybe was a model of them all. The only special feature of the reputed Mosaic Code is that it was never obeyed, except in its most cruel and vicious precepts. In the supplementary legislation that followed, death was made the bloody penalty for the slightest work on this voodooed seventh day (Ex. xxxi, 15; xxxv, 2).

Other Divine Mosaic Laws

The very next Law after the Decalogue is a brutal law of human slavery for this nation of slaves but three months escaped from 400 years of slavery,—just as the very first edict after their escape from slavery treated of slaves of these fugitive slaves (Ex. xii, 44). Saith Yahveh: Now these are the judgments which thou shalt set before them: If thou buy a Hebrew servant, so and so; if the slave be married and have children, they may be torn apart and separated; if the slave loves his wife and children and does not want to be torn away from them, "his master shall bore his ears through with an awl," and hold him in perpetual slavery. A man may sell his own daughter to be a slave (Ex. xxi, 7), and it is broadly hinted that her master might indulge his lusts upon her with impunity. If a Child of Yahveh kills his slave, "he shall not be punished, for he is his money" (v. 21). No God of Mercy ever gave these execrable laws. The brute ex-slaves, now turned brutal slave-masters, framed them up to justify their own inhumanity, and to give them "Divine" sanction accused them upon their God.

The Bloody Code, with its key-stone *Lex Talionis*—of "life for life, eye for eye, tooth for tooth, hand for hand, foot for foot, burning for burning, wound for wound, stripe for stripe" (Ex. xxi, 23–25), reads as if dictated not by a just and merciful God, but rather by the spirit of Devils incarnate or of Apache Indians. Every man was made his own bloody avenger: "The revenger of blood himself shall slay the murderer: when he meeteth him, he shall slay him" (Num. xxxv, 19):—there was not a criminal court known among these barbarian Children of their barbarous God. And dice, or sanctified craps, were the God-prescribed method of detecting the unknown criminal (Ex. xxviii, 30; Lev. viii, 8; Num. xxvii, 21; 1 Sam. xiv, 41) to be revenged upon, as well as for deciding civil lawsuits (Num. xxvi, 55–56; Prov. xvi, 33). The "Law of God" superstitiously and wickedly commands the murder of harmless old women: "Thou shalt not suffer a witch to live" (Ex. xxii, 18);

though God knows there was no such thing as a witch! Countless
cruel priestly and judicial murders have resulted through the ages
from this "inspired" Bible mandate—which one sentence alone totally
discredits and disproves the whole Hebrew Bible as being the "Word
of God."

The Holy Law is a reeking bloody priestly Code, decreeing
death and maiming for every violation of its superstitious Voodoos.
Abject subjection to the priest is riveted upon the people by this
inspired ukase: "The man that will do presumptuously, and will
not harken unto the priest, even that man shall die" (Deut. xvii,
12),—a bloody enactment reiterated in scores of variations of
fiendishness. If one's nearest and dearest, even "the wife of thy
bosom," entice to worship some milder Deity than Yahveh, "thine
eye shall not pity, neither shalt thou spare; but thou shalt surely
kill; thine hand shall be the first upon him to put him to death,
and afterward the hand of all the people" (Deut. xiii, 6–10). But
why pursue these revolting atrocities further? They are not the
"Law of God," but the savage enactments of the priests of crude
and barbarous Tribes of primitive people, branded with the name
of their Pagan God Yahveh to give them greater terror to ignorant
and superstitious heathens.

These priests were supreme and final judges of all crimes and
civil controversies: "by their word shall every controversy and every
stroke be tried" (Deut. xxi, 5); though this seems to contradict
the "*lex talionis*" and adjudications by sacred dice just noticed.
Beautiful women captives of war might be forced to shave their
heads and become the lust-slaves of their holy captors; if these holy
ones did not find the expected "delight in her," she might be turned
out of doors after being "humbled" (Deut. xxi, 10–14). Of stub-
born sons, gluttons or drunkards, it is commanded that their fathers
accuse them to the elders, "and all the men of his city shall stone
him with stones, that he die; . . . and all Israel shall hear, and
fear" (Deut. xxi, 18–21), as well they might. Other undefined
deeds judged by the priests "worthy of death," are ordered to be
punished by hanging to death on a tree (v. 22).

If one of the Children finds a bird-nest, Yahveh ordains that
the mother bird and her eggs or young must not be taken together,
but these may be robbed from the mother bird with Divine approval
(Deut. xxii, 6–7). If a man marries a woman and "go in unto her,"
and is disappointed and reports "I found her not a maid," the
father and mother of the young woman must hale her before all
the elders in the public gate of the city, bringing along "the tokens

of their daughter's virginity"; these holy wiseacres must then hold a sort of solemn ogling "*inquisitio de ventre inspiciendo*," and if the "tokens" incite their condemnation, "the men of the city shall stone her with stones that she die" (vv. 13–21); and so in cases of adultery, if the woman be married (vv. 23–24). A man having the misfortune to be sexually crippled, and an unfortunate *filius nullius* are forever excommunicated from the holy Congregation of Yahveh unto the tenth generation (Deut. xxiii, 1–2). The whole races of Ammonites and Moabites are accursed for fanciful reasons; "thou shalt not seek their peace nor their good all thy days forever" (vv. 3–6).

Yahveh established Trial by Ordeal for cases of suspected infidelity of a woman to her husband. The priest before whom the lady was accused was to make up a holy horrid concoction of "holy water," filthy dust from the floor of the Tabernacle, and a lot of barley meal, mixed up with "bitter water that causeth the curse," into a "jealousy offering"; the priest then makes some conjurations "unto the woman, if no man hath lain with thee," and "charge the woman with an oath of cursing," saying, "Yahveh make thee a curse and an oath among thy people, when Yahveh doth make thy thigh to rot and thy belly to swell; and this water that causeth the curse shall go into thy bowels, to make thy belly to swell and thy thigh to rot." To all this holy incantation the woman shall complaisantly say "Amen, Amen." The holy priest then makes the woman drink the loathsome concoction; "then it shall come to pass, that if she have done trespass against her husband, that the water which causeth the curse shall enter into her, and become bitter, and her belly shall swell, and her thigh shall rot. . . . But if the woman be not defiled, then she shall be free, and shall conceive seed. This is the Law of Jealousies" (Num. v, 11–29). One would think this noxious dosing would be very efficacious to cause swell belly whether guilty or innocent, and the test worse than the suspicion.

Such are samples of the holy Laws of the Infinite Wisdom of Yahveh. For enlightened legislation some might prefer even the Tennessee Legislature to Yahveh and Moses.

Moses Not the "Law-giver"

From the innumerable "internal evidences" in the Hebrew Bible itself which we have pointed out here and there, it is shown to demonstration that Yahveh did not "give the Law" to Moses on Sinai, or anywhere else, and that Moses did not write the "Book

of the Law"; that Moses never even heard of the "Law" attributed
to him. In a word, that the Books containing the "Law" were not
written until many centuries later, and were never in existence at
all, until the "Law" was framed up, by the Priests, many hundreds
of years after the time Moses is supposed to have lived, if ever such
person lived at all, outside of legendary tradition.

We have abundantly seen by the many instances cited, that the
so-called "Five Books of Moses" relate many supposed historical
facts which occurred, if they ever at all occurred, hundreds of years
after the traditional time of Moses, who is said to have died 1451
years B.C. And we have seen many other such "anachronisms" in
the other Books of the Hebrew Scriptures, as Joshua, Judges,
Samuel: thus proving that they were not written until after those
alleged facts had supposably occurred, long after their times. A
better kind of proof than that so plentifully furnished could hardly
be desired to refute and disprove the claims of "inspired" or of very
ancient origin of these Books.

The "Law" of Late Priestly Origin

What is true of the Books containing the "Law" is equally true,
by Bible "internal evidences" of the late and priestly origin of the
"Law" itself. The "Book of the Covenant," we are first told, in
Exodus, XXIV, 4, was written by Moses; later, in Deuteronomy (Ch.
XXIX), Moses several times (vv. 20, 21, 27, 29) denounces upon the
Chosen People "all the curses of the Covenant which are written in
this Book of the Law"—because they had "served other gods." Then,
in Chapter XXXI, just before his death, he seems to have gotten
out a new edition of his "Compiled Laws" for permanent record:
"For Moses wrote this Law, and delivered it unto the priests, the
sons of Levi, which bare the Ark of the Covenant of Yahveh, and
unto all the elders of Israel" (v. 9); and he commanded them: "Take
this Book of the Law, and put it by the side (inside) of the Ark of
the Covenant of Yahveh your God, that it may be there for a witness
against thee" (v. 26).

Moses also particularly commanded them, that they assemble
all the people every seven years, and read to them all the words of
this Law (vv. 10–13). This "Book of the Law" was evidently a very
sizable tome. And, as if foreseeing, with prophetic eye, a time when
the Chosen would have kings over them (though the thing was written long afterwards), Moses orders that every such king, "when
he sitteth upon the throne of his kingdom, he shall write him a copy

of this Law in a book, and he shall read therein all the days of his life: that he may learn to fear Yahveh his God, and to keep all the words of this Law and these statutes, to do them" (Deut. xvii, 19). And it is decreed that every such king shall not "multiply wives to himself, neither shall he greatly multiply to himself silver and gold." But, by the clearest negative evidences of the texts, no king (until Josiah) ever had or read such Book or ever saw or heard of or read this wonderful "Law," which positively forbade under terrible penalties everything which was their common and daily practice and idolatrous cult; and all the kings, following the example of David and Solomon, did very greatly "multiply wives unto themselves," and with all their people, habitually did every thing which is so fearfully forbidden in the "Book of the Law." This clearly proves their entire ignorance of it, and that it could not have been in existence during all the ages from Moses to the futile "reforms" of the "good king" Josiah, when the Book of the Law was "discovered" by the Priests of Judah, as we shall shortly examine.

It was at Sinai, in the first year of the Exodus, that Moses, it is recorded, wrote the first edition of his "Book of the Covenant"; and forty years later that he made his revised edition and ordered the bulky tome laid up as a testimonial against the people in the Ark of the Covenant. Yet, when next we hear of it, Joshua built an altar unto Yahveh, of *unhewn stone*, "over which no man hath lift up any iron"; and on this very rough surface, "he wrote there upon the stones a copy of the Law of Moses" (Josh. viii, 32); and "afterward he read all the words of the Law, the blessings and cursings, according to all that is written in the Book of the Law" (v. 34), to all the people. This is about the last word in all the Hebrew Scriptures, for about a thousand years, until Josiah, of this famous "Law of Moses." When Solomon had built the Temple, he put into it the ancient "Ark of the Covenant" made by Moses; and it is said: "There was nothing in the Ark save the two Tables of Stone, which Moses put there at Horeb, when Yahveh made a Covenant with the children of Israel" (1 Kings viii, 9; 2 Chron. v, 10). And of this Solomon more explicitly says: "the Ark, wherein is the Covenant of Yahveh" (1 Kings viii, 21; 2 Chron. vi, 11). This "Covenant" was clearly the Covenant of Circumcision, or regarding the Sabbath and other gods; not the "Ten Commandments" or the "Law," so unanimously unknown and unobserved until the "Find" of Josiah. Never once again is it mentioned, or a single command of it observed or knowledge of it seemingly suspected, in a thousand years, till the Book of the Law was "found" by Hilkiah the Priest.

THE "FINDING" OF THE LAW

All are familiar with the celebrated "finding" by the late lamented Joseph Smith—led thereto by the Angel Moroni—of the wonderful golden plates containing the text of the famous Book of Mormon, in nineteenth century United States. History repeated itself. In 2 Kings xxii, is the relation of an equally notorious discovery. In the eighteenth year of the "good King" of Judah, Josiah, while some repairs were being made in the Temple, Hilkiah, the Priest of a sudden "found the Book of the Law of Yahveh given by Moses," and by him ordered to be preserved in the Ark of the Covenant" (Deut. xxxi, 24–26). Hilkiah announced his "discovery" to Shaphan the Scribe, and they took the great "find" to Josiah the King. This remarkable "discovery" was made in the year 623 B.C., or 828 years after the death of Moses. So the first proof that this "Book of the Law" never existed until it was "found" by the Priest, is that for 828 years nobody had ever heard of it, nor is it once mentioned in Hebrew Holy Writ, and not a one of its many holy laws and commands had ever been observed, by Priest, King, Prophet, or people of Yahveh.

This fact is expressly proven by the positive statement of King Josiah, to whom the Book was at once taken and read: "When the King heard the words of the Book of the Law, he rent his clothes"; and he sent to "inquire of Yahveh concerning the words of this Book that is found: for great is the wrath of Yahveh that is kindled against us, *because our fathers have not hearkened unto the words of this Book*, to do after all that is written in this Book" (v. 13). So Huldah the Priestess, who was consulted, reported that Yahveh was very angry, "because they have forsaken me, and have burned incense unto other gods" (v. 17), exactly as they had done during their whole history. This is highly significant:—It never once occurred to this lady Prophet, nor to any of the many inspired Prophets who infested all the history of Israel, to "prophesy" that the Book of Law was laid away there in the holy Ark and could be found for the looking! So Josiah at once called all the people and Priests together, and read to them the Book of the Law, and pledged them to keep and perform all the laws and commandments thereof, which their fathers had never before known or observed.

Josiah then at once began a great series of "reforms," related in 2 Kings XXIII and in 2 Chronicles XXXIV; each one of which corresponds exactly with the various commands of the Book of the Law, as may be verified by consulting the marginal references and the texts referred to. Even the great celebration of the Passover, purporting to commemorate the wonderful Exodus from Egypt, was quite unknown; the King especially ordered: "Keep the Passover unto Yahveh your God, as it is written in the Book of this Covenant"; and it is added: "Surely there was not holden such a Passover from the days of the Judges that judged Israel, nor in all the days of the Kings of Israel, nor of the Kings of Judah" (xxiii, 22).

Among the reforms made by the King, he destroyed the idols, the "pillars and groves," the "high places" which filled the land, the places where children were sacrificed to Moloch, the chariots of the sun and all the accessories of the worship of the sun, moon and stars. "He brought out the Asherah from the house of Yahveh (Solomon's Temple); and he brake down the houses of the Sodomites, that were in the house of Yahveh" (xxiii, 6–7); he destroyed even the holy altar which Jacob himself had erected to Yahveh at Beth-el (v. 15); and he removed the wizards, and those that had familiar spirits, and the teraphim, and all such: in each instance carrying out the detailed commands of the "Law" as contained in the Book just "found" by the Priest: or as it is recited in the record: "that he might confirm the words of the Law which were written in the Book that Hilkiah the Priest found in the House of Yahveh" (xxiii, 24). This tallying of "reforms" with the new-"found" Law may be verified at a glance by checking the Laws against the reforms, as set out in 2 Kings xxiii. The verses cited of Chapter xxiii show the reforms carrying out the Laws of the "Book of the Law" in Deuteronomy: v. 7, as to Sodomites, in Dt. xxiii, 7 seq.; v. 9, as to Levites, in Dt. xviii, 8; v. 10, as to passing through fire, in Dt. xviii, 10; v. 11, as to horses and chariots of the sun, in Dt. xvii, 3; v. 14, as to phallic images and groves, in Dt. xvi, 21 seq.; v. 21, as to the Passover, in Dt. xvi, 5–6; v. 24, as to wizards, etc., in Dt. xviii, 11. In a word, Josiah essayed to destroy at a blow the ancient religion and worship of the people, and to introduce quite a new and novel system of worship devised by the Priests, as described in the new Book, a system never known or practiced in all the history of Israel from the days of Abraham, some 1500 years previously.

Now, it is quite impossible that this wonderful "Law of Yahveh," said to have been given to Moses on Sinai, should have been in existence, right there in the Ark of the God, in the great Temple, in the constant custody and care of the Priests, and never have been known or observed, by any of the good Judges, Kings, or Prophets of Yahveh, for over 800 years. And the Hebrew Scriptures are full of proofs conclusive, and innumerable instances of practice, that every precept of this "Law" was totally unknown to and unobserved by, all the holy "Men of God," Prophet, Priest and King, from Moses to Josiah, every one of whom continuously violated some or all of the most dreadfully prohibitory and penalized articles of the so-called Mosaic Code of Laws, as we have seen and shall further see.

POSITIVE PROOFS AGAINST MOSES

We will very briefly pass in review some of these proofs that this "Law" was not instituted by Yahveh "by the hand of Moses," but was a priestly scheme written up about the time the "Book of the Law" was "found" by the High Priest of Josiah, quite a millennium after the time of Moses.

The first and most cogent proofs are to be found in the "Book of the Law" itself; this Book, said to have been laid down by Yahveh on Mt. Sinai, and written by Moses in the wilderness, and deposited in the Ark of Yahveh for a perpetual memorial and Law to the Chosen People in all their generations.

In the first place, the "Book of the Law" itself expressly declares there was no such body of Law in existence during the forty years wandering in the wilderness; though the "Law" is supposed to have been given at Sinai in the very first year of the Exodus from Egypt. And this declaration of the non-existence of the "Law" is curiously put into the mouth of Moses himself, in the fortieth year, just before the Chosen were to pass over Jordan into the Promised Land. Moses says: "And ye shall observe to do all the statutes and judgments which I set before you *this day* (Deut. xi, 32). These are the statutes and judgments which ye shall observe to do in the land, which Yahveh thy God giveth thee to possess it (Deut. xii, 1). . . . Ye shall *not do* after all the things *that we do here this day, every man whatsoever is right in his own eyes*" (v. 8). A more positive evidence that the "Law" had not been enacted forty years previously on Sinai could not be; for that "Law" left nothing to be done according to "right in his own eye," but minutely prescribed and regulated every act of life of the Chosen.

But there are a couple of specific instances of non-existence of "Law" which may be cited for particular proof. Notice first the words introducing the first instance: "And *while* the Children of Israel *were in the wilderness*," the thing happened. If Moses spent forty years rambling around in the wilderness, and wrote his wonderful "Five Books" of Law there in the wilderness, it is preposterous that he would relate an incident specially as occurring "while in the wilderness"—it all occurred there, according to inspiration. Evidently some scribe of many ages later wrote an old tale and inserted it in the general collection, and to give it good standing and currency, fathered it upon Moses "while the Children of Israel were in the wilderness."

So, while thus in the wilderness, "they found a man that gathered sticks upon the sabbath day. And they brought him unto Moses and Aaron, and unto all the congregation. And they put him in ward (jail), *because it was not declared what should be done unto him*. And Yahveh said unto Moses, The man shall surely be put to death: all the congregation shall stone him with stones without the camp" (Num. xv, 32–36), and so they did. God never ordered a man to be murdered for picking up sticks, sabbath or no sabbath; and especially by a barbarous *ex post facto* law, which was not in existence when the offense was committed; the Constitution of every State in this Union forbids such an infamy. But the text says there was *no law* on the subject when the man offended, so that he was held until Yahveh ordered his judicial murder. But the statement is wholly error, according to the recitals of the Books. For, two years before, at Sinai, it was barbarously enacted: "Whosoever doeth any work in the sabbath day, he shall surely be put to death" (Ex. xxxi, 15). Of course, neither is true; and the two statements are totally contradictory; but the instance shows that the writer knew there was no "Law" of Sinai for the murder of sabbath workers.

Again, a man "blasphemed the name of Yahveh"; he was put in ward, "that the mind of Yahveh might be shewed them"; Yahveh decreed: "He that blasphemeth the name of Yahveh, he shall surely be put to death," by stoning; and this was done (Lev. xxiv, 16). This shows there was no "Law"; though the Stone Tables of Sinai decreed: "Thou shalt not take the name of Yahveh thy God in vain" (Ex. xx, 7).

HEBREW BIBLE HISTORY DISPROVES "LAW OF MOSES"

That the "Law of Moses" was not given on Sinai and preserved in a Book kept by the High Priest in the Ark of the Covenant, and that it did not exist until "discovered" by the priests of Josiah, and was in fact unknown and unobserved by all the holy "Men of God," priests, prophets and kings, from Moses to Josiah, may be further instanced. We will briefly pass in review some of these manifold proofs.

Idols and idolatry were terribly forbidden in the "Law of Moses." We may take the word of the Prophet Ezekiel for proof of unbroken idol-worship of the Chosen People from the day they left Egypt with Moses to his own time—all in violation of the pretended but non-existent "Mosaic" Law. Ezekiel thus testifies: "Neither did they forsake the idols of Egypt" (Ezek. xx, 8); "their eyes were after their fathers' idols" (v. 24); and he quotes the Chosen as declaring: "We will be as the nations, as the families of the countries, to serve wood and stone" (v. 32). This is conclusive that the "Book of the Law," proscribing idolatry under terrible penalties of punishment and death, was non-existent through all those ages until it was "found" by the Priests of Josiah; that idolatry was the "orthodox" religion of Israel from the Exodus to Josiah—(as of course it was from the days of Abraham and before till the Exodus); and was practiced, with full approval of Yahveh himself, by all his holy "Men of God," as we shall see, in utter oblivion of any "Law" proscribing it.

We will make brief résumé of the proofs from the unbroken practices of the Chosen People from the time of the Patriarchs, that the primitive worship of Yahveh was nothing else than the sensuous phallic idolatry of the peoples about them—the old pagan, patriarchal system of Abram the heathen Chaldean. In the next chapter we will see in detail of instances, that the Patriarchs, from Abraham to Moses, were ordinary idolators and phallic worshipers of Yahveh and Baal, with their teraphim, ephods, mazzebahs, asherahs, high-places of Baal-worship and Moloch child-sacrifice and their simple earth or stone altars, where Yahveh "put his name" as a local Baal or Lord. Never once, until the "Book of the Law," pretended to be given to Moses on Sinai, was "found," is there the slightest hint against all these popular heathen practices. After Moses and the pretended "Law" of Sinai, the identical practices continued unabated and unrebuked, though the "Book of the Law" denounced them one and all in scathing terms, and threatened every imaginable human woe and destruction for disobedience to them.

Moses himself for the first thing he did after descending from Sinai and writing the "Law" in his Book and swearing the people to it, erected the twelve phallic "pillars" or mazzebahs for the twelve tribes of Israel, and sent young men to offer sacrifices on earth-made altars (Ex. xxiv, 4–5); though the very "Law" he is said to have just that day revealed, enacts: "Thou shalt not plant an asherah nor set thee up a mazzebah, which Yahveh thy God hateth"; and which time and again decrees that no sacrifice shall be offered except by the holy monopoly of Priests, and upon the wonderful altar in the Tabernacle of the congregation. His successor Joshua erected phallic pillars of stone, and built an altar of unhewn stone, on which he is said to have written the very "Laws of Moses" forbidding such practices, and although Joshua was not a Priest, he "offered thereon burnt offerings unto Yahveh, and sacrificed peace offerings" (viii, 30–31), in violation of the "Law." Joshua conjured the people to "put away the gods which your fathers served beyond the river (Euphrates), and in Egypt, and serve ye Yahveh" (xxiv, 14); which proves the unbroken idol-worship from Abraham to the last days of Joshua, and he repeated, "put away the strange gods which are among you" (v. 23); and the people promised they would, but they never did. Under the Judges, continuously, "the people served Baalim, and followed other gods, the gods of the people that were round about them; and served Baal and the Ashteroth. They hearkened not unto their Judges, for they went a-whoring after other gods" (ii, 11–17, and all through the Book).

The story of Gideon and the fleeces, and the contest between Baal and Yahveh, is further proof of the popular cult persisting (Ch. VI), contrary to "Law." Even the "good" Judges continued the forbidden sacrifices; and private persons, as Manoah, father of Samson; and Yahveh sent down fire from heaven upon the altars to consume the acceptable sacrifices (Ch. XIII). Micah's golden ephod was a god in Israel served by Levites for priests, "until the day of the captivity of the land" (Ch. XVIII).

The great and good Samuel, when first met by Saul as he was hunting the lost asses, was coming "for to go up to the high-place," where the phallic "pillars and groves" were set up and Baal was worshiped, and where, on that day, the people were holding a sacred feast; "and the people will not eat until he come, because he blesseth the sacrifice" (I Sam. ix, 13–14); practices utterly banned by the "Law" of Moses.

Samuel sent Saul to meet and join "a band of prophets coming down from the high-place (of Baal on the "hill of the gods")—and they shall be prophesying (raving), and the spirit of Yahveh shall come mightily upon thee, and thou shalt prophesy [rave] with them" (x, 5–6); thus showing the unity of the worship of Baal and Yahveh, and the entire "orthodoxy" of high-places and phallic worship. And all the days of his life, Samuel "went from year to year in circuit" to the principal "high-places," or Baal-altars of the country, and

judged all Israel (vii, 16); and though no Priest, he continuously
made sacrifices and offered up burnt-offerings, all as fearfully forbidden by "the Book of the Law."

Saul, made King over the Chosen People by Yahveh's own special
selection, continued the same practices (1 Sam. xiii, 9–10; xiv, 25,
passim), and consulted Witches, and was troubled with an "evil
spirit from Yahveh." David was a "man after Yahveh's own
heart"; he is the most murderous, adulterous, lustful, perfidious,
mendacious character in the Hebrew Scriptures; he practiced the
phallic rites of divination with ephods and teraphim, and danced
naked in public the phallic Baal-dance before the Ark of Yahveh;
and when Michal, his wife, who was herself a heathen and kept a
phallic teraphim for her private use and worship, rebuked him for
it, he shamelessly retorted: "I will be yet more vile than thus, and
will be base in mine own sight" (2 Sam. vi, 22); and he served
notice on her then and there that she should never have a child by
him, but that he would bestow his amorous favors upon "the hand-
maids of his servants."

For many years, and during the time of David, Yahveh's special
delight, "The Tabernacle of Yahveh, which Moses made in the wilderness, and the altar of the burnt offering," and presumably the holy
Ark containing the "Law" banning all such things, "were in the
high-place at Gibeon" (1 Chron. xxi, 29), in charge of "Zadok the
Priest, and his brethren the priests" (xvi, 39). David built an altar
on the threshing-floor of Ornan, or Araunah, and offered sacrifices
to Yahveh, which were so acceptable to Yahveh that he sent down
fire from heaven upon the altar of burnt offering (xxi, 26); and
David christened it: "This is the house of Yahveh ha-Elohim, and
this is the altar of the burnt offering for Israel" (xxii, 1): all which
is fearfully forbidden in the "Book of the Law," which was required
to be copied and read by every King: but no King of all Jewry, until
Josiah read the new-found Book in his eighteenth year, ever saw or
heard of "the Book of the Law of Yahveh." It was clearly not in
existence.

Solomon was a worthy chip off the old block; he "loved Yahveh,
walking in the statutes of David his father; only he sacrificed and
burnt incense in the high-places" (1 Kings iii, 3); and he "loved
many strange women," besides his 700 wives and 300 concubines,
all pagan heathen; and he built high-places, and burned incense
and sacrificed to all the gods of his women; though Yahveh was
"jealous" and mad about all this, and threatened him trouble. And
Solomon built the famous Temple of Yahveh, erected by the heathen

Hiram King of Tyre, which was adorned with the two notable phallic pillars, Jachin and Boaz, hung about with the phallic pomegranates, and built around with houses of Sodomites and Temple-whores, and abundantly provided with "pillars and groves" right in "the House of Yahveh"; and there they remained and were worshiped by all Israel till temporarily removed by Josiah, in accordance with the new-found "Book of the Law," right at the end of Hebrew national existence.

The great Prophet Elijah himself built up the ruined heathen altar at Carmel (1 Kings xviii, 30); and mourned to Yahveh because impious hands had "thrown down thine altars" in the land (xix, 10),—all such altars being utterly taboo by the "Book of the Law," as heathen Canaanitish devices. The great Isaiah himself declared, as a token of the triumph of Yahveh over the nations and their gods: "In that day there shall be an altar to Yahveh in the midst of the land of Egypt, and a mazzebah at the border thereof to Yahveh" (Is. xix, 19).

The other Prophets, as Amos, Hosea, Micah, while they deplored the Canaanitish Baal practices performed at the altars of Yahveh, never a single time declared them illegal, as contrary to the "Law of Moses," or sought to abolish them. Their efforts were solely directed toward bringing the Chosen People to devote these practices to Yahveh alone as a special God of Israel, to be worshiped by his Chosen to the exclusion of the gods of the other peoples. The Kings of Israel and of Judah, from Solomon to Josiah, set up many other gods, and mazzebah and asherah, and the worship of the sun, and moon, and stars, in the very Temple of Yahveh at Jerusalem and in Samaria; and the people continuously and unquestioningly worshiped them.

All this could not have been rationally possible if any sort of monotheistic worship of "one God Yahveh," sole God of all the earth, had been the anciently established religion of Israel, decreed in a God-given "Book of the Law" to Moses, and if such Book had existed as a holy legacy to the people, sanctioned by the fearful threats it contains against disobedience to its dread and holy commands.

It is needless to remark, with respect to the elaborate and intricate system of priestly functions and sacrifices, contained in the "Book of the Law," and said to have been practiced in the forty-year wandering in the wilderness, that all this would have been utterly impossible in such surroundings, and during the centuries of struggling warfare and very partial conquest of the Promised

Land. It was all a Priest-devised system, adopted late in the history of the Kingdom, and sought to be given authority and sanction by attributing it all to the direct command of "Yahveh by the hand of Moses."

Many other nations and peoples have had sacred "Books of Law," revealed by gods or angels to pretended Prophets: the Koran of Mohammed and the Book of Mormon may be mentioned as very well known and more modern instances. This should suffice to demonstrate that the religion of the Hebrew Bible was none other than the universal phallic pagan worship centered to a certain extent around a "Jealous" Yahveh as the special, tribal El of his Chosen Isra-el and forbidden by no extant "Law of Yahveh" given to Moses on Sinai.

CHAPTER VII

THE "CONQUEST" OF THE PROMISED LAND

THE foregoing sketch of the Exodus of Yahveh's Chosen People from Egypt, and their wonderful forty years in the wilderness, with the exemplification of all their Yahveh's marvelous providences in their behalf, must serve to give us a very keen appreciation of the authentic historicity of the inspired Word of God.

Having been duly impressed with the Divine promises reiterated by Yahveh to his Chosen People, let us turn our attention to the wondrous manner of their fulfillment, as recorded in the inspired History.

The Promise is repeated so often, from Abraham to Moses, and with so many varient ifs, buts, conditions, provisos, circumlocutions, and contradictions, that it is difficult to select the most representative one. But a fair and comprehensive sample proceeds from amid the smoke and fire of Sinai:

"Behold, I send an Angel before thee, to keep thee in the way, and to bring thee into the place, which I *have prepared*. . . .

"For mine Angel shall go before thee, and bring thee unto the Amorites, and the Hittites, and the Perizzites, and the Canaanites, and the Hivites, and the Jebusites; and I will cut them off: thou shalt *utterly overthrow them.*

"And I will send my fear before thee, and I will *destroy all the people* to whom thou shalt come, and I will make all thine enemies turn their backs unto thee.

"And I will send Hornets before thee, which shall *drive out* the Hivite, the Canaanite, and the Hittite from before thee.

"I will not drive them out from before thee in one year; lest the land become desolate, and the beast of the field multiply against thee.

"By little and little I will drive them out from before thee, until thou be increased, and inherit the land.

"And I will set thy bounds from the Red Sea even unto the Sea of the Philistines, and from the Desert unto the River: for I will deliver the inhabitants of the land into your hand; and thou shalt drive them out before thee.

"Thou shalt make no covenant with them, nor with their gods.

161

"They *shall not dwell in thy land*, lest they make thee sin against me: for if thou serve their gods, it will surely be a snare unto thee" (Ex. xxiii, 20-88).

Under both the Old and the New "Dispensations," promises are always coupled with threats of penalties. There is a difference in favor of the Old: its penalties and punishments are always temporal and temporary; those of the New are eternal as Hell-Fire. It is the earthly body alone that suffers according to Yahveh's Old Will, and that has an end with life: in the New Testament of the gentle and loving Jesus, the penalty only attaches and begins when life ends, and the immortal soul writhes out its expiation in the Fires of Hell through all Eternity. But even the Old is not wanting in picturesque detail of torture that does high credit to a God of distinguished reputation for long-suffering, forgiveness, and mercy. Here is one typical hint to the Chosen:

"If ye will not hearken unto me, and will not do all of these commandments, I will do this unto you: I will even appoint over you terror, consumption, and the burning ague, that shall consume the eyes, and cause sorrow of heart. And I will set my face against you, and ye shall be slain before your enemies. Then I will punish you seven times for your sins. I will make your heaven as iron, and your earth as brass; and your strength shall be spent in vain; for your land shall not yield her increase, neither shall the trees of the land yield their fruits.

"And I will bring seven times more plagues upon you according to your sins. I will also send wild beasts among you, which shall rob you of your children, and destroy your cattle, and make you few in number; and your highways shall be desolate.

"And if ye will not be reformed by me by these things, but will walk contrary unto me, then will I also walk contrary unto you, and will bring a sword upon you, that shall· avenge the quarrel of my Covenant: and I will send the pestilence among you, and ye shall be delivered into the hand of the enemy.

"And I will walk contrary unto you in fury; and I, even I, will chastise you seven times for your sins. And ye shall eat the flesh of your sons, and the flesh of your daughters shall ye eat. And I will cast your carcasses upon the carcasses of your idols, and my soul shall abhor you!" (Lev. xxvi).

Verily the olden Priests of Yahveh were excellent prototypes of those of the New Dispensation of Love and Mercy. Truly, "It is a fearful thing to fall into the hands of the Living God!" (Heb. x, 31)!

Incited and encouraged by the pre-cited Promises, and thus lovingly admonished to the Fear of Yahveh—the even impartial balancing of Promise and Penalty—such was the situation of the parties to this Promised Land project when at last, after 685 long years since Abraham of hopeful, watchful, waiting, of slavery and affliction, of suffering and of destruction, the Chosen People of Yahvah, in Yahveh's own leisurely way, finally

> "On Jordan's stormy banks did stand,
> And viewed the landscape o'er."

Now might they have some hopeful reason to expect, from the explicit terms of the Divine Covenant, that the Almighty Grantor would put them into immediate, quiet and peaceable possession of the long Promised Land. He had covenanted to send an Angel and some Hornets on before them, to put "the fear of Yahveh" into the rightful inhabitants on the Land, and to drive them all out well in advance of the arrival of the new and "peculiar" occupants "into the place which *I have prepared*," as Yahveh had just described it. But now it appeared that the place was not "prepared" at all; the old inhabitants were all tenaciously yet there in their walled cities and by their domestic vine and fig-tree, undisturbed by Angel or Hornets. The newcomers must yet do their own "preparing," driving out, and cleansing the Land, by fire and sword, before they could even begin to possess and enjoy the promised Possession. And this must be thorough; this was Yahveh's Motto: "When I begin, I will also make an end" (1 Sam. iii, 12). Yahveh, who was a "Man of War" (Ex. xv, 3), would see to that, and even help to it, with the angel and hornets,—as he had not done already, as promised.

Let us now contemplate the task which confronted the new-comers: Six Hundred-odd Thousand Soldiers of Yahveh, all mighty men and valiant, marching armed with scavenger-paddle-tipped spears (Deut. xxiii, 13), and with impedimenta of a couple of million or more of old men, women, children, and camp-followers, to war of extermination against "seven nations more and mightier" than they; seven highly civilized and powerful peoples, aggregating, according to the Mosaic estimate, at least twenty-odd millions of people, inhabiting a country of about 11,000 square miles, just about the size of immortal Belgium, practically the most densely populated country in the world, with its less than 8,000,000 people. Palestine then was near three times more densely populated. The God who had wrought such fearful wonders in Egypt, and brought out his Chosen with a "mighty hand and an outstretched arm," is under contract now to send one Angel and some hornets to help his Soldiers drive these seven greater and mightier nations out of their Land! But they must not be all driven out or destroyed at once, so that the wild animals should not multiply against the new arrivals too rapidly (Ex. xxiii, 28–29),—in a country about as sparsely populated as New York City!

Well, the Chosen People began at last their Heraklean task to "conquer and possess the Land." Yahveh, Man of War, the Merciful God, as Generalissimo of the Armies of Israel, thereupon issued these notable Orders of the Day:

"When Yahveh thy God shall bring thee into the Land whither thou goest to possess it, and hast cast out many nations from before thee— (naming again the "seven nations more and mightier than thou"); and when Yahveh thy God shall deliver them before thee;

"Thou shalt smite them and *utterly destroy them;* thou shalt make no Covenant with them, nor show mercy unto them;

"And thou shalt *consume all the people* which Yahveh thy God shall deliver thee; *thine eye shall have no pity upon them*" (Deut. vii, 1–16).

These Divine War Orders, issued by the Hebrew War God, which are possibly even more drastic and diabolic than some more modern and really brutal ones issued by a modern Hun War-Lord, are repeated time and again in the inspired texts, but this sample is stated here once for all. These were about the only commands of Yahveh which his Chosen People ever so much as partially obeyed, and executed heartily so far as they were able. For we shall see in the sequel, that the Almighty Yahveh did not deliver and drive out so completely as the Chosen had possibly the right under the Covenant to expect; nor were they able, despite the Divine allies of Angel and Hornets, to massacre the home-defenders of the Land to the degree of extermination and annihilation which Yahveh ordered and promised. But scores of times the official report of battle after battle, and massacre after massacre, reads like this first one: "And they *utterly destroyed* all that was in the city, both men, and women, young and old, ox, ass, etc., with the edge of the sword, and they burnt the city with fire" (Josh. vi, 21).

A little later the original Orders were modified so as to give play to the holy lust and greed of Yahveh's Chosen, it being ordered: "Thou shalt smite every male with the edge of the sword; but the women, and the little ones, and the cattle, and all that is in the City, even the spoil thereof, shalt thou take unto yourself" (Deut. xx, 13–14).

The Chosen were encouraged and urged forward with this

repeated Divine assurance: "There shall no man be able to stand before you: for Yahveh your God shall lay the fear of you and the dread of you upon all the land that ye shall tread upon" (Deut. xi, 25). And just before Moses passed to his reward—or was afflicted with his promised punishment—above but not across Jordan, he put on record Yahveh's final reassurance: "Yahveh thy God, he will go over *before* thee, and *he will destroy these nations from before thee,* and thou shalt possess them" (Deut. xxxi, 3). With this illusory promise on his lips, Moses died.

Joshua succeeded to the command next under Yahveh; and he proceeded to cross over Jordan under the circumstances that are told two ways. Beginning his campaigns of quasi-conquest with the famous fall of Jericho, where he "utterly destroyed all that was in the city, both man and woman, young and old, and ox, and sheep, and ass, and they burnt the city with fire," but kept the gold and silver and other loot for the Treasury of Yahveh (Josh. vi, 21–22), he swept on from massacre to massacre, city after city being taken and burned by Joshua: "he left none remaining, but *utterly destroyed all that breathed,* as Yahveh God of Israel commanded" (Josh. x, 40).

Here we may begin to see in what fashion the preceding glittering, sweeping Promises of Yahveh were kept and performed. A brief mental retrospect will recall to us the original simple Promise of 685 years previously to Abram, to give to him and his seed "the Land to possess it." Later the "Covenant of Circumcision" was superimposed as a single condition; then 400 years of abject slavery in a strange land was imposed as a dismal preliminary, lengthened into 430 years by a bit of forgetfulness on the part of Yahveh. At last he "remembered" his People and his Covenant, and he commanded Moses to lead the hosts of Israel out of Egypt into the Promised Land. This looked like a tardy start towards performance. But because the People got hungry and thirsty while camping for a year in the wilderness around Sinai, the fierce anger of Yahveh was kindled against them, and untold numbers of his Children were massacred by plague, fire and sword, and fiery serpents, and the entire millions of them were condemned to wander forty years in the wilderness until their carcasses were all scattered in the wilderness —or were not, as the case may be. Then, at length, the Children, or the children of the Children, as the case again may be, were sent across into the Promised Land, which had been promised to be made all ready and waiting for their undisputed and undisturbed possession.

Their mighty Yahveh had repeatedly promised them that he would "put his fear" upon the seven "greater and mightier" nations, and that not a man of them would be able to stand against them; that he would completely drive them out of their country, even using hornets to rout out those that hid in the mountain recesses; and Yahveh commanded and assured that every single inhabitant, male and female, young and old, should be all exterminated, so that not one of them should be left alive to vex and lead astray his holy People. Yahveh repeatedly promised to accomplish this annihilation of the nations, and to help his Chosen People to execute this program of universal extermination. The Chosen of Yahveh were to possess the Land completely, with no one to share it with them or to molest them in it, or to corrupt their holy lives by wicked examples of idolatry and whoredom. This precise reason, as justification for the wholesale murders and extermination of millions, was expressly stated by Yahveh himself: "They shall not dwell in thy Land, lest they make thee sin against me" (Ex. xxiii, 33). The Land was to have rest.

But: after a number of preliminary, and prevaricated, massacres of extermination as above noticed, Yahveh and his Chosen seem to have slacked their murderous zeal, or in their ability to perpetrate it, or the exaggeration of their chroniclers toned down. Joshua did not exterminate the Hivites, but made peace with them and spared the lives of the people, in direct disobedience of Orders, and made them "hewers of wood and drawers of water to Yahveh" (Josh. ix, 27). He then helped these Hivites in a war made against them by the Five Kings, this being the famous occasion when the sun stood still upon Gibeon and the moon in the valley of Ajalon (Josh. x, 12–13), so that the massacre might be completed. Then the kings of the Canaanites—already totally exterminated, (in Num. xxi, 3)—Amorites, Hivites—(already enslaved "unto this day")— Hittites, Perizzites, Jebusites, and others, leagued and went to fight against Israel. And the inspired record assures us as positive and fatal fact, that Joshua and his Israelites "smote them, until they left them none remaining; and all the cities of those kings, and all the kings of them, did Joshua take, and smote them with the edge of the sword, and he *utterly destroyed* them, as Moses the servant of Yahveh commanded" (Josh. xi, 1–12). But the Jebusites continued to inhabit "Jebus, which is Jerusalem" (Jud. xix, 10), until, at least, when part of the city was taken by David, and Jerusalem was certainly not destroyed until by the Assyrians. So of the Canaanites, and others, who for centuries afterwards occupied the

Land. But it is solemnly declared: "So Joshua took the *whole land*, according to all that Yahveh said unto Moses; and Joshua gave it for an inheritance unto Israel" (Josh. xi, 23).

This sounds like the thorough fulfillment of Yahveh's sacred Promise and Covenant. I quote again the formal and inspired assurance: "So Joshua took the whole Land, according to all that Yahveh had said unto Moses; and Joshua gave it for an inheritance unto Israel, according to their divisions by their Tribes. *And the Land rested from war*" (Josh. xi, 23).

And for further specification of assurance, Inspiration itemizes the muster-roll of Conquest of lands and kings:

"And these are the kings of the country which Joshua and the Children of Israel smote . . . which Joshua gave unto the tribes of Israel for a Possession according to their divisions;

"In the mountains, and in the valleys, and in the plains, and in the springs, and in the wilderness, and in the south country;

"The *Hittites*, the *Amorites*, and the *Canaanites*, the *Perizzites*, the *Hivites*, and the *Jebusites*" (Josh. xii, 7–8).

Thus indeed, by iterated Inspiration, "Joshua took the whole Land, and gave it for an inheritance unto Israel; and the Land rested from War." The Canaanites, Jebusites, and all the seven "more and mightier" nations were utterly destroyed and dead.

So Yahveh had kept his sacred Promise and had redeemed his Everlasting Covenant. The Chosen People of Yahveh had inherited the Land of Promise: of the seven nations of its former inhabitants, "greater and mightier" than all Israel, the Soldiers of Yahveh, "all the cities of those kings, and all the kings of them, did Joshua take, and smote them with the edge of the sword, and he utterly destroyed them; . . . every man they smote with the edge of the sword, until they had destroyed them, neither left they any to breathe. . . . And the Land rested from war" (Josh. xi, 12; xiv, 23). And time and again the inspired historian repeats the refrain, reckless of its verity: "And Yahveh gave unto Israel all the Land which he sware to give unto their fathers; and they possessed it and dwelt therein. And Yahveh gave them rest round about: there stood not a man of all their enemies before them; Yahveh delivered all their enemies into their hand" (Josh xxi, 43–44). A long list of countries and their kings which Joshua took and smote, on both sides of Jordan, of whom 31 were on the west side, is given in Joshua xii,

But Not Conquered

What is then our honest and legitimate surprise to read, in the very next chapter of the Sacred History, that Yahveh himself negatives this whole solemn record. In Joshua xiii, Yahveh says to Joshua: "Thou art old and stricken in years, and *there remaineth yet very much land to be possessed*" (v. 1); and a good part of Chapter XIII is taken up with a recital of "the land that yet remaineth" to possess—being precisely the lands and cities just recited as taken. Nor had a single one of the Seven Nations been destroyed and driven out, as so often promised, commanded, and proclaimed to have been totally accomplished.

It is a number of times expressly declared: "Nevertheless, the Children of Israel drave not out" the very several peoples named, "but they dwell among the Israelites unto this day" (e.g. Josh. xiii, 13; xv, 63; xvi, 10; xvii, 12–13). And as Joshua came on to die, he gave this remarkable warning, and admission: "That ye come not among the nations, these that remain among you . . . but they shall be snares and traps unto you, and scourges in your sides, and thorns in your eyes, until ye perish off this good land" (Josh. xxiii, 7, 13). Nearly the whole of Judges I (vv. 19–34) is a schedule of peoples whom the Chosen "*could* not drive out—but they dwell among Israel to this day"—of course very long afterwards. And wonderful to relate—it is by Divine Inspiration related: "Now these are the Nations which Yahveh *left*, to *prove Israel by them*, . . . namely . . . "All of the *Canaanites* . . . and the *Hivites*. And they were to *prove* Israel by them, to know whether they would harken unto the commandments of Yahveh (!). And the Children of Israel *dwelt among* the *Canaanites*, *Hittites*, and *Amorites*, and *Perizzites*, and *Jebusites*;—(the precise seven nations who were so annihilated that "not a man was left of them to breathe"):—And they took their daughters to be their wives, and gave their daughters to their sons, and served their gods" (Jud. iii, 1–6)! What a rare bit! One wonders what was the matter with Yahveh and his famous Hornets.

This admission that the Children of Israel "*dwelt among*" the seven Nations proves that the 600,000 Soldiers of Yahveh had not exterminated the 20-odd millions of inhabitants of Canaan Land, but remained a small, and as now follows to be seen, conquered minority among their vengeful enemies.

For these several nations, so often totally destroyed that "not a man of them was left alive to breathe," but whom the Chosen

Warriors "*could* not drive out," quickly took turn in conquering and subjected Israel. First, the King of Mesopotamia kept them in subjection for 8 years (Jud. iii, 8); then the Moabites for 18 years (v. 14); then the oft-destroyed Canaanites enslaved them for 20 years (iv. 3); then the Philistines for 18 years (x. 8); and again for 40 years (xiii, 1), and so on all but continuously until the time of David. Though Yahveh had divinely assured and promised: "Ye shall reign over them, but they shall not reign over you" (Deut. xv, 6).

All these oft-exterminated but ever conquering Seven Nations continued for centuries to possess and dwell in the Promised Land "unto this day," though Yahveh had so often vowed, "They shall not dwell in thy Land, lest they make thee sin against me" (Ex. xxiii, 33). Thus the performance of the reiterated Promise of complete possession and inheritance is seen to be a complete and dismal failure. The Covenant of quiet and peaceable possession is seen to be equally illusory and unperformed. War between the Soldiers of Yahveh and the Seven Nations was continuous under Joshua; was hardly interrupted during the 400-odd years of the Judges; was Saul's chief occupation and the occasion of his death; and was so incessant and sanguinary during David's whole reign that he had no time and was too bloody-handed to build the celebrated phallic Temple of Yahveh. As late as Solomon, 600 years after the "Conquest" and extermination by Joshua, these Nations still dwelt in "thy land"; Solomon levied tribute on six of these same Nations who "were left to prove Israel," and whom Israel had not been able to destroy or drive out (1 Kings, ix, 15–23).

The Abject Subjection of Israel

The sacred record contains many instances, of which but a sample or two will be cited here, of the desperate straits to which Yahveh's Heroes of the "Conquest" were reduced by their exterminated enemies. In the days of Samuel the Judge, the Philistines beat the Chosen so badly that the latter sought recourse to miracle or magic, and brought up the wonder-working Ark of the Covenant of Yahveh out of Shiloh, so that, they said, "when it cometh among us, it may save us out of the hand of our enemies" (1 Sam. iv, 3). It is recorded that the Philistines were afraid when they heard of the advent of the Ark, and said, "Woe unto us, for Gods (Elohim) (*is*) come into the Camp." Nevertheless, they attacked the Soldiers of Yahveh at Ebenezer (which was not then in existence—vii, 12), killed 30,000 of them, and, to their own great misfortune, they captured the wonder-Ark, which they kept until, to get well rid of it, they sent it back to the Chosen accompanied by suggestive golden images of emerods and mice.

When Saul was King, the Ammonites besieged Jabesh-Gilead, a city of the Benjaminites, and the Chosen were so abjectly terrified that they immediately offered to surrender and become slaves of the Ammonites. Nahash, the Ammonite leader, replied that he would accept—"on this condition, that I may *thrust out all your right eyes*, and lay it for a reproach on all Israel" (1 Sam. xi, 2). The elders of Jabesh begged seven days' time in order to send throughout Israel for aid; and, they said, "If there be no *man*"—(what of Yahveh or his Hornets?)—"to save us, we will come out to thee" (v. 3),—and suffer their eyes to be punched out and themselves to be made slaves! They then sent out a wild call for aid to Saul; and when the tidings became known throughout Israel, "all the People lifted up their voices and wept" (v. 4). King Saul sent swift couriers from Dan to Beersheba, commanding every man in Israel, under pain of being "hewed to pieces," to report at once for war. And, it is said, "the fear of Yahveh fell upon the People" (as well, maybe, the fear of Saul's dire threats); and they "came with one accord," to the goodly number of 330,000 men, it is said; and the next day they defeated and drove off the Ammonites—who are reported to have waited there a whole week till a force could be raised in all Israel to destroy them!

How the Israelites could do this, an *unarmed mob*, as the following inspired account proves, is one of the standing wonders of non-revelation. It will be noted, that Saul's threat of death could raise in all Jewry but 330,000 men, just about one-half of the alleged armed Host that crossed the Jordan with Joshua. The truly abject and God-forsaken condition of the Chosen People of their God, despite the celebrated "Everlasting Covenant" of Yahveh, is shown by the following graphic picture drawn by the inspired Historian, within two years after Saul was made King:

"The Philistines gathered themselves together to fight Israel, 30,000 chariots, and 6000 horsemen, and the people as the sand which is on the seashore for multitude, and pitched in Mishmash.

"When the men of Israel saw that, then the People did hide themselves in caves, and in thickets, and in rocks, and in high places, and in pits; and some of the Hebrews went over Jordan to the land of Gad and Gilead. As for Saul, he was yet in Gilgal, and all the People followed him trembling" (1 Sam. xiii, 5–7).

This is the inspired revelation of the utterly abject state of subjugation and misery of the Chosen People of their Yahveh:

"Now, there was no smith found throughout all the land of Israel; for the Philistines said, Lest the Hebrews make them swords and spears. But all the Israelites went down to the Philistines, to sharpen every man his plowshare, and his coulter, and his ax, and his mattock, and to sharpen the goads.

"So it came to pass in the day of battle, that *there was neither sword nor spear* found in the hand of any of the People that were with Saul and Jonathan" (1 Sam. xiii, 19–22).

From bad to worse the Chosen People had gone and yet went. Saul, under threat of death, had gathered an unarmed rabble of 330,000. Later, when another of their incessant wars was upon them, Ahab the King "numbered all the Children of Israel, being 7000" (1 Kings, xxix, 15, 27)—this all the People, not the fighting men only.

Thus we see the Chosen People of Yahveh, the redoubtable Soldiers of El, whom he had brought with a mighty hand and an outstretched arm—and some Hornets,—and hedged about with an "Everlasting Covenant," reduced by the inhabitants of the land which was to be perfectly "prepared" for their sole inheritance and possession, to even direr state of misery and oppression than was a certain little heroic Land by the Huns and Vandals of later History. And Israel was the "peculiar treasure" unto Yahveh, and his Chosen People; so warlike that only the "men of war" were ever numbered, and they were captained in person by their Yahveh, the "mighty Man of War." While little Belgium was civilized, peaceable, industrious, neutral, and neutralized by International Treaty.

The "Everlasting Covenant" of Yahveh may have been the original "Scrap of Paper."

CHAPTER VIII

THE HEBREW-HEATHEN RELIGION.   SEX WORSHIP AND IDOLS

THE first that we know of the Hebrew Yahveh, after the fabled Flood of Noah and the fabulous Tower of Bab-el, is his appearance to the Chaldean Heathen Abram at Haran, telling him to move on West to the Land of Canaan, which Yahveh then and there promised to give to Abram and his descendants as an inheritance and possession forever (Gen. xii, 1–3).

With Abram we get our first Biblical initiation into the religion of the Semitic peoples and knowledge of the forms and ceremonies of their worship of El, Bel, or Baal, as the form of speech might render the same term for the same Deity in their respectively closely allied vocabularies.

It is highly important to fully understand this common Semitic religion and its forms of worship, which we shall see continued unchanged all through Bible times down to the very end of the Hebrew record.   The Hebrew Scriptures, in this respect, are certainly a revelation, in a sense all too little known to the casual reader or hearer of the Word of God, as we shall abundantly see as this search of the Scriptures progresses.

PHALLISM, OR SEX-WORSHIP

The first notion of the early peoples as to a supreme Creator, was the great and glorious Sun, giving light and heat and life; so all the early peoples, including the Hebrews, worshiped the Sun, the beautiful, visible, shining Agency of Creation, as they did to the end, and as some primitive peoples do to this day.

Life was a wonderful thing to them and Creation the great miracle.   Man discovered in himself the power to reproduce this miracle of creation, to recreate life; and the organ of this wonderful procreation became from the earliest times an object of wonder, of veneration, and of worship, as the human representative of the divine Creator and Life-giver.   The woman, too, or "womb-man,"—(as is the Anglo-Saxon derivation of the word)—was an indispensable cooperator in this work of wonder, and almost equal veneration and worship were paid to the wonderful organ by which she participated in the creative work, and brought forth life: "Eve" was "Life" from the beginning of the human species—"And the man called his wife's name Havvah (Eve), because she was the mother of all living" (Gen. iii, 20).

Hence, the human organs of life, symbolized as the "staff of life" and the "door of life," through which life entered and issued, were all through ancient history, Biblical and profane, and into the present, among many peoples, sacred objects of human worship. This capital fact should be borne in mind throughout this phase of the revelation: for it is the personification of the Hebrew and Semitic religion, a thousand times verified in the Hebrew Scriptures. Not only, it may be remarked, was it the soul of the Hebrew and Semitic religion, but of the religions of Egypt, India, Greece, Rome, all Europe, and all primitive America. Its emblems have been unearthed right here in Missouri, and can be "shown" to any curious inquirer.

We have early, and many, Biblical instances and illustrations of this ancient, Hebraic, Semitic, universal, Phallic worship. Let us examine this matter a moment in its beginnings, under the light of Hebrew Scripture: all the ancient monuments testify the same customs. In Genesis x, of the reputed sons of Shem, son of Noah, one was Asshur (v. 22). This phallic name signifies, more or less, happy, fortunate, upright, erect—*unus cui membrum erectus est, vel fascinum ipsum.* Asshur went forth, we are told, out of that land, "and builded Nineveh," and founded the great kingdom of Assyria, which perpetuates his name, for its name in Assyrian, and in the Bible is "Asshur." Asshur, or Asher, as the Triune-God was called in their mythology, became deified; he represented the virile male agency of creation, and was the special Divinity of the Assyrians. His divine consort, Ishtar or Ashtoreth, was the deified personification of the female principle of creation. The idolic symbol under which they were represented and worshiped was the "Asherah," —the creative union of Bel, or Baal, and Ashtoreth, and typified "happiness," of which we shall have occasion to hear more as we proceed to search the Scriptures during this phase of our discussion.

The Primitive Trinity

The Assyrians, no less than the Egyptians, the Hindus, the Canaanites, the Israelites, the Christians, and many other religious peoples, had and have their Trinity, purely phallic in origin and significance. The virile male phallus was noted to be not alone efficient in the great and divine work of procreation: its creative labors were shared by two coefficient mates, the two *testes*, or tests of efficient manhood. Hence these were likewise honored, personified, and deified, with distinctive names: the right-side one, supposed to be prepotent in the generation of a man-child, was named Anu, or On,—that is, "strength, power"; while the left-side, or female-producing test was called Hoa or Hea. When Jacob's youngest son was born, his mother Rachel with her dying breath "called his name Ben-oni,"—"but his father called him Ben jamin"—"son of my right hand" (Gen. xxxv, 18). Thus Anu and Hoa completed the Assyrian, and Hebrew, Trinity, side by side with Asshur. This triad of the miracle of human procreation was represented by the triune symbol of the phallic cross in its most primitive—and natural —form:

HO-A-NU
S
S
H
U
R

a universal religious symbol perpetuated under many variations of form, but always with the identical phallic significance: its most conspicuous adaptations

to-day are the sacred "Cross of Christ," and the Christian Temple with its towering steeple and lateral transcepts.

The Assyrian supreme masculine Creator, Bel, was manifested in this male Triad of Asshur-Anu-Hoa, with the female creative consort, Ashtoreth, the whole symbolized and worshipped under the symbolic "Asherah," which will be more graphically pictured a little further along. Bel, Ashtoreth, and the "Asherah" were integrally part and parcel of the fervent worship of the Hebrew Semites in the Land of Canaan, just as they had been in the Land of Chaldea whence they came, and so continued from first to last, as their Scriptures vividly portray.

The Assyrian Asshur was not the only one of the name to whom the Hebrew Scriptures introduce us. One of the sons of Jacob and of his other wife Leah, was given the selfsame name of his old Semitic ancestor: "and she called his name Asher, for, she said, Happy am I" (Gen. xxx, 13); and this Asher gave his phallic name to one of the twelve Tribes of Israel.

A few more instances of identity of the Semitic peoples may be noted very briefly. Of the offspring of the reputed triplet sons of Noah set out in Genesis x: from Cush came the Ethiopians; from Mizraim the Philistines and the Egyptians; from Canaan the Canaanites; from Shem the Hebrews, the Assyrians, the Ishmaelites or Arabians, the Elamites, etc. From Lot sprang the Moabites and the Ammorites (Gen. xix, 30–37). Thus we see pretty well connected up all the Semitic peoples, and see the Biblically identical origin, traditions, deities, religion, and worship of the Hebrews and all their Semitic neighbors and kindred.

Phallic Emblems

The universality of the Phallus Worship,. and the peculiar significance and sanctity of its emblems, especially the Cross, the Triangle, the Spire, and the Oval, are indicated in the universality of the use of these sacred emblems in nearly all lands and among nearly all peoples, both ancient and modern. The very Christian emblem, the "cross of Christ," is simply the ancient conventional emblem of the "phallus" and "testes," and of the phallus in conjunction with the female "door of life," represented in every land and age, and very especially in almost every hieroglyphic Egyptian record, where the "ankh"-Cross—(Cross and Oval)—♀-is the emblem of, and means, "life." .This is exemplified in the now well-known name of Tuk-ankh-amen, or "Life-image of Amen." The Cross, in diverse forms, but with ever the same phallic significance of "life," age-long antedates Christianity, and is found on the ancient religious monuments of many far-scattered peoples, even in prehistoric America.

Another very favorite Hebrew and universal emblem is the Triangle, the perfect representation of the pubic hairs on man and woman. The famous "Six-pointed Star of David," the National Emblem of Israel, and always and today blazoned on the banners of Zion, is formed by superimposing the male on the female pubic "triangle," and is of very sacred significance. The Pyramids of Egypt, as of Central America, are faced by four triangles, representing in Egypt the "Four Great Gods," purely phallic and very sacred.

Of like origin and significance are the Jewish manner of holding the hands in priestly blessing; the oval windows of Gothic Churches; the heaven-pointing Spires of Christian temples; all purely phallic devices, though to-day seemingly formal or conventional, as the sacred Pagan origins are forgotten. We will now observe some other Phallic devices of universal Heathen, and Hebrew, usage, out of the inspired records of the Scriptures.

The Patriarchal Phallic Idolatry

Abraham, the Chaldean of Ur, and the patriarchal family and tribes which he is said to have established, were in common with all their Semitic kindred, ordinary Semitic idolators; he and his descendants worshiped phallic idols; and they retained and worshiped these same common Semitic idols through all their history down to the times of the last of the Prophets, as the Hebrew Bible a thousand times makes evident. We will make some review of this phallic cult, so that the interested reader may appreciate what was this Hebrew Religion and its God, now taken over by the Christian Religion.

The Phallic Symbols of Scripture

Principal among the idols or images of their Yahveh were, throughout Hebrew History, the phallic objects of worship mentioned a thousand times in the sacred pages under the euphemistic but very misleading terms "pillar" and "grove." These so popular and venerated emblems were nothing more or less than the phallic reproductions of the virile and erect male organ of procreation, the symbolic "staff of life," and the receptive and fecund female "door of life," to ourselves euphemize them. In the English translations the term "pillar" is used for the representation, called in Hebrew "mazzebah," of the male organ; and "grove" for the "asherah" or female organ of reproduction of the species. For public and outdoor worship these images were of large size and bold design, often actual, sometimes conventional or symbolic, representations of the living sex-organs. Smaller idols of the same nature, more for household worship, were images of Yahveh, the peculiarly sacred *alias* of the Hebraic "El," with an enormous "phallus," or male organ, erect *in situ*. The names given to these household images were "ephods" and "teraphim," words constantly occurring together throughout the Hebrew Bible to as late as Hosea iii, 4. These phallic idols, as we shall see, were used for worship, and for the purposes of divination or oracular consultation of the God Yahveh, in seeking his advice and receiving his awful decrees, as appears from many instances.

Thus the religion and worship of the Hebrews and their Semitic neighbors were frankly and purely phallic. I will illustrate this fact by a few instances from among hundreds in the inspired and sacred Hebrew Scriptures. And first of the "pillars" and "groves" of almost universal worship.

The "Pillars" or Mazzebahs of Yahveh

The first mention of the mazzebah or "pillar," as it is deceptively rendered in the English translation, is the one piously set up by Jacob at the place where he dreamed of the Ladder, in Genesis XXVIII; where he "took the stone which he had used for a pillow and set it up for a mazzebah ("pillar"), and poured oil on the top of it. And he called the name of that place Beth-El—the House of God (vv. 18–19); and he said, This stone which I have set up for a mazzebah shall be God's house" (v. 22). The same or a similar incident is recorded of Jacob at Padan-aram, when his name was changed to Israel (xxxv, 14). Now, Beth-El was a very sacred "high place" and holy shrine throughout Hebrew history. It was a center of phallic idol worship; and as such was railed against by the later Prophets, who were trying to reform the religion of Israel. They "cried against the altar in Beth-El" (1 Kings xiii, 4, 32); and Amos quotes Yahveh as commanding, "Seek not Beth-el, Beth-el shall come to nought" (v, 5); and Josiah, as one of his "reforms" in abolishing the phallic heathen practices of the Chosen, destroyed this holy phallic altar of Beth-El (2 Kings, xxiii, 15), and burned the bones of its prophets and priests upon the polluted altar. This proves that the very sacred Beth-el was, from its beginning to its end, a place of heathen phallic Yahveh-worship, and somewhat discounts the eulogies heard upon it from modern Christian pulpits. Jeremiah declared: "the house of Israel was ashamed of Bethel their confidence" (Jer. xlviii, 13).

Again, following the hot family quarrel between Jacob and Laban over the stealing of Laban's phallic teraphim gods by Rachel, and as an emblem of peace, "Jacob took a stone and set it up for a Mazzebah; and said, 'This is witness between me and thee this day; and he called it Mizpah, for he said, Yahveh watch between me and thee when we are absent one from another" (Gen. xxxi, 48–49). This mazzebah was a representative of the sacred phallus, for which a tall or pointed stone, or even a heap of stones, was used when nothing else was available.

In another chapter of Genesis, when Rachel died, in pious grief "Jacob set up a mazzebah (pillar) upon her grave: the same is the mazzebah of Rachel unto this day (xxxv, 20). And for a very

notable instance, which disproves an important claim of Inspiration:
Moses, when he came down from flaming Sinai where he is said to
have received the fearful Law of Yahveh, straightway, in celebration,
"builded an altar under the Mount, and twelve mazzeboth (plural),
according to the twelve Tribes of Israel" (Ex. xxiv, 4). This proves
that Moses did not receive the Law there, for, but a few verses
previously, that Law expressly declares: "Thou shalt utterly overthrow them, and break in pieces *their* mazzeboth" (xxiii, 24). But
this maybe, as is said, means the mazzeboth of the other Peoples, the
seven nations named in verse 23, not those of Yahveh, which were
not then prohibited, as Moses' act in erecting the twelve pillars
(mazzeboth) would indicate.

So all through the Hebrew Scriptures runs the relation of this
popular phallic practice, as perfectly proper and "Orthodox." A
thousand years later, the raptured vision of the great Prophet
Isaiah foresaw the glory of Yahveh in the heathen lands, and this is
his ideal of the supreme emblem of that glory: "In that day there
shall be an altar to Yahveh in the midst of the land of Egypt, and
a *Mazzebah* at the border thereof to Yahveh" (xix, 19). A further
proof, thus, that there was yet no "Law" of Yahveh condemning this
phallic cult of the Mazzebah, which Yahveh is quoted as having so
fearfully denounced through Moses: "Neither shalt thou set thee
up a Mazzebah, which Yahveh thy God hateth" (Deut. xvi, 22).
Hosea speaks of the "goodly mazzeboth" (x, 1); and bewails that the
Chosen shall be deprived of them (iii, 4).

These phallic pillars or "mazzeboth" were regarded as being the
actual abiding-place of the deity who "put his name" on them; he
verily lived in the stone, and it became sentient and possessed of
human or divine faculties, as of sight, hearing, understanding, the
power of protection. We have noticed the mazzebah which Jacob
set up "for God's house" (Gen. xxviii, 22); and the mazzebah and
stone heap which Jacob and Laban set up as a "witness" and "watch
tower" between them, saying "this heap be witness and this pillar
(mazzebah) be witness," to keep them from harming each other
(Gen. xxxi, 45–52). And Joshua set up a great stone, and said
unto all the People: "Behold, this stone shall be a witness unto us;
for *it hath heard* all the words of Yahveh which he spake unto us"
(xxiv, 26–27). Samuel set up the famous "Stone of Help" (Eben-
ezer; 1 Sam. vii, 12).

This superstition that deity, or spirits, or jinn resided in the
sacred stones, was almost universal among ancient peoples, and persists today among low tribes from Alaska to equatorial Africa.

And not only did the deity reside in the stones, but "Stone" or "Rock" was, and yet is, a favorite name or appellation of the Deity: Jacob calls Yahveh "Stone of Israel"; Moses "the Rock of our Salvation"; "the Rock that begat me"; "he is a Rock"; and so says Samuel; and David: "Yahveh is my Rock; Elohim is my Rock; my high tower, in whom I trust"; Jesus says "on this Rock will I build my church," etc. All these inspired allusions are purely phallic in terms and in signification; and so of our "Rock of Ages, cleft for me." There could be no clearer evidence that the phallus, and the stone representation of it, was regarded religiously as the emblem of Deity.

The "Groves" or Asherahs

The "grove" or graven representation of the female "door of life," also makes a very early Scriptural appearance, and runs hand in hand, or in phallic parlance, "linga in yoni," with the mazzebah, through the whole record of the Hebrew Bible. In Genesis XXI, 33 it is recorded: "And Abraham planted a grove (asherah) in Beersheba, and called there on the name of Yahveh, the everlasting (El) God." It is another instance of the many of "pious fraud" on the part of the Bible translators to use the deceptive euphemism "planted a grove," as if it meant the commendable horticultural work of setting out trees, instead of the actual truth of the original, "erected an Asherah," or visual phallic image of the female "door of life" penetrated by the male "staff of life," as is the truth of fact.

The idea of planting out a grove of trees, besides being actually false, is negatived by so many expressions in sundry passages even in the oft-falsified English Version of the Bible, that the "pious fraud" to hide it, of the translators becomes absurd. A few instances suffice to illustrate this: "And Ahab served Baal, and made a grove" (1 Kings xvi, 33); under Jehoahaz "there remained a grove in Samaria" (2 Kings xiii, 6); "The Children of Israel set them up pillars and groves in every high hill and under every green tree" (2 Kings, xvii, 10); while, previously, the Prophet Abijah had declared, "Yahveh shall smite Israel because they have made their groves, provoking Yahveh to anger" (1 Kings xiv, 15). A grove of trees could not be planted under a tree, nor would such innocent and useful work of forestation provoke the Lord Yahveh to anger to the extent of smiting his chosen Israel. In every one of the passages cited, and hundreds of others, the word used in the Hebrew Scriptures is "Asherah" or the plural "Asherim," which was the name in

Hebrew for the universal Semitic object of phallic idol-worship representing the conjunction of male and female sex-organs.

The proof in the concrete is close at hand and easy of verification. In the entrance hall of the Mercantile Library at St. Louis (where this is written), is an ancient stone slab from the walls of the Assyrian palace at Nippur. It is the Semitic, the Hebrew Scripture, Asherah. The slab is so sawn, for removal from its original place, as to split the principal object, the female "door of life," vertically into two parts; but one half of it is very plainly shown. The oval vulva is here represented, with a fanciful fan-shaped clitoris within its upper arched point, divided into seven whorls representing the days of the week; around the edge of the vulva are thirteen conventionalized tufts of the pubic hairs of the Mons Veneris, representing the thirteen "periods" of a woman in a year; while penetrating erect within the female "yoni" is the male "linga" or phallus in static conjunction. Beside this phallic Asherah altar stands the wingèd Genius or "Jinn" of the shrine; in his outstretched hand he holds the usual offering of the pine-cone, emblematic of fecundity, while in his other hand he holds the conventional bag filled with like emblems, for votive offerings to this Phallic Assyrian, Canaanitish, and Hebrew Divinity.

It is this selfsame phallic device, the Asherah, which, not in wall-carvings but in practical altar-form, filled the Holy Temple of Solomon at Jerusalem, for the worship of Ashtoreth, Baal and Yahveh, and there remained in constant and fervid "orthodox" Hebrew worship until Josiah "cleansed the Temple," and "brought forth out of the Temple of Yahveh all the vessels which were made for Baal, and for the Asherah (groves), and for all the host of heaven" (2 Kings xxiii, 4).

YAHVEH'S PHALLIC EPHODS AND TERAPHIM

Besides the mazzebahs and asherahs which so abounded in "orthodox" Hebrew worship, the ephods and teraphim, before described as being smaller household idols of Yahveh with great standing phalli, were very popular objects of the worship of Yahveh, and very potent for conjure and oracular prophecy, as we will briefly notice.

The first mention of "teraphim" is in the interesting passage in Genesis XXXI, between Jacob and his Pagan father-in-law Laban, and involving the modest Rachel, Jacob's wife and Laban's daughter. Inspiration tells us that "Rachel stole the teraphim which were her father's"; and Laban was very wroth because, as he accused Jacob, (v. 30), "Thou hast stolen my gods (elohim)." But Jacob protested and said, "With whomsoever thou findest thy gods, he shall not live; for Jacob knew not that Rachel had stolen them" (v. 32). So Laban instituted search through all the household tents, and finally came into Rachel's tent. "Now, Rachel had taken the terephim," says verse 34, "and sat upon them." Considering the phallic manner in which these idols were ornamented, with the erect male phallus, it is suggestive of the form and manner of devotion that Rachel was engaged in, "sitting on" the gods, and explains the naïve excuse which she gave to her father for not rising politely when he came into her tent (v. 35). So Laban "searched, but found not the teraphim" (v. 35).

Gideon, the Man of Gods, "made an ephod of gold and put it in his City; and all Israel went thither a-whoring after it" (Judges viii, 27). And this phallic idol was, at the time, expressly recognized as an entirely proper and "orthodox" form of worship of Yahveh, who was personified by the image. The People had requested Gideon to set himself up as King and rule over them; but Gideon replied, "I will not rule over you; *Yahveh* shall rule over you." So he called on the People for all of their golden ornaments, and of these he made the golden Ephod, which he set up to Yahveh in his city Ophrah, where all Israel resorted to worship it. The ephod was thus Yahveh or his idol. It was evidently the writer of "Judges," centuries later, who used the opprobious term "went a-whoring after" this sacred statue or idol of Yahveh, which he says "became a snare unto Gideon and his house" (Judges viii, 22, 27).

In Judges XVII and XVIII is the account of the idols of Micah the Ephramite, which became famous: "The man Micah had an house of gods, and he made an ephod, and teraphim, and consecrated one of his sons, who became his priest" (xvii, 5). Afterwards he secured a Levite for this office, and said, "Now I know that Yahveh will do me good, seeing that I have a Levite to my priest" (v. 13). And the Danites came and consulted the ephod, or phallic image of Yahveh, in regard to their expedition against Laish; and they said to the Levite-priest, "Ask counsel, we pray thee, of the gods (Elohim)" whether they should be successful, and the priest consulted the idol and reported "Yahveh is with you" (xviii, 1–6), again proving that Yahveh was worshiped and consulted through idols. And when they had captured the city and changed its name to Dan, and dwelt there, "they set up Micah's graven image all the time that the house of the gods was in Shiloh" (v. 31)—and there it remained and was worshipped "until the day of the captivity of the land" (v. 30), several hundred years still later. This also proves that the Book of Judges was not written until after "the captivity of the land."

When David was on a foray against Saul, and had no weapon, he went to Abiathar the priest, in the house of Yahveh (1 Sam. xxi, 9) and got the sword of Goliath, which was "wrapped in a cloth behind the ephod," or phallic statue of Yahveh. When Saul sought for David one time to kill him, the fair Michal, Saul's daughter and David's first wife, who "loved him," put one of her big phallic tera- phim in the nuptial bed and covered it, while David, who was thus supposed to be in the bed asleep, escaped.

That these teraphim were idols used in divination or the oracular consultation with Yahveh, is plain from the passage of the Prophet Zechariah: "For the Teraphim have spoken vanity, and the diviners have seen a lie, and they have told false dreams" (x, 2). The Authorized Version in English uses the word "idols"; but the He- brew, and the Revised Version, more honestly, both use the word "Teraphim."

The Sacred Dice of Yahveh

The pious Hebrews had another very sacred device, common to the heathen peoples of those regions, and which is said to have been revealed by Yahveh himself to Moses on Sinai. This was the sacred oracular dice, Urim and Thummim, by which Yahveh revealed his holy will and counsel to his Chosen; which dice the priest must carry in his "breast-plate of judgment before Yahveh continually" (Ex. xxviii, 30). These oracular dice or "lots" were "cast" before Yah- veh, and answered "Yes" or "No" just as the Assyrian "Tablets of Destiny" did before Marduk, or Bel.

Some random instances of the use of these sacred dice may be cited. Moses first dedicated Aaron (Ex. xxviii, 30), later Joshua (Num. xxvii, 21), to use the Urim and Thummim dice; yet later, he consecrated the sons of Levi, the Levites, for this office in perpetuity (Deut. xxxiii, 8). Joshua used these dice "lots" to detect Achan for his theft at the taking of Ai (Josh. vii). Samuel used them to select Saul to be King (1 Sam. xxiii, 9)—Saul said unto Yahveh, "Shew the right; cast lots between me and Jonathan my son," to detect the person who had eaten during a battle with the Philistines, and the lot fell upon Jonathan, who then confessed (1 Sam. xiv, 41–42). Sometimes this device failed, as in XXVIII, 6; for, "when Saul enquired of Yahveh, Yahveh answered him not, neither by dreams, nor by Urim, nor by prophets" (the three methods of "divination" or "fortune-telling" used to secure the will of Yahveh); so it was that Saul then made his famous visit to the Witch of Endor, to consult the shade of Samuel.

The pious King David "enquired of Yahveh" several times, through the dice Urim and Thummim and by the phallic ephod image of Yahveh. When he wished to know whether he should attack Saul, he said to Abiathar the priest, "Bring hither the ephod," and David inquired of it, saying, "O Yahveh, God of Israel, tell thy servant," and Yahveh replied to the satisfaction of David (1 Sam. xxiii, 9–12). This practice David followed on a number of occasions.

As late as the Prophets Nehemiah (vii, 65), and Ezra (ii, 63), questions were not decided "till there stood up a priest with Urim and Thummim," to consult Yahveh for the answer—just like Greek oracle-mongers and the Roman augurs. These superstitious and idolatrous Hebrews used these consecrated dice even to decide law-suits and legal controversies, a practice instituted on Sinai in Exodus XXVIII, 30, and followed with the express approval of the Wisest Man, in two of his Proverbs. For Solomon says, "The lot is cast into the lap; but the whole disposing thereof is of Yahveh" (Prov. xvi, 33); and again, he records this maxim of legal practice: "The lot causeth dissentions to cease, and parteth between the mighty" (Prov. xviii, 18). As if the "God of all Wisdom" would reveal himself and his will through such superstitious and childish devices, a sort of sacri-monious craps-shooting. Dreams, dice, and prophets—certainly a convincing triad of revelation of the oracles of God! And witches, and wizards, and necromancers, and charmers, and dealers with familiar spirits, to assist!

OTHER HEATHEN RITES OF YAHVEH

Besides all the phallic worship and idolatrous practices above noticed, and which were throughout their history associated with the cult of Yahveh, as a sort of specially Hebraic Super-El or Baal, the Chosen People never even for a season gave up the common heathen idolatry into which they were born and bred and with which they were everywhere surrounded among their kindred peoples. We remember that Aaron made the Golden Calf right at the foot of Sinai while Moses was up there with the new-found god Yahveh (if he ever was); and Aaron proclaimed to the People, then but three months out from Egypt: "These be thy gods, O Israel, which brought thee up out of the land of Egypt," this Golden Calf being the reproduction of the sacred bull, Apis, of Egypt. Little wonder, for the Chosen People had never before known any other gods or forms of worship than those of Egypt, for 430 years, and were common Chaldean idolators before that time; and ever after leaving Egypt they followed the practices of their kindred peoples among whom they lived, and refused to pay any very particular attention to the new "Jealous God" Yahveh, as we shall abundantly see.

Moses himself, in addition to the "twelve mazzeboth" which he set up just after receiving a "Law" against them, also made the famous brazen image of the Fiery Serpent, which healed the plague-stricken Children, and was preserved and worshipped as a god by the Chosen until it was finally destroyed by King Hezekiah; "for unto those days the Children of Israel did burn incense unto it" (2 Kings xviii, 4).

Gideon, as we have seen, also encouraged idolatry; his other and proper name was Jerubbaal, showing his dedication to the Canaanite-Hebrew Baal; he "made an ephod of gold, and all Israel went a-whoring after it" (Judges viii, 27). The holy King David worshipped Baal religiously, and in public and near-naked, as the custom was in the Baal-worship, danced the Baal-dance "with all his might" before the Holy Ark of the Covenant of Yahveh; and his wife "Michal, looking out the window saw King David leaping and dancing amain before Yahveh; and she despised him in her heart"—as is graphically related in 2 Samuel, vi, 14–17. Absolam "reared up for himself a mazzebah (or phallic "pillar"), for he said, I have no son to keep my name in remembrance; and he called the mazzebah after his own name" (2 Sam. xviii, 18). The Wise Man, Solomon, it is recorded, "loved Yahveh: only he sacrificed and burnt incense in high-places" (1 Kings iii, 3); the Bamah or "high-place" being the popular shrine of Baal-worship universal through-out Israel. King Solomon also "loved many strange women," having 700 wives and 300 concubines, of all the heathen peoples; and im-partially he built a phallic Temple for Yahveh (constructed by the Pagan Hiram of Tyre), and "an high-place for Chemosh the abomi-nation of Moab, and for Molech the abomination of Ammon," and went after Ashtoreth the goddess of the Zidonians; "and so did he for all his strange wives, which burnt incense and sacrificed unto their gods" (1 Kings xi, 1–8). Jeroboam, the son of Solomon, King over Israel, made two golden calves and set them up, one in Bethel and the other in Dan, saying, as did Aaron, "Behold thy gods, O Israel, which brought thee up out of the land of Egypt" (1 Kings xii, 28).

These "heathenish" practices were not confined to sundry "bad kings" who backslided from Yahveh: they were universal and constant throughout the rank and file of the Chosen; and these practices were part and parcel of the "orthodox" worship of Yahveh: "For they also built them high-places, and mazzeboth and Asherim, on every high hill, and under every green tree; and there were also sodomites in the land: they did according to all the abominations of the nations which Yahveh drave out before the Children of Israel" (1 Kings xiv, 23–24)—only Yahveh never did drive them out, but they stayed there until the Chosen were themselves driven out into captivity.

The whole Books of Kings and Chronicles, and the "Prophets" are filled with these records of continuous idolatry under the successive Kings of Israel and Judah, to the very end of the national record. Even under the few and scattering so-called "good Kings" (i.e., Yahveh devotees), who made some reforms, it is always related, as of Joash: "But the high-places were not taken away; the People still sacrificed and burnt incense in the high-places" (2 Kings xii, 3). Asa "took away the sodomites out of the land, and removed all the idols that his fathers had made;" he also removed his mother Maachah from being queen because she had made "an abominable Asherah"—"but the high-places were not taken away" (1 Kings xv, 12–13), where the People continued their idolatrous worship of Yahveh—Baal. The Kings, however zealous for Yahveh they are reported, never once attempted to disturb the public idol worship of the People. Although these few "good Kings" held personally maybe, to only Yahveh, and some Prophets thundered against other Idols and other idolatry, in favor of the "Jealous God" Yahveh, the universal idol-worship of the Chosen People was never once interrupted. Elijah, Prophet of El-Yahveh, murdered the 450 prophets of Baal and 400 "prophets of the groves" (1 Kings xviii); and wailed, in his solitude, "I, even I only, am left," of all the Prophets of Yahveh. Later Jehu massacred every worshipper of Baal, although he continued the worship of the two Golden Calves in Bethel and Dan (2 Kings x). Still the idol-worship throve, and the Chosen People "did not believe in Yahveh their God."

This recital of instances must end; and will be brought to a close with some panoramic views of the Idolatry throughout the history of the Chosen People. In 2 Kings XVII this striking picture is presented:

"(9) And the Children of Israel built them high-places in all their cities, from the tower of the watchman to the fenced city. (10) And they set them up *Mazzeboth* and *Asherim* in every high hill, and under every green tree: (11) And there they burnt incense in all the high-places (Bamoth); and wrought wicked things to provoke Yahveh to anger: (12) For they served idols, whereof Yahveh had said unto them, Ye shall not do this thing. (14) *Notwithstanding they did not believe in Yahveh their God.* (16) And made them molten images, even two calves, and made Asheroth, and worshipped all the host of heaven, and served *Baal.* (17) And they caused their sons and their daughters to pass through the fire (to Moloch), and used divinations and enchantment."

This picture is drawn just at the close of the national existence, in the year in which the Children were first carried away into Captivity. It is declared: "Yet Yahveh testified unto Israel and unto Judah, by the hand of every prophet, and of every seer, saying, Keep my commandments and my statutes, according to all the law which I commanded your fathers, etc. Notwithstanding they would not hear, like to their fathers, who *believed not in Yahveh their God*" (vv. 13–14).

This clearly proves that the few "Prophets" who "raved" against the "gods of the nations," which were also the gods of the Chosen People, were but as "a voice crying in the wilderness" against the popular religion, and were wholly without effect upon the prevalent popular practices, from Moses to the conquest by the Assyrians. The Prophet Hosea (iii, 4), in bewailing the desolation coming upon his country, either bewailed or exulted—it does not clearly appear which—the destruction of the national religion: "For the Children of Israel shall abide many days without a king, and without a prince, and without a sacrifice, and without a mazzebah, and without an ephod, and without teraphim"—which indicates the habitual prevalence and entire "orthodoxy" of these national customs and objects of popular worship.

The Temple an Idol House

Just before the Captivity we find (2 Kings xxiii) the "good King" Josiah, he who "found" the "Book of the Law," making a crusade against the idols. Solomon's great Temple to Yahveh was the consecrated shrine of the Hebrew idolatry and Sex-Worship. Josiah "brought forth out of the Temple all the vessels which were made for *Baal,* and for the Asherah, and for all the host of heaven, and he brought forth the Asherah from the house of Yahveh; and he brake down the houses of the sodomites, that were by the house of Yahveh, where the women wove hangings for the Asherah" (vv.

4–5). "And he put down the idolatrous priests whom the Kings of Judah had ordained to burn incense in the high-places in the cities of Judah, and in the places round about Jerusalem; them also that burnt incense to Baal, to the Sun, and to the Moon, and to the Planets, and to all the (starry) Host of Heaven."

This is a graphic description of the polytheistic and phallic idolatry of the Hebrews, identical in every respect with that of all the other Semitic peoples around them and among whom they lived. These records prove to demonstration that the Hebrew People never, at any time, before the "Return from Captivity," knew or worshiped any such God as we are taught in modern Sunday Schools as the "One True God" of Israel; but the same El or Baal, and the same Elohim, or gods, exactly, as all their neighbor heathen nations. It is preposterous to pretend that the Hebrews as a nation were not "heathen" or "pagan," like all their kindred and neighbors, but were worshipers of some "only one true and living God" such as we are erroneously taught was their great, peculiar worship. We will presently study the Hebrew conception and "revelation" of their Yahveh at close range.

THE TEMPLE HARLOTS OF YAHVEH

There remain several phases of the Hebrew phallic worship which we will briefly notice. One feature which was common to all the ancient religions, was the consecrated women, or priestess-prostitutes, who were always in attendance in the temples and at the Asherah "groves," to participate in the worship with the True Believers who had the price of this oblation. Their earnings in this sacred calling went into the "Treasury of Yahveh," and were a large part of its legitimate income. True, the "Law" prescribed: "There shall be no harlot (kedeshah) of the daughters of Israel, neither shall there be a sodomite (kadesh) of the sons of Israel. Thou shalt not bring the hire of a whore, or the wages of a sodomite, into the house of Yahveh thy God for any vow" (Deut. xxiii, 17–18). But then, this "Law" was very much *ex post facto,* and totally unobserved, for the practice prevailed even in the Holy Temple of Solomon, which was planned by Yahveh himself (1 Chron. xxviii, 19) and built with particular reference to this phallic practice, with small "chambers" all around (1 Kings vi, 5–6, 10) for the Temple-whores and their sportive cult. It may be mentioned, that the Hebrew word *"kadesh"* which was the name for these consecrated devotees of Phallism, is exactly the same word as "holy" or "consecrated," or "sanctified":

in the "Ten Commandments" it is recited "wherefore Yahveh blessed the sabbath day and hallowed (*kadesh-u*) it" (Ex. xx, 11); and so wherever this idea is expressed.

The first Bible mention of this sportive cult is some 500 years before the time of Moses, when the fair young widow Tamar, despairing of getting the man so often promised her, dressed herself in the garb of a "Kedeshah" or Temple-harlot, with a veil over her face, and went and "sat in an open place" where she knew that her father-in-law Judah would pass by; and Judah came by, and fell into her trap, which led to an interesting sequel, as related in Genesis XXXVIII. Later Moses, in instituting (as recited) the religious observances of the Chosen People of Yahveh, thought it amiss that Hebrew young women and young men should engage in this religious prostitution, and hence the "Law" above quoted, prohibiting the Children from acting the rôle of Temple-prostitution. So these sacred offices were usually filled by "the stranger within thy gate," and particularly by the Moabitish maidens and young men. While yet in the midst of their wanderings in the wilderness, "the People began to commit whoredom with the daughters of Moab, and bowed down to their gods; and Israel joined himself to Baal-Peor" (Num. xxv); that is, to "Baal the hymen-breaker," so-named because the Moabitish maidens were wont to break their hymens on the Idol-phallus before becoming "kedeshoth," or religious prostitutes, for the holy People of Yahveh. As to the "kadeshuth," or official sodomites, which abounded among the Chosen People, as attested by the verses I have cited, and by many other Scriptural passages, the less said about these detestable objects of the worship of Yahveh, the better.

When Solomon erected the magnificent Temple of Yahveh (built by the Pagan Hiram of Tyre), from plans drawn by Yahveh himself (1 Chron. xxviii, 19), he made liberal arrangements for the comfort of these consecrated Temple-attendants, and for the convenience of the phallic worshippers. In 1 Kings vi it is recorded: "(5) And against the wall of the Temple Solomon built side-chambers round about, both of the temple and of the oracle; (16) even the most holy place." These side-chambers (tselaoth), the small size of which is stated (vv. 6, 10), were the habitations of the "kedeshoth" and the "kadeshuth," the Temple-whores and sodomites, whose sacred earnings went into the "treasury of Yahveh." When the Holy Temple needed repairs, the "good King" Jehoash said to the Priests, "All the money of the kadashim (translated 'dedicated things') that is brought into the House of Yahveh" (2 Kings xii, 4), use it for the work of repairs; but the priests stole it and made not the repairs (v. 6). These chambers, "where the women wove hangings for the Asherah," which were even in the Temple itself, were broken down by Josiah: "And he brake down the houses of the sodomites, that were in the house of Yahveh, where the women wove hangings for the Asherah" (2 Kings xxiii, 7). Notwithstanding, so profitable, as well as pleasurable, a form of worship continued unabated in Israel, as in the rest of the heathen world.

PHALLUS HOMAGE

Of another phallic practice of the Hebrew religion, of universal sanctity among them and their Semitic neighbors, we have frequent testimony, from first to last, in their sacred Scriptures. This was the solemn phallic form of oath prevalent among them. As the "phallus" was the object of most sacred reverence in Israel, as every elsewhere, the most solemn oaths and vows were taken upon it; the form of ceremony being for the person to be obligated to take in his hand the sacred member of the person to whom he swore (euphemistically translated "under the thigh"), and register thus his oath. Thus in Genesis XXIV, Father Abraham called his major-domo, and said to him: "Put, I pray thee, thy hand under my thigh: and I will make thee swear by Yahveh (v. 2). And the servant put his hand under the thigh of Abraham his master, and sware to him "concerning this matter" (v. 9). So Jacob, in Genesis xlvii, when he came on to die in Egypt, called his son Joseph to him, and said: "Put, I pray thee, thy hand under my thigh; bury me not, I pray thee, in Egypt, etc. And he sware unto him" (v. 29).

This phallic practice was not confined to the ancient Patriarchs: it prevailed throughout Bible history. When Solomon was crowned King over all Israel, the ceremony of taking the oath of allegiance is related in 1 Chronicles XXIX, 24: "And all the princes, and the mighty men, and all the sons likewise of King David, gave the hand under Solomon." In other words, the interesting spectacle was presented of all the mighty men of Israel lined up like at a Presidential New Year's reception, and filing by before the Wise King; as each came up he would take the Royal Phallus in his good right hand, and with low obeisance pronounce upon it the solemn oath of fealty. In Lamentations, the Weeping Prophet bewails the dire distress of the Chosen People, and declares: "We have given the hand to the Egyptians and to the Assyrians, to be satisfied with bread" (v, 6)—taking the phallic oath of fealty to those foreign nations in return for protection and provisions. Other instances might be cited, but these suffice to show the time-honored phallic practice, in private and in public, of all Israel. In modern times, we evidence the solemnity of an official or judicial oath by putting the hand on the Bible, as a sacred thing, and kissing it. It is all the same in effect as the older custom, except somewhat different in esthetic taste.

SANCTITY OF THE PHALLUS

The sanctity attached by the Hebrew religion to the male organs of generation, is clearly recognized by various passages of the Law. These phallic organs must not be profanely touched or injured, and the injury or loss of any of them wrought an excommunication from the worship of Yahveh. In Deuteronomy xxv, 11–12, the rigorous Law enacts, that when two of the Chosen are engaged in a street fight together, "and the wife of the one draweth near for to deliver her husband out of the hand of him that smiteth him, and putteth forth her hand, and taketh him by the secret parts (a very élite performance for a lady): then thou shalt cut off her hand, thine eye shall have no pity." While in Chapter xxiii, 1, excommunication is pronounced against the unfortunate one: "He that is wounded in the stones, or hath his privy member cut off, shall not enter into the assembly of Yahveh." These two barbarous laws discredit the theory that a true and merciful God had anything to do with their enactment, or with the barbarous "scriptures" which attribute them to him. But the One True Church of God to-day holds to this phallic prohibition yet; and while it pretends to deny to its asexual ministers the natural exercise of these organs, its canons decree that its consecrated ones, from Yahveh's Vicar down, must be "perfect in all their parts"; and before the sacred ceremonial and public "laying on of hands," it exacts a private and thorough examination, to satisfy Yahveh's and Peter's phallic requirements.

THE SUPERSTITION OF WITCHCRAFT

A brief reference to some other superstitions of the Hebrew Bible religion may be permitted. Witches, wizards, familiar spirits, and demons, were as plentiful and popular as angels and devils in modern Christianity,—and as real. Yahveh, on Sinai, enacted (Ex. xxii, 18), "Thou shalt not suffer a witch to live." This one sentence, among all the inspired unrealities of the Bible, is in itself sufficient to utterly discredit the whole Book as "the Word of God."

If Yahveh was the real all-wise God of Heaven, he could never have uttered such an ignorant superstition, for he would have known that there is no such thing as a witch; yet on the strength of this "revelation of the will of God," countless helpless and miserable persons, mostly old women, have perished in torture at the hands of the pious persons who fondly believed these inspired old witch tales.

When Saul was King, after the death of Samuel, he got a virtuous spell, and "banished those that had familiar spirits, and the wizards, out of the land," on pain of death. This of course proves the existence of such unrealities. The Philistines came up against Saul, and he was very much afraid, and inquired of Yahveh what to do about it; but, as we have seen, "Yahveh answered him not, neither by dreams, nor by Urim (the sacred dice), nor by prophets" (1 Sam. xxviii, 6). So Saul said unto his servants, "Seek me a woman who hath a familiar spirit, that I may go to her and inquire of her" (v. 7). Thus a Witch was as good an oracle of Yahveh as another, or better, judged by the results. And they told Saul, "Behold, there is a woman who hath a familiar spirit, at En-Dor"; and Saul disguised himself and went to her by night, and he said to her "Divine unto me, I pray thee, by the familiar spirit, and bring me up whomsoever I shall name unto thee"; proving the immortality of the soul, and that witches can call up the dead from Sheol to earth; and Saul ordered her: "Bring me up Samuel." After some bargaining, the Witch of En-Dor consented; and when the spirit was on her, she cried out, "I see gods (Elohim) coming up out of the earth"; and Samuel came up, and talking as well as ever, said, "Why hast thou disquieted me, to bring me up?" This is precious sacred lore to be recorded as inspired truth in the "Holy Word of God." It is a ridiculous superstition; but it proves that the Chosen People of God reverenced and believed in witches; that the witches had the same supernatural powers as their Yahveh, and could also through Yahveh, prophesy the future,—"as Yahveh spake by me" (v. 17); and that the great El was, in their concept, nothing other or better than a sort of chief spirit among the many Elohim (gods or spirits) which peopled their perfervid superstitious imaginations. Indeed, Yahveh is frequently called, "El, Elohe of spirits," as in Numbers xvi, 22 and xxvii, 16; and in Joshua xxii, 22, "El Elohim," the "God of Gods, or spirits"; elsewhere he is "the El above all Elohim," the "God above all Gods or spirits"; and Paul calls him expressly "the Father of Spirits" (Heb. xii, 9).

Hundreds of years later, old Isaiah vapored about "the familiar spirits and the wizards that peep and that mutter" (viii, 19); and others of the inspired holy Prophets share the same superstition. Yahveh is "jealous" of these competitors; and in Deuteronomy makes a sweeping prohibition of them all: "There shall not be found with thee one that useth divination, one that practiseth augury, or an enchanter, or a sorcerer, or a charmer, or a consulter with familiar spirits, or a wizard, or a necromancer" (Deut. xviii, 10–11): all these practices were reserved for the priests and prophets of Yahveh alone. To cite but one other out of many instances, Manasseh, King of Judah, "used enchantments, and used witch-craft, and dealt with a familiar spirit, and with wizards" (2 Chron. xxxiii, 6). These pious superstitious beliefs and practices existed all through old Bible times and all through the New Testament.

The Bible a Great "Dream Book"

As for dreams, it is idle to go into any mention of them: the whole Bible, Old and New, is little more than a superstitious "Dream-Book," all the way from Abram's dream to sacrifice his only son Isaac, to the Apocalyptic nightmares of John on Patmos. One of these latter was indeed a Vision unique in inspired Scripture: "Behold, there appeared a great wonder in Heaven, a Woman" (Rev. xii, 1).

Most of the principal inspired events in the Hebrew Scriptures were dreamed,—all its miraculous happenings were of such stuff as dreams are made. Abraham dreamed the Promise and the Covenant, as did Jacob at the Ladder; Joseph was a "Baal of dreams." Yahveh himself prescribes dreams as his predilect medium of revelation of his awful Will: "If there be a Prophet among you, I, Yahveh, will make myself known to him in a *Vision*, and will speak unto him in a *Dream*" (Num. xii, 6). David dreamed, Solomon dreamed, Ezekiel dreamed, Daniel was the premier dreamer of them all. Jeremiah derides the whole horde of self-styled Prophets gadding about the land crying "I have dreamed, I have dreamed; and they prophesy (Heb. *rave*) lies" (Jer. xxiii, 25). That Jesus Christ was "conceived by the Holy Ghost" is an admitted dream (Matt. i, 20). The Book of Revelation is all a dream.

The superstition of dreams being sent by Gods as a revelation of their will was not limited to ancient Hebrew "revelation" of Yahveh; it pervaded antiquity, and prevails yet among low-civilized tribes. Great Zeus lay awake all one night on high Olympus devising trouble for the Greeks:—

"At last, this counsel seemed the best,—to send
A treacherous *Dream* to Agamemnon, son
Of Atreus. Then he called a Dream, and thus
Addressing it with wingéd words, he said:
Go, fatal Vision, to the Grecian fleet,
And, entering Agamemnon's tent, declare
Faithfully what I bid thee. . . . At his head the Dream
Took station in the form of Neleus' son. . . . In such a shape
The Heaven-sent Dream to Agamemnon spake . . .
He spake, and disappearing, left the King
Musing on things that never were to be" (Iliad, Bk. ii, 1–47).

This false Dream from Jove for the undoing of the Greek Hero is
tallied by the "lying Spirit" sent by Yahveh falsely to "entice Ahab,
King of Israel, that he may fall at Ramoth-Gilead" (2 Chron. xviii,
18–22).

CHAPTER IX

THE PAGAN GOD—AND GODS—OF ISRAEL

THERE is no doubt, a God, the Great Architect of the Universe, the Creator of the earth and of the fullness thereof, and of the wondrous "finite but unlimited" universe. Lord Bacon has profoundly said, "I had rather believe all the fables of the Legend, of the Talmud, and Al-Koran, than that this universal frame is without a mind." The Fool, only, hath said in his heart, "There is no God." Truly, and beautifully, has the Psalmist sung, "The heavens declare the glory of God, and the firmament sheweth his handiwork. Day unto day uttereth speech, and night unto night sheweth knowledge." The works of God in Nature are the veritable revelation of the Creator God to Man.

Many times and places, in the later Hebrew Scriptures, there are found sublime outbursts of the highest and noblest concepts of Yahveh, as Creator God, as the Supreme Being, infinitely great and infinitely good. These, all of them, will be found to be simply fervid pious declamations; the occasional visions of a few ecstatic souls, denouncing the prevailing idolatrous practices of the whole People, and thundering their unheeded appeals for the worship of this ideal and "one true" God. This was very late, however, in the history of Israel, maybe a little preceding but mostly after the tribulations of the Babylonian Captivity. But this late-evolved rhetoric God is very far from being the "Lord God" (Yahveh Elohim) of the Hebrews, as revealed in the Hebrew Scriptures and worshiped throughout their Bible history. "Yahveh" was but a Mythological Tribal God, as non-existent as Bel or Baal, or Zeus.

In speaking of this Bible Hebrew Deity, and for the purpose of clearly distinguishing between this Hebrew Tribal Deity, and the ideal but "unknown" God of our more refined concept, the Hebrew names "El," "Elohim," and "Yahveh" are used in all references to the "revealed" Deity of the Hebrew Scriptures. This Yahveh, this God—or plurality of Gods—as revealed in the Hebrew Sacred Writings, will now be examined as revealed in the inspired texts.

Pagan Origins of the Hebrews

Whatever later they may have become, indisputably the people known as Hebrews were a derived People, not always Hebrews, and not always votaries of the God Yahveh: both had a beginning. It is needful, therefore, to go back to this beginning in order to get a proper perspective of this People and of their Deity.

The name "Hebrew" is derived from Heber, a reputed descendant of Noah and ancestor of Abraham; just as the appellation "Semite," applied to the whole family of kindred peoples of whom the Hebrews are one branch, derives from Shem, one of the triplet sons of Noah, and reputed common ancestor of the Semitic nations.

Abraham, when he first comes to our knowledge, was as we have seen, a nomadic Chaldean Semite, of "Ur of the Chaldees," and speaking, of course, only the Chaldean language. Naturally, like the rest of his people, he shared their religion, and was thus a "heathen" or "pagan." He came with his father and family into the land of the Canaanites, descended from Canaan, one of the sons of Ham, another son of Noah, to follow the Scriptural genealogies. So, according to Genesis, all these peoples were of like origin and close kindred, living together in the same section of the country between Mesopotamia and the Mediterranean.

These peoples, the Babylonians, the Assyrians (originally a Babylonian colony), the Syrians, the Canaanites, the Hebrews and Arabians when they came along, and the peoples generally of Palestine and Western Asia, were all akin; they spoke practically the same language, and had practically the same religion and forms of religious worship—the same God or Gods. These historical facts, gathered from the Hebrew Scriptures themselves, and confirmed (except as to the Noachian traditions) by ethnological knowledge, are stated for the purpose of showing the common origin and kinship of these peoples, and expressly to disabuse the mind of the common notion that the Hebrews were in some racial or practical sense a "peculiar people" and different from their kindred nations and neighbors. They "had Abraham as their Father"; and Abraham was a native Chaldee who left his country and became the reputed father and founder of a branch of his people called Hebrews. Thus their racial and cultural identity is established.

The Hebrews (so named from Heber, fore-father of Abraham), were also called Israelites; because Jacob, the grandson of Abraham, after fighting all night, according to their legend, with the God ("El"), had his name changed to Israel. Now this is very significant of the whole nature and history of the Israelites. The word "Israel" is formed of the two Hebrew words "sarah," to fight, and "El," God: Jacob's new, name meant "fighter or soldier of God"; and, as we shall see, this same "El" or Yahveh was very often called, in the Hebrew Scriptures, a "mighty man of war," and was indeed their War-God.

So, in keeping with their religion, the Hebrews, throughout their history, were simply a nation of fighters or semi-barbarous soldiers, with Yahveh as their War-Lord, and with very primitive instincts of humanity or civilized culture. They took their characteristics from their notions of their God, for like all primitive peoples, they were very religious in their way; or, their notion of their God took its form from their own characteristics: it is the same either way. Their Isaiah had the idea when he said, "Like people, like priest; like servant, like master; like maid, like mistress" (Is. xxiv, 2); and he could exactly as well have added, "like God, like people," or "like people, like God"—the terms are convertible.

Indeed, it is error to say "the God of the Hebrews," for "El" or "Yahveh" was but one of their many gods: the Hebrews had the same gods as their kindred and neighboring nations, and never did, in Bible times, abandon their "false gods" for the worship of the "one true and living God of all the earth," as Yahveh was ultimately "evolved" by some of the later Prophets of Israel, after the Captivity. This is abundantly proven by all the Hebrew Scripture writers and Prophets without exception, as we have seen and will proceed to further verify.

The Hebrews were "Heathens"

That the Hebrews had the same God and gods as their kindred peoples around them, and were thus pagan idolators or "heathen," their own Scriptures abundantly prove, and so declare a thousand times. The proof may first be made in negative form.

Up to the reputed times of Moses, indeed, this fact is indisputable, on the face of the record. Until the traditional "giving of the Law" to Moses on Sinai, there is not the slightest hint in the Hebrew Scriptures, covering a space of 2500 years, that the El or Yahveh of the Patriarchs was different from any other El, or had or claimed any different cult or form of worship. He never made any such intimation, in all his reputed appearances and talks with men, from Adam to Abraham, and from Abraham to Moses.

That the "Patriarchs" down to the time of Moses were ordinary idolatrous heathen is perfectly apparent from the inspired texts.

As we have noted, Father Abraham was of Ur of the Chaldees "the land of his nativity" (Gen. xi, 28); and from the silence of the record, had never heard of Yahveh until the God appeared to him at Haran and told him to emigrate to Canaan (Gen. xii, 1); though he had already voluntarily done so (Gen. xi, 31). The Chaldeans were "Syrians," and certainly not "peculiar" votaries of the God Yahveh; but were ordinary idol-worshiping heathens, as were also naturally the ancestors and family of Abram, and all their fellow "Syrians," as they are expressly called. Laban, the father-in-law of Isaac, is called "Laban the Syrian" (Gen. xxxi, 20, 24), and he and his family worshiped teraphim-idols (Gen. xxxi, 30). Laban was "son of Bethuel the Syrian" (Gen. xxviii, 5); the name Bethu-el shows that "El" was a common Syrian or Chaldean God, who continued as God of the three "Patriarchs." Abram's grandson Jacob, in the third generation, is called "a Syrian about to die" (Deut. xxvi, 5), when he migrated to Egypt, 250 years after Abraham. It was therefore 70 Syrians who went into Egypt, speaking the Chaldean tongue, and becoming in 430 years good Pagan Egyptians. After Jacob and his family of 70 Syrians migrated to Egypt, he and all his people continued regularly to worship "the gods which your fathers served on the other side of the flood (i.e. in Syria or Chaldea), and in Egypt" (Josh. xxiv, 14). After 430 years in Egypt, worshiping their ancient and the local gods, Moses had never even heard of the El-Yahveh: when he first met the strange God, there at the Burning Bush, Moses had to ask, "What is thy name?" (Ex. iii, 13), so that he might report it back to the elders of the People in Egypt. Nearly a millennium after the death of Moses, we are expressly told that the Chosen People persisted up to date in the worship of the foreign gods: "they did not forsake the Gods of Egypt" (Ezek. xx, 8),—of which fact the Hebrew Scriptures present an unbroken record: a fact which is a thousand times declared to be the cause and reason for their being "carried away into Captivity."

In a word, until the "Book of the Law" was promulgated, in the time of Josiah, there was never a hint even that Yahveh was a "Jealous God," nor that "thou shalt have no other gods" before (i.e. in preference to) him,—though this admits the fact of "other gods." The whole world, in other words, in those parts, had the same gods and one common form of religion and worship; and the Israelites were identical in this respect with all the other kindred peoples, and so persisted until the Return from Captivity, as the record proves.

"El"—"Bel" and "Baal"

The word usually applied by the Hebrews to designate God,— any god, true or false, Hebrew or Heathen, was the common noun "El," as the word was pronounced among them. With the Babylonians, the name of God in general was called Bel; with the Canaanites the form of the name was Baal: they are identical, the same common name for the same idea of God or Lord. It was simply a Semitic word meaning "Lord." This word for deity,— (*El*, god, spirit, lord; plural, *Elohim*, gods, spirits, lords), persists to-day: more millions of Mohammedans than there are millions of Christians and Jews combined, prostrate themselves to the earth five times a day and cry the Arabian words, "Lo Illah, il Allah,"— "there is no God but Allah,—and Mohammed is his Prophet." This is the selfsame "El," "Ilu," Bel, Baal, of the Hebrews, Canaanites, Babylonians and Assyrians. The Arabians are reputed as descended from Ishmael ("God heareth"), the bastard son of Abraham and Hagar and half-brother of Isaac; they to-day hold Abraham as their father, and speak a language nearest to the Hebrew; their "Allah," the Aramaic "Elah," is the Hebrew "El" or "Ilu," God, Lord. And yet, the Hebrew-God Christians say that Allah is a false god, and Bel and Baal heathenish abominations.

But God is God in whatever language his name is named: we in English say "God"; the Teutons and their kindred call him "Gott"; the French call him "Dieu"; the Spanish "Diós"; the Italians "Dío"; the Portuguese "Deus,"—exactly the Latin word for God; this in its turn came from the Greek "Theós," and it from the Sanskrit "Dyaus": but all the same God; while the Hebrew, again, was "El" or "Ilu," the Babylonian-Assyrian "Bel," the Canaanite "Baal," the Arabian "Il": all again the same God, or God-name. But these names were all but the common or generic name applied to deity, any god, even to departed spirits, or even as a title of respect, "Lord" or "master," to living persons, by these several kindred peoples; though the Bible and the Christians say that the El Yahveh was the only one real and true God. But the Bible usage is quite to the contrary.

"Baal" is "Lord"

In the Hebrew Bible, the ancient Semitic word "Baal," the same as Hebrew "Adon," or the English "lord," in every sense, is constantly employed as a common noun meaning "lord," "master," or owner of this or that. Joseph is called by his brothers "this baal (master) of dreams," translated "this dreamer" (Gen. xxxvii, 19); and again of Joseph it is said, "the archers—baalim of arrows—have shot at him" (Gen. xlix, 23). A man is called "baal" or "master of the house" (Ex. xxii, 7); again the "owner" of the house is "baal" (v. 10). Certain "sons of Belial spake to the master (baal) of the house, an old man" (Jud. xix, 22); the Law says that "the ox shall be stoned and his owner (baal)" shall be free of blame (Ex. xxi, 28); Job speaks of the owners (baalim) of a field (xxxi, 39). A "baal of hairs" is a "hairy man" (2 Kings i, 8); "baalim of oaths" are "conspirators" (Neh. vi, 18); "baal of wings" is "winged creature." The lord and master of a wife is her "baal" or husband. Yahveh tells Abimelech that Abraham is "baal" of Sarah—"for she is married to a baal" (Gen. xx, 3); and the Law says "if he be married—(a baal)—then his wife shall go out with him" (Ex. xxi, 23). In the very next verse *"adon"* is used for "master,"—"if his master (*adon*) give him a wife" (Ex. xxi, 4). As a verb "baal" means "to marry"; the feminine form of the noun, "baalah" is "mistress" or a married woman.

As the term is applied to deity, the word Baal, which is then always used with the definite article,—the-Baal, the-Baalim,—the word Baal retains its idea of lordship or ownership. The-Baal was the local deity or "lord" who had "put his name" in this or that place, as the-Baal of Tyre, to whom Solomon's friend Hiram built a magnificent Temple in his capital; the-Baal of Lebanon, the-Baal of Heaven; also often, Baal-zebub, lord of flies; Baal-peor, the Lord Hymen-opener. Jerub-baal, "who is Gideon," died, "and the Children of Israel went a-whoring after the-Baalim, and made Baal-Berith' (the Lord-of-the-Covenant) their gods—elohim" (Jud. viii, 33); and it is revealed that the hosts of Israel went into the house of this their Lord of the Covenant—now called Beth-El-Berith (Jud. ix, 46): this clearly shows "El" and "Baal" to be identical and interchangeable terms. David's son Beeliada (1 Chron. xiv, 7) elsewhere appears as Eliada (2 Sam. v, 16), again showing that El, God, was regarded as equivalent of Baal; and as so clearly appears in the name Bealiah, meaning "Yahveh is Baal, or Lord" (1 Chron. xii, 5). Crowning proof is the victory-tokening name given by David to a place where, he said, "Yahveh hath broken forth upon mine enemies . . . therefore he called the name of that place Baal-perazim"—"that is, Baal, the Lord of Breaches" (2 Sam. v, 20). El-Yahveh-Baal was all one and the same, in those good old Hebrew Bible days. See the "Dictionary of Bible Proper Names" in any well-edited Bible for scores of corroboratory instances.

Exactly so was it with the other word "El" Yahveh, as the local Lord or Baal of sundry places or things rendered sacred by his "putting his name" there or thereon. As on Sinai, Yahveh said to Moses, "in all places where I record my name I will come unto thee, and will bless thee" (Ex. xx, 24; Deut. xii, 5; 1 Kings viii, 29, etc.). Thus, Jacob said of the place where he dreamed that he saw the Ladder (Gen. xxviii, 17), "this is none other but the house of the gods (Beth-Elohim)"; and he set up a phallic "pillar" or "mazzebah," and called it "Beth-El—the house of God" (vv. 17–19). And Elohim (gods) came to him in a dream and said, "I am the El of Beth-El" (Gen. xxxi, 13); and Jacob built there an altar and called the place Beth-El, "because there Ha-Elohim—*The-Gods—were revealed* unto him" (Gen. xxxv, 7). Here the Hebrew text expressly uses the *plural*, noun and verb—"the-gods were revealed"; but the Authorized Version falsely translates as "God appeared unto him," while the Revised Version correctly reads "revealed," but uses wrongly the singular "was."

The Pagan Jebusite Melchizedek ("King of Righteousness"), was "priest of El-Elyon—God Most High" (Gen. xiv, 18),—which also proves again that "El" was a common term of deity, Pagan and Hebrew alike; and Yahveh himself is frequently called "El-Elyon"—God Most High"—the word "elyon" being an adjective simply meaning "high" or "lofty." Yahveh tells Moses that he is "El-Shaddai"—God my Daemon" (Ex. vi, 3), as he is often very peculiarly called, as will be noticed in its place; and in Joshua he is called "Yahveh-El-Elohim," translated "the Lord God of gods" (Josh. xxii, 22), and so on, scores of times; proving that Yahveh was just one El or God of or over the other gods or spirits which abounded in the Hebrew and neighboring Pagan mythologies.

Gradually, towards the close of the Hebrew Sacred History, particularly after the return from Captivity, out of all this jumble of confused local Baalim and Elohim, evolved a more or less definite idea of the Hebrew Yahveh as a higher or super-El or Baal of and above all the others; then as a supreme El or Baal or Lord of Heaven and earth; and then as One and Only True God, to the exclusion and proscription of all others as "false gods" or worse— "all the gods of the heathen are Devils" (Ps. xcvi, 5, Vulgate).

Ha-Elohim Yishrael—The Gods of Israel

This brings us to the climax of "revelation" of the Hebrew Scriptures, which to many good Christians and Hebrews alike, brought up on professional translations, may well seem startling; but which will now be fully proven by the literal words of the Hebrew Scriptures in their original texts—the patent and admitted plurality of Hebrew Gods in their wonderful Revelation to man.

The English, Latin, Greek, and other Versions "diligently compared and revised" by professional Divines, with which texts only the vast majority of people are familiar from youth up, diligently and persistently conceal this cardinal Fact under a form of "pious fraud" of translation designed to give us a belief of an Only One God of Israel from "in the beginning," who created heaven and earth, and performed the many wonders therein related as revealed. But this is a pious false pretense; for, according to the texts of the Hebrew Scriptures, in their original Hebrew language, the fact is luminous, that not to any One God, but to *The Gods*," are attributed all the works of Creation and the many acts and wonders appearing in translation and in Theology as the wondrous work of a One and Only God.

THE ORIGINAL HEBREW WORDS

It is no work of pedantic erudition, but a simple and easy accomplishment for any one who will take the pains to learn the 22 consonantal letters of the Hebrew Alphabet, to recognize by sight and distinguish between four Hebrew words—the holy but very variable words applied to the Hebrew God and Gods,—plainly printed in the original texts of the "Word of God." First we learn their word "El" (Heb. אל), meaning God or spirit-shade; the plural forms of that word, "Elohim" (Heb. אלהים and "elohe" (Heb. אלהי), which are simply the plural for god·· then their name-word "Yahveh" (Heb. יהוה), or Jehovah, w. ¿h name is persistently falsely concealed and rendered in translation by simply the *title* "Lord"; then we learn the actual Hebrew Chaldeán word for "Lord," which is "Adon" (Heb. אדן). Equipped with this easy and elementary learning, we will proceed to pick out and examine these four words in some of the principal instances where they occur in the Hebrew texts, and ourselves "diligently compare" them with the pious mis-translations of the English "versions,"—asking any scholarly Doctor of Divinity to deny the result if he truthfully can.

"THE GODS CREATED"

Here we have the "Word of God" in the sacred Hebrew language in which it was first written and edited. We scan the venerable pages of Genesis, the Book of Beginnings.

In the very first sentence we find the "revelation" of the plurality of Gods—Elohim: "In beginning created ELOHIM (gods) the-heavens and-the-earth" (Gen. i, 1). The forms of the sentences show the order of the Hebrew words, and the hyphens indicate the combination of the particles "and," "the," etc., which are joined to the noun in Hebrew and written as one word, e.g. "theheavens," "and-theearth." And, v. 2, "And-the-spirit (*ruach*, wind) of-Elohim (gods) moved upon-the-face of-the-Abyss"; and, v. 3, "And-said Elohim (gods), Let-there-be light." And thus, for 33 times in the first Chapter of Genesis, we read "ELOHIM" (Gods): always plural, always "gods," but always translated "God."

In undeniable proof of plurality, which even translation cannot in this instance conceal: "And-said ELOHIM (Gods), Let *us* make man (*adam*) in-image-*our*, after-likeness-*our*" (v. 26). And the words of the text indicate there must have been female gods, too; for it is recited: "And-created Elohim the-adam (man); in-the-image of-Elohim (gods) created-he-him; male-and-female created-he-*them*." This is reiterated for positive assurance in the opening verses of Chapter v: "In-the-day that Elohim created adam (man), in-the-likeness of-Elohim (gods) made-he-*them*; male-and-female created he them; and-blessed them, and-called their-name adam (man), in-the-day when they-were-created" (Gen. v, 1–2).

Not one God, but a plurality of *gods*, from the very start of Hebrew-Scripture "revelation," is further proven to demonstration by the familiar dialogue between the Serpent and the Woman: "And the Serpent said unto the Woman, Ye shall not surely die; for Elohim (gods) doth know that in the day ye eat thereof, then your eyes shall be opened, and ye shall be as gods (Elohim), knowing good and evil" (Gen. iii, 5). And the Serpent spoke true; and when Yahveh-Elohim heard that the-man and the-woman had eaten the Forbidden Fruit of the Tree of Knowledge, he, they, said: "Behold, the man is become as *one of us*, to know good and evil" (v. 22). Here certainly is one God speaking to another God or a whole assembly or Olympus of Gods.

In the second, or Jahvistic, Chapter, we first encounter the varients "Yahveh" and "Yahveh Elohim," (Yahveh being abbreviated "), which distinguish, plainly as the Gulf Stream in the Ocean, the use of a second and very often conflicting source-record of the events narrated in the composition-work of Hebrew Scriptures, and very uncritically worked together into the composite Books which have come down to us, as is elsewhere pointed out. The Elohist account of Creation, using the word "Elohim," ends with the third verse of Genesis II; immediately the totally different "Jahvistic" narrative begins: "In *the day* (not six days of Elohim) that YAHVEH ELOHIM made the earth and the heavens" (v. 4). And so, we find "Yahveh Elohim" 13 times through the second Chapter, doing a totally different work of Creation; but always Yahveh-Elohim, always plural, always "gods," but always misrendered "Lord God."

Chapter iii is composite, and we find sometimes Elohim, sometimes Yahveh Elohim; but always plural; and so in Chapter iv. Even more explicit are the words of Chapter v, where it is twice recited: "And Enoch walked with THE-GODS (eth ha-Elohim); and Elohim (gods) took him" (vv. 22, 24). And so of Noah, in Chapter vi, "And Noah was a just man; he walked with the-Gods" (ha-Elohim; v. 9). Chapter vi is a veritable medley of composition, and of plurality of deity, beginning the Fable of the Flood: "The "SONS OF THE GODS (Beni ha-Elohim—a Hebraism for "the Gods") saw the daughters of men" (v. 2), and (v. 3) "Yahveh said." And again (v. 4), "THE SONS OF THE GODS (*Beni ha-Elohim*) came in unto the daughters of men, and they bore children unto them"; and (v. 5) "Yahveh saw." And (v. 11) "the earth was corrupted before THE GODS" (ha-Elohim); and (v. 12) "Elohim (gods) saw the earth"; and (v. 13) "Elohim (gods) said to Noah"; and (v. 22) "Noah did all that Elohim commanded him." Here again, always plural (except where we have the Yahveh reading), always THE GODS, but always rendered "GOD."

And "the sons of the gods" (*Beni ha-Elohim*—a Hebraism for Gods)—are of frequent mention in the Hebrew Scriptures: in Job i, 6 and ii, 1, "the sons of the gods came to present themselves before Yahveh"; and in xxxviii, 7 "all the sons of the gods shouted for joy." The God of the Hebrews was thus plainly not one God, but a plurality of gods and goddesses, who had children (or the-Gods themselves) of so sporty a nature that they corrupted the earth and brought on its fabled destruction by the fabled Flood of Noah.

Now we have a singular confirmation of the plurality of the Hebrew Elohim (gods), and that they were identical with the Elohim (gods) of the other heathen tribes and peoples thereabouts. In Genesis xx, Abraham takes Sarah his wife and journeys to Gerar, in the Philistine country, of which Abimelech was King: his name is "Moloch (or the King) is my Father"—certainly a heathen who knew not the supposed One-God, Yahveh, of Abraham. Abimelech, according to a jovial custom of the country, took Sarah and slept with her, thinking she was Abraham's sister, as he had falsely stated.

Lo (v. 3) "Elohim (gods) came to Abimelech in a dream" and
warned him of the error of his way; and (v. 6) "The Gods (ha-
Elohim) said unto him in the dream." Being a heathen, Abimelech
would hardly dream foreign Hebrew gods: they were all clearly the
same Elohim that he was familiar with. Abimelech was scared sick;
but Abraham "prayed unto the gods (ha-Elohim), and Elohim
healed Abimelech" (v. 17). Oddly enough, many years later
(Chapter xxvi), Isaac also visits Gerar, takes his wife Rebekah
along, passes her off as his sister, and our same old friend Abimelech
repeats the same sportive hospitality with Rebekah.

In Genesis xxii, 1, "it came to pass that the Gods (ha-Elohim)
tempted Abraham"—(as he dreamed)—to offer up Isaac as a sacrifice; and Abraham (v. 3) rose up and took Isaac and "went unto
the place which the gods (ha-Elohim) told him"; but fortunately,
at the critical moment, (v. 11) "an angel of Yahveh" called out and
checked his hand from the pious human sacrifice. When Isaac came
on to die, and Jacob, camouflaged to feel like Esau, came in to
receive the stolen blessing, Isaac (xxvii, 27) said: "You smell like
a field which Yahveh has blessed"; (v. 28) "May the gods (ha-
Elohim) give thee," etc. Then, in Chapter xxviii, Isaac further says
to Jacob: (v. 3) "And El-Shaddai (God my Daemon) bless thee";
(v. 4) "mayst thou inherit the land which Elohim (Gods) gave unto
Abraham." Here, again, all through, plural, "the gods," always
rendered "God"; and a fairly clear distinction always made between
the particular El "Yahveh" and the plural "Elohim" gods in general.

Yet a little more, "to make assurance doubly sure" that the
God of the Hebrews was "the gods" of the other heathens among
whom they lived. Jacob had played his notorious cattle-breeding
tricks on his heathen father-in-law Laban, who got mad and broke
up the family arrangements. Thereupon (Gen. xxxi, 11), "an angel
of the gods (ha-Elohim)" spoke unto Jacob in a dream; and (v.
13) said, "I am the god of Beth-El (ha-El-Beth-El)," and advised
him to take secret leave of Laban, and return to his own country;
and Jacob's wives, who were plain Chaldee heathens, said to him,
(v. 16) "all that Elohim (gods) said unto thee, do." Then Rachel,
one of his heathen wives, daughter of the heathen Laban (v. 19)
"stole the teraphim (phallic idols) which belonged to her father,"
and the Jacob family fled. Laban pursued after them for a week
before he caught them; and (v. 24) "Elohim (gods) came upon
Laban the Syrian in a dream, and said," etc. And (v. 30) Laban
said to Jacob, "Why hast thou stolen my gods? (Elohim); and
Jacob told Laban to search for them, and said (v. 32), "Whoever

hath THY GODS (Elohim) shall not live." Laban searched, but Rachel had hidden the idols, and Laban could not find them. After a quarrel betwen them, Jacob invoked "THE GODS" (Elohe) of his father Abraham for making peace between them; and he set up a phallic mazzebah (pillar) for a testimonial (v. 45), and invoked the GODS (Elohe) of Abraham, Nahor, etc., to "judge between us" (v. 53). Then Jacob went on his way, "and angels of THE GODS met him" (xxxii, 1), and Jacob called them "the Hosts of THE GODS" (v. 2). Thus all through these chapters and following ones, we find nothing but "Elohim," "ha-Elohim" and "Elohe" (gods) for heathen Laban's teraphim-gods and Jacob's gods just alike.

At Jabbok (xxxii, 28) Jacob fought with a stranger, who asked him his name; and the stranger changed Jacob's name to Israel, for "thou hast fought with GODS (Elohim) and with men"; and Jacob called (v. 31) the place Peni-El ("face-of-God"), for, he said, "I have seen GODS (Elohim) face to face." In xxxiii, 20, Jacob erected an altar and called it "El-Elohe-Israel"—"GOD OF THE GODS of Israel"—a very positive proof of plurality of gods.

In Chapter xxxv the plurality of GODS, Hebrew and "strange" is further clearly shown: (v. 1) "Elohim (gods) said to Jacob, Go to Beth-El, and make there an altar unto THE GOD (*ha El*) who appeared to thee when thou fleddest"; then (v. 2) "Jacob said unto his household, Put away the strange GODS (Elohe) which are in your midst"; and (v. 3) "I will make there an altar to THE GOD (*ha El*) who," etc.; and (v. 4) "they gave unto Jacob all the strange gods (Elohe), and Jacob came to Beth-El and built an altar which he called (v. 7) "El-Beth-El, because there THE GODS (*ha-Elohim*) appeared unto him." Thus clearly is distinction made between a particular "El," and the generality of plural "Elohim" or "Elohe" common to the heathen peoples of those parts.

Pharaoh dreamed a dream, and called on Joseph to interpret it. This "Baal of Dreams" (dream-master), as his brothers called him (Gen. xxxvii, 19), said to Pharaoh, "What ha-Elohim (the gods) is about to do, he has told Pharaoh" (Gen. xli, 25); and "the thing is settled by ha-Elohim (the gods, v. 28); and ha-elohim (the gods) is hastening to do it" (v. 33). Pharaoh certainly knew of no Hebrew only-one God, but all the gods of Egypt, and of them clearly he spoke, saying to his servants: "Can we find such a one as this is, a man in whom is the spirit of *Elohim?*—gods (v. 38); and to Joseph he said, "Forasmuch as *Elohim* has shewed thee all this" (v. 39). The "elohim" of Pharaoh and the ha-elohim of Joseph were clearly one and the same gods to whom they both appealed. To his brothers

Joseph said, "it was not you that sent me hither, but ha-elohim—the gods" (Gen. xlv, 8); and "Elohim (gods) has made me lord (*adon*) of all Egypt" (v. 9)—two of our words appearing in this verse.

That the Egyptian Pharaohs by "elohim" spoke only of their own myriad gods, the same "elohim" and "ha-elohim" of the Hebrews, who knew no other gods, is made evident by the incident of 430 years later, when the Pharaoh of that time commanded the Hebrew midwives to kill all the male Hebrew children as they were born; and it is twice said, "but the midwives feared ha-elohim" (the gods; Ex. i, 17, 21). Surely these were none other than the gods of Egypt, for after 430 years in Egypt the Hebrew slaves knew of no other gods; even their Moses knew not Yahveh and had to ask his name, that he might tell it to the equally ignorant elders (Ex. iii, 13); and it is expressly declared by Joshua that in Egypt, and long after, the Hebrews "served the gods of Egypt" (Josh. xxiv, 14); and even for centuries down to the time of Ezekiel, "they did not forsake ha-elohim—the gods—of Egypt" (Ezek. xx, 8). So that it cannot be gainsaid, that "Elohim" is plural, and means and reveals more gods than one, wherever used of Hebrew "ha-elohim" or "ha-elohim" of Egypt and other heathen lands round about Israel.

Plurality of Gods Betrayed

Plural Nouns and Plural Verbs

We have gone through the wonderful Book of Genesis, and all through we see reflected "the-*gods*" of the ancient Hebrews, who are throughout just like the-gods of their Heathen neighbors.

It is but fair and bounden to say, for what it is worth, that the verbs used, for the most part, in the Hebrew texts with this plural "Elohim" of the noun El referring to the Hebrew Deity, are generally found in the singular number. The verb-forms "is" and "are" are not used in Hebrew; as any one may verify by glancing down any page of the Authorized Version of the Old Testament, where these words are always written in italics, signifying that they do not occur in the original. Thus a very large verb-iage is missing in the Hebrew texts.

But the actual verb plural-form (which in Hebrew is the tiny "u" tacked on to the end, as we add "s" in English to form the singular), although mostly missing, is a number of times to be found, and is undeniable proof of plurality of "ha-elohim." Father Abraham himself avows this plurality: "When Elohim—gods—caused (plural: *hith-u*) me to wander from my father's house" (Gen. xx, 13). And Jacob built an altar at Luz, "and called the place El-beth-el"; because there Ha-elohim *were revealed* (plural: nigl-u) unto him" (Gen. xxxv, 7). And David the King makes the self-same open avowal of the plural gods of Israel: "Israel, whom gods—elohim—went (plural: *halk-u*) to redeem . . . from the nations and their gods—elohim" (2 Sam. vii, 23).

The Law says, "at the mouth of two witnesses, or at the mouth of three witnesses, shall the matter be established" (Deut. xix, 15). Here then is the fulfillment of the Law: three witnesses, of the chiefest of Israel, have declared by word of Inspiration the plurality of the *gods* of Israel. But there is more textual proof of plurality of the-gods of Israel. Moses uses the plural adjective with elohim: "hath heard the voice of the living gods (elohim hayyim) and lived" (Deut. v. 26; *Heb.* v. 23). And twice David threatens Goliath, for that he should "defy the armies of the living gods (elohim hayyim—1 Sam. xvii, 26, 36). Six times here we have the textual admission of the plurality of elohim—the editorial blue-pencil slipped, and overlooked to kill the little "u" plural-sign of the Hebrew verbs and the inobtrusive "im" of the adjective. As, on the recently discovered Throne of Tut-ankh-amen, the zealous orthodox priests of the whilom heretic King undertook to change the numerous heretical "Aten"-signs blazoned thereon to "Amen"-signs of the orthodox Faith; but in a single instance the "Aten-sign" was overlooked, and left unchanged through the ages, a silent but potent witness to the "One-God" heresy of Amen-hotep IV and the youthful Tut-anhk-Amen.

The "Plural of Dignity"

The apologists for the plural-gods usage, "Elohim" and "Elohe," reason that this is a "plural of dignity"—a sort of Divine "editorial we"; they even go to the length to say that "Elohim" connotes the awful sense of "Godhead." If so, there were scores of Pagan God-heads—Elohim.

But then, the Hebrew Deity—when Yahveh only speaks or is particularly spoken of or quoted, does not hide behind the anonymous "editorial plural," but always says forthright "I" (Heb. *ani*, *anoki*), with the singular "El-God," or the personal name Yahveh. A few instances out of many hundreds must suffice.

Time and again the chief Tribal Baal says, "anoki El" and "anoki Yahveh," "anoki El-Shaddai" (Gen. xvii, 1; Ex. iii, 6), "Anoki ha-el beth-el—I am the God of Beth-el" (Gen. xxxi, 13), "anoki El, and there are no other elohim" (Is. xlvi, 9); "I am El" (id. xlv, 22). Yahveh descended in a cloud upon Sinai and proclaimed, "Yahveh, Yahveh El" (Ex. xxxiv, 5–6). Moses often quotes Yahveh as saying, "Thou shalt worship no other El: for Yahveh, whose name is Jealous, is a jealous El" (Ex. xxxiv, 14; xx, 5; Deut. iv, 24; v, 9; *passim*). Again, "there is none like El" (Deut. xxxiii, 26): "This is my El" (Ex. xv, 2). Hagar said, "Thou art a god—El—of seeing" (Gen. xvi, 13). Balaam said to Balak, "El is not a man—*ish*, that he should lie, nor the son of man —*ben adam*, that he should repent" (Num. xxiii, 19). "God—El— who brought them forth" (Num. xxiii, 22); "see what El—God— hath wrought" (Num. xxiii, 23); "when El does this" (Num. xxiv, 23); "who hears the words of El" (Num. xxiv, 4). "El is my salvation; Yah Yahveh is my strength" (Is. xii, 2). "Verily, thou art an El that hidest thyself" (Is. xlv, 15); "This is my El" (Ex. xv, 2). Joshua says, "Hereby ye shall know that El is among you" (iii, 10).

This usage of "El" for a particular God, Hebrew or other— Pagan; of "Elohim" and "Elohe" for Hebrew and other-Pagan Gods indiscriminately, as in hundreds of instances in this Chapter and elsewhere noticed, quite explodes the pious "editorial we" and "plural of dignity"; and demonstrates the common polytheism of Israel and their neighbor Heathens.

YAHVEH—GOD "E PLURIBUS UNUM"

MANY "OTHER GODS" ARE ACKNOWLEDGED

No one thing is admitted, proved and established in the ancient Hebrew Sacred Books more and more undeniably than the factuality, the reality and actuality of existence, genuineness and power of many "other" and "strange" gods—of "all the gods of the peoples," as so often mentioned and named, by the Hebrew Yahveh and his inspired Holy Men of old who "spake as they were moved by the Holy Ghost," to admit and record this unimpeachable fact. Thousands of times the actual existence of the gods of the surrounding peoples is declared and vouched for by Inspiration; and no one thing in Holy Writ is more frequent or more positive than the affirmance and recognition of "other gods" as living actual beings, save only the like existence and the asserted superiority of Yahveh God of Israel. So numberless are the inspired Texts voicing this unquestioned fact that sundry instances only, picked almost at random, can be cited here.

Yahveh was only God of Israel, as time and again is averred; his holy Covenant, as it was first proclaimed with Abraham, was: "I will establish my Covenant between me and thee and thy seed after thee in their generations, for an everlasting Covenant: to be a God (Elohim) unto thee, and to thy seed after thee" (Gen. xvii, 7); and ever after he called himself and was simply called, "The God of Abraham, the God of Isaac, and the God of Jacob," as, for example, he declared himself to Moses at the Burning Bush (Ex. iii, 6). Yahveh chose the "seed of Abraham" to be his "Chosen People," he to be their special, national God: "For thou (Israel) art an holy People unto Yahveh thy God; Yahveh thy God hath chosen thee to be a People for his own possession, above all the peoples that are upon the face of the earth" (Deut. xiv, 2)—as to whom Yahveh made no claims at all. But the Hebrew Yahveh, though a "Jealous God," and demanding that his Chosen People worship him preferably or alone, and though he claims his superiority over all "other gods," yet admits the existence and divine personality of these "other gods," and recognizes their rights and powers, all but equal to himself.

On Sinai Yahveh solemnly commands: "I am Yahveh thy God, which have brought thee (Israel) out of the land of Egypt: Thou (Israel) shalt have no other gods before (i.e., in preference to) me" (Ex. xx, 3)—but in perfect recognition of the other nations and their gods: "thou shalt make no covenant with them, nor with their gods" (Ex. xxiii, 32); and, "thou shalt worship no other god; for Yahveh, whose name is Jealous, is a Jealous God" (Ex. xxxiv, 14).

The holy Law of Yahveh, promulgated amid the fires and thunders of Sinai, commanded reverent respect for all other gods. It is enacted by Yahveh: "Thou shalt not revile *the* GODS—ha-Elohim—nor curse the ruler of thy people" (Ex. xxii, 28)—thus a solemn, positive recognition by Yahveh's divine Law of the fact of other living gods. Again, the Law confesses the gods and their activities: "Thou shalt not bow down to their gods—elohim, nor serve them, nor do after their works; ye shall serve Yahveh thy God" (Ex. xxiii, 24). Never once, in the Law of Sinai, nor for a thousand years after, is there the avowal or the hint, that "there is no other god"; but "other gods" galore are confessed. In the face of the commands of the "Jealous God," his holy Chosen "feared Yahveh, and served their own gods" (2 Kings, xvii, 33, *et seq.*).

Moses, "the man of the Gods—ish ha-Elohim" (Deut. xxxiii, 1), himself, in his famous Song of Triumph, asserts only superiority for his Yahveh, and proclaims vauntingly, "Who is like unto thee, O Yahveh, among the gods"? (Ex. xv, 11). His father-in-law, Jethro,

Pagan priest of the gods of Midian, seeing some of the wonders of
Sinai, admits to Moses, "Now I know that Yahveh is greater than all
the Gods" (Ex. xviii, 11). Again, in his celebrated Swan Song,
Moses exults to Israel: "For Yahveh thy God is God of Gods—
Elohe ha-elohim—and Lord of lords—adonai ha-adonim—the great
El" (Deut. x, 17). Again, Moses surveys the gods of the nations
around, and appeals to Israel: "What nation is there so great, who
hath GODS—(Elohim)—so nigh unto them as Yahveh our God is?"
(Deut. iv, 7). By Joshua the God of Israel is proclaimed, "Yahveh
God of Gods, Yahveh God of Gods—El Elohim Yahveh, El Elohim
Yahveh" (Josh. xxii, 22)—admitting the "other gods" and simply
Yahveh's superiority to them all.

The godly Psalmist takes up the refrain, making it the burden
of many a sweet song: "O give thanks to the God of Gods—elohe
ha-elohim; O give thanks to the Lord of lords—adonai ha-adonim"
(Ps. cxxxvi, 2–3); "For Yahveh is a great God—El; he is to be
feared above all gods—elohim" (Ps. xcvi, 4); and "Yahveh is exalted above all gods" (Ps. xcvii, 9). Again he sings, "For Yahveh is
a great God—El, and a great king above all gods—elohim" (Ps. xcv,
3); "among the gods—elohim—there is none like unto thee, O
Adonai—Lord" (Ps. lxxxvi, 8). Again he sings, "All the gods—
elohim—of the nations are DEVILS—*elihim;* but Yahveh made the
heavens" (Ps. xcvi, 5)—confessing again the living "other gods"
but declaring them only devils. But gods or devils, they are living
actualities; and David calls on them as immortal beings to render
homage to the Yahveh of Israel: "Worship him, all ye ELOHIM—
gods" (Ps. xcvii, 7)—not now *elilim,* devils. And the Wise Man
Solomon echoes the refrain, "For great is our El above all elohim"
(2 Chron. ii, 5).

So a thousand times the tongue and pen of Inspiration declare
the verity and living reality of "all the gods of the nations," that
Yahveh is simply a God "*e pluribus unum*"—a "God above all the
other gods"; not any "One God of all the earth," not until the idea
and later Dogma of Judaism evolved out of the tribulations of the
Captivity. But, "out of nothing nothing is made." In the view of
the reiterated admissions above noted, and thousands others in the
sacred Texts, to otherwise contend is an ostentation of unscriptural
Theology.

The God of Israel and the Gods of the Nations

That Yahveh was only, and claimed only to be, the Tribal God
of Israel, and recognized "all the gods of the nations" as his con-

temporaries and fellow, though inferior, Deities, is true as anything in the Bible may be taken as true. All these tribal or national Divinities were strictly territorial, and their sphere of activity, power and jurisdiction was local and limited by the national boundaries, and to the "Chosen People" of the respective God. Two interesting illustrations of this primal fact of Biblical Mythology are recorded by inspiration in the Book of Kings.

Ahaziah, King of Israel, was sick, and he sent messengers to "Go, inquire of Baal-zebub, the God of Ekron, whether I shall recover of this disease. But the angel of Yahveh said to Elijah, Arise, go up to meet the messengers of the King of Samaria, and say unto them, Is it because there is no God in Israel, that thou sendest to inquire of Baal-zebub the God of Ekron?" Elijah delivered the message, and repeated the query about the God of Israel, adding an unreported message from Yahveh to Ahaziah: "Therefore thus saith Yahveh, Forasmuch as thou hath sent messengers to inquire of Baal-zebub the God of Ekron, is it not because there is no God in Israel to inquire of his word? Therefore thou shalt surely die." And it is solemnly recorded, "So he died according to the word of Yahveh which Elijah had spoken" (2 Kings i).

Shalmanezer, King of Assyria, destroyed the nation of Israel, or Samaria, in 721 B.C., and he carried away bodily the whole "Ten Tribes" into perpetual captivity, leaving their land bare; he then re-peopled Samaria with colonies of other nations subdued by Assyria (v. 24). Yahveh, who had not saved his Chosen People, took it upon himself, as local Baal of the land, to harass the newcomers by sending lions among them, which slew some of them. The new colonists sent word to the Great King, saying, "The nations which thou hast removed, and placed in the cities of Samaria, know not the manner of the God of the land; therefore he hath sent lions among them," etc. (v. 26). The King therefore commanded, "carry thither one of the priests whom ye brought from thence, and let them go and dwell there, and let him teach them the manner (Heb. mishpat) of the God of the land. Then one of the priests whom they had carried away from Samaria came and dwelt in Beth-el, and taught them how they should fear Yahveh" (2 Kings, xvii, 26–27). But this first recorded missionary expedition (barring Jonah's) failed, for the newcomers "feared Yahveh, and served their own gods" (v. 31), who are named in vv. 30–31.

Here it is recorded, that "every nation made gods of their own" (v. 29); the colonists from each nation, towit, Babylon, Cuth, Hamath, etc., established the worship of the gods of their respective countries, now acclimated in Israel. As in the days of Moses the Chosen also "feared Yahveh," and worshipped the gods of Egypt and of "beyond the flood," and of the "seven nations" among whom they dwelt. In the days of the Judges, "the Children of Israel served the Baalim, and Ashtaroth, and the gods of Syria, and the Gods of Zidon, and the gods of Moab, and the gods of the children of Ammon, and the gods of the Philistines, and forsook Yahveh, and served him not" (Jud. x, 6); they also "made Baal-Berith (Lord of the Covenant) their god" (Jud. viii, 33, ix, 4). Hundreds of foreign, "strange gods" are named, and their activities indicated, far too many to relate; in a word, "all the gods of the nations" (Deut. xxix, 18). These gods, even like Yahveh, were "the Rock in whom they (their Chosen Peoples) trusted"; and it is averred, as of Yahveh, these other gods "did eat the fat of sacrifices, and drink the wine of their offerings" (Deut. xxxii, 37–38), as only actual living beings can eat and drink—a very superstitious belief, but pertinent confession of their supposed divine reality.

Jeremiah complains that "the women make cakes to the Queen of Heaven, and pour out drink offerings to other gods" (Jer. vii, 18). The gods of Hamath and of Arphad, the gods of Sepharvaim, asks Rabshakeh, "have they delivered Samaria out of my hand?" (Is. xxxvi, 19); and he taunts Hezekiah of Judah, "Who among all the gods of these lands hath delivered their land out of my hand, that Yahveh should deliver Jerusalem?" (v. 20); and none could answer him a word (v. 21). Jeremiah accuses Judah, "according to the number of thy cities are thy gods" (Jer. ii, 28, xi, 13). Ahaz "sacrificed unto the gods of Damascus, which smote him; . . . but they were the ruin of him and of all Israel" (2 Chron. xxviii, 23), as they are expressly credited with actually doing. Yahveh threatened to "smite all the gods of Egypt" (Ex. xii, 12)—proving their existence to be smitten. "Woe unto thee, Moab, people of Chemosh," cries Yahveh (Num. xxi, 29); "against Moab thus saith Yahveh Sabaoth, Elohe of Israel, Woe unto Nebo" (Jer. xlviii, 1); "Chemosh shall go forth into captivity, with his priests and his princes together" (Jer. xlviii, 7). "Bel boweth down, Nebo stoopeth," avers Isaiah (xlvi, 1). Jephthah, "on whom was the spirit of Yahveh," said to the King of the Ammonites, "Yahveh Elohe Israel had dispossessed the Amorites, . . . wilt thou not possess that which Chemosh thy Elohe giveth thee to possess it?" (Jud. xi, 23–24). "Dagon our God hath delivered Sampson into our hands" (Jud. xvi, 23). Thus the existence and power of the "other gods" is time and time admitted, declared and illustrated.

Time and again inspiration couples and distinguishes the rival Deities: "I am Yahveh thy Elohe; fear not the elohe of the Amorites" (Jud. vi, 10). "Chemosh thy elohe and Yahveh our elohe" (Jud. xi, 24). Full patent of authenticity is vouched for "Dagon our elohe" (1 Sam. v, 7); for "Ashtoreth, elohe (goddess) of the Zidonians, and Chemosh, elohe of Moab, and Milcom, elohe of the children of Ammon" (1 Kings xi, 33); for "Baal-zebub, elohe of Ekron" (2 Kings i, 2); for "the elohe (gods) of Sepharvaim" (2 Kings xvii, 31); for "the star of your elohe Moloch" (Amos v, 26); all "true and living gods" during all the centuries of the national life of Israel and Judah.

Allegiance could be transferred from one god to another, upon removing from one country to another; as where Ruth would go with Naomi, and said, "thy people shall be my people and thy god my god" (Ruth i, 16).

Regular "tournaments" or contests of power were staged between Yahveh of Israel and some of his rival Gods. The conjure-contests between Yahveh and the magicians of Egypt are well known, and elsewhere herein admired. Gideon staged an effective duel between Yahveh and Baal, in honor of which Gideon was nicknamed Jerubbaal (Jud. vi). The Philistines captured the "Ark of the Gods" (aron ha-elohim) of Israel, and deported it to Ashdod "into the House of Dagon, and set it by Dagon"; and for several nights Yahveh knocked Dagon off his perch and broke his hands and head off (v. 4). When the Philistines saw this, their priests deserted their temple, saying, "the ark of the gods (ha-elohim) of Israel shall not abide with us; his hand is sore upon us, and upon our god Dagon" (v. 7). The Philistines sent the ark back to the Chosen, with sundry suggestive tokens; and the Holy Ones of Yahveh carted the holy Ark to the very heathen "Beth-Shemesh"—the House of the Sun-god Shamash, and parked it there (1 Sam. v–vi). The notable contest between Yahveh, represented single-handed by Elijah, against Baal and his four hundred priests (1 Kings xviii), is another well-known instance. In all these Yahveh was triumphant, thus proving "there is none like unto thee, O Yahveh, among the gods" (Ex. xv, 11; 2 Kings xviii, 35; Ps. lxxvii, 13, lxxxvi, 8, passim.)

Moses even quotes Yahveh as having brought Israel up to be his own "people of inheritance," while he, Yahveh "divided (i.e., set apart) unto all nations under the whole heaven," to be their gods, "the sun, and the moon, and the stars, even all the host of heaven" (Deut. iv, 19–20).

In all the national existence of the Chosen, until after the Captivity, always is Yahveh only called and calls himself, "Yahveh, God of Israel," "the God of thy Fathers," "the God of Abraham," never once the One God of all the earth. The "gods of the nations" lived and ruled in their respective bailiwicks, with the benevolent "live and let live" of Yahveh Elohe Israel.

From the inspired "revelation" foregoing, the conclusion is obvious and inevitable: all these "other gods" were, or were regarded by the inspired authors of the "Word of God" to be as actually real and existent as was Yahveh's self; convertibly, Yahveh was no more real and existent than any other of the "gods of the nations." All actually lived and existed as gods of their respective nations, or, none of them had any existence outside the invention of their priests and the fond beliefs of their respective votaries. The "Word of God" inspiredly vouches equally for them all; with respect to all it is equally either true or not true. This is unescapable.

If these gods ever once existed, they all yet exist, for according to all accounts, Gods are "ever-living" or immortal. To deny Baal, Chemosh or Dagon is to deny Yahveh; to admit Yahveh is to confess "all the gods of the nations": the same inspired record vouches for the one and the others.

It may be here suggested, though out of its orderly place: Yahveh, as simply the Tribal God of Israel, no more real and existent than Baal, Chemosh, Dagon, and all the "other gods of the nations," never himself existed except in imagination and Hebrew Mythology; he never therefore lived and existed as an actual Divine Being: therefore Yahveh could not have had and never had a son, Joshua or Jesus; and therefore Joshua-Jesus, as Son of God-Yahveh, is a non-existent and Mythological Personage. This too is unescapable.

Pagan Bible Names

All through the Old Scripture record these two names appear—El and Yahveh, some preferring the one, and some the other; and both inextricably connected with the Canaanitish form "Baal." The names of the Bible Worthies are the clearest proof of this sometimes preference, sometimes combination, of titles of their Deity. The votaries of El bore his name: as Israel, soldier of El; Reuel, Friend of El; Samuel, Daniel, Ezekiel, Emmanuel, Elisha, Elihu, Elizabeth; the adorers of Yahveh or Jehovah chose his name, as: Isaiah, Jeremiah, Hosea, Joshua, Jehoahaz, Jehoshaphat, Jehu; while such as Elijah and Joel combined the two.

The names of Baal and Bel shared the same honors among the

devout Soldiers of El: Gideon was but a nickname of Jerub-baal, which seems to combine Jehovah and Baal. A son of Gideon was Abimelech, who set himself up briefly, during the days of the Judges, as first king over Israel, his name meaning "Moloch is my father." One of the sons of Saul was named Eshbaal, "son of Baal"; one of the sons of David was Beeliada, "whom Baal has known" (1 Chron. xiv, 7), while the same name is given under the form Eliada (2 Sam. v, 16), showing that El and Baal were interchangeable names—as also occurs in the name of one of the "mighty men" of David, Bealiah, "Yahveh is Baal" or Lord, and in Jezebel, both perfect combinations of the two heathen (Israelite and Canaanite) names for "Lord."

That Baal, Bel, and El were equivalent names for "Lord," but that Yahveh preferred the figurative term "my husband" to the more formal "Lord," and that a customary name for Yahveh was "Baal," he himself is quoted as declaring in Hosea ii, 16: "And it shall be in that day, saith Yahveh, that thou shalt call me Ishi ("my husband"); and shalt call me no more Baali ("my Lord").

Not only the Hebrews, but all the Semitic peoples had this custom of compounding their names with that of their favorite deity, in the desire to thus secure the protection of the local Baal for their children. We may recall such names of Belshazzar, Hasdrubal, Hannibal. In more modern and Christian lands the names of Saints, and often a long string of them, are fondly bestowed on helpless infants with the like motive: just as others are named after rich uncles and other important relatives—all in the hope of favors, divine or human. The names cited and their significance are none of them fanciful; they are all, but the last two, taken from among many others from the "Dictionary of Scripture Proper Names," printed in the back of every well-edited copy of the "Holy Bible." They serve to further prove that the El or Yahveh of the Hebrew Bible was nothing more or less than a heathenish Semitic Deity or local god, or "Baal," and was not in any sense a "One God of Israel" or of the whole earth.

CHAPTER X

YAHVEH—THE "TERRIBLE GOD" OF ISRAEL

THE revelation which is made in the inspired pages of the Hebrew Scriptures, of the personality and characteristics of the Hebrew God, cannot but be amazing and even revolting to those whose concept of the God of the Bible is of a God of Mercy and Truth. The portraiture of their Deity, which the Chosen People draw by inspiration in the sacred pages, will be here exposed to candid view, in the very words and lines in which it is drawn by inspired pens; the candid reader must be left to formulate his own convictions of the result. The revelation is written by inspiration of this selfsame God, and not by this reviewer of the record. We will examine this revelation of Yahveh, the great Hebrew Deity, as given by himself through his own inspired biographers.

YAHVEH AS A SUPER-MAN

First of all, the Hebrew God was to his Chosen People merely a man, or Superman, human altogether in form, functions, and attributes, with some attributes of a spirit or Jinn added, such as changing shape at will, like the gods of Homer.

As for his human or "anthropomorphic" form and functions, this appears unequivocally from the Beginning: "Elohim created man in his own image, in the image of Elohim created he him," indeed, it is positively added: "male and female created he them, and said unto them, Be fruitful, and multiply, and replenish the earth" (Gen. i, 27–28). This, indeed, would imply an hermaphroditic sexuality in the person of Elohim (as a single deity), or a female consort, or a plurality of Elohim or gods, male and female, like the gods and goddesses of Olympus. In truth, Yahveh Elohim is very often represented as having many off-spring, referred to as "the sons of God" (or, of the gods—*beni ha-Elohim*). It is early recorded by the inspired texts, that "the sons of God" (*beni ha-Elohim*) saw the daughters of men that they were fair, and they took them wives (*nashim*) of all which they chose" (Gen. vi, 2), and thus produced a race of giants and provoked the Flood.

This primitive Hebrew God-man, named Yahveh, used to come down to the very near-by earth and walk about, and talk to the people he had created, and he made coats of skins for Adam and Eve. He came down as a man and watched the Tower of Babel abuilding (Gen. xi, 5); and a thousand times he came in man-form to earth, to talk with people and to do this and that. At Horeb he stood on the Rock and watched Moses smite it for water (Ex. xvii, 6); and on Sinai "Yahveh descended in the cloud, and stood with him there" (Ex. xxxiv, 5); and he came down as an angel and had an all-night wrestling-match with Jacob. To Moses he always appeared on Mt. Sinai in man-form—"and Yahveh spake unto Moses face to face, as a man speaketh unto his friend" (Ex. xxxiii, 11); although in the same Chapter this is contradicted, for Moses asked Yahveh to let him see him, and Yahveh replied, "Thou canst not see my face: for man shall not see me and live" (v. 20). But the God wished to be complaisant, as far as possible without danger of death; so he put Moses into a little cleft in the rocks, and placed his (Yahveh's) hand over Moses's face, and paraded by and showed Moses his man-like "back parts" (vv. 21–23). Though previously Yahveh was more sociable and seeable; for after writing the Tables of Stone with his *finger*, he celebrated the occasion by inviting Moses and Aaron, Nadab and Abihu and seventy Elders of Israel, to a big banquet up on the "Mountain of the Gods"; and there "they saw the Gods (*ha elohim*) of Israel," whose *feet* were upon a paved work of sapphire stone; and they all "beheld the Gods, and did eat and drink" (Ex. xxiv, 10–11).

But there would seem to be some mistake about all this somewhere. For we have the positive assurance of John that "No man hath seen God at any time" (John i, 18); though St. John the Divine contradicts this by his own claim to have made a personal visit to highest Heaven, where he saw both God himself and his Son (two wholly distinct Persons), sitting side by side on the Throne of Glory, circled around by a rainbow; and John gives minute personal description of one or the other, or both—it is all so mixed and fairy-tale-like: "His head and his hair were white as wool, and his eyes were as a flame of fire, and his feet like unto burnished brass, and out of his mouth went a sharp two-edged sword" (Rev. i, 14–16)—very much like a grotesque idol-image in a Hindu Temple. This description must be intended for Yahveh himself, as it is very like that given by Daniel when he too visited Yahveh (Dan. vii, 9), when

the Son was not recorded as there; but Daniel does not mention the
two-edged sword sticking out of his mouth, but he does tell us that
Yahveh "had wheels," which were as burning fire (Dan. vii, 9).
Isaiah also either visited Heaven or had a good long-distance view
right into it, for he assures us, "I also saw Yahveh sitting upon a
throne" (Is. vi, 1); and he reports that "the breath of Jahveh is like
a stream of brimstone" (Is. xxx, 33). And, says Job (a Heathen),
"Now mine eye hath seen thee" (Job xlii, 5); while Amos saw him
in quite a belligerent mood: "I saw Yahveh standing upon the altar,
and he said, Cut them in the head, all of them; and I will slay the
last of them with the sword" (Amos ix, 1). Also, Ezekiel toured
around Jerusalem with Yahveh, whom he calls a man, measuring the
City, Yahveh being in his usual man-form: "The man (Yahveh)
stood by me" (Ezek. xliii, 6), and "Yahveh said unto me" (Ezek.
xliv, 2)—this arrangement of the texts identifying the man with
Yahveh.

All this certainly proves, so far as any wonder in the Bible may
be taken as proven, that many of the Holy Chosen did see the dread
Yahveh in very person, and yet lived to tell the tale. But, whether
seated on his Throne or parading around on earth, he was always
and everywhere "very man" as well as "very God," as the all-knowing
Doctors of Divinity assure us. And it proves, as do hundreds of
sacred texts, that Yahveh was "revealed" and seen as having every
bodily part, function, faculty and attribute of mere Man, though,
like Jove, in very godly degree.

Yahveh is throughout the Book credited explicitly with human
body and all its parts: head, hair, face, beard, eyes, lips, mouth,
tongue, nostrils, breath, arms, hands, horns on his hands, fingers,
legs, feet, loins, heart, "back parts," even wheels; he wears garments,
and makes them for our First Parents; he has voice, uses words, talks
and speaks: "We have this day seen that Yahveh doth talk with
men" (Deut. v, 24); he laughs, sleeps, loves, hates, is pleased, de-
lighted, angry, in wrath, in fury, takes vengeance, is grieved, jealous,
weary, promises, threatens, repents, changes mind, forgets, remem-
bers, swears, takes oaths, lies, swears he will not lie to David, has a
soul. He is a "man of war," and fights, and slays, and throws down
stones (like Jove) from Heaven, and fights with a sword, bow and
arrows, a quiver full of arrows, and has a whole armory of weapons
from which to equip himself for war; he walks, marches, "and he rode
upon a cherub, and did fly: he was seen upon the wings of the wind"
(2 Sam. xxii, 11, Ps. xviii, 10); "Yahveh rideth upon a swift cloud"
(Is. xix, 1), and he also rides in a chariot. So throughout this

Hebrew "revelation" of their God, El or Yahveh was a man in all his form and parts, actions and passions; although like Zeus and the Gods of Olympus, he could and often did change himself into other forms, and often appeared as an "atmospheric" divinity, as in the Burning Bush, in the pillar of cloud and of fire, in thick clouds, in darkness, in smoke, in storms and winds, as a still small voice; he has his favorite abode upon the Mt. of Sion (Ps. lxxiv, 2; lxxvi, 2).

And over in the New Testament throughout, the Hebrew-Christian Yahveh is still represented as in form and act a man. The Evangelist Mark, who is the only one to mention the circumstance, says that at the Ascension, Jesus was received up into Heaven, "and sat down on the right hand of God" (Mark xvi, 19); he represents Yahveh and Jesus as two entirely separate and distinct persons, both of human form and having separate hands and seats and as sitting separately on a seat. In Acts vii, Stephen, becoming very ecstatic and clairvoyant, "saw the heavens opened, and the Son of Man (whether Jesus or Ezekiel he does not specify) standing on the right hand of God" (55–56)—no doubt meaning on the right-hand side. John also, in his Apocalypse, beheld a Throne in Heaven, and "One sitting on it," and he "saw in the right hand of him who sat on the Throne a book" (Rev. v, 1).

The "Apostles' Creed" likewise is inspired to advise us that Jesus, after rising from the dead and ascending into heaven, "sitteth on the right hand of God the Father, from whence *he* (Jesus) shall come to judge the quick and the dead"—evidently leaving his Father Yahveh back home in Heaven: which sounds to the ordinary understanding very much like two Gods instead of one God, as we have been taught to understand it. The Evangelist John, alone of all the Bible biographers (except for a side remark of Paul in 2 Corinthians iii, 17), is unique in declaring that "God is a Spirit"; but his notion must be doubted as contrary to all the rest of the inspired authority from Genesis to Revelation, inclusive; and even the Creed does not credit him.

Ex Nihil Nihil

The God "revealed" in the Bible is therefore, by its every text and test, altogether a sort of magnified Man, created by his votaries —as were all the "gods of the nations" about them—in their own form and image, with all their own traits and qualities, but magnified.

There is, therefore, nowhere to be found a word of Biblical authority or precedent for the Article of Faith of all the great

Christian Creeds, affirming in their all-knowledge of things unknowable, that "God is a Being without form, parts, or passions, and invisible" (Vide Westminster Confession; Calvin's French Confession; 39 Articles; Methodist Articles of Religion; Baptist Declaration of Faith, *et id omne genus*)—and therefore, a perfect Nonentity or Nothingness, if possible it be to conceive such: the antithesis of Milton's shapeless "Shape, if Shape that can be called which shape hath none."

If the Pope himself or any curious one should think that these Protestant Creeds are crazy and reduce the "revealed" Godhead to Nihility, they may perfectly be matched with these incomparable, and incomprehensible, mystic Dogmas of the One True Faith, admitted to be directly inspired and revealed by Yahveh himself for our faith and wonder:

"The Divinity is transcendentally One, *absolutely free from composition*. The Divine Being is not, and may not be conceived as, a fundamental substrate in which qualities or any other modal determinations inhere." (Cath. Encyc., II, 63).

If this be considered a bit "ultra" for ordinary lay minds to grasp, relief may be found for the dazed understanding in the simpler affirmance of Nonentity revealed out of the celebrated Deposit of Truth for our wonder:

"God is a simple Being or substance excluding every kind of composition, physical or metaphysical" (Cath. Encyc., VI, 614);

or the Divine assurance, from the same source:

"The Three Persons of the Trinity are distinguished from all creatures by the three following characteristics: Absolute IMMATERIALITY; Omniscience, and *Substantial* Sanctity" (Id. XI, 309).

If this does not spell NOTHING, the human mind may despair of reconciling "absolute *immateriality*," which is one ineffable "quality" or "characteristic," with "sanctity of *substance*," which is another and a "material" one; or to unravel how one "Person" of an absolutely immaterial Triad of Nothing can be "*consubstantial*" with two other fractions of the same "Absolute Immateriality." But this is a question for the learned Divines who invented it all; though common mortals may find comfort in their assurance: "It is manifest that a Dogma so mysterious presupposes a Divine Revelation" (Id.)—

which frees it all from the suspicion that it were the product of a pious human of dethroned reason. However, one and all, True Faith and Heretic, are in this particular totally mistaken and un-Biblical. The God of the Bible, El or Yahveh, is, upon all Bible revelation and authority, a man-god exactly the same as Bel, Baal, Zeus, Jupiter or Thor, in the Pagan Mythologies.

Yahveh a Local Deity

Like Zeus and the Gods of Olympus, Yahveh had his special habitat on a high mountain, Horeb or Sinai (the seat of the Pagan Moon-God Sin), which is in Hebrew Scripture always called "the mountain of the Gods" (Har Ha-Elohim: Ex. iii, 1; xxiv, 13, *passim*). He also lurked in the Ark of the Covenant, carried about in tents: "For I have not dwelt in an house since the day that I brought up Israel unto this day; but have gone from tent to tent, and from one tabernacle to another" (1 Chron. xvii, 5); though later he took up his abode in Mt. Sion (Ps. lxxvi, 2). When the Chosen came into the Promised Land, Yahveh lodged wherever the Ark happened to get stranded; later he was localized as having his chief seat of presence and worship, first at Shiloh, afterwards in the Temple at Jerusalem, on Mt. Sion. This was the express command of Moses (Deut. xii, 5, 10–11, 14), and all other places were forbidden. The dispute about worshipping at another place (Mt. Gerizim) instead of at Jerusalem was the crux of the schism of the Samaritans (John iv, 20–21). But this command was evidently not of Moses but by the priests much later; for in Canaan, or the Promised Land, Yahveh was essentially a local Baal, or Lord, and was worshipped, as we have seen and shall see, with all the Canaanitish phallic accessories, "on every high hill and under every green tree."

On Sinai Yahveh himself declared: "In all places where I record my name I will come unto thee and I will bless thee" (Ex. xx, 24); there at the simple "altars of earth" which were then enjoined by Yahveh, but later prohibited by the monopoly of priests. So all through the record, Yahveh would "put his name," or *numen*, here or there, in stone, or earth altar, or mazzebah—"pillar," and was the recognized Baal, or land-Lord, of that locality, as Beth-el, Mizpah, or Eben-ezer.

Yahveh a King Elohim

The Hebrew El or Yahveh was also in a vague sense conceived as a sort of spirit, or king-spirit, or king of departed spirits—the "El of the Elohim." Yahveh was himself known and worshipped by the Patriarchs as "El Shaddai" (El my Daemon—translated as "God Almighty")—as himself tells Moses (Gen. xvii, 1, Ex. vi, 3, *passim*). This seems very curious, for the word means, or is often used as meaning, demon or devil, as in many instances: "They provoked him (Yahveh) to jealousy with strange gods (*elohim*); they sacrificed unto devils (*shaddim*), which were no gods (*elohe*); to gods (*elohim*) whom they knew not, to new gods (elohim) that came newly up" (Deut. xxxii, 16–17). "They sacrificed their sons and their daughters unto devils (shaddim; Ps. cvi, 37); "And he ordained him (Rehoboam) priests . . . unto the devils" (*shaddim;* 2 Chron. xi, 15). Ezekiel speaks of the "voice of the Almighty—kol shaddai —kol el-shaddai" (i, 24, *passim*); the form "shaddai" being a sort of genitive, "my-daemon."

Moses and Aaron address the Deity Yahveh directly as El Elohe —O God, the God of the spirits of all flesh" (Num. xvi, 22); and again, Moses calls him, "Elohe ha-Elohim" ("God of the gods," Deut. x, 17). And in Joshua he calls himself "El Elohim Yahveh" (xxii, 22). In Exodus (xxii, 28), Yahveh is himself quoted as saying, "Thou shalt not revile the gods" (spirits—*Elohim*). This term, *Elohim,* was likewise applied to departed spirits. The Witch of En-dor says, "I see Elohim (gods, spirits) ascending out of the earth" (1 Sam. xxviii, 13).

Oracles or supposed declarations of Yahveh's will were pretended to be received from these "familiar spirits," subject to the King El, Yahveh, and Elohim, as in the case of the Witch of En-dor; and as is recognized by Isaiah, "And when they shall say unto you, Seek unto them that have familiar spirits, and unto the wizards: should not a people seek unto their (*Elohe*) God? On behalf of the living should they seek unto the dead?" (Is. viii, 19); an assumed fact stated scores of times in the sacred texts. Frequently the King-El sent "evil spirits from Elohim" on this or that mission; as when "an evil spirit from God (Elohim) came mightily upon Saul, and he raved" (1 Sam. xviii, 10). The term "*Elohim*" was likewise applied to "other gods": as in the "First Commandment" (Ex. xx, 3); to Chemosh, to Dagon, to Ashtoreth, to Baalzebub, and all the others.

YAHVEH AS A WAR-GOD

The celestial Yahveh was also par excellence "El Sabaoth—the Lord of the (starry) Hosts." These, personified, were considered as his personal retinue; and they "fought on high for Israel." In

Judges v, 20, "They fought from heaven; the stars in their courses fought for Sisera." In 2 Kings (vi, 17), when the King of Syria came to war against Israel, "Behold, the mountain was full of horses and chariots of fire round about." The warlike Psalmist sings that "the chariots of Yahveh are twenty thousand, even thousands of Angels; Yahveh is among them" (Ps. lxviii, 17). While in Joshua (x, 11), "Yahveh cast down great stones from heaven" upon the Amorites, and killed more of them than the Chosen Warriors slew by the sword, while the Sun stood still to watch and aid the slaughter —"For Yahveh fought for Israel" (x, 14). All this is exactly as if lifted bodily from the Iliad of Homer, describing the battles of Zeus and the gods of Olympus on behalf of their favored Greeks or Trojans.

YAHVEH, WAR-GOD OF ISRAEL

These latter references introduce what was, of all, the most definite and dominant concept of Yahveh found in the Hebrew Scriptures from the Exodus until the end of the inspired record. Yahveh was par excellence the War-God of the semi-barbarous Soldiers of El, as was Zeus of the Greeks, and Thor and Odin of the barbarian Teutons, and as was their Gott till but yesterday. In Exodus (xiv, 14), Moses tells the fleeing Soldiers to hold hands off the pursuing Egyptians (of whom they were scared nearly to death (v. 10), for "Yahveh will fight for you"; and in xv, 3, jubilant over the destruction of the Pharaoh and his army, drowned in the Red Sea, he sings, "Yahveh is a man of war: Yahveh is his name." Miriam, sister of Moses, and the women take up the exultant refrain, "Sing ye to Yahveh, for he hath triumphed gloriously" (v. 21). Moses tells the Soldiers of El, that when they go to battle against their enemies, "be not afraid of them, for Yahveh your God is he that goeth with you to fight for you against your enemies, to save you" (Deut. xx, 1-4). In Numbers (xxi, 14) and sundry other places, several heroic exploits of the War-God Yahveh are mentioned as being recorded, among evidently a whole history of them, "in the Book of the Wars of Yahveh." When Joshua went up against Jericho, Yahveh himself came down "as captain of the Hosts of Yahveh," with a drawn sword in his hand, and he gave in person the orders for the famous conduct of the siege by marching around the city seven days blowing trumpets (Josh. v, 13-15).

"When David went out to fight Goliath, he called upon "Yahveh Sabaoth (the Lord of (starry) Hosts), the Elohe of the armies of

Israel" (1 Sam. xvii, 45), and he said "for the battle is Yahveh's" (v. 47). In Psalms he sings of "Yahveh strong and mighty, Yahveh mighty in battle" (xxiv, 8); and again, "he breaketh the bow and cutteth the spear in sunder" (xlvi, 9). Isaiah says "Yahveh Sabaoth mustereth the host for the battle" (xiii, 4); and he prophesies: "so shall Yahveh of Hosts come down to fight for mount Zion" (xxxi, 4), evidently with the celestial hosts, for, he says, "As birds flying, so will Yahveh of Hosts defend Jerusalem" (v. 5); prophecies, by the way, failed to be fulfilled.

Nehemiah encourages the returning exiles with the assurance, "Our Yahveh shall fight for us" (iv, 20); and Zechariah declares, "Then shall Yahveh go forth, and fight against those nations, as when he fought in the day of battle" (xiv, 3); and he says, "Yahveh shall be seen over them, and his arrow shall go forth as the lightning" (ix, 14). The battle-cry of the band of Gideonites, when they attacked the hosts of Midian, was "The sword of Yahveh and of Gideon." The phrase "the sword of Yahveh" is one of the most frequent phrases in the sacred texts; while the title "Yahveh Sabaoth" ("Lord of Hosts") is of infinite recurrence. The most potent conjure of the Soldiers of El was the miracle-working "Ark of the Covenant," within which the numen of Yahveh-Elohim dwelt, and which they constantly carried before them into battle. The Egyptian and Babylonian monuments frequently show similar "Arks" of their war-gods, which they also carried into battle as the source of potent "Voodoo" against their enemies. Thus we have seen that Yahveh, as the War-God of Israel, is the dominant note of their conception of their warlike Deity: "Yahveh Sabaoth is with us, the El of Jacob is our refuge," (Ps. lxvi, 7) was their battle-aegis.

PERSONAL TRAITS OF YAHVEH

This Hebrew El-Elohe-Isra-El, as he is dubbed by Jacob (Gen. xxxiii, 20), is beyond all odds the most hateful and execrable character in all literature, sacred or profane, according to the divine attributes of his Godhead ascribed to him by his own inspired biographers. The Pagan Gods of Greece are sung by the Poet as—

"Gods partial, vengeful, changeable, unjust,
    Whose attributes were rage, revenge, and lust."

The Hebrew-Pagan God Yahveh has all the gods of Greece and of every other known Theogony paled into innocuous shades of villainy in comparison. Yahveh, to credit his inspired Biography, is the greatest criminal on record: he reeks with the blood of murders unnumbered, and is personally a murderer and an assassin, by stealth and treachery; a pitiless monster of bloody vengeances; a relentless persecutor of guilty and innocent alike; the most rageful and terrifying bully and terrorist; fickle and changeable as chameleon Fortune; a synonym for partiality and injustice; a vain braggart; a false promiser; an arrant and shameless liar; and he has repeated fornications and adulteries to his credit; a shameless procurer, as well as being the premium agent of the White Slave Traffic of all time.

Every particular of this, maybe to many shocking, description, is right out of the inspired Bible—as I shall verify and prove by the Book. It is wholly out of the question, in this sketch, to review a tithe of the proofs of these divine attributes of Yahveh, his Holy Word is too replete with them. But I promise to produce amplest "proofs of Holy Writ" for each and every one of these attributes, picked almost at random from the inspired and sacred pages which lie open before me. Many instances of these several attributes of Yahveh have already been recounted, or will appear in other connections in this review; so I wish to avoid repetition as much as may be. Listen first to some generalities glittering with fiery terror.

Yahveh a Deity of Terror

Moses, who had occasion to know him quite intimately, if he is to be believed at all, declares, "Yahveh thy God is a mighty God and terrible" (Deut. vii, 21); and "Yahveh is a great God, mighty and terrible" (Deut. x, 17): a description repeated in nearly every Book of Hebrew Scripture: by Nehemiah (i, 5); by Isaiah many times; by David very often; by Jeremiah, as "a mighty, terrible one" (xx, 11); by Daniel, as the "great and dreadful God" (ix, 4); and so times without number.

In fierce and fatal wrath Yahveh surpasses gods and men: one of the most iterated phrases in the whole "Word of God" is "and the anger of Yahveh was kindled." Yahveh's own solemn words and acts belie altogether his own vainglorious boastings, as for instance, when, on Sinai, Yahveh paraded himself in review before Moses hid in a cleft of the rock, and proclaimed, "Yahveh, Yahveh El, merciful and gracious, long-suffering, and abundant in goodness and truth" (Ex. xxxiv, 6).

But at the very first encounter between Yahveh and Moses, there at the Burning Bush, when Moses did not want to go to Egypt and

head the' get-away of fugitive slaves, and asked to be excused, "the
anger of Yahveh was kindled against Moses" (Ex. iv, 14); and a
little later, as he reluctantly went, Yahveh ambushed him behind a
wayside inn "and sought to kill him" (v. 24)—which scores one for
Yahveh as an assassin. And long before that, to say nothing of the
Garden of Eden and the Flood, "Er was wicked in the sight of
Yahveh, and Yahveh slew him" (Gen. xxxviii, 7); and then, because
"the thing that his brother Onan did displeased Yahveh, he slew him
also" (v. 10): from which name, a "conventional offense"—a well-
known term of race-suicide—is derived. Yahveh "came unto Balaam
at night, and said unto him, If the men come to call thee, rise up,
and go with them. And Yahveh's anger was kindled because he
went" (Num. xxii, 22); and even Balaam's Ass had some remarks
to make about the unjustness of it all (v. 28). In 1 Kings xxii,
Yahveh entered into a conspiracy of murder in heaven, and sent
"a lying spirit" to deceive Ahab and entice him to his death in
battle (vv. 20–23).

A God of Bloody Murder

The alleged atrocities which Yahveh wilfully and maliciously
perpetrated by the universal destruction of the Flood, and on the
Egyptians with his inhuman Plagues, and the wholesale massacre
of the firstborn of Egypt, and the drowning in the Red Sea of the
Pharaoh and his army, also score for his alleged inhumanities and
murders. He is pictured as no less atrocious and murderous in his
treatment of his own Chosen People, condemned to a miserable
wandering in the howling wilderness for forty years and to entire
extinction in death, because simply the People were frightened at
the majority report of the Spies sent to prospect in Canaan, and
they wept all night, and wanted to go home to Egypt (Num. xiii–
xiv). So Yahveh was "provoked," and his "anger kindled," and he
said: "I will smite them with a pestilence, and disinherit them";
but Moses again held up the spectre of "what the Egyptians would
say—because Yahveh was not able to bring this People into the
land which he sware unto them, therefore hath he slain them in
the wilderness" (xiv, 16); so Yahveh sees the point and relents, a
little; but "Yahveh's anger was kindled against Israel, and he made
them wander in the wilderness forty years: As I live, your carcasses
shall fall in this wilderness."

Just after the departure from Sinai, the People for some reason
murmured, "and when Yahveh heard it, his anger was kindled; and

the fire of Yahveh burnt among them, and devoured in the uttermost part of the Camp" (Num. xi, 1). And then a little later, the People lusted for meat to eat, "the anger of Yahveh was kindled greatly, and Moses was displeased" (xi. 10); and Yahveh sent the holy oily Manna, also a lot of quails; and when the Children started to eat them, "the anger of Yahveh was kindled against the People, and Yahveh smote the People with a very great Plague" (v. 33). Later, because the People got tired of eating Manna, Yahveh in his anger "sent fiery serpents, and they bit the People, and much People of Israel died" (xxi, 5-6). Because his Chosen took up with the Moabitish maidens, "the anger of Yahveh was kindled against Israel," and he murdered 24,000 of them (Num. xxv, 9). Against the man who should worship any other god, "the anger of Yahveh and his jealousy shall smoke against that man, and all the curses that are written in this Book shall lie against him"; and the People must do this and do that, or not do this or that, all through the Book of Curses, "that Yahveh may turn from the fierceness of his wrath."

Because Achan kept out a little of the spoils at the battle of Ai, "the anger of Yahveh was kindled against the Children of Israel"; and Yahveh ordered Achan, and his sons, and his daughters, to be murdered by stoning them to death. The sons of Eli "lay with the women that assembled at the door of the Tabernacle," and Eli reproved them; "notwithstanding they harkened not to the voice of their father, *because Yahveh* would slay them" (1 Sam. ii, 25); and Yahveh said, "*because* he restrained them *not*," and he murdered them, and brought ruin on the whole house of Eli (iii, 13-14). Because Uzzah put forth his hand and touched the malignant Ark to keep it from jolting off the ox-cart when it struck a rut, "the anger of Yahveh was kindled against Uzzah, and Yahveh smote him, and he died by the Ark of Yahveh." And "again the anger of Yahveh was kindled against Israel," for what reason I cannot clearly gather, "and *he moved* David to number Israel and Judah," and because David did so, Yahveh sent his holy Angel and murdered 70,000 of his Chosen, from Dan to Beersheba, in one daylight (2 Sam. xxiv, 15).

Time and again Yahveh repeats the infernal commands of Deuteronomy vii, ordering the indiscriminate murder of men, women and children, the total extermination of the teeming populations of the Promised Land by the savage Soldiers of El: "thou shalt smite them, and utterly destroy them; nor shalt thou show mercy unto them; thou shalt not spare; thine eye shall have no pity; lest the anger of Yahveh be kindled against you, and he destroy thee suddenly" (v. 2–4); and his brutal soldiers execute his holy will to the letter, pitilessly, though totally ineffectively, for they never did succeed in exterminating the populations.

These ebullitions of Jahvistic temper and terror, with their trains of frightful murder, might be multiplied indefinitely; but these suffice to prove our point of constant rage, terrorism, and murder against the Hebrew Yahveh. For murderous "Schrecklichkeit" the crimes of the War-Lord of the leagued Huns and Turks in the World War were trivial brutalities in comparison.

Yahveh the Vengeful

As for vengeance,—"Vengeance is Mine, I will repay," is the crown-jewel of Yahveh's Gorgonic Godhead. "Yahveh, whose name is Jealous, is a jealous God" (Ex. xxxiv, 14), "and Jealous for my holy name" (Ezek. xxxix, 25). Again, "Yahveh he is an holy God; he is a jealous God; he will not forgive your transgressions, nor your sins" (Josh. xxiv, 19); "Yahveh is Jealous, and Yahveh revengeth" (Nahum, i, 2). One must not dare to even dislike him: "Yahveh repayeth them that hate him to their face, to destroy them" (Dt. vii, 10). In his Holy Ten Commandments he stigmatizes himself to infamy with: "I Yahveh am a Jealous God, visiting the iniquity of the fathers upon the children unto the third and fourth generation" (Ex. xx, 5). This is Yahveh's own Law of relentless vengeances and persecutions of innocent and guilty alike. Fortunately it is simply a monstrous terroristic "bluff," for, despite all its repetitions, in multiplied blood-curdling iteration, it was perfectly innocuous. The Jahvistic decree against "other Gods" is repeated scores of times, and thus in Leviticus xxvi, 1: "Ye shall make you no idols, nor mazzebahs (graven images)", etc.; and vv. 16 to 39 are a perfect hell of sulphuric penalties denounced against the poor idolator, as all the Hebrews were, who naturally would prefer some milder deity to the terrible Jealous Yahveh: "I also will do this unto you: I will even appoint over you terror, consumption, and the burning ague, that shall consume the eyes, and cause sorrow of heart: and I will set my face against you, and ye shall be slain before your enemies; and I will bring seven times more plagues upon you; and I will send wild beasts among you, which shall rob you of your children; I will walk contrary unto you also in fury, and ye shall eat the flesh of your sons, and the flesh of your daughters also shall ye eat" (Lev. xxvi, 16–21); so spake the long-suffering and Merciful God. While most of these things did, quite deservedly, one might think, befall the Chosen People, it certainly "just happened," as it did to all the other nations about them, from their incessant bloody warfares, as the Sacred History itself makes perfectly evident.

The Changeful Yahveh

There was no fulfillment of these fearful brutal threats, which no kind of idolatry could justify; and this chronic "crime" of Israel was never punished, nor had anything to do with the disasters which befell the Chosen People. It would require a review of their whole miserable history to fully demonstrate this; but one humorous instance must suffice, in proof of the false promises and threats of Yahveh, and his constant fickleness. After several hundred years of unbroken idolatry, Solomon worshiped quite a variety of "strange gods" imported by his seven hundred strange wives, and "Yahveh was angry with Solomon" (1 Kings xi, 9). But Solomon was not stoned to death, as Yahveh's awful "Law" commanded; he was not even "utterly destroyed"; Yahveh only says to Solomon, "I will rend the kingdom from *thee;*—but in *thy* days I will not do it, for David thy father's sake: but I will rend it out of the hand of *thy son*" (vv. 12–13). And after the death of Solomon, when it did not much matter to Solomon anyhow, and when the Kingdom was divided, not because of idolatry, but of the ambitious rivalries of his sons, both the successors of Solomon, who divided the kingdom, were far worse idolators than Solomon; and the kingdom was not rent from them at all; and their respective successors kept up unrestrained idolatry for several hundred years, until the end. And Yahveh also told Solomon, "for this I will afflict the seed of David, but not forever" (v. 39); but which he did, or at least they were afflicted, by incessant wars and captivities, till the end of the record, so we will give Yahveh the credit for it.

Way back in Judges, four or five hundred years before Solomon, Yahveh declared his patience to be exhausted, "and Yahveh said unto the Children of Israel, Ye have forsaken me and served other gods: wherefore I will deliver you no more" (x, 13); but we find this same Yahveh saying through Samuel: "Yahveh will not forsake his People for his great name's sake; because it hath pleased Yahveh to make you his People" (Sam. xii, 22); it being added, however, out of force of savage habit, "but if ye shall still do wickedly, ye shall be consumed!" (v. 25). But they continued to do the same as ever, and were not consumed. Yahveh gave his plighted word to David, referring to Solomon: "He shall build an house for my name, and I will establish the throne of his kingdom forever; my mercy shall not depart away from him" (2 Sam. vii, 13). Which Yahveh never did; for immediately on Solomon's death the kingdom was split by secession from his son Rehoboam, incessant civil wars followed, and both factions were finally wiped out by the Assyrians and other powerful enemies.

This was not because the Chosen served idols and had their Jealous Yahveh to punish them; the other nations around them were not inflicted with Yahveh, yet they all went the same way of destruction. For as King Hezekiah, in terror of the Assyrians, wails to Yahveh: "of a truth, Yahveh, the kings of Assyria have laid waste all the nations, and their countries" (Is. xxxvii, 18); and as Rabshakeh, in his warning to Hezekiah, points out: "Hath any of the gods of the nations delivered his land out of the hand of the King of Assyria?" (Is. xxxvi, 18–20).

The truth is, that Israel worshiped the same Gods as the Assyrians and the other nations, and *never believed* in or worshiped Yahveh, except as a local phallic Baal, one of their many gods. Just at the time of the first Captivity this fact is admitted: "They served idols, as did the heathen whom Yahveh carried away before them" (2 Kings xvii, 11); and although Yahveh "testified against them by every prophet and by every seer, notwithstanding, they did not believe in Yahveh their God" (vv. 13–14); but they persisted in idolatry and departed not therefrom, "until Yahveh removed Israel out of his sight" (v. 23).

And this idolatry is admitted to have been continuous from first to last, some seven hundred years: "Because they have done that which was evil in my sight, and have provoked me to anger since the day their fathers came forth out of Egypt, even unto this day" (xxi, 15). Therefore, says Yahveh,—in total disregard of his "everlasting Covenant" with Abram, and the interation *ad nauseum*, "I will not forsake my People for my great name's sake,"—therefore, said Yahveh, "I will forsake the remnant of mine inheritance, and deliver them into the hand of their enemies; and they shall become a prey and a spoil to all their enemies" (v. 14).

And yet the farce-comedy goes merrily on: in the last chapter but one of the old Jewish Folk Book, the curtain is rung down to this same old tune: "For I am Yahveh, I change not; therefore ye sons of Jacob are not consumed. Even from the days of your fathers ye have gone away from mine ordinances and have not kept them. Return unto me, and I will return unto you, saith Yahveh of Hosts" (Mal. iii, 6–7),—though to an unprejudiced observer it might seem that both parties would be glad for a mutual good riddance of each other. And Yahveh takes this humorous parting loathing longing fickle fling at his "lying Children": "Ye are cursed with a curse; and I will open the windows of heaven, and pour you out a blessing; and all the nations of the earth shall call you blessed"! (Mal. iii, 9–10). All this, and so much more with which the sacred and truth-inspired record is full, is a perfect see-saw of fickle inconstancies, and proves that, and several other points, against the Hebrew-Bible Yahveh.

YAHVEH REPENTANT

This same and some other points may be further illustrated, taking as our text Numbers xxiii, "Yahveh is not a man that he should lie; neither the son of man, that he should repent: hath he said, and shall he not do it? Or hath he spoken, and shall he not make it good?" (v. 19). From the foregoing, and some to follow, out of his own Word, it would seem not. We have seen all these instances of fickleness, threats, changings, and repentings. Yahveh several times, as we have seen, in the Wilderness, "repented of the evil which he thought to do unto his People"; in Genesis "it repented Yahveh that he had made man on earth" (vi, 6); in 1 Samuel Yahveh says, "It repents me that I have set up Saul to be king" (xv, 11); in 2 Samuel, when Yahveh's murdering Angel had slain 70,000 men, and had stretched out his hand upon Jerusalem to destroy it, "Yahveh repented him of the evil," and stayed the Angel's massacring hand (xxiv, 16). And so on throughout, with this fickle Deity who boasts "For I am Yahveh, I change not." But after so many instances of it, Yahveh himself complains to Jeremiah, "I am weary with repenting" (Jer. xv, 6).

THE FATHER OF LIES

With respect to bald lies attributed to Yahveh by his inspired biographers and votaries, and lies instigated by this *soi-disant* God of Truth, we have several edifying instances. In Exodus, Yahveh told Moses to lie to the Pharaoh, as a pretext for escape, by saying that the People wanted to go "three days' journey into the wilderness, that we may sacrifice unto Yahveh our God" (iii, 18); but as Yahveh was quite new to Moses, and totally a stranger to the People and to the Pharaoh, the latter, when the inspired lie was repeated to him, was skeptical, and retorted, "Who is Yahveh, that I should hearken unto his voice to let Israel go? I know not Yahveh" (v, 2). This hypocritical religious excuse seems to have been a favorite with Yahveh, or with the holy men who wrote his biography, for it is the same lie that Yahveh suggests to Samuel, when he told this Prophet to go to Bethlehem and find Jesse, and pick one of his sons for King; "and Samuel said, How can I go? If Saul hear of it, he will kill me. And Yahveh said, Take an heifer with thee, and say, I am come to sacrifice to Yahveh" (1 Sam. xvi, 2). We recall the "Lying Spirit" sent by Yahveh to put a lie into the mouths of the four hundred prophets, in order to lure Ahab to death in a fatal battle (1 Kings xxii, 20–23).

His own Prophet Ezekiel attributes all prophetic lies directly to Yahveh, and quotes Yahveh as shamelessly declaring, "If the prophet be deceived when he speaketh a thing, I Yahveh have deceived him" (xiv, 9); and with outrageous injustice Yahveh inflicts this punishment upon the deluded prophets whom he himself has deceived: "and I will stretch out my hand upon him, and will destroy him." Several times Jeremiah frankly taxes Yahveh to his face with deception and lies, to wit: "Then I said, Ah, Yahveh, surely thou hast greatly deceived this People and Jerusalem" (iv, 10); and again, "O Yahveh, thou hast deceived me, and I am deceived" (xx, 7); and Jeremiah is so mad with Yahveh that he declared, "I will not make mention of him, nor speak any more in his name" (v. 9); and for the climax, he puts it straight into the teeth of Yahveh: "Wilt thou be altogether unto me as a liar?" (xv, 18). All this would seem to make Yahveh a rival with Baalzebub as the "Father of Lies,"—a glorious conception of the boasted "God of all Truth."

We will close this hasty but too lengthy review of Jahvic virtues. In Genesis Yahveh gets mad and threatens a general destruction, and Abraham expostulates with him, "Shall not the Judge of all the earth do right? Wilt thou destroy the righteous with the wicked?" (xviii, 23, 25). But this is a constant form of injustice of Yahveh—to believe his Book, many instances of which we have seen. In Exodus Yahveh tells Moses that the fleeing Hebrew slaves shall rob the homes of their masters, and steal all their jewelry and clothes, "and ye shall spoil the Egyptians" (iii, 22).

The Lusts of Yahveh

There is not much of detail in the sacred record in regard to the "sportive tricks" of the Hebrew Jove, but what there is reveals the constant practice. Yahveh had so many "sons," as is apparent from Genesis vi, who were amorous with the fair daughters of men, that this is given expressly as the reason for the monstrous injustice of Yahveh in destroying the whole of his creation in the Flood, instead of keeping his lustful sons at home in heaven with him.

But more explicit instances of Jahvistic paternity are recorded. Yahveh had promised a son to Abraham by his wife Sarah; but she laughed when she heard it, and said to Yahveh: "After I am waxed old shall I have pleasure, and my lord being old also?"; but Yahveh replied, "Is anything too hard for Yahveh?" (Gen. xviii, 12–14); "And Yahveh visited Sarah according as he had said, and Yahveh did to Sarah according as he had spoken. And she conceived and bore to Abraham a son" (xxi, 1–2), Isaac being the result; and the favorite phrase, "and so-and-so begat" is not spoke of Abraham. In the other instance, five offspring are credited to Yahveh by one human woman: "And Yahveh visited Hannah, so that she conceived, and bare three sons and two daughters" (1 Sam. ii, 21). Besides all which, we have the well-known instance of Jahvic potency projected into the Virgin Wife of Joseph, thereby arousing his natural suspicions of carnal, rather than Holy Ghostly agency, until he dreamed that Yahveh was the paternal author of the pregnancy. And Yahveh admitted: "Thou art my son; this day have I begotten thee" (Heb. i, 5; v, 5).

YAHVEH THE WHITE-SLAVER

But it is as the premium Procurer on record that Yahveh is a shining example for the White Slavers of all time. After first commanding that all men, women and children of the peoples of the Promised Land should be massacred and their property and cattle destroyed, Yahveh withdrew this proviso of his barbarous rules of war, and substituted: "Thou shalt smite every male thereof with the edge of the sword: but the women, and the little ones, and all the spoil of the city shalt thou take unto thyself" (Deut. xx, 13–14); and the women and children were consigned to debauchery and slavery for the "holy nation" of Yahveh. The most signal single instance of Yahveh's utter depravity as a monster of murder and debauchery is on the occasion of the battle with the Midianites, where Master Procurer Yahveh delivered 32,000 tender captive maidens to the holy lusts of his holy People (Num. xxxi).

I call attention to the lying sophistry of the inspired "justification" for this particular wholesale rape. When Moses saw the women and little ones brought captive into Camp, "Moses was wroth with the officers of the Host, and Moses said unto them, Have ye saved all the women alive? Behold, these caused the Children of Israel to commit trespass against Yahveh in the matter of Peor," where, because "the People began to commit whoredom with the daughters of Moab," Yahveh massacred 24,000 of his "Holy People" (Num. xxv). But the women of Midian, several hundred miles away across the Arabian deserts, could have had nothing to do with the sportings of the daughters of Moab with the Holy Ones. However, we should naturally expect that Yahveh's command through Moses to the derelict captains of the Host would be, "smite all these women," and thus prevent further sin of whoredom on the part of the holy Chosen.

But his brutal order is naïvely sophistical, and knavishly diabolic: "Now therefore kill every male among the little ones, and kill every woman that hath known man by lying with him. But all the women children, that have not known a man by lying with him, keep alive for yourselves"! (Num. xxxi, 17). The inspired devilish illogic of Yahveh: "Ye have sinned against me by whoring with the Moabitish women; *ergo*, after killing all the male little ones, and their mothers, and all "sporty" girls—"every woman that hath known man,"—the others, the best of them, the fresh and yet virtuous young Midianite maidens, 32,000 of them, keep for your holy selves, and whore with them all your holy lusts may please"! Verily, as the Psalmist sang, "the commandment of Yahveh is pure, enlightening the eyes"! (Ps. xix, 8). And Job pertinently queries: "Shall mortal man be more just than Yahveh? Shall a man be more pure than his Maker?" (iv, 17). With such an example as Yahveh to enlighten human eyes, and to piously imitate, the wonder is that there are any Saints in the Calendar or virgins left alive, ever since. And we will notice later along how Yahveh kindly acted as Go-between for his holy Prophet Hosea (p. 254).

Here, astonished Reader, hangs before you a pen-and-ink outline sketch of the Bible Yahveh. Every line of it is drawn in, it is pretended, by a divinely inspired pen, at the infallible dictation of the Great Subject himself, and it is said to bear his own sacred seal of accuracy and authenticity. That there might be no mistaking it for a lurid portraiture of the Devil-in-Hell, read Yahveh's own "pinxit" signature label upon it: "I am Yahveh which exercise lovingkindness, judgment and righteousness, in the earth, for in these things I delight" (Jer. ix, 24). But for this Divine Certificate of

Authenticity and good character, the casual observer of this inspired work of Art must inevitably, on seeing it, have taken it to be the life-portrait of the Devil Incarnate, and have recalled, as applicable to its Original, the horrible words of the Veiled Prophet of Khorassan, as he tore the silver veil from his blasted face before his deluded votaries:

> "Here, see, if Hell, with all its powers to damn,
> Can add one blot to the foul thing I am!"

But, No; it is the auto-portrait of the dread Yahveh, God of Israel. True, the braggart words of the Certificate, and many others scattered through the sacred Biography, sing perfervid praises of him as "the Holy God," and "glorious in Holiness" and in Righteousness, *etcetera*, and ascribe manifold goodnesses and mercies to him. But these are mere words of exaltation by fervid partisans. As they are *ad nauseum* recorded, his

> "Deeds are bigger things than words are;
> Actions mightier than boastings";

and from "In the beginning" of Genesis, to the closing blast, "Lest I come and smite the earth with a Curse," of Malachi, there is not be to found—I challenge its production—one single good, honest, true, faithful, decent or righteous action or thing which it is even alleged, as matter of accomplished fact, that this Hebrew Yahveh ever did or even thought of doing, in his whole recorded life and acts. On the contrary, every act and deed of Yahveh, as recorded by his inspired Biographers, brings us back to, and fully vindicates, our opening couplet describing the Gods of Greece,—as perfectly descriptive of the Hebrew Yahveh:—

> "God partial, vengeful, changeable, unjust,
> Whose attributes are rage, revenge, and lust."

CHAPTER XI

THE HOLY PRIESTS AND PROPHETS OF YAHVEH

TURNING from the self-portraiture of the Hebrew chief God, let us view the system of holy Priests and Prophets of Yahveh, the votaries of this Hebrew War-God, and the representatives of this Hebrew Religion, which we have seen to be none other than the heathen beliefs and practices common to Chaldea and Canaan. This will show the vague and shadowy notions of Pagan Deity which they held, as well as the cardinal characteristics of the whole priestly and prophetic hierarchy of Israel.

The system of priests will be seen to have been founded on the basic principle of idle life and greedy graft; while that of the prophets was in most cases the same, plus a crazed or "meshuggah" fanaticism such as distinguishes the holy Fakirs of India and the Howling Dervishes of Arabia up to the present time. This priestly-prophetic gentry existed from the earliest times, always and in all (olden) countries the objects of special privilege and rapacious greed and graft. When Joseph, son of Jacob-Israel, organized the first "corner" in food-stuffs, during the grievous seven-year famine in Egypt, he first profiteered the people out of all their money, and next extorted all the lands in Egypt from their starving owners in exchange for food, until "all the land became Pharoah's; . . . except the lands of the priests only, which became not Pharaoh's" (Gen. xlvii, 20, 26). And they have escaped all fiscal obligation to the civil State ever since.

PRIESTS BEFORE MOSES

The earliest Scripture mention of a priest is a curious instance of confused Theology, and may be cited as illustrating the fact, already proven, that the Hebrew El Yahveh was common property of the Semitic Heathenism, and was none other than one of the many recognized heathen divinities.

Abram, during his wanderings into Canaan, came to the heathen Jebusite City of Salem, later become Jerusalem; and there he met

236

Melchizedek, King of Salem, who is described as "priest of El-Elyon —the Most High God" (Gen. xiv, 18). The name Melchizedek signifies "King of Righteousness"; he was a foreign Canaanite Heathen, and of course was no priest of the Hebrew El Yahveh, and knew nothing of any special El or Yahveh of Abram. Yahveh himself had first appeared and become known to Abram at Haran as he set out on his family migration to Canaan (Gen. xii, 1), since which time Yahveh had not further been heard of or further appeared upon the scene.

Melchizedek, "priest of El-Elyon," at once recognized Abram as a brother-Pagan of the same God or gods as himself, and greeted him warmly: "Blessed be Abram of El-Elyon" (v. 19),—which proves the identity of the common Deity of Chaldea and Canaan. It may be explained, that the word "Elyon" added to the name "El," is no part of that common noun at all; but is simply a common Semitic adjective, meaning "lofty, very high," and is frequently used in the Hebrew texts in qualifying many other "high" things other than El or God.

Further curious proof of identity and of common possession of the same "El" by all the Semitic Heathens follows. For the very Pagan King of Sodom joins the friendly group, and began bargaining about spoils of the battle; and Abram swore to him by their common God El-Elyon that he would justly close the bargain (vv. 21–22). Thus, clearly, El, exalted as El-Elyon, was just a common Semitic deity, which the Pagan Melchizedek served as Priest just as Abram did, and the very Pagan King of Sodom shared the same religious cult. As Melchizedek was altogether a Pagan Priest, and is never shown to have been "converted" to Yahveh, it is curious that Paul several times avers that Jesus Christ was "called of God an high priest after the order of Melchizedek" (Heb. v, 5, *passim*).

A "Kingdom of Priests"

During the so-called Patriarchal times, and down to the traditional "giving of the Law" on Sinai—and for a thousand years afterwards—every man who pleased was his own priest and made his own bloody sacrifices. Thus did they all: Cain, Abel, Noah, Abraham, Isaac, Jacob, including Moses and Aaron, before and after the "Law" on Sinai; and so continued to do Joshua, Gideon and all the Judges, Samuel, David, Solomon, and other Kings, after the "Law": not one of them was a priest. No sooner had the fleeing Chosen arrived at Sinai, than Yahveh himself is recorded as having proclaimed: "Ye shall be unto me a kingdom of priests and an holy nation" (Ex. xix, 6); that is, every man should be at liberty to act for himself as priest and make his own altars and sacrifices "for the atonement of his soul" unto Yahveh.

And right under the shadow of Sinai, the very next day after the first giving of Law to Moses, Moses came down from the Mount, and himself "builded an altar under the hill, and twelve pillars (phallic mazzebahs) according to the twelve tribes of Israel; and he sent young men of the Children of Israel, which offered burnt offerings and sacrificed peace offerings unto Yahveh" (Ex. xxiv, 4–5).

Revelation of Priestly Monopoly

But Moses had been brought up in the royal-priestly court of Egypt and was "learned in all the wisdom of the Egyptians" (Acts vii, 22); and he knew the priestly game full well. So, Moses gets a "revelation" from Yahveh that Brother Aaron should be High Priest, and the four sons of Aaron should be priests: "it shall be a statute forever throughout their generations" (Ex. xxvii, 21; xxviii, 1),—just as Mohammed afterwards successfully imitated for his own family. And Yahveh complaisantly again decreed: "And thou shalt anoint them, as thou didst anoint their father, that they may minister unto me in the priests' office: and their anointing shall be to them an everlasting priesthood throughout their generations" (Ex. xl, 15).

Having gotten this divine commission in perpetuity for Brother Aaron's family, it was necessary to sanction it with awful Jahvistic pains and penalties, so as to prevent sacrilegious meddling with the monopoly. The penalty of death was therefore decreed for any interference with the priestly monopolists: "Thou shalt appoint Aaron and his sons, and they shall keep their priesthood: and the stranger that cometh nigh shall be put to death"! (Num. iii, 10). And it was reiterated: "The man that will do presumptuously, and will not harken unto the Priest, even that man shall die" (Deut. xvii, 12). The priests of Yahveh were as jealously exclusive as was their God whose name was Jealous; and they were protected in their monopoly by the fatal enactment on Sinai: "He that sacrificeth to any god, save unto Yahveh only, he shall be utterly destroyed" (Ex. xxii, 20); and these deadly priestly penalties were as deadly enforced by their beneficiaries.

Of course, none of this ever historically happened; it was put into mouth of "Yahveh by the hand of Moses" many centuries later, by Ezra or his priestly successors after the return from Captivity, when the ritualistic priestly system was established in the restored remnant of Israel, to give sanction and sanctity to their exclusive system. Of this the proof is evident: none of the many priests named in the whole history after Aaron, from Eli to Hulda the Priestess who officiated at the "finding of the Law," was of the monopolistic priesthood of Aaron; and none of them, nor of the many non-priestly sacrificers, as Samuel, David, and the kings of Judah and Israel, and who sacrificed to many "other Gods" than Yahveh, was ever "utterly destroyed" or put to death for either of these flagrant violations of "the Law"; which is good proof that "the Law" prohibiting these practices under penalty of death was not existent through all those centuries. The inspiredly recorded instances of infliction of these penalties, as now to be noticed, were therefore clearly anachronistic and apochryphal, related to terrify the "strangers who should come nigh" to question or to meddle with the "restored" priesthood.

Two of the new-made priestly sons of Aaron, Nadab and Abihu, who seem not to have been well initiated into the mysteries of their new office, "put strange fire into their censers, and offered strange fire before Yahveh"; and, Lo, "there came forth fire from before Yahveh, and devoured them, and they died before Yahveh" (Lev. x); and Moses commanded Brother Aaron, in the name of Yahveh, that he and his family should not mourn for the murdered dead, "that ye die not, and Yahveh be not wroth with all the Congregation" (v. 6). Thus decreed the God of all Compassion—"even as a Father pitieth his children."

In Numbers xvi we are given a "horrible example" of the jealousy of Yahveh in favor of his priestly monopolists, which is worth while to cite somewhat fully. Yahveh had declared, we have seen, that the whole holy nation of Chosen should be "a kingdom of priests" (Ex. xix, 6). So, taking Yahveh at his word, three of the renowned representatives of the Chosen, Korah, Dathan, and Abiram, with 250 of the "Princes of the Congregation," rose up before Moses and Aaron, and said unto them: "Ye take too much upon you, seeing all the Congregation are Holy, every one of them, and Yahveh is among them: wherefore then lift ye up yourselves above the Assembly of Yahveh?" Moses was very wroth, as was his wont, at this challenge of his family monopoly, and he taunted them, saying, "Seek ye the priesthood also?" and Moses challenged them to a contest of incense-offering, saying, "Yahveh will show who are his, and who are Holy." And Moses the meek "was very wroth, and said unto Yahveh, Respect not their offerings."

Yahveh at first told Moses and Aaron to stand aside, and threatened to smite and consume the entire balance of the millions of the holy Congregation in a moment. But Moses evidently reflected that there would be nothing to the priestly monopoly if all the Faithful were consumed; so he expostulated with Yahveh, saying, "O El, Elohe of Spirits, shall one man sin, and wilt thou be wroth with all the Congregation?" and Yahveh-El-Elohe saw the point, and he told Moses to have all the Congregation keep away from the tents of "these wicked men"; and he put a taboo upon all their possessions, saying, "touch nothing of theirs, lest ye be consumed." Such Taboos, of the perfect Hottentot type, riot throughout the holy pages of the Hebrew Bible.

The contest of incense-burning to which Moses had first challenged the anti-monopolists was called off; and Yahveh, after the People had stood aside out of the way, caused "these wicked men" to stand forth in the doors of their tents, with "their wives, and their sons, and their little ones," all doomed to a common massacre by the Merciful Yahveh who benignly avows that he "visits the iniquity of the fathers upon the children of the third and fourth generation." Then stood forth Moses and proclaimed: "Hereby ye shall know that Yahveh hath sent *me* to do all these works"; and, behold the righteous judgments of Yahveh: "the ground clave asunder that was under them; and the earth opened her mouth, and swallowed them up, and their households, and all the men that appertained unto Korah, and all their goods; so they went down alive into Sheol; and the earth closed upon them, and they perished from among the Assembly" (vv. 31–33). And the wrath of Yahveh being not yet satiated, "fire came forth from Yahveh, and devoured the 250 men that offered the incense" to their Compassionate God. And at the further command of Yahveh, and as a fearful warning for all who should dare to meddle with the priestly monopoly, the censers in which these "sinners" had offered their incense were beaten out into a brazen covering for the awful bloody altar of Yahveh, "to be a memorial unto the Children of Israel, to the end that no stranger, which is not of the seed of Aaron, come near to burn incense before Yahveh" (v. 40).

Even yet the wrath of Yahveh was not yet appeased with deaths. For on the morrow all the Congregation of the Children of Yahveh murmured against Holy Moses and Brother Aaron, saying, "Ye have killed the People of Yahveh." So Yahveh ordered Moses to stand aside, "that I may consume them in a moment"; and he sent a Plague and killed 14,700 more of them (v. 49). Yahveh is indeed a merciful and a jealous God. One tiny extenuation of the crime, and one admitted falsity of the record, mitigates a bit this wholesale murder, for inspiration records the flat contradiction of the inspired assertion that "all their households" were swallowed up alive into Sheol, for "notwithstanding, the children of Korah died not" (Num. xxvi, 11).

Then (Chapter xvii), to confirm further the priestly monopoly of the Aaron family, Yahveh resorted to another rod-conjuring contest reminiscent of the conjure-contests of Egypt. He ordered Moses to take twelve rods, according to the twelve tribes, and write the name of the chief of each tribe on the respective rods, putting Aaron's name on the rod of the tribe of Levi, and to lay the rods up overnight, "and it shall come to pass, that the man whom I shall choose, his rod shall bud; and I will make to cease before me the murmurings of the children of Israel, which they murmur against you,"—but they never did cease. So Moses took the twelve rods, representing the phallic "staff of life," and laid them up overnight in the tent where the phallic "Ark of the Covenant" was housed; and, lo, on the morrow, "the rod of Aaron for the house of Levi was all budded forth and bare ripe almonds"! Thus vindicated, Yahveh told Moses, "Put back the rod of Aaron before the testimony, to be kept for a token against the Children of Rebellion; that thou mayest make an end of their murmurings against me, that they die not." Who would not love such a benign Deity, and be filled full of the "fear of Yahveh"? And the Chosen were filled with godly fear, saying unto Moses, "Behold, we perish, we are all undone. Everyone that cometh near unto the Tabernacle of Yahveh dieth." Then, to cap the climax of divine sanction for the priestly monopoly, and everlastingly secure them in their power and profit, Moses cajoled from Yahveh on Sinai this fatal and priestly decree: "The man that will do presumptuously, and will not hearken unto the Priest, even that man shall die" (Deut. xvii, 12). Thus were the priestly fetters firmly riveted on the neck of the superstitious People of Yahveh—where they have galled and impaled humanity until this very year of his Son Christ. But, humanity is coming to know the truth, and the truth shall make men free.

THE PRIESTLY PERQUISITES

A large part of the "Five Books of Moses" is taken up with sacred prescriptions by Yahveh for the holy incantations and bloody ceremonials of the sect of Priests, and for the enforcement of their sacred perquisites. The Mighty Yahveh himself fully initiated Moses into the sacred mysteries of smearing blood of victims on the right ear-tips and big toes of Brother Aaron and his sons, and in teaching them to dip their fingers in the blood of the victims and do the most potent conjure (Ex. xxix, 20; Lev. xiv). But, naturally, the most important feature of the holy ministry was the rules and regulations of their sacred rights.

This was indeed a gigantic guerdon; for when the priestly assistants (Levites) were "numbered at the commandment of Yahveh, all the males of the Levites were twenty and two thousand" (Num. iii, 39). It was ordained amid the fires and thunders of Sinai, that "No man shall appear before me empty when he cometh to make atonement for his soul" (Ex. xxiii, 15).

It would be impossible, in this outline, to go into the details of this priestly system of tribute. Every act of life, from the cradle to the grave, must be accompanied by sacrifices and offerings, at which the priests must officiate, and receive their holy pay. There were kinds of offerings too numerous to catalogue: sin-offerings, peace-offerings, trespass-offerings, and what-not other revenue-producing offerings and sacrifices. In most instances, Yahveh got the "sweet savor" of the burnt smell of them, and the holy priests got the solid nourishment which the sacrificed animals afforded apart from the smell. These offerings were frequently simply "waved before Yahveh," after which ceremony, "it shall be thine, and thy sons" with thee, as a due forever, as Yahveh has commanded" (Lev. x, 15).

Chapter vii of Numbers, with 89 verses, is a marvel of rich donations made to the Priests by the principal leaders of the Chosen; these just-escaped slaves could only have stolen these things when, a few weeks before, they "spoiled the Egyptians,"—unless indeed, as the truth is, it never happened at all, or occurred ages later, when the Priestly System was well established and the "Law" was "found" by Hilkiah the Priest. Numbers xviii gives a precious view of this whole scheme of priestly rewards ordained to Aaron and his kith; a few lines must suffice: "The first-fruits of all that is in their land, which they bring unto Yahveh, shall be thine. Everything devoted in Israel shall be thine. All the best of everything have I given thee; whatsoever is first ripe in the land shall be thine. Everything that openeth the womb (first-born) of all flesh which they offer unto Yahveh, both of man and beast, shall be thine: nevertheless the first-born of man, and the firstling of unclean beasts, shalt thou redeem," at a fixed money rate, which the priests got. "And unto the Children of Levi, behold, I have given all the tithe in Israel for an inheritance." Everytime the People were "numbered," every one of them, over twenty years old, had to pay a half-sheckel "for a ransom of his soul unto Yahveh, that there may be no plague among them, when thou numberest them" (Ex. xxx, 12),—a very fruitful source of inspired income.

The first-fruits of all the Land, and the best of everything else, "without spot or blemish," and a tenth of everything the Children possessed, was, in a word, the perpetual income of these holy servers of Yahveh. It is related in 1 Samuel, as a common resort of shiftless loafers of Israel, to come to a Priest and bow down to him for a piece of silver and a loaf of bread, saying, "Put me, I pray thee, into one of the priests' offices, that I may eat a morsel of bread" (ii, 36). The custom has ever since been popular and yet prevails in the world.

THE HOLY FAKIR PROPHETS

The Prophets, as described by Inspiration, were a precious set of lazy and worthless vagabonds of Israel: they were the exact counterpart of the howling dervishes and divination-mongers of their cousins Ishmael. In speaking of Prophets one thinks naturally of Isaiah, Jeremiah, Ezekiel, and such reputed "holy men of God": these are but a few signal ones out of thousands of these unkempt and unclean loafers, who went publicly naked—as Isaiah, Aaron, Saul, Samuel, David—or wore old bran-sacks for clothes,—as John the Baptist and others—and wandered about begging, and selling sorceries and conjure, and talking in a wild sing-song jargon which they themselves did not know what it meant. The usual term to describe them was in the Hebrew language "meshuggah," or "frenzied," and they wandered about "prophesying" or as the Hebrew word actually signifies (see R. V.)—"*raving*" through the land; they were fortune-tellers and diviners, through pretended dreams and trances, and by the use of sacred dice and arrows, and armed with phallic ephod images of Yahveh, of which we will see abundant instances in proof.

The job of prophet was a free-for-all occupation, which any one who pretended to feel the "divine afflatus," or was a fluent liar, could take up at will and without license. A shining example, Samuel, will be noted in another connection. The Prophet Amos frankly states his own case, which was typical, and has passed into a proverb:

"I was no prophet, neither was I a prophet's son; but I was a herdsman; and Yahveh took me from following the flock, and said unto me, Go, prophesy unto my People Israel" (vii, 14). Elisha, the Bald-Pate, was a farmer, and was out plowing one day when Elijah passed by, and Elisha dropped his plow and ran after him, and became a prophet too. After this manner are many modern "Divines" self-"called" unto this day.

Jeremiah, who was a big one among them, describes their single qualification: "every man that is mad (*ish meshuggah*) and maketh himself a prophet" (xxix, 26). Hosea also declares the same truth: "The prophet is a fool, the man that hath the spirit is mad—meshuggah" (ix, 7). Elisha is called "this mad fellow—meshuggah" (2 Kings ix, 11). A thousand instances prove the truth of these candid admissions—that the prophets were a rabble of "meshuggah" or frenzied fakirs. We have seen the example of Saul, when "the spirit of Yahveh came mightily upon him, and he prophesied" (Heb. *raved*), along with the whole band of howling, naked prophets (1 Sam. xix, 6); and frequently afterwards it is recited of him, "an evil spirit from God came upon Saul, and he prophesied" (*Raved:* xviii, 10). Like the Devils that came down from among the tombs, their name was Legion; they infested the land like the locusts of the Egyptian Plague, and like the priests and Levites of Israel, and like the priests and monks of more modern times. Jeremiah describes them gadding about the country, crying, "I have dreamed, I have dreamed," and, saith Yahveh, "prophesying (*raving*) lies in my name" (xxiii, 25).

THE FRENZIED PROPHETS

The word "Prophet," as a name for these nomadic conjurers and fortune-tellers, is a Biblical late term; they were originally called—just as the fortune-tellers and trance-mediums of to-day describe themselves in their advertisements—"Seers";—people who "see things" in their imaginations, or pretend for pay to see them. This is testified in 1 Samuel—who also well describes the grafting fortune-telling character and practices of this gentry: "Beforetime in Israel, when a man went to inquire of the Gods (ha-Elohim), thus he said, Come, let us go to the Seer (*Roeh*): for he that is now called a Prophet (*Nabi*), was beforetime called a (*Roeh*) Seer" (1 Sam. ix, 9). We may note here another sidelight on Bible editorship: As the word "*Roeh*" (Seer) is used all through the Books of Samuel, and elsewhere, it is evident from this philological explanation, that these books were compiled long afterwards, when "*Nabi*"—(raver, hence prophet)—was the word in current use, so that the original and then obsolete word, "*Roeh*" (Seer) had to be explained, in parentheses, as appear in the authorized text.

THE DIVINE TEST OF PROPHECY

The ear-marks and badge of authenticity of a prophecy-monger are prescribed in the Law—in terms of vagueness sufficient to allow considerable latitude of practice in the craft: "If there be a prophet among you, I Yahveh will make myself known unto him in a vision, and I will speak unto him in a dream" (Num. xii, 6)—a test obviously lending itself to the objection afterwards made by Yahveh himself, through Jeremiah: "I have heard what the prophets said, that prophecy lies in my name, saying, I have dreamed, I have dreamed" (Jer. xxiii, 25).

Again, the illusive credential is thus prescribed by Yahveh: "If there arise among you a prophet, or a dreamer of dreams, and giveth thee a sign or wonder, and the sign or the wonder come to pass, whereof he spake unto thee, saying (things idolatrous and mischievous).; Thou shalt not hearken unto the words of that prophet, or that dreamer of dreams: for Yahveh your God proveth you, to know whether ye love Yahveh your God. . . . And that prophet, or that dreamer of dreams, shall be put to death" (Deut. xiii, 1–5). Certainly an odd sort of roving commission of general deception.

But a more comprehensive and soul-satisfying test of authenticity and veracity of the Prophet is again laid down by Yahveh. This was the prescribed and accepted, but precarious and much *ex post facto* test of a Prophet, whereby to know whether he spake by Yahveh or was simply lying. Yahveh himself expressly decreed this peculiar test of prophecy in his Siniatic Law:

"And it shall come to pass, that whoever will not hearken unto my words which he (the Prophet) shall speak in my name, I will require it of him.

"But the prophet which shall presume to speak a word in my name, which I have not commanded him to speak, or shall speak in the name of other gods, even that prophet shall die.

"And if thou say in thine heart, How shall we *know* the word which Yahveh hath *not* spoken?

"When a prophet speaketh in the name of Yahveh, *if the thing follow not, nor come to pass,* that is the thing which Yahveh hath *not* spoken, but the prophet hath spoken it presumptuously: thou shalt not be afraid of him" (Deut. xviii, 19–22)!

That this latter is the really true and infallible, though negative
and *ex post facto*, test of true prophecy, is not only thus averred
by Yahveh in precept, but he gives a remarkable practical example
of its efficiency in practice. When from the Burning Bush Yahveh
ordered Moses to go unto Pharaoh and bring the Children of Israel
out of Egypt, and Moses demurred, Yahveh reassured him divinely:
"And this shall be a token unto thee, that I have sent thee: When
thou hast brought forth the People out of Egypt, ye shall serve
the Gods (*ha-Elohim*) upon this mountain" (Ex. iii, 12). Though,
by the same Divine Token, Isaiah prophesied "presumptuously" and
falsely when he told Ahaz that the two Kings would fail before
Jerusalem (Is. vii); for the City was captured by them and nearly
destroyed (2 Chron. xxviii).

This same sagacious and safe test of the truth or falsity of
prophecy is stated in its affirmative form by the shifty Meshuggah
Jeremiah: "When the word of the prophet shall *come to pass*, then
shall the prophet be known, that Yahveh hath truly sent him" (Jer.
xxviii, 9). For a wonder under the sun. For how long, O Yahveh,
must the expectant and impatient Votary wait into Futurity to
know whether the "man of the Gods" (*ish ha-elohim*) has missed his
guess or not, and his message was or was not of Thee? Isaiah
prophesied a "sign" in the Virgin-born son Immanuel (Is. vii, 14),
and not till 750 years later, as Matthew says, was it "fulfilled which
was spoken of Yahveh by Isaiah" (Matt. i, 22); whereas Jesus himself prophesied that his *second coming* would be in the life-time of
those hearing him speak (Matt. xvi, 28)—and in near two thousand
years the event has not proven the truth of the prophecy. However,
full faith and credit may charitably be awarded to these prophecy-
mongers, at least until the event proves that "they speak lies in my
name," as we shall soon inquire.

Having thus seen and satisfied our minds, if not our souls, as
to the official character and tests of veracity of this guild of
prophets, we will return to the revelations of their inspired methods
of plying their sacred trade.

Samuel, Dean of the Profession

The great "Meshuggah" Samuel was stark frenzied, like all of
the howling bands of Fakir-prophets with whom he paraded naked
up and down the land, raving-prophesying. A graphic picture of
them is given by Samuel himself, or whoever wrote his biography,
in 1 Samuel xix. David had fled from the wrath of Saul, and Saul

"sent messengers to take David"; but as each squad of messengers came upon "the company of the prophets prophesying (*raving*), and Samuel standing as head over them, the spirit of God came upon the messengers of Saul, and they also raved (prophesied)." So after three details of messengers had "gone bad" in this way, Saul himself went on his own mission; and as he went, "the spirit of the Gods came upon him also, and he went on, and he (*raved*) prophesied until he came" to where all the others were assembled. The whole outfit were stark naked and raving; and "Saul also stripped off his clothes, and he also prophesied (raved) before Samuel, and he fell down naked all that day and all that night" (vv. 18–24). And by this token of rank insanity and phallic idolatry, was "Saul also numbered among the prophets," to the derision of the public.

Samuel himself was a well-known "Seer," or fortune-teller and prophecy-monger, as appears from the sacred History, 1 Samuel ix. It is here related, by divine inspiration, that Kish, the father of Saul, had several asses which had strayed, and he sent young Saul and one of the family servants to go "seek the asses." After beating the country-side for several days without success, Saul was on the point of giving it up and returning home, when the servant said: "Behold now, there is in this city a man of the gods (*Ish-ha-Elohim*), and he is a man that is held in honor; all that he saith cometh surely to pass: let us now go thither; peradventure he can tell us" about finding the lost asses. But Saul replied—an answer showing that he well knew the *raison-d'étre* of the fortune-telling craft— that he had no money, nothing to pay,—"there is no present to bring to the man-of-the-gods" (Ish-ha-Elohim)—which shows that fortune-telling by "men of God" was a paying business.

But the servant came to the rescue from this difficulty, and said, "Behold, I have in my hand the fourth part of a shekel of silver: that will I give to the man of God, to tell us our way" (vv. 7–8). So they went into the city; and as they went they met some girls, and asked them, "Is the Seer (Heb. Roeh) here?": and the girls told them that Samuel was in town that day, having come to town expressly to attend a big picnic sacrifice held by the people of the town in the baalic high-place of the city, "for the people will not eat until he come, because he doth bless the sacrifice" (vv. 12–13). Which, incidentally, proves the very heathenish practices of this holy Man of the Gods, and of all the people; and proves that the "Law" as pretended to have been promulgated by Moses long previously, did not yet exist; for this "Law" a thousand times denounces the "high places" as a heathenish abomination, and prohibits under penalty of death, the performance of sacrifices by any but the holy monopoly of priests.

So Saul and his servant started on their search for Samuel; and as they went along they met a man, and Saul said to him: "Tell me, I pray thee, where the seer's house is"; and it was Samuel himself, for he replied, "I am the seer." Samul then invited them to dinner with him; and without waiting to be asked about the asses, he said, "As for thine asses which were lost three days ago, set not thy mind on them; for they are found." After several other matters which need not be related, Samuel told Saul a number of things which he should see as he returned along the road, among which was a "band of prophets coming down from the high place" (of phallic Baal worship), playing a diversity of musical instruments, "and they shall be (raving) prophesying" (x, 5). This proves precisely the wild and incoherent nature of this "meshuggah" practice. And Samuel said to Saul, "the spirit of Yahveh will come mightily upon thee, and thou shalt (rave) prophesy with them" (v. 6). And so it came to pass; and when the people who knew Saul saw him "prophesying (raving) among the prophets," they said, "What is this that is come unto the son of Kish? Is Saul also among the prophets?" (v. 11). Then they all went up to the phallic high place together. All this I have stated at some length, in order to give a graphic idea, from the Sacred Scriptures, of what manner of men were these holy prophets of Yahveh, and what the manner of their practices. There is some more yet.

ELIJAH

Elijah the Tishbite was a typical "meshuggah"; he was "an hairy man and girt with a girdle of leather about his loins" (2 Kings i, 8); he lived in deserts and caves, and angels and ravens fed him; he saw and talked with Yahveh in great and strong winds which rent the mountains and brake in pieces the rocks, in earthquakes, in fires, and in a still small voice. He had a wonder-working phallic staff, with which he parted the waters of rivers so that he could walk across dry-shod; and he is said to have raised a dead child to life by laying the stick upon him (2 Kings iv, 29).

Elijah murdered two companies of fifty soldiers and their captains by calling down fire from heaven to consume them in order to prove "if I am a man of Yahveh" (2 Kings i, 12); and he murdered the 450 priests of Baal and the 400 "priests of the groves"

(Asherah), for the same purpose. As Elijah himself admits, "I, even I only, remain a prophet of Yahveh" (1 Kings xviii, 22); and as there were at that time only seven thousand persons in all Israel who "bent not the knee to Baal" and kissed not the Baalic phallus, as the sacred text says, it would seem that this mighty "meshuggah" of Yahveh used very drastic means to vindicate his very minor dignity and importance.

Elisha

Even old Elisha, he of the bald pate, who had a double portion of the spirit of his partner Elijah shed upon him, could not get his prophetic conjure up until he was put into a trance by music,—the instrument of prophetic trance being preferably (and appropriately) the lyre, as is instanced in 2 Kings iii, 15; and he had Yahveh to murder forty-two little children because, in their childish simplicity and want of good manners they said, "Go up, thou Bald Head." As these two old cronies, Elijah and Elisha, walked along and talked one day, "behold there appeared a chariot of fire, and horses of fire, which parted them both asunder; and Elijah went up in a whirlwind into heaven,"—something more than 1,000,000 light years distant. How these fiery objects could have side-swiped so close to Elisha without burning him, or the mantle of Elijah which fell from him as he went up, is not explained in the sacred history of the incident. Elisha organized a posse and beat the woods hunting for Elijah for three days (2 Kings ii, 17), thinking evidently that the driver of the fiery chariot had kidnaped his side-partner Elijah;—which would seem to discount the inspired averment that Elijah was visibly whisked away into heaven right before the eyes of Elisha, who evidently did not believe so at the time.

And Elisha continued to go about alone and do much potent magic, such as "healing" some water that tasted bad, by casting salt into it; and going into a wierd trance until "the hand of Yahveh came upon him," in order to be able to "prophesy" to the Kings, during a drought, that they could get water by digging the low valley of the Jordan full of trenches,—a trick that any farmer's prentice could have told them just as well, without bothering Yahveh about it.

Isaiah

The great Isaiah was a "Meshuggah of the Meshuggahs," if that is good grammer in Hebrew. He admits it himself, and everything which he uttered attests it: he appears never to have had a lucid interval. He was certainly stark mad when, as he says, at Yahveh's dread command, he took the old bran-sack from off his loins and the shoes from his feet, and "walked *naked and barefoot three years* for a sign and a wonder (as indeed it must have been!) upon Egypt and upon Ethiopia" (Is. xx, 2–3); and he had not recovered when he wrote about it, or he would never have told it on himself.

Isaiah had chronic intestinal trouble, which may have been what caused him to go so "meshuggah"; for he groans "my bowels sound (or, will boil) like a harp" (Is. xvi, 11), and he tells how "my loins are filled with pain: pangs have taken hold upon me, as the pangs of a woman that travaileth; my heart panted, fearfulness affrighted me" (Is. xxi, 3–4); and he despairingly avowed, "therefore I will weep bitterly; labor not to comfort me" (Is. xxii, 4). No wonder that he saw and said things which even Aristotle could not unriddle. His Dream-Book is entitled "The Vision of Isaiah"; and his raving "prophecies" are divided up into paragraphs headed, in the English translation, as "the burden of Jerusalem," of Egypt, of Babylon, etc. The Hebrew word of the original means "the Oracle concerning"; they are no more or less, throughout,—as are the "prophesies" of all the meshuggahs,—than the incoherent jargon of the Greek Oracles of Apollo or the Pythoness, and just as pellucid in style and innocent of intelligent meaning.

In the year that King Uzziah died, Isaiah says he "saw Yahveh sitting on a throne; above him stood six seraphim: each one had six wings: with twain he covered his face, and with twain he covered his feet, and with twain he did fly" (though they were all standing), and the whole place was filled with smoke, until Isaiah cried, "Lord, how long!" (Is. vi, 2, 11). Afterwards he saw Yahveh riding upon a swift cloud going to Egypt; it was on this trip that Yahveh was to be received triumphantly with an "altar to Yahveh in the midst of Egypt, and a mazzebah-pillar at the border thereof,"—a phallic device which he says "shall be for a sign and a witness unto Yahveh Sabaoth in the land of Egypt."

In his frenzy, Isaiah calls upon the ships of Tarshish to howl (Is. xxiii, 1); and says that the earth shall reel to and fro like a drunkard, and the moon shall be confounded, and the sun ashamed; that Yahveh with a great and strong sword shall punish Leviathan the Serpent, and shall slay the Dragon that is in the sea. He displays his inspired notions of cosmical geography by speaking of the "ends of the earth" and the "four corners of the earth,"—a bit of inspired ignorance which held the world benighted for centuries, to the great credit of inspired infallible Church and its holy Inquisition of Truth, until heretic Columbus proved that uninspired Pagan Pythagoras, Aristotle, Seneca, and Ptolemy were better diviners of the truth than was Yahveh's own inspired meshuggah-Prophet. The sweet singer of the Ever Verdant Isle, hotbed of ever-verdant Faith, using his finest imagery descriptive of the great Prophet of Prophets, poetically sang of his peculiar style of "meshuggah" as "rapt Isaiah's wild seraphic fire"; it is all that, and some less poetic appreciations besides.

JEREMIAH

The Wailing Prophet, Jeremiah, was little less "meshuggah" than Isaiah himself. He says, "Since I spake, I cried violence and spoil" (xx, 8). He also was diseased inside: he agonizes and cries out, "My bowels, my bowels! I am pained at my very heart; my heart maketh a noise within me" (iv, 19); he cries aloud, "I am full of the fury of Yahveh; I am weary with holding in!" (vi, 11). He avers that "Yahveh put forth his hand and touched my mouth, and said unto me, Behold, I have put my words in thy mouth," and told him to "Go, cry against Jerusalem." Jeremiah fulfilled his divine mission to the letter; and then, for good measure, added his weeping Lamentations, in which he again complains, "Behold, O Yahveh, I am in distress: my bowels are troubled" (xxxi, 20). And yet after these two pitiful appeals, the "Great Physician" did not so much as prescribe any Stomach Bitters for his poor sick Meshuggah.

EZEKIEL

The most perfectly frenzied of the whole troupe of Meshuggah-Prophets, so far as the record goes, is Ezekiel. His regular diet seems to have been bread made of human dung; but for some reason, unrevealed, Yahveh indulgently gave him a substitute of cow's dung, and thus commanded him: "Lo, I have given thee cow's dung for human dung, and thou shalt prepare thy bread therewith" (iv, 15). And he assures us that Elohe Yahveh "put forth the form of a hand, and took me by a lock of mine head (viii, 3); and the spirit lifted me up between the earth and the heaven"; and that "the heavens were opened, and I saw visions of Yahveh" and things unspeakable.

It beggars me of wit to even describe what Ezekiel tries to describe that he saw: man nor beast ever looked like those things before or since, except maybe in heaven: "every one had four faces, and every one had four wings (Isaiah, vi, 2, 11, says each one had six wings; but probably he couldn't see to count well for the smoke); they four had the face of a man, and the face of a lion, on the right side: and they four had the face of an ox on the left side; they four also had the face of an eagle: thus were their faces. Their appearance was like burning coals of fire, and like the appearance of lamps; and the fire was bright, and out of the fire went forth lightning"; and they had wheels (or maybe it was Ezekiel himself), and works inside like a wheel within a wheel"; and they had four rings full of eyes round about, etc. (Ezek. i).

Ezekiel too had awful cramps of the stomach, even worse than Jeremiah, if may be, for Yahveh made him "eat the roll of a book, and fill his belly with it" (iii, 1–3); and it tasted in his mouth as honey for sweetness. The apoplectic John of Patmos had to eat a similar book (or maybe it was the same one rehashed), which also tasted like honey, but he says it made his belly bitter (Rev. x, 10): in both instances it was a divine proof of the Shakespearean prophecy —"things sweet to taste are to digestion sour." And their dyspepsia must have been something awful, to judge from the nightmare visions they had and the excruciating things they saw and uttered.

DANIEL

The greatest single Dream-book extant is that of Daniel, to which those of Isaiah and Ezekiel are only close seconds. Daniel avows that Yahveh endowed him with "understanding of all visions and dreams"; so that he was "ten times better than all the magicians and astrologers" in all the king's realm (i, 20). He several times relates, as in viii, 18, that "as he (Yahveh) was speaking with me, I was in a deep sleep on my face, with my face toward the ground," —his favorite attitude for wooing nightmare revelation.

He certainly saw some fearful and wonderful things: he describes his "control" as having a "face as the appearance of lightning, and his eyes as lamps of fire, and his arms and his feet like in color to burnished brass, and the voice of his words like the voice of a multitude" (x, 6). No wonder that when Daniel saw such as this, all his "comeliness was turned into corruption" within him and he was scared so that all his strength left him (v. 8); and that he had abdominal disorders and pains in his head, as he says, "I was grieved in my spirit in the midst of my body, and the visions of my head troubled me" (vii, 15).

Poor Daniel spent much time in "prayer and supplications, with fasting, and sackcloth, and ashes" (ix, 3), and would mourn for three full weeks of days at a time, without eating or making his toilet (x, 2–3). It was enough to derange anybody. And he would hear the terrible voice of Yahveh as he was in his deep sleep on his face, with his face towards the ground; and Yahveh would "set me upon my knees and upon the palms of my hands" (x, 9–10); and while in this graceful but uncomfortable all-fours posture, Yahveh told him many wonderful and incomprehensible things, which Daniel himself frankly admits, "I heard, but understood not" (xii, 8). Nor has anyone else ever since. And these visions which he had, of "all the wonders that would be," were very explicitly scheduled to happen and come to pass within the very precise period of "a time, times, and a half" (xii, 7)—whenever that is. I leave the interpretation thereof to more orthodox, or more credulous, Scriptural scholars.

Only I remark, that among the myriads of Babylonian monuments and records which have so far been unearthed and deciphered, thanks to modern Science, the one which records how good old King Nebuchadnezzar, a Heathen special friend of the Yahveh of Israel, to whom he gave the dominion of the earth (Jer. xxvii, 6–8), turned ox and ate grass for seven years out in the pasture in the dews of heaven, has not yet appeared, nor is the name of the Prince Regent during that interregnum yet recovered. And no monument preserves the name of their wonderful inspired Prime Minister Daniel, or records the incidents of the Lion's Den or the burning Fiery Furnace. Maybe all this awaits the next monument or court record to be translated by the scholars. Let us so hope, for dear old Meshuggah Daniel's veracity's sake.

YAHVEH'S HOWLING DERVISHES

The so-called Prophets, major and minor, are one and all typical examples of the Howling Dervish of the desert. Hear them howl; and what a string of them from the great Howl-Master Isaiah: "Howl ye, for the day of the Lord is at hand"! (xiii, 6); "'Howl, O gate; cry, O City!" (xiv, 31); "Every one shall howl!" (xvi, 7); "Howl, ye inhabitants of the isle!" (xxiii, 6); "Ye shall howl for vexation of spirit!" (lxv, 14). Jeremiah swells the refrain: "Lament and howl, for the fierce anger of Yahveh!" (iv, 8); "All the inhabitants of the land shall howl" (xlvii, 2). Ezekiel, he who saw things inexplicable, joins in: "Cry and howl, son of man!" (xxi, 12); "Howl ye, woe worth the day!" (xxx, 2). And the "Minor League" joins the chorus: "Howl, ye inhabitants!" cries Zephaniah (i, 11);

"Howl, ye oaks of Bashan!" bellows Zechariah (xi, 2); "The songs of the Temple shall be howlings!" howls Amos (viii, 3). Joel not only howls himself, but wants everybody else to howl: "Awake, ye drunkards, weep and howl! Lament, ye priests! Howl, ye ministers of the altar! Alas, for the day of Yahveh is at hand! How do the beasts groan! Yahveh also shall roar out of Zion!" (*passim*). Poor Job—but then he was not a Prophet, but a Pagan, and it is not known how he got into the Bible—Job is the only one who does not howl; for, he wails, "My bowels boiled; the days of affliction prevented me!" (xxx, 27). Micah exults in his frenzy, and cries: "I will wail and howl; I will go stripped and naked: I will make a wailing like the Dragons, and mourning as the Owls!" (i, 8).

PROPHETIC EROTICISM

These "meshuggah" Prophets had other peculiarities which we may notice, which are not overly to their credit nor to that of their Yahveh. Hosea was apparently the subject of neuropathic erotomania. His induction into prophecy was a vision in which Yahveh commanded him: "Go, take thee a wife of whoredoms" (i, 2), which he proceeds to do without any recorded reluctance. He has by her a couple of children, without being married to the Lady Gomer, who is very sportive, for he has to make these children "plead with your mother, plead: for she is not my wife, neither am I her husband," begging her to "put away her whoredoms and her adulteries" (ii, 2), so as to indulge them only with this Holy One, who threatens to "strip her naked" (v. 3), if she doesn't quit it. But she kept it up; for Hosea tells us, she "went after her lovers and forgat me"; and Yahveh tried to help him out and win her back, for Yahveh says, "Behold, I will allure her, and bring her into the wilderness" (v. 14). This kindly Divine Go-between seems to have failed of success, for Yahveh tells Hosea, "Go yet, love a woman beloved of her friend, yet an adultress" (iii, 1); which also he does without delay. This new Lady Love seems to have highly pleased the amorous Hosea, for he tells her, "Thou shalt abide for me many days; thou shalt not play the harlot and be for another man; so will I also be for thee" (iii, 3). The erotic visions of Hosea quite rival the amatory Canticles of Solomon, and take all the romance out of Don Juan Tenorio.

Amos had visions beliking Yahveh to a choleric fisherman, swearing by his holiness unto his People, "that he will take you away with hooks, and your posterity with fishhooks"; and while they didn't wear pants in those days, he swears (maybe of the posterity in pants), "and ye shall go out at the breaches" (iv, 2–3). And he promises that Yahveh will break out like a fire and devour Israel, and there will be none to quench it; and he says that Yahveh says he will command the serpent and it shall bite them (ix, 3).

Jonah should be passed with a sympathetic tear; for surely he had great disappointment, after all his vicissitudes, and then Nineveh being spared after all, and had some reason to complain to Yahveh, "it is better for me to die than to live"—which nobody these days doubts; so he should not be expected to tell us about his experiences with much calmness of reason.

The rest of the herd of "minor" prophets likewise gadded about, with their various "burdens" sore upon them, preaching divine wrath and destruction in like frenzied and incoherent fashion, dealing damnation round the land on each they deemed thy foe, O Yahveh. Malachi reaches the climax of low-comedy vengeance with the holy Yahveh's picturesque threat, "I will corrupt your seed, and spread dung upon your faces" (ii, 3); and he winds up with the promise or threat of the "great and dreadful day of Yahveh," that shall burn as an oven, and shall burn up as stubble all those who do wickedly, " and Yahveh shall smite the earth with a curse" (iv, 6). As if the infliction of the whole of Yahveh's dread and inspired Word upon Humanity were not curse enough already.

This ends the unprofitable tale of the Prophets, told in their own frenzied, incoherent, fury-breathing jargon; and proves their just right to their title of Meshuggah.

All the foregoing is inspired revelation of what "prophesying" was in the Holy Hebrew fraternity of Prophets. We have an awesome idea of "prophecy" as the speaking by Divine inspiration of the truths of God and the inspired revealing of the hidden things of the future, for so our Sunday Schools teach, and pious "Divines" and preachers preach. But "God's Word" reveals quite otherwise. All the frenzied Fakirs whom we have seen wander up and down Israel naked and crazed and "raving," were not "prophesying" truths of God nor revelations of the future; but crazed to start with, and worked into a howling frenzy by wild "Jazz" music of a barbarous kind, they truly "raved" frothy and incoherent *non*-sense; for in the Revised Version, more honest than the King James, the word "raved" is given in the margins as the correct sense of "prophesied" used in the text, as where Saul "prophesied (raved) in the midst of the house" when "an evil spirit from the Gods came upon him" (1 Sam. xviii, 10).

Prophetic Lying Factions

With the division of the kingdom after the death of Solomon, followed by constant civil war and partisan hatreds, the prophets split into factions filled with all the hatreds of their respective factions—just like some Christian Churches at the time of the American Civil War; and they prophesied lies against each other right patriotically.

At one time Jehoshaphat, king of Judah, and Ahab, king of Israel, made common cause against the common enemy, the king of Syria; a story which illustrates several tricks of the prophetic trade (1 Kings xxii). Jehoshaphat asked Ahab to "inquire at the word of Yahveh today" about the expedition; and Ahab "gathered the prophets together, about four hundred men, and said, Shall I go up to battle, or shall I forbear? And they said, Go up." But these 400 were prophets of Israel, and the king of Judah mistrusted them, and wanted one of his own party; so he asked, "Is there not here a prophet of Yahveh besides, that we might inquire of him?" Ahab replied that there was one, Micaiah, "but I hate him; for he doth not prophesy good concerning me, but evil" (v. 8).

However, Jehoshaphat insisted, and Micaiah was sent for. The messenger told him that all the other prophets had "declared good unto the king with one mouth," and asked him to speak good likewise. But Micaiah replied that he would speak only "what Yahveh saith unto me." So when Micaiah came before the kings, he prophesied also, "Go up, and prosper; for Yahveh shall deliver the city into the hand of the king." Then King Ahab, mistrusting, said to him, "How many times shall I adjure thee that thou speak unto me nothing but the truth in the name of Yahveh?" Micaiah then retorted with this lying prophecy of conspiracy, which is a blasphemy against any real God of Heaven: "Therefore hear thou the word of Yahveh: I saw Yahveh sitting on his throne, and all the Host of Heaven standing by him. And Yahveh said, Who shall deceive Ahab, that he may go and fall in the battle? And there came forth a spirit and stood before Yahveh, and said, I will deceive him. And Yahveh said, Wherewith? And he said, I will go forth, and will be a lying spirit in the mouth of all his prophets. And Yahveh said, Thou shalt entice him, and shalt prevail also: go forth and do so"! What precious revelation of God! And, said Micaiah, "Behold, Yahveh hath put a lying spirit in the mouth of all these thy prophets; and Yahveh hath spoken evil concerning thee" (vv. 19–23).

Curious that after Yahveh had framed up this conspiracy, and inspired 400 of his holy Prophets to lie and entice Ahab to his death, Yahveh should be so careless as to let one other of his holy Prophets "spill the beans" by revealing the conspiracy.   All that Micaiah got for his word of truth was the kingly order, "Take this fellow to prison and feed him with the bread and water of affliction" (v. 27). As Micaiah was led away to his doom, he fired this parting Parthian shot at Ahab: "If thou returnest at all in peace, Yahveh hath not spoken by me" (v. 28).   And this time the event proved the case for Micaiah, for Ahab was struck by an arrow shot at a venture, and was killed (vv. 35–37), and the other 400 holy prophets of Yahveh were proved wholesale liars by the "lying spirit from Yahveh."

This scene between Micaiah and the 400 prophets whom Yahveh inspired with the "lying spirit" to encompass the death of Ahab, is not the only instance of unbecoming jealousy and Tribal hatred between these Holy Ones of Yahveh.   The kings of Judah and Israel together besought the "word of Yahveh" from Elisha, and this venerable Bald-pate, being of the faction of Judah, scorned to deal with the king of Israel, saying: "What have I to do with thee?   Get thee to the prophets of thy father, and to the prophets of thy mother."   But after expostulation by the king of Israel, Elisha spit back, "As Yahveh liveth, before whom I stand, were it not that I regard the presence of the king of Judah, I would not look toward thee, nor see thee" (2 Kings iii, 14).

An interesting instance of personal altercation and recrimination between two of the holy men of Yahveh is related by Jeremiah, xxviii. This holy Wailer had prophesied that the king of Babylon, in the pending war, would finish the destruction of Jerusalem; while a rival Prophet, one Hananiah, had declared, "Thus speaketh Yahveh Sabaoth, the Elohe of Israel, saying, I have broken the yoke of the king of Babylon."   The altercation proceeds through the chapter to this comical and fatal climax: "Then said the Prophet Jeremiah unto Hananiah the Prophet, Hear now, Hananiah, Yahveh hath not sent thee; but thou makest this People to trust in a lie.   Therefore thus saith Yahveh, Behold, I will cast thee forth from off the face of the earth: this year thou shalt die.   So Hananiah died the same year"!   An edifying instance this, of *post hoc, ergo propter hoc;* and a first-class illustration of prophetic ethics, and the *modus vivendi* of the whole holy class.

It is impossible to relate all the trumperies and lies and false prophecies of these holy inspired Prophets of Yahveh: the Holy Bible is too full of them.   Elisha, in 2 Kings vi, told a bare falsehood, saying, "this is not the way: follow me, and I will bring you to the man whom ye seek," and he led the blinded messengers astray to capture and all but to their death. The false prophecy of Isaiah as to the outcome of the war between the kings of Israel and Syria against Judah, warped into a foretelling of Jesus Christ, will in due order be fully shown (Is. vii).

Jeremiah tells several patent lies and false prophecies, besides being a traitor to his country. For instances: his agreement with the King to make a false report about their conference together (xxxviii, 25); his false prophecy to Zedekiah, that he should die in peace (xxxiv, 2–5); when he himself unblushing relates that the king of Babylon captured Zedekiah, put out his eyes, and kept him languishing in prison until the day of his death (lii, 10–11). Every one of these Meshuggah "prophets" seems to have considered himself as the only one who spoke the truth of Yahveh, and all the others were impostors and liars, as they unanimously and eloquently testify, in the only "honest-to-God" truthful utterances which grace their gibberish, mendacious "ravings" of non-sense.

Confessions of the Prophets

The as-it-were death-bed confessions of the Prophets of Israel of the truth about their sacred profession and co-professionals, priests and prophets, are extremely enlightening, and have the unique merit of being the only honestly true things any of them ever said. It is like the fleeing thief's cry of "stop thief!" pointing to another; or the cordially mutual recriminations of Catholic and Protestant, and sect and sect, denouncing the lies and heresies of all the others—all alike false and mendacious, while each one for itself, Pharasaically, like old Elijah, says: "I, even I only, remain a Prophet of Yahveh"!

Isaiah denounced the Chosen of Yahveh as a whole: "This is a rebellious people, lying children" (xxx, 9); and then he said, "as with the People, so with the Priest." And we shall see there is no difference in favor of the Prophet. Ezekiel had a special divine mission by the word of Yahveh which came to him, saying, "Son of man, prophesy against the prophets of Israel that prophesy, and say thou unto them that prophesy out of their own hearts, Hear ye the word of Yahveh; Thus saith Yahveh: Woe unto the foolish prophets, that follow their own spirit, and have seen nothing! O Israel, thy Prophets are like the foxes in the deserts. They have seen vanity and lying divination, saying, Yahveh saith: and Yahveh hath not sent them" (xiii, 1–6); and "Thus saith Yahveh Elohim, and Yahveh hath not spoken" (xxii, 28). These confessional exposures and de-nunciations run through the whole gamut of Prophets, major and minor, embracing priest and prophet in the same sweeping, scathing anathema.

Hear the word of Yahveh out of the mouth of his holy prophets, each telling the truth on all the others. The Master-Meshuggah Isaiah makes this confession of their drunkenness and befuddled wits: "The priest and the prophet have erred through strong drink, they are swallowed up of wine, they are out of the way through strong drink; they err in vision, they stumble in judgment" (xxviii, 7). Jeremiah confesses the rapacity, mendacity, and fraud of the whole fraternity: "From the least of them even unto the greatest of them every one is given to coveteousness; and from the prophet even unto the priest every one dealeth falsely" (vi, 13); and again, in xxiii, is an entire chapter of inspired invective against them for the whole teeming catalogue of their crimes: "(11) For both prophet and priest are profane; yea, in my house I have found their wicked-ness, said Yahveh. (13) And I have seen folly in the prophets of Samaria; they prophesied in Baal, and caused my people Israel to err. (14) I have seen also in the prophets of Jerusalem an horrible thing: they commit adultery, and walk in lies: they strengthen also the hand of evildoers. (16) Thus saith Yahveh of Hosts, Hearken not unto the words of the prophets that prophesy unto you: they speak a vision out of their own heart, and not out of the mouth of Yahveh. (32) Therefore, behold, I am against the prophets that prophesy false dreams, saith Yahveh, and do tell them, and cause my people to err by their lies: therefore they shall not profit this people at all, saith Yahveh. (34) And as for the prophet, and the priest, and the people, that shall say, The burden (oracle) of Yahveh, I will even punish that man and his house; for ye have perverted the words of Yahveh." Yet again (v. 31), he indicts the whole tribe of impostors and people: "The prophets prophesy falsely, and the priests bear rule by their means, and the people love to have it so"— a God's truth to this very day!

In Lamentations (iv, 13) is a lament "for the sins of her prophets, and the iniquities of her priests, that have shed the blood of the just." Hosea confesses their bloodiness and immorality: "The company of priests murder in the way by consent; they commit lewdness" (vi, 9). Micah confesses the bribery and corruption of all Jewry: "The heads of Israel judge for reward, and the priests thereof teach for hire, and the prophets thereof divine for money" (iii, 11). Zephaniah confesses that "her prophets are light and treacherous persons: her priests have polluted the Sanctuary, they have done violence to the law" (iii, 4). For they are all idolators, admits Jeremiah: "The prophets prophesied by Baal" (ii, 8); and again: "Their priests and their prophets say to a stock, Thou art our Father; and to a stone, Thou hast brought me forth" (v. 26). While Malachi, the last of the Meshuggahs, conjures by Yahveh the whole tribe: "O Priests, that despise my name" (i, 6)!

The revolting record closes not with the Hebrew Scriptures, but continues into the Gentile Era: it was the Priests of Yahveh and the Elders of the People who (it is said) delivered the Christ to the martyrdom of the Cross.

THE CHRISTIANITY PROPAGANDISTS

That doughty Pillar of Christianity, Simon Peter, he whose "ministry" was founded on the hope of exceeding great reward: "Behold, we have forsaken all, and followed Thee; what shall we have therefor?" (Matt. xix, 27); he who like a braggart swore that although all others should desert his Lord, he would stay by him to the end; who like a bully carried a sword to the place of prayer and smote off the ear of one of the Lord's captors—maybe or maybe not; then cowardly ran away from the scene of capture, and like a thief in the night sneaked along far behind to the place of trial; then like a craven thrice lying denied his persecuted Master; and then hypocritically wormed himself into the highest seat in the new priestly. propaganda, and falsely wrested a self-serving meaning into several meaningless mummeries of pretended "prophecy"—this Peter delivers himself of this solemn bit of Inspiration: "Prophecy came not in old time by the will of man; but holy men of God spake as they were moved by the Holy Ghost"! Oh, Innocence!

This seems highly inept in view of the many other inspired definitions and characterizations of prophecy by those who were Prophets and knew what they were confessing, as we have just heard, and who knew a good deal more about it than Fisherman Peter did. There was no Holy Ghost on record in those pre-Petrean days; but those old Meshuggahs confessedly "followed their own spirit," as Ezekiel avers (xiii, 2), and Jeremiah confirms, "They prophesy a false vision and divination, and a thing of naught, the deceit of their heart" (xiv, 14); so that Yahveh himself declares, through Jeremiah; "I will bring an everlasting reproach upon you, and a perpetual shame, which shall not be forgotten" (xxiii, 40). This book helps Yahveh to that end. Thus Peter is seen to have erred again in his Scripture;

which is not to be marveled, but rather excused, seeing that he was an "unlearned and ignorant man" (Acts iv, 13).

This Peter, this "Rock" upon which the Christ punningly assured that he would build his Church, was later expressly and scathingly repudiated by the Christ: "He turned, and said unto Peter, Get thee behind me, Satan: Thou art an offense to me: for thou savorest not the things that be of God, but those that be of men" (Matt. xvi, 23). It was this same Peter who scoffed the Resurrection reports as "idle tales, and believed them not" (Luke xxiv, 11), yet later Peter himself, and to this day through his self-styled Successors (the same term as the Caliphs of Mohammed)—is the prime sponsor of the alleged truth of these same idle tales.

Such as we have seen are confessedly the Holy Prophets of Israel, as pictured by Inspiration. These are the meshuggah old Fakirs and Howling Dervishes of Israel over whom for a score of centuries the credulous Christian world has ecstasized and called inspired of God, and the almost divine oracles and ambassadors of their fictitious Pagan Yahveh—Jehovah. Upon their frenzied incoherent "ravings" the Dogmatists of Christian Theology, errantly, as we shall more than amply see, citing and perverting their "ravings" into inspired "prophecies of Jesus Christ," have founded and built up the labored system of Dogmas and Creeds, sanctioned by dire threats of hell fire and eternal damnation to him who believes not their Holy Word.

CHAPTER XII

BIBLE THEOLOGY AND MODERN TRUTH

BEFORE assaying frankly, in the search of Truth, to "search the Scriptures" of the New Testament, wherein, says the Christ, "ye *think* ye have eternal life" (Jno. v, 39), it is of prime importance to consider briefly the relations of those Scriptures to the Church and to Theological Christianity. Obviously, Bible and Church are vitally related and unseverable; they stand or fall, live or die together, inevitably. The total inspiration and truth of the "Holy Bible, Book Divine," is the first postulate of every Christian Creed. The "Apostle's Creed" enshrines and recites for belief every "fundamental" of the Christian Bible Faith. Not to attempt to cite every Christian Creed in corroboration of this cardinal fact—for all Christian Sects it is a basic fact—I quote only the highest and most ancient Authority in some of its most modern reaffirmations.

The Sacred Vatican Council thus states the Dogma of Infallible Truth of Scripture: "These Books are sacred and canonical because they contain revelation without error, and because, written under the inspiration of the Holy Ghost, they have God for their Author." And more recently, Pope Leo XIII, in his Encyclical *Provid. Deus*, thus reaffirms the Christian Credo of the plenary inspiration of Scripture: "It will never be lawful to restrict inspiration merely to certain parts of the Holy Scriptures, or to grant that the sacred writers could have made a mistake. . . . They render in exact language, with infallible truth, all that God commanded and nothing else; without that, God would not be the Author of the Scripture in its entirety." Says the Catholic Encyclopedia: "The Church, according to St. Paul's Epistle to Timothy, is the pillar and ground of truth; the Apostles, and consequently their Successors, have the right to *impose* their Doctrine; whosoever refuses to believe them shall be condemned, whosoever rejects anything is shipwrecked in Faith. This authority, called the *Magisterium*, or teaching authority, is therefore INFALLIBLE" (Vol. xv, 8). That is the inspired Doctrine of the Church concerning the Bible and concerning its "sacred Deposit of Truth" or "Tradition."

This same dogmatic assertion of Plenary Inspiration and total

Infallibility of Scripture—which sounds oddly assured after the examinations of the preceding Chapters—is more anciently expressed in a couple of precious excerpts, among many others, from the Fathers: "Nothing is to be accepted save on the authority of Scripture, since *major est Scripturae auctoritas quam omnis humani ingenii capacitas*—greater is the authority of Scripture than all the powers of the human mind," says St. Augustine in his Commentary on the Book of Genesis. Equally credent and more graphic is the assurance of the great Church Father St. Ambrose: "Moses opened his mouth and poured forth what God said to him."

Credulous as may be all four of the precited Churchly dogmatisms, their conclusions are of the highest logical validity and truth —if their Scriptural premises be true. This is Orthodox Faith; it is essential Christian Belief; and departure one iota from it is not only heretical in Faith, but un-Christian in fact. "Whosoever rejects anything is ship-wrecked in Faith."

The Modern "Liberalists" are sadly errant in their vaunted Liberalism. They hold to Jesus as son of Yahveh and his mission to "redeem mankind from the sin of Adam," while they deny that Adam existed and repudiate the Virgin-birth of Jesus and throw Hell into the discard. This is Scriptural anarchy, and its votaries are wholly "shipwrecked in Faith," and cannot be Bible Christians, however good as citizens.

These Modernists decry and deride what they term "Mediaeval Theology"; but Mediaeval Theology is Bible Theology and the only orthodox and true Theology—if Theology could be true at all. With no more logical truth and reason can "Modern" Theology repudiate Mediaeval Theology, than could Mediaeval Theology logically accept Copernicus and Galileo, and the long brilliant line of God's true Prophets whom the inspired Church has persecuted and martyred through the past Ages of Faith for daring to proclaim God's truths which have impeached and destroyed its dogmas of the inspired truth of Hebrew and Christian Scriptures.

Briefly, and inadequately, I am going to recall here just a few of the precious things of God "poured out through the mouth of Moses," to which the inspired Church, fatuously but with unimpeachable logic and Scripture-truth, had clung through the ages of Faith, and with these shibboleths of Revelation has opposed every revelation of God in Nature through the powers of the human mind. These are only a few of the manifold phases of the eternal and triumphant "conflict between Science and Religion"—between Knowledge and the outpourings of God through Moses.

It is the celebrated aphorism of Huxley: "Every path of Natural Science is closed with the sign: 'No Thoroughfare, Moses.'"

Moses, inspired by Yahveh, declared that the heaven and earth, and all the fullness thereof, were created by Yahveh out of Nothing in six (or one) days; that Adam ate the Forbidden Fruit of Knowledge in Eden, whereby, avers the Apostolic Founder of the Faith and its Church, "sin and death entered into the world," and damned all humanity. Father Luther, with all the assurance of an eye-witness, avers: "Moses spoke properly and plainly, and neither allegorically nor figuratively; and therefore the world with all creatures was created in six days." The Westminster Confession of Faith—in full force and effect today—specially lays it down as "necessary to salvation to believe that all things visible and invisible were created not only out of nothing but in exactly six days." The Catholic Father Peter Martyr clinched the whole matter by declaring, and with inexorable logic and truth:—"So important is it to comprehend the work of Creation that we see the Creed of the Church take this as its starting point. Were this Article taken away, there would be no Original Sin; the Promise of Christ would become void, and all the vital force of our Religion would be destroyed."

This is, indeed, the enormous fatal significance of the Six Days and the Fall; emphasized, and explained, by the alarmed outcries of the Church against the wonderful discoveries of the human mind in the fields of Astronomy, Geology, Anthropology, and Natural Science, which wholly negatived and disproved their cherished Dogmas of Revelation, and discredited forever the basic tenets of the whole fabric of the Christian Religion. Calvin wrote a "Commentary on Genesis," in which he argues that the Genesis account of Creation is literally true, and warns those who dare to believe otherwise, and thus "basely insult the Creator, to expect a Judge who will annihilate them."

But Modern Knowledge, Science, has proved beyond all contradiction of inspiration, that all these inspired truths, right out of the "infallible annals of the Spirit of God," are contrary to the facts; and makes it impossible for Adam and Eve and Eden to have ever existed. So here alone, with one great crash, the whole Christian Plan of Salvation, founded on the Fable of Adam and the Forbidden Fruit, collapses to utter ruin.

Moses again, by inspiration of Yahveh, avers this goodly earth to be flat and square, of "four corners," and that all its vari-colored inhabitants are directly descended from his First Man, Adam, through Noah and his three Sons. The great Pagan Philosophers, by the power of their genius of Reason, happily untrammeled by Hebrew Revelation and Christian Inspiration, declared with true inspiration God's Truth of the rotundity of the earth, and that the "antipodes" could be and were inhabited by races of men. Centuries before Christ and before Columbus, the "Christ-bearer," Pythagoras taught the spherical form of the earth. Aristotle went further and demonstrated the roundness of the earth by his famous Three Arguments, concluding: "So that from this it is manifest, not only that the form of the earth is round, but also that it is part of not a very large sphere" (Arist. De Coelo, 11, 14).

Seneca the Younger, who died in 65 A.D., in his *Naturales Questiones*, thus poses the sublime idea: How great a way is it, he asks, which lies from the furthest shores of Spain to India? and answers himself: that it is a space of a very few days if a fair wind drives the ship. One of his great tragedies gives striking expression to his famous prophesy:

> "Venient annis, saecula seris,
> Quibus Oceanus vincula rerum
> Laxet, et ingens pateat tellus,
> Tethysque novos detegat orbes;
> Nec sit terris ultima Thule." (Medea, ii, 375.)

"There will come a time," he says, "in later years, when Oceanus shall loosen the bonds of things, and a huge land shall lie revealed, and Tethys shall disclose new worlds, and Thule shall no longer be at the end of the earth." This is one of the most notable un-"inspired" prophecies on record, and was wonderfully fulfilled: in a copy of the Tragedies of Seneca, belonging to Ferdinand Columbus, now in the Biblioteca Colombina, there is attached to these prophetic verses this marginal note: "Haec prophetia expleta et per patrem meum Cristoforo Colon, Almirante, anno 1492."

But no, this is impious heresy, contradictory of Holy Moses, and destructive of the Holy Church! "Scripture," avers the all-knowing Father St. Augustine, "speaks of no such descendants of Adam as the Antipodeans. Men could not be allowed by the Almighty to live there, since if they did they could not see Christ at his second coming descending through the air"; and, he avers, the supporters of this geographical heresy "give the lie direct to King David and to St. Paul, and therefore to the Holy Ghost"! The Antipodeans, argues Father Procopius, according to a text of Luke, are theologically impossible; "If there be men on the other side of the earth, Christ must have gone there and suffered a second time to save them; and therefore there must have been, as necessary preliminaries to his coming, a duplicate Adam, Eden, Serpent, and Deluge"! We see again, how the Christian "Plan of Salvation" depends confessedly and utterly upon Adam, the Garden, and the Talking Snake!

Father St. Boniface appealed to Yahveh's Vicar Pope Zachary to combat this heresy of the antipodes, of men who were beyond the appointed means of salvation; and the Pope, inspired of the Holy Ghost, issued his "Bull," embellished and fortified with passages from Job and the apochryphal "Wisdom of Solomon," against the heretical doctrine, declaring it "perverse, iniquitous, and against the soul" of whoever maintained it. And the Holy Ghost, speaking further through this "Bull," harshly condemned the good Saint Vergilius, who heretically held the earth to be round; declaring that such doctrine involved errors as to Original Sin and the universality of Redemption; for, averred the Holy Ghost, if there were antipodes, the "other race of men" could not be descendants of Adam and were not redeemed by Christ. In this conclusion I must confess that the Holy Ghost and His Holiness are right for once.

The Holy Council of Salamanca solemnly decided against Columbus' theory of the rotundity of the earth and the antipodes, declaring that texts of Scripture and "the Fathers" were opposed to such an idea; that, as Father St. Augustine said, "If there were any antipodes, the Bible would have said so"; that the earth was actually a flat disc with a dropping-off place; and that if the world were round they would slide off! But Columbus persisted in his immortal heresy; and his epochal voyages, and the circumnavigation by Magellan, proved once again that it was not safe to trust Scriptures and the "Fathers" for inspired scientific knowledge.

Shortly after the return of Columbus from his first Faith-shattering voyage, the Holy Church set itself up as the self-appointed dispenser of the New World which it had just declared through the Holy Ghost never existed; and God's Vicar Pope Alexander VI, of savory memory, perpetrated his celebrated Bull "*Inter caetera Divinae Majestati*," in May, 1493, partitioning the New World between Spain and Portugal. As this touches a highly interesting event in American History, of far-reaching consequences, I will quote from the notable "Bull," quite fairly turned into the vernacular from the original Latin published in Volume I of "American Charters, Constitutions and Organic Laws," published by the U. S. Government. From page 42 I translate and transcribe the Papal Grantor's inspired claim to Divine power and infallibility in making the Partition:

". . . Out of Our mere liberality, and of Our certain knowledge, and the plenitude of Apostolic power . . . and by the authority of Omnipotent God to US in Blessed Peter granted, and the Vicarship of Jesus Christ which we exercise on earth——"

by these plenipotentiary credentials and Divine powers of attorney, His Holiness granted to Spain all the new lands discovered and to be discovered, west of a line, dictated by the Holy Ghost, drawn one hundred leagues west of the Azores and Cape Verde Islands. But Portugal angrily protested and made threats, basing its protests and claims not upon the geographical "certain knowledge" of the Holy Ghost but upon sundry human discoveries in geography, which demonstrated such a line to be impossible, as there are about ten degrees of longitude difference between the two groups of Islands. So the two rival Powers, by the Treaty of Tordesillas, amended the inspired but impossible geography of the Holy Ghost, and established the famous "Line of Demarcation" at 370 leagues west of the Cape Verde Islands, a line corresponding to the 50th degree of longitude west of Greenwich, and striking the mainland of South America across the mouth of the Amazon River; thus making Brazil Portuguese, while the remaining half of the continent, west of "the Line" became Spanish, as both so remain to this day.

Even after Magellan's triumphant voyage of 1519 around the globe had proven to demonstration the errancy of Scripture, Fathers, and Infallible Church, such redoubtable Churchmen as Luther, Melancthon and Calvin, stuck to Scriptural "revelation" and roundly denied sphericity; as do the holy followers of "Moses II" Dowie at Zion City, Illinois, right today. Another bit of geographical Bible lore may be mentioned just here. Calvin, in 1553, persecuted and burned to death Servetus, because in his edition of Ptolemy's "Geography," he spoke of the Holy Land as not a "land flowing with milk and honey," but as mainly barren and inhospitable; Calvin declared that such language "necessarily inculpated Moses, and grievously outraged the Holy Ghost"!

But "the infallible annals of the Spirit of God" were not only discredited by Geography and Geology and the Sciences named; the Divine Science of Astronomy gave it a blow under which it has writhed for three centuries, and from which only the fatuous fidelity of Faith, which reasons not nor doubts, enables it to yet sustain a precarious credit among those who do not think adequately. The Holy Ghost, through Yahveh's Vicar Pope Alexander III, in 1163, in a "Bull" forbade to ecclesiastics "the study of Physics or the Laws of the World," and decreed that any one violating this inspired command of Yahveh "shall be avoided by all and excommunicated."

There were immortal Heroes of Science who dared defy such Inspired Ignorance. Copernicus, truer Prophet of God than Moses or Pope, wrote his inspired Revelation of God in the Heavens, "The Revolutions of the Heavenly Bodies," which in terror of Yahveh's Holy-Ghost-inspired Church he withheld from publication till the day of his death, May 24, 1543; when with his dying breath he gave to the world the revelation that the Sun is the center of the solar system, and that the earth and other planets revolve around it; and from the security of the border of the grave he defiantly dedicated his immortal work to His Holiness the Pope.

The Inspired Roman Church instantly denounced the work as heresy, and condemned it to suppression "until his statement should be corrected" to conform to the Bible and to Ptolemy, who was a Pagan; but whose "Geography" was held almost inspired by the Church. Father Luther screeched at Copernicus, calling him "an upstart astrologer," and vamped: "This fool wishes to reverse the entire science of astronomy; but Sacred Scripture tells us that Joshua commanded the sun to stand still, and not the earth." Melancthon, another great luminary of Reformed Inspiration, declared: "It is a want of honesty and decency to assert such notions publicly, and the example is. pernicious." Calvin, in his "Commentary on Genesis," which precious work I have mentioned, condemned all who asserted that the earth is not the center of the Universe, and triumphantly appealed to Psalms xciii, 1: "The world also is established, that it cannot be moved"! defiantly asking: "Who will put the authority of Copernicus above that of the Holy Spirit?" The Methodist Founder, John Wesley, averred that these new ideas "tend towards infidelity"; and with acute logic he demonstrated how the Dogmas of the Christian Religion must perish before this one stupendous Revelation of God in Science—please note well his reasoning, for it is unanswerably true:

"His pretended discovery vitiates the whole Christian Plan of Salvation. It casts suspicion on the Doctrine of the Incarnation. It upsets the whole basis of Theology. If the earth is a Planet, and only one among several planets, it cannot be that any such great things have been done for it as the Christian Doctrine teaches. If there are other planets, since God makes nothing in vain, they must be inhabited; but how can their inhabitants be descended from Adam? How can they trace their origin back to Noah's Ark? How can they have been redeemed by the Saviour?"

Upon what as string of "silly fancies" the whole "sacred science of Christianity" hangs and the so-called "Church of God" dangles and precariously exists!

In 1618 and 1619 God's Prophet Kepler published his immortal works "Epitomy of the Copernican System" and "The Harmonies of the World." He lived in a Protestant country, where the Roman Church couldn't get at him. But the Protestant Consistory of Stuttgart solemnly warned him "not to throw Christ's Kingdom into confusion with his silly fancies," and ordered him to "bring his theory of the world into harmony with Scripture"—as if Truth could be harmonized with ignorant Fables! A direr fate befell the illustrious Giordano Bruno, an Apostole of Learning and of the Copernican System. Right in the face of the Holy Church he flung his immortal Satire ridiculing it, *Lo Spaccio della Bestia Trionphale* ("The Expulsion of the Triumphant Beast"); and after seven years in its foul dungeons, the "Beast" threw his heroic but heretic body and his books to the flames of its Holy Inquisition, in Rome, in 1600; but his soul and Truth go marching on!

All the world knows and blushes in shame at the ignominious spectacle which the Inspired Church made of the venerable, truly inspired Galileo, haled before the Holy Inquisition, dressed in the penitential sackcloth robe of a repentant criminal, there forced upon his knees before God's Vicar Pope and his assembled Cardinals, laying his hands upon the "Holy Evangels," and invoking Divine aid in "abjuring and detesting the infamous doctrine of the earth's motion and the sun's stability"! This Holy Inquisition, presided over in person by Yahveh's Vicar, Pope Paul V, after a month's deliberations in solemn session with the Holy Ghost, in 1615, rendered its inspired unanimous decision: "The first proposition, that the sun is the center and does not revolve around the earth, is foolish, absurd, false in theology, and heretical, because expressly contrary to Holy Scripture. The second proposition, that the earth is not the center but revolves around the sun, is absurd, false in philosophy, and from a theological point of view at least, opposed to the true Faith." Galileo was therefore commanded, "in the name of His Holiness the Pope and the whole Congregation of the Holy Office (i.e., the Inquisition), to relinquish altogether the opinion that the sun is the center of the world and immovable, and that the earth moves; and henceforth not to hold, teach, or defend it in any way whatsoever, verbally or in writing." A couple of weeks later the Congregation of the Index, at the instigation of the Pope, rendered its decree that "the doctrine of the double motion of the earth about its axis and about the sun is false, and entirely contrary to Holy Scripture," and must not be taught or advocated. The decree condemned all the works of Copernicus and "all writings which affirm the motion of the earth," and placed them, and those of Kepler and Galileo on the "Index of Prohibited Books," from which they were only removed in 1835!

In 1633 Galileo was again haled before the Inquisition, by order of Pope Urban VIII, threatened with torture, and subjected to imprisonment by order of the Pope. Forced again by the Holy Terror to abjure, he was forced to pronounce publicly and on his knees this monstrous Recantation: "I, Galileo Galilei, being in my seventieth year, being a prisoner and on my knees, and before your Eminences, having before my eyes the Holy Gospel, which I touch with my hands, abjure, curse, and detest the error and heresy of the movement of the earth"! And from this cringing attitude of Terror to which he was forced by the inspired Vicar of Yahveh, the broken old Prophet of the Architect God rose in righteous rebellion of spirit, and muttered back at his Holy Inquisitors the immortal "*Ma pur' si muove!*" (But it does move, for all that!) and tottered out to his hastening death. The world knows, too, whether Holy Ghost or Galileo was right. In 1664, the Pope Alexander VII, issued his inspired "Bull," in which he "finally, decisively and infallibly" condemned "all books teaching the movement of the earth and the stability of the sun"; all works in which the arch heresy was taught or proposed were put upon the Index of Prohibited Books, and True Faith was again triumphant on earth.

It is a curious commentary on Inspiration and Infallibility: the catalogue of the Papal Index shows every single book, published during all the Dark Ages of Faith, in which the genius of man sought to reveal God's true knowledge of Himself through His works of Nature, and to enlighten the human mind and spirit steeped in the dark superstitions of the Bible and the Church, to have been banned and cursed and burned by the dictates of the Holy Ghost operating through its Inspired Infallible Church! Because, forsooth, God's Facts of Nature contradicted and rendered ridiculous the ancient Tales of Yahveh and "Revelation"! Besides the epoch-making works of the great Physicists and Philosophers, by the hundreds, scores of others, and quite modern, too, such as those of the great Naturalists, of Linnaeus, of Geoffrey Saint-Hilaire, of Cuvier, of Lyell, of Buffon, appear in that Catalogue of inspired ignorance. The latter, Buffon, just at the time of our Revolution for Independence, was forced by the inspired Vice-gerent of Yahveh to subscribe and swear to this debasing formula of recantation: "I declare that I had no intention to contradict the text of Scripture; that I most firmly believe all therein related about the Creation, both as to order of time and the matter of facts. I abandon everything in my book respecting the formation of the earth, and generally all which may be contrary to the narrative of Moses"! And his monumental "Histoire Naturelle" of 44 wonderful volumes was put under the Anathema of the Church in its Holy Index. Such are a few instances of the enlightenment of the Holy Spirit to its inspired Expounders.

These unhappy instances of human ignorance are of no importance as such, for every day we learn things which were ignorance to us the day before, and thus we grow in knowledge. But the awful significance of these instances and all their kind is, that the "Word of God" is the inspired source and fountain of all this ignorance and teaches it as "revelation" of truth of God; and the "Church of God," which claims to be daily taught and guided by the Spirit of Yahveh, perpetuated humanity in this ignorance under the pretense that the "Holy Ghost" advised it that all this mass of ignorance was the very truth of God, to doubt or deny which meant the terror of Churchly curses and prison and rack and stake. That Bible and Church have in every single instance of conflict been defeated and proved in error, proves that the Church is mistaken in its claim to be possessed of infallible Scriptures and Inspiration.

The Bible throughout, Old and New, and particularly the latter, teaches that sickness and disease are due directly to devils and demoniacal possession; Christ and his Disciples cast out devils and the sick were thereupon cured. Never a word or hint of medicine or surgery in all the Bible, except the fig-poultice for Hezekiah's boil, and the spit-salve in the blind man's eyes; and never a hint of the prevention or rational cure of disease. The Divine Prescription is, "Go, cast out Devils in my name and heal the sick." According to the Bible and the Church all plagues are specifically sent by God in punishment of sin. Yes, Sanitary Sin! against which there is not a single word in all Scripture, though it abounds in incantations and exorcisms and "purifications." The holy unwashed Saints of Holy Church were very active agents of God in invoking and propagating these God-sent Plagues. The Canon Law, given by the Holy Ghost to its Infallible Church, declared "the precepts of Medicine are contrary to Divine knowledge," for, says Holy Writ: "Is any sick among you? let him call for the elders of the Church, and let them pray over him, anointing him with oil in the name of the Lord." And so declares Father St. Ambrose: "The precepts of Medicine are contrary to celestial science, watching and prayer"; a maxim re-iterated throughout the Ages of Faith (id est, the Dark Ages).

The great Father Origen thus instructs us in celestial science: "It is demons which produce famine, unfruitfulness, corruptions of the air, and pestilences; they hover concealed in clouds in the lower atmosphere, and are attracted by the blood and incense which the heathen offer to them as gods." God save the mark for celestial science! The quasi-Divine Father St. Augustine adds for our faith in celestial science: "All diseases of Christians are to be ascribed to these demons; chiefly do they torment fresh-baptised Christians, yea, even the guileless, new born infants"! The great Father St. Bernard warned his monks that "to seek relief from disease in medicine was in harmony neither with religion nor with the honor and purity of their Order." The use of the crude pain-reducing "anesthetics" of the times was opposed by the Inspired Church; especially its use in child-birth was objected to as an attempt "to avoid one part of the primeval curse on women"; and in 1591, Lady Macalyane was burned alive on Castle Hill in Edinburgh for seeking aid for relief of pain in the birth of her two sons! The "Apostles' Creed," regarding resur-rection of the body, discouraged anatomical study, and the Church forbade surgery to Monks; all dissection was forbidden by Decretal of Pope Boniface VIII, and excommunication was threatened against all who presumed to practice it.

An awful case of belly-ache suffered by a pious Nun is solemnly avowed by the Holy Father, Pope Gregory the Great, to have been caused by her having swallowed a devil along with a piece of lettuce which she was eating, she having omitted to make the sign of the cross (which is potent conjure as a scare-devil); and this devil, when commanded by a holy Monk to come out of her, derisively replied, "How am I to blame? I was sitting on the lettuce, and this woman, not having made the sign of the cross, ate me along with it!" And Gregory the Great was Yahveh's own Anointed Vicar on earth, full of the inspiration of truth; he is the same through whom the Holy Ghost made the formal revelation of Purgatory; the same who stopped a pestilence in Rome by marching at the head of a procession of Priests, and saw Michael the Archangel shooting fiery darts of death into the Holy City.

All this is illuminating evidence of the truth and inspiration of Bible and Church; and is all of a piece with the inspired "Bull" in which Pope Calixtus, moved by mortal fear and the Holy Ghost, excommunicated Halley's Comet. In 1618, "a comet caused an eruption of Mt. Vesuvius, which would have destroyed Naples, had not the blood of the Invincible St. Januarius withstood it" (see Cath. Enc., Vol. VIII, p. 295). Thousands of like inspired relations of the Holy Ghost and the Holy Church abound, too numerous to mention, for it would take whole volumes to contain them and be too impracticable for modern consumption. Read the Catholic Encyclopedia.

WITCHCRAFT AND INSPIRATION

One of the most piteous and murderous superstitions in all the inspired "infallible annals of the Spirit of God," is the inspired revelation of Witches. A thousand times it is assured in this "Word of God poured forth by Moses," that Witches, witchcraft, and sorcery exist and have wrought much wonders on earth; and that God himself commanded that witches and sorcerers should be put to death without mercy. All the world but a Bible Christian knows that the persons who wrote down that God told them by inspired revelation to state such things were mistaken, and truth was not in what they wrote. This is the alleged direct and positive enactment of Yahveh on Sinai: "Thou shalt not suffer a witch to live" (Ex. xxii, 17)—"or a charmer, or a consulter with familiar spirits, or a wizard, or a necromancer"—what a string of "inspired" superstitious, cruel errors.

The Founder of Methodism was so saturated in this "inspired Word of God," that he declared with all the assurance of credulous intellectual darkness: "Unless Witchcraft is true, nothing in the Bible is true"—and I admit he told the truth, though in a contrasense. And hear his solemn science of natural history, spoken as if by full inspiration, about primitive wild animals: "Before Adam's sin none of these attempted to devour or in any wise hurt one another; the spider was as harmless as the fly"! He hadn't ever heard what Science has of late revealed about this little filth-laden, disease-disseminating imp of the Devil. So they are—for Father Luther is positive that "Flies are the image of heretics and Devils"! But to stick to inspired witchcraft for a moment—not indeed that witches fly in an age of electric light, but to illustrate the darkness of Holy Inspiration.

Wesley may be doubted to have been fully inspired. But the Bible is admitted so to be; and the Holy Church admits that itself is. Several of its Divinely Inspired Vice-gerents of Yahveh, "by virtue of the teaching power conferred by the Almighty, and under the Divine guidance against any possible error in the exercise of it" (such is their holy formula), have from time to time during the Ages of Faith (*id est,* the Dark Ages), emitted God-inspired fulminations against the unholy practices of witchcraft and sorcery, so often avowed as fact and denounced as the work of the Devil, in Old and New Testaments alike. To mention but a few out of many for samples of the infallible teachings of the Holy Ghost on this subject, by which we may judge of other like inspired teachings on other subjects: remembering "*falsus in uno,*" etc.

Yahveh's Vicar Pope John XXII, in 1317, in his "Bull"—(odd about the Holy Church speaking, like the classic Irishman, always "Bulls")—"*Spondent Pariter,*" and others of like tenor, complains that both he and his Flock (i.e. of "Sheep") are in danger of their lives by the arts of sorcery and witchcraft; he declares that such sorcerers can send Devils into mirrors and finger rings, and kill men and women by a magic word; that they have tried to kill him by piercing a waxen image of him with needles in the name of the Devil. He therefore called upon all rulers, secular and ecclesiastical, to hunt down the miscreants who thus afflicted the Faithful, and he especially increased the powers of the Inquisitors in various parts of Europe for this pious purpose. Yahveh's Vicar Pope Eugene IV, in 1437, in another "Bull" exhorted the Holy Inquisitors of Heresy and Witchcraft to use greater diligence against these human agents of the Prince of Darkness, and especially against such of them as have the power to produce bad weather! Yahveh's Vicar Pope Innocent VIII, on December 7, 1484, perpetrated the famous "Bull *Summis Desiderantes,*" inspired by the Divine command "Thou shalt not suffer a witch to live," exhorting the clergy to leave no means untried to detect sorcerers, and especially those who "by evil weather destroy vineyards" (he was evidently not a Prohibitionist,—as have been none of his Inspired Successors, this being the unique instance in Ecclesiastical History when these Vicars of Yahveh have ever pretended to champion "personal liberty" of conduct or conscience). Armed with his Manual "*Malleus Maleficarum,*" of "Witch Hammer," his Witch-hunting Inquisitors scoured Europe for victims, extorting confessions by torture, and murdering wholesale victims of their fanaticism.

Similar "Bulls" were inspired by the Holy Ghost and issued by Yahveh's Vicars Pope Julius II in 1504, and by Pope Adrian VI in 1523; tens of thousands of unhappy—and innocent—persons were thus perpiously destroyed because of the inspired but ignorant Scriptural and priestly Witchcraft and Sorcery. James I of England, "By the Grace of God, King, Defender of the Faith,"—he who instigated the "Authorized Version" of this old Jewish Witch Book, and to whom it is dedicated in terms of most disgusting adulation,—wrote a famous book of Demonology, and used torture to get *evidence* of witchcraft with which to adorn its veracious pages. On the occasion of his august Bride being driven back by a storm at sea, Dr. Fian, under torture, confessed that several hundred witches had gone to sea in a sieve from Leith and had raised storms and tempests to drive back the Princess! Sir Matthew Hale, in burning two witches to death, judicially declared that he based his judgment on the direct testimony of Holy Scripture! But both Bible and Church are in evident error in teaching this miserable Witch-superstition.

ANCIENT FAITH YET FULLY VALID

Yet all the foregoing outpourings of Yahveh through Moses are of the most essential "fundamentals" of the Christian Religion. It is Catholic and Protestant "Truth" alike, and by the Creeds of them all, are "necessary to salvation," to be professed and believed: it is Christianity. The truth is admirably, if presumptuously, expressed by the great Father St. Augustine: "Neither in the confusion of Paganism, nor in the defilement of Heresy, nor in the lethargy of Schism, nor yet in the blindness of Judaism, is Religion to be sought; but among those *alone* who are called Catholic Christians, or the Orthodox, that is, the custodians of sound doctrine and followers of right teaching" (*De Vera Religione*, Chap. v). The famous Athanasian Creed, of the Council of Nice, A.D. 325,—reaffirmed by the Papal Encyclical "*Pascendi Dominici Gregis*," in 1907, avers: "Whoever will be saved, it is necessary above all else that he hold to the Catholic Faith."

Faith is the "substance of things hoped for, the evidence of things not seen," defines the great Dogmatist of the Faith. The preceding pages have shown much of this "substance" very unreal, and as "evidence" of factuality to be less than nil. Indeed, some progressive and "modernist" Theologians, would wave away all this as old stories, as ignorant superstitions of credulous Faith, long since abandoned and forgotten by the Holy Church, as shining but discarded vagaries of "Mediaeval Theology." But Truth is of all time; Bible and Church, in all of truth they ever had, are—if ever they were—as infallible and hence as eternal as Truth—the same yesterday, to-day, and forever. The same "Holy Ghost" inspires the Bible and presides over and inspires its infallible Church to-day as did in its beginning and through all the precious Dark Ages of Faith.

As if fearful that this sacred truth might be discounted, if not impiously laughed quite out of countenance in this modern Age of Reason and of Knowledge, the Holy Ghost has very recently and repeatedly gone to much pains and suffered no little skeptical ridicule, to reaffirm the eternal truth of all its Dogmas, and its own and its inspired Vicars' total Infallibility in all matters of Faith or Belief—or Credulity, as we shall notice with interest.

In the year 1870, the Sacred Vatican Council, convoked by Pope Pius IX and presided by the Holy Ghost itself, expressly avowed the immutability—the stagnation—the fossilization—of Religious Truth in all its ancient and hoary Dogmas and Beliefs, which some threatened to reject as discredited Superstition, averring: "The Doctrine of Faith, which God (i.e. Yahveh) has revealed, has not been proposed as a philosophical discovery to be improved upon by human talent, but has been committed as a Divine Deposit to the Spouse of Christ, to be faithfully guarded and infallibly interpreted by Her." It embalms its petrified "Sacred Science of Christianity" as the eternal and unchangeable revelations of truth of Yahveh, asserting: "The Successors of St. Peter have been promised the Holy Ghost, not for the promulgation of new doctrines, but only for the preservation and interpretation of the Revelations committed by the Apostles." All this was a sort of Socratic leading up to the climacteric formulation in writing of the terms of the inspired Mandate granted of old orally by the Holy Ghost to its Vicar General on earth, and reiterating the venerable Dogma of its own Infallibility:

"Faithfully adhering, therefore, to the Traditions inherited from the beginning of the Christian Faith, *we*, with the approbation of the Sacred Council, for the Glory of God our Savoir, for the exaltation of the Catholic Religion, and the Salvation of Christian peoples, teach and define, as a Divinely revealed Dogma, that the Roman Pontiff, when he speaks *ex cathedra*, that is, when he, in the exercise of his Supreme Apostolic Authority, decides that a doctrine concerning *faith and morals* is to be held by the entire Church, he possesses, in consequence of the Divine Aid promised him in *St. Peter*, that *infallibility* with which the Divine Savoir wished to have his Church furnished for the definition of Doctrine concerning Faith and Morals; and that such definitions of the Roman Pontiff are of themselves, and not in consequence of the Church's consent, *irreformable*."

All this is as lucid of expression and inspiration as one could reasonably expect; and it expressly and solemnly, in A.D. 1870 puts the Great Seal of Yahveh on all the "Bulls" and claims of ecclesiastical Inspiration and Infallibility from the New Testament and the Witch Bulls, to the celebrated Encyclical *"Pascendi Dominici Gregis"* ("Feeding the Lord's Flock") of his inspired Successor Pius X.

This monumental emanation of Inspiration, put forth on September 8, 1907, reiterates the "Bull" axiom of Holy Church: "Faith has for its object the *unknowable"*; and at great lengths proceeds to aver its own Infallible Knowledge of all these things Unknowable; puts its ineffable Anathema or Churchly Curse upon all the priceless Truths of human knowledge acquired through the ages in defiance of Holy Church, and upon the precious boon of liberty of thought and conscience attained fearfully in spite of the Church,—all which this Popish Encyclical sneeringly dubs "Modernism," averring that this "Modernism embraces every Heresy against the inspired revelations of Bible and Church" (which, indeed, is true); and winds up with a sweeping formula of abjuration, to which all priests and clerical persons "are obliged to swear, reprobating the principal Modernist tenets"—which, of course, include the utter denial of witches and sorcery, possession by Devils, flatness and stability of the earth, Miracles, the Inspiration of Revelation, the Virgin Birth and Divinity of Jesus Christ, the validity and justice of the Plan of Salvation, and a thousand like relics of ancient Faith, incompatible with modern Knowledge of the Truth.

Thus in full XXth Century, the Holy Ghost itself, if Pius X—, now about to be canonized by his Church for his own miracles—is to be credited with authentic knowledge of its true sentiments—harks back with conscious pride through the Dark Ages of Faith to its original fountains of inspired Verity, and puts its seal of approval on the classic Formula of Faith: *"Illa sola credenda est Veritas quae in nullo ab Ecclesiastica et Apostolica discordat Traditione"*— "That only must be believed as Truth which in nothing disaccords with the Ecclesiastic and Apostolic Tradition"!

Oh, Fratres Ignorantiae!

CHAPTER XIII

THE "PROPHECIES" OF JESUS CHRIST

THROUGHOUT the four Gospel biographies of Jesus, the Christ, there are very frequent references to and quotations of sundry passages in the Hebrew Old Scriptures, which are appealed to as "prophecies" concerning Jesus Christ, and are avowed to foretell his birth and death, as well as many incidents of his life; and are asserted to have been fulfilled by these several incidents.

The Jews had for centuries, ever since their Captivity, lived in the fervent belief and expectation of a Messiah, an anointed King of the race and lineage of David, who should at last arise, overthrow all their enemies, restore the Kingdom of Israel, and "reestablish the Throne of David forever." Many "Pretenders" to the yet vacant Messiahship had from time to time arisen and asserted their false pretenses to be the Promised Messiah; and even Jesus was not the last who arose to proclaim himself the Messiah or Christ. This Jesus himself declared: "For many shall come in my name, saying I am Christ; and shall deceive many. . . . Then if any man shall say, Lo, here is Christ, or there, believe it not. For there shall arise false Christs, and shall show great signs and wonders; insomuch that, if it were possible, they shall deceive the very elect" (Matt. xxiv, 5, 23–24; Mark xiii, 6, 21–22). And the intervening verses between those cited, are filled with a long catalogue of "great signs and wonders" which these Pretenders shall work in proof of their false claims.

How and why these false Pretenders to Messiahship could "come in my name"—in the name of Yahveh's genuine Messiah, who had already come and by his own "signs and wonders" had demonstrated to the satisfaction of all who believed them, that he thus "fulfilled all the law and the prophets" and was indeed the Messiah and thus closed the lists, is not at this day very evident. But, admittedly, the working of such "great signs and wonders"—miracles—was no authentic badge of Messiahship, but was the common stock in trade of any bogus Pretender. Of this fact there are many Scriptural assurances and instances, besides the admission just made by Jesus.

278

A very curious instance of Pretended Messiahship noted in the New Testament, was Simon Magnus, the Sorcerer, who notoriously "used sorcery, and bewitched the people of Samaria, from the least to the greatest," so that all the people said, "This man is the great power of God," and "of a long time he had bewitched them with sorceries" (Acts viii, 9–11),—which seems a very silly superstition to be vouched for by the Bible, and does not much credit to its inspired truth. The case of Elymas Bar-Jesus is also somewhat in point (Acts xiii, 6, 8); as is also that of the "damsel possessed with a spirit of divination, which brought her masters much gain by sooth-saying" (Acts xvi, 16), or common fortune-telling. And even greater "signs and wonders" were worked by common charlatans. Thus even total strangers to Jesus Christ, uncommissioned by him, disbelievers in him, common Fakirs and false Pretenders, could exercise the divine power of "casting out devils" in his name, to the great scandal of the Disciples (Mark ix, 38; Luke ix, 49).

Yet all these miraculous powers, these "great signs and wonders," were clearly not of God, and prove no divine mission or authority of the wonder-workers: although Nicodemus declares, "No man can do these miracles that thou doest except God be with him" (Jno. iii, 2). Howbeit, Jesus himself appealed to this very power of working "signs and wonders" as the culminating proof and Patent of his divine authority and Messiahship: "For the same works that I do, bear witness of me, that the Father hath sent me" (Jno. v, 36); and, "though ye believe *me* not, believe the works" (Jno. x, 38); and again, "Believe me for the very works' sake" (Jno. xiv, 11). But such "works," such "great signs and wonders," are proven by Bible proofs to prove nothing—as Jesus himself had just averred and admitted—except great credulity of people to believe them. The proof of the divine mission and authority of Jesus as the Christ must, therefore, derive from some more valid evidences than that of mere popular wonder-working: though Jesus himself considered his "signs and wonders" as greater and more persuasive proof than the inspired assurances of his only human witnesses, the Gospel-writers: "But I receive not testimony from man. . . . But I have greater witness than John; for . . . the same works that I do, bear witness of me, that the Father hath sent me" (Jno. v, 34, 36). And Jesus himself wholly discounts his own claims for himself, for he declares: "If I bear witness of myself, my witness is not true" (Jno. v, 31).

Therefore, with the testimony of "man," John and other Gospel-biographers discounted; with his own testimony for himself declared "not true"; with the "witness of the works" discredited as being the common arts of charlatans and false Pretenders, we must needs, in seeking proofs and satisfying evidences of the truth of claims that Jesus Christ is the true "Promised Messiah" of the Hebrew Prophets, turn to and examine these "prophecies," and the "internal evidences" of the Gospels, if haply they may prove themselves worthy of the high credit of truth.

The Gospel Records

The Jews, the People who lived in the devout expectation of the coming of the Messiah, and who are said to have seen all the "great signs and wonders" of Jesus,—as well of the numerous "false Christs" whom Jesus decried—the Jews believed not in Jesus as Messiah and King. Some fifty years after the death of Jesus, when a new generation, which had not seen these "great signs and wonders," had come on, the Gospel biographies and propaganda-Epistles began to be written, to further the propaganda of the new Faith.

The Jews still looked for their "promised" Messiah, promised and prophesied, it is said, in their ancient Scriptures. Obviously, there could be no Messiah who did not fit into and fulfill these various prophecies. Hence, the very first necessity for any Pretender for credence as Messiah—for the "false Christs" who, as Jesus avers, abounded—was to make himself, or be made out by his propagandists, to fit into the "prophecies" and thus fill the rôle of Fulfiller of Messianic Prophecy.

Ample stores of alleged "prophecy of Messiah" were at hand, in the ancient Scriptures of Israel. Of these prophecies the most curious feature, as the review of them to follow will remarkably verify, betraying a blood-relationship to Delphic Oracles, is their utter meaninglessness, or their capacity to mean anything or everything, according to the necessities of the person invoking them to serve his own purposes or the cause he seeks to promote. One would think, it may be remarked in passing, that an Allwise real God, intent upon revealing his awful purposes for the future of his Chosen People—and in the instance of the Christ, for the redemption of all the human race—would speak not in "dark sayings" but in plain, intelligible Hebrew, so that every one might know of a certainty and understand the Prophecy and recognize clearly its wonderful fulfillment. Thus only, would one think, could Yahveh's own test of true prophecy be intelligently and certainly applied, when a question arose: "If the thing follow not, nor come to pass, that is the thing which Yahveh hath not spoken, but the prophet hath spoken it presumptuously" (Deut. xviii, 22). Rather, as we will see, the chief characteristic of Prophecy as of Oracle is lack of precision of intelligent meaning; which gives it quite a latitude of interpretation and lends itself admirably to even maladroit manipulation by every one who raises the cry, "Lo, here is Christ, or there." But the Prophecies of the Messiah, and the Gospel interpretation of them, may be let now speak for themselves, and bear their own testimony.

The Jews knew their Scriptures and what sort of "Messiah" they were promised and expected: a lineal descendant of David King of Israel, who should himself be King of Israel and "establish the throne of David forever" in the restored national Land. Most special of all qualifications of Promised Messiahship was: "he shall deliver us from the Assyrian, when he cometh into our land" (Micah v, 5–6). None of the "false Christs" had met any of the "prophetic" prescriptions; and Jesus was hailed by the rabble as King but for one day. In beginning his campaign among the People, he sent forth his adjutants or Disciples, and straitly commanded them: "Go not into the way of the Gentiles; but go rather to the lost sheep of the house of Israel" (Matt. x, 5–6): so "he came unto his own, but his own received him not" (Jno. i, 11). But when his own received him not, but repudiated both his claim of Messiahship and his claim to be the actual Virgin-born Son of God (which was not an attribute of the prophetic Messiah),—"Lo, we turn to the Gentiles" (Acts xiii, 46), says Paul, who had now turned from being the chiefest persecutor of those who believed to become the Chief Propagandist of the new Faith of Dogma, formulated by himself.

The Gentiles were the superstitious Pagans of Palestine, Asia Minor and parts thereabouts; they were steeped in credulity in all the fables of all the gods of the heathen world. They knew nothing of the Jewish Scriptures or of the promised Messiah; they had no critical sense in religion, but "believed all things and hoped all things." A new God was to them just one more God among many: the Greeks had even an altar erected "To the Unknown God" (Acts xvii, 23). The Gentiles believed already in virgin-born gods and in resurrections from the dead: the Myths of Attis, Adonis, Isis, and Tammuz were accepted articles of their Pagan Faiths. Fertile ground for a new Faith with little or nothing new or strange about its beliefs and dogmas. So to the Pagan Gentiles the Propagandists turned, and fortified their propaganda with marvelous tales of venerable "Prophecies" wonderfully fulfilled: "and when the Gentiles heard this they were glad, and glorified the Word of Yahveh" (Acts xiii, 48).

It was among these Pagan Gentiles that the propaganda of the new Faith was chiefly conducted and mostly successful; and for these Gentile Pagans was it that the Gospel "Good News" and Epistles were chiefly written and published—a whole generation and more after the death and disappearance of the Divine Subject about whom it all was. Pagans whose Articles of Faith were the Myths of Jove and the Gods of Greece, Egypt and Rome, and all the Pantheon of the Orient, had little difficulty or scruple to "convert" from these crude superstitions and to accept full Faith of the new God, whose "Coming" had been prophesied in the ancient Books of Israel, and was wonderfully fulfilled—they were told—in the miraculous birth, life, death, and resurrection of Jesus of Nazareth, Son of Yahveh, Elohe Israel.

The inspired Formula of the new Faith is Paul's own Confession of Faith: "Believing all things which are written in the Prophets" (Acts xxiv, 14); and "believing all things, hoping all things" (2 Cor. xiii, 7); their Faith was to them "the substance of things hoped for, the evidence of things not seen" (Heb. xi, 1),—and not knowable:— "Hope that is seen is not hope: for what a man seeth, why doth he yet hope for?" (Rom. viii, 24).

We will now respectfully view the Divine Comedy—the Supreme Tragedy—of the "Promised Messiah," and briefly review the wonders of "Prophecy fulfilled in Jesus Christ."

1. The Miraculous "Virgin Birth" of Jesus

Matthew, whose Gospel was written later, comes first in the order of Gospels in our printed collections, rather naturally for the reason that he gives a detailed "revelation" of the manner of miraculous conception and virgin-birth of the Subject of his inspired Biography. He begins his Book with the genealogy of Jesus, which we elsewhere take notice of. He then proceeds with inspired pen to record:

"Now the birth of Jesus Christ was on this wise: When his mother Mary was espoused to Joseph, before they came together, she was found with child of the Holy Ghost (v. 18). Then Joseph her husband, being a just man, and not willing to make her a publick example, was minded to put her away privily (v. 19). But while he thought on these things, behold, the angel of Yahveh appeared unto him in a *dream*, saying, Joseph, thou son of David, fear not to take unto thee Mary thy wife: for that which is conceived in her is of the Holy Ghost (v. 20). (21)

And she shall bring forth a son, and thou shalt call his name *Jesus:* for he shall save his people from their sins."

The foregoing is pure Fiction; here follows the crowning instance wherein "the false pen of the Scribes hath wrought falsely"—

(22) "Now all this was done, that it might be fulfilled which was spoken of the *Lord*—(Heb. Yahveh) by the prophet, saying, (23) *Behold, a virgin shall be with child, and shall bring forth a son, and they shall call his name Emmanuel,* which being interpreted is, *God with us.*"

For this wonderful "prophecy" of the Virgin-birth of the Child Jesus, the marginal reference is to the Old Testament, Book of Isaiah, Chapter vii, v. 14, as the inspired "source" of the assertion made by Matthew. True, it says nothing of any miraculous pregnancy of any woman by the Holy Ghost, who was wholly unknown in the Old Testament; but this we do find, as rendered by the "false pen of the Scribes" who translated Isaiah:

"Therefore the Lord himself shall give you a sign: *behold, a virgin shall conceive, and bear a son, and shall call his name Immanuel*" (Is. vii, 14).

The King James, or Authorized Version or Translation, puts into the margin opposite this verse, the words "Or, Thou, O Virgin, shalt call" etc. Nothing like this is in the Hebrew text.

We turn to the Hebrew text of this most wonderful of the "prophecies"; and may well be amazed to find that it is falsely translated. The actual Hebrew words, read from right to left, and transliterated into English letters, so that the reader who knows not Hebrew may at least "catch" some words, the sacred words are:

"laken yittan *adonai* hu lakem oth hinneh *ha*-almah harah ve-yeldeth *ben* ve-karath shem-o immanuel."

Literally translated into English, in the exact order of the Hebrew words, the original "prophecy" truly reads:

"Therefore shall-give my-lord he (himself) to you sign behold *the*-maid *conceived* (*is* pregnant) and-*bear-eth* son and-*call-eth* name-his immanuel."

Here the word "harah" (conceived) is the Hebrew Perfect tense, which as in English represents past and completed action; there is not the remotest hint of future tense or time.   No Doctor of Divinity or scholar in Hebrew can or will deny this.

Moreover, this is confirmed by the more honest, yet deceptive Revised Version.   In its text of Isaiah vii, 14, it copies word for word the false translation of the King James; but it inserts figures in the text after the words "a virgin" and "shall conceive," and puts into the margin opposite, in small type, which not one in many thousands ever reads or would understand the significance of the true reading: "*the* virgin" and "*is with child*."   It was thus not some indefinite "a virgin" 750 years *in futuro*, who in the future "*shall* conceive" and *shall* bear a son, and "*shall* call" his name Immanuel; but it was some present, known and designate maiden, to whom the "prophecy" referred, who had already conceived, or was already pregnant and with child; and whose offspring should be the "sign" which "my lord" would give to Ahaz.   The honesty of the Translators and of Matthew in perverting this text of Isaiah into a "prophecy" of Jesus Christ is apparent.

The "Sign" of a False Prophecy

What really was Isaiah "prophesying" about and whereof was the "sign" which he persisted in thrusting upon Ahaz after the King had flatly refused to listen to it and had piously protested that "I will not ask (for a sign), neither will I tempt Yahveh"?

No lawyer or other intelligent person would for a moment jump at the meaning of a document from an isolated paragraph; would stultify himself if he should pretend to form or render an opinion without a careful study of the whole document.   The passage on which the opinion is sought must be taken with all its context or other contents of the document.   Knowledge of the whole must therefore be had before the meaning of any pertinent passage can be understood.

As this of the "prophecy" of the alleged "Virgin-birth of Jesus Christ" is the key-stone of the arch of the whole scheme of Christianity, it is of the highest importance to know and clearly understand, from the context, what Isaiah is recorded as so oracularly delivering himself about.   The whole of Chapter vii, or its material verses bearing upon the subject-matter of his "prophecy" must of necessity be presented to the reader.

In a word, Isaiah was speaking of a then pending war waged against Ahaz and Judah by the Kings of Israel and Syria, who were besieging Jerusalem; Isaiah volunteered his "virgin-born sign" in proof of his "prophecy"—shown false by the sequel—that the siege and war would fail by the defeat of the allied Kings. Here is the inspired text with its full context:

"1. And it came to pass in the days of Ahaz, son of, etc., King of Judah, that Rezin the King of Syria, and Pekah the King of Israel, went up toward Jerusalem to war against it, but could not prevail against it. 3. Then said Yahveh unto Isaiah, Go forth now to meet Ahaz, 4. and say unto him, Take heed, and be quiet; fear not, neither be faint-hearted. 7. Thus saith Yahveh Elohim, It shall not stand, neither shall it come to pass. . . .

"10. Moreover Yahveh spake again unto Ahaz (here Isaiah is not the medium), saying, 11. *Ask a sign* of Yahveh thy God; ask it either in the depth, or in the height above. 12. But Ahaz said, I will not ask, neither will I tempt Yahveh. 13. And *he* said, Hear ye now, O house of David; Is it a small thing for you to weary men, but will ye weary *my* God also? (here apparently Isaiah or some unknown medium is again speaking).

"14. *Therefore my Lord* (Heb. adonai, my lord) himself shall give you a *sign;* (honestly translated): *behold, the maid is with child,* and beareth a son and calleth his name Immanuel."

"15. Butter and honey shall he eat, that he may know to refuse the evil, and choose the good. 16. For *before the child* shall know to refuse the evil, and choose the good,—(that is, quite soon after its birth)— *the land that thou abhorest shall be forsaken of both her kings.*"

This about eating butter and honey, so that the Child should know good from evil, is none too lucid of meaning; nor the assurance that before this should come about, "the land which thou abhorest shall be forsaken of both her kings," is hardly more intelligible. But if meaning it has, it means—as elucidated in Chapter viii—that very soon after the promised "sign," Samaria, the land of Israel and its king Pekah, under the suzerainty of Rezin king of Syria, should be overthrown; and that the two kings should not prevail in their war against Judah.

The following vv. 17 to 24, to the end of Chapter vii, and which give the unique information that "Yahveh shall hiss for the fly that is in Egypt and for the bee that is in the land of Assyria" (v. 18), and assure us that "Yahveh shall shave with a razor which is hired" (v. 20), are altogether too oracular and cabalistic for modern understanding; but their perusal is recommended as a rare bit of inspiration.

Isaiah carries his peculiar line of "prophecy" over into Chapter viii, and after several verses utterly unintelligible, strikes the trail of his war prophecy again, thus:

"5. Yahveh also spake unto me again, saying, 6. Forasmuch as this people . . . rejoice in Rezin and in Remaliah's son (Pekah): 7. Now, therefore, behold, Yahveh bringeth upon them the King of Assyria, and all his glory; 8. And he shall pass through Judah; he shall overflow and go over; and the stretching out of his wings shall fill the breadth of thy land, O Immanuel."

No clearer proof could be that Isaiah, whatever he was trying to say, was not speaking of Jesus. In Chapter vii, he spoke of the war of the kings Rezin and Pekah, son of Remaliah, and offered a "sign" that their expedition would fail, this sign being the virgin-born child Immanuel. Immediately afterwards he predicts a further war upon Judah by the King of Assyria, and addresses his allocution to this same unborn or infant Immanuel, and says that Assyria will overrun "thy land, O Immanuel." Isaiah spoke simply, and falsely, of a "sign" to King Ahaz, as to the then pending war. Yet Matthew says that this Immanuel was a prophecy of Jesus; but how Jesus could be Immanuel and a "sign" of the result of a war 750 years previously, or the subject of the remarks of Isaiah about the Assyrian war of the same period, is not explained in any revelation I have yet come across. This pretense by Matthew is clearly unfounded and false.

Moreover, as this "sign" of the virgin-born child Immanuel, was proclaimed by Isaiah as a proof of the truth of his prophecy, I call special attention to the historical record of the result of this expedition of the Kings of Syria and Israel against Jerusalem and Ahaz. This is from the second volume of the Chronicles of Israel and Judah, Chapter xxviii, as follows:

"(1) Ahaz reigned sixteen years in Jerusalem: but he did not that which was right in the sight of Yahveh. (5) Wherefore Yahveh his God delivered him into the hand of the king of Syria; and they smote him, and carried away a great multitude of them captives, and brought them to Damascus. And he was also delivered into the hand of the king of Israel, who smote him with a great slaughter. (6) For Pekah the son of Remaliah slew in Judah an hundred and twenty thousand in one day, which were all valiant men: because they had forsaken Yahveh Elohim of their fathers. (8) And the children of Israel carried away captive of their brethren two hundred thousand women, sons, and daughters, and took also away much spoil from them, and brought them to Samaria."

So the "prophecy" is seen of itself to be false.

2. Where the King was Born

The second statement made by Matthew, in which he appeals to the prophets, is in Chapter ii, vv. 1 to 6, that when the "Wise Men" came from the East to Jerusalem in search of the newborn "King of the Jews," Herod sent for the chief priests and scribes and "demanded of them where Christ should be born." How Herod could call a baby a few days old, of whom he knew nothing, "Christ," is beside the present issue. "Christ" means "anointed," and Jesus was not "anointed" in any sense until thirty-odd years later, the woman broke the box of ointment over him just before his death. But Matthew asserts, in vv. 5 and 6:

"And they said unto him, In Bethlehem of Judea; for thus is it written by the prophet, (6) And thou Bethlehem, in the land of Judah, art not the least among the princes of Judah; for out of thee shall come a Governor, that shall rule my people Israel."

The marginal source reference of this prophecy is the Book of Micah, Chapter v, v. 2. This, with its pertinent context, reads as follows:

"(2) But thou, Bethlehem Ephratah, though thou be little among the thousands of Judah, yet out of thee shall he come forth unto me that is to be *ruler in Israel;* whose goings forth have been from of old, from everlasting. (5) And this man shall be the peace, *when the Assyrian shall come into our land:* and when he shall tread in our palaces, then shall we raise against him seven shepherds and eight principal men. (6) And they shall waste the land of Assyria with the sword, and the land of Nimrod: *thus shall he deliver us from the Assyrian, when he cometh into our land,* and when he treadeth within our borders."

Now, whatever this may have referred to, it referred to some leader who should arise to oppose the Assyrians. Nineveh, "that great city," the capital of Assyria, was destroyed, and Assyrian power ceased to exist, 606 years before Christ. This makes it most evident that Micah had no reference to Jesus; and it may seem an oddity that the chief priests and scribes, who always opposed and denied Jesus during his life, and sent him to his death, should have wittingly furnished Matthew with so potent a prophecy concerning him, when Jesus was but a few days old. If the chief priests and scribes knew that the infant Jesus was the Messiah, the fulfillment of Micah's prophecy, some may wonder why they did not help him to become indeed "a ruler in Israel" and its great deliverer.

3. "Out of Egypt"

Matthew's third invocation of the prophets, although the matter referred to was a past fact and not a prophecy of future fact, is also found in Chapter ii, when the Angel is said to have appeared to Joseph in a dream and told him to take Jesus to Egypt in order to escape Herod. I quote verses, where Joseph,

"(14) When he arose, he took the young child and his mother by night, and departed into Egypt: (15) And was there until the death of Herod: that it might be fulfilled which was spoken of Yahveh by the prophet, saying, Out of Egypt have I called my son."

The marginal reference for the source of this prophecy is to Hosea (xi, 1). This chapter is entitled by the Bible editors, "The ingratitude of Israel unto God for his benefits," and refers entirely to the past record of the people of Israel. I quote v. 1, supplemented by v. 5, which read:

"(1) When Israel was a child, then I loved him, and called my son out of Egypt. . . . (5) He shall not return into the land of Egypt, but the *Assyrian shall be his king,* because they refused to return."

Now, there is a marginal reference at this passage (v. 1), which refers to Exodus, iv, 22–23, as the source of Hosea's allusion to the people called "Israel" as the "son" of Yahveh, and refers to the fact of this "son" being in Egypt, and being "called" out of Egypt by Moses. Never once does the text say "I will call"—but "*called.*" The historical allusion, with its context, is as follows:

"(21) And Yahveh said unto Moses, (22) thou shalt say unto Pharaoh, Thus saith Yahveh, Israel is my son, even my first born; (23) and I say unto thee, Let my son go, that he may serve me."

From this it is clear that Hosea was looking into the far past and speaking of the exodus of the children of Israel out of Egypt; and was not peering into the dim future and speaking of the flight of the Joseph family into Egypt. So Matthew makes another false appeal to "prophecy."

4. "Out-Heroding" Herod

The fourth venture of Matthew citing the prophets is in the same Chapter (ii, 17–18), after relating the "Massacre of the Innocents" by Herod in his effort to murder the infant Jesus. I quote those verses, in which Matthew states:

"(17) *Then was fulfilled* that which was spoken by Jeremy the prophet, saying (18) In Rama there *was* a voice heard, lamentation, and weeping, and great mourning, Rachel weeping for her children, and would not be comforted, because they are not."

The marginal reference opposite this citation is to the Book of Jeremiah (xxxi, 15). The weeping Prophet was speaking of the utter desolation of the people on account of the Babylonian captivity, and threats of further destruction by Nebuchadnezzar, as any one reading the Chapter may see. I quote the verse referred to, which is as follows:

"(15) Thus saith Yahveh: A voice was heard in Ramah, lamentation and bitter weeping; Rachel weeping for her children refused to be comforted for her children, because they were not."

Jeremiah speaks of an event already happened, and quotes Yahveh as speaking in the past tense—"a voice *was* heard," because of the great afflictions caused by the Babylonians over 600 years before the episode related of Herod. The reader may draw his own conclusions as to the honesty of Matthew's use of this "prophecy" and its fulfillment under Herod. And not a word of uninspired human history records such an impossible massacre by the Roman King.

5. The "Nazarene"

The fifth in order occurs in the same Chapter (ii, 23), referring to their residence upon the return of Joseph and Jesus from Egypt. I quote it as follows:

"(23) And he came and dwelt in a city called Nazareth: that it might be fulfilled which was spoken by the prophets, He shall be called a *Nazarene.*"

This is a bit of fancy falsehood. There is not a word of mention in the Old Testament of such a place as Nazareth nor of *Nazarenes.* The marginal references to this v. 23 are two, Judges xiii, 5, and 1 Samuel, i, 11. These verses, and their context, refer to matters so far removed from Matthew's alleged "prophecy," that it is idle

to quote them. But here they are. In the first instance, the wife
of Manoah was childless; an Angel of Yahveh appeared to her, and
said:

"(5) Lo, thou shalt conceive, and bear a son; and no razor shall
come on his head: for the child shall be a *Nazarite* (Heb. Nazir) unto
God from the womb: and he shall begin *to deliver Israel out of the hand
of the Philistines.*"

The product of this angelic visitation was the giant-killer Samson, and he was to fight the Philistines; Jesus never did. The second
reference has to do with a like angelic aid to Hannah, who made
a vow to never let a razor come upon the head of her prospective
son Samuel. Those unkempt offsprings of angelic intercourse were
called *Nazarites*. This is the closest that the Old Testament gets
to Nazareth, and its inhabitant *Nazarenes*. So Matthew's invocation of the "prophets" is far afield both in form and substance.

6. THE GREAT LIGHT

The sixth so-called "prophecy" relating to Jesus, which Matthew
invokes in this behalf, is in Chapter iv, 12–16, a paragraph standing
unrelated to anything else in the Chapter. I copy the verses as
follows:

"(12) Now when Jesus had heard that John was cast into prison, he
departed into Galilee; (13) And leaving Nazareth, he came and dwelt
in Capernaum, which is upon the sea coast, in the borders of Zabulon
and Nephthalim: (14) That it might be fulfilled which was spoken by
Esaias the prophet, saying, (15) The land of Zabulon, and the land of
Nephthalim, by the way of the sea, beyond Jordan, Galilee of the Gentiles; (16) The people which sat in darkness saw a great light; and to
them which sat in the region and shadow of death light is sprung up."

We are given as marginal reference of authority for this, Isaiah
ix, 1–2. As Matthew so mutilates and distorts his quotation, I shall
have to direct attention of the reader to the several marked discrepancies and contortions which he makes of his texts, and explain,
by their context, what Isaiah was really saying:

"(1) Nevertheless the dimness shall not be such as was in her vexation, when at the first he lightly afflicted the land of Zebulun, and the
land of Naphtali, and afterwards did more grievously afflict her by the
way of the sea, beyond Jordan, in Galilee of the nations. (2) The people
that walked in darkness have seen a great light: they that dwell in the
land of the shadow of death, upon them hath the light shined,"

It will be noticed that Matthew entirely omits all the words which show that Isaiah was speaking of some past and accomplished historical fact, relating to the afflictions which the tribal sections mentioned had already suffered. These explanatory and historical words, to repeat them for the reader's better catching their significance, are: "Nevertheless, the dimness shall not be such as (was) in her vexation, when at the first he lightly afflicted Zabulon and Naphthali, and afterwards did more grievously afflict her." After thus depriving the verse of all sense, Matthew retains the simple geographical names as follows: "the land of Zabulon, and the land of Nephthalim, by the way of the sea, beyond Jordan, Galilee of the Gentiles." And he converts these meaningless words, taken out of their sense in a historical past context, into a prophecy, which he says was fulfilled because Jesus went to the town of Capernaum in that part of the country.

But there is more to it, to which I will briefly call attention, for better understanding. The verse opens with the words "nevertheless the dimness." Necessarily this refers to something which has preceded in the text. This is found in Chapter viii, of which Chapter ix is simply a continuation. But Chapter viii is so incoherent, speaking of "seeking unto them that have familiar spirits, and unto wizards that peep, and that mutter," that it is hardly possible to know what Isaiah is "raving" about. However, in the last v. 22, he denounces such seekers after wizards, and delivers himself of this: "(22) And they shall look unto the earth; and behold trouble and darkness, dimness of anguish; and they shall be driven to darkness." Then Chapter ix opens with the words quoted, "Nevertheless, the dimness shall not be such as was in her vexation, when at the first he lightly afflicted the land of Zebulun and the land of Naphthali, and afterwards did more grievously afflict her," etc. Isaiah then continues, in v. 2: "The people that walked in darkness have seen a great light," etc. All this, whatever unapparent sense there may be in it, refers to past facts and events, and the reader may judge of Matthew's accuracy in calling it a "prophecy" fulfilled by Jesus going to Capernaum.

7. He Bore Our Infirmities

The seventh appeal of Matthew to "prophecy" is in Chapter viii, 16–17, which are as follows:

"(16) When the even was come, they brought unto him many that were possessed with devils: and he cast out the spirits with his word, and healed all that were sick; (17) That it might be fulfilled which was spoken by Esaias the prophet, saying, Himself took our infirmities, and bare our sicknesses."

For this the marginal reference carries us to Isaiah liii, 4, which I copy as follows:

"Surely he hath borne our griefs, and carried our sorrows: yet we did esteem him stricken, smitten of God, and afflicted."

All this is in the past tense, showing Isaiah lamenting over some "departed friend," who was esteemed to have been "smitten of God," and now dead. It can have no possible reference to Jesus Christ, Yahveh's "beloved son in whom I am well pleased," engaged in the divine work of casting out devils and healing the sick and smitten; never was Jesus at any time "smitten of God." So Matthew again uses a few words out of their context, misquotes them at that, and calls a lamenting statement over some past fact a "prophecy" of future event.

8. The "Bruised Reed"

The eighth instance of Matthew in adapting what he calls "prophecy" to his own uses, as proof that his account is the truth, occurs in Chapter xii, vv. 14 to 21. The passage is long, but as it is necessary to compare it with the reputed "prophecy" in order to show Matthew's singular misquotation, and misuse, I copy it entire as follows:

"(14) Then the Pharisees went out, and held a council against him, how they might destroy him. (15) But when Jesus knew it, he withdrew himself from thence: and great multitudes followed him, and he healed them all; (16) And charged them that they should not make him known; (17) That it might be fulfilled which was spoken by Esaias the prophet, saying, (18) Behold my servant, whom I have chosen; my beloved in whom my soul is well pleased: I will put my spirit upon him, and he shall shew judgment to the Gentiles. (19) He shall not strive, nor cry; neither shall any man hear his voice in the streets. (20) A bruised reed shall he not break, and smoking flax shall he not quench, till he send forth judgment unto victory. (21) And in his name shall the Gentiles trust."

The marginal reference for the source of this is Isaiah, xlii, 1–4, as follows:

"(1) Behold my servant, whom I uphold; mine elect, in whom my soul delighteth; I have put my spirit upon him: he shall bring forth judgment to the Gentiles. (2) He shall not cry, nor lift up, nor cause his voice to be heard in the street. (3) A bruised reed shall he not break, and the smoking flax shall he not quench: he shall bring forth judgment unto truth. (4) He shall not fail nor be discouraged, till he have set judgment in the earth: and the isles shall wait for his law."

Who "my servant" upon whom "I have" put my spirit, here spoken of is, Isaiah does not tell us; but certainly the description does not in the least fit Jesus. Jesus was discouraged, and he enjoined secrecy on all his followers and fled to Gethsemane, where he collapsed in despair, as the whole unhappy scene in the Garden shows, and he never saw "victory"! And Isaiah never at all said what Matthew attributes to him in v. 21: "And in his name shall the Gentiles trust"; this is entirely new, made of the whole cloth, and the whole "prophecy" is misquoted and misapplied.

9. "The King Cometh"

The ninth resort by Matthew to this method of proof that things done by Jesus were fulfillment of ancient prophecy, is found in Chapter xxi, vv. 1 to 5, which are as follows:

"(1) And when they drew nigh into Jerusalem, and were come to Bethphage, unto the mount of Olives, then sent Jesus two 'disciples, (2) Saying unto them, Go into the village over against you, and straightway ye shall find an ass tied, and a colt with her: loose them, and bring them unto me. (3) And if any man say ought unto you, ye shall say, The Lord hath need of them; and straightway he will send them. (4) All this was done, that it might be fulfilled which was spoken by the prophet, saying, (5) Tell ye the daughter of Sion, Behold, thy king cometh unto thee, meek, and sitting upon an ass, and a colt the foal of an ass."

This is an "ass" misquotation of alleged prophecy, as is shown by turning to the marginal reference, Zechariah, ix, 9, which I quote as follows:

"(9) Rejoice greatly, O daughter of Zion; shout, O daughter of Jerusalem: behold, thy King cometh unto thee: he is just, and having salvation; lowly, and riding upon an ass, and upon a colt the foal of an ass."

The Book of Zechariah treats of the return of parts of the Jewish tribes from captivity in Babylon, by leave of King Darius;

and Zechariah is very jubilant over it, and indulges in some very flighty exultations about it. In the previous Chapter viii, Zechariah declares:

(8) "Thus saith Yahveh of hosts: behold, I will save my people from the east country, and from the west country; (9) And I will bring them, and they shall dwell in the midst of Jerusalem."

And, in Chapter ix, after the "ass entry of the King," and amid other exultations, Zechariah exclaims, in further evidence that he was speaking of the "return from captivity," and not of Jesus entering Jerusalem:

"(12) Turn you to the strong hold, ye prisoners of hope: (16) And Yahveh their God shall save them in that day: (17) For how great is his goodness, and how great is his beauty! corn shall make the young men cheerful, and new wine the maids."

Zechariah is not here very lucid, but in any event he was exulting over the "return of the captivity," and not over Jesus Christ, as Matthew would have believe.

10. What is this One?

Matthew's tenth appeal to the prophets, Chapter xxvi, 51–56, is too general to permit of specific contradiction by comparing his authority. I refer to those verses, but will simply state their substance. It is the story of Peter cutting off the ear of the high priest's servant with a sword on the night of the arrest of Jesus. Jesus told him to put up his sword, and said that he could call down twelve legions of angels to his defence if he should pray for them. And he asks:

"(54) But then how shall the scriptures be fulfilled, that thus it must be?"

Then Matthew puts in, and says:

"(56) But all this was done, that the scriptures of the prophets might be fulfilled."

He does not say which scriptures nor which prophets; but the Bible editors come to his aid and give a marginal reference to the much abused Isaiah (liii, 7), which we have above referred to and shown to be all in the past tense, in which Isaiah bewails his anonymous "departed friend" who was "smitten of God." Another editorial reference is far afield to the Book of Lamentations, iv, 20, which may be offered for what it is worth:

"(20) The breath of our nostrils, the anointed of Yahveh, was taken in their pits, of whom he said, Under his shadow shall we live among the heathen."

The Lamentator is here bewailing the desolation of Jerusalem under the captivity of the "heathen" Babylonians, as appears from the entire epic of woe, but particularly in the preceding verses 11 and 12, which I quote in this connection.

"(11) Yahveh hath accomplished his fury; he hath poured out his fierce anger, and hath kindled a fire in Zion, and it hath devoured the foundations thereof. (12) The kings of the earth, and all the inhabitants of the world, would not have believed that the adversary and the enemy should have entered into the gates of Jerusalem."

So it is plain that the writer was speaking of the ruin of Jerusalem. But it further appears of whom he was speaking by the terms "the breath of our nostrils, the anointed of Yahveh." All the Jewish Kings were the "anointed of Yahveh"—just as modern ones also are said to be. A marginal reference opposite these words of Lamentations is to Jeremiah, lii, 9, which I will quote together with the preceding verse 8, so as to get the full context.

"(8) But the army of the Chaldeans pursued after the king, and overtook Zedekiah in the plains of Jericho; and all his army was scattered from him. (9) Then they took the king, and carried him up unto the king of Babylon to Riblah in the land of Hamath, where he gave judgment upon him."

And for full measure of the woe which moved the Lamentations, I add verse 10:

"And the king of Babylon slew the sons of Zedekiah before his eyes: he slew also all the princes of Judah in Riblah."

Hinc illae lacrimae! So Matthew is seen again twisting historical past facts into pretended prophecies fulfilled by Jesus,

11. The "Potter's Field"

For the eleventh time Matthew tells us something, and invokes the prophets, the passage being the story of Judas and the thirty pieces of silver, in Chapter xxvii, 3–10, which I refer to, and state the substance. Matthew says that Judas repented of his bargain of betrayal and took the money back to the chief priests; and threw the money at their feet and went and hanged himself. The holy priests who had paid the thirty pieces for the "betrayal of innocent blood," were punctilious about putting the price of the blood back into the treasury of Yahveh, so

"(7) They took counsel, and bought with them the potter's field, to bury strangers in.

(8) Wherefore that field is called, The field of blood, unto this day. (9) Then was fulfilled that which was spoken by Jeremy the prophet, saying, And they took the thirty pieces of silver, the price of him that was valued, whom they of the children of Israel did value; (10) And gave them for the potter's field, as Yahveh appointed me."

If I were arguing this as a case in court, I would indict this in strong terms. But as I am simply offering appeals to "prophecy" with a little necessary comment, I merely let the reader compare it with Jeremiah's words, in his Chapter xxxii, 6–15, to which I refer the reader. But as they have no more to do with the high priests' buying the potter's field with the thirty pieces of silver, than they have to do with my buying my house in this City, I will not copy them into the record. They simply refer to Hanameel coming to Jeremiah in prison, "according to the word of Yahveh," and saying to him,

"(8) Buy my field, I pray thee, that is in Anathoth; (9) And I bought the field of Hanameel, my uncle's son, that was in Anathoth and weighed him the money, even seventeen shekels of silver."

This is all there is to "that which was spoken by Jeremy the prophet," pretended to be fulfilled by buying the potter's field with the blood-money of Judas Iscariot.

But the Bible editors give another marginal reference, not to "Jeremy the prophet," but to Zechariah, Chapter xi, 10–14, for the reason, presumably, that a "potter" and "thirty pieces of silver" are mentioned. So that no opportunity to let Matthew and his editors vindicate themselves even once may be denied them, I quote these incoherent verses, without comment, as they are not worth it—only to say, what the reader can readily see, that they have no earthly connection with Iscariot's thirty pieces, or with any thing else sanely imaginable:

"(10) And I took my staff, even Beauty, and cut it asunder, that I might break my covenant which I had made with all the people. (11) And it was broken in that day: and so the poor of the flock that waited upon me knew that it was the word of Yahveh. (12) And I said unto them, If ye think good, give me my price; and if not, forbear. So they weighed for my price thirty pieces of silver. (13) And Yahveh said unto me, Cast it unto the potter; a good price that I was prized at of them. And I took the thirty pieces of silver, and cast them to the potter in the house of Yahveh. (14) Then I cut asunder mine other staff, even Bands, that I might break the brotherhood between Judah and Israel."

Judas Hanged Himself?

Before passing from Matthew's story of Judas, who, he says, (verse 5) "departed, and went, and hanged himself," I may call attention to the fact that Matthew is flatly contradicted on this point by whoever wrote "The Acts of the Apostles" (supposed to be the Evangelist Luke). This authority, also indulging in some dubious references, makes Peter tell a different story from Matthew, as appears from Chapter i, 15–18, as follows:

"(15) And in these days Peter stood up in the midst of the disciples, and said, (16) Men and brethren, this scripture must needs have been fulfilled, which the Holy Ghost by the mouth of David spake before concerning Judas, which was guide to them that took Jesus. (17) For he was numbered with us and had obtained part of this ministry. (18) Now this man purchased a field with the reward of iniquity; and falling headlong he burst asunder in the midst and all his bowels gushed out."

As is seen, according to this delicate gloat over the ill-fate of an apostate brother apostle, it was Iscariot himself that bought a field —and not a "potter's field"—but an estate—with the thirty pieces which he had received as "the reward of iniquity"; he did not, therefore, "repent" and return the money to the priests, and go hang himself; but he accidentally fell and ruptured himself fatally.

Peter's reference to David as speaking, one thousand years previously, of Judas, is of a piece with some of the false pretenses of Peter's pretended "successors" ever since. The side reference for

David's reputed remarks about Judas, is to Psalms xli, 9, which I quote:

"Yea, mine own familiar friend, in whom I trusted, which did eat of my bread, hath lifted up his heel against me."

Now, David had troubles of his own, without bothering himself with Judas a thousand years ahead. The whole Psalm xli shows that Peter ignorantly or wilfully falsified. David was pleading with Yahveh for himself alone, as appears by the verses which I will quote:

"(4) I said, Yahveh, be merciful unto me: heal my soul; for I have sinned against thee. (5) Mine enemies speak evil of me, When shall he die, and his name perish? . . . (9) Yea, mine own familiar friend, in whom I trusted, which did eat of my bread, hath lifted up his heel against me. (10) But thou, Yahveh, be merciful unto me, and raise me up, that I may requite them."

No words are needed to show that David was speaking of his own present troubles, and nothing else. And he prays his Yahveh to be merciful and raise him up, so that he could take vengeance on his enemy. And David says no such thing as "he was numbered among us, and had obtained part of this ministry." This is a pure invention of Peter, often imitated by his "Successors" since.

In this connection, read Acts i, v. 19, about the "field of blood," which flatly contradicts Matt. xxvii, 7–8, as to the origin of the term; and the finish of Peter's false appeals to "prophecy" by David regarding Judas, "and his bishoprick let another take" (Acts i, 20), is shown absolutely false and ridiculous by the reference cited, (Ps. cix, 8), as the context of the whole Psalm makes clear as day.

12. PARTING HIS GARMENTS

The twelfth and last of Matthew's appeals to the prophets—which we will here notice—is indulged at the time of all others when the occasion would seem to have led him to quote accurately and to tell the truth. In Chapter xxvii, 35, right under the shadow of the Cross, he says:

"(35) And they crucified him, and parted his garments, casting lots; that it might be fulfilled which was spoken by the prophet, They parted my garments among them, and upon my vesture did they cast lots."

The reference is to Psalm xxii, 18, where David is again made responsible for a pretended prophecy—though David is not usually, like Saul, "numbered among the prophets." Matthew misquotes the words of David, spoken in the present tense, and puts them into the past tense, and changes the pronoun "my" to "him," to make it apply to the acts of the Roman soldiers. I quote the words of David:

"(18) They part my garments among them, and cast lots upon my vesture."

Again David is bewailing his own troubles, in the fanciful imagery of Oriental poetry. He begins the Psalm, which is a song inscribed "to the Chief Musician Aijeleth," with the same words quoted by Jesus on the Cross: "My God, my God, why hast thou forsaken me!" and proceeds in language which he himself calls "the words of my roaring." Among the many "roaring" things he says about himself, I quote a very few:

"(12) Many bulls have compassed me; (13) They gaped upon me with their mouths, as a ravening and roaring lion. (14) All my bones are out of joint: my heart is like wax; it is melted in the midst of my bowels (David evidently wasn't up on anatomy, and didn't know of the diaphragm). (16) For dogs have compassed me: the assembly of the wicked have inclosed me: they pierced my hands and my feet (Wonder that Matthew didn't use this apt phrase as a prophecy of what they did to Jesus!) (17) I may tell all my bones: they look and stare upon me." Then follows the casting of lots over his clothes.

How far these "words of roaring" applied to Jesus on the Cross, as Matthew avers one verse of them did, and how correct Matthew is in his use of so-called prophecy, I leave now with the reader, for this is the end of Matthew's dealings with the Prophets. I pass now to Mark.

MARK'S APPEALS TO PROPHECY

Mark is quite sparing of prophecy, but no less unsuccessful in its use.

1. TO "PREPARE THE WAY"

His book opens with a very fanciful vision of the Day of Judgment converted into a prophecy concerning John the Baptist as the herald of Jesus. In Chapter i, 1–2, Mark says:

"(1) The beginning of the gospel of Jesus Christ, the Son of God;

(2) As it is written in the prophets, Behold, I send my messenger before thy face, which shall prepare thy way before thee."

The marginal reference here is to the Book of the last of the Prophets, Malachi, Chapter iii, 1, which, together with its context, shows what it was that Malachi was beholding:

"(1) Behold, I will send my messenger, and he shall prepare the way before me: and Yahveh, whom ye seek, shall suddenly come to his temple, even the messenger of the covenant, whom ye delight in: behold, he shall come, saith Yahveh of hosts. (2) But who may abide the day of his coming? and who shall stand when he appeareth? for, he is like a refiner's fire and like fullers' soap. (3) And he shall sit as a refiner and a purifier of silver; and he shall purify the sons of Levi, and purge them as gold and silver, they may offer unto Yahveh an offering in righteousness."

Malachi carried his vision over into Chapter iv, which Chapter is of only six verses, and is headed by the Bible editor's "Elijah's coming and office." I copy the pertinent verses, 1 and 5:

"(1) For behold, the day cometh, that shall burn as an oven; and all the proud, yea, and all that do wickedly, shall be stubble: and the day that cometh shall burn them up, saith Yahveh of hosts, that it shall leave them neither root nor branch. (5) Behold, I will send you Elijah the prophet before the coming of the great and dreadful day of Yahveh."

It is thus clear that Malachi was "seeing things" concerning the "great and dreadful day of Yahveh," and said that Elijah would be sent ahead as sort of press-agent and preparations committee. This vision certainly has nothing to do with John the Baptist or with Jesus, who both denied that they were Elijah (Jno. i, 20–21; Matt. xvi, 13); though Matthew makes Jesus say that John *is* Elijah (Matt. xi, 14).

In this connection, to show a contradiction of inspiration, it may be mentioned that Matthew makes a similar claim of prophecy in behalf of John the Baptist, in Chapter iii, 3, but cites a different source. He says:

"(1) And in those days cometh John the Baptist, preaching in the wilderness of Judea; (3) For this is he that was spoken of by the prophet Esaias, saying, The voice of one crying in the wilderness, Prepare ye the way of Yahveh, make his paths straight."

Matthew's reference is to Isaiah, xl, 3, which reads a little differently:

"The voice of one that crieth, Prepare ye in the wilderness the way of Yahveh, make straight in the desert a highway for our God."

In verse 6 he adds: "The voice of one saying Cry. And one said, What shall I cry? All flesh is grass," etc. John the Baptist is not reported as having made any such cry in the wilderness: it is all simply poetic frenzy, the meaning of which, if any it have, being not yet revealed or unraveled.

2. "Numbered among Transgressors"

The second and last reference by Mark to "prophecy" is in Chapter xv, 27–28, which read as follows:

"(27) And with him they crucify two thieves; (28) And the scripture was fulfilled, which saith, "And he was numbered with the transgressors."

Here again we are referred to that inexhaustible source of pretended prophecy, Isaiah liii, which throughout is in the past tense, and is a lamentation and eulogy over some dead friend. Any righteous man who is put to death unjustly or upon false accusations, may be said to be "numbered with the transgressors." There is no "prophecy" in this.

This ends the references to alleged prophecies of Jesus by Mark. The two other Evangelists, Luke and John, mention very few "prophecies" as being fulfilled in Jesus, but they are as true as the balance. One or the other mentions such instances as riding on the ass and casting lots for the garments, which we have already introduced from Matthew, and will not repeat. The few remaining instances will now be considered.

Luke Cites Prophecy

The first of Luke's is in Chapter i, 67 to 80. Luke does not himself invoke the so-called prophecies, but puts them into the mouth of Zacharias, the father of John the Baptist. In offering this remarkable reference to "prophecy," I call attention to some very singular features. Luke says that when the child John was born (v. 67), "his father Zacharias was filled with the Holy Ghost, and prophesied, saying." Now, what Zacharias said related exclusively to his own child John, but he cites the exact same "prophecies" as applying to John which are always invoked as applying to Jesus. The Bible editors recognized this, and straddled by heading the Chapter, "The prophecy of Zacharias, both of Christ, and of John." But John was born *six months before* Jesus was born. It was on the *eighth day after* the birth of John, and at his "christening," that Zacharias, having been stricken dumb as a "sign" of John's birth to the old and barren Elizabeth, wrote "his name is John," then recovered his voice, and "was filled with the Holy Ghost, and prophesied." Being "filled with the Holy Ghost," he was consequently fully "inspired," and must have spoken knowingly and truly. Being so filled, he "prophesied"—of his own son John—saying:

"(68) Blessed be Yahveh God of Israel; for he hath visited and redeemed his people, (69) And hath raised up an horn of salvation for us, in the house of his servant David: . . . (76) And *thou* child, shalt be called the *Prophet of the Highest,* for thou shalt *go before the face of Yahveh* to *prepare his ways:* (77) To give knowledge of salvation unto his people, by the remission of their sins, (78) Through the tender mercy of our God; whereby the day-spring from on high hath visited us, (79) To give light to them that sit in darkness and in the shadow of death, to guide our feet into the way of peace. (80) And the child grew, and waxed strong in spirit, and was in the deserts till the day of his shewing unto Israel."

Zacharias clearly speaks all this only of his son John. But whether of John or Jesus, or both, the result is the same: they apply to neither, as is very plain to see. The marginal references to "prophecy" on behalf of his son John, together with their respective contexts, are:

Chapter i, verse 69, refers to Psalm cxxxii, 17: "There will I make the horn of David to Bud: I have ordained a lamp for my anointed." This "anointed" is pretended to be John or Jesus. A few anterior verses will show who the "anointed" was—King David himself. He begins the Psalm,

"(1) Yahveh, remember David, and all his afflictions. (10) For thy servant David's sake turn not away the face of thine anointed. (11) Yahveh hath sworn in truth unto David: he will not turn from it: Of the *fruit of thy body* will I set upon thy throne. (12) If *thy children* will keep my covenant and my testimony that I shall teach them, their children shall also *sit upon thy throne for evermore.* (13) For Yahveh hath chosen Zion; (14) This is my rest forever: here will I dwell; (17) There will I make the horn of David to bud: I have ordained a lamp for my anointed."

All this is about a long line of kingly successors of the house of King David: nothing of Zacharias' son John or of Jesus, neither of whom ever sat on the throne of David.

"Genealogies" of Jesus

In entire disproof of this reference to Jesus as being a "bud of the horn of David," or, as in the next "prophecy" which I have to offer, a "Branch of David," I wish to offer a bit of collateral evidence proving that Jesus was in nowise "of the house of David," as is so often assured in the New Testament. Matthew and Luke both give detailed reputed "genealogies of Jesus Christ, the son of David." Matthew, Chapter i, verses 1 to 17, and Luke, Chapter iii, verses 23 to 38, record these "genealogies," which are totally and with but few exceptions, different and contradictory, except only the name of David at one end and of Joseph at the other. These two sections of verses are referred to for comparison. Matthew records twenty-eight generations between David and Joseph, while Luke avers and records forty-three generations, every name but three intermediates in each "genealogy" being totally different. Matthew derives Joseph from David through Solomon and Bathsheba; then on through Rehoboam, son of Solomon, down to "Joseph the son of JACOB." But Luke derives the ancestry from David through "Nathan, the son of David" down to "Joseph, the son of Heli," with but three intermediate ancestors of the same name as those vouched by Matthew. But, in either event, and from whichever "genealogy," Jesus could not be the son of Joseph, and hence of David, if it is true, as Matthew quotes the Angel as having said to Joseph in a dream:

"(20) Joseph, thou son of David, fear not to take thee Mary thy wife: for that which is conceived in her is of the Holy Ghost. (21) And thou shalt call his name Jesus."

For as "Joseph, thou son of David" was not, according to this dream, the father of Jesus, either line of descent from David, whether Matthew's or Luke's, was broken, and the rather attenuated blood of David did not at all pass into Jesus. It is as if the first husband of some woman had been the son of George Washington, but died without child, and the widow married a Mr. Smith, and they had a little George Washington Smith: certainly this offspring would not be a "son" of the Father of his Country, not even by the "bar-sinister" or left-handed.

2. The first reference for verse 70 is to Jeremiah xxiii, 5–6; their context in verses 7 and 8, which I add, might honestly have been also referred to. They are as follows:

"(5) Behold, the days come, saith Yahveh, that I will raise unto David a righteous Branch, and a King shall reign and prosper, and shall execute judgment and justice in the earth. (6) In his days Judah shall be saved and Israel shall dwell safely: and this is his name whereby he shall be called, Yahveh Our Righteousness. (7) Therefore, behold, the days come, saith Yahveh, that they shall no more say, Yahveh liveth, which brought up the children of Israel out of the land of Egypt; (8) But, Yahveh liveth, which brought up and which led the seed of the house of Israel out of the north country, and from all countries whither I had driven them; and they shall dwell in their own land."

All this refers to a righteous King of the dynasty of David, who "shall reign and prosper"; and "in his days" Judah and Israel shall be saved and live in safety; for under this King Yahveh "led the seed of the house of Israel out of the north country and from all the countries" where they were scattered, "and they shall dwell in their own land." No language could be plainer than that this "Branch of David," was to be a secular King who should, as Zachariah himself says, "save us from our enemies, and from the hand of all that hate us" (70). Neither son John nor Jesus was this man, nor was a King, or did any of these heroic things. And Jeremiah's "prophecy" failed, for no such deliverance ever came. So much for all this.

But Zacharias, filled with inspiration, applies these prophecies to his son John; others apply them to Jesus, the "Branch of the Stem of David," so often referred to; they refer to neither. Another marginal reference is to Daniel ix, 24; but Infinite Wisdom alone could tell what this is about, so I pass it.

This disposes of and discredits Luke; so we take up John.

John Appeals to Prophecy

1. A Prophecy Puzzle

The first "prophecy" noticed is in Chapter i, verse 45, in which John says:

"Philip findeth Nathaniel, and saith unto him, We have found him, of whom Moses in the law, and the prophets, did write, Jesus of Nazareth, the son of Joseph."

This brings on such an intricacy of reference and cross-reference, that merely to read them and try to disentangle such meaning as they may have, would certainly affect one's mind, as was Don Quixote's from a like exercise with his books of knight-errantry. So I shall give only a few samples, and leave any reader who has nothing better to do, and is willing to take the risk, to unravel the rest.

The first reference is to Genesis, iii, 15, the story of Eve and the Serpent, and Yahveh's saying that there should be enmity between her seed and the Serpent's seed. As nobody rationally believes that such a scene and colloquy ever occurred, what was not said does not signify; it means nothing anyhow, as demonstrated elsewhere. A *bona fide* God could speak more to the point than this jargon, if he wanted to make a "prophecy" of anything, and especially of so fateful an event.

The next reference is to Genesis xlix, 10, which I will quote with its context:

"(10) The sceptre shall not depart from Judah, nor a law giver from between his feet, until Shiloh come: and unto him shall the gathering of the people be. (11) Binding his foal unto the vine, and his ass's colt unto the choice vine; he washed his garments in wine, and his clothes in the blood of grapes: (12) His eyes shall be red with wine, and his teeth white with milk."

Whatever this red-eyed drunkard was, it can hardly be believed to be a prophetic portrayal of Jesus, who was neither a wine-bibber nor held a sceptre as King of Judah. The next reference is to Deuteronomy xviii, 18, which, as Jesus himself is made to refer to this later by John, I will pass it until we reach it in regular order. This ends these references to Moses as having written of Jesus; the other references are to the prophets, many of which we have already "weighed in the balances and found wanting" in truth. All the others will be found of exactly the same stripe, or even more meaningless and inapplicable to Jesus.

2. "For Moses Wrote of Me" (Jesus)

The second of John's appeals to prophecy occurs in Chapter v, verse 46, where John puts into the mouth of Jesus a false statement of pretended "prophecy" concerning himself; which verse, with others explanatory of it, I quote. John makes Jesus say:

"(46) For had ye believed Moses, ye would have believed me: for he wrote of me. (47) But if ye believe not his writings, how shall ye believe my words."

This latter verse, 47, is reserved for future consideration; we will run down the statement of verse 46—"for Moses wrote of me." In the course of discussion we may make some allusion to the point of fact as to whether Moses wrote anything at all which is attributed to him. We will connect this statement by cross-reference with a similar statement of Acts, Chapter iii, verse 22, to get the full force of the combined declarations:

"(22) For Moses truly said unto the fathers, A prophet shall Yahveh your God raise up unto you of your brethren, like unto me; him shall ye hear in all things whatsoever he shall say unto you."

The reference opposite these companion verses take us back to the citations we have last reviewed, and particularly to the so-called "Fifth Book of Moses," or Deuteronomy, Chapter xviii, verses 17 and 18. And Jesus and the author of Acts call this a "prophecy" concerning Jesus; saying that "Moses wrote this of me." I offer in evidence what "Moses" wrote:

(17) And Yahveh said unto me, (18) I will raise them up a Prophet from among their brethren, like unto thee and will put my words in his mouth; and he shall speak unto them all that I shall command him."

Who, then, was this prophet whom Yahveh was to raise up out of "thy brethren" like unto Moses, and to whom they were to hearken in all things which he commanded them? Moses if he wrote the Five Books, himself tells us, or whoever wrote them tells us. For, in Numbers, Chapter xxvii, verse 12, Yahveh told Moses to go up into Mt. Abarim, "and see the land which I have given unto the children of Israel":

"(13) And when thou hast seen it, thou shalt be gathered unto thy people. (15) And Moses spake unto Yahveh saying, (16) Let Yahveh set a man over the congregation, (17) Which may go out before them, and lead them. (18) And Yahveh said unto Moses, Take thee Joshua the son of Nun, a man in whom is the spirit, and lay thine hand upon him; (19) And set him before all the congregation; and give him a charge in their sight. (20) And thou shalt put some of thine honor upon him, that all the congregation of the children of Israel may be obedient. (22) And Moses did as Yahveh commanded him: and he took Joshua," etc.

It is plain from this and the other alleged "prophesies" referred to by Jesus and the Evangelists, that Moses did not write of Jesus, nor did the prophets speak of him; but of Joshua as the immediate successor of Moses as leader of the Chosen People.

3. Who Hath Believed? And Why Not?

The third essay of John to fulfill "prophecy" is a two-horned affair and a double imposition on Isaiah, as usual. I quote John, Chapter xii, verses 36 to 40, where he says:

"(36) These things spake Jesus, and he departed and hid himself from them. (37) But though he had done so many signs before them, yet they believed not on him: (38) that the word of Isaiah the prophet might be fulfilled, which he spake:—Yahveh, who hath believed our report? And to whom hath the arm of Yahveh been revealed. (39) For this cause they could not believe, for that Isaiah said again, (40) He hath blinded their eyes, and he hardened their heart; Lest they should see with their eyes, and perceive with their heart, and should turn, and I should heal them."

The first reference, about believing our report, is to that mine of "near-prophecy," Isaiah liii, verse 1. I can see no connection between "not believing our report" which would be of things past and unknown to the persons to whom the report is told, and not believing in a person and things seen with one's own eyes, some seven centuries later, as was the case with those "before" whose eyes Jesus did "so many signs." And further, Isaiah is speaking about the "report" of himself and other prophets: "Who hath believed *our* report?" It is idle to say more about this phase of it.

The other horn of this dilemma is utterly false, and implies an abhorrent proposition. John says that the Jews who saw the many signs of Jesus "believed not on him." But why not? John tells us why, saying positively: "For this cause they *could not* believe," for that, as Isaiah (vi, 9–10) said again, "He (Yahveh) hath blinded their eyes and hardened their heart, lest they should turn (repent), and I shall heal them." It is discouraging to have to point out time and again, that Isaiah was speaking of his own times and people. A few verses will make this evident even to a learned Theologian; so I quote several from these introductory Chapters:

"(i, 1) The vision of Isaiah, which he saw concerning Judah and Jerusalem, in the days of Uzziah, Jotham, Ahaz, and Hezekiah, kings of Judah. (2) For Yahveh hath spoken: they have rebelled against me: (3) Israel doth not know, my people doth not consider. (4) Ah, sinful nation. (21) How is the faithful city become an harlot! (ii, 5) O House of Jacob, come ye, and let us walk in the light of Yahveh. (8) For Jerusalem is ruined, and Judah is fallen: because their tongue, and their doings are against Yahveh. (v, 3) And Now, O! inhabitants of Jerusalem and men of Judah, judge, I pray you. (5) And now go to; I will tell you what I will do: I will break down and I will lay waste, etc. (25) Therefore is the anger of Yahveh kindled against his people. (vi, 9) And he (Yahveh) said (to Isaiah), Go, and tell this people, Hear ye indeed, but understand not; and see ye indeed, but perceive not. (10) And make their ears heavy, and shut their eyes; lest they see with their eyes, and hear with their ears, and understand with their heart, and turn again, and be healed."

John, maybe inadvertently, omits even the opening words of Isaiah's verse 9, which of itself shows that Isaiah was told by Yahveh to "go and tell *this* people" those things, which John then claims that Isaiah said as the reason why other Jews 750 years later would not believe Jesus! And the preceding scraps of verses which I have picked from each of the preceding five chapters, to connect the whole together, further prove what Isaiah was talking about, and to whom he was speaking.

The "abhorrent thing" which I mentioned is John's remarkable excuse for Jesus not being believed by the Jews: "For this cause they *could not* believe"—because Yahveh had "blinded their eyes and hardened their hearts," so that they could not believe and turn and be healed; that is, repent and be saved! Yet, if this same John and all his colleagues in inspiration are to be believed: Yahveh sent his own "Beloved son" into the world that the world through him might be saved; he called all to repentance, saying, Believe on me and ye shall be saved, and if ye believe not ye shall be damned!

4. A COOKING LESSON AS "PROPHECY"

After this, we pass now to the last reference by John to alleged "prophecy" of Jesus, for a wholesome laugh as we finish this preposterous line of "prophecies" re Jesus Christ. This is also a double-barreled blunderbuss, and scatters all through the Law and the Prophets.

As Jesus hung on the Cross between the two thieves, says John, Chapter xix, verses 32 to 37:

"(32) Then came the soldiers, and brake the legs of the first, and of the other which was crucified with him. (33) But when they came to Jesus, and saw that he was dead already, they brake not his legs. (34) But one of the soldiers with a spear pierced his side;

(36) For these things were done, that the scripture should be fulfilled, A bone of him shall not be broken. (37) And again another scripture saith, They shall look on him whom they pierced."

These two jokes with pretended prophecy, cracked under the shadow of the Cross where their God died, are a new shame on the joker. He appeals to these spurious "prophecies" with great solemnity, and as he admits, for the express purpose of making himself believed: "(35) And he that saw it bare record, and his record is true: and he knoweth that he saith true, that ye might believe"— for, he adds, "these things were done that the scripture should be fullfilled." What scripture? The references for verse 36 are to Exodus xii, verse 46; Numbers ix, verse 12, and Psalms xxxiv, verse 20. I quote these in full, to show the straits of the Evangelist and his editors to find something to fit; and their context to show what they really refer to: a Passover cooking lesson to the fugitive slave Jews!

1. Exodus xii, established the Passover feast, consisting of unleavened bread and a male lamb or kid (v. 5). This was to be prepared and eaten:

"(8) And they shall eat the flesh in that night, roast with fire, and unleavened bread; and with bitter herbs shall they eat it. (9) Eat not of it raw, nor sodden at all with water, but roast with fire; his head with his legs, and with the purtenance thereof. (11) And thus shall ye eat it; with your loins girded, and your shoes on your feet, and your staff in your hand; and ye shall eat it in haste; it is Yahveh's passover. (46) In one house shall it be eaten; thou shalt not carry forth ought of the flesh abroad out of the house; *neither shall ye break a bone thereof*"!

John wonderfully misquotes this last sentence out of a whole Chapter of minute directions as how to cook and eat the Passover lamb or kid; and changes the neuter "a bone thereof," that is, "*of it*"—of the lamb or kid—so as to make it apply to a man: "a bone *of him* shall not be broken," and calls it a "prophecy" of Jesus Christ fulfilled!

2. The second reference, to Numbers ix, verse 12, is practically identical in words; it is identical in subject; and its application to Jesus is identical in falsity:

"(2) Let the children of Israel also keep the passover at his appointed season. (11) The fourteenth day of the second month at even they shall keep it, and eat it with unleavened bread and bitter herbs. (12) They shall leave none of it unto the morning, nor *break any bone of it;* According to all the ordinances of the passover shall they keep it."

3. The third reference in trying to make this break-bone cookery recipe apply to Jesus on the Cross is to Psalm xxxiv, verse 20: "He

keepeth all his bones; not one of them is broken." This does not even squint at the misused "prophecy"—"A bone of him shall not be broken." David is in a better humor with himself and his Yahveh this time, and he sings:

"(1) I will bless Yahveh at all times: his praise shall continually be in my mouth. . . . (19) Many are the afflictions of the *righteous:* but Yahveh delivereth him out of them all. (20) He keepeth all his bones: not one of them is broken."

This clearly irrelevant last appeal to wholly impertinent antiquities of "prophecy," exhausts the series of remarkable attempts of the Four Evangelists to torture Old Testament "ravings" of the Prophets of Yahveh into inspired foretellings of the Jesus Christ of the New; and may well exhaust the patience of the reader in unraveling these "old odd ends stolen out of Holy Writ" by the propagandists of the new Faith to give credence and currency to their miraculous Histories of Jesus the Carpenter, whom they proclaimed King of the Jews, Son of Yahveh, and Saviour of the World. It is more than evident from this review of misused "Prophecy," that not a single word of the scores of so-called "prophecies" culled from the old Hebrew Scriptures in the remotest degree hints or squints at the humble Man of Galilee.

If a lawyer, pleading his cause before any Court in any civilized country of the world, should resort to the device of citing records, precedents and authorities in support of his contentions, and these should be discovered by his opponent or the Court to be of the ilk of these appealed to for credence by the Gospel-writers, such lawyer would be disgraced and infamous, would be branded as charlatan and shyster, a base impostor, and would be driven from the honorable profession which he had thus dishonored, and exposed forever after to the scorn and contempt of honest mankind.

But Gospel Writers are yet haloed as inspired and holy Saints, and Preachers of the "Word of God" are yet Sacred "Divines," who go about with the odor of sanctity redolent about them, and are listened to with rapt awe when they teach and preach these "prophecies" and their "fulfillment" to those who have been taught to believe them and have never thought for themselves or "searched the scriptures" for the wonders of their Most Holy Faith.

CHAPTER XIV

THE INSPIRED "HARMONY OF THE GOSPELS"

OF THE LIFE OF JESUS CHRIST

THE Life and Times of Jesus of Nazareth, the Messiah, the King of the Jews, the Savior of the World, is preserved in four short Monographs, called after their Greek title Gospels, which means in English "Good News." The first and earliest of these Biographies, "The Gospel according to Mark," was written about the year 70 of the new Era, some forty years after the death of Jesus, when a whole new generation of men had come upon the scene of the therein reported events of his life and death.

In these biographies their Subject is claimed by the writers to be the "Son of God,"—the Hebrew Yahveh; as "conceived by the Holy Ghost, born of the Virgin Mary," working wonders, crucified to death, and rising again from the dead, ascended into Heaven, where he sitteth on the right hand of his Father God, until he shall "come again to judge the quick and the dead"—which he asserted would be very shortly, in the life-time of his hearers.

In his brief life-career, between three Jewish Passovers only, he is recorded to have wrought "great signs and wonders"—miracles: to have raised the dead, cured incurable diseases by a word or a touch or the simple healing faith of the cured person or of his friends, or by his potent command "casting out devils" which caused the ailments; to have been tried and condemned by a Roman Magistrate, and crucified to death by Roman Law; on his death to have caused a great eclipse of the sun; to have rent in twain by earthquake the veil of the Holy Temple; which caused innumerable graves to open and their sheeted dead to come forth and walk the streets of the Holy City, in full view of the populace; to have himself resurrected from under the eyes of an armed Roman guard, specially stationed at his grave to prevent all tampering; and to have—on the same or the next day or forty days afterwards, ascended to Heaven —five different times and places, before the eyes of five different sets of spectators, and under five totally different sets of surrounding facts and circumstances. (*Vide* Four Gospels and Acts.)

Not a word of all or any of these transcendent Wonders is to be found in all the historic records or contemporary annals of that great City and Age. The Roman Philosopher Pliny, some forty years later, just about the time the first Gospel was written, lost his life seeking to investigate the very minor event of an eruption of Vesuvius which destroyed—and preserved for future confirmation— the minor Roman town of Pompeii, of which event ample contemporary historical records abound. Flavius Josephus, a contemporary, the greatest Historian of Jewry, records the minutest facts and even myths of Hebrew History from the earliest ages down to his own times. But there exists not, nor has ever existed, a word of any record, human or Divine, concerning this God made Man and all his wondrous works—outside of a supposedly forged and meagre reference stuck between incongruous paragraphs of one of the works of Josephus (Antiquities of the Jews, Bk. XVIII, Ch. iii, 3), and outside the pages of these so-called Gospels and Epistles, with the Apocalypse or Revelation, thrown in for full measure of the meagre and contradictory records.

This Jesus was Incarnate God on earth, or he lived as a man and Teacher, if ever he did, in one of the most brilliant ages and cultured societies in ancient History: in the reign of Caesar Augustus, an epoch illustrious as the Augustan, the Golden Age, of Roman imperial, legal, literary, and cultured Civilization.

Judea then was a Roman Province, Jerusalem a Roman capital. Its ruler, at the time of the traditional Advent of the Nazarene, was Herod the Great, celebrated by the Jewish Historian Josephus as one of the great if wicked men and rulers of the age; learning and literature, of the elegant Roman and brilliant Greek types, flourished. But nowhere a scrap of papyrus even whereon the name of this God, or of this miracle-working man, is so much as mentioned, except in the passage referred to in an old MSS. of Josephus, and by most scholars held to be spurious.

These tales of the Christ are marvelous and incredible, impossible, according to all human standards of reason, as shown in every detail and circumstance of the confused and contradictory records of the four Gospels—as the simple comparison of their texts will demonstrate them to be. We have seen their Subject stripped of every vestige of claim to "fulfillment of Prophecy," appealed to by his four posthumous Biographers, in support of their accounts of the most salient features of his life and acts. No less unreal will be found the much-heralded "Harmony of the Gospels" with respect to the most signal events of his life and deeds, his trial, crucifixion, death, resurrection, ascension, related of this Jesus by the spirit and pen of inspiration. Such things, so contradictorily chronicled and vouched for, could not be accepted as truth, if testified on oath before a Court of human justice. But where, as here, it is assured that every word of the record is inspired of truth by God—the inevitable rule of logic and of law: "Of two contradictories, one must be false," makes their "harmony" and truth incredible and impossible.

We will take up these several diversely recorded incidents one by one in their order, and submit them to candid judgment.

The "Blessed Name" of Jesus

It may be noted first, in passing, that the name of the "Christ," whether God or Man, was not, to himself and his own family and people, Jesus at all. His name, christened upon him in Hebrew, or Aramaic, the language in which he spoke, is plain Joshua—exactly the same as the old Heathen Worthy for whom the sun and moon stood still upon Gibeon. The meaning of this name is "Yahveh is salvation": Jesus is the later Greek form of the name Joshua.

As for the added title "Christ," this is another Greek translation or substitute; the translation of the Hebrew Scripture word "Messiah," which simply means "anointed." The Gospel-writer John, himself a Hebrew, but writing in current Greek, correctly explains this, when he tells of Andrew coming to his brother Simon Peter, and announcing, "We have found the Messias, which is to say, being interpreted, the Christ" (Jno. i, 41); both the words, the Hebrew *Masshiach* and its Greek equivalent *Christos*, meaning simply, The Anointed.

Again, as to his name, Hebrew Joshua, Greek Jesus: its Galilean bearer, by this token, cannot be the Virgin-born subject of the "prophecy" of Isaiah, as claimed by Matthew: for Isaiah declares that his virgin, bearing a son, "shall call his name Immanuel" (Is. vii, 14), as quoted by Matthew (i, 23); this name, as Matthew explains in the same verse, "being interpreted is, God (El) with us" (Matt. i, 23); whereas Joshua (Jesus) means, as we have seen, "Yahveh is salvation." So the Virgin-born Joshua or Jesus of Matthew cannot be possibly—all other proofs aside—the same infant as the Virgin-born Immanuel of Isaiah.

It has already been abundantly proven, that Isaiah's unfulfilled "prophecy" regarding his virgin-born "sign" of the outcome of the war of the two Kings against Jerusalem, does not at all refer to the Virgin-born child of Mary, 750 years later. It is apparent and faith-compelling in the context of the "prophecy" itself, by the simple reading of Isaiah's Chapter vii, that this pretended "prophecy" of Isaiah did not, could not, and was not intended by

Isaiah, to refer to any such Joshua or Jesus of 750 years in the future. Matthew is thus seen to be in error in this particular—as in so many others, as convincingly demonstrated in the review already made of all of his alleged "prophecies fulfilled" in Jesus Christ. So we need not dwell again here on this prophecy of miraculous birth; but will proceed to other as compelling proofs of the persistent errancy and inconsistency of Matthew and his fellow Propagandists of this Jesus as the Christ.

The great national Hero who would come to revenge the Chosen People of Yahveh against the Assyrians and other oppressors, is not once intimated in the Hebrew Scriptures to be any other than a human being, "of the seed of David," who should reestablish the throne of David on earth, as so often promised and proclaimed by Yahveh. Never once is it hinted that Yahveh himself, "Man of War" though he was, would come in person to accomplish the liberation and restoration of his Chosen People, after having so signally failed to save them from destruction and captivity. Nor is there so much as an ambiguous or doubtful bit of revelation that Yahveh had a son by the name of Joshua, whom he would send some time in the future to fill the role of the promised Hero, and either reestablish the throne of David on earth, as so oft-promised, or set up a new Religion promising a Kingdom in Heaven to the disappointed expectants of the renewed earthly Kingdom of Israel.

Genealogies of Jesus

The Pedigree of Jesus is the next notable conflict between Matthew and one of his colleagues, Luke, who contradicts him. The chief of the essential qualifications of the expected Jewish Messiah was that he should be of the house and lineage of David the King, and should as such "reestablish the Throne of David forever." So this descent in unbroken line must be proven upon Jesus the Son of Joseph or of Yahveh, or upon any other, who would successfully claim to fulfill the Promise of the Messiah as a Davidic earthly King. Matthew therefore begins his Biography with "The Book of the Generation of Jesus Christ, the son of David, the son of Abraham" (Matt. i, 1). Beginning with Abraham, he comes in direct line of "begettings" to David, and from David in further unbroken line of begettings, through Solomon and Roboam, to one Jacob: "And *Jacob begat Joseph* the husband of Mary, of whom was born *Jesus*, who is called the Christ" (Matt. i, 16); and he declares specifically, after naming all by name, that from David to Christ there are twenty-eight generations (v. 17).

Here Luke begins his inveterate contradictions of Matthew (as well as of the others); and in Chapter iii of his equally inspired and credible Biography, he produces the genealogy of his Subject, but in inverse order from Jesus to David, instead of as in Matthew from David to Jesus. But Luke carries the line of begettings directly back to David *via* one Mattatha, "which was the son of Nathan, which was the son of David" (v. 32), instead of David, Solomon, Roboam, as says Matthew—as the progenitors of Jesus. And Luke names and specifies forty-three generations from David to Jesus, instead of Matthew's twenty-eight: and only three names of the two contradictory lists are the same, except David at one end and Jesus at the other, and the immediate ancestry at both ends is totally different. For comparison, here are the Sacred Genealogies as vouched for by the two inspired Biographers:

MATTHEW (i, 6–16)	LUKE (iii, 23–31)	
1. David	1. David	29. Mattathias
2. Solomon	2. Nathan	30. Maath
3. Roboam	3. Mattatha	31. Nagge
4. Abia	4. Menan	32. Esli
5. Asa	5. Melea	33. Naum
6. Josaphat	*6. Eliakim	34. Amos
7. Joram	7. Jonan	35. Mattathias
8. Ozias	8. Joseph	36. Joseph
9. Joatham	9. Juda	37. Janna
10. Achaz	10. Simeon	38. Melchi
11. Ezekias	11. Levi	39. Levi
12. Manasses	12. Matthat	40. Matthat
13. Amon	13. Jorim	41. HELI
14. Josias	14. Eliezer	42. JOSEPH
15. Jechonias	15. Jose	43. JESUS
*16. Salathiel	16. Er	
*17. Zorobabel	17. Elmodam	
18. Abiud	18. Cosam	
*19. Eliakim	19. Addi	
20. Azor	20. Melchi	
21. Sadoc	21. Neri	
22. Achim	*22. Salathiel	
23. Eliud	*23. Zorobabel	
24. Eleazar	24. Rhesa	
25. Matthan	25. Joanna	
26. JACOB	26. Juda	
27. JOSEPH	27. Joseph	
28. JESUS	28. Semei	

* Indicates names which occur in both lists.

This proves entire want of inspiration of truth in one or the other of these contradictory Genealogies; and curiously, both at the most critical point break the circuit of direct lineage of descent of Jesus from David. For, if Jesus was not the carnal son of Joseph, but the incarnate Son of Yahveh by the Holy Ghost and the yet Virgin Mary, he could not, by any possibility of human descent, be a blood descendant of David, whose line of generation ended with Joseph, if Joseph was not the carnal father of Jesus. So in no sense could Jesus be a direct descendant and "Son of David," and so could not fill the first essential requirement of the Promised Messiah.

And Jesus himself denies positively that he is any "son of David." For, "While the Pharisees were gathered together, Jesus asked them, saying, What think ye of Christ? Whose son is he? They say unto him, The son of David. He saith unto them, How then doth David in spirit call him Lord: If David then call him Lord, how is he his son?" (Matt. xxii, 41–45). This was a good deal of a conundrum, for "no man was able to answer him a word" (v. 46). Nor can I.

Virgin Birth of Jesus

The reputed Virgin-birth of Jesus we have already fully disproved as having been prophesied by Isaiah, Matthew to the contrary notwithstanding. We will briefly inspect the miraculous pregnancy of the Ever-Virgin-Mother (who had more than half a dozen children), and the circumstances of the birth of her first-born Joshua or Jesus.

Matthew again is our inspired Historian. He relates that, "When as his Mother Mary was espoused to Joseph, before they came together, she was found with child of the Holy Ghost" (i, 18); that Joseph felt quite naturally disposed to "put her away privily"; but that he dreamed that an Angel of Yahveh told him to fear not to accept his wife Mary, "for that which is conceived in her is of the Holy Ghost" (v. 20). This dream seems to have quite satisfied Joseph, though he had never heard of any Holy Ghost, and no such Person of the Christian Trinity is recorded in the Hebrew Scriptures. So Joseph, "being raised from sleep," did as—(he dreamed that)—the angel of Yahveh had bidden him, and "took unto himself his wife: And knew her not till she had brought forth her first-born son" (vv. 24–25).

Thus we learn, from Matthew, that the news of this pregnancy of his wife by the Holy Ghost was first broken to Joseph in a dream, or he dreamed that the Holy Ghost was the author of it. When, Inspiration vouchsafes not directly; but it is readily deducted that it was not till at least three months after the secret Visitation by the Holy Ghost took place, as will appear below. Also, that it was several months after is indicated by the fact that Joseph then took her unto himself, "and knew her not *till* she had brought forth her first-born son"—thus evidently a considerable space of time, as the fact of Joseph's marital self-restraint is specially noted by inspiration.

This, too (parenthetically), disproves the Dogma that Mary remained immaculate and Ever-Virgin: for, that Joseph knew her not "till" she had given birth to her *first*-born son, argues that he *did* "know her" carnally thereafter; and her "*first*-born" son argues others born thereafter. So a very favorite Fallacy of the Fathers Celibate is exploded; to say nothing of the virginity-destroying effects of the births of half a dozen brothers and sisters of Jesus: "his brethren, James, and Joses, and Simon, and Judas, and his sisters," (Matt. xiii, 55–56; Mark vi, 2–3); and Paul tells us of seeing his Apostle friend "James, the Lord's brother" (Gal. i, 19).

But here again Luke as usual contradicts Matthew's story of Joseph's dream-revelation by the Angel to himself of the origin of his wife's pregnancy. Luke goes into much detail relating that the Angel Gabriel, in the sixth month after his like mission to Mary's cousin Elizabeth, was sent from Yahveh to Nazareth, "to a virgin espoused to a man whose name was Joseph, and the virgin's name was Mary" (Luke ii, 26–27). Gabriel announced to Mary that "the Holy Ghost shall come upon thee," and that she should "bring forth a son, and shalt call his name Jesus." And Gabriel told her that the same kind of a thing had already happened to her Cousin Elizabeth, six months previously; and he departed. Mary, with true womanly instinct, arose and went with haste into the hill country, to the town of Elizabeth, to congratulate her and to break the news of her own like expectation; they both celebrated exultantly "with a loud voice" (v. 42); and Mary remained with Elizabeth for three months until John Baptist was born to Elizabeth. It may, in a word be wondered how any sort of "divinity" or odor of sanctity could be attached by intelligent and modern people to this John, surnamed the Baptist. He was a wild, uncouth dirty Desert Dervish, dwelling in the Judean wilderness, of the Nazarite type, with never a haircut or shave in his life; he wore old bran sacks strapped to his waist for his scanty clothes, and for regular diet ate desert grasshoppers, evidently raw (Matt. iii, 4). He spent his life and

his voice idly in the wilderness crying "prepare the way for Yahveh"
—not for Yahveh's Son and his own cousin Jesus. That his cousin
Joshua-Jesus was any different from the family type does not
appear, except that he lived in an adobe town and was of the rude
carpenter class. Over two such Christians indulge in holy ecstasy.

That Mary had not told Joseph of the "visitation" of the Holy
Ghost to her, and that he was ignorant of it for at least three
months, is very evident from Matthew's inspired record. The
promise was no doubt performed to Mary at the same time of the
"visitation" of the Angel, related by Luke, who told her that "the
Holy Ghost shall come upon thee," and that her Cousin Elizabeth
had been similarly visited six months before. Mary at once went
to Elizabeth and remained until after John was born three months
later; then Mary returned to Joseph. It was then, or later, that
Joseph, by some means not revealed, "found" that Mary was "with
child of the Holy Ghost." Really, this of the Holy Ghost was not
what Joseph found, but simply that his wife "was with child,"
without his knowing by whom or what. For Joseph was thereupon,
and naturally, "minded to put her away privily," so as not to
"make her a publick example" and create a scandal, as related by
Matthew. So Joseph could not have known, at the time of his
discovery of the pregnancy, who was its author. It was only later,
when he was sleeping on the matter, that he had the dream in which
he dreamed that he was told that "that which is conceived in her
is of the Holy Ghost," and that therefore he should "fear not to
take unto thee Mary thy wife" (Matt. i, 20). That the suspicions
of Joseph should have been so easily allayed by a dream may appear
to some to be queer; though both Joseph and Mary, as Luke elsewhere relates, positively disclaim the whole story of the intervention
of the Holy Ghost in the conception of Jesus, and themselves assert
their own human and natural parenthood of the Child (Luke ii,
48–50).

We may here note, for what it is worth in support of the orthodox
Faith, that there was no novelty at all in Virgin Births from Gods
in the ancient religions. It was a commonplace happening enough,
which any superstitiously inclined Pagan or Hebrew would readily
accept in fullness of faith. Even the Hebrew Yahveh, who is not
revealed to have had any Heavenly Spouse, is credited with numerous
offspring—the "beni ha-Elohim, sons of the-Gods," of Genesis and
Job, who sported with the daughters of men, producing the demigod
Giants.

The great God of the Greeks, Zeus, Heaven Father, was also

prolific author of virgin births; of which we may cite only the well known and highly accredited instances of his Swan-form copulation with Leda, the miraculous product of which were the holy twins Castor and Pollux; and his intrigue with Io, which resulted in the son Epaphus. The Roman War God Mars likewise kept amorous tryst with the Vestal Virgin Rhea Silvia, of which the celebrated twins Romulus and Remus resulted. The great Hero Achilles was also the by-product of the amours of, this time, a human father and the immortal Sea-Goddess Thetis. God hybrids in human form resulted. The Son of Yahveh and Mary could not thus have been altogether "Very God," but was half-human. Virgin births by Gods are thus seen to have been either very frequent actualities in the good old Hebrew-Pagan times, or priestly assurance and popular credulity passed them as miraculous events worthy of the most holy faith and credence. It is all the same, so far as they may serve for precedents for faith in the Virgin Birth of the reputed Son of Yahveh.

The only authentication which we have of this highly interesting and much controverted Event, are sundry "proofs of Holy Writ," consisting of very contradictory scraps of inspiration in the New Testament. The much vaunted "harmony of the Gospels" and perfect inerrancy of Scriptures are sadly wanting in this capital phase of Divine revelation.

Paul, the most dogmatic Theologian of them all, avers and admits that Jesus Christ was *altogether human* in origin, for that he "was made of the seed of David according to the flesh" (Rom. i, 3), and was simply "declared to be the Son of God (Yahveh) with power, according to the spirit of holiness" (v. 4). Mark, the first and earliest of the Gospel biographers, mentions no miraculous or Virgin birth at all, either of Jesus or of John; Mark is therefore a potent witness *ab silentio* against the controverted fact. Luke, although quoting Gabriel in Chapter i (vv. 28–36), seems to forget all about it in Chapter ii, where he simply relates that Joseph went from Nazareth to Bethlehem "to be taxed, with Mary his espoused wife, being great with child; . . . and she brought forth her first-born child" (Luke ii, 5, 7). According to all human standards of possibility and of propriety, this indicates that the Child was legitimate fruit of human husband and wife.

John says not a word of miraculous or Virgin birth; he says, "I saw, and bare record that this is the son of God (Yahveh; Jno. i, 34). But what John meant by "son of God" he has previously defined, and the expression is clearly shown by his own words to

be used in a metaphorical, or Pickwickian, sense,—for that all believers are even sons of God: "But as many as received him, to them
gave he the power to become the sons of God, even to them that
believe on his name—('even the devils believe and tremble') which
are born, not of blood, nor of the will of the flesh, nor of the will
of man, but of God" (vv. 12–13).

Thus two of the four Gospel biographers wholly ignore, and thus
tacitly deny, any pretense of miraculous or Virgin birth—the most
transcendent Dogma of later Christian Faith; and Paul, the greatest
author of Dogma of them all, expressly declares Jesus to have been
of purely human procreation and birth—"made of the seed of David
according to the flesh,"—which he could not have been if of Yahvistic
paternity.

The "Star of Bethlehem"

The signs and portents attendant upon the miraculous birth of
Joshua-Jesus give occasion to another clash between the inspirations
of Matthew and of Luke, and lead into several tangles of truth.
Matthew alone of the Four Gospel Historians, relates that mysterious phenomenon of the sidereal heavens—the "Star of Bethlehem"; and so relates it that, all other negations aside, we know that
it never was seen by eye of Wise Man or foolish, but was only a
vision of inspired imagination. The "East" was celebrated for its
zeal and science of Astronomy; but never an Astronomer of Eastern
antiquity ever saw or recorded that extraordinary Star. Nor did
anyone else ever see it, outside the mind's eye, as is evident enough
from the inspired account of it into which we will briefly inquire.

In his second Chapter Matthew essays to tell how that certain
"Wise Men from the East," but from where in the East he says
not, came to Jerusalem "when Jesus was born in Bethlehem of
Judea," and went about asking "Where is he that is born King of
the Jews?" for, they explained, "we have seen his Star in the East,"
and are come to worship him (vv. 1–2).

Clear it is therefore that this "Star" was no bright and flaming
sidereal Luminary: it was not visible on the meridian of Jerusalem;
no one but the Wise Men is recorded to have seen it at all; and they
saw it only "in the East"; but at Jerusalem it was not seen or
seeable by naked human eye. Proof of this is, that "Herod and all
Jerusalem with him was troubled" (v. 3), when they heard about
the strange Star. Herod "gathered all the chief priests and scribes,"
and inquired about the alleged new King of the Jews (v. 4); then
he "privily called the Wise Men, and enquired of them diligently

what time the Star appeared" (v. 7). Thus Herod nor any of "all Jerusalem" had seen this marvel of a Pilot Star anywhere around Jerusalem, or there would be no need to so "diligently enquire" as to the when and where of the Phenomenon, which now had entirely disappeared from human view,—else Herod could have seen it for himself.

Clear too it is that this "Star" was not the guiding Pilot that it is popularly supposed to have been, leading the Wise Men from the East to Jerusalem, or to the new-born King. We have seen that it was not visible in Jerusalem; the Wise Men only claimed to "have seen his Star in the East," some where far away. And they came to Jerusalem (*not* "to Bethlehem where the child was"), wholly ignorant of his whereabouts; so that they had to go about asking anybody they met on the streets, just as a stranger in town these days asks the corner policeman,—"where is he that is born King of the Jews?" (v. 2). How these Pagan down-Easters were inspired to know or care anything about an unheard-of baby King of the Jews, or to know what the alleged "Star in the East" signified with respect to the mangered Kingling, and should journey across the burning deserts to come "worship" a baby pretended King, is curious to inquire, but it is not revealed. Nor was the miraculous "Star" itself very revealing. Though hung up there in the Eastern skies for their own special benefit and guidance, it led them not to the Babe King in Bethlehem, nor even to Jerusalem where he had not been heard of at all; so that they had to go about and ask all comers, "Where is he that is born King of the Jews?" But no one in all Jerusalem had seen the Star or knew of the new-born King.

When Herod the King heard of these ignorant Wise Men and their quest, he and all Jerusalem were troubled. The sequel proves that wicked Herod was now himself to be "numbered among the Prophets": for "he gathered all the chief priests and scribes together, and demanded of them"—(a very curious and "inspired" sort of question)—"where *Christ* should be born?" (v. 4). Surely Herod never asked such a question. It was thirty-odd years afterwards, that (to believe the story at all) the Jesus was first "Christ"-ened, or "anointed," and thus first became "Christ" or "The Anointed." Unless Herod was inspired of prophetic vision, and could foresee thirty-odd years into futurity, and behold in his mind's eye the very variously related incident of the Woman breaking the Alabaster Box of Ointment over the head—or the feet—of the then Mangered Babe of Bethlehem, he could not know to ask such a question; and we may be sure that he did not. So we will return to our "Star"-

gazing with the Wise Men, who were stranded in their quest in Jerusalem, asking "Where do we go from here?"—which their Star had not revealed to them.

As the Star had not led them right, they had to pursue their street inquest for the Object of their search. Herod himself had to come to their help; and it required the whole assemblage of priestly wiseacres of Jerusalem to answer, by the aid of an errant prophecy, that the "Governor" was to be born in Bethlehem of Judea (v. 5–6). And it was not even now that the "Star" helped or guided them to their goal. It was Herod himself, when he got the report of the priestly conclave, Herod then "privily called the Wise Men" who did not know; "and *he sent them to Bethlehem*" (v. 8), to find the young Child, and return and report to him. These Wise Ones then, "when they had heard the King, they departed" (v. 9) on their now well-directed way; and *mirabile dictu*, "lo, the Star, which they had seen in the East, went before them, till it came and stood over where the young child was" (v. 9). Thus the wonderful Star, till now wonderfully inefficient as a Guide to the Wise Men, when they needed guidance across the deserts, now when it was no longer needed as a Guide, Herod himself having located the place, flares up before their eyes and flits along before them on their journey to Bethlehem, a little suburban town just across the creek from Jerusalem, which needed no Star to point it out.

This fabled "Star of Bethlehem" was evidently just a sort of flighty Will-o'-the-Wisp affair, specially arranged for the private and unneeded uses of the Wise Men who now were humanly told where they wanted to go, and was not a regular Star; for the nearest Star in the Heavens is some twenty trillions of miles away from earth, where it can be seen of all men, Wise or otherwise, and neither goes before people, to guide them where they do not need a guide to go, nor comes nor stands for their accommodation when they get there. However, it is curious to note, the Wise Men, who are said to have seen the Star way back there "in the East" before coming to Jerusalem, now seem to have "seen" it for the first time as they left Jerusalem and as it "went before them" Bethlehem-ward; for, "when they saw the Star, they rejoiced with exceeding great joy" (v. 10).

When the Wise Men had at last, thanks to Herod and their Star, found the Young Child, they duly worshiped it, and delivered their gifts; then, dreaming of some Heavenly warning not to return to Herod, they "departed into their own country another way" (v. 12),—so as to fool Herod, who was said to be awaiting their return to go himself and worship the baby King to be (v. 8). This is the faithful record of Matthew, in his Chapter ii.

The Shepherd Choir

But, according to the record of Luke, it did not happen this way at all. There was no Star of Bethlehem; there were no Wise Men from the East; simply a group of lowly "Shepherds abiding in the field, keeping watch over their flocks by night" (Luke ii, 8). To them an anonymous Angel came, scaring them very badly, and told them that "a Savoir, which is Christ the Lord" (thus again anticipating the Anointing Scene), was born unto them that day. And of a sudden a whole Angel Choir, a "multitude of the heavenly host," winged down to earth from the Heavens over 1,000,000 Light-years away, and sang wonderously there in the cold night air of "Glory to God in the Highest, and on Earth peace, good will toward men" (vv. 13–14);—an Angelic prophecy never yet realized on this war-wracked, hate-filled Earth. And it was the Shepherds, according to the Gospel according to Luke, who came with haste to Bethlehem to investigate the Angelic report; and when they had verified "the Babe lying in the Manger," they straightway broadcast the news throughout all those parts (vv. 16–17). The interested Reader may choose whether to accept Matthew's Star or Luke's Angel Choir.

The Nocturnal Flight to Egypt

Another highly important conflict of inspiration occurs right here, in connection with the early Life of the Child Jesus. Mark, who wrote first of them all, omits all the Child-Life of his Subject, beginning his Biography with "the beginning of the Gospel of Jesus Christ, the Son of God" (Mark i, 1). But Matthew seeks to supply many childlife items,—as is not infrequent with Biographers, as instance the Cherry-Tree episode of the youthful Father of his Country. But Matthew's "sources" were not ample, or his imagination lagged at childish details; so he sends the Holy Family and the Child to Egypt for some years, as he says in fulfillment of another "prophecy," which we have elsewhere seen was not one at all; but it may as well have been to avoid recording many things he did not know. In any event, Luke says it was not true, as we will presently verify.

According to Matthew, immediately after the Wise Men had

departed for their own country, as a result of their dream of warning (Matt. ii, 12), another dream caused another Hegira, thus related:

"When they had departed, behold, the angel of the Lord appeared to Joseph in a dream, saying, Arise, and take the young child and his mother by night, and flee into Egypt; and be thou there until I bring thee word: for Herod will seek the young Child to destroy him. When he arose, and took the young child and his mother by night,—(that same night)—and departed into Egypt. And was there until the death of Herod: that it might be fulfilled which was spoken of the Lord by the Prophet, saying, Out of Egypt have I called my Son" (vv. 13–15).

And there they stayed until after the death of Herod, some unknown time later. But this is not so at all, says Luke.

We have already examined this so-called "Out of Egypt" prophecy of Hosea (xi, 1); and have seen that it meant nothing whatever about Jesus. It is pleasing to know from Luke that we are right on this point; as such a meaningless "prophecy" was not fulfilled anyhow, according to the Gospel of Luke. For Luke goes inspiredly into the young life of the Child, and relates it in no little detail. We see Luke's Shepherds find the Babe in his Manger (Luke ii, 16); then still there, eight days afterwards the Child is circumcised and named Jesus (v. 21); then the Virgin-Mother, dogmatized as Immaculate and Ever-pure, remained right there for another thirty-three days, purging herself for her "purification according to the Law of Moses" (v. 22; Lev. xii, 2–4); then followed the several visits of Simeon (vv. 25–35), and of Anna (vv. 36–38), how long their visitations lasted being unrevealed. However, here on these exact figures we have at least forty days—before either of the visits—that the Child remained in his lowly Bethlehem Manger, instead of flitting to Egypt the night of the visit of the Magi. All this time, too, the Immaculate Mother of God was "unclean" by the holy Law, and could not so much as touch her own Holy Child (Lev. xii, 4)—a truly Godly prohibition to a Mother with a news-born babe, especially a God-baby. And then, Luke literally assures us: "When they had performed all things according to the Law of Yahveh, *they returned into Galilee,* to their own city Nazareth" (v. 39).

So they did not flee into Egypt, as Matthew records. Not when Matthew says, nor at all, according to the Gospel of Luke. For upon returning directly to their home in Nazareth, there they remained all the child and youth life of their young son Jesus, and there "the child grew and waxed strong" (v. 40), right there in

Nazareth, never leaving home except once a year to go to Jerusalem with his parents, says Luke:

> "Now his parents *went to Jerusalem every year* at the feast of the Passover (v. 41).
> "And when he (Jesus) was twelve years old, they went up to Jerusalem after the custom of the feast (v. 42).

And they took the young Jesus along with them, at least on this occasion, for "when they had fulfilled the days, as they returned, the child Jesus tarried behind in Jerusalem, and Joseph and his mother knew not of it" (v. 43); and the parents did not discover the fact that the child was missing until the next day: "But they, supposing him to have been with the company, went a day's journey" (v. 44); and not finding him "they turned back to Jerusalem, in anxious search of the lost child; and "after three days" of search, "they found him in the Temple" arguing with the Doctors (vv. 43–46). So for at least twelve years there was no midnight flight to Egypt to escape Herod; and they could not have remained there "until the death of Herod" (Matt. ii, 15), for Herod died in the year 4 A.D., during the twelve years that the Holy Family remained at home in Nazareth, as testified by Luke. That Jesus was not born in the year 1 of his Era, but some 6 to 10 years B.C., is now generally known.

And right there in the Holy Temple, when the Child was found, Mary herself positively denies the Holy Ghost paternity of her Child, and rightly credits Joseph as its father; for when she found the Child, she cried: "Son, why hast thou dealt thus with us? Behold, *thy Father* (Joseph) and I have sought thee sorrowing" (v. 48). Though Jesus here seems to deny the paternity of Joseph, saying, "Wist ye not that I must be about my Father's business?" (v. 49). But both Joseph and Mary "understood not the saying which he spake unto them" (v. 50)—thus proving that they knew him for their own flesh-and-blood Child, and had no thought or knowledge of the Holy Ghost Paternity Dogma.

And they did not go to Egypt even now, for "he went down with them, and came to Nazareth, and was subject unto them" (v. 51). And there he remained until he began to teach and preach when he "began to be about thirty years old," after his baptism by John. So the "I have called my Son out of Egypt" prophecy is shown to be another instance of errant Inspiration.

The "Massacre of the Innocents"

This amazing narrative of Matthew, that when "Herod saw that he was mocked of the Wise men, he was exceeding wroth, and sent forth and slew all the children that were in Bethlehem, and in all the coasts thereof, from two years old and under" (Matt. ii, 16), may be dismissed with mentioning this bit of inspiration, on which peg is hung another "fulfillment of prophecy"—"Rachel weeping for her children." That a Roman King, under the great Roman Peace of the Golden Age of Augustus, could execute such a wholesale massacre of the subjects of the Empire—why, it proves itself impossible. No human history records such a massacre in Judea; not even Josephus, who retails the most trifling details of the life and reign of Herod, has a word of this tremendous murderous event. But why argue such a statement of even an inspired Author? The story, moreover, involves other serious contradictions, which further discredit it. Matthew says that Herod commanded the massacre of all the children of the District "from two years old and under": thus Jesus was at least two years old at the time, and, curiously enough, Herod must have patiently waited quite two years after being "mocked of the Wise Men" before he got so "exceeding wroth" as to commit this amazing, and unrecorded, crime. But, what is more serious, it proves that the Massacre never occurred at all; for Luke expressly assures, that immediately after the forty days "purification" of the Immaculate Virgin, and after the visits of Simeon and Anna, Joseph and Mary "returned into Galilee, to their own city Nazareth," and remained there continuously. This wholly discounts Matthew's visit of the Magi, the Flight to Egypt, the "mocking" of Herod, and Herod's Massacre of the Innocents. So this bloody blot is removed from wicked Herod's escutcheon.

We pass on to more important events recorded, and contradicted, by inspiration.

John and the Baptism of Jesus

The first thing recorded by inspiration in regard to Jesus,—after his return from Egypt, or after he did not go to Egypt but "began to be about thirty years old" peaceably at home in the carpenter shop of Nazareth,—is his reputed Baptism by his cousin John the Baptist, in the Jordan. John himself is the subject of much inspired uncertainty, into which we may for a moment inquire. His paternity is involved in curious obscurity, very like that of ancient Isaac. His parents were "both now well stricken in years," and his Mother was "barren," like olden Sarai. Angels, too, had to come and prophesy a child to them; and some sort of Divine agency is apparent in its fulfillment, for the child was "filled with the Holy Ghost, even from his mother's womb" (Luke i, 5–15). By special orders of Gabriel the child was named John; but he wasn't really John, but miraculously was the old-time Prophet Elias, *alias* Elijah,—if his cousin Jesus is to be believed as against the positive denial of the Baptist. For Jesus, inspired with all Truth, says and repeats explicitly, of John: "this is Elias, which was for to come" (Matt. xi, 14; xvii, 11–13); and Matthew invokes a prophecy of Malachi (iv, 5) to prove it, as if the word of Jesus needed proof. But John as positively, and categorically, twice denies the imputation:

"And he confessed, and denied not; but confessed, I am not the Christ. And they asked him, What then? Art thou Elias? And he saith, I am not. Art thou that Prophet? And he answered, No" (John i, 20–21).

So with this positive "He is," of Jesus, and the equally positive "I am not," of John, who ought to know, we must leave the identity of the Baptist in doubt, and pass to the proofs of the Baptism and some of its contrary incidents. Matthew, Chapter iii, again tells us:

"In those days came John the Baptist, preaching in the wilderness of Judea (1); (and many came), and were baptized of him in Jordan (5–6). Then cometh Jesus from Galilee to Jordan unto John, to be baptized of him (13). But John forbad him, saying, I have need to be baptized of thee, and comest thou to me? (14). But Jesus answering said unto him, Suffer it to be so now. . . . Then he suffered him (15). And Jesus, when he was baptized, went up straightway out of the water: and, lo, the heavens were opened unto him, and he saw the Spirit of God descending like a dove, and lighting upon him (16): And, lo, a voice from heaven, saying, This is my Beloved Son, in whom I am well pleased (17)."

So for a surety of inspiration, John knew and recognized Jesus, talked with him, and modestly protested against baptizing the Son of Yahveh, "whose shoes I am not worthy to bear" (v. 11); and John saw the dove from heaven, and heard the voice from heaven proclaiming the God-Man. Mark (i, 9–11), Luke (iii, 21–22), and John (i, 25–32), all relate the same inspired incident. And John, whose "record is true," as he himself admits, emphasizes the knowledge of the Baptist of the Divine identity of Jesus; that the Baptist knew that it was the Christ whom he baptized:

"John answered them (some Pharisees who were watching the baptism), saying, but there standeth One among you, whom ye know not; He it is, who coming after me is preferred before me, whose shoe's latchet I am not worthy to unloose" (vv. 26–27). . . .—And, "The next day (after the baptism) John seeth Jesus coming unto him, and saith, Behold the Lamb of God, which taketh away the sin of the world. This is he of whom I said, After me cometh a man which is preferred before me: for he was before me (John i, 29–30); And I saw (the Dove descending), and bare record that this is the son of God" (v. 32).

But withal this very explicit testimonial, inspiration contradicts it all; makes it clear that John did not baptise or even know Jesus, and makes John have to send a special embassy from prison to inquire about it all:

"Now when John had heard in the prison the works of Christ, he sent two of his disciples, And said unto him, Art thou he that should come, or do we look for another?" (Matt. xi, 2–3; Luke vii, 19–20).

Which proves by the clearest inference that the Baptist did not baptize the acknowledged Son of God, and did not "bare record" that "this is he who cometh after me—this is the Son of God"; in fact, seems to indicate that the Baptist did not even know Jesus, his own cousin, with whom he is painted together in many Madonna pictures. So whether Jesus was ever really baptized at all is a very open question. John the Baptist certainly, on the Gospel word of two of the four Gospel Biographers, did not baptize him; for he could not have done so and borne such witness, and then forget all about it, and send to inquire as about a total stranger to himself.

THE APOSTLES CHOSEN

The "calling of the Apostles" should, it would seem, be one of the simplest narratives that truth-inspired Gospel Historians could relate—if they knew or were inspired of what they were talking about. But it is as sadly mixed and muddled as any narrative in the Books, when there is more than one inspired recorder of the same alleged fact,—for no two ever tell the same thing the same way— as we shall see throughout.

Matthew is inspired to relate, that immediately after the baptism by John, and the wonderful "temptation in the wilderness" by the Devil, Jesus, "leaving Nazareth, he came and dwelt in Capernaum"

(Matt. iv, 13),—in order to fulfill another pretended prophecy, which we have seen never was. And, "from that time Jesus began to preach" (v. 17). And Jesus, "walking by the sea of Galilee," (evidently alone), saw two fishermen, brothers, Simon called Peter, and Andrew his brother, "casting a net into the sea"; and he saith unto them, "Follow me, and I will make you fishers of men"; and the two "straightway left their nets, and followed him" (Matt. iv, 18–20). Then, the three "going on from thence"—or, as Mark says, "when he had gone a little further thence" (Mark i, 19)—showing that it was some material distance further on, and not together with Peter and Andrew,—he saw two other fishermen brothers, James and John Zebedee, "in a ship mending their nets"; and "he called them; and they immediately left the ship, and their father, and followed him" (vv. 21–22), and they "went all about Galilee teaching" (v. 23).

Thus we have two separate and distinct pairs of fishermen, found successively some distance apart, both pairs expressly "called" by Jesus, and straightway leaving their jobs and following a total stranger on a novel kind of man-fishing expedition.

But Matthew's persistent contradictor Luke, relates it totally differently, but by the same inspiration. In his Chapter v, Jesus, now evidently in a big crowd, "as the people pressed upon him to hear the word of God," he "stood by the Lake of Gennesaret (v. 1). And saw two ships standing by the lake: but the fishermen had gone out of them, and were *washing* their nets" (v. 2)—not here "casting their nets into the sea," as Matthew tells. So Jesus "entered into one of the ships, which was Simon's, and prayed him that he would thrust out a little from the land. And he sat down and taught the people out of the ship" (v. 3). And James and John, the Zebedees, were right there with Peter and Andrew—"their partners, which were in the other ship" (v. 7); and it is repeated, for our greater credence—"James and John, the sons of Zebedee, which were partners with Simon" (v. 10). And here, all together on one shipboard it was, that "Jesus said unto Simon, Fear not; from thenceforth thou shalt catch men" (v. 10); and then—(after a fish story extraordinary which we will tell soon)—"when they had brought their ships to land, they (all four together) forsook all, and followed him" (v. 11)—this time without being "called" or asked at all. So Matthew and Luke here again inspiredly contradict each other, and it is certainly bad and sad enough; but this time John breaks into the narrative and flatly contradicts them both.

For John tells us himself, that "his record is true: and he knoweth that he saith true, that ye might believe" (xix, 35); so on this admission we must accept him in preference to even inspired Matthew and Luke. And this is the "record true" of the "calling"—which was not a calling at all, and happened very differently from what we have diversely learned already by the two other inspired Recorders. John was beside the Jordan, baptizing all comers; and as "John stood, and two of his disciples" (John i, 35),—there by Jordan, and not on the Sea of Galilee or Lake Gennesaret at all,—when Jesus walked by—evidently all alone this time; and John "looking upon Jesus as he walked, he saith, Behold the Lamb of God" (v. 36). And John's "two disciples heard him (John) speak, and they followed Jesus" (v. 37). Then "Jesus turned, and saw them following, and saith unto them, What seek ye? They said unto him, Rabbi, where dwellest thou? He (Jesus) saith unto them, Come and see" (vv. 38–39). And the two went home with Jesus "and abode with him that day."

Now here comes the most surprising feature of this inspired true record: "One of the two which heard John speak, and followed him (Jesus), was *Andrew, Simon Peter's brother*"! (v. 40)—here following John by the Jordan, not fishing with Brother Simon, on the Sea of Galilee at all. And Simon Peter was not there fishing either. For Andrew, says John, then went off somewhere and "findeth his own brother Simon, and saith unto him, We have found the Messias. *And he brought him to Jesus*" (vv. 41–42). No truly inspired and true records could possibly be more diverse than these three, and two of them must undeniably be wholly untrue. But it is a safe assertion that Andrew did not say to Peter, as he is quoted to have said, "I have found the Messiah." It was on the very next day (v. 35) after the baptism of Jesus by John, at the very beginning of the public activities of Jesus, that this scene is laid; Jesus was not Messiah, or Christ (v. 41), until he was "anointed" on head or feet long afterward, as we shall soon curiously see. Inspiration is here sadly at loggerheads with itself, even on the highly important point, which would make Simon Peter the Fisherman "called" to be the Founder of the whole Apostolic Succession, installed at Rome, Italy, even to this xxth Century.

"The Twelve"

Before leaving the Apostles to shift for themselves, we may briefly notice several other flaws of inspiration relating to them. Matthew was one of them, and surely ought to know his own name, and how he came to be numbered among the Chosen Twelve. We have seen already the conflicting accounts given by him and by Luke and John, as to the "calling"—or volunteering—of Andrew, Peter, James and John. As for himself, Matthew says modestly: "And as Jesus passed forth from thence," (where he had healed the man with the palsy), "he saw a man, named Matthew, sitting at the receipt of custom; and he saith unto him, Follow me. And he arose, and followed him" (Matt. ix, 9). But Mark tells us, that "as he (Jesus) passed by (after the palsy cure), he saw *Levi*, the son of Alpheus sitting at the receipt of custom," and called him (ii, 14). And Luke (v, 27) for once corroborates Mark, while as usual contradicting Matthew, even as to his own name.

But this little tangle does not end here: Matthew gives a list of the Twelve Apostles; among the others he lists "Matthew the Publican; two Simons, one surnamed Peter, and one The Canaanite —(the whole race of Canaanites having been exterminated by Joshua); two James, son of Alpheus and son of Zebedee; and one Lebbeus, whose surname was Thaddeus" (x, 2–4). Luke (Ch. vi) quite omits Lebbeus, and substitutes a second "Judas, brother of James," together with Judas Iscariot (v. 16). So we do not really know who composed the famous Twelve.

Again, Matthew and John, as we have seen, represent the Twelve picked up, one, two, or four at a time, at various times and places; but Mark and Luke say that they were all chosen together at one and at the same time, from out a large number of Disciples: "he (Jesus) went out into a mountain to pray, and continued all night in prayer; and when it was day, he called unto him his disciples, and of them he chose Twelve, whom also he named Apostles" (Mark iii, 13–14; Luke vi, 12–13); and then follows the list of names we have just seen to differ from the other two lists. So the whole matter of the Apostles is left a puzzle by inspiration. Except in one point, the personal character of these Apostles and Gospel Propagandists, which we will now reveal from the inspired record.

APOSTOLIC GREED AND STRIFE

Two of them, Peter and John, are expressly declared to be "unlearned and ignorant men" (Acts iv, 13); all twelve were of the same type and well matched. They were variously picked up from among the humblest and most superstitious of the Jews of the time, naked fishermen and peasants, "called" personally, we are told, by the Son of Yahveh, the King of the Jews, to be his counselors, guides and friends, in the establishment of his earthly and heavenly Kingdoms. They saw this Carpenter's Son of Nazareth—this man proclaimed as prophesied king—acclaimed by the Desert Dervish John as the Son of Yahveh, the long-promised and never-realized Messiah, the King of the Jews. This John was the own cousin of Jesus, born within six months of each other, and raised in intimate association; yet John avers and repeats, "I knew him not," until the dove flew down and lighted on him (Jno. i, 29–34),—and thus gave Godsent "sign" of the truth of his claim. But any signs are good to the ignorant and superstitious; and none at all are needed to gather followers for curiosity or hope of reward.

The hope of reward was the inspiredly recorded motive of these peasants who left their petty crafts for greater profit by following the lowly King-to-be. The greed and zeal for personal aggrandizement of the Chosen Twelve is constantly revealed throughout their inspired record. Hardly had the Twelve gotten organized and into action, before the cunning and crafty Peter, acting as spokesman for the craft, boldly advanced the itching palm: "Then answered Peter and said unto him, Behold, we have forsaken all, and followed thee; *what shall we have therefor?*" (Matt. xix, 27). Here for once in Holy Writ is complete "harmony of the Gospels"; all three record the demand and the promise of reward, though still variantly (Mark x, 28; Luke xviii, 28)—as is their inveterate custom. And the Master came back splendidly with the Promise: "And Jesus said unto them, Verily I say unto you, That ye which have followed me, in the regeneration, when the Son of Man shall sit in the throne of his glory, ye also shall sit upon twelve thrones, judging the twelves tribes of Israel" (Matt. xix, 28)—which would seem, too, to indicate that those Ten Tribes were not so lost as generally supposed. But still, this reward of reigning in future glory was naturally dampening to the spirits of those who had abandoned fish-nets and such to follow one proclaimed as King of the Jews, whose earthly throne on which he was to reign, was to be established forever, right there on earth. Although the other two inspired recorders assure that the promise was for reward both on earth and in the Hereafter: that the followers "shall receive a hundredfold now in this time, . . . and in the world to come eternal life" (Mark x, 29); Luke xviii, 30). But even these brilliant rewards could not satisfy the greed of the Holy Ones, and led not to gratitude, but to greater greed and strife.

The Mother of James and John, probably inspired by them, and zealous for their greater glory, came secretly, with her two sons, to Jesus, "worshiping him, and desiring a certain thing of him" (Matt. xx, 20); and when Jesus asked her what it was, "She saith unto him, Grant that these my two sons may sit, the one on thy right hand, and the other on the left, in thy Kingdom" (v. 21). But Mark contradicts the assurance of Matthew that it was Mrs. Zebedee who came and made the request; and avers that "James and John, the sons of Zebedee, come unto him, saying, Master, we would that thou shouldst do for us whatsoever we shall desire," and stated their own modest demand for preferment (Mark x, 35–37). But, in either contradictory event, both agree that "when the (other) ten heard it, they were moved with indignation against the two brethren" (Matt. xxix, 24; Mark x, 41).

Nor during the whole two years of association with their Master, did these holy Apostles abate their greed and strife. Several times are recorded disputes among them as to "who should be greatest among them" (Matt. xviii, 1; Mark ix, 33–34; Luke ix, 46) —here again the "harmony of the Gospels" assuring the constant inharmony of the Apostles. And even at the Last Supper, when Jesus had announced that one of them would that night betray him to death, "there was also strife among them, which of them should be accounted the greatest" (Luke xxii, 24). And great was the disgust of the Master at his miserable Apostles, and especially at the craven and crafty Peter. When first Jesus began to foretell that he must be put to death—thus putting an end to their hopes of reward, Peter, more knowing than his own Lord, "began to rebuke him, saying, Far be it from thee, Lord: this *shall not be* unto thee"; and Jesus turned on him with blasting scorn, "and said unto Peter, Get thee behind me, Satan: thou art an offense to me" (Matt. xvi, 23); and again the Gospels are in Harmony (Mark viii, 33). Such are the Holy Apostles of Jesus Christ, painted by some of themselves through inspiration. This "Satan" Peter, later self-appointed "Saint" Peter, may deserve our mention again.

We will return now to point out some other of the more glaring contradictions and obviously impossible truths of the inspired Gospels. All such with which they abound, and all their fables and superstitions are impossible for number to even mention. We limit instances now to reputed incidents of the Life of Christ, as so variously related.

The Sermon on the Mount—or Plain

The Sermon on the Mount is the most beautiful and lofty Discourse in Christian History. Very little of it is original;—as the marginal references show, and reference will verify, a great part of it is the stringing together odd scraps of moralizing taken bodily from the Old Testament Books. Matthew sets it out in extenso; and lays the scene just after the Temptation in the Wilderness, and the "calling" of Peter, Andrew, James and John, according to his version of the latter event. He declares, that Jesus, "seeing the multitudes, went up into a mountain: and when he was set, his disciples came unto him: And he opened his mouth, and taught them, saying" (Matt. v, 1–2), here following in three Chapters the justly celebrated Sermon.

But Luke tells the whole affair totally differently. It was not on the mountain, where Jesus spoke seated; it was down in the plain, where Jesus stood and spoke: it was after all the Twelve had been chosen and commissioned, which, according to Luke, as we have seen, was while up on the Mount in prayer all night (Luke vi, 12–16). Then, with the Twelve, "He *came down* with them, and *stood in the plain*, and the company of his Disciples, and a great multitude of people" (v. 17). Then, standing, "He lifted up his eyes on his disciples, and said" (v. 20): and here follows the self-same but abbreviated Sermon—not on the Mount but after coming down from the Mount onto the Plain. Again inspiration clashes with inspiration, and we are left in doubt of truth.

The Lord's Prayer

A beautiful part of Matthew's Sermon on the Mount is the Lord's Prayer. Jesus told of the vain public prayers of the heathen and of the hypocrites, and said, "Be not ye, therefore, like unto them; after this manner therefore pray ye: Our Father which art in heaven," etc. (Matt. vi, 8–9). Luke again belies this cherished story of its origin; lays the scene long after the Sermon on Mount or Plain; and under totally different circumstances; a prayer delivered as a model, on request. As by plenary inspiration Luke says: "And it came to pass, that, as he (Jesus) was praying in a certain place, when he ceased one of his disciples said to him, Lord, teach us to pray, as John also taught his disciples. And he said unto them. When ye pray, say Our Father, etc. (Luke xi, 1–2). Every single circumstance of the two origins is in conflict. Even this Gem of devotion is in two totally different settings,—and like the whole Sermon, is a composite of quoted ancient sayings of the Scriptures.

Christ Anointed

Let us witness the much celebrated "Christ-ening" or Anointing of the Messiah-King of the Jews. Inspiration is strangely at variance as to when and where it happened, and how. If the great Yahveh of Heaven had sent his only begotten Son on special Mission to earth as the long-prophesied Messiah, to re-establish the Throne of David forever and sit upon it as King—it was a very sorry sort of ceremonial, at best, for the anointing of a King, earthly or heavenly.

Matthew avers, in his Chapter xxvi, that "two days before the Passover" (at which he was to be betrayed)," Jesus was in Bethany, in the house of *Simon the leper*" (v. 6); and "There came unto him a woman having an alabaster box of very precious ointment, and poured it on his head as he sat at meat" (v. 7); whereat "his disciples had indignation" for the waste (v. 8). Mark relates the same, in substance (xiv, 1–4), but specifies that the box of ointment was "of spikenard, very precious" (v. 3), and that only "some" of the disciples were peeved at the waste. Both lay the scene, as we have seen, *two days before* the last Passover at which Jesus was ever present, just before his betrayal and death, and in the house of Simon the Leper.

But Luke (Chap. vii) makes a very different story of it: the time was just after John Baptist had sent two of his disciples to Jesus, in the earliest days, to inquire "Art thou he that should come, or look we for aonther?" (vv. 19–20). Then, "one of the Pharisees desired him that he would eat with him. And he went *into the Pharisee's house*, and sat down to meat" (v. 36). Now and here it was, "Behold, a woman of the City, which *was a sinner*" (v. 37), came in with the alabaster box of ointment; and she "washed his feet with tears, and did wipe them with the hairs of her head, and kissed his *feet*, and anointed *them* (his *feet*) with the ointment" (v. 38). And nobody said anything about the waste—the disciples were not even invited to the dinner; but the Pharisee is here called Simon, but could not of course have been the Leper, for lepers were "unclean," and no one would have given a dinner or been present with them; moreover this dinner was *two years before* the last Passover;— and it was feet and not head which were anointed.

But the greatest surprise comes from the inspired record borne by John, Chapter xii. The event takes place *"six days before* the Passover," and *in the house of Lazarus* "which had been dead, whom he had raised from the dead" (v. 1): "There they made him a supper: and Martha served: but Lazarus was one of them that sat at the table with him" (v. 2): "Then took *Mary* a pound of ointment of spikenard, very costly, and anointed the *feet* of Jesus, and wiped his feet with her hair" (v. 3); and it was "one of his disciples, Judas Iscariot" (v. 4), who alone complained about the waste, and that the ointment should have been sold and the proceeds given to the poor (v. 5). And in Chapter xi, John tells of a "sick man named Lazarus" and of "Mary and her sister Martha" (v. 1); and makes the positive identification: "It was *that* Mary which anointed the Lord with ointment, and wiped his feet with her hair" (v. 2),—though she did not do it until the next Chapter. So we are pardonably surprised to learn that it was this well-known lady friend of Jesus, who was the "woman of the city, which was a sinner" (Luke vii, 37), for we had not previously suspected her virtue, and thought it was Mary Magdalene who was the "soiled dove" out of whom he had "cast seven devils" (Mark xvi, 9; Luke viii, 2). Inspiration is here again at odds.

Jesus—King of the Jews

The saddest, sorriest mockery in the reputed Life of the humble Nazarene, was his tawdry, burlesque, ass-back Entry into Jerusalem as the arrived Messiah—the King of the Jews. Great must have been the obsession, the possession, the delusion, of the poor Wayfarer, who had nowhere even to lay his head, and had to catch a fish to find a penny to pay his pittance of a poll-tax—and must needs filch an ass's colt to make his mock-triumphal entry into his Kingdom—for a one-day stand. It is too trifling almost to mention here—and the discrepancies of the four inspired accounts of it are rather trifling, but they exist, and may be noted in passing the pitiful scene.

In Matthew xxi, Jesus having arrived, with disciples and a rabble, to Bethphage, by the Mount of Olives, "sent two disciples, Saying unto them, Go into the village over against you, and straightway ye shall find an ass tied, and a colt with her; loose them, and bring them unto me" (vv. 1–2). And the two disciples went and brought the ass and the colt (v. 7),—*two* animals. The disciples "put on them (both animals) their clothes, and they set him thereon" (v. 7), —thus riding both ass and colt. And the rabble followed behind, shouting Hosannas to their King,—"and clapping their chopped hands, and threw up their sweaty nightcaps, and uttered such a deal of stinking breath, as had almost choked Caesar there upon the Lupercal, the time when he thrice refused the crown, and would not be King." But our poor Nazarene, the man who would be King, jogged ass-colt-wise with his shouting rabblement into Jerusalem, and all the City wondered, saying, "Who is this?" and for answer the rabble accompaniment replied, "This is Jesus, the Prophet of Nazareth of Galilee" (vv. 10–11). And with his inveterate habit of warping ancient sayings into "prophecies fulfilled by Jesus," Matthew says: "All this was done, that it might be fulfilled which was spoken by the prophet, saying: "Behold thy King cometh unto thee, meek, and sitting upon an ass, and a colt the foal of an ass" (vv. 4–5). But after a big flourish of mock authority by driving the money-changers from the Temple, the very same day, the uncrowned King "left them, and went out of the City into Bethany; and he lodged there" (v. 17). Years later, another King made a like grand flourish, and

> ". . . with four thousand men,
> Rode up the hill, and then rode down again."

So, the God-sent King who was to establish his Kingdom and reign forever over Israel, did not fulfill the principal part of the Prophecy.

Mark, who wrote the story first, says, that Jesus said: "Go your way into the village . . . and you will find a colt tied; bring him; . . . and they brought the colt to Jesus" (xi, 7); but as this would not fulfill the prophecy of "an ass and a colt," Matthew, in copying Mark, added the ass and the prophecy. Luke tells only of the colt and omits the ass (xix, 29–40). John, who tells us that he always tells the truth, says, in Chapter xii, that the thing happened just the other way around; it was "on the next day" (v. 12) after the "six days before the Passover" (v. 1) when Harlot Mary anointed the feet of Jesus; "much people that were come to the feast, when they heard that Jesus was coming to Jerusalem, took branches of palm trees, and went forth to meet him, and cried, Hosanna, Blessed is the King of Israel," etc.—thus the City rabble took the initiative in the farce-comedy, instead of Jesus himself, as told by the other Three. And John assures us, "These things understood not his disciples at the first" (v. 16), whereas the other Three make it the disciples who brought the ass, or ass and colt, or colt, and put their own clothes "thereon," and themselves started the whole scene. Until another revelation, we will never know exactly how the whole affair did start, and who is to blame for the distressing farce.

Secrecy Enjoined

But however it was, it is singular that the Messiah, so often proclaimed by long-distance voices of his father Yahveh from

Heaven, "This is my Beloved Son . . . hear ye him"—and now making
a public parade of the fact, should have so often denied it and
enjoined silence and secrecy about it. Time and again, as in the
anguish of fear, "he charged his disciples that they should tell no
man that he was Jesus the Christ" (Matt. xvi, 20); and even he
suffered not his very active and efficient witnesses, the Devils, to
testify for him, "for they knew that he was Christ" (Luke iv, 41).
Before Caiaphas and Pilate, who questioned him, "Art thou the
Christ" (Matt. xxvi, 63), "Art thou the King of the Jews?" (Matt.
xxvii, 11), he hesitated, and equivocated, and answered solely, "Thou
hast said." Even his disciples, who had fled and abandoned him
in his hour of dire distress and death, heard the news of his resurrection as "idle tales and they believed them not" (Luke xxiv, 11).

Superstitions of Jesus Christ

A very curious and discrediting phase of the personality of the
proclaimed Son of Yahveh, who knew all things, even the hidden
thoughts of men, is that he believed and declared so many things,
which were current beliefs among the ignorant of his times, but are
known by all school-children to-day to be fables and superstitions,
and which the all-knowing mind of a God would always, even then,
know to be impossible and untrue. Multiplied instances abound in
the four inspired Biographies.

The Christ warns against all others who should claim to be
Christs, offering his own proofs of credit: "If any man shall say
unto you, Lo, here is Christ, or there, believe it not. For there shall
arise many false Christs, and false prophets, and shall show great
signs and wonders; insomuch that, if it were possible, they shalt
deceive the very elect" (Matt. xxiv, 23–24). We all know that
miracles do not happen; that, as Hume justly said: "No testimony
can prove miracles, for it is more probable that the testimony is
false than that the miracles are true." But, even otherwise, how
could "great signs and wonders" be worked, great and deceptive
miracles be wrought, by Impostors in whom is not the power of
God? Signs and wonders, miracles, were the very sign-manual proof
of the identity and authenticity of Jesus as the Christ: "for no man
can do these miracles that thou doest, except God be with him"
(Jno. iii, 2). "Believe me for the very works' sake" (Jno. xiv, 11),
is the Christ's special challenge for Faith to the Doubting. Yet he
concedes to impostors and to devils the very same power to work
miracles which is his own special patent of Divinity.

It is this same token of his authentic Divinity that he sends to the doubting Baptist, who sent to inquire: "Art thou he that should come, or look we for another?"—and the only answer which Jesus returned, and the only proof he deemed necessary, was a report of his miracles: "Go and shew John again those things which ye do hear and see,"—reciting a list of the miracles he had done (Matt. xi, 4–5). And it is the same all-sufficient answer which he flung back at Herod: "Go ye, and tell that Fox, Behold, I cast out Devils," etc. (Luke xiii, 32); and throughout, the "signs and wonders" which he worked are the test and certain authentication of the Divinity of the Christ: "except ye see signs and wonders, ye will not believe" (Jno. iv, 48)—Jesus himself declared.

Yet, a thousand times, the "false Christs" and the Devils do the miracles of Yahveh—quite as fluently and as powerful as Yahveh, and are in this respect his very successful rivals. The instances are too many to more than mention a few: The Devil leads the Christ into the Wilderness, upon a high mountain, and onto the pinnacle of the Temple, and "tempts" him, claiming undisputed dominion over the kingdoms of the world (Matt. iv, 1–11); he "cast out devils" by the Legion from disordered persons, and held argument with the Devils, recognizing their existence, intelligence and power (Matt. viii, 28–32, *passim*); he enjoins to "fear him which is able to destroy both soul and body in Hell" (Matt. x, 28); he proclaimed that there is "everlasting fire prepared for the Devil and his angels" (Matt. xxv, 41); he declared that "false Christs and false prophets" should arise who could and would perform "great signs and wonders," deceiving even the elect (Mark xiii, 22); and as the badge of their Divine mission and authority, he gave to his Disciples "power and authority over all Devils" (Luke xi, 1)—and so *ad infinitum*: though God and intelligent humans know there are no Devils and no Hell of Fire—and that Devils and false Christs cannot work miracles, all as so often declared as verities by the Son of God.

Scores of other superstitions he also constantly uttered, which we know are legends and fables, but to which he appeals as living truths: Abel, Noah and the Flood, Lot and his wife turned to the fabled pillar of salt, Moses and the Burning Bush, Jonah swallowed by the Fish—a whole congeries of ancient Scripture Fables which the Son of Yahveh takes as Gospel Truth—and which God knows never were.

THE "SECOND COMING" OF CHRIST

The crowning disproof of the Divinity, even of the common sense of truth of the Christ, and a sad proof of the serious delusion which he suffered, is the stupendous assertion which he made of his *immediate second coming* to earth in all the glory of his triumphant Kingdom. A more positive and explicit thing—incapable of misunderstanding or double meaning—he never said than this:

"Verily I say unto you, There be some standing here, which shall not taste of death, till they see the Son of Man (*Ben-adam*) coming in his Kingdom". (Matt. xvi, 28; Mark. ix, 1).

"Verily I say unto you, that this generation shall not pass, till all these things be done" (Mark xiii, 30).

"But I tell you of a truth, that there be some standing here, which shall not taste of death, till they see the Kingdom of God" (Luke ix, 27).

And Caiaphas, the High Priest, before whom Jesus was led after his capture in the Garden, solemnly appealed to him for truth:

"I adjure thee by the Living God, that thou tell us whether thou be the Christ, the Son of God."

"Jesus saith unto him, Thou hast said: nevertheless, I say unto you, Hereafter shall *ye see* the Son of Man sitting on the right hand of power, *and coming in the clouds of heaven*" (Matt. xxvi, 63–64; Mark xiv, 61–62).

And in these Nineteen Hundred years this supreme avowal of the Son of Yahveh has gone unverified. No more is needed to convict the inspired records of utter fallacy and discredit; to prove to demonstration that the lowly Nazarene was no God, was no Promised Messiah—was himself a "false Christ," who has deceived the Very Elect of those who have had a misplaced Faith in his Holy Word.

CHAPTER XV

MORE "HARMONY OF THE GOSPELS"

THE CLOSING SCENES OF THE DRAMA

WE have thus reviewed the salient features of the recorded events of the birth and career through life of the Man of Nazareth, and thus have been enabled to form an intelligent, if amazed, judgment as to their inspired and historical verity.

Let us regard now the closing scenes of the sacred Tragedy of the Son of Yahveh made Man, in the distressing episodes of his betrayal, condemnation, and ignominious death, and in his glorious triumph over death, his resurrection from the dead, his varied subsequent appearances to the living, and his transcendent ascension into Heaven to sit with his Father Yahveh—until his prophesied speedy Coming Again in glory to establish his promised Kingdom—which he was indeed to establish on the first trip to earth; no return appearance for this purpose is once prophesied.

This review will cap the climax of inspired Verity of the sacred Record, and show new phases of the Harmony of the Gospels.

THE BETRAYAL AND ARREST

First we note the affecting incident of the betrayal and capture of Jesus, by night, in the Garden of Gethsemane. But first, of the *posse comitatus* which effected the capture, its source, its personnel, its matériel.

Matthew thus records:

"And while he (Jesus) yet spake, lo, Judas, one of the twelve, came, and with him a great multitude with swords and staves, from the Chief Priests and the Elders of the people" (xxvi, 47).

Mark records it thus:

"And immediately, while he (Jesus) yet spake, cometh Judas, one of the twelve, and with him a great multitude with swords and staves, from the chief priests and the scribes and the elders" (xiv, 43).

Luke thus relates:

"And while he (Jesus) yet spake, behold a multitude and he that was called Judas, one of the twelve, went before them. Then Jesus said unto the chief priests, and captains of the temple, and the elders which were come to him" (xxii, 47, 52).

John says:

"Judas then, having received a band of men and officers from the chief priests and Pharisees, cometh thither with lanterns and torches and weapons" (xviii, 3).

The discrepancies in the foregoing four accounts of the "posse" may seem slight; but for a narration of inspired truth they are significant. Matthew says the "posse" was *sent* by "the chief priests and elders"; Mark, by the "chief priests, scribes and elders"; Luke, that the chief priests, and captains of the Temple, and the elders" *went* in person with the "posse"; John says that it was *sent* by the "chief priests and Pharisees." Matthew and Mark say, that Judas took along "a great multitude"; Luke, simply a "multitude"; John, much more orderly, says "a band of men and officers." This whole proceeding having been by night, may naturally be somewhat in the dark, notwithstanding the lanterns and torches of John.

Secondly, as to what happened when Judas and his "posse" arrived at the Garden. Matthew, vv. 48–50, relates:

"Now he that betrayed him gave them a sign, saying, Whomsoever I shall kiss, that same is he: hold him fast. And forthwith he came to Jesus and said, Hail, Master, and kissed him. And Jesus said unto him, Friend, wherefore art thou come? Then came they, and laid hands on him, and took him."

Mark, vv. 44–46, relates:

"And he that betrayed him had given them a token, saying, Whomsoever I shall kiss, the same is he; take him, and lead him away safely. And as soon as he was come, he goeth straightway to him, and saith, Master, Master; and kissed him. And they laid hands on him, and took him away."

Luke, vv. 47–48, relates:

"Judas went before them, and drew near unto Jesus to kiss him. But Jesus said unto him, Judas, betrayest thou the Son of man (ben-adam) with a kiss"?

John, vv. 4–8, 12, relates; that as the "posse" approached at some distance:

"Jesus, therefore, knowing all things that should come upon him, went forth, and said unto them, Whom seek ye? They answered him, Jesus of Nazareth. Jesus saith unto them, I am he. And Judas also, which betrayed him, stood with them. As soon then as he had said unto them, I am he, they went backward, and fell to the ground. Then asked he them again, Whom seek ye? And they said, Jesus of Nazareth. Jesus answered, I have told you that I am he: if therefore ye seek me, let these go their way. Then the band and the captain and officers of the Jews took Jesus, and bound him."

The conflicts of testimony are much more glaring in this portion of the inspired reports. Matthew and Mark are substantially agreed, declaring that Judas had given his posse a prearranged "sign" by which he would point out Jesus to them, kissing him; and they both say, that Judas went straightway to Jesus, hailed him "Master," and kissed him. But Luke testifies that Judas did not kiss Jesus; that he only "drew near unto Jesus to kiss him"; and that Jesus, telepathically knowing his purpose, checked him; saying: "Judas, betrayest thou me with a kiss?" John contradicts the contradictory reports of all three of the others, and gives his version: That as Judas and the posse, at some distance, approached, Jesus, "knowing all things," went forth to meet them, and asked, "Whom seek ye?" And "they" answered him "Jesus of Nazareth." And Jesus replied, "I am he." Judas, instead of going "before them," as Luke says in v. 17, simply "stood with them"; and as soon as Jesus had said "I am he," the whole posse, terrified, "went backward, and fell to the ground." Jesus, then, a second time, asked "Whom seek ye?" and upon being again told Jesus of Nazareth," replied, "I have told you that I am he; if therefore ye seek me," do your duty and take me. No contradictions in human language could be more contradictory than these.

The little incident of Peter cutting off the ear of one of the posse may be related in passing. Matthew (vv. 51–52), tell it thus:

"And behold, one of them that were with Jesus stretched out his hand, and drew his sword, and smote the servant of the high priest, and struck off his ear. Then saith Jesus unto him, Put up again thy sword," etc.

Mark, vv. 47 and 48, tells it thus:

"But a certain one of them that stood by drew his sword, and smote the servant of the high priest, and struck off his ear. And Jesus answered and said unto them, Are ye come out as against a robber, with swords and staves to seize me?"

Luke, vv. 49–51, tells it thus:

"When they which were about him saw what would follow (the kissing), they said unto him, Lord, shall we smite with the sword? And one of them smote the servant of the high priest, and cut off his right ear. But Jesus answered and said, Suffer ye thus far. And he touched his ear, and healed him."

John, vv. 10–11, thus relates it:

"Simon Peter therefore having a sword drew it, and struck the high priest's servant, and cut off his right ear. Now, the servant's name was Malchus. Jesus, therefore, said unto Peter, Put up the sword into the sheath; the cup which the Father hath given me, shall I not drink it?"

Little as this incident is, these four inspired historians cannot tell just how it happened. Matthew relates the smiting by "one of them which were with Jesus," and Jesus simply said, "Put up again thy sword." Mark tells of the sword-play by "a certain one of them that stood by"; and Jesus said nothing about putting up thy sword, but said to the posse, "Are ye come out as against a robber?" Luke tells us that "they which were about" Jesus, seeing what was going to follow the undelivered kiss by Judas, asked permission as for a general affray, saying, "Lord, may we smite with the sword?" and one of them without waiting reply, smote the servant's ear. Jesus, when too late, answered in the negative; then Luke, the physician, puts in a word for his profession, and tells us that Jesus performed a miracle and stuck the ear on again and healed it. No one else relates this, the only remarkable thing of the whole evening. John goes into his usual detail and gives us the name of Peter as the aggressor, says nothing about the asking permission for a general assault, and gives the name of the wounded servant. And he reports that Jesus told Peter to put up his sword, for he, Jesus, must take his medicine out of the cup prepared for him. Each reader may take his choice as to how it happened or did not.

PETER'S DENIAL OF JESUS

We will now take up and review the records of the trial of Jesus as recorded by his four inspired reporters. I omit, of course, all reference to Jewish or Roman law and legal practice, as the Bible account must stand or fall on its own internal consistency.

First, we will consider the incident of Peter's denial, as the beginning of the incident precedes the trial. This takes us back a moment for our authority. Jesus is reported to have predicted this of Peter, in rebuke of his vain boasting of unfailing fidelity.

Matthew, Chapter xxvi (vv. 30–34), states the events thus:

"And when they had sung a hymn, they went out (from the Last Supper) unto the Mount of Olives. Then said Jesus unto him (Peter), Verily I say unto thee, that this night, before the cock *crow*, thou shalt deny me *thrice*."

Mark, Chapter xiv (17, 30–32), relates the events thus:

"And when it was evening he (Jesus) cometh with the twelve. And Jesus saith unto him (Peter), Verily I say unto thee, that thou to-day, even this night, before the cock *crow twice*, shalt deny me *thrice*. And they came into a place which was named Gethsemane."

Luke, Chapter xxii (vv. 14, 34, 39), relates the events thus:

"And when the hour was come, he sat down, and the apostles with him. And he said, I tell thee, Peter, the cock shall *not crow* this day, until thou shalt *thrice* deny that thou knowest me. And he came out, and went, as his custom was, unto the mount of Olives."

John, Chapter xiii (vv. 2, 38), relates the events thus:

"And during supper, Jesus answereth, Verily verily, I say unto thee, the cock *shall not* crow, till thou hast denied me *thrice*."

Here we have some more conflicting truths. Matthew says that the accusation of Peter was made by Jesus *after* the Last Supper and in the Garden of Gethsemane on the Mount of Olives. Mark, Luke and John deny this, and assert that it occurred *during* the Last Supper, and that they then, afterwards, went to the mount. Matthew, Luke and John report Jesus as saying, "before the cock crows once" Peter would deny him thrice; while Mark makes him say "before the cock crows twice" Peter would make the three denials. The reader may accept either of these two cock-tales which he most relishes.

Now, how did these denials of Peter's work out, with their attendant circumstances?

Matthew, Chapter xxvi, relates the story thus:

"(57) And they that had taken Jesus led him away to the house of Caiaphas the high priest, where the scribes and the elders were gathered together. (58) But Peter followed him afar off, unto the court of the high priest, and entered in, and sat with the officers to see the end. (The trial was proceeding,—vv. 59-68). (69) Now Peter was sitting *without* in the court (i.e. courtyard), and a *maid* came unto him saying, etc. (70) But he denied before them all, saying, etc. (71) And when he was gone out into the porch, another *maid* saw him, and saith, etc. (72) And again he denied with an oath, saying, etc. (73) And after a little while they that stood by came and said to Peter, etc. (74) Then began he to curse and swear, I know not the man. And straightway the cock crew. (75) And Peter remembered the word which Jesus had said, Before the cock crow, thou shalt deny me thrice."

Mark, Chapter xiv, reports the matter with important variations:

"(53) And they led Jesus away to the high priest, and there came together with him all the chief priests and the elders and the scribes. (54) And Peter had followed him afar off, even *within*, into the court of the high priest; and he was sitting with the officers and warming himself. (The Trial then progressed:—vv. 55 to 65). (66) And as Peter was beneath in the court (i.e. court-yard), there cometh one of the *maids* of the high priest, (67) and says to Peter, etc. (68) But he denied, etc.; and he went out on the porch; and the cock crew (69) And the *maid* saw him, and began again to say, etc. (70) But he again denied it. And after a little while again they that stood by said to Peter, etc. (71) But he began to curse and to swear, etc. (72) And straightway the second time the cock crew. And Peter called to mind the word, how that Jesus said unto him, Before the cock crow twice, thou shalt deny me thrice."

Luke, Chapter xxii, relates the incident with marked differences —and as occurring *before* the Trial on the next day:

"(54) And they seized him (Jesus) and led him away, and brought him to the high priest's house. But Peter followed afar off. (55) And when they had kindled a fire in the midst of the court (i.e. court-yard), and had sat down together, Peter sat in the midst of them. (56) And a certain *maid* seeing him as he sat in the light of the fire, said, etc. (57) But he denied saying, etc. (58) And after a little while, another saw him and said, But thou art one of them. (59) But Peter said, *Man,* I am not. And after the space of about one hour, another said, etc. (60) But Peter said, *Man,* I know not what thou sayest. And immediately, while he yet spake, the cock crew. (61) And the Lord turned and looked upon Peter. And Peter remembered the word of the Lord, how that he said unto him, Before the cock crow this day, thou shalt deny me thrice."

John, Chapter xviii, gives a totally different "true record" report:

"(15) And Simon Peter followed Jesus, and so did another disciple; the disciple entered in with Jesus into the court of the high priest, (16) but Peter was standing at the door without; (later the maid that kept the door let Peter in). (17) The maid that kept the door said to Peter, etc., and he denied. (18) The servants and officers and Peter were standing there warming themselves.—(The Trial, apparently before Annas, is proceeding, vv. 19–24).—(25) Now Simon Peter was standing and warming himself. They said therefore unto him, etc. He denied, etc. (26) One of the servants saith, etc. (27) Peter therefore denied again: and straightway the cock crew."

The conflicts and contradictions in the relation of this trifling incident are astonishing. It is very difficult to untangle the twisted narrative into its several warped strands. Matthew, Mark and Luke lay this incident of denials and cock-crowing at the house of the high priest, Caiaphas; John lays it partly at the house of Caiaphas and partly at the house of Annas. Matthew and Mark say that it took place during the night trial of Jesus at the house of Caiaphas; Luke says that it occurred during the night, but during no trial, as Jesus was simply held a prisoner in the courtyard overnight, and his trial was next day; John says—well, Aristotle himself could hardly tell what John says, it is so mixed: I will pass this puzzle till we come to the account of the Trial.

To whom the denials were made, and where, is a matter of much conflict. As to the first denial; Matthew says, Peter was sitting without in the court, and a maid came unto him saying. Mark says, as Peter was *within* the court, and as he was beneath *in* the court, one of the maidens came and said to him. Luke says, a certain maid seeing him as he sat by the fire, said. John says, The maid that kept the door of the court and who let Peter in, said.

As to the second denial: Matthew says, when Peter was gone out into the porch, *another maid* saw him and said. Mark says, when Peter was out on the porch, the *same maid* as at first saw him and began again to say. Luke says Peter was still by the fire and that it was a *man*, Peter replying, "Man, I am not." John says, they (*officers and servants*) said unto him.

As to the third denial: Matthew says, after a little while "*they that stood by*" came and said. Mark says, the same thing. Luke says, after the space of about one hour, "*another man*" said. John says, "one of the servants" said.

Matthew, Luke and John report the cock as crowing only *once*, and *after* the *third* denial; Mark says that the cock crowed *twice*, *after* the *second* and after the *third* denials. Matthew, Luke and John record Peter as thereupon remembering that Jesus had said to him, "before the cock crows (once) thou shalt deny me thrice"; Mark makes Peter remember that Jesus had said "before the cock crow *twice* thou shalt deny me thrice."

The Trial of Jesus

This brings us now to the scene of the famous Trial of Jesus Christ.

Matthew, (xxvi, 57–67 and xxvii, 1–2) thus relates the trial scene:

"(57) And they that had laid hold on Jesus led him away to Caiaphas the high priest, where the scribes and the elders were assembled. (59) Now the chief priests, and elders, and all the council sought false witness against Jesus, to put him to death; (60) But found none: yes, though many false witnesses came yet found they none. At the last came two false witnesses (61) And said, This fellow said, I am able to destroy this temple of God, and to build it in three days. (62) And the high priest arose, and said unto him, Answerest thou nothing? what is it which these witness against thee? (63) But Jesus held his peace. And the high priest answered and said unto him, I adjure thee by the living God, that thou tell us whether thou be the Christ, the Son of God. (64) Jesus saith unto him, Thou hast said: nevertheless I say unto you, Hereafter shall ye see the Son of man sitting on the right hand of power, and coming in the clouds of heaven. (65) Then the high priest rent his clothes, saying, He hath spoken blasphemy; what further need have we of witnesses? Behold, now ye have heard his blasphemy. (66) What think ye? They answered and said, He is guilty of death. (67) Then did they spit in his face, and buffeted him; saying, Prophesy unto us, thou Christ, Who is he that smote thee? (xxvii–1) When the morning was come, all the chief priests and elders of the people took counsel against Jesus to put him to death; (2) And when they had bound him, they led him away, and delivered him to Pontius Pilate, the governor."

Mark (xiv and xv, 1) relates the trial scene in substantial identity with Matthew, as just copied in full into the record; therefore I do not repeat it.

Luke (xxii and xxiii, 1) records the scene entirely differently. To get the connection I shall have to repeat a few verses offered in connection with the "denial" story.

"(56) But a certain maid beheld him (Peter) as he sat by the fire, and said, etc. (57) And he denied, etc. (60) And the cock crew. (61) And the Lord turned and looked upon Peter. (63) And the men that held Jesus, mocked him, and smote him. (64) And when they had blindfolded him, they struck him in the face, and asked him, saying, Prophesy, who is it that smote thee? (65) And many other things blasphemously spake they against him. (66) And as soon as it was day, the elders of the people, and the chief priests and the scribes came together, and led him into their council, (67) Saying, Art thou the Christ? tell us, And he said unto them, If I tell you, ye will not believe. (68) And if I also ask you, ye will not answer me nor let me go. (69) Hereafter shall the Son of man sit on the right hand of the power of God. (70) Then said they all, Art thou then the Son of God? And he said unto the, Ye say that I am. (71) And they said, What need we any further witness? for we ourselves have heard of his own mouth. And the whole multitude of them arose, and led him unto Pilate."

John, (xviii) gives a very different account of the trial scene:

"(12) Then the band, and the captain, and officers of the Jews took Jesus, and bound him, (13) And led him away to Annas first, (for he was father-in-law to Caiaphas which was the high priest that same year). (19) The high priest then asked Jesus of his disciples, and of his doctrine. (20) Jesus, answered him, I spake openly to the world; I ever taught in the synagogue, and in the temple, whither the Jews always resort; and in secret have I said nothing. (21) Why askest thou me? Ask them which heard me, what I have said unto them: behold, they know what I said. (22) And when he had thus spoken, one of the officers which stood by, struck Jesus with the palm of his hand, saying, Answerest thou the high priest so? (23) Jesus answered him, If I have spoken evil, bear witness of the evil: but if well, why smitest thou me? (24) (Now Annas had sent him bound unto Caiaphas the high priest.)"

The first two Evangelists, Matthew and Mark, practically tally in their accounts of the trial: it was before *Caiaphas;* it was *during the night* when Jesus was captured; some false witnesses testified; Jesus made statements which were considered blaphemous, and was judged worthy of death; on the *next morning* he was carried before the Roman Governor, *Pilate.* But Luke completely discredits the reports of Matthew and Mark. For Luke makes it plain that there was no trial during the night, but Jesus passed the night in the courtyard with his guard and Peter; and the next morning, "as soon as it was day," the council assembled, "and they led him into their council." The proceedings are related with some minor differences which need not be noticed. John says that Jesus was first taken to Annas, where some proceedings and one of Peter's denials seem to have passed: then "Annas sent him (Jesus) bound unto Caiaphas the high priest." But whether by night or day does not appear. The proceedings are related with some differences of detail.

After the proceedings before Caiaphas, Jesus was taken to Pilate for final sentence. There are many variants in the four records of the proceedings before Pilate, but I shall pass them; the result was that Pilate very unjustly delivered up "this just man" to the chief priests to be crucified. Now we take up the tangle of contradictions again. Instead of quoting all these accounts in full, I will simply state the points of contradiction, where this can be done with full justice to the exact truth.

THE CRUCIFIXION

The immediate scene of the Crucifixion offers several points of conflict of narrative. Let it be remembered that we now have to do with the most stupendous series of events in all Time—if any of them ever happened at all. The Jewel of Consistency should crown the inspired record of these World Wonders. Amidst all the miracles appealed to to accredit the story of the death and resurrection of a God, the seal of God's Truth upon the inspired histories should blaze upon this Supreme Miracle for the Faith of Mankind. Let us offer these four records, and look for the Miracle of Truth in the Bible!

BEARING THE CROSS

Matthew, (xxvii, 32), Mark (xv, 21), and Luke (xxiii, 26), say that on the way to Golgotha with Jesus, one Simon a Cyrenian was "compelled to go with them, that he might bear his cross"; John, who says he was there, declares (xix, 17) that Jesus himself, "bearing the cross for himself went forth to Golgotha."

THE INSCRIPTION

Jesus was crucified with a Legend above his head. With respect to this: Matthew (xxvii, 37) makes it read:

"And they (the soldiers who crucified Jesus) set up over his head his accusation written, This is Jesus the King of the Jews."

Mark (xv, 26) makes it read:

"And the superscription of his accusation was written over, The King of the Jews."

Luke (xxiii, 38), makes it read:

"And a superscription also was written over him in letters of Greek, and Latin, and Hebrew, This is the King of the Jews."

While John (xix, 19), says it read:

"And Pilate wrote a title, and put it on the cross. And the writing was, Jesus of Nazareth, the King of the Jews."

And John, who says he was there throughout, adds (v. 21), a totally new incident:

"The chief priests of the Jews therefore said to Pilate, Write not, The King of the Jews; but that he said, I am King of the Jews." Pilate answered, "What I have written, I have written."

So interesting an inscription as this reads four different ways; not so very different, but different. The inspired writers differ in greater contradictions as to the circumstances of the inscription: Matthew (v. 37), says that after casting lots for his garments, "the *soldiers* set up over his head" the inscription; Mark (xv, 26) and Luke (xxiii, 38), simply say the superscription "was written," quoting it divergently; while John (xix, 19) avers that *Pilate wrote* it and put it on the cross." This latter is clearly incredible in itself, and it contradicts Matthew flatly, that the soldiers set it up.

THE WITNESSES

The incident of who was present at this awful scene, and what was said and done, is very important, one would think; and it is very variently and contradictorily related. Matthew (xxvii, 39–44) says that "they that passed by" railed at him, taunting him to come down from the cross; adding, "And the robbers also that were crucified with him cast upon him the same reproach." Mark (xv, 29–32), says that not only they that passed by, but "in like manner also the chief priests," as well as they that were crucified with him. According to Luke (xxiii, 35–39) "the people stood beholding"; the "rulers scoffed at him; and the soldiers also mocked him, saying"; also that but "one of the malefactors which were hanged railed on him." John, who was right there on the spot, and so he says "his record is true," relates several things, saying "these things the soldiers did"; but not a word of passers-by, chief priests, rulers, scoffing, or mocking.

And John, who was "standing by," says only that "there were standing by the cross of Jesus his mother" and the two other Marys; and that Jesus said "Woman, behold, thy son," pointing out John. Matthew (vv. 55–56) says that the mother of Jesus, the Marys, and many women," were there beholding from afar"—therefore not "standing by the cross," as John assures; Mark (xv, 40) says the three Marys and the other women "were beholding from afar"; while Luke (xxiii, 49) joins the chorus asserting positively that the women "stood afar off, seeing these things."

THE LAST WORDS

Matthew and Mark relate not a word said by Jesus on the cross except the expiring cry at the ninth hour, "*Eli, Eli, lama sabachthani*" (a quotation from David; Ps. xxii, 1), meaning "My God, my God, why hast thou forsaken me," but not a single precious "dying word" of his Man-God. Luke (v. 43) tells of a single remark, to one of the thieves, "To-day thou shalt be with me in paradise"; and then, at the ninth hour, the expiring cry, "Father, into thy hands I commend my spirit" (v. 46). While John relates only one remark by Jesus, to his mother, concerning John, and "Woman, behold thy son"; and Jesus merely said, "it is finished," and "bowed his head and gave up the ghost," without either of the expiring cries. Surely all this is unsatisfactory for such a scene.

THE WONDERS AT DEATH

Wonderful miracles attended the death of a God on a cross, as related by one or another of the Reporters.

Matthew (v. 45), Mark (v. 33) and Luke (v. 44) say that "from the sixth hour there was darkness over all the earth unto the ninth hour," when, with or without the expiring cry, Jesus, "gave up the ghost." But John, who was there, "and saw and bears true witness, that ye may believe," did not see the darkness, nor other of the wonderful phenomena. Matthew gives a whole catalogue of wonders, which is found in no other history of that period:

"(51) And behold, the veil of the temple was rent in twain from the top to the bottom; and the earth did quake, and the rocks rent; (52)

And the graves were opened; and many bodies of the saints which slept arose, (53) And came out of the graves *after his resurrection,* and went into the holy city, and appeared unto many."

How there could have been "saints" already dead and buried, ages before the Holy Church was started and set up its saint calendar, is not clear; and what they did between the "ninth hour" when they "arose," and three days later when they "came out of their graves after his resurrection," is not revealed. But Mark does not credit this "ghost-walk," nor the earthquake, any more than I do, for he simply says (v. 38) the "veil of the temple was rent in twain," as also only says Luke (v. 45), adding the remark of the centurion, to be quoted in a moment; and John, who was there and says "his record is true," discredits every word of the three others, for he says nothing of all these wonders.

These inspired writers are also in hopeless conflict as to what the Roman centurion said when Jesus "gave up the ghost." Matthew and Mark say that when those present "saw the earthquake," etc., the centurion said "Truly this was the Son of (Yahveh) God"; but Luke is not so ambitious for a confession of Christian faith from the Pagan Roman, and declares that he simply said, "Certainly this was a righteous man"; while John, who was there at the foot of the cross, did not hear any remark from the centurion, or did not record even the testimonial which Luke affirms.

The Burial Scene

We will omit the burial scene, except to call attention to the remarkable claim of Matthew (xxvii, 62–66, and xxviii, 11–15), with regard to sealing the sepulchre and setting a watch of Roman soldiers, and bribing them to say that the body of Jesus was stolen away while they slept; all the others discredit this myth. We pass on to the Resurrection Morn.

The Resurrection

Jesus was buried Friday evening; the Jewish sabbath, our Saturday, passed, and the next morning, Lo, "He is risen from the dead"! We will take up the resurrection record "line upon line and precept upon precept," and see how this wonder was:

Matthew (xxviii, 1), states the time and persons thus:

"In the end of the sabbath, as it began to dawn toward the first day of the week, came Mary Magdalene and the other Mary to see the sepulchre."

Mark (xvi, 1–2) states the time and persons thus:

"And when the sabbath was past, Mary Magdalene, and Mary the mother of James, and Salome, had bought sweet spices, that they might come and anoint him. And very early in the morning the first day of the week, they came unto the sepulchre at the rising of the sun."

Luke (xxiv, 1) states the time and persons thus:

"Now upon the first day of the week, very early in the morning, they (i.e., the women which came with him from Galilee; ch. xxiii, 55) came unto the sepulchre, bringing the spices which they had prepared, and certain others with them."

John (xx, 1) states the time and person thus:

"The first day of the week cometh Mary Magdalene early, when it was yet dark, unto the sepulchre."

The conflicts here are very apparent, even upon seeming trifling points: but nothing is trifling when concerning inspired truths of the single Event surpassing everything in history, human or divine. The time varies: Matthew, "as it began to dawn toward the day"; Mark, "very early in the morning at the rising of the sun"; Luke, "very early in the morning"; John, "when it was yet dark." Now, it could not be sunrise and dark at the same time.

The conflict continues as to the persons who came, at sunrise or by dark: Matthew, two persons, "Mary Magdalene and the other Mary"; Mark, three persons, "Mary Magdalene and Mary the mother of James, and Salome"; Luke, a number of persons "the women, which came with him from Galilee, and certain others with them"; and, John, one person, "Mary Magdalene," single and alone; and nothing about "spices and anointing"; and it might be wondered how any of them could expect to anoint a body already buried three days, sealed in a grave with a great stone before the door, and with an armed Roman guard, specially posted to prevent tampering.

Now we will see if we can disentangle what happened when one, two, three, or a number of persons came to the sepulchre at sunrise, or by dark:

Matthew (xxvi, 2–5) asserts that this happened:

"And, behold, there was a great earthquake: for the angel of the Lord descended from heaven, and came and rolled back the stone from the door, and sat upon it. His countenance was like lightning, and his raiment white as snow. And for fear of him the keepers did shake, and became as dead men. And the angel said," etc.

Mark (xvi, 4–5) asserts that this happened:

"And when they looked, they saw that the stone was rolled away: for it was very great. And entering into the sepulchre, they saw a young man sitting on the right hand side, clothed in a long white garment; and they were affrighted."

Luke (xxiv, 2–4) asserts that this happened:

"And they found the stone rolled away from the sepulchre. And they entered in and found not the body of the Lord Jesus. And it came to pass as they were much perplexed thereabout, behold, two men stood by them in shining garments."

John (xx, 1–5; 10–12) asserts that this very different thing happened:

"Cometh Mary Magdalene unto the sepulchre, and seeth the stone taken away from the sepulchre. Then she runneth, and cometh to Simon Peter, and to the other disciple (John) whom Jesus loved, and saith unto him, They have taken away the Lord out of the sepulchre, etc. Peter therefore went forth, and that other disciple, and came to the sepulchre. So they ran both together, (but John was a better sprinter and arrived first); And he (John) stooping down, and looking in, saw the linen clothes lying. Then cometh Peter, and went into the sepulchre, and seeth the linen clothes lie: Then John came in. Then the disciples went away again into their own home. But Mary (Magdalene) stood without weeping, and stooped down and looked in: And seeth two angels in white, one at the head, and the other at the feet, where the body of Jesus had lain."

The contradictions here are very glaring, and are of the highest importance. Matthew avers that after the two Marys arrived at the sepulchre, a lightning-faced Angel descended before their eyes, accompanied by an earthquake, and rolled away the stone and sat on it outside the sepulchre; this second edition of his "great earthquake," which none of the others saw or felt or mention, leaves the armed Roman keepers stretched out as dead men; the angel speaks to the scared women; neither of Matthew's two women enters the sepulchre, but the angel announces the Resurrection and sends them away to tell the news. Mark brings his three women and they see that the stone is already rolled away, and they enter into the sepulchre and find one young man sitting on the right hand side.

Luke brings his whole troupe of women, and they find the stone removed, and they all entered into the sepulchre, and find two men standing by. John, who was there himself after Mary Magdalene called him, avers that Mary Magdalene went alone to the sepulchre, and found the stone taken away; but no angel of Yahveh, nor one young man sitting, nor two men standing by, were there at all; and she fetches Peter and John, and they find the sepulchre empty except for the grave-clothes. When Peter and John had found nothing and gone home, then the Magdalene looked in and saw two angels, one at each end where the Body had been. But none of all these saw a guard of keepers scared by a great earthquake till they were as dead men.

Breaking the Resurrection News

The happenings immediately after the arrival at the sepulchre of the one, two, or three women, or the troupe of women, and their finding an angel sitting outside on the stone, or one young man sitting, or two men standing by, inside, or none of these at all, is thus related by the four inspired recorders:

Matthew, vv. 5 to 8, tells this story, abbreviated but exact:

"(5) The angel said to the women: Fear ye not; (6) for he is risen, as he said. (7) Go quickly, and tell his disciples that he is risen from the dead; he goeth before you into Galilee; there shall ye see him. (8) And they departed quickly, and did run to bring his disciples word."

Mark, vv. 6 to 8, abbreviated but exact, tells this story: The young man sitting on the right side said:

"(6) He is risen. (7) But go tell his disciples and Peter that he goeth before you into Galilee; there shall ye see him. (8) And they went out quickly, and fled; neither said they anything to any man; for they were afraid."

Luke, vv. 6 to 12, abbreviated but exact, tells a different story thus: The two men standing by said to the several women, who were "Mary Magdalene and Joanna, and Mary the mother of James, and other women that were with them" (v. 10):

"(6) He is not here, but is risen; remember how he spake unto you, etc. (8) And they remembered (9) And they returned from the sepulchre, and told all these things unto the eleven, and to all the rest. (12) Then arose Peter, and ran unto the sepulchre; and stooping down, he beheld the linen clothes laid by themselves."

John, vv. 6 to 10, abbreviated but exact, tells a very different story: Peter and John, as above related, ran together to the sepulchre after Mary Magdalene had told them, and John, arriving first, stooped down and looked in, and found nothing and both went home.

The same character of contradictions is found in these short lines. Matthew's angel announces the resurrection, as he sits outside on the stone, and sends the two women to tell the disciples, and that Jesus had gone ahead into Galilee, where he would see them; and the women did run to bring the disciples word. Mark has his young man, sitting inside, make the announcement, and tell the three women to go tell the disciples; but being afraid they told no man. Luke says his two men, standing by, told the troupe of women that Jesus was risen, and they went, without being told, and told all the disciples; and Peter and John, upon being told by the troupe, went and looked in and both entered the sepulchre. While John says, that Mary Magdalene alone went to the sepulchre, found it empty and saw no one, and then went and told him and Peter, and they went running, looked in, entered, and found nothing and saw no one, and went home. Then it was that Mary Magdalene a second time looked in and saw two angels, standing at opposite ends, who spoke to her, asking what she sought, but they did not announce the resurrection, for the reason which will next appear.

POST-RESURRECTION APPEARANCES OF JESUS

This brings us to the first Appearance of the Risen Lord to any of his acquaintances, after his resurrection.

Matthew (xxviii, 9–10) after stating that "Mary Magdalene and the other Mary" left the sepulchre at the behest of the lightning-faced Angel to go tell the disciples that Jesus had gone to Galilee, relates the first Appearance thus:

"(9) And as they went to tell his disciples, behold, Jesus met them, saying, "All hail. And they came and held him by the feet, and worshipped him. (10) Then said Jesus unto them. Be not afraid: go tell my brethren that they go into Galilee, and there shall they see me."

Mark (xvi, 9–10) after telling that "Mary Magdalene and Mary the mother of James, and Salome" had "fled from the sepulchre," and told no man, "for they were afraid," relates the first Appearance thus:

"(9) Now when Jesus had arisen early the first day of the week, he appeared first to Mary Magdalene. (10) And she went and told them that had been with him, as they mourned and wept."

Luke (xxiv, 13–15) after relating how "Mary Magdalene, and Joanna, and Mary the mother of James, and other women that were with them," had returned from the sepulchre and told all these things to the eleven and to all the rest, and that Peter had then run to the sepulchre alone and seen only the grave-clothes laid by, relates the first Appearance very differently, thus:

"(13) And, behold, two of them (disciples) went that same day to a village called Emmaus. (14) And they talked together of all these things that had happened. (15) And it came to pass, that while they communed together and reasoned, Jesus himself drew near and went with them. (25) Then he said unto them, O fools, etc. (30) He tarried and took supper with them."

John (x, 14–18), after telling of Mary Magdalene going alone to the sepulchre, and finding the body gone but seeing no one, and her telling Peter and John, and they went and found nothing but the grave-clothes, and saw no one and went home, and how Mary stood weeping, and looked in and saw two angels sitting at either end where the body had lain, and the angels asked her, "Woman, why weepest thou?" then declares:

"(14) And when she had thus said, she turned herself, and saw Jesus standing; (after some conversation during which she did not know him), (17) Jesus saith unto her, Touch me not, etc. (18) Mary Magdalene came and told the disciples."

Thus we have the four conflicting different accounts. Matthew says that Jesus first appeared to the two women as they went to tell the disciples, and they at once recognized him; Mark says that he first appeared to Mary Magdalene early the first day without any of the intermediate occurrences; Luke says that Jesus first appeared to the two disciples as they went to Emmaus; John says that Jesus first appeared to Mary there by the sepulchre as she turned from speaking with the two angels, and she did not recognize him; and she says that Jesus forbade her to touch him, "for I am not yet ascended"; while Matthew says that his two Marys "came and held him by the feet."

THE SECOND APPEARANCE

The Second Appearance is as diversely narrated. Matthew, (xxvii, 16–18, 20) after relating that Jesus had told the two Marys to tell his disciples to meet him in Galilee, says the Second Appearance was thus:

"(16) Then the eleven disciples went away into Galilee, into a mountain, where Jesus had appointed them. (18) And Jesus came and spake unto them, saying, etc. (20) And, lo, I am with you alway, even unto the end of the world. Amen."

Mark (xvi, 12) after telling that "Jesus appeared first to Mary Magdalene," on the first day, tells of the Second Appearance thus:

"After that he appeared in another form unto two of them, as they walked, and went into the country."

Luke (xxiv, 33 *et seq.*) after relating how Jesus first appeared to the two on their way to Emmaus, and that he went with them, and took supper with them, tells:

"(33) And they rose up the same hour, and returned to Jerusalem, and found the eleven gathered together, and them that were with them, (36) And as they thus spake, Jesus himself stood in the midst of them, and saith unto them, Peace be unto you. (37) But they were terrified, and supposed they had seen a spirit. (38–40) and Jesus showed them his hands and feet, and asked for meat, and he ate broiled fish and honeycomb before them, and spoke with them at length."

John (xx, 19) after relating how Jesus had first appeared on the first day to Mary Magdalene at the sepulchre, says of the Second Appearance:

"Then the same day at evening, being the first day of the week, when the doors were shut where the disciples were assembled for fear of the Jews, came Jesus and stood in their midst, and saith unto them," etc.

The contradictions as to the Second Appearance are notorious. Matthew says that it was on a mountain in Galilee, "where Jesus had appointed them." Mark says that it was "in another form" (what he does not say) "unto two of them as they walked in the country." Luke says that it was in Jerusalem, unto the eleven "and them that were with them," and greatly terrified them all. John says that it was on the evening of the first day in a closed room "where the disciples were assembled for fear of the Jews," but he does not say where.

Tʜɪʀᴅ Aᴘᴘᴇᴀʀᴀɴᴄᴇ

There were some other Appearances, the accounts of which are equally conflicting. Matthew relates only the two Appearances already credited to him. Mark (xvi, 14) after telling of the Second Appearance, to the two walking in the country, tells of a third:

"Afterwards he appeared to the eleven as they sat at meat, and upbraided them with their unbelief."

Luke is satisfied with his two, which differ entirely from Matthew's two, as we have seen. John (xx, 26) after relating his Second Appearance, to the disciples in the closed room, at which event he says that Thomas Didymus, the Doubter, was not present, and stating that Thomas said, when he heard about it, that it was a case of "show me" with him, then tells of a Third Appearance, at which Thomas was shown:

"And after eight days again his disciples were within, and Thomas with them: then came Jesus, the doors being shut, and stood in the midst, and said, Peace be unto you,"—and showed Thomas, etc.

Thus we see that Matthew and Luke relate only two Appearances, and, if we believe Luke, as we shall see, there were no more; while Mark and John relate three. All Appearances are different in time, place and circumstance.

Fourth Appearance

John (xx, 1, 14) relates a fourth Appearance, although he calls it the third, thus:

"(1) After these things Jesus showed himself again to his disciples at the sea of Tiberias; and on this wise shewed he himself. . . . (14) This is now the third time that Jesus shewed himself to his disciples after that he was risen from the dead."

This is the occasion where the disciples were fishing, and fishing was not good and they had caught nothing; and Jesus told them to throw their net on the other side of the boat, and they landed 153 so large that they broke the net. And when they landed, lo a nice fire of coals was there, with fish already broiling thereon, and bread, though apparently no butter or coffee, and they all had breakfast.

Sundry other Appearances

This would seem to complete the very contradictory relations of the two, three, or four Appearances of the Crucified after the Resurrection. But the end is not yet, as we discover other witnesses, who say there were, at least, forty and maybe more, appearances.

We call the anonymous author of the "Acts of the Apostles," supposed to be Luke, who has already, and quite differently, testified in his Gospel. In Acts, Chapter i, vv. 1 and 2, this witness now testifies that Jesus, "before the day in which he was taken up," gave commandments to the Apostles,

"(13) To whom he also shewed himself alive, etc., being seen of them *forty* days."

This would be at least forty several appearances, to the Apostles, on forty several days after the Resurrection. But with the lapse of time wonders grow, and Paul writing to the Corinthian late Pagans adds prodigiously to the throng of witnesses for the verity of his Risen Lord. After telling of the death and burial of the Christ, he proceeds:

"He rose again the third day according to the scriptures; that he was seen of Cephas, then of the twelve; after that he was seen of *above 500* brethren at once. . . . After that he was seen of James; then of all the Apostles. And last of all he was seen of *me* also, as of one born out of due time" (1 Cor. xv, 3–8).

James, own brother of Jesus, nowhere makes claim to have seen him after the Resurrection; nor is there any corroboration for the 500 eye-witnesses all at once; and only Paul vouches for his own peculiar vision, "as of one born out of due time." But the point is, that both the last cited witnesses totally contradict the contradictory histories of the four Gospel writers, above quoted; and leave the whole matter of post-mortem and pre-Ascension Appearances much more confused and more in doubt than even the Gospels leave it.

THE ASCENSION

We will now consider this Phenomenon, whether and how it so variously happened or not.

Matthew, the most prolific wonder-teller, knew nothing of any "Ascension," and there was none, if we stop with him, for he does not mention it. On the contrary, Jesus assures his hearers that he was going to stay right there with them—"I will be with you always, even unto the end of the world, Amen" (xxviii, 20 and last).

Mark xvi, after relating three Appearances, the third being to the eleven as they sat at meat, which was evidently in a room in a house, and Jesus talked with them, declares:

"(19) So then after the Lord had spoken unto them, he was received up into heaven, and sat on the right hand of God. (20) And they went forth, and preached," etc.

Luke xxiv, after relating his second and last Appearance, to the eleven in Jerusalem, when Jesus ate the broiled fish and honey-comb, and finshed supper, says:

"(50) And he led them out as far as Bethany, and he lifted up his hands, and blessed them. (51) And it came to pass, while he blessed them, he was parted from them, and carried up into heaven."

John, like Matthew, knows nothing, or says nothing, of any Ascension.

We have recourse now to our new and fifth witness, the "Acts of the Apostles." Chapter i, after assuring that Jesus remained on earth with the apostles and "and was seen of them forty days," and being assembled together with them on the Mount of Olives, speaking with them, the writer says:

"(9) And when he had spoken these things, while they beheld, he was taken up, and a cloud received him out of their sight. (12) Then returned they unto Jerusalem from the mount called Olivet."

The evidence for the wonderful event of Ascension is quite as contradictory and conflicting both as to time and place, as all the rest which we have examined. Matthew and John record no Ascension at all. The Resurrection is laid by all on the first day of the week. As to the time of the Ascension, Mark is indefinite; he makes the first Appearance of Jesus on the same first day; says "after that" he made the second Appearance, and "afterward" the third. This third Appearance was indoors, at a mealtime, with the eleven, and probably in Jerusalem, their headquarters; and, then and there, "the Lord was received up," right through the roof of the house.

Luke, in his Gospel, lays the time immediately after the second and last Appearance, at a meal with the eleven in Jerusalem, and asserts that when the meal was ended, Jesus led them out as far as Bethany, and there "was separated from them and carried up into heaven," from the open country side. But, in the "Acts" Luke tells a different story: he explicitly says that the time was after forty days and at least forty Appearances, and that the place was "the mount called Olivet." As stated, John does not record any Ascension; but he relates the second Appearance of Jesus, to the eleven on the evening of the Resurrection Day, and says "after eight days" Jesus again appeared to them when Thomas Didymus was also present; so that, according to John, The Ascension, if any such there were, must have been at least eight days after the Resurrection; and longer, for John records that "after these things Jesus shewed himself again to his disciples at the sea of Tiberias," on the occasion of the fish-fry.

NOBODY BELIEVED THE "IDLE TALES"

In concluding our review, we may pause for a moment, and satisfy a natural curiosity, as well as adduce important evidence, by inquiring what effect all these "miracles and wonders and signs" had upon the loyal disciples and close associates of Jesus. They were with him throughout his career, and as Jesus said to them, "Ye are witnesses of these things"; and Jesus gave them the fair and gentle admonition, "he that believeth not shall be damned" (Mark xvi, 16). This inquiry affords pertinent evidence on behalf of one who, twenty centuries after,—when "seeing is believing"—not having seen these thing himself, and having them only on the credit of the four inspired biographies and one "Acts," which we have just examined, may be so bold as not to be obtrusively credulous of them.

Matthew guards a discrete silence, although he says (xxviii, 17) that when Jesus met his disciples in Galilee, "some doubted."

Mark, after saying that Jesus first appeared to Mary Magdalene and she had told the others, says (Chapter xvi):

"(11) And they, when they had heard that he was alive, and had been seen of her, believed not. (12) After that, he appeared in another form unto two of them, (13) And they went and told it unto the residue: neither believed they them."

Luke (xxiv, 11), after relating that his group of women returned from the sepulchre and told the apostles of the resurrection, says:

"And their words seemed to them as idle tales, and they believed them not."

John quotes Jesus as saying, "Ye also have seen me, and believe not"; and John tells the story of "Doubting Thomas," who said "Show me, or I will not believe."

This summary review of the reputed life and acts of Jesus of Nazareth, as set forth in the only human documents in which they are by any pretense of inspiration recorded, has more than abundantly shown, to even the most reverently credulous, the degree of inspired Truth in the Gospel Stories. The favorite asseveration of veracity, "true as the Gospel," is become quite maladroit and lost force as a convincing assurance. On Word of Honor is to be recommended as a more persuasive formula for men of truth and honor.

Sad maybe it is to discover that the long-cherished Gospels are totally wanting in that "Harmony" which has been regarded as their most potent assurance of Truth, which is the soul of Harmony. But the simple process of attentively comparing their records, and pointing out their contradictions, has stripped them of all pretense of inspired Truth. The fault is theirs, not mine. These Gospels prove themselves—as historical records—to be clumsy fabrications of impossibilities, palmed off upon an ignorant and credulous populace—a whole generation and more after the pretended events, by maybe well-meaning persons, pretending, like Paul admits of himself, by their "lies to make the glory of God the more to abound" (Rom. iii, 7).

But shown not to be true, shown to be a "strong delusion," no God of Truth would have a reasonable mind to believe it for Truth.

CHAPTER XVI

THE SACRED "DOCTRINES" OF CHRISTIANITY

The Creeds, says a Poet, in number are some seventy-three. Of Christian sects or denominations, each founded upon some chosen texts differing specifically from all others, there are in fact a much greater number, some hundreds, each quite out of harmony with all the others. Each, by its sectarian votaries is fondly held to be the sole inheritor of saving truth; and can point with pride to the inerrant texts of the Testament where the legacy of truth is made to it alone. But every other disputes this reading, and with equal assurance and no less pride can point to yet other texts of the true Testament, which nullify the pretensions of all the others, and leave itself the sole and universal heir to saving truth.

For are not the Christian Sects, seventy-three though be their conflicting Creeds, one and all of them founded upon the "impregnable Rock of the Holy Scripture," as Mr. Gladstone terms it, and the revealed truth that this Book is divinely inspired in its every word: that it is the "Living Word of God," the faithful revelation of His Divine will to man, and that it is inerrantly harmonious and true?

But Christian zeal of sect has found totally divergent texts, doctrines and dogmas enshrined for Faith in the Sacred Word; and, selecting some, rejecting others, has built up dissentient Creeds and Faiths, as far apart as the poles, as Catholicism and Christian Science, with the infinity of contrary "isms" between. On these divergent texts of Holy Writ have been founded the Holy Inquisition, with its rack and stake, and the counter-fires of Episcopacy and Calvanism. Each "ism" repudiates all the other "isms."

Outside the sacred Tome itself, no higher authority can be invoked for the inspired Dogma of inerrant truth of Holy Writ, and the utter unity of that truth, than the recent (A.D. 1870) Spirit-illumined Declaration of the Sacred Vatican Council:

"These Books are sacred and canonical because they contain revelation without error, and because, written by the inspiration of the Holy Ghost, they have God for their author."

365

Howbeit, we have in the foregoing pages seen very great parts of this God-written Book sadly discounted for inspiration and truth; and to explain or attenuate this, some might be led to suspect that such parts of it may be excepted from the general rule of inspiration. But in this they err, to believe the Holy Ghost speaking lately through Pope Leo XIII, in his encyclical *Provid. Deus*, where this error is roundly refuted:

"It will never be lawful to restrict inspiration merely to certain parts of the Holy Scriptures, or to grant that the sacred writers could have made a mistake. . . . They render in exact language, with infallible truth, *all* that God commanded and *nothing* else; without that, God would not be the Author of the Scripture in its entirety."

This settles it, for—"*Roma locuta est, causa finita est*"—as all know. And to this dogma of infallibly inspired truth *in toto*, all the otherwise protestant and dissentient members of the Body of Christ chorus unanimously Amen.

The trouble with the Dogma of inspired infallible truth is in the utter riot of diversity of truth in the sacred Tome; in the infinite variancy of doctrinal truth, each inferentially and necessarily discounting or discrediting all the others. For is it not the truth, that between two or more contradictory dogmas or doctrines, while none may be true, not more than one of them can possibly be?

"All Scripture is given by inspiration of God" (2 Tim. iii, 16). The truth of this inspired dogma, and of the Papal complements to it, above quoted, is so easily tested and proven—or disproven—by the simplest and most infallible of tests—that an honest mind can but candidly apply the test—comparisons. The simple expedient of pairing off Bible texts one against another, or, as it were, "matching inspirations," is an infallible way of testing the truth and harmony of inerrant revelation—and its revelations will be found astounding.

No single dogmatic doctrine, or inspired truth of Christian Creed, will thus be found in all the New Testament, which is not contradicted, denied, refuted, repudiated, and made ridiculous, by some equally inspired truth, uttered ofttimes by the same, or by some other equally inspired, dogmatist of the Christian Faith.

The fault lies not in the reader and searcher, but in the Book, that such amazing results should follow so simple and conscientious a search of the Scriptures. We will simply turn the pages of the inspired and inerrant Word, and note the inspired utterances of the principal dogmas and doctrines of the Christian Creeds—and leave the result to speak for itself.

THE FORMULA OF FAITH

The inspired formula of credulity of the New Faith is Paul's own Confession of Faith: "Believing all things which are written in the law and in the prophets" (Acts xxiv, 14). Faith cares not for facts or proofs, but boasts that it—"believeth all things, hopeth all things" (1 Cor. xiii, 7). Their Faith is to them all sufficient in lieu of Fact:—"the *substance* of things *hoped* for, the *evidence* of things not seen" (Heb. xi, 1), not known, and altogether unknowable.

In this confessed absence of certain knowledge, we will see what the inspired dogmatists and doctrinairies so solemnly posit for our most holy Faith.

REDEMPTION FROM THE CURSE

The dogma of soul-death and damnation through the "Sin of Adam" is variously stated and elaborated by its Protagonist Paul, first as follows:

"Wherefore, as by one man sin entered into the world, and death by sin; and so death passed upon all men; . . . therefore, as by the offense of one judgment came upon all men to condemnation; even so by the righteousness of one the free gift came upon all men unto justification of life" (Rom. v, 12, 18).

Thus Paul propounds the doctrine of death and damnation to all by the sin of one, Adam, and of salvation by the "free gift unto all men" by the atonement of another one. More directly and positively he repeats this:

"For as in Adam all die, even so in Christ shall all be made alive" (1 Cor. xv, 22).

And with the utmost of assurance he avers:

"Christ hath redeemed us from the curse" (Gal. iii, 13–14).

These well-argued texts carry the positive, as well as perfectly logical and just assurance,—if true—that as the fearful "Original Sin" of Adam entailed the "Curse" of inevitable involuntary sin and damnation upon all mankind ever since, now the great Sacrifice and propitiation of Jesus Christ would, must, have the effect of wiping out that old score utterly, and redeeming all mankind without more ado.   Indeed, the nearest and dearest to Jesus of his four Biographers several times in his Epistle justifies this interpretation and confirms this reasonable expectation:

"And sent his Son to be the propitiation for our sins" (1 John iv, 10; iii, 5).

Repeating and amplifying this assurance of universality of free and common redemption for all mankind:

"And he is the propitiation for our sins, and not for ours only, but for the sins of the whole world" (1 John ii, 2).

The same is likewise certified by Peter:

"For Christ also hath once suffered for sins, the just for the unjust, that he might bring us to God" (1 Pet. iii, 18).

And he asserts the complete efficacy of the vicarious atonement once and for all:

"Who in his own self bare our sins in his own body on the tree, that we, being dead to sins, should live unto righteousness: by whose stripes we are healed" (1 Pet. ii, 24).

These plain texts surely seem to mean what they with such reiteration say—that as all were damned *nolens volens* through the Old Adam, willy-nilly all should have free, unconditional, and universal redemption and salvation through the expiation of the New Adam—"for the sins of the whole world." But our well justified confidence is by a variety of limitations disappointed: redemption and salvation are found to be quite partial, precarious, and then impossible.

Free for All or Limited?

The universality of free redemption is assured in gracious terms by the Master's own words:

"For the Son of Man is come to save that which is lost" (Matt. xviii, 11).

And again, those appealing, soothing words of assurance of free grace and salvation to all, Believer or not:

"Come unto me, all ye that labor and are heavy laden, and I will give you rest" (Matt. xi, 28).

Even broader and freer is the offer of the Apocalypse:

"And whosoever will, let him take of the water of life freely" (Rev. xxii, 17).

Surely these repeated passages prove free and general "redemption from the Curse" and salvation from sin, to all mankind, without condition and without price—the "free gift of grace." All were cursed and damned: all are redeemed and saved.

But the Beloved Disciple strikes a chord whose fatal dissonance alarms the hopeful soul even under the beautiful words in which it is clothed—it is the Believer only for whom the supreme Propitiation is made, who only is thus "redeemed from the Curse":

"For God (i.e., Yahveh) so loved the world that he gave his only begotten Son, that whosoever believeth in him should not perish, but have everlasting life" (Jno. iii, 16).

"Salvation is of the Jews"

Even this limitation of redemption and salvation to "whosoever believeth" has yet another limitation: it is not all mankind damned in the Curse that is to be redeemed, whom Christ came to redeem from the Curse—but the Jew only Christ was *sent* to redeem and to save—if the Jew believed. The Christ himself so positively asserts:

"But he answered and said, I am *not sent* but to the lost sheep of the house of Israel" (Matt. xv, 24).

This was the Divine Commission given by the Master to the Twelve upon their very first mission:

"These twelve Jesus sent forth, and commanded them, saying, Go *not* into the way of the Gentiles, and into any city of the Samaritans enter ye not; but go rather to the lost sheep of the House of Israel" (Matt. x, 5-6).

The Christ told the Woman of Samaria,—

"Salvation is of the Jews" (Jno. iv, 22).

Thus, by his own iterated assertion and admission, the Christ gainsays all the assurances we have seen of free and universal redemption "for the sins of the whole world," and explicitly the assurance that God sent his Son that "whosoever believeth" should be saved: the Believer must be a "Lost Sheep" of Israel; all others remained yet under the universal Curse. But then, Jewry was safe —and that too without condition of belief:

"And so all Israel shall be saved: as it is written, There shall come out of Sion the Deliverer, and shall turn away ungodliness from Jacob: For this is my Covenant unto them, when I shall take away their sins" (Rom. xi, 26–27).

But this is known to have not yet been wholly verified; and also is expressly repudiated by the Chief Apostle after the total failure of the Christ to realize his Special Mission to the "Lost Sheep" of Israel. The Jews had been so often deceived by "false Christs"— by self-proclaimed promised Messiahs—by the fatuous cry, "Lo, here is Christ, or there" (Matt. xxiv, 23), that they were not in a receptive or deceptive mood towards this One.

So Paul, who had taken up the Propaganda of the Faith that failed at the Cross, hopeless of the sophisticated "Lost Sheep of Israel," denounced them as "unworthy of everlasting life" (Acts xiii, 46); and he proclaimed: "Lo, we turn to the Gentiles" (v. 46)— who were not so schooled in Hebrew traditions and lore, and might thus more readily be taken in to the Fold—as Paul thus assures them:

"For so hath the Lord (Yahveh) commanded us, saying, I have set thee for a light to the Gentiles. And when the Gentiles heard this, they were glad, and glorified the Word of Yahveh" (Acts xiii, 47–48).

But it is the Hebrew God Yahveh, way back in Isaiah xlix, 6, who is quoted as saying this: it was no part of the mission or purpose of the Christ to redeem or save any but the Jews—"I am *not sent* but to the Lost Sheep of the House of Israel." So the God-sent Mission of the Christ had been a confessed failure; and the Gentiles, to whom the "free gift" was now promised, and who were glad, were yet to learn the conditions and limitations of the gift.

Believe and be Saved—or Stay Damned

God so loved the World that he sent his only begotten Son, that whosoever believeth on him should not perish, but should be redeemed from the Curse, and have everlasting Life; but

"He that *believeth not* the Son shall not see life, but the Wrath of God abideth on him" (Jno. iii, 36).

The *sine quo non* of Belief as the alternative to continued eternal damnation is reiterated throughout the Gospels and the Epistles of the God of Love, who came "that the world through him might be saved." At the border of the grave after the Resurrection, the Crucified Christ thus challenges the unredeemed by his Sacrifice:

"He that believeth and is baptized shall be saved; but he that believeth not shall be damned" (Mark xvi, 16).

And the culmination of all repudiations of the doctrine of unconditioned free grace and salvation is this of Paul:

"And he that *doubteth* is damned" (Rom. xiv, 23).

REPENTANCE AS A CONDITION

To the requirement for belief, the Master has just added that of "and is baptized," otherwise the soul is damned and the wrath of Yahveh God abideth on him as since Adam's time. Following this fearful intimation, come Peter's words of exhortation, adding yet another condition to the Free Gift:

"Repent ye therefore, and be converted, that your sins be blotted out" (Acts iii, 19).

While Paul flatly contradicts the proposition and denies the need for repentance:

"For the gifts and calling of God are without repentance" (Rom. xi, 29).

Which is also a flat contradiction of the explicit words of his Master:

"I tell you, Nay: but except ye repent, ye shall likewise also perish" (Luke xiii, 3).

While the need of repentance, or of any other act on the part of the individual—(damned through Adam without act or volition on his part),—seems to be entirely obviated by the explicit avowal of Divine responsibility for Unbelief—which seems hard to believe of a good God:

"For God hath concluded them all in Unbelief, that he might have mercy upon all" (Rom. xi, 32).

But the assurance of gratuitous mercy to all, even in unbelief, is contradicted by the same inspired Dogmatician in the selfsame

Epistle, wherein he imputes to God the wilful turning of human souls to damnation, destroying their power of escape:

"Therefore hath he mercy on whom he will have mercy, and whom he will he hardeneth" (Rom. ix, 18).   .

Elected or Eclectic?

The fatal text last quoted contains the hint of what may be termed election to involuntary damnation, which is the effect of God's "hardening" of a pre-damned soul which may desire to believe and be saved.   But the fatal doctrine—which is the total repudiation of "propitiation for the sins of the whole world," finds many more explicit assertions—as well as bald denials, in the inspired texts. When Paul "turned to the Gentiles," in Acts xiii, and the Gentiles were glad, and glorified, and apparently were all zealous to accept the new Faith, it is fatally recorded:

"And as many as were *ordained* to eternal life believed" (Acts xiii, 48).

This fatal phrase "ordained to eternal life," limiting the possibility of belief, and hence of salvation, to an unknowable select number of the Gentile Elect, seems like the explosion of a sapper's mine under the hope in the Promise of "whosoever will."   But hope is raised by the Apostolic assurance:

"For whoever shall call upon the name of the Lord (Yahveh) shall be saved" (Rom. xix, 13).

Which however is dashed by the counter-assurance of the same inspired author, in quite a contrary sense:

"According as he hath chosen us in him before the foundation of the world, having *predestined* us unto the adoption of children by Jesus Christ to himself according to the good pleasure of his will" (Eph. i, 4–5).

But John gives us renewed hope:

"And he is the propitiation for our sins, and not for ours only, but also for the sins of the whole world" (1 John ii, 2).

But the doctrine of Free Will to choose to be saved—if not saved without choice, as damned without choice,—is denied by the Stone on which the Church is founded:

"Elect according to the foreknowledge of God the Father, through sanctification of the Spirit" (1 Pet. i, 2).

These words of renewed hope greet us:

"For when we were yet without strength, in due time Christ died for the ungodly" (Rom. v, 6).

But the hope is sadly jarred by these others of the same Dogmatician:

"Because God hath from the beginning chosen you to salvation through sanctification of the Spirit and belief of the Truth" (2 Thess. ii, 13).

The colloquy between the Jailer of Philippi and his prisoners Paul and Silas, raises again the hope of salvation to all who will believe:

"Sirs, what must I do to be saved? And they said, Believe on the Lord Jesus Christ, and thou shalt be saved, and thy house" (Acts xvi, 30–31).

The Jailer would seem to be an "Elect," and the reasonable hopes of other willing believers seem rudely curtailed, by the discouraging Ipse Dixit of the Master:

"Then said one unto him, Lord, are there few that be saved? And he said unto them, Strive to enter in at the strait gate: for many, I say unto you, will seek to enter in, and shall not be able" (Luke xiii, 23–24).

Which seems strangely at variance with the inspired assurance, so oft repeated:

"And whosoever calleth upon the name of the Lord (Yahveh) shall be saved" (Acts ii, 21; Romans xv, 13).

While all hope of free choice of salvation is quite upset, and only those foreordained by Divine Providence are given any chance to escape the Wrath of God, by these other words of his Son:

"All that the Father (Yahveh) giveth me shall come unto me; and him that cometh to me will I in no wise cast out" (Jno. vi, 37).

The dismal doctrine of "Election" to redemption from the Curse and of salvation for those only whom the Father Yahveh giveth to be saved (and of the Lost Sheep of Israel only), is reaffirmed in the very words of the Father of Life, as quoted by the inspired Epistle of Paul:

"For the children being not yet born, neither having done any good or evil, that the purpose of God according to election might stand, not of works,

but of him that calleth. . . . For he saith to Moses, I will have mercy on
whom I will have mercy, and I will have compassion on whom I will have
compassion. So then it is not of him that *willeth,* nor of him that runneth, but of God that sheweth mercy. . . . Therefore he hath mercy on
whom he will have mercy, and whom he will he hardeneth" (Rom. ix,
11, 15–16, 18).

Which doom of Election to salvation and damnation, by Yahveh
himself, regardless of the poor human striving, receives solemn confirmation in the practical workings of the Plan, as recorded in its
early operations:

"And the Lord added to the Church daily such as *should* be saved"
(Acts ii, 47).

Those who have never taken the pains to match Bible verses and
to compare doctrinal texts, must naturally prick their ears in curiosity when struck by the discordant notes of inspired contradiction
between the sacred texts of salvation. The one doctrine is set off
against and flatly denied by the other, each, therefore, alike discredited, or at least inextricably confused; so that no man can guess
whether "salvation" was for the Jew only, or to the Jew first and
then, upon his rejection of the chance, to the Gentile, to keep the
legacy of the "Free Gift" from failing entirely; or in any event,
whether Jew or Gentile might be saved by believing and willingly
seeking salvation, or whether only those "elected" by Yahveh in
Heaven before the foundation of the world might ever attain to
Heaven; and, if only the "Elect" are to be saved, and these be saved
willy-nilly, what then is the use for any one, who cannot possibly
know whether he is of the "Elect" or not, to make any effort or worry
at all about salvation; which efforts, in the one event, are quite unnecessary, and in the other event would be wholly unavailing? Such
and many like thoughts must assail the curious mind in reading these
sacred texts, maybe seriously disturbing some, while merely amusing
others. But childlike Faith is likely to be jarred in either event.

Faith or Works?

However we may solve or not the foregoing problem of contradictions, we are at once met with another series of conflicting inspirations, on that interesting subject of salvation by grace through
faith or without either by works—both contrary to the theorem of
salvation through election. Paul asserts:

"For by grace we are saved through faith; . . . not of works" (Eph.
ii, 8–9).

But James, the brother of Jesus, flatly denies and contradicts Paul:

"What doth it profit, my brethren, though a man say he hath faith, and have not works? Can faith save him? Even so faith, if it hath not works, is dead, being alone" (Jas. ii, 14, 17).

While this in turn is denied and the previous one confirmed:

"As it is written, The just shall live by faith" (Rom. i, 17).

But the Brother of Jesus returns to the conflict with array of ancient instance—and a contemptuous slur at his antagonist Paul:

"But wilt thou know, O Vain Man, that Faith without Works is dead? Was not Abraham our father justified by Works, when he offered Isaac his son upon the altar?" (Jas. ii, 20–21).

But the status of Father Abraham himself is not quite so free from uncertainty in view of the labored retort of the doughty Paul:

"What shall we then say that Abraham our father, as pertaining to the flesh, hath found? For if Abraham were justified by works, he hath whereof to glory; but not before God. For what saith the Scripture? Abraham believed God, and it was counted unto him for righteousness" (Rom. iv, 1–3).

The bone of Apostolic contention over the good old Patriarch is not yet gnawed bare, as appears by the next bit of inspiration:

"Even as Abraham believed God, and it was accounted to him for righteousness. Know ye therefore that they which are of faith, the same are the children of Abraham" (Gal. iii, 6–7).

While the next text of the Lord's Brother plays off faith against works and makes a combination of both to be essential to the free grace of salvation, or a prerequisite to election, as the case may be:

"Seest thou how faith wrought with his works, and by works was faith made perfect? And the Scripture was fulfilled which sayeth, Abraham believed God, and it was imputed unto him for righteousness: and he was called the friend of God. Ye see then that by works a man is justified, and not by faith only. For as the body without the spirit is dead, so faith without works is dead also" (Jas. ii, 22–26).

The contradictory doctrine of justification by faith alone receives a decided boost in the labored argument of the great apostle:

"Knowing that a man is not justified by the works of the law, but by the faith of Jesus Christ, even we have believed in Jesus Christ, that we might be justified by the faith of Christ, and not by the works of the law: for by the works of the law shall no flesh be justified" (Gal. ii, 16).

Which proposition is further apparently clinched by the next:

"Therefore we conclude that a man is justified by faith without the deeds of the law. Do we then make void the law through faith? God forbid: yea, we establish the law" (Rom. iii, 28, 31).

Though the same high authority contradicts himself and harks back to the "deeds of the law" in the text which follows:

"For not the hearers of the law are just before God, but the doers of the law shall be justified" (Rom. ii, 13).

Which would seem to negative the hope of reward to the believer, as is next in order:

"Receiving the end of your faith, even the salvation of your souls" (1 Pet. i, 9).

While the whole muddled disputation seems left in a bewilderment of non-sensical puzzle, both for the inspired dogmatician and for the perplexed seeker after truth, by the confused ratiocinations of the Apostolic Chief:

"And if by grace, then is it no more of works; otherwise grace is no more grace. But if it be of works, then is it no more grace: otherwise work is no more work" (Rom. xi, 6).

All which produces in the mind a certain querulous and questioning state which finds very apt expression in the query of the Chief Apostle and leader in the above debate:

"And if the righteous scarcely be saved, where shall the ungodly and the sinner appear?" (1 Pet. iv, 18).

LAW OR NOT LAW?

While such jumble of ideas is fomenting in the mind of the reader, the effect may be heightened by considering this:

"And by him all that believe are justified from all things, from which ye could not be justified by the law of Moses" (Acts xiii, 39).

But the unequivocal words of the Master would seem to be in express denial of the text last quoted as well as of several of those cited just previously, for he said:

"Think not that I am come to destroy the law, or the prophets: I am not come to destroy but to fulfill. For verily I say unto you, Till heaven and earth pass, one jot or one tittle shall in nowise pass from the law, till all be fulfilled" (Matt. v, 18).

A Divine utterance of policy and purpose which is quite negatived by the assertion of the Apostle of Grace:

"For sin shall not have dominion over you; for ye are not under the law, but under grace" (Rom. vi, 14).

Who, however, in one of his next breaths contradicts himself most egregiously:

"The law hath dominion over a man as long as he liveth" (Rom. vii, 1).

Though almost immediately he "renigs" his own assertion and avers contrawise:

"But now we are delivered from the law, that being dead wherein we were held" (Rom. vii, 6).

But he again reaffirms the permanency of the law and the obligation to do its full works:

"For as many as are of the works of the law are under the curse: for it is written, Cursed is every one that continueth not in all things which are written in the Book of the Law to do them" (Gal. iii, 10).

Which is specifically contradicted in his own words:

"For if they which are of the law be heirs, faith is made void, and the promise made of none effect: Because the law worketh wrath: for where no law is, there is no transgression" (Rom. iv, 14–15).

But Paul in the verse next below quoted, makes a curious refutation of the latter clause of the one just preceding, which, quite truly one would think, declared that in the absence of previous law there could be no violation or transgression of law; but the new verse works backwards and makes out the law to be dependent upon and a consequence of previous transgression:

"Wherefore then serveth the law? It was added because of transgressions" (Gal. iii, 19).

Though John takes issue with this anomaly of Paul, and states the rule more reasonably in the next quotation:

"Whosoever committeth sin transgresseth also the law; for sin is the transgression of the law" (2 John iii, 4).

This Paul answers by now lauding the Law, forgetful apparently that he had twice just told the Galatians that the Law was a thing of curse:

"Wherefore the law is holy, and the commandment holy and just, and good, For we know that the law is spiritual" (Rom. vii, 12, 14).

And then returns to the Galatians with the assurance that the Law has them all bound in sin, from which they might be relieved by Faith which has done away with the Law: heedless that this is a flagrant denial of the words of the Master previously quoted, as well as of his own to the Romans:

"But the Scripture hath concluded all under sin, that the promise by faith of Jesus Christ might be given to them that believe. But before faith came, we were kept under the law, shut up unto the faith which should afterwards be revealed" (Gal. iii, 22–23).

While the verse which follows next asserts that Yahveh God of Israel gave the Law for the express purpose of working the ruin of all those subject to that Law:

"Now we know that what things soever the law saith, it saith to them who are under the law: that every mouth may be stopped, and all the world may become guilty before God (Rom. iii, 19).

The effect of these added bits of inspiration can be but to increase yet the more the wondering feeling of the "hearers of the Word," a feeling much akin to that produced by the celebrated snake in Hudibras, which—

> "Wriggled in and wriggled out,
> Leaving the people much in doubt,
> Whether the snake that made the track
> Was going east or coming back."

CIRCUMCISION OR UNCIRCUMCISION?

An effect which is heightened even to amazement by the series of inspired texts which follow, which touch upon the hotly debated question raised, but adroitly dodged of solution, in Acts xv:

"Is any man called being circumcised? Let him not become uncircumcised. Is any called in uncircumcision? Let him not be circumcised.

Circumcision is nothing, and uncircumcision is nothing, but the keeping of the commandments of God" (1 Cor. vii, 17, 19).

But Paul himself quite denied the assurance of the one just preceding:

"For circumcision verily profiteth, if thou keep the law" (Rom. ii, 25).

While the next makes a flat contradiction of both the preceding:

"Behold, I Paul say unto you, that if ye receive circumcision, Christ will profit you nothing. Ye are severed from Christ" (Gal. v, 2).

And the next, uttered by the self-same Paul, flings a denial into the very teeth of his immediately preceding inspired assertion:

"What profit is there of circumcision? Much every way" (Rom. iii, 1–2).

Though the next was a flagrant gainsaying of several of the preceding:

"For in Jesus Christ neither circumcision availeth anything, nor uncircumcision" (Gal. v, 6).

And in spite of our Paul, in the verses quoted, having assumed to preach on both and every side of the question, which did or did not matter anyhow, according to whom he was addressing, whether Jew or Gentile, he claims a special revelation of Yahveh to himself and to his side-partner Peter to split the question and take opposite and contradictory sides of it:

"The gospel of the uncircumcision was committed unto me, as the gospel of the circumcision was unto Peter" (Gal. ii, 7).

FORGIVENESS OF SIN

The Master said:

"If thy brother trespass against thee, rebuke him; and if he repent, forgive him. And if he trespass against thee seven times in a day, and seven times in a day turn to thee, saying, I repent: thou shalt forgive him" (Luke xvii, 3–4).

Which is supplemented by an even more liberal version of the same divine injunction, never known to have been acted upon since:

"Jesus saith unto him, I say not unto thee, Until seven times: but, Until seventy times seven" (Matt. xviii, 22).

But this beautiful precept of conduct of man to man finds no place in the stricter dealings of Yahveh with man, to believe Paul:

"For if we sin wilfully after that we have received knowledge of the truth, there remaineth no more sacrifice for sins" (Heb. x, 26).

Which harsh denial of the comfortable and saving principle of "back-sliding" is reaffirmed by the same dogmatician:

"For as touching those who were once enlightened and tasted of the heavenly gift, and then fell away, it is impossible to renew them again unto repentance" (Heb. vi, 4–6).

RESURRECTION

We now may cite a series of conflicting texts touching upon a new subject, that of the resurrection of the body, a doctrine much in dispute in the early days, and which here appears to be stated by Paul rather as a pious hope than as a dogmatic fact:

"And I have *hope* toward God, which they themselves also allow, that there shall be a resurrection of the dead, both of the just and unjust" (Acts xxiv, 15).

But at another place the apostle seems to put the matter even more in doubt, as possibly an unattainable aspiration:

"If by any means I might attain unto the resurrection from the dead" (Phil. iii, 11).

While again, we have the impression of a rather facetious reason for the hope within the inspired Evangelist:

"For in the resurrection they neither marry, nor are given in marriage, but are as the angels of God in heaven" (Matt. xxii, 30).

The preceding sentiment, which is quite worthy of the lady-hating Paul, is followed by one from that Worthy in his typical vein:

"But some man will say, How are the dead raised up? and with what body do they come? Thou fool, that which thou sowest is not quickened, except it die" (1 Cor. xv, 35–36).

Besides exposing himself to the "danger of hell fire" denounced by the Master himself against whoever calls his brother a fool (Matt. v, 22), and being a rather unbecoming exhibition of Apostolic spleen, the Apostle seems, to any one who has done "war-gardening" or otherwise acquired the rudiments of agricultural biology, to show himself entitled to the appellation, for a tyro in farming knows that the inspired argumentation is fallacious: the seed sown which dies is not "quickened," but rots and is lost; only the seeds which live, in the ground, and germinate, are "quickened" and grow up to reproduce their kind.

The next verse is from the same ill-inspired source, and some may think that if the inspired author was so ignorant of natural things he might be at some error with respect to things supernatural:

"It is sown a natural body; it is raised a spiritual body. There is a natural body, and there is a spiritual body" (1 Cor. xv, 44).

The argument is laboriously resumed in the next passage:

"Now this I say, brethren, that flesh and blood cannot inherit the kingdom of God; neither doth corruption inherit incorruption. Behold, I shew you a mystery: We shall not all sleep, but we shall all be changed, in a moment, in the twinkling of an eye, at the last trump; for the trumpet shall sound, and the dead shall be raised incorruptible, and we shall be changed" (1 Cor. xv, 51–52).

These last verses seem quite to deny the proposition of the resurrection of the body such as it is laid in the grave, but to be of something quite entirely different which is manufactured "in the twinkling of an eye at the last trump," out of nothing, for in many instances the original body would be quite destroyed in a material sense. And certainly, as would occur to any one more versed in Theological lore, this theory is wholly opposed to the proposition of the so-called "Apostles' Creed" (of origin several centuries after the Apostles), concerning the material "resurrection of the body." This Creed, however, finds some support in the text of the Beloved Disciple:

"Marvel not at this: for the hour is coming, in which all that are in the graves shall hear his voice. And shall come forth; they that have done good, unto the resurrection of life; and they that have done evil, unto the resurrection of damnation" (John v, 28–29).

The Final Judgment

These texts may appear to any thoughtful person to raise the curious question as to what becomes of the human soul between the time of the death of the body and the magical blasts of the Resurrection Trumpet, countless ages in the future, at the Day of Judgment. In popular concept, as in Scriptural representation, the soul goes to its final reward or punishment immediately that it leaves the body at death. Lazarus died, and quite shortly Dives, and both souls sped at once to their respective eternal billets; for we are told, that upon the death of Lazarus, "he was carried by the angels into Abraham's bosom"; and Dives, "in Hell lift up his eyes, being in torment," and engaged in an instructive dialogue with Lazarus across the immeasurable great gulf fixed between their diverse spirit habitats. And the death-bed repentant thief on the Cross was on the same day transported permanently to Paradise, with other instances *id omne genus.*

If this be true, what then, one may curiously ask, is the use or need of a general Final Judgment, which could not alter the status of the souls already for unnumbered ages basking in Heaven or broiling in Hell? On the other hand, if the above be not true, it appears very incongruous that souls, after leaving the body, should flit around in a sort of Limbo of empty space for untold time awaiting the playing of the last trump which should decide their fate, calling up their discarded and destroyed bodies for judgment "according to the deeds done in the flesh," some of the judgment of salvation, the luckless ones to the judgment of damnation. For thus is the situation declared by One who was snatched up into the Third Heaven, and verily "saw the vision of the future and the wonders that would be"; for he says,—in rapt clairvoyance:

"And the sea gave up the dead which were in it; and death and Hell delivered up the dead which were in them: and they were judged every man according to their works" (Rev. xx, 13).—But why—in Hell—judge one who already for ages was in Hell?—a reversal of his decree would be like reversing the sentence of a man already hanged.

This Final Judgment Day theory is for some upset by the very words of the Master, containing the assurance that the soul went straight-away to its final award, as he told the dying thief:

"And Jesus said unto him, Verily I say unto thee, To-day shalt thou be with me in Paradise" (Luke xxiii, 24).

Though all this is apparently negatived by another gospel text, which seems to represent both soul and body as lying mouldering in the grave, not until a Trumpet-call, but the voice of the Master, should awaken such only as were "elected" to awake to a new life:

"Verily, verily, I say unto you, The hour is coming, and now is, when the dead shall hear the voice of the Son of God; and they that hear shall live" (John v, 25).

But a plain contradiction of this theory, and an averment that the dead are raised to life at once without waiting for any general Resurrection Day, comes in the Master's own words (misquoting his source), in yet another verse:

"Now that the dead are raised, even Moses showed at the bush, when he calleth the Lord (Yahveh) the God of Abraham, and the God of Isaac, and the God of Jacob. For he is not a God of the dead, but of the living; for all live unto him" (Luke xx, 37–38).

As this argument of proof is, however, based on the "burning bush" incident, which no one believes ever happened, and is also a misstatement of the alleged fact, as it was Yahveh himself, and not Moses (Ex. iii, 6), who made use of the words quoted, Moses not even knowing Yahveh at all and asking his name (v. 13), some may not be very much persuaded thereby. But a contradiction by the Master himself of the theory of his just previous utterance is contained in the verse next quoted, which postpones to his "second coming" the adjudication of rewards and punishments, during the interval preceding which both body and soul are apparently quiescent in the common grave:

"For the Son of Man (ben-adam) shall come in the glory of his Father with his angels; and then he shall reward every man according to his works" (Matt. xvi, 27).

But the next verse is in a tone of dubious argumentation, suggesting a possible negation of the major premise of its final sentence, as well as begging the whole resurrection question:

"Now if Christ be preached that he rose from the dead, how say some among you that there is no resurrection of the dead? But if there be no resurrection of the dead, then is Christ not risen" (1 Cor. xv, 12–13).

While yet a deeper note of potential despair echoes in the next following text of the great Dogmatist:

"And if Christ be not raised, your faith is vain; ye are yet in your sins. Then they also which are fallen asleep in Christ are perished" (1 Cor. xv, 17–18).

So the questions of the resurrection of the body and the Final Judgment of the soul, and the why and wherefore of both, are left in a nebulous state in the mind. The Lord only knows just exactly how it will all happen, as it is not very clearly revealed so far.

THE "SECOND COMING"

The most unequivocal and positive of the teachings and assurances alike of Jesus and of his several Apostles, is the immediate visible notorious "Second Coming" of Christ, the end of the world, the Final Judgment, and the prompt establishment of the Messianic Kingdom of Yahveh and David on the new earth,—all this being the most potent propaganda of the new religion. The Master commanded:

"And as ye go, preach, saying, The Kingdom of Heaven is at hand" (Matt. x, 7).

The immediacy of the Coming is proclaimed by the Master in the most positive and unmistakable terms in the repeated avowals:

"Verily I say unto you, There be *some standing here,* which shall not taste of death, *till they see* the Son of Man coming in his Kingdom" (Matt. xvi, 28),

He adds reassurance to make assurance of the Coming and the Kingdom doubly sure:

"Verily, I say unto you, *this generation shall not pass away till all these things be accomplished*" (Matt. xxiv, 34).

The same doctrine, in almost identical words, is repeated in texts of Mark ix, 1 and Luke ix, 27, and again indicated in the reply of Jesus to the jealous passage between Peter and John:

"Jesus saith unto him, If I will that he tarry till I come, what is that to thee? Follow thou me" (John xxi, 22).

The assurance of the speedy fulfillment of the prophesied end of all things is reaffirmed, somewhat tardily howbeit, in the Apocalyptic revelation—written some 100 years after Christ:

"The revelation of Jesus Christ, which God gave unto him, to show unto his servants things which must *shortly come to pass;* and he sent and signified it by his angel unto his servant John, for the time is at hand" (Rev. i, 1, 3).

And again:

"Behold, I come quickly" (Rev. iii, 11).

And repeated by the Apostle:

"For yet a little while, and he that shall come will come, and will not tarry" (Heb. x, 37).

And reiterated by the Beloved Disciple:

"Little children, *it is the last time:* and as ye have heard that Antichrist shall come, even now are there many Antichrists; wherefore *we know that it is the last time*" (1 John ii, 18).

While Paul declares that the Great Day is so close at hand that he enjoins total carnal abstinence as a sort of preparatory purification:

"But this I say, brethren, *the time is short:* it remaineth that both they that have wives be as though they had none" (1 Cor. vii, 29).

And again he tells the same Corinthians, who were evidently getting impatient, that the Coming was to be during the very lives of themselves; that they would not die, but should hear the Fateful Trump sound in their living ears; that those already dead should be promptly resurrected, and the yet living would be "changed" into the Kingdom:

"Behold, I show you a mystery: we shall not all sleep, but we shall all be changed, in a moment, in the twinkling of an eye, at the last Trump; for the trumpet shall sound, and the dead shall be raised incorruptible, and *we (the yet living)* shall be changed" (2 Cor. xv, 52).

The Master again preaches preparedness for his early Advent:

"Be ye therefore ready also: for the Son of Man cometh at an hour when ye think not" (Luke xii, 40).

Peter joins in the refrain of Watchful Waiting:

"But the end of all things is at hand: be ye therefore sober, and watch unto prayer" (1 Pet. iv, 7).

And paints a lurid picture of how it is all to happen:

"But the day of Yahveh will come as a thief in the night; in which the heavens shall pass away with a great noise, and the elements shall melt with fervent heat, the earth also and the works that are therein shall be burned up" (2 Pet. iii, 10).

While Paul, with his chronic cock-sureness about everything which he is totally ignorant of, tells us explicitly and fully just how it is all going to happen, and very promptly,—as it has *not* happened even until this day:

"For Yahveh himself shall descend from Heaven, with a shout, with the voice of the archangel, and with the trump of God: and the dead in Christ shall rise first: then *we that are alive,* that are left, shall together with them be caught up in the clouds, to meet Yahveh in the air: and so shall we ever be with Yahveh. Wherefore comfort one another with these words" (1 Thess. iv, 15–18).

But as the brethren, despite all these assurances of quick dividends of glory, were apparently getting restless for the grand catastrophe and spectacle which was so tardy in being verified, James, own brother of Jesus, cajoles with them:

"Be patient, therefore, brethren, unto the coming of Yahveh. Behold, the husbandman waiteth for the precious fruit of the earth, and hath long patience for it, until he receive the early and latter rain" (Jas. v, 7).

As Paul also finds himself under the necessity to do in order to save his own face and reputation as an inspired prophet:

"And Yahveh direct your hearts into patient waiting for Christ" (2 Thess. iii, 5).

And yet again, to those of the Hebrews who had fallen into the Faith and were chafing at its unfulfillment, he repeats the coaxing and the assurance:

"For ye have need of patience, that, having done the will of God, ye may receive the promise. For *yet a very little while, he that cometh shall come, and shall not tarry*" (Heb. x, 36–37).

But the clamor for fulfillment of these "Second Coming" promises ever became louder and more insistent, threatening the total discredit of the inspired promisors; the disappointment of the saints over the non-fulfillment of the reiterated assurances, promises and prophecies, and the nature of their taunts, being voiced with very pertinent directness by what the crafty Peter dubs "scoffers":

"And saying, Where is the promise of his Coming? For since the fathers fell asleep, all things continue as they were from the beginning of the creation" (2 Pet. iii, 4).

This same crafty Peter, first Jew-Pope of the New Faith, himself makes a shifty "bluff" of a pretended answer to these "scoffers," whereby he tries to squirm out of the situation created by the palpable failure of all the inspired declarations of himself and his confreres of the predicted immediate end of all things:

"But, beloved, be not ignorant of this one thing, that one day is with the Lord as a thousand years, and a thousand years as one day" (2 Pet. iii, 8).

Which however did not seem to any to be at all disingenuous and honest, and hardly to meet the positive and plain repeated assurances to the effect that "some standing here shall not taste of death" until the quick and immediate "Second Coming," promised by Christ himself, should be an accomplished fact;—that "this generation shall not pass away till all these things be accomplished"; —when "we that are alive" should be "caught up" into glory. There seems to be a sad want of inspiration of truth, and even a lack of common honesty, both in the Master and in his Apostles, in solemnly declaring such awful events, which scared thousands into belief, and then deceived their terrified expectation. And it may be wondered how any of them ever persisted in their new faith after the proof of such patent deception. If inspiration is so out of joint of Truth in this most positive of the declarations of Christ and his propagandists, the whole congeries of their preachings and predictions may well be subject to some discount of credibility, if not entire discredit.

From this dangerous train of thought we will arouse to the next series of Dogma, concerning

DEVILOLOGY

A flood of inspired texts illustrates one of the most curious and persistent superstitions of the whole Scriptures: the belief in devils and demoniac possession, in Hell and its malign ruler Satan, almost if not quite equal in power and in some respects even superior to Yahveh Almighty, which is the English rendering of the Hebrew El Shaddai, the "God of Demons," as the Supreme God is called in the Hebrew Bible. The Devil appears early and holds fast: .

."And Jesus was led by the Spirit into the Wilderness, being forty days tempted of the Devil. . . , And the Devil, taking him into a high mountain, showed him all the kingdoms of the world in a moment of time, and the Devil said unto him: All this power will I give thee, and the glory of them; for all that is delivered unto me; and to whomsoever I will I give it. If thou, therefore, wilt worship me, all shall be thine" (Luke iv, 1–7).

These verses clearly recognize the Devil as a Divine Being, with full power of possession, dominion and disposition over this mundane world, having miraculous powers quite on a par with those of Yahveh's Godhead: indeed, Paul gives him this exalted title:

"In which the *God of this world* hath blinded the minds of them which believed not" (2 Cor. iv, 4).

A designation of rank and power confirmed by the Master himself:

"For the *Prince of this world* cometh, and hath nothing in me" (John xiv, 30).

And repeated, among many others, by the Chief of the Apostles:

"According to the Prince of the Power of the Air, the Spirit that now worketh in the children of disobedience" (Eph. ii, 2).

The Master himself avers the Divine origin of the Princely Devil:

"And he said unto them, I beheld Satan as lightning fall from Heaven" (Luke x, 18).

In the nightmare visions of the Apocalypse a fearful and wonderful pen picture is drawn of this great Potentate of Heaven, rebel against Yahveh his King, conquered by the great Michael Archangel, and ousted from the realms of light:

"And the great Dragon was cast down, the Old Serpent, he that is called the Devil and Satan, the deceiver of the whole world; he was cast down to the earth, and his angels were cast down with him" (Rev. xii, 9).

So great was the awe in which the Satanic power was held by even the highest in the hierarchy of Heaven, that it is declared:

"Yet Michael the Archangel, when contending with the Devil he disputed about the body of Moses, *durst not* bring against him a railing accusation, but said, Yahveh rebuke thee" (Jude i, 9).

While the miraculous power of Satan and his minor devils is attested by the Apostle in Chief:

"The working of Satan, with all power and signs and lying wonders" (2 Thess. ii, 9).

As is affirmed by the Apocalypse:

"For they are the Spirits of Devils, *working miracles*" (Rev. xvi, 14).

And their powers are quite equal to Yahveh's and defiant of his Allmightiness:

"And no marvel; for Satan himself is transformed into an angel of light. Therefore it is no great thing if his ministers also be transformed as the ministers of righteousness" (2 Cor. xi, 14–15).

The Master himself accredits the doctrines of Zoroaster touching the two great Powers who disputed the government of the Universe, one the creator and purveyor of Good, the other of Evil:

"Ye are of your Father the Devil. He was a murderer from the beginning. He is a liar, and the father of it" (John viii, 44).

The following verse recognizes the same principle, but impresses one with a feeling of disappointment that the purpose expressed in its second sentence has seemingly as yet failed of complete success:

"He that committeth sin is of the Devil; for the Devil sinneth from the beginning. For this purpose the Son of God was manifested, that he might destroy the works of the Devil" (1 John iii, 8).

Again this divinely purposed triumph over the Evil One is expressly declared, admitting at the same time the extraordinary powers possessed by His Satanic Majesty:

"That through death he might destroy him that hath the power of death, that is, the Devil" (Heb. ii, 14).

And the success of the project is assured by the Christ in person:

"Now is the judgment of this world: now shall the Prince of this world be cast out" (John xii, 31).

But Paul trims down the promise of destruction of the Devil and his works, substituting a milder form of discipline, which though assured for prompt accomplishment, does not appear to have been yet verified:

"And the God of Peace shall bruise Satan under your feet shortly" (1 Cor. i, 20).

Considerable puzzlement is caused after all the foregoing texts descriptive of the activities of the Prince of Devils and his Legions, and the Divine assurances of his early capture and destruction, or at least bruising, by the official keeper of the keys of Hell, who makes the surprising revelation of assurance that his Satanic Majesty and his Devil hosts were already in captivity and chains in Hell, and had indeed always been so since they were first cast out of Heaven:

"For God spared not the angels that sinned, but cast them down to Hell, and delivered them into chains of darkness, to be reserved unto judgment" (2 Pet. ii, 4).

Though such captivity is again revealed as being simply an Apocalyptic vision *in futuro*, and for a term of imprisonment which, with Yahveh is, as we are elsewhere told, but as one day:

"And he laid hold on the Dragon, that Old Serpent, which is the Devil, and Satan, and bound him for a thousand years" (Rev. xx, 2).

And even this millennial period, so confidently assured, not only has not eventuated in these two thousand years, but it is expressly admitted to be but a temporary makeshift of restraint, after which the Devil was to be freed to resume his operations:

"And cast him into the Abyss, and shut it, and sealed it over him, that he should deceive the nations no more, until the thousand years should be finished: after this time he must be loosed for a little time" (Rev. xxix, 3).

Which causes the thought that it was odd for the All-Mighty Yahveh of Heaven to permit the release of the Arch Fiend to prey upon his creatures, after once he had gotten him safely chained down and sealed up in the Bottomless Pit; and it even seems that Yahveh himself would thus make himself accomplice of the malignant works of the Devil thus voluntarily permitted by him. And one wonders upon what compulsion "must he be loosed" from Hell, which would seem to imply a serious limitation upon the All-Mightiness of the All-Mighty Yahveh. And in any event, the confused and conflicting texts about the Devil and his status, past, present and prospective, leads to the thought that the inspired Writers did not really know what they were talking about anyhow; that either the Devil was a Myth, or the revelations made concerning him were altogether mythical so far as their inspiration and show of true knowledge were concerned.

Paul himself admits the besetting activities of the Devil, and acknowledges himself, despite all his boasted power over Devils, to be a victim of the powers of their Chief:

"We fain would have come unto you, but *Satan hindered* us" (1 Thess. ii, 18).

While Peter, evidently despairing of the promised victory over the Devil and of his effective restraint, from which he was broken loose, issues a warning to the faithful against his continued activities:

"Be sober, be vigilant; because your adversary the Devil, as a roaring lion, walketh about, seeking whom he may devour" (1 Pet. v, 8).

Fighting the Devils

That a very active campaign was, however, waged against the hosts of Devils, who were evidently as plenty as blackberries in those days, and very mischievous, is made apparent by the scores of texts of Devilology which make up so large a part of Gospel Truth, that only a few can be here reviewed. The fight against devils was apparently the principal occupation of the Master, and the highest patent of his Divine personality and mission:

"And he preached throughout all Galilee, and cast out devils" (Mark i, 39).

He cites this knack as the first and most potent proof of his Divine mission:

"And he said unto them, Go ye, tell that Fox, Behold, I cast out Devils" (Luke xiii, 32).

So likewise of the Twelve, it was their badge of commission:

"Then he called his twelve disciples together, and gave them power and authority over all Devils, and to cure diseases" (Luke ix, 1).

As also of the Seventy:

"And the Seventy returned again with joy, saying, Lord, even the Devils are subject to us through thy name" (Luke x, 17).

This Devil-exorcism was also the badge and working tool of all true believers:

"And these signs shall follow those that believe: In my name they shall cast out Devils" (Mark xvi, 17).

Paul reaches the apex of the superstition in the startling assertion not only of the very reality of Devils galore, but, without giving credit of originality to the Vulgate Version of Ps. xcvi, 5, that "all the Gods of the Heathen are Devils," asserts their Gentilic Divinity with his usual omniscient assurance:

"But I say, that the things which the Gentiles sacrifice they sacrifice to Devils, and not to God (Yahveh); and I would not that ye should have fellowship with Devils" (1 Cor. x, 20).

While the inspired historian of the Acts makes our Paul the hero of an episode which attributes to these Devils the Divine faculties of foreknowledge and prediction, the same as the acknowledged Prophets of Yahveh:

"And it came to pass, as we went to prayer, a certain damsel possessed with a Spirit of Divination met us, which brought her masters much gain by soothsaying: and this did she many days. But Paul, being grieved, turned and said to the Spirit, I command thee in the name of Jesus Christ to come out of her. And he came out the same hour" (Acts xvi, 16, 18).

The Great Physician graciously busied himself in healing all kinds of diseases, but made a specialty of casting out Devils, which in those days, before Materia Medica was well developed, were regarded, even by the Son of Yahveh, as being the active agents of all the ills to which human flesh was heir:

"Jesus of Nazareth went about doing good, and healing all that were oppressed of the Devil" (Acts ix, 38).

Some texts seem to distinguish between ordinary diseases, and those caused by the possession of Devils in the inner works of the body, and cases of lunacy:

"And they brought unto him all sick people that were taken with divers diseases and torments, and those which were possessed with Devils, and those which were lunatic, and those that had the palsy; and he healed them" (Matt. iv, 24).

But the Devils were evidently the efficient cause of even sore cases of mental alienation, according to the Master Physician's own diagnosis:

"Lord, have mercy on my son: for he is a lunatick, and sore vexed; And Jesus rebuked the Devil; and he departed out of him" (Matt. xvii, 15, 18).

As likewise of sundry female troubles:

"And, behold, a woman of Canaan came out of the same coasts, and cried unto him, saying, Have mercy on me, O Lord, thou son of David; my daughter is grievously vexed with a Devil" (Matt. xv, 22).

And again:

"And ought not this woman, whom Satan hath bound, lo, these eighteen years, be loosed from this bond on the Sabbath day?" (Luke xiii, 16).

And especially in the celebrated case of Mary Magdalene:

"Mary, called Magdalene, out of whom went seven Devils" (Luke viii, 2).

Also of dumbness:

"As they went out, behold, they brought him a dumb man possessed with a Devil and when the Devil was cast out, the dumb man spake" (Matt. ix, 32).

These Devils had a way, in those Bible days, of entering into people and causing them a devil of a time, to their great suffering and distress; and the Devils were quite intelligent in their way, as appears:

"And he healed many that were sick of divers diseases, and cast out many Devils; and he suffered not the Devils to speak because they knew him" (Mark i, 34).

The perversity of the Devils is indicated by the fact that they did not at all heed the command of the Master not to speak:

"And Devils came out of many, crying out and saying, Thou art Christ the Son of God: And he rebuking them suffered them not to speak: for they knew that he was Christ" (Luke, iv, 41).

And the Devils were even saucy and talked back:

"Saying, Let us alone; what have we to do with thee, thou Jesus of Nazareth? art thou come to destroy us? I know thee who thou art: the Holy One of God" (Luke iv, 34).

Which, if the Devils ever really said it, proves that they themselves are Children of Yahveh and joint heirs of Salvation with the best of the believers—for

"Every Spirit that confesseth that Jesus Christ is come in the flesh is of God" (John iv, 2).

And, by every principle of the Gospel promises, are entitled to share in the joys of the Lord Yahveh:

"That through his name whosoever believeth in him shall receive remission of sins" (Acts x, 43).

That the Devils would seem to have had a firm Christian faith, evidenced by their unanimous confessions, is avowed in express terms:

"Thou believest that there is one God; thou doeth well: the Devils also believe, and tremble" (James ii, 19).

But they are seemingly doomed to a disappointment of their just hopes as True Believers:

"Then shall he say also unto them on the left hand, Depart from me, ye cursed, into everlasting fire, prepared for the Devil and his angels" (Matt. xxv, 41).

All the Devils were apparently not of Satan, but some seem to have been celestial, a point to be tested by some means not explained:

"Beloved, believe not every Spirit, but try the Spirits whether they are of God" (1 John iv, 1).

These and a hundred or more other verses dealing with various phases of Devilology, establish the high record for inspired Bible texts on a single subject, it being apparent that no other name or subject in all the Bible, hardly excepting the Divine Father Yahveh and his Son, is more often mentioned, or held in higher faith or fear than that of the Devil, and the teeming hosts of Devils which infest the sacred pages. Belief in Devils and in Demoniac possession was an article of the profoundest faith and credulity of all the inspired writers as of the uninspired ignorant masses, and in none stronger than in the Son of Yahveh; a fact so apparent that one indeed can but wonder how the belief in such an ignorant myth and superstition was possible to one who claimed to be the very Son of Yahveh God of Truth, and by those claiming to be divinely inspired by Yahveh to be the Apostles of Truth on earth.

THE PENALTIES OF UNBELIEF

As some may be tempted to question the eternal verity of it all, let them take warning from the fearful threat against unbelief which the chief apostle hurls at the Incredulous:

"That they might all be damned who believed not the truth" (2 Thess. ii, 12).

Which same dire fate is denounced against him who even hesitates in his faith:

"And he that doubteth is damned" (Rom. xiv, 23).

This is that to which they are damned:

"Are set forth for an example, suffering the vengeance of eternal fire" (Jude vii).

To which is added the Master's fearful admonition:

"Fear him which is able to destroy both soul and body in Hell" (Matt. x, 28).

And the *ad terrorem* fulmination of the ex-Persecutor of the Faithful, Persecutor now of the Faithless:

"He that despised Moses' Law died without mercy: Of how much sorer punishment, suppose ye, shall he be thought worthy who hath trodden under foot the Son of God" (Heb. x, 28–29).

Followed by the warning of the horrible example of the past:

"The Lord, having saved the people out of the land of Egypt, afterward destroyed them that believed not" (Jude i, 5).

And the very pertinent warning for the future:

"For which things' sake the wrath of God cometh upon the children of disobedience" (Col. iii, 6).

And the yet more terrifying threat in the gentle Jesus' own words:

"Ye serpents, ye generation of vipers, how can ye escape the damnation of Hell!" (Matt. xxiii, 33).

As the Chief Apostle again says:

"For the wrath is come upon them to the uttermost" (1 Thess. ii, 16);

And the Apocalyptic terror:

"For the great day of his wrath is come; and who shall be able to stand?" (Rev. vi, 17).

Augmented by the Apostolic animadversion of yet more wrath to come:

"But a certain looking for of judgment and fiery indignation, which shall devour the adversaries" (Heb. x, 27).

The argument of terror and its efficiency is again urged by the same specialist, who admits he uses it for "moral suasion" of converts:

"For we must all appear before the judgment seat of Christ; that every man may receive the things done in his body, according to that he hath done, whether it be good or bad. Knowing therefore the terror of the Lord, we persuade men" (2 Cor. v, 10–11).

While the climax of terrorism on the part of this great Persecutor of the early Believers now the Apostle of Persecution of the Unbeliever:

"Seeing it is a righteous thing with God to recompense tribulation to them that trouble you; And to you who are troubled rest with us when the Lord Jesus shall be revealed from Heaven with his mighty angels, in flaming fire taking vengeance on them that know not God, and that obey not the gospel of our Lord Jesus Christ: Who shall be punished with everlasting destruction from the presence of the Lord, and from the glory of his power; When he shall come to be glorified in his saints" (2 Thess. i, 6–10).

All which tends to induce the mind to yield a very ready assent to the total truth of the same apostle's warning—if truth it were at all:

"It is a fearful thing to fall into the hands of the living God!" (Heb. x, 31).

Many may well wonder, how it could be that a reputed kind and loving Heavenly Father of us all should make such terrible threats or inflict such fearful penalties upon his human children for simply not believing so many unbelievable things so contrary to the most Godlike faculty He had endowed them withal, divine Reason; and that a Hell-fire enforced belief should be sought to be imposed by such blood-curdling threats and penalties, more consonant with the practices of Apache Indians than with the principles of a just and merciful God.

Intolerance and Destruction

But evidently, from what follows, it was not sufficient sanction *ad terrorem* for the new Religion to wait for the awful things that the wrathful Yahveh was said to have in store for the hapless Unbeliever in a next world after death. His Apostolic vicars and vice-gerents here on earth hold Divine commission of Yahveh to anticipate upon the body here and now the fearful tortures which their Yahveh should inflict upon the soul hereafter and eternally. The nefast principle of priestly intolerance, and the torch which lit the Hellish fires of their Holy Inquisition, have both their certain warrant and Divine command in the inspired texts which now follow.

The Christ himself, to say nothing of numerous impostors who had preceded him, declared that others too after him should claim to be Messiah, and should have miraculous powers like himself, so that even the inspired Chosen could hardly tell the difference between the genuine and the spurious Christs:

"For there shall arise false Christs, and false prophets, and shall show great signs and wonders; insomuch that if it were possible, they shall deceive the very elect" (Matt. xxiv, 24).

And Peter, the Rock upon which the Church Persecutrix was founded, true to his traditions of violence, breathed deadly vengeances against all who presumed to differ with his dogmas. Peter cites Moses as predicting Jesus Christ as the Prophet to be raised up "like unto me," and quotes Yahveh as denouncing death to all who would not heed his word:

"Every soul that will not hear which Prophet, shall be destroyed from among the people" (Acts iii, 22–23).

And he devotes to swift destruction all who do not think as he thinks—a murderous program followed by his Apostlic Successors for as long as they dared and could:

"There shall be false teachers among you, who privily shall bring in damnable heresies, and bring upon themselves swift destruction" (2 Pet. ii, 1).

Even the Beloved Disciple preaches denunciation and intolerance:

"Who is a liar but he that denieth that Jesus is the Christ? He is an antichrist" (John ii, 22).

But then we recall the admission that this is the bluster of ignoramuses:

"Now when they saw the boldness of Peter and John, and perceived that they were unlearned and ignorant men, they marvelled" (Acts iv, 13).

Against those who were indisposed to receive the ministrations of the zealous crusaders of the New Religion, summary destruction is invoked of Heaven:

"And when his disciples James and John saw this, they said, Lord, wilt thou that we command fire to come down from heaven, and consume them, even as Elias did?" (Luke ix, 54).

The next verse gives the earliest, and very characteristic, glimpses of him who became the Chief of the Apostles:

"And Saul, yet breathing out threatenings and slaughter against the disciples of the Lord, went unto the high priest" (Acts ix, 1).

And thus vents his Apostolic intolerance against free speech and liberty of discussion of the novel dogmas—the cardinal polity ever since followed by the Holy Church which he founded:

"For there are many unruly and vain talkers and deceivers, whose *mouths must be stopped*" (Titus i, 10).

Ostracism and the boycott are proclaimed as the first steps in the ascending scale of suppression of those who disagree with the new doctrines:

"Now I beseech you, brethren, mark them which cause divisions and offenses contrary to the doctrine which ye have learned; and avoid them" (1 Cor. i, 17).

He then boldly preaches the Gospel of Priestly Anathema against man or angel who should presume to contradict the Apostolic Dogmas:

"But though we, or an angel from heaven, preach any other gospel unto you than that which we have preached unto you, *let him be accursed.* As we said before, so say I now again, If any man preach any other gospel unto you than that ye have received, let him be accursed" (Gal. i, 8–9).

And caps the climax of consecrated bigotry with a pious exhortation to the murder and annihilation of all who dare disbelieve his inspired pretensions of truth:

"He that troubleth you shall bear his judgment, whosoever he be. I would that *they were even cut off* which trouble you" (Gal. v, 10, 12).

To the credulous he even adopts a tone of terroristic authority to hold them in the thrall of their credulity:

"For though I should boast somewhat more of our authority, which the Lord hath given us, I should not be ashamed: That I may not seem as if I should *terrify you* by letters" (2 Cor. x, 8–9).

And modestly claims for his self-assumed authority no limitations of law human or divine except sacerdotal notions of expediency:

"All things are lawful for me, but all things are not expedient" (1 Cor. x, 23).

INSPIRED PRIESTLY PRESUMPTIONS

The Bigot Paul hedges himself about with autocratic near-divinity and warns away presumptious mortals from all profane contact or interference with his awful personality, while he vainglories in the mutilation of person which distempers him into a zealot celibate:

"From henceforth let no man trouble me: for I bear in my body the marks of the Lord Jesus" (Gal. vi, 17).

Heedless of the infinite contradictions of his variant Dogmas, he modestly asserts in their behalf and for himself the infallible verity of direct inspiration, not, however, from the Father Yahveh, but from his Son Jesus:

"I certify you, brethren, that the gospel which was preached of me is not after man. For I neither received it of man, neither was I taught it, but by the revelation of Jesus Christ" (Gal. i, 11–12).

Which inspired veracity he lays claim to in the fullest measure:

"As the truth of Christ is in me" (2 Cor. xi, 10).

He vaunts his self-assumed title and claims all the credit for the results of his pious propaganda:

"Am I not an Apostle? Am I not free? Have I not seen Jesus Christ our Lord? Are ye not my work in the Lord?" (1 Cor. ix, 1).

Though he admits that he is not a free agent in this propaganda, but claims to be under some sort of mysterious "control," or maybe under the spell of his own terroristic doctrines:

"For though I preach the gospel, I have nothing to glory of: for necessity is laid upon me; yea, woe is unto me, if I preach not the gospel" (1 Cor. ix, 16).

He claims precedence over all other propagandists of the new faith, and makes (parenthetically) an interesting personal though braggart admission:

"Are they ministers of Christ? (I speak as a Fool) I am more" (2 Cor. xi, 23).

Which gospel truth he reaffirms, claiming to be proud of the fact:

"I am become a fool in glorifying; ye have compelled me" (2 Cor. xii, 11).

And ostentates it so patently and publicly that Festus declares *ex cathedra:*

"Paul, thou art beside thyself; much learning doth make thee mad" (Acts xxvi, 24).

But he justifies it all by the special plea that it is for the good of the cause:

"For whether we be beside ourselves, it is to God: or whether we be sober, it is for your cause" (2 Cor. v, 13).

ADMITS AND JUSTIFIES LYING

And in his zealot exaltation justifies, on true Jesuistic principle, the preaching of falsehood, and really feels aggrieved that honest men should take exceptions to such a mendacious propaganda:

"For if the truth of God hath more abounded through my lie unto his glory; why yet am I also judged as a sinner?" (Rom. iii, 7).

With unusual tolerance in this instance, while justifying mendacity in himself he allows fraud to others, though he does not explain how one may consent to be so defrauded:

"Defraud ye not one the other, except it be *with consent* for a time" (1 Cor. vii, 5).

With the inflation of pretended plenary inspiration he assures us of his perfect knowledge of all the divine mysteries, which, however, he does not very plenarily reveal to the rest of us:

"Whereby, when ye read, ye may understand my knowledge in the mystery of Christ" (Eph. iii, 4).

And reaches the superlative of obsessed egoism by boldly ousting Jesus Christ from his own gospel and erogates it all to himself:

"Remember that Jesus Christ of the seed of David was raised from the dead according to *My gospel*" (2 Tim. ii, 8).

Even setting up his own notions as the *ratio decidendi* of the Last Judgment:

"In the day when God shall judge the secrets of men by Jesus Christ according to *My* gospel" (Rom. ii, 16).

And would even supplant his old friend and partner Peter as the Purveyor General of Pardons, in a childish tangle of tautology:

"To whom ye forgive anything, I forgive also: for if I forgave anything, to whom I forgave it, for your sakes forgave I it in the person of Christ" (2 Cor. ii, 10–11).

And boastingly claims commission as the true Adjutant of the All-Mighty Yahveh to give human utterance to His Holy Will, and makes acceptance of this pretense the one test of the true prophet and of the genuine gift of the Spirit—whatever that is:

"If any man think himself to be a prophet, or spiritual, let him acknowledge that the things that *I write* unto you are the commandments of the Lord" (1 Cor. xiv, 37).

Claiming again that the Deity speaks right through him:

"And I command, yet not I, but the Lord" (1 Cor. vii, 10).

While he pretends to rely upon moral suasion rather than to impose belief by Yahveh's Divine authority:

"Not for that we have dominion over your faith, but are helpers of your joy: for by faith ye stand" (2 Cor. i, 24).

Although he certainly had the divine right and authority to command boldly and to impose his own will as that of the Lord Yahveh:

"Wherefore, though I might be much bold in Christ to enjoin thee that which is convenient" (Phil. i, 8).

And again he returns to a warning against any who may not even yet be quite persuaded by all his strained arguments and terrifying threats:

"Take heed, brethren, lest there be in any of you an evil heart of unbelief" (Heb. iii, 12).

An Infamous Accusation

But aside from the difficulty, or stark impossibility, of knowing what to believe of all the contradictions and conflicts of Dogma, or of believing any of it at all under such conditions, our inspired Dogmatist, with very odd logic, tells us that it is impossible to believe at all, as his God Yahveh has himself closed the human heart to belief, so that he could save men whether they believed or not:

"For God hath *concluded all men in unbelief,* that he might have mercy upon all" (Rom. xi, 32).

Though he contradicts himself in this by his dogmatic assertion that the promise of salvation is only to those who do believe:

"But the Scripture hath concluded all under sin, that the promise by faith of Jesus Christ might be given to them that believed" (Gal. iii, 22).

While again the same "artful Dodger" Apostle denies both of his former bald assertions, and wonderfully avers that we are to be saved actually through *not* believing at all:

"For as ye in times past have not believed God, ye have *now obtained mercy through their unbelief*" (Rom. xi, 30).

Straightway he contradicts all this medley of contradictions, and with amazing assurance imputes to the God of Truth and Mercy the total depravity of making men believe lies in order that they might be damned for their God-imposed Unbelief:

"And for this cause *God shall send them a strong delusion, that they should believe a lie: that they might all be damned* who believed not the truth"! (2 Thess. ii, 11–12).

And then, as if conscious of being adjudged into this class himself, and before any one has time to accuse him of it, he hastens to deny it and to proclaim his own inspired veracity—though with respect to which of his manifold contradictions of Dogma he does not explain, so leaving us in the darkness of doubt as to them all:

"I say the truth in Christ, *I lie not*" (Rom. ix, 1; Gal. i, 20; 2 Cor. xi, 31).

Though he has just a little before confessed to the Romans, with a show of pious pride in his adroitness of mendacity, that he was accused and "judged as a sinner," because of his abounding *lies* "to the glory of God" (Rom. iii, 7).

John of Patmos, from the Third Heaven, illumined by the great white light of Yahveh's throne, caught a good bird's-eye view of them all—"Thou hast tried them which say they are Apostles . . . and hast found them *liars*" (Rev. ii, 2)!

Childish Faith for Salvation

When a person of any God-given intelligence has read and pondered these correlated contradictions, so solemnly uttered for our Faith, then can such person better appreciate the subtle significance of the oft-repeated prime qualification for Christian Faith and Salvation. The Master himself avers:

"Except ye become as little Children, ye shall not enter the Kingdom of Heaven" (Matt. xviii, 3). "For of *such* is the Kingdom of Heaven".! (Matt. xix, 14).

Little children have such childish simplicity and credulity,—believing Santa Claus, fairies, elfs and ghosts in full faith. Continuing into adult child-mindedness, Yahveh and Jesus Christ are added to their holy faith.

Damnation for Unbelief

Such childlike belief in all these things is enjoined upon us—along with the most fearful threats of eternal death and damnation if one is not so childish as to believe it all:

"Except ye become as little children, ye shall not enter the Kingdom of Heaven" (Matt. xviii, 3).

And for him who will not be childish and believe, the Master himself decrees his fate:

"He that believeth not is damned already, because he hath not believed in the name of the only begotten Son of God; but the wrath of God abideth on him" (John iii, 18, 36).

And after reading all the Divine and inspired assurances which we have just wonderingly reviewed, even

"He that *doubteth* is *damned*"! (Romans xiv, 23).

Fatuous Fanaticism

When under the influence of the inspired and contrary preachments above dinned, coaxed and threatened upon one, he forswears his reason and becometh so like a little child as to believe, these are the pious duties and obligations to which he is devoted, by the Master's own avowal, and for his own sweet sake and that of the holy Christian Religion:

"The brother shall deliver up the brother to death, and the father the child: and the children shall rise up against their parents, and cause them to be put to death" (Matt. x, 21).

A Christian ideal untold times realized during the long dark Ages of Faith, and which yet today, in dark realities short of death, flourishes, dividing the Christian World into hostile camps of bigoted and intolerant Factions. And the promise of reward for so great inhumanity is very incentive to those who believe it:

"Every one that hath forsaken houses, or brethren, or sisters, or father, or mother, or wife, or children, or lands, for my name's sake, shall receive a hundredfold, and shall inherit everlasting life" (Matt. xix, 29).

And in millions of homes and hearts, blighting the tenderest passion of Love, has the curse of the inspired Ban been felt:

"Be ye not unequally yoked together with unbelievers: . . . for what part hath he that believeth with an Infidel?" (2 Cor. vi, 14–15).

The "Prince of Peace"

Of all the inspired Words, preachments and prophecies which in these Chapters we have quoted and commented, the only provably and proven true ones are those of the last few paragraphs, and the sinister, cruel and fearful sentences of the Man of Nazareth, fondly called the "Prince of Peace"—words which have borne the bitterest harvest of blood, and blight, and Hell-on-Earth through all the Ages since they were uttered:

"Think not that I am come to send *peace* on earth; I came not to send peace, but a *sword*. For I am come to set a man at variance against his father, and the daughter against her mother, and the daughter-in-law against her mother-in-law. . . . And a man's foes shall be they of his own household. . . . He that loveth father or mother more than me, is not worthy of me: and he that loveth son or daughter more than me, is not worthy of me" (Matt. x, 34–37; Luke xii, 51–53).

The Christian Creeds and Dogmas of Faith, as laid down with such inspired assurance—and so criss-cross—in the Holy Bible may here be left, conveniently thus assembled and matched, for the easier work of radical revision of opinion regarding them, which some haply may feel them worthy of.

CHAPTER XVII

THE CHRISTIAN "PLAN OF SALVATION"

ORIGINAL SIN AND ETERNAL DAMNATION

"REDEMPTION FROM THE CURSE"

THE whole philosophy of what is fondly known as the "Sacred Science of Christianity" is evolved around two extremes of inspired Bible History: the "Curse on Man" through Adam, and the "Redemption from the Curse" through Jesus Christ. The Second Council of Orange (A.D. 529), thus declares and defines the deadly Dogma: "One man (Adam) has transmitted to the whole human race not only the death of the body, which is the punishment of sin, but even sin itself, *which is the death of the soul*" (Cath. Encyc. XI, p. 314). St. Augustine, profoundest apologist of the Church and its Dogmas, truly states the Christian Scheme: "The whole Christian Religion may be summed up in the intervention of two men, the one to ruin us, the other to save us" (*De Pecc. Orig.* xxiv; Cath. Encyc. XI, p. 314). This is but a paraphrase of the proposition as formulated by the directly inspired Originator of the Dogma, St. Paul, who states it very explicitly:

"For as in Adam all die, even so in Christ shall all be made alive" (1 Cor. xv, 22).

So thus, by the express utterance of Inspiration, the Christian Religion rests totally upon, is inextricably and fatally involved with, the inspired historicity of the Garden of Eden, of Adam and Eve, of the Talking Snake, and of the "Curse" and the "Fall"—for upon the verity of these events depends utterly the validity of the Divine Mission of Jesus Christ, Son of Yahveh God, sent by Yahveh to "redeem the world from the sin of Adam." It was the "Original Sin" of Adam which brought on the fearful Curse of Yahveh which clings to every since-born human soul, until and unless "redeemed" by Faith in Jesus the Christ.

The frightful conception of this Sin and its tremendous consequences, is thus defined by inspiration of the Holy Ghost in the Sacred Council of Trent: "Original Sin is described not only as *the death of the soul*, but as the *privation of justice that each child contracts at its conception*" (Coun. Trent, Sess. vi, Chap. iii; Cath. Encyc. XI, 314). If this, in the mercies of a just and merciful God, is not true, it is the most fearful and blasting infamy of Untruth which Priest has ever inflicted on mankind. Let us examine the Dogma with the fearful attention which it challenges.

Inevitably, if Genesis is not true, Jesus Christ, as God and "Savior," is not, cannot be, true: both stand or fall together; if one, then the other, must be relegated to the same Limbo of exploded Myth. Adam, says Paul, "is the figure of him that was to come" (Rom. v, 15); Jesus Christ, again he says, is the "last Adam" (1 Cor. xv, 45): if the "first Adam" goes into the discard of Myth, the "last Adam" must needs follow suite.

In a previous Chapter we have examined a score or more of pretended "prophecies" of the Hebrew Scriptures averred to predict Jesus Christ and sundry of the acts of his life and death, and tolled over into the Gospel Biographies where they are alleged to have been "fulfilled" in him and in the events described: each and every one of these we have found to be apochryphal and untrue. In addition to these score or more of ineptly invoked "prophecies" which we have seen to be none such, there are many other—some one hundred and forty-nine—jumbles of words scattered through the Hebrew Scriptures, which the pious Bible Editors, or the inspired Church, proclaim to be other "prophecies of Jesus Christ"—of like quality with the former. We deal here with the first of this new crop.

The very first of these 149 editorially-designated "prophecies" is that of the "Curse" and "Fall," with its pretended "Promise of the Redeemer." How priest ever proclaimed, and human intelligence ever believed, that a good and loving Father God (as Yahveh is naïvely described), for whom not a sparrow, it is said, could fall without his anxious concern, would damn throughout eternity the errant masterpieces of his creation, on the very first day of their existence, for a simple disobedience, and involve all creation and all future humanity in a deadly curse on the soul of man, until his Son should come, maybe, four thousand years later to "redeem" this humanity from the damnation of this "Original Sin," and then leave damned or redamn all those who would not believe the Word of God about it, or who never heard of it and so never had a chance to disbelieve it—this I leave to more knowing or more credulous minds to try to explain. I simply read the texts of the Word of God where this is all said to be revealed, haply to discover whether an unprejudiced lay mind can see it that way.

THE REVELATION OF THE FALL

Out of this utterly exploded Adam-Eden Myth—for such candor forces even common intelligence to call it—let us read what it is that is accused against Yahveh, and by him supposed to be cursed against his creation Man and humanity, to the death and eternal torture of their souls in the fires of Hell.

Chapter III of Genesis begins with the Revelation of the Talking Snake, who is praised as being more subtile than any beast of the field which Yahveh had made. The Serpent meets, for the first time, Mother Eve under the shade of the wondrous Tree of Knowledge which flourished in the midst of the Garden of Eden, with respect of which Yahveh had benignly threatened: "In the day that thou eatest thereof thou shalt surely die." The Serpent tells Eve that this is really not a true statement of Yahveh, for the fruit of the Tree was good to eat, and that if eaten, "your eyes shall be opened, and ye shall be as *the gods*, knowing good from evil." Here again the verity of a plurality of Gods is asserted.

This was Eve's first day on earth; she was totally inexperienced with the ways of the world or of serpents; so she was "beguiled" by the Serpent and did eat of the fruit, and gave some to Adam. While the trio were yet together, but too late to do any good by way of prevention, Yahveh appears upon the scene, learns of the incident, flies into the most damning of all the rages recorded of him in all his Book of Curses, and immediately damns every person and thing in being and yet to come.

THE "CURSE" IN EDEN

This "Curse" is a triple-plated damnation—against the Serpent, against the Woman, and against the Man. It is well worth the while for enlightenment to pause a moment to dissect it, Curse by Curse, as set out in Genesis III:

THE SNAKE CURSE

"*To the serpent* Yahveh Elohim said: Because thou hast done this,
  "(1) cursed art thou above all cattle, and above every beast of the field;

"(2) upon thy belly shalt thou go, and dust shalt thou eat all the days of thy life;

"(3) and I will put enmity between thee and the Woman, and between thy seed and her seed;

"(4) it shall bruise thy head, and thou shalt bruise his heel" (vv. 14–15).

While this is quite a blustering Curse, it seems of slight practical consequence,—though the Bible Editors and the inspired Church assure us that this really and truly is a pellucid and positive Divine Promise of Jesus Christ. As the Serpent naturally went on his belly anyhow, one may wonder where is the point in cursing him to continue to "wriggle in and wriggle out" as usual; and as to eating dust for a steady diet, this must be a mistake, if the "curse" applied to snakes generally, as some insist, for snakes are not known to eat dirt, but they suck eggs, and eat birds and rabbits and rats and other snakes, and such; not even Barnum's Circus at its heydey ever had a snake addicted to such unusual and economical diet as dirt.

However, in truth, this dust diet is prescribed to this particular Serpent during his own life only; and there seems no just reason to read into the plain language of Yahveh the curse of a perpetual dirt diet for all snakes for all time, which they do not do anyhow; and it would hardly be just in Yahveh to condemn all snakes in the world for the wrong of one snake only. Certainly, "Shall not the Judge of all the earth be just?" And should the "just suffer for the unjust?" We will consider the wonderful words "enmity between thee and the woman" and about "snake seed," when we have noticed the other Curses in their order.

The Curse on Woman

."*Unto the woman* he said:

"(1) I will greatly multiply thy sorrow and thy conception;

"(2) in sorrow shalt thou bring forth children;

"(3) and thy desire shall be to thy husband, and he shall rule over thee" (v. 16).

Here the choleric Yahveh simply inflicts poor Eve in her own single person with increased pangs in child-birth and a multiplication of sorrows, which would do no credit to any kind and loving God. As for the rest, a desire or love only to her own husband, instead of running off after affinities and soul-mates—this would seem to be a blessing and a good thing rather than a curse; and the subjection to her husband as the head of the household, is no such accursed thing within reasonable limits of equality of personal privilege.

This woman-curse was also evidently limited to Eve alone; and there is no justice or reason in claiming, as some expositors insist, that Yahveh cursed all women for the simple act of one woman, any more than in the case of the Serpent. However, this is all that was really cursed against Eve: pain and sorrow in giving life, not eternal damnation after death.

The Curse on Man

"*To Adam* he said: Because thou hast harkened unto the voice of thy wife, and hast eaten of the tree, of which I commanded thee, saying, Thou shalt not eat of it:

"(1) Cursed is the ground for thy sake;

"(2) in toil shalt thou eat (of) it all the days of thy life;

"(3) thorns and thistles shall it bring forth to thee;

"(4) and thou shalt eat the herb of the field;

"(5) in the sweat of thy face shalt thou eat bread, till thou return unto the ground;

"for out of it wast thou taken: for dust thou art, and unto dust shalt thou return" (vv. 17-19).

This was Adam's share in the tremendous Curse; and just what was it? Let me state its terms again: 1. The ground is accursed; 2. in sorrow shalt *thou*—"Adam"—eat *it* all the days of thy life; 3. thorns and thistles shall grow from the ground; 4. *thou* shalt eat the herbs of the field; 5. *thou* shalt eat bread in the sweat of thy face until *thou* return unto the ground, that is, until thy death.

This is every single solitary item of the fearful and wonderful "Curse on Man." It is no curse upon Adam or man at all, except the one single item as to having to work for an honest living: all the rest of the "Curse" is upon the harmless and helpless *earth* which Yahveh had just created with such a deal of pains that he had to rest a whole day,—which with him is as a thousand years (2 Pet. iii, 8). But there is not a single word or remotest hint at sin or death or eternal damnation. If Yahveh ever said, as he is quoted (ii, 17), "in the day that thou eatest thereof thou shalt surely die," he either "repented" as usual—of his direful threat, or it was all a brutal Jahvic bluff; for Adam continued to live, after that fatal day, for just nine hundred and thirty years, if the vital statistics of Genesis are to be credited. But I repeat that there is not one word in the whole record, of sin or death or damnation as a penalty against Adam himself, much less against his posterity and all humanity.

The "Curse" Innocuous

Several details may be noticed for a moment. The "Curse" as we have seen, is principally against the ground itself, not upon the Man: "accursed is *the ground* for thy sake." The Man is humorously condemned to *eat ground*, as was the Snake; there is no "*of* it" in the original Hebrew. The ground also should grow thorns and thistles: yet, according to Genesis I, every kind of herb and plant and tree, including, of course, thorns and thistles, had already been created and "the earth brought forth" the same, on the third day (v. 12). The Man was further condemned as part of the "Curse," to eat "the herb of the field"; but, already, and as a Divine providence for man, these same herbs of the field had been already graciously bestowed upon him for food; for it is recorded: "And Elohim said, Behold, I have given you every *herb*, and every tree on which is fruit; to you it shall be for food" (i, 29). As for eating bread in the sweat of his face, or working to make the ground bring forth its produce of food, why, that was the express purpose for which man was created in the first place—(in the second version of his creation)—and put into the Garden of Eden,—again a blessing of healthful work instead of idle existence. For, after the earth was created, and before man was put upon it, it is recorded, "and there was not a man to *till the ground*" (ii, 5). So Yahveh proceeded to form man out of the dust of the ground, then laid out and planted the celebrated Garden of Eden; then Yahveh Elohim took the man, and put him into the Garden of Eden "*to dress it and to keep it*" (ii, 15),—thus providing for him useful and healthful work, so that "by the sweat of his face" he should eat of all the varied products of Nature which Yahveh had given the man for food, until his return to the dust from which he was taken.

So we see that every single clause of the wonderful "Curse" on Man, was no "curse" at all; every single item of it, except about "eating dirt" all his life like the Snake, and which he never acquired the habit of doing, was already provided by the bounteous Creator Yahveh as particular blessings for his masterpiece of Creation. And the statement about his death and return to dust, was no part of the "Curse" at all, for man was never designed to live on earth forever, but was mercifully to be released, in due time, from that intolerable Fate. The pretense of some pious persons that but for this awful "Original Sin," man would have lived always without tasting death, besides being utter absurdity, is distinctly denied by the inspired record; for, in a very curious passage, Yahveh Elohim is represented in a colloquy with some of the other Gods, anonymous in the record, and, says Yahveh: "Behold, the man is become as one of *us*, to know good and evil: and now, lest he put forth his hand, and take also of the Tree of Life, and eat, and *live forever*, therefore Yahveh Elohim sent him forth from the Garden of Eden, to till the ground from whence he was taken" (iii, 22–23). Thus the man was driven away from the Tree of Life, which had the magic property of *giving* earthly life everlasting, expressly for the purpose of preventing him from acquiring immunity from death and living forever, by eating of the magical Tree of Life.

And he was driven forth from the Garden expressly "to till the ground from whence he was taken" (iii, 23),—which was exactly the purpose for which he was originally put into the Garden, "to dress it and to keep it" (ii, 15). So the "Curse" is seen to be quite innocuous; and I will pledge my word of honor that there is not another word nor the remotest allusion in all the Hebrew Bible to the whole incident of the Garden and the Snake: the Old Testament is as silent as Sheol (the grave) about any pretended "Original Sin" and "Curse" and "Fall," and of eternal damnation on account of the same or of anything else.

THE "CURSE" LIFTED

And just here one very singular circumstance may be mentioned, which is also another falsehood imputable to Yahveh, for he never kept his promise. Just after the Flood, when pious reckless old Noah destroyed one-half of all his breeding stock for a burnt sacrifice to Yahveh, we are told (Gen. viii, 21), that "Yahveh smelled a sweet savor; and Yahveh said in his heart, I will not *again curse the ground* more for man's sake." This would certainly seem to indicate that Yahveh was appeased and the "Curse" was lifted, and the new race of mankind would now have a fair new start in life. But this is evidently a mistake; for the "Curse" of Eden yet rests upon the ground. Indeed, "all things continue as from the beginning of the world";—for the ground still brings forth thorns and thistles, and in toil man still eats of it in the sweat of his face; for, as the Poet sings—"How salt with sweat is the laborer's bread!"; snakes still wriggle through life on their belly; and in pain do women yet bring forth children. So Jahvistic injustice is still universal and his Holy Word is broken, believe either phase of it one may prefer.

This then, is the whole of the fearful and wonderful "curse" and "Fall of Man," whereby, we are told, all humanity was placed under the "Curse of God," and Jesus Christ had to be sent by his Father Yahveh, after four thousand years of weary "watchful waiting," into the world to suffer and die ignominiously, in order "to redeem mankind from the sin and curse of Adam." But one may wonder and say to himself, "Why, I don't see any eternal death and damnation in all this, or any scheme of redemption; where is the joke?" I will reveal it.

The Riddle of the Serpent Seed

The utterly all of the "Plan of Salvation" is revealed, or concealed, in one fatal Verse of Genesis III. The whole trick is in the Riddle of Yahveh and his Talking Snake: "I will put enmity between thee and the woman, and between thy seed and her seed: it shall bruise thy head, and thou shalt bruise his heel" (v. 15). Yahveh Almighty, Maker of Heaven and Earth, in his Infinite Wisdom, said those few cabalistic words about snake-and-women-seed, and about bruising heads and heels, to his Talking Snake; and, Lo! the inspired Oracles of the New Dispensation, over four thousand years afterwards, have conjured out of this inspired sentence this fearful and wonderful combination Curse and Prophecy, clear as mud: Mankind is damned through the sin of Adam to the last generation; but the merciful and loving Yahveh will send his son Jesus Christ, the Lord knows when, to "redeem and save" all those who believe this childish Jewish Fable, and to Re-damn in Hell Fire, not then invented, all those who do not and will not believe a word of it.

Of course, Yahveh did not say this in words that anybody but a Talking Snake or a Priest could understand. The mystic remark was made to the Serpent; it does not appear that Adam and Eve even heard it or understood it to mean anything, and certainly not the tremendous Curse of death, damnation, and salvation, four thousand years afterwards evolved out of it.

Nor did a single Patriarch, Priest, Prophet, or Seer of Israel, with all their frenzied visions and fiery cursings, ever imagine or mention anything of the sort. Of all persons on earth, these Old Testament Worthies surely would not have overlooked so momentous and terrific a Curse, in the very beginning of their own Book of

Curses, if either by inspiration or ingenuity they could have unriddled such a sense out of these seemingly senseless words. Those Holy Ones of Israel surpassed all human skill of those ages in devising curses and terrors to terrify the Chosen People into abject submission to the Priests and to Yahveh; but, fearfully effective as it was afterwards made, not a word of the awful "Curse of Adam," with eternal Hell Fire and Damnation, do they utter or even hint, or suspect.

A Big Chance Missed

Moses is Yahveh's Arch Terrorist: he piles Pelion on Ossa of threats and curses throughout all of his reputed Five Books, and fearfully and wonderfully sums them all up in his Schedule of Curses in the closing chapters of Deuteronomy. He elaborates the most frightful and blood-curdling Catalogue of Curses ever framed or imagined prior to the Gentle and Loving Jesus and his Apostles and to Mediaeval Churchly Anathemas,—all which he threatens "shall come to pass if thou wilt not hearken unto the voice of Yahveh, to observe and to do all his commandments; all these curses shall come upon thee and overtake thee": Cursed shalt thou be in this and cursed shalt thou be in that;

"Yahveh shall send upon thee cursing, vexation, and rebuke, until thou be destroyed; Yahveh shall make the pestilence cleave unto thee, until he have consumed thee off the land; Yahveh shall smite thee with a consumption, and with a fever, and with an inflammation, and with an extreme burning, and with the sword, and with blasting, and with mildew, and thou shalt eat the fruit of thine own body, the flesh of thy sons and of thy daughters shalt thou eat,"—and countless other blood-curdling and diabolic horrors; and when old Moses has exhausted his powers of invention of terrors and his vocabulary of horrors, and is choked off by an apopleptic fit of rage, he sputters and spits forth a residuary clause of curses: "Moreover, also every sickness, and every plague, which is *not written* in the Book of this Law, them will Yahveh bring upon thee, until thou be destroyed" (Deut. xxviii, 15–68).

These gentle admonitions to belief and obedience, be it remembered, are by Moses himself,—the same inspired author of the Riddle of the Serpent Seed, supposed by Christian propagandists to signify eternal damnation in Hell Fire; and thus, read in the light of such Hell Fire, this "Curse of Adam" would have been the most potent terror of all the terrors of the Priests of Yahveh, just as it always has been, until lately, of those of the later Yahveh Triplex Deity.

Moses imposed the yoke of the Priest upon the People by the threat of mortal death: "The man that will do presumptuously, and will not hearken unto (obey) the priest, . . . even that man shall die" (Deut. xvii, 12); and he exhausts the vocabulary of terrorism to instill the abject fear of the Hierarchy into the minds and souls of the deluded Chosen: but never once does he hurl at them: "Doubt and be damned"—"Fear him who hath power to destroy both soul and body in Hell"! What a chance he missed—if he had just known, or could foresee.

But Moses, in all his fluency of frightfulness and fury of invention of terror, never once includes the "Curse of Adam" in the Catalogue of "All the Curses that are written in this Book"; he evidently did not read his own Riddle that way; and no other Priest or Prophet from Moses to Malachi, even hints at Adam's Curse, or Fall, or eternal damnation in Hell Fire. Hell and its Fire are totally non-existent in the entire Hebrew scheme of penalties and punishments.

Again, let it be noted in the reader's mind, and written in indelible impress upon his memory: that from the first "Curse" in Genesis III, until the final "lest he come and smite the earth with a Curse" in the last verse of Malachi, amid all the fearful cursings and ravings of the Prophets of Yahveh denouncing death and destruction upon his Chosen People, there is not one single mention or remotest reference again in all the Hebrew Bible to the Snake Story, or to the Curse of Adam, or to the "Fall of Man," or to the necessity or propriety of Redemption from "Original Sin" and from the Fires of Hell. All the furies of the dread Yahveh, denounced by all his holy Prophets, are temporal terrors; all his pains and penalties are satiated with the death of his miserable victims. In the grave (*Sheol*) they are at rest; they are never pursued into any Hell in the original Hebrew, on account of Adam's sin or of their own. We must give even their Yahveh his due.

DAMNATION A CHRISTIAN DOGMA

Whence then, for a wonder of the world, comes this fearful Doctrine of "Original Sin," of the "Fall of Man," of Eternal Death and Damnation, of this curious and accursed "Plan of Salvation"? It is all a fiendish invention of the Apostles and Priests of the New Dispensation, as will now be very easily seen and understood. Hell Fire and Damnation in it are simply the genial sanction of the Religion of the Gentle and Loving Jesus. But Jesus Christ never once even mentioned Adam or the pretended Curse and Fall; he never once intimated that his Mission was due to the pretended Talking Snake scene in the Garden of Eden. More than that, not a one of the four writers of the so-called Gospels, utters a word about Adam, or the Curse, or the Fall, or of "redemption" by Jesus Christ for any sin of Adam, which is never even remotely referred to throughout their gospels. The single reference by the Gospel Writers to any Mosaic antecedent for any of the events of Jesus Christ, (except some pretended "prophecies" elsewhere examined), is by John, "the disciple whom Jesus loved," and his dearest and closest friend; and he only says: "As Moses lifted up the serpent in the wilderness, even so must the son of man be lifted up" (Jno. iii, 14). But this is not because of the Serpent in Eden, or of the "Curse" on Adam and mankind; but simply, as John says, "that whosoever believeth in him should not perish, but have everlasting life." Thus neither Jesus, not any of his inspired biographers, makes the remotest allusion to the very cornerstone of the wondrous "Plan of Salvation."

PAUL THE APOSTLE

The awful Dogma was inflicted upon suffering superstitious humanity by one who never knew Jesus; who was the most malignant of the early persecutors of the believers in Jêsus; one Saul of Tarsus, a Jew, a Pharisee, a doctrinaire, a garrulous tergiversant Zealot, who admits that he "profited in the Jews' religion above many" (Gal. i, 14); then changed his name to Paul, and with the zeal of a new convert became perfectly frenzied as a propagandist of the new religion,—admittedly "lying to the glory of God,"—to such extent that he came to be called "the second Founder of Christianity," the creator of its Dogma, and deviser of its dogmatic system, both self-contradictory in most or all of their muddled propositions.

This Paul was so "meshuggah," that in a fit of his frenzy about himself he gives vent to this: "I knew a man in Christ above fourteen years ago (whether in the body I cannot tell; or whether out of the body I cannot tell: God knoweth:—but certainly out of the mind;—such an one caught up into the Third Heaven; and heard unspeakable words, which it is not lawful for a man to utter" (2 Cor. xii, 2). Notwithstanding this pretended side trip to the very Fount of Inspiration, our Paul is so uninspired of truth that he takes the meshuggah Prophets of old seriously, and assures us that "God at sundry times and in divers manners (i.e. by dreams, dice, and phallic ephods) spake in time past unto the Fathers by the Prophets" (Heb.

i, 1),—heedless that this same God himself had said, as he is quoted, "I sent them not; they speak lies in my name" (Jer. xiv, 14).

The grossness of his superstition, and the proof of his total discredit to be believed in anything he utters as very "oracles of God," lies not only in his incessant contradictions of himself, but also in his own boasting confession before Felix: "But this I confess unto thee, that after the way they call 'Heresy,' so worship I the God of my Fathers (Yahveh), *believing all things* which are written in the Law and the Prophets" (Acts xxiv, 14). We have just seen the portraiture of this Yahveh "God of my Fathers," and heard the maudlin "ravings" and monstrous lies of the Meshuggah Prophets, of whom Paul's old side-partner and rival Peter fatuously vouches: "Prophecy came not in old time by the will of man; but holy men of God spake as they were moved by the Holy Ghost" (2 Pet. i, 21). But these "holy men of Yahveh" have abundantly admitted the sources of their "inspiration," and are totally discredited for truth and belief.

Now it is that this Paul inflicts his cruel and accursed "Original Sin" Infamy on humanity. If he had been inspired of truth by God, he would have known that Adam, Eve, the Garden of Eden, the Talking Snake, the "Curse," Moses and his "Genesis," all were Myths and Fables without one word of fact or truth in a single one of them. But he had been whisked into the Third Heaven, wherever that is, and this may have been one of the things which he heard "which it is not lawful for a man to utter," at least, for an honest and truthful man; but why a man who was the chief advance agent of "revelation" should deem it unlawful to reveal things which he saw in Heaven with his own eyes, and take it out in peddling ancient and phony "prophecies" of the old Meshuggahs of Israel, is curious to wonder. So when he comes back to earth, (but not to his senses), he maunders through some pages of myth and wrath of God and blood, and delivers himself of the solemn, oracular and gratuitous utterances on his novel Propositions of "Original Sin" and the "Plan of Salvation," which we shall quote in a moment.

The "Plan of Salvation"

The whole of Theology, founded on these Fables of Dogma, is aptly summed up in those memorable opening words of Milton's Immortal Epic:

"Of man's first disobedience, and the fruit
Of that Forbidden Tree whose mortal taste

> Brought death into the world and all our woe,
> With loss of Eden, till one Greater Man
> Restored us and regained that blissful seat,
> Sing, Heavenly Muse."

But truly inspired of Poesy as was Milton, let us turn to yet higher Inspiration for the more authoritative Theory of Original Sin and for the inspired originals of the Plan of Salvation. The great Dogmatist of the New Faith, Paul, thus states and restates his fearful and wonderful Doctrine of "Original Sin," of the "Fall of Man," and the Scheme of Salvation,—of all which he is the great Originator and Inventor:

"For as in Adam all die, even so in Christ shall all be made alive" (1 Cor. xv, 22).

And this Theorem he elaborates at great length and with much iteration, in others of his Letters, too many to quote, of which this is a fair example:

"Therefore, as by one man sin entered into the world, and death by sin; and so death passed upon all men, even over them that had not sinned after the likeness of Adam's transgression. . . . By the trespass of one many died" (Romans v, 12–15).

"For as by one man's disobedience many were made sinners, so by the obedience of one shall many be made righteous" (Romans v, 19).

And to cap and crown his direful Dogma, this positive and dogmatic assurance he emits:

"Christ redeemed us from the curse of the law" (Gal. iii, 13).

Human language is inadequate to qualify the fearful fatality of these fatuous sentences. The fairest part of the earth has been under their blight for nearly twenty centuries; but of this not at this time and place: it suffices to demonstrate their awful enormity of falsehood.

A childish Fable of a Talking Snake and a muddled "Curse," about as pregnant of the sense of "Original Sin" and eternal damnation as "chops and tomato sauce" are of breach of promise of marriage, is warped and twisted and tortured by the adroit Sergeant Buzfuz of Christianity into the priestly doctrine of eternal damnation in Hell Fire for all humanity! As there never was any Adam, it cannot be true that "in Adam all die"; therefore its corollary cannot follow that "even so in Christ shall all be made alive." As

it consequently is not true that "by one man sin entered into the
world, and death by sin," the superstition of "Original Sin" is
therefore false, as it is likewise false that "so death passed upon
all men," in the sense of the Soul's "death by sin" of Adam inflicted
upon all succeeding generations by a "Curse" that was never cursed
by God upon snake or man.

From this fatuous torturing of an idle and meaningless Fable,
purely personal and temporal in its every fanciful term, of a Talking
Snake, comes the monstrous cardinal Tenet of the Christian Church,
that a Great and Glorious God damned all the countless millions
of yet unborn Humanity to eternal damnation and Hell Fire because
one non-existent man in a Fable ate a Fabled Apple, at the instigation of a fabled Talking Snake; and for punishment was told that
he must work for his living thereafter, and "in the day that thou
eatest thereof thou shall surely die," and which he leisurely enough
is said to have done just 930 years after the fatal incident.

Based on this inspired Talking Snake Story, and on the amazing
deductions from it by the inspired and enthused Doctor of Dogma,
Paul, is the inspired Doctrine thus formulated by the Original One
True Church of Yahveh, and fondly adopted by every however otherwise Dissentient Sect in Christendom, as the very Corner-Stone of
the Ecclesiastical Plan of Salvation:

"The souls of those who depart in Mortal Sin, or only in *original sin,*
go down immediately to Hell" (Second Council of Lyon; and Decree
Unionis, Council of Florence; Cath. Encyc. VII, p. 208).

The climax of this deadly Doctrine being found in the awesome
aphorism of sundry of the Christian Creeds, that "Hell is full of
infants a span long," roasting in the torments of everlasting Hell
Fire, all because of the "original sin" of Father Adam, who never
lived, in a Garden of Eden that never was.

"Redemption from the Curse"

The culminating Doctrine of the whole series, a perfect type of
untruth of it all, is Paul's astonishing assurance: *"Christ has
redeemed us from the curse"* (Gal. iii, 13). Let us apply a moment's
thought to this Dogma of Paul and the Priests.

According to the infamy imputed to Yahveh, he damned all
future humanity into Hell for the sin of the fabled First Man.
Awful, if true: all babes, however innocent, all men and women, however nobly good and virtuous in life, all damned in Hell irretrievably

because of One—for "in Adam all men die" (1 Cor. xv, 22)—"and so death passed upon all men" (Rom. v, 12).

But, after four thousand years, Yahveh, who had done this, relenting, sent his only Begotten Son to die and so save the world from this Curse: "Christ died that all might live: He redeemed us from the Curse" (supra). Just and righteous this, however tardy, if true. As all were damned, whether they knew it or not, whether they believed it or not, whether they had sinned or not,—surely, in righting the wrong, all should be saved whether or not, in the same terms, quite as universally and effectively.

But, No, the Christian Plan of Salvation does not work that way. Its terms and conditions are: "Believe, and ye shall be saved; believe not, and ye are damned already" (Mark xvi, 16; Jno. iii, 18). Damned *nolens volens:* undamned only *volens* and credulous. Be born and be damned; believe unbelievable things and be saved, or remain damned: such is the "Sacred Science of Christianity."

Of course, if the sacrificial death of Jesus Christ is given full credit and effect, its efficacy is, must be, universal. He was proclaimed from Heaven: "Behold, the Lamb of God, which taketh away the sin of the world" (Jno. i, 29); and Inspiration explicitly avers: "And he is the propitiation for our sins: and not for ours only, but for the sins of the whole world" (1 Jno. ii, 2). Therefore, by every token of truth and reason, if the Sacrifice of the Cross really and truly "redeemed us from the Curse," as generously and universally as Adam's reputed sin damned every one in the whole world regardless, then are all saved by that atoning act alone, just as sure as all were damned by that one act of Adam. But there would be then no use for Priest and Church and Theology; and threats of Hell Fire would be as innocuous as water on the proverbial goose's back. So the zealous soul-savers, inventors and propagandists of Hell Fire, have "made the sacrifice of Christ of no avail," by limiting its effective redemption strictly to the microscopic minority of True Believers alone, leaving the countless majority of mankind yet damned forever. Indeed, millions of Dissentient Believers who cherish the heretic hope of Salvation, are doomed to infernal disappointment and eternal damnation for their un-Orthodox way of belief; for the venerable Athanasian Creed of the One True Church thus assures us: "Whoever will be saved, it is necessary above all things that he hold to the Catholic Faith. Unless each one keep this whole and unbroken, he shall without doubt perish into eternal death. . . . This is the Catholic Faith: unless each believe it rightly and firmly, he cannot be saved" (Cath. Encyc. II, p. 34).

THE CURSE NOT 100% REDEEMED

There are yet other curiosities of the Plan of Salvation—of this wondrous "redemption" from the fearful and wonderful "Curse"— even for the True Believers. If by the Sacrifice of the Cross the "Curse" is taken away, even for only those who believe it all, then, why not all the Curse? Why is the wondrous work of redemption so partial and incomplete? For the Snake yet goes pronely upon his belly, under the Curse; the believing Woman yet brings forth her yet damned child in birth pains, under the Curse; the yet accursed ground yet brings forth thorns and thistles, under the Curse, and yields its fruits, even to the True Believer, only by dint of "the sweat of his face," under the Curse; even the True Believer yet eats his bread in the sweat of his face—all exactly as pronounced in the "Curse" from which his Christ "redeemed" him two thousand years ago. Surely, "the wisdom of Yahveh is foolishment to men." And all this Wisdom is the legitimate fruit of the Tree of Knowledge in the Garden of Eden. Such is the Sacred Science of Christianity.

Thus we see that the whole of the Christian Faith, the entire Christian Plan of Salvation,—the sole and only apology for Christian Theology—hangs like a Dead Sea Apple from the fabled Serpent-entwined Tree of Knowledge in the mythical Garden of Eden. And, like the Dead Sea Apple, the "Sacred Science of Christianity," with its labored "Plan of Salvation," turns to vain ashes at the touch of Truth and is blown away with a breath of Reason.

The whole fabric of the Christian "Faith"—not its admirable moral precepts and maxims, which are not new or exclusive to it at all, but its laboriously built up Theology of Dogma, forged by Paul and his associate propagandists into a Priestly system of Beliefs and Practices enforced by terrific threats of eternal damnation hereafter through Eternity—and so long as was possible by torture and death here on earth—is seen to be totally dependent, as it was falsely founded, upon the idle Fables of Yahveh of the primitive, superstitious, heathen Hebrews, and falls into vacuous Nothingness with the disproof of the truth of the fabled Eden and its Fall.

This enthused forger of Dogma, Paul, admits, "Beyond measure I persecuted the Church of God, and wasted it" (Gal. i, 13), and he admits that he found his profit in the bloody business (v. 14). When he saw the "great light" on Damascus way, and took up the new Faith, he became a much more bigoted persecutor of all unbelievers in his labored ludicrous Dogmas. Time and again he screams,

"If any man love not the Lord Jesus Christ, let him be Anathema-Maranatha"—a frightful Churchly Curse; "If any man preach any other gospel unto you than that we have preached, let him be accursed"; and he pledges eternal Hell Fire to the skeptically inclined: "He that doubteth is damned" (Rom. xiv, 23)—"suffering the vengeance of eternal fire" (Jude vii). This is the nearest that Ecclesiastical Terrorism could get to inflicting torture and death upon Disbelievers, while the mighty Roman Empire stood on guard of human rights: the rack and the stake for Unbelief came later, when the debased and Christianized State had entered into a Priest-imposed League of Hell and Covenant of Death with the Holy Church, which this Paul and his Arch-Adjutant Peter had created and established "*Ad Majorem Dei Gloriam*," and for their mutual profit and aggrandizement and that of the whole race of Apostolic Succession and even dissenting Protestants ever since.

On a play on words, a Pun of Jesus Christ, the Church of Christ is founded: "Thou art Peter (Greek, *Petrus*, a stone), and on this Rock I will build my Church"—and the assurance is fondly added, "and the gates of Hell shall not prevail against it" (Matt. xvi, 18). Hell and the Church are thus cut from the same piece by the Grand Master of both Superstitions. The Hell-Myth has long since been exploded, and the Church was shaken to its foundations by the explosion. When the Key-stone of the arch, Ecclesiastic Theology, is knocked out, great will be the fall of the whole structure, "and great will be the fall thereof," to the universal boon of true spiritual uplook and the brotherhood of man on earth.

CHAPTER XVIII

REVELATIONS OF THE HEREAFTER

Heaven, Hell, and Purgatory

In the XXth Century after the traditional Advent of the Son of Yahveh on earth, the Religion which is built around that Event persists fundamentally upon a congeries of primitive cosmological notions, which modern Knowledge has made totally obsolete. The Hebrew, and ancient primitive, notions of the construction, or architectural scheme, of their very limited Cosmos or universe, was intimately related to, and an integral part of, their scheme of Theology and of Eschatology, or after-life affairs as they conceived them. Their notions of God, of Heaven, of Hell, and of after-life, were adapted, and were adaptable only, to the narrow scheme of things bounded by the very narrow limits of the universe as known to and imagined by the Ancient Theologians. And the present-day Christian Theology adopts wholly and wholly rests upon the ancient Hebrew Revelation of Earth, and Heaven, and Hell—with Fire later kindled in the latter.

According to this ancient Hebrew Revelation: the earth is flat and four-cornered; the sun moves around it as a center, and on occasion can be made to stand still in its course. No great distance above the flat surface of the earth is a solid arched "firmament," in which the sun, moon and stars are somehow set and on which they move. Just within this firmament, which is a solid something which "divides the waters which were under the firmament from the waters which were above the firmament" (Gen. i, 7), is Heaven, where their Yahveh and sundry other beings, angels, seraphim, the "Sons of the Gods," and others of the "heavenly hosts" have their abode.

This Heaven is quite close to the earth: so close that men could propose and attempt to build a Tower which should reach into it and enable them to scale right up among the gods; so close that a Ladder resting on the earth actually reached into the Heaven, on which angels passed to and fro. Yahveh and his messengers can easily and quickly pass back and forth from earth to heaven;

the "sons of the Gods" can come to earth among the daughters of
men. The voice of Yahveh can easily be heard when he cries from
heaven, and from heaven he can hurl stones and thunder-bolts when
he fights, like Jove, in the battles of his Chosen warriors. The
Spirit of Yahveh can flit dove-like from heaven to earth to accredit
the Son of Yahveh to men. The living bodies of Enoch and Elijah
can be "translated" into heaven, the latter before onlooking human
eyes, in a chariot and horses of fire; the flesh-clothed shades of
Elijah and Moses can swoop down upon the Mount of Transfiguration and back again like flashes of lightning. The human eye in
ecstasy can see into heaven and behold Yahveh seated on his Throne.
Dives in Hell can look right up into Heaven and see Lazarus "in
the bosom of good old Abraham," and hold converse with him there.
Satan, King of Hell, was wont to pass readily to Heaven to hold
Yahveh its God and King in challenging argument and defiance and
to plot evil to Job. While, too, under the "new dispensation," the
souls of the newly dead found instant lodgment in Heaven or Hell,
as the case might be, according to the deeds done in the flesh.

What Heaven Is and Where

In the beginning *Elohim* (gods) created Heaven and the earth,
reads the ancient Hebrew Revelation, and made the Firmament, "and
called the Firmament Heaven" (Gen. i, 8).

About maybe the same time Marduk, Babylonian Sky-God and
Creator of Heaven and earth, forged the immense dome of Heaven
out of the hardest metal, resting it upon a wall surrounding the
earth. For the Egyptians, the Heavens were an arched iron ceiling
from which the stars were suspended by cables. To the ancient
Greeks and Romans, the Sky-Father (Zeus-Pater, Jupiter) had set
up a great vault of crystal, to which the fixed stars were attached,
the sun and planets being suspended movably by brazen chains.
Olympus' high head pierced the visible sky, and on its lofty summit
awful Zeus held his court in Heaven. The Romans called it "Coelum,"
the vaulted ceiling or covering of the earth.

Ah, "How do the heathen rage and the peoples imagine vain
things." Fatuous notions these, of childish Heathen cosmogony, of
Pagan superstition. Only the Hebrews in their hoary Holy Writ,
had the true Revelation of Creation by their True God(s); they
only, inspired with truth by their Yahveh, truly knew what or where
Heaven is and whereof it is really wrought, for their Yahveh himself
only wrought it, as is revealed: "I am Yahveh that maketh all

things; that stretched forth the Heavens alone; that spreadeth abroad the earth by Myself" (Is. xliv, 24). Which Heaven, avers Job, "is strong, and as of molten brass" (Job. xxxvii, 18).

This was the Heaven of the Hebrew: in his consonantal language SHM, "to be high"; in Anglo-Saxon English, Hoeven, "heaved, lifted up." It is the "Firmament of Heaven"—"and Elohim called the Firmament heaven"; a solid something which was fixed "in the midst of the waters, to divide the waters from the waters" (Gen. i, 6)—thus a sort of great vaulted bulkhead or retaining-wall for the vast celestial reservoir above, through which the upper waters poured in Noah's Deluge when "the windows of Heaven were opened" (Gen. vii, 11). The Firmament (RQY) of Hebrew Revelation, is something "beaten or hammered out," something "made firm or solid—hence Firm-amentum" in the Vulgate. How strangely alike the Pagan Fables and the Inspired Revelation. Howbeit, the revealed Hebrew-Christian Heaven so closely girded the four-cornered flat Bible earth that Jacob's somewhat elongated Ladder could comfortably span the intervening space and lean up against the open "Window of Heaven," so that, as Amos assures, living people might "climb up to heaven" (ix, 2). And it is common knowledge that the departed soul "in the twinkling of an eye" flashes from earth to its home in Heaven, so near is Heaven unto us, according to Paul.

But the profane revelation of human Knowledge points otherwise. By processes wonderful as they are precise, the primitive Heaven of Hebrew Revelation has been pushed back beyond the tiptop of Jacob's dreamed Ladder and the storied snow-capped peaks of Olympus, and has been translated so far into fathomless sidereal Space, that the journeyman departed Soul needs much more liberal allowance of time to span.

Delicate instruments devised by the genius of man, and the Divine powers of Trigonometry, while not yet attaining the exact triangulation of Heaven, have amazingly shown where Heaven is not yet. The unwritten revelations of the real Creator God through Divine Astronomy have made manifest for our wonder and reverence the farflung extent of His work of the Universe: the Sun at 93,000,000 of miles from its tiny planet Earth; Neptune, most distant of his planets, 2,793,000,000 miles further into space; the nearest of the fixed Stars, which "God set in the Firmament" just where Jacob's Ladder reached, 20,000,000,000,000 miles from the base of that wonderful Ladder on earth. But this is the first and very nearest Star.

Not to pause at others which have yielded the secret of their distance to the eye of Science, we plunge in thought upward and onward to those wonderful "Star Clusters," so thick-studded and so far away that their glorious separate bodies are mingled to the sight of the most powerful sidereal telescope so as to be in appearance almost as identical and inseparable as are in Dogma the Ineffable Persons in the Mystery of the Three-in-One Godhead, Yahveh, Logos and Paraclete—Bel, On and Hea; Osiris, Isis and Horus, or Brahma, Siva and Vishnu, one has a liberal choice of Trinities. And there is revealed, away on the very frontiers of the yet fathomed Universe—a truly Divine Revelation—the Star-cluster known only by its Number "N. G. C. 6822," which lies in profound depths of Space distant so far that the blaze of light from it reaches this mundane sphere only after a flight through Space of 1,000,000 years! (Int. Encyc. Year Book, 1924, p. 66). Those true Prophets of the God Creator known as Astronomers measure sidereal distances not by miles or leagues but by "light-years," or units of the distance in miles that light travels through space in a year of time; and 1,000,000 such light-years measure the stupendous and unexpressable distance from earth to somewhere this side of Heaven where Star Group No. N. G. C. 6822 answered the Divine Fiat "Let there be Light," and burst into glorious being.

But we have not yet defined this stretch of Space Heavenward; so we will at least resolve it into its arithmetical elements. Light flashes through space at the dizzy speed of 186,300 miles in one second of time. In one year there are 31,566,926 seconds. Thus one light-year is equal to 5,883,928,333,800, or approximately 6 trillions, of miles of travel per year. This number of miles multiplied by the 1,000,000 years the light of this Star Group requires to reach our eyes, gives us a number that no man can apprehend and only the mind of God can comprehend—5,883,928,333,800,000,000 miles! And Heaven—since we can see with uninterrupted, though telescopic, sight right up to that Star Cluster, is Somewhere on Beyond, with its myriads of mansions, its jasper walls, its golden streets and pearly gates, its wondrous River of Life which flows by the Throne of Yahveh; elsewise it would intercept and shut off the blaze of light from the Divine Star Group N. G. C. 6822.

Nowhere by Inspiration is it revealed unto man the speed of a Soul in flight nor how long it takes to flit "from earth to Heaven's immortal day." Indeed, a near-revelation is near-made in one well-known Scripture passage, when about the Sixth Hour of a memorable day One Crucified is reported as saying to one of his companions in passion: "Verily, this day shalt thou be with me in Paradise." It was not until the Ninth Hour that that immortal Spirit gave up the

Ghost, leaving only three hours of the day remaining for the Paradisiac journey; so that this remark may be interpreted as a suggestion of very rapid ascent to the Kingdom of Heaven. But the data are quite too meagre to allow of so exact computations as we are enabled to make in the calculations just above submitted.

Inspiration and Science have here yet another point of friendly contact, in their processes. "Believe not every spirit, but try the spirits whether they are of God" (Jno. iv, 1), is the thumb-rule of Revelation. Science, applying this same principle to test its own revelations, tries out every possible hypothesis before it puts the seal of Infallibility upon its really Heavenly Dogmas. So until it is revealed or otherwise satisfactorily shown that a departed Soul has, as it were, a muzzle-velocity on leaving the body, and a constantly maintained flight through space, far excelling the speed of light, and quite equal to that of Thought, our conclusions from irrefragible figures that three hours is too narrow a margin of time for a Soul to span the gap from earth to Heaven, must stand, at least on as firm a foundation of verity as that of the revelation of the efficacy of priestly prayers—at so much per—for the relief and ultimate release of the Souls in Purgatory, which we are now approaching in our inquiry.

So, scientific methods of research for Truth, as well as certain precepts of inspired Dogma, compel us to examine the reluctant hypotheses of Purgatory and Hell, against the possibility that perchance, after all, the soul of the Repentant Thief did not, in sad reality, bend its flight Heavenward, but, in virtue of sin, original or acquired, or both, it were barred from that Kingdom of Glory, and must perforce seek its temporary or eternal habitat in one or another of the Spirit Realms which are conveniently provided for unshriven Souls by inspired Revelation or equally inspired Tradition. Such an inquiry is not only demanded by scientific candor, as just explained; but as the problem of the destiny of the Soul, when disembodied, is both quite germane to our theme, and is not without a curious interest of its own, the subject justifies a brief excursus in the spirit to explore the hypotheses of these two other Christian Provinces, or Providences, or Properties.

So This Is Hell

HELL, as it comes first in venerable time of discovery, or revelation, or invention, claims first our fearful attention. In the genial Doctrine of the Gospel of Love, Hell is the Gehennic goal of the

Soul which even dares to doubt, which is the Unpardonable Sin. Here we are not vexed with scientific or mathematical speculations of time of transit. Dogma, which so admirably complements the shortcomings of Revelation, has set its fatal sanction on the assured fact of instantaneous translation, and sundry other congenial incidents, which we must notice for what they are worth.

Thanks to the inspired infallible Decree *"Unionis"* (Council of Florence; Cath. Encyc., VII, p. 208), we now know just when and where we arrive and what to expect upon arrival: "The souls of those who depart in Mortal Sin, or only in Original Sin, go down *immediately* into Hell." And patching out this precious piece out of the Sacred Deposit with a scrap from the Creed, we learn that it is "into everlasting fire" that we land; and once landed safely in it, "the torments of the damned shall last forever and ever," as Holy Writ of the Dispensation of God's Love and Mercy for our warning so often reassures us.

The "Sacred Science of Christianity," even as our acquisition of other facts of profane knowledge, is a progressive Science, and Hell has evolutionized fearfully and wonderfully with the process of the Suns and of Revelations. In the Babylonian "Lay of Ishtah"—whence Hebrew Revelation would seem to have plagiarized some of its inspiration on this and other matters of revelation—the Underworld to which the shade of the departed, Sinner or Saint alike, sank after death, is described in appropriately gloomy colors. It is variously and poetically called "The Pit," the "House of Darkness," the "Land of No Return"—metaphors strangely reminiscent of "Pluto's gloomy realm" of Homer, of the "go down to the Pit" of the Psalmist, of Isaiah, and of Job; of the "Bottomless Pit" of Apocalypse; of the "outer darkness" and "Pits of darkness" of the Evangelists; of the "Land of Forgetfulness" of the Sweet Singer of Israel (Ps. lxxxviii, 12); of "Death, and the House appointed for all living" of the Man of Boils and Patience" (Job xxx, 23)—of that "Bourne from whence no traveler returneth," of Another of high inspiration.

Wherever in the old Hebrew Revelation the place of dim life after death is named, its name is "Sheol" (the Cave, dug-out); it is equivalent to and often rendered as "the grave" in our English versions: "Oh that thou wouldst hide me in the grave (Sheol)," cries Job (xiv, 13), "until thy wrath be past"; Korah and his band "went down alive into the grave (Sheol) and the earth closed upon them" (Num. xvi, 30, 32, 33); "Thou hast brought my soul from Sheol," sings the Psalmist (Ps. xxx, 3). It is identical in every sense with the "Hades" of Pagan and Christian Greek: "Thou wilt not leave

my soul in Sheol," sings again in Hebrew the Psalmist (Ps. xvi, 10)
—quoted: "Thou wilt not leave my soul in Hades" (Acts ii, 27).
Good and bad alike found there their rest after life's fitful fever
o'er; it was truly for all "the house appointed for all living" (Job
xxx, 23). The soul of the Psalmist we have just seen there, though
his hope is that it will not remain alway. "Out of the belly of Sheol
I cried," wails the godly Jonah (ii, 2). In grief for Joseph reported
dead, the good Patriarch Jacob rent his garments and cried: "I will
go down to Sheol to my son mourning" (Gen. xxxvii, 35). There
in the same Sheol was the shade of the Holy Samuel, conjured up to
earth at King Saul's behest by the uncanny Witch of En-Dor (1
Sam. xxviii).

Moreover, the place and locality of the Hebrew Sheol is fixed
with a precision unusual to Revelation: "I will make thee dwell in
the nether parts of the earth, in the places that are desolate of old,
with them that go down to (Sheol) the Pit" (Ezek. xxvi, 20). Nor
is it so far down but that reasonable efforts of excavation may not
lay it bare: "Though they dig into Sheol" (Amos ix, 2); indeed
there are things and places which are "deeper than Sheol" (Job xi,
8). And in all this: not one fleck of Hell Fire; not one whiff of
Brimstone; not even the sound of "weeping and wailing and gnashing
of teeth!" (Luke xiii, 28). By all original Revelation, therefore,
Sheol is simply "the place desolate of old," bereft merely of the
"glory set in the land of the living" (Ezek. xxvi, 20). The Books
of the Law and the Prophets, major and minor, are silent as Sheol
(the grave) on the whole Christly-Apostolic-Churchly Doctrine of
future rewards of Good and punishment of Evil. There is no Fire
or eternal Damnation about it at all. Their Hell is on earth, in life;
the nearest approximation in Hebrew Revelation to the notion of
Heavenly reward is death and the ensuing "sinking down into Sheol,"
away from the awful wrath of their Jealous Yahveh.

Had our Repentant Thief then, by Luck or in Providence, lived
and passed from life under the *post-mortem* régime of the Old Dispensation, his worthy spirit would have found its lasting abode in a
cheerless, maybe, but not fiery habitat, where it would have enjoyed
the congenial companionship of the shades of Adam and Eve and Noah,
of the Patriarchs (but not of the Prophets, as we shall see, except
Samuel), of Kings David and Solomon, of the Queen of Sheba, and
Jezebel, and the Harlot of Jericho, and other Worthies, good, bad
and indifferent of Israel; of Homer, Ulysses, Socrates, Xantippe,
Sappho, of unnumbered other great and good spirits of those olden
times. The Worthies of Israel we have seen were there, as vouched

by their own inspired revelation; while a newer revelation, not indeed of the Scriptures but of the Sacred Deposit of equal inspiration, vouchsafes to us the real reason for their seclusion in that House of Darkness: "The souls of the Just who died before Christ awaited in Hell (Limbo) their admission to Heaven; for in the meantime Heaven was closed against them in punishment for the sin of Adam" (Cath. Encyc., VII, p. 207). Which is to weep, and which is very interesting; and also proves there was no Fire in Hell prior to the New Dispensation—and also that Purgatory was not yet discovered; for it would not have been fair to broil the Just along with the Unjust for four thousand years, while they waited for transfer to Heaven. It also proves that Mohammed spoke the Truth, "God is Just," as the event also proves.

If our Repentant Thief Ghost had been immured in the Old Dispensation Sheol-Hades, it would undoubtedly have been an interested spectator, if not a beneficiary, of the very remarkable act of Justice, however tardy, rendered to these poor imprisoned Spirits—that goal-delivery unequaled, or Hell-delivery unparalleled, which Inspiration, at first rather hazily, afterwards with the most soul-satisfying assurance, relates to us. To St. Paul we are indebted for the first glimmer of inspired light on this affair, in the lucid passage where he is said to say, in substance and effect, that in the three-day *entre-acte* between the Crucifixion scene and the Resurrection scene, the Redeemer of Mankind put in his time in a side-trip to Hell (Eph. iv, 10); which valuable information, if such it be, is illumined by further light supposed to be shed on this same incident, by St. Peter, who relates, that while there, the Master "preached unto the spirits in prison" (1 Pet. iii, 19). Which must mean the same thing, though by the context of both SS. they might as well have been discussing chops and tomato sauce or the sort of stuff dreams are made of. But between the two, supplemented and made intelligible by more positive revelation out of the inexhaustible Sacred Deposit, we have the assurance, that as the result of this Infernal excursion, "Christ conducted to Heaven the Patriarchs who had been in Limbo," as it is euphemistically termed.

Captivity Captive

The inspired History of all this is deserving our profound ponderation; the logic which demonstrates its factuality is as unique as it is faith-compelling. The great Logician of the Faith, St. Paul, speaking to the Ephesians (Ch. iv), of any or every thing else or of nothing pertinent whatever, springs upon them without warning this wonderful inspired Syllogism:

"But unto each one of us was the grace given according to the measure of the gift of Christ; . . . Wherefore he saith, When he ascended on high, he led captivity captive, and gave gifts unto men; . . . Now this He ascended, what is it but that he also descended into the lower parts of the earth? He that descended is also the same that ascended"!

Which is almost as convincive of his conclusion as the ditty-axiom:

"Whatever goes up is bound to come down,
On somebody's head or on the ground."

And it naturally proves all about the aforesaid side-trip to Hell, which, we have seen, is undoubtedly in "the nether parts of the earth." And this sententious surplusage mixed in with the Syllogism, about "leading captivity captive," by every postulate of Reason, as of Faith, means that the Spirits of the Patriarchs and Worthies which were in the "captivity" of Sheol these four thousand years, were now led "captive" into Heaven! The wonders of Grace, as of inspired Logic, are beyond comprehension.

These Ephesians were only new-hatched Pagan-Christians, and unread in the Hebrew Scriptures, so the foregoing probably sounded to them familiarly like an Orphic Oracle, and therefore worthy of all acceptation. But to one more Scripture-sophisticated, reading this "he saith, 'When he ascended on high, he led captivity captive,'" this of "captivity captive" jingles in the memory like a half-forgotten quotation, like an ill-remembered "old odd end stolen out of Holy Writ" of olden time. Pricked by the curiosity of verification, let us then "search the Scriptures," whether perchance we may locate this alluring alliteration. Our reward is as great as our surprise: there is naught of "ascending on high" nor of saying anything on the ascent; it is the Jubilation Song of Deborah and Barak over the "down and out" of Sisera, him against whom the "stars fought in their courses"; but we capture the captivity, and here it is:

"Awake, awake, Deborah;
Awake, awake, utter a song:
Arise, Barak, and lead thy captivity captive!" (Judges v. 12).

All of which greatly increases our wonder at the wonderful Syllogism of Paul the Logician—and of course proves wonderfully the captivity in Hell and the leading captive into Heaven.

The Sermon-to-the-Spirits incident is revealed by equally cogent and inspired Logic of St. Peter (1 Pet. iii, 18–20), equally assuring to our spirits:

"It is better that ye suffer for well-doing than for evil-doing; . . .

"Because Christ also suffered, being put to death in the flesh, but quickened in the spirit;

"In which he also went and preached unto the spirits in prison,

"Which aforetime were disobedient, when the long-suffering of God waited in the days of Noah, while the Ark was a-preparing,

"Wherein a few, that is, eight souls, were saved through water." ·

So, after this preachment, addressed clearly only to the disobedient pre-Noachians, the whole of "captivity captive" was led, like the rats in the Pied Piper, out of Hell into Heaven; for this Truth, if not entirely deducible from the two inspired Syllogisms supra, is vouched by the inspired Logic of the Deposit, above cited: "Christ conducted to Heaven the Patriarchs who had been in Limbo."

But how this side-trip to Hades during the three-days between Crucifixion and Resurrection was possible, does not appear, in view of the assurance of the Crucified One to the Repentant Thief: "This day shalt thou be *with me in Paradise*," which shows that they "ascended" together, and not "descended" into Hell at all.

But just here we seem to strike a snag in Inspiration. Fathers Abraham, Isaac, and Jacob certainly were Patriarchs of the Patriarchs; but unfortunately they were not in Sheol to share in this Patriarchal delivery, or captivity, which happened, according to Inspiration, just post-crucifixion. For, some time prior to this Event, Christ Himself, yet in life, speaks positively of "Abraham, Isaac and Jacob in the Kingdom of God" (Matt. viii, 11). Too, Beggar Lazarus died, and he was "carried away by the angels into Abraham's bosom" (Luke xvi, 22); a fact confirmed by the fact that Dives, in Hell, "lifted up his eyes, and seeth Abraham afar off, and Lazarus in his bosom"; and Dives cried to Father Abraham to please send Lazarus with a drop of water, "for I am in anguish in this flame" (Luke xvi, 24)—which proves that the Fire had now been kindled in the olden Hades, and it was now the Christian Hell. But Abraham called back, No, there is a great gulf fixed between Heaven and Hell, "so that they which would pass from Heaven to you, cannot; neither can they pass to us, that would come from Hell" (v. 26); though evidently it was no trick at all for people in either place to see well into the other and talk, like by wireless telephony, across the gulf of space; however there was "No Thoroughfare" nor corporeal

passing back and forth; which causes wonder how Christ managed
to "conduct to Heaven the Patriarchs (minus Abraham, Isaac and
Jacob) who were in Limbo"—though Satan fell from Heaven into
Hell, and often used to go back to Heaven to visit with Yahveh
regarding Job.

Nor were these the only absentees from the roster of Patriarchs
in Limbo. The godly Enoch was not there, for he had been "translated" from the original Hebrew into Heaven alive; nor was Elijah
in Hell, for he had been whirled alive in the fiery chariot right into
Heaven; nor was Moses, for he and Elijah appeared there to Peter
and company on the Mount of Transfiguration, and they must have
come down from Heaven together, not one down from Heaven and
the other up from Hell. So here we have to record some very distinguished absentees from the Patriarchal captivity, they being
already captive in Heaven long since. Morever, "all the Prophets"
were on the absent-list of Hell, for they were right there "also with
Abraham, Isaac and Jacob in the Kingdom of Yahveh" (Luke xiii,
28).

A Damnèd Place Is Hell

But all these wonders and this good and godly company our
Repentant Thief must have missed. His departure from life was
under the New Dispensation of Love and Mercy, after the fires of
brimstone had been kindled by Christ himself in the olden Sheol, and,
in Providence, it had become the Christian Hell. So if, according
to the hypothesis which we are examining, having missed Heaven,
our Repentant Thief's soul was doomed to the Christian Hell, what
a Hell of a doom awaited it! It is all so horrid—and we know so
much about it already from the Hell-reeking inspired pages of the
Gospels of Love, and from the blood-curdling "Inferno" as it really
is, described as an eyewitness by the "man who has been in Hell" on
a personally conducted tour with a good old Pagan guide, there resi-
dent, who pointed out all the sights of special horror, and also by
the glimpse we have just caught of Dives "in anguish in this flame"
—that we turn away with a shudder of soul from the spectacle, and
will not look for even a Thief in any such a damned place—or "place
of the damned," if that sounds less profane, as it is more Scriptural
and Theological. And surely the gentle reader would not endure to
witness the Apocalyptic vision revealing the genial Repentant Soul
among all those poor sinners (either of original or mortal sin), who
are there "tormented with fire and brimstone in the presence of the

Holy Angels and in the presence of the Lamb," who all look on complacent and unqualmed while "the smoke of their torment goeth up for ever and ever, and they have no rest day and night—from the fierceness of the wrath of Almighty God" (Rev. xiv, 10–11). Which is inspired Revelation of the God of all Love.

What a horrid caricature of the Christian Yahveh's mercy is that of the abominable Koran of the Infidel, with its crude brutal bullying Fate of the Unbeliever: "Verily, those who disbelieve our signs, we will surely cast to be broiled in Hell Fire; so often as their skins shall be well burned, we will give them other skins in exchange, that they may taste the sharper torment; for Allah is Mighty and Wise!" (Ch. iv). Oh, the holy mercies of the Christian Faith, wherein no such fiendish skin-grafting is practised for our greater torment! Turning away in holy horror and Godly fear from such a Hell, we would fervently utter in spirit the prayer "God have mercy on the souls in Hell"; but are checked by the remembrance that this our prayer would not do them any good anyhow, for it is revealed that "the wrath of God *abideth* on the damned"—and "the torments of the damned shall last for ever and ever," without even any graft of new skin (the "graft" comes in Purgatory in the next paragraph)—as the brutish Koran God provides. Besides, the equally inspired revelation of the Sacred Deposit warns us that the souls of the Christian Damned in the Christian Hell, "are never released, notwithstanding the Mass for Dead Souls" (probably meaning souls of the dead)—no, "the soul that sinneth it shall surely die." Why then torment dead souls? one would wonder—which is otherwise quite efficacious, if properly paid. This brings us up with a sudden jerk right in Purgatory, whither we have been steering our course for since some pages back. Let us look around for our Crucified Thief here.

Purgatory and Pay

This Purgatory is surely the strangest place this side of Hell. Curiously it is not in the Inspired Bible at all; as is negatively proven by there not being jot nor tittle of remotest hint of it from "In the Beginning" of Genesis to the final "Amen" of Apocalypse, search for it who will; and its proof positive is in the two Syllogisms we have just reviewed and in the Depository Revelation quoted, that "the souls of the Just who died before Christ awaited *in Hell* their admission to Heaven," there being thus evidently no Purgatory open for occupation at that time.

This omission of Purgatory from the earlier Christian "properties" is the more curious for that we have admirable and elaborately defined Purgatories in a number of contemporary Heathen Hereafter-systems; as to wit, the Twelve Cycles of Purgation of Zoroaster, the seven of the very near-Christian Mithraism, and the refined "Empyrosis" of the Stoics; from which ancient but Diabolic Religions, and several others, the Hebrew-Christian Sacred Science had so many apparently borrowed revelations that the Holy Fathers were much put to it to explain away the identities of the Pagan and Christian Rituals, by averring that "the Devil had blasphemously imitated the Christian rites and doctrines"—which would be very persuasive, if not conclusive, but for the fact that all of these plagiarized Pagan systems predated Christianity by many centuries.

Curious, too, that not for several centuries after the close of the Canon Revelation was this serious omission of Purgatory ever officially noticed by the inspired regular Guardians of the Sacred Deposit. Whereupon they held a hasty Council session with the "Keepers of the Sacred Deposit," at Lyons in the year 1274—reiterated (on the well-known principle that by frequently repeating a thing one often comes himself to believe it) at Florence in 1439, and in the famous Council of Trent in the 1500's, and resoluted:

"Whereas, the Catholic Church, instructed by the Holy Ghost has from the Holy Scriptures (Chapter and verse not cited) and the ancient Tradition of the Fathers taught in Councils (unspecified), and very recently in this Ecumenical Synod, that there *is* a Purgatory, and that the Souls therein detained are helped by the suffrages (i.e., paid prayers) of the Faithful, but principally by the acceptable Sacrifice of the Altar; the Holy Synod enjoins on the Bishops that they diligently *endeavor* to have the sound doctrines of the Fathers in Council regarding Purgatory everywhere taught and preached, held and *believed* by the Faithful"—which proves that the Faithful did not very much believe it, so that Tetzel & Co.'s famous bargain sales of Indulgences from Purgatorial pains were not so remunerative as in greater Faith they really should have been.

In honor of Truth, however, it must be admitted that much earlier efforts to "graft" this Purgatory onto the True Faith had often been made, though not with so plenary instruction of the Holy Ghost as could be invoked by the Holy Councils referred to. For instance, the Holy Father Pope Gregory the Great, in the neighborhood of 600 A.D., was the first to formulate the hitherto vacuous doctrine into good Latin and to "call a spade a spade," as it were, by naming the place Purgatory, though its latitude and longitude in Ecclesiastical Cosmogony have never been adequately defined.

Here we may pause to do a paragraph of honor to the memory and spiritual illumination of this Great Man, Pope Gregory, in noting another amusing incident for which he vouches with the same infallible inspiration as that which attests his discovery and definition of Purgatory. When elected Pope in 590 A.D., the Eternal City Rome was threatened with being wiped out by a dreadful Pestilence sent by the Hebrew God Yahveh who had supplanted Jupiter in the Roman Theogony. The pious new *Pontifex Maximus* (another Heathen institution appropriated by the Christians) at once determined to propitiate (an euphemism for "bribe") the angry God, who was flinging fiery darts into the devoted City. So Yahveh's inspired Vicar-general Gregory headed a Monkish parade through the unclean streets (maybe an indirect adjunct of the Pestilence), when suddenly he saw (he tells it himself, just as he told about the nun swallowing the devil on the lettuce leaf) the Archangel Michael hovering right over the great Pagan Mausoleum of Hadrian, just in the act of sheathing his flaming sword, while three angels with him chanted the "Regina Coeli"—a Monkish Hymn to the "Queen of Heaven." The great Pope made the sign of the Cross and broke into hallelujahs (Heb., "Praise Yahveh"), whereupon the plague promptly ceased; in commemoration of which notable event, the Pope built a Christian chapel dedicated to S. Michael on the top of the Pagan monument, and over it erected the colossal statue of the destroying Archangel in the act of sheathing his bloody sword; thus the Pagan Mausoleum became the Christian Castel Sant' Angelo, which stands there to this day in proof of infallibility of Papal narratives, and thus corroborative of his Dogma of Purgatory.

To resume where we interrupted ourselves for this momentary act of reverence to the inspired Vicar of Yahveh, we were going on to say that the holy Council of Trent, for the better procuring that its inspired Doctrine of Purgatory, and the superior efficacy of paid prayers, might the better be believed by the Faithful, who might be curious to know just where their money went in this direction, and what good it did anyhow, solemnly warned and commanded the said Bishops "to exclude from their preaching difficult and subtle questions which tend not to edification, and from the discussion of which there is no increase either of piety or devotion"—though there might thereby be a decrease of Churchly revenues. Some of these unedifying questions which are taboo might, to some of the inquisitive Faithful, be, for instance—but then, why should there be any "difficult and subtle questions" at all about so interesting and important a Revelation of Faith, especially when the Holy Ghost was right there in Person in at least three Councils, and could be called into any other at a moment's notice, to "instruct" them on these very points? And, too, it is idle to ask questions as to what good paid prayers do for the souls of the dead, when the answer to such questions is ever the very ready silencer retort of "the Angelic Doctor" St. Thomas: "Unless they (*id est*—the souls of the dead) *know* that they are to be delivered, they would not *ask* for the prayers" (Cath. Encyc., XII, p. 578)—which cinches it; though the source or means of the dead souls' knowledge is not revealed, nor are their messages of request, in their own spirit handwriting, ever exhibited for confirmation of Faith in them, to the interested or curious public, in proof of their pious petitions.

But the real question for a Faith up a tree, as it were, is how there *can be* any Purgatory at all, in which slightly soiled and faded souls may be burnt free from earthly dross and renovated for Heaven —even if the Holy Ghost did very tardily instruct the Holy Councils that there *is* such a place—when the same Holy Ghost had assured other Councils, including these same Councils of Lyons and Florence, that there was in effect no such place, for that "the souls of those who depart in mortal sin, or only in *original* sin (which is such an extenuated 'trail of the Serpent' as defiles even the souls of just-born babes and of Ecclesiastical Persons), go down *immediately* into Hell, to be visited, however, with unequal punishments" (Cath. Encyc., VII, p. 207); and from which latter place, as Abraham told Dives, there was no come back at all? Such a clash of inspirations —or rather slip in promulgating the last one before repealing, or concealing, the former—illustrates the convenience of keeping a well regulated card-index system as an adjunct of the Depository of Faith, so as to enable a ready check to be kept on revelations, and thus avoid possible future embarrassments of Faith, due to their conflicts.

Here we must confess an error in our quest, induced by friendly zeal for the comfort of our ex-Thief's soul, in suggesting the possibility of finding it in this Purgatory of the Orthodox (*id est*, "right-believing") Faith. For, as is evident, in life he was either a Jew or a Pagan, hence a Heretic, who could have no part in the Orthodox Christian pangs of Purgatory; and he would no doubt have added to his Heresy by sharing with the Great Faith-Splitter in the Doctrine of the 27th of his 95 Theses nailed up on the Wittenberg Church-door: "They preach man who say that the soul flies out of Purgatory as soon as the money thrown into the chest rattles." As it is thus only the Orthodox who are permitted to share the flambent discomforts of the Papal Purgatory (pending the propitiatory pay), vain it is that we seek for a Heretic soul in this Orthodox Christian community. That this Splitter of the Faith was a gross uncultured person is apparent from the prosaic statement he makes, as above quoted, of this cardinal Tenet of the Orthodox Faith; much more chaste and ornate is the poetic version of the same inspired truth:

"As soon as the gold in the casket rings,
The rescued soul to Heaven springs"!

Though even this sins of poetic licentiousness in the adverbial phrase "as soon as," and is thus unorthodox; for the true orthodox rule of payment is, that the suffering soul "is not released until the last farthing be paid"—which suggests an instalment-plan of payments. This is indeed just and as it should be. For if the well-to-do heirs of a just-dead Christian sinner were to make an immediate lump-sum payment for prompt prayers, the soul might escape from Purgatory into Heaven before the penitential flames had done their perfect work of preparatory purification: the Great Idea being, as defined by Father Origen, that "the Purgatorial fire burns away the lighter materials of faults, and prepares the soul for the Kingdom of God, where nothing defiled may enter"; and so agree all the Fathers Celibate.

The instalment-plan of payments, and their fear-compelled obligation, is distinctly recognized and enjoined by the Father Tertullian, who advises a widow lady "to pray for the soul of her husband, begging repose for him, and participation in the *First Resurrection*"; he commands her also to make Oblations (euphemism for priestly "tips") for him on the anniversary of his demise, and charges her with infidelity (whether spiritual or corporal is not explicit)—if she neglect to succor his soul" (Cath. Encyc., XII, 577). Evidently this good Father, and the great Father St. Augustine, pinned no faith on the efficacy of such paid prayers to hurry up the escape of the soul from the fires of Purgatory; for the former only suggests such escape at the "first resurrection," while the latter postpones it till the last (whenever either of these should be)— declaring that "the punishment of Purgatory is temporary, and will cease, at least at the Last Judgment" (*De Civ. Dei*, lib. XXI, cap. xiii and xvi). Which is an awful long time to wait, writhing in such terrible torment; for as we are assured by the Holy Pope Gregory the Great, taking the cue from St. Augustine if not from the Holy Ghost, that "the pain of those who after this life expiate their faults by Purgatorial flames, will be more intolerable than any

one can suffer in this life": which is certainly considerable, judging
by the excruciating tortures which this Holy Church, by rack and
wheel, by flaying alive, by the slow burning at the stake, and other
perpious like practices, inflicted upon the sensitive bodies of thousands who dared to disbelieve her inspired Dogmas, and despise the
source, and defy her prostituted powers.

Here we may digress a moment to do tribute to that ancient and
cherished Precept of Mosaic Law, generously observed through the
ages, and become the chief stone of the corner of the Church Universal—"None shall appear before Me *empty* (Deut. xvi, 16)—when
they give the Offering of the Lord to make atonement for your souls"
(Ex. xxx, 15)—but shall *pay*, rich and poor alike, to "*buy* Atonement"; and this pious work is to the Churchman, like Faith to
Father Abraham, accounted to him for righteousness. Curiously,
while the New Dispensation quite overthrew and repealed the whole
Code of Laws and Ceremonies of the Old, this one thrifty exception
escaped the general repealing clause of the Divine new Ordinance;
and the Holy Church of the Dispensation of Free Grace, with a wisdom truly of this world worldly, preserved it and diligently incul-
cated, that in the Article of Tithes the Mosaic Law is still "of Divine
obligation and cannot be abrogated" (Cath. Encyc., XVI, p. 741,
742). Further yet it went, inciting the Faithful to outdo even the
quota of the Tenth commandeered by the ancient Law, by yet more
liberal donatives exhorted by the Master, who commanded to "give
all that ye have" (Mark x, 21), in order to be His true disciples.

This inspired tolling over by Divine command of the retained
"pay" precept of the Law into the New Dispensation of the Gospel,
is expounded with his usual naïve (an orthographic peculiarity of
our language omits the "k" in this word when used of things ecclesiastic) and cogent (*Lat. cogens, taking*) logic by the dogmatic
Second Founder of the Faith:

"Know ye not that they which minister about sacred things live of the
things of the Temple, and they which wait upon the altar are partakers
with the altar? Even so did the Lord ordain that they which proclaim
the Gospel should live of the Gospel" (1 Cor. ix, 13–14).

While among the devotional gems of the Sacred Litany of Holy
Church a predilect place is ever held by the doggerel Latin Chant
of the "Collect," celebrant of this mystic union of the Law and the
Gospel:

> "Cum summa cura est fratribus,
>   (Ut sermo testatur loquax)

Offere, fundis venditis
Sestertiorum millia.
Addicta avorum praedia
Foedis sub auctionibus,
Successor exheres gemit,
Sanctis egens parentibus.
Haec occulantur abditis
Ecclesiarum in angulis,
Et summa pietas creditur
Nudare dulces liberos! (Prudentius, Hymn II):

all which is the poetry of the Scriptural injunction to "sell and give all," with the added prosaic truth that the denuded children and disinherited heirs of the Giver groan as naked beggars for that their prodigal parents may have the odor of pious Saints. *O Tempora! O Mores!* Thus a goodly portion of their heirs' expectancies our good Churchmen often obediently dispend in this pious form of mundane Vanity, leaving their families sensibly less of worldly goods, but buying withal their soul's atonement in truly Churchly fashion, and earning incidentally the approving plaudits of the Clergy of all Cloths of the Cult, who hold them up before their Flocks for the emulation of this admirable and Godly example—of Giving.

In parentheses, how striking and faith-compelling is that wonderful system of Types and Symbols of the Oriental Scriptures—wherein everything typifies or symbolizes something or other else—one knows not what—which the inspired scrivener nine times in ten never really thought of or heard about in his life; but which, all perplexed delvers into the "hidden things of Scripture" assure us, meant some mysterious something or other other than it actually says in ordinary Hebrew or Greek words of usual plain and ordinary meaning. But for once in all Scripture, Type and Typified are here readily identified, even to unimaginative Occidental minds. In New Dispensation Typeology or Symbolicology, or whatever it is canonically called, the groups of True Believers are always figured forth as "Flocks"; the older and dyed-in-the-wool Bell-wethers of the Flocks are dubbed "Sheep"; the tender and wholly innocent of any sense are affectionately termed "Lambs"; while all are herded and driven by venerable "Pastors" (Postors, or in some old readings, Im-postors) called "Shepherds," always allegorically pictured as going about armed with "Crooks," to hook the stragglers into the "Fold," and to keep them there when once hooked in. Verily, the imagery of the Oriental mind is singularly appealing at times and persuasive of a sure-enough inspiration of ironic Truth under its Symbols!

Even in a prosaic Standard Lexicon of the Century XX we may discover the persistence of this bit of Oriental imagery in the accepted definition of "Sheep," in the figurative sense: "The Flock of the Good Shepherd; simple-minded and silly persons"; while to be "sheepish" is to "resemble a sheep in silliness or dullness"! The Sheep is yet to this day the Symbol of the vacuous herd, all blindly following some equally stupid old Bell-wether which heads the Flock this way or that as his inner lights may lead, or the crook of the Shepherd pulls. So much for Scriptural Symbology, which also symbolizes the feeding of the Flock on the New Doctrine under the figure of "Feed my Sheep." All which we now dismiss from mind, and return to what we were saying in the paragraph preceding the digression of this parenthesis.

The diminution of patrimonial expectancies occasioned by such worthy emulation of contributions to the "Lord's Treasury" is often, we blush to say, measureably retrieved by the excellent income which the good and generous Givers derive from the rental of some of their best corner buildings down town for saloons, and in some exceptional instances of houses owned by them in the "restricted districts" for uses which are as well understood as need be, without being more specific. True, the fine sense of Churchmanly propriety and of Christian rightmindedness often does not allow our good Churchmen to make these leasings directly to the degraded occupants. They piously salve their conscience by giving their agents carte-blanche and asking them no inconvenient questions. We all know that "Yahveh loveth a cheerful Giver"; and Yahveh commands his People— "Thou shalt remember Yahveh thy God: *for* it is he that giveth thee power to get wealth" (Deut. viii, 18), which we must acknowledge is a potent appeal to sacred cupidity.

This delicacy of scruple on the part of some good Churchmen, which does them honor, and which is a refinement upon the Scriptural injunction to let not the right hand know (or let be known) what is left-handedly done (a sanctimonious custom much imitated by the Godly of these cultured times), is one of the most eloquent testimonies to the cultural influence of our professed Religion in refining the grosser practices of earlier forms of worship on the practical side. Every one who is not blinded by prejudice against the Christian Faith and is not a chronic scoffer at its cherished practices, must recognize the (relative) purity of thus replenishing by discrete indirection, of the Lord's Treasury from the toll of Sin, as compared with the unblushing system of Temple Harlotry of ancient Pagan-Hebrew worship, and the quasi-gross but lucrative scheme of relatively recent times when Brothels of pious prostitution were recognized adjuncts of holy Nunneries, and the Virgins of Christ hallowed as pious alms the wages of Sin earned for them by their sisters whose virginity was a welcome sacrifice, if not a savory odor, on the Altar, not of Cupid, but of Churchly Cupidity. So all praise to those worthy Churchmen who, in returning a pittance of their gifts from Yahveh, reject such unrefined practices, and find ready means to obey the Divine command to "Give to the Lord," without openly offending the more refined feelings of modern Churchianity, though indeed the productive source is the same, one and immutable, as are many other equally pious and worthy practices.

To return from this sympathetic digression on the theme of pious paying enjoined by Holy Writ, and come back to the post-mortem Purgatorial Payment Plan of Holy Church. A Revelation which would make believe of some commutation of this penitential torment, and of final escape therefrom some time this side of that First Resurrection or Final Judgment, even at considerable cost to the harrowed and terrified survivors, would thus be regarded a good thing for the tormented soul, its family and friends, and incidentally net a handsome Church revenue. So, or however it may be, the Holy Ghost is said to have instructed the Holy Council of Trent as to the famous instalment-pay-plan, revealing that "Indulgences (at so much per) are most salutary for Christian people, and may be applied to the souls in Purgatory" (Cath. Encyc., XII, p. 578).

It betrays a darkened understanding, or a malevolent wit, of course, to imagine that this pay-as-you-enter plan of priestly prayers for the souls in Purgatory smacks even remotely of buying Yahveh's Grace or of bribery to the Holy Church. The refined distinction, if not difference, is acutely defined by an approved Theological apologist, thus: "The celebration of the Mass for money would be sinful; but it is perfectly legitimate to accept a Stipend offered on such occasion for the support of the Celebrant. The amount of the Stipend, varying for different times and countries, is usually *fixed* (in advance, you see) by Ecclesiastical Authority" (Cath. Encyc., XIV, 1). Very lucidly it is thus the Stipend which must be paid, and not the Prayers. Though the corollary thereof— "No stipend, no prayers," just as effectively deprives the paining soul of the prayers, and of any benefit they might do it. But the Scheme testifies to the refining influence of the Holy Ghost working upon greedy humanity. Simon the Magician, the earliest Christian exponent of the offense stigmatized with his name, Simony, grossly offered money outright for the Gift of the Holy Ghost; and was justly rebuked by St. Peter, "because thou hast thought to obtain the gift of God with money" (Acts viii, 20). The boasted Successors of St. Peter, being more practical, piously shun such gross venality and take the money, but do not sell the Gift at all. With the utmost delicacy of discriminating propriety, they simply withhold the free gift of the Gift until the pre-stipulated Stipend is paid. This, when paid, on the analogy of the coin-in-the-slot, loosens the mechanism of the Mass, and the Prayers begin to ascend for the writhing tenants of the Christian near-Hell. Only in this roundabout, de-Simonized, and eminently legitimatized left-handed sense should the reasonable mind understand the otherwise ribald jibe of Father Luther, that only "when the money thrown into the chest rattles," does the tortured soul begin to shake loose its singeing wings for flight from the flames of Purgatory, being thereunto "aided by the acceptable sacrifice of the altar," prepaid according to the Schedule of Stipends prescribed by Holy Church. *Honi soit qui mal y pense* after so adroit an explanation.

This near-Hell-Fiery habitat of the near-Blessed being exclusively a resort of the Orthodox Christian, we are precluded thus— not by Doubt (which is damnable), but by Dogma (which is infallible)—from the possibility of encountering our Repentant Thief's soul in the Christian Purgatory. And our compassion is already seen in revolt against the Doctrine of Hell Fire, common alike to Orthodoxy and to Heterodoxy (said terms signifying *my* Doxy or "right-think," and *your* "Doxy" or "wrong-think," reciprocally according as one is the speaker or the spoken to or of in any Theological controversy). So being evidently in neither of these habitats, and as it must needs be somewhere, though not yet arrived at Heaven, we have thus an added and cogent reason in support of our original conclusion that the soul of our crucified Thief is indeed still wending its way Heavenward through the fathomless reaches of sidereal space, and may yet confidently be expected to present itself and its credentials to the Celestial Concierge, St. Peter, in due course of Heaven-transit, as we have it figured out, *supra.*

If some should be disposed to question this, on the faith-founded theory, above indicated, that no soul clogged with the material dross of earthy fault may be suffered to enter in at the Golden Gates, but that the same must first be burnt and purged away by the Purgatorial fires, we oppose a very reasonable, and equally effective, counter-theory, suggested by more modern Science, to wit: That the upper interstellar regions are infested with inconceivably intense cold, a degree of cold even greater maybe than the fires of Purgatory are hot; that heat and cold, in intense degree, have often a similar effect, particularly in point of desiccation or drying up of sundry substances, rendering them friable or brittle and easily crumbled or broken away; therefore, that the earthly material dross of venial faults yet clinging to the departed Soul, being subjected for somewhat upward of the 1,000,000 light-years of its trajectory Heavenward, to such ultra-cold, may thus be either frozen quite off, or at least rendered so brittle and crumbly that either the simple violent swish of the air caused by the rapidity of flight would flip it off en route, or at any rate enable it to be very easily flipped or scraped off just outside the pearly Gates of Heaven upon ultimate arrival, and the Soul thus present itself quite as freed from such Dross as if it had done its very indeterminate fiery Penance amid the flames of Purgatory.

Thus the same result is attained, and by a process quite as uncomfortable—which is a very great desideratum in Theology; and enormous time would be saved, as the Soul could begin its purging flight Heavenward immediately on its corporeal release, instead of first doing infinite Time until the "first Resurrection" or the "Last Judgment" in Purgatory, before beginning its million-light-year flight Heavenward. Moreover, sidereal spatial Cold is a Scientific Fact, while Purgatorial Fire is only a Theological "speculation," though a highly successful one as the source of a fine Church revenue. As it doesn't cost anybody anything to accept our new "cold storage" revelation, and as we vouch for it as as good as any on the market, we trust that it may have ready credence, and in time even supplant some of the ancient and more costly nostrums of Credulity.

In the long meanwhile, let us bid Good-speed to the fleeting Soul on its Heavenward flight, with the classic *ex voto:* "Let it R. I. P."!

CHAPTER XIX

CESSET SUPERSTITIO! AND THEN?

"But if the salt have lost his savor, wherewith shall it be salted? It is thenceforth good for nothing, but to be cast out, and to be trodden under foot of men" (Matt. v, 13).—"It is neither fit for the land, nor yet for the dunghill; but men cast it out. *He that hath ears to hear, let him hear*" (Luke xiv, 35).

PAUL's naïve confession that he told lies that the truth of God might the more abound (Rom. iii, 7), we have found to be about the only true thing he is recorded as saying. The same is true of all his confrères of Holy Writ and Theology, as our examination has shown. We have found, no doubt with amazement, that in now classic phrase, lies are "the mostest things there isn't nothing else but" in all Bible and Dogma, to the pretended glory of God—and to the great profit of Priestcraft. Paul also spoke true when he admitted that he "profited in the Jew's religion above many" (Gal. i, 14),—showing that it was for many a profitable occupation; he lost no gains when he apostatized to become the propagandist in chief of the new Faith. But "strong delusion that men should believe lies" of religious superstition propagated by him and his confrères, was not, as he avers, sent by God; it is just another of Paul's own admitted mendacities; the conscious—and unconscionable work of professional Priestcraft.

That otherwise intelligent thinking people should be yet under this strong delusion to believe priestly lies, is because they do not know their Bible and its derived Theology; they take their fore-shortened beliefs about it "on faith" from the parsons and from such choice fervent texts as they hear expounded or casually read. That this is true—that the vast majority of Christians are rankly know-nothings of Bible and Theology, is evidenced by the gasps of surprise and shock which no doubt many readers of this book have gasped at the disclosures of what really "God's Word" is, as revealed in the preceding pages. Brought from youth up on the "strong delusion" that it is all verily "God's Word," and that "he that

444

doubteth is damned—suffering the vengeance of eternal fire," they reason not nor dare to doubt; they hear believingly, if not heed, the preached word.

Some good and scholarly "Divines" too, educated to Theology and its sophistries, even no doubt believe yet, in simplicity of faith, quite innocently. The distinguished Bishop Colenso, Church of England "Divine," may be instanced. Being appointed, in the good mid-Victorian Era, as Bishop of Natal, so great was his zeal to spread the saving truth in "Darkest Africa," that he learned the Zulu language, wrote a grammar and dictionary of the idiom, and then taught English to a number of bright native converts to the Christian Faith. With their aid he then began the work of translating the Bible into Zulu, for the conversion of the heathen natives to the Truth. Ere long the good Bishop's troubles began—and he began to "see a great light." His intelligent Zulu collaborators—who had been converted to Christianity by hearsay and not upon knowledge, would come to him in great amazement and point out to him things encountered in the Bible as they worked in translating, which to their untutored minds seemed shocking contradictions of text, absurdities and untruths, in what they had been taught was the inerrant inspired Word of God. The Bishop's attention being thus for the first time challenged to the subject, he thoroughly studied the whole matter of inspiration and revelation, in this new light: the result was his monumental 7-volume work "The Pentateuch and Book of Joshua Critically Examined" (1862–1879), in which the inspiration and truth of the Old Testament were denied and disproved. The Bishop's "conversion" caused great sensation and scandal in England; he was excommunicated and deposed by his indignant Church, and his salary stopped; but the Courts held this action invalid and decreed full payment of salary with all arrears. Many such cases have been known.

But many instances no doubt abound, in these more recent times, like to that of the good Parson in St. Louis who urged the writer to become a member of his Church and congregation. In answer to the frank objection, that for the reasons in this book now exposed, he could not without hypocrisy go back into the Church which he had abandoned, the good Pastor as frankly replied, that all that was no sound objection; that "If your ideas about the Bible and mine were put into a bag and shaken up and poured out, you could not tell which were yours and which mine"! How many good parsons, reading this book, would not—at least to their own inner selves—make a like "confession of faith"!

The Christ, in the text on salt of lost savor, above quoted, was inveighing against the superstitious old Hebrew Law, in himself now fulfilled, said to have been handed down by word of mouth of his own putative Father, Yahveh God of Israel. In all the Bible there is no God but Yahveh and the Christ is his Son.

The description and condemnation thus voiced by the Christ are found to fit perfectly the ancient fables and superstitions both of the Old and the New "Revelations." The long and fondly-held theories of the Divine revelation, inspiration and inerrant truth of these old Jewish Books as the unimpeachable "Word of God," have lost their savor, and must be cast out and discarded.

The most and worst that follows from this discovery that the Bible is *not* the "Word of God"—but only Jewish Fables of Yahveh —is, that God has not seen fit or necessary to deliver any written "Word" or "Law," neither to the ancient Hebrews, nor to the more modern Christians, nor to any body else. Possibly—the Supreme Architect of the Universe, who framed all this wonder of the world, and established its immutable laws, could, and maybe would, if he so pleased and saw fit and needful, find some way and means to make written revelation of himself and of his will and wish, for the behoof of the human race. But he who ordered the harmony of the worlds and ordained their divine laws, would in such event, we may do him credit to believe, so reveal and state his will and laws to man, that man would know veritably two things: that the God did it, and what he said and meant. It would be certain and unmistakable, so that it could be known for sure to all men. It would be simple, too, as sure, like two and two are four; so simple and sure that the way-faring man, though a fool, could not err therein. There would be no danger of losing one's soul through impossibility to understand the revelation so made; no occasion for "heresies" of different and discordant interpretations of it, as with the present revelations of Yahveh and Son by the mouth of priests and clergy. In such a true God-given revelation would there be no occasion for the apologetic casuistry of Peter—himself an "ignorant and unlearned" person— for the Jewish revelation, "in which are some things hard to understand, which they that are unlearned and unstable wrest unto their own destruction" (2 Pet. iii, 16); and Paul would not be so put to it to make believe that "the foolishness of God (Yahveh) is wiser than men" (1 Cor. i, 25).

The supreme destiny of the human soul would not be left, by a true and intelligent God, to the clouded, mystic, mythic jangling jargon of professional priests and prophets and apostles and theologians such as in small part in the preceding pages we have curiously examined. A God who could not or would not reveal his awful will for the eternal destiny of man better and truer than in these "inspired revelations" of Bible and Theology, is fit not to be a God or to be entrusted with the fate of a human soul. A man's last Will and Testament, so dubiously authenticated, would never be admitted to probate; and with such darkened and contradictory dispositions, would by any competent court be held "void for uncertainty," and the testator declared intestate.

Since, evidently, the true, all-wise Creator God has *not* revealed thus autobiographically his Word, his creature man is evidently in need of no such revelation and is none the worse off without it.

The mythic Yahveh of Israel, exactly as all ancient and some more modern mythic deities, was by his professional prophets and priests pretended to have spoken and commanded through them. But in truth, as admitted, "the prophets prophesy falsely, and the priests bear rule by their means, and the people love to have it so"—then, and all through human history, until right modernly. Professional priests undeniably devised all "revealed" gods and religions; professional clergy are yet the propagandists of these ancient myths as "religion" of God, as "articles of faith necessary to salvation"—personally purveyed by themselves, with damnation as the alternative.

Priests ruled the ancient world and kings superstitiously did their cunning bidding. For centuries priests dominated the modern world and made kings superstitiously grovel before them and don and doff their crowns at their suzerain command. Priestcraft to-day proclaims itself Vicar and adjutants of Yahveh God on earth, and strives yet mightily to impose itself on the minds and consciences of men, through their superstitious fears, invented and imposed by Priest and Clergy, and by the awful but anachronistic authority of the "Keys of Heaven and Hell." It is all the same old priestly game, very little modernized.

The Hebrew Scriptures are seen to be an inextricable complex of ancient cosmological legends, of primitive folklore, of rude tribal chronicles, of some actual historical events, of superstitious religious fables, of pagan Hebrew concepts of their primitive mythological tribal Yahveh, God of Israel. Later the fabled Yahveh of Israel was slowly and dubiously evolved into a—no less mythological—One God Yahveh of all the earth. A mythological god cannot evolve into a real living true God—*ex nihil nihil fit*. A myth cannot be imagined into a reality. The "revelation" is all one, from Moses to Ezra and his Priests—they hang and fall together. False premises cannot produce true conclusion, possibly.

Seizing upon the patent myth of Yahveh as God of all the earth
as its basic point of departure, and retaining fully and without
reserve all the primitive fables and mythology of ancient Jewry, the
Jewish Christian "revelation" builds up a fabulous fatuous scheme
of Theology of mystery and casuistry fondly called The Sacred
Science of Christianity—founded upon the Yahveh Myth, his curse
on mankind for the Original Sin of the fabled "first Adam," atoned
by the sacrifice of the "last Adam," Virgin-born Son of the mythic
Yahveh, sent to redeem the world from that mythic Adamic sin, and
culminating in the Dogma of Three Gods in One—Yahveh the
Father, Joshua-Jesus his only-begotten Son, and the joint Holy-
Ghostly "procession" of the other Two—all Three very Gods in their
own divine right, but the Three only One God. Such is the holy
Christian Faith—"which except a man believe faithfully and firmly,
he can not be saved" (Athanasian Creed, Cath. Encyc. Vol. II,
p. 34).

The theology of this is rather mystifying. Each of these Triune
Persons is all Yahveh but only a part of Yahveh. According to the
Creed above cited, "The Father (Yahveh) is God, the Son is God,
and the Holy Spirit is God," and yet there are not three Gods but
one God" (Yahveh); but "these Three Persons being truly distinct
one from another." And the Sacred Deposit lays it down: "In this
Trinity of Persons the Son is *begotten* of the Father by an *eternal
generation*, and the Holy Spirit *proceeds* by an *eternal procession*
from the Father and the Son. Yet notwithstanding this difference
as to *origin* (Gods are supposed to be *without origin*, but "from
eternity"), the Persons are co-eternal and co-equal: all alike are
uncreated and omnipotent" (Cath. Encyc., Vol. XV, p. 47). If three
persons are co-eternal, or all existing from the same time, or eternity,
there is difficulty to perceive how one should be *begotten* by another,
which implies *previous existence* of the begetter, or how another
could "*proceed*" from the other two, which implies the previous co-
existence of the other two. This is too subtle for any but professional Theologians. But they seem to be contradicted by the positive Yahvic declaration of relative modern begetting of the Son, only
about 1000 B.C.; for David quotes some one, apparently—but quite
impossibly—the Son himself, on his very first day of existence:
"Yahveh hath said unto me, Thou art my Son; *this day have I
begotten thee*" (Ps. ii, 7). For positive assurance of identity it is
thrice averred by Paul, "God (Yahveh) . . . hath raised up Jesus
again; as it is also written in the second psalm, Thou art my Son,
this day have I begotten thee" (Acts xiii, 33; Heb. i, 5, and v, 5).

So Yahveh the Father and his Son can hardly, on this revealed record, nor naturally, be "co-eternal"; and if the Holy Ghost "proceeds" from Yahveh and Son, the "procession" must have begun since the date the Son was *begotten* by Yahveh.

Yahveh was wholly a mythological deity existent only in a very primitive pagan imagination; a mythological deity could by no possibility, except imaginative, have had an actual begotten and incarnate son; it is a very attenuated Ghost that could "proceed" from such mythic sources. This simple consideration, with its unescapable logic, leaves nothing of the Triune-Yahveh but Myth and a pious perplexity at the one-time faith-accepted Dogma of the Theologians.

It may be commented, in passing, that the "Three Persons" of the Yahvic godhead—or at least two of them, these being the only ones recorded as ever saying anything—are indeed, on all Bible authority, to be taken as "being truly distinct one from another," and therefore difficult to regard as "not three Gods but one God." Yahveh is just heard as assuring his Son "this day have *I* begotten *thee*"; a thousand years later the Son comes to earth while the Father Yahveh remains in Heaven; the Father Yahveh calls from Heaven "this is my beloved Son," and the Son prays to the Father— all which is odd if both are the Same Person; the Son is specially said to be "an advocate with the Father" (1 Jno. ii, 1), who "is at the right hand of God (Yahveh), and who also maketh intercession for us" (Rom. viii, 34), as also "the Spirit itself maketh intercession for us with groanings that cannot be uttered" (Id., v. 26); and so often are we told that the Son sitteth or standeth "on the right hand of the Father" (Yahveh). The Bible speaks of "God the Father, God the Son, and God the Holy Ghost," but never once does it say that these three distinctly named and designated Gods are all One God or a Triune God at all. The word "Trinity" is totally unknown in Holy Writ.

All this clearly corroborates the fact of three Gods "truly distinct one from another"; but their distinctive functions and activities leave more questionable the theory of "not three Gods but One God" (Yahveh alone). As fact this seems inexplicable; as fable it needs no explanation: it is Theology.

As the Bible and its Yahveh-God are wholly mythological, no less so must be the elaborate and intricate Theology founded on them: the stream can rise no higher than its source. This simple truth quite destroys the whole congeries of conflicting Creeds and wrecks their exhaustless Fount, the "Sacred Deposit of Truth." The disclosed want of inspiration and truth of the Bible makes grimly humorous the dogmatic assurances of the inspired truth of the Deposit, for which it is claimed: "All revealed truth is not consigned to Holy Scripture, but Christ gave to his Apostles to be transmitted to his Church—or they received from inspiration or revelation—divine instructions which they transmitted to the Church and which were not committed to the inspired writings. Thus Christ instituted his Church as the official and authentic organ to transmit and explain in virtue of divine authority (of Yahveh) the revelation made to men. Holy Scripture is therefore not the only theological source of the revelation made by God (*i.e.*, *Yahveh*) to his Church. Side by side with Scripture there is Tradition, side by side with the Written Revelation is the Oral Revelation. This *granted*, it is impossible to be satisfied with the Bible alone for the solution of all dogmatic questions" (Cath. Encyc., Tit. Tradition, Vol. XV, pp. 6, 7). The premises of the above ratiocination not being now maybe so readily granted, there may be appreciably less satisfaction with either Bible or Tradition with respect to the Verity of Theological Dogmas.

The Bible, though thus all true, is not all the truth—so says the Sacred Deposit. Let us now again—in the light of our study of Bible and Deposit—read a couple of precious excerpts from the Deposit vouching modernly for the Bible, both put forth as *ex cathedra* utterances of the Holy Ghost of Yahveh God: "These Books are sacred and canonical because they contain *revelation without error*, and because *written by the inspiration of the Holy Ghost, they have God* (Yahveh) *for their Author*" (Vatican Council, Sess. III, ch. ii, 1870; Cath. Encyc., Vol. II, p. 543). And: "It will *never be lawful* to restrict inspiration merely *to certain portions* of the Holy Scriptures, or *to grant that the sacred writers could have made a mistake . . . They render in exact language, with infallible truth, all that God* (Yahveh) *commanded, and nothing else*"!—"Wherever the sacred writer makes a statement as his own, *that statement is the word of God and infallibly true, whatever be the subject-matter of the statement*"! (Pope Leo XIII, Encyclical *Prov. Deus*, 1893; Cath. Encyc., Vol. II, p. 543). To be impartial, and for example of stark presumption of uninspired ignorance of theology, take this of the 13th of the XXXIX Articles of Religion: "Good works done before the grace of Christ *are not pleasant to God; but they have the nature of Sin*"! *Sancta Simplicitas!*

The old Roman Augurs, when they performed the sacred mysteries of the auspices upon the vatic fatal livers and entrails of the sacrifices, and delivered to the superstitious kings and people their solemn oracular mummeries of the awful will of the God so revealed, were wont to stick their tongues in their cheeks and wink the other eye at one another, in mirthful self-appreciation of their own ingenuity in "getting away with it," thanks to the crass ignorance and superstition of their pious dupes. The Pagan augurs must have felt as self-conscious of base imposture, as are of Yahveh's own true power of miracle the Christian priests who with mystic signs and mutterings "make God with three Latin words," and metamorphose ordinary bread and wine into the veritable body and blood of a God who never was—and who, being a "spirit" (Jno. iv, 24), so could not have body and blood or other "corporeal elements" to be thus anthropophagistically consumed, thousands of millions of times a year through twenty centuries, and still be non-existent as ever. When the Theologians and "Divines," in full Twentieth Century, read in their Bibles the self-same things we have just wonderingly reviewed, then give utterance to the above quoted and other like outpourings of the Holy Ghost, and stand forth to proclaim all this to intelligent modern men as God's own truth—to disbelieve which is eternal death and damnation—probably they restrain themselves from outward visible indications of their inner reactions; or maybe, knowing no better, they have none. The charitable imputation of deception of ignorance is all that saves from the guilt of conscious imposition; though ethically it is all one to assert as true what one does not know is true and to assert as true what one knows to be untrue. Whether ignorant or conscious, Theology and Dogma savor none the less inevitably of imposture and superstition.

Superstition is thus defined by a high lexicographic authority:

"A belief founded in irrational feelings, especially of fear, and characterized by credulity; also any practice originating in such belief; excessive and unreasonable scruples due to ignorant dread of the supernatural. Specifically, a belief in a religious system regarded *by others than the believer,* as unreasonable and without support; a false religion, or any of its rites" (New Standard Dictionary of the English Language).

With this accurate definition of Superstition, and with the preceding revelations of Holy Writ fresh in mind—the Hebreo-Christian creeds, dogmas and theologies, of Bible as of Deposit, are they not superstitions all? The question is submitted in all candor to the answer of every candid mind.

The supernatural myths and superstitions of Bible and Theology are no part and parcel of real Religion; they have no portion in the inheritance of righteousness such as exalteth a man and a nation. Rather are they a degrading concept of God and his intelligence;

and betray a strange contempt for the dignity of mind and common sense of men to impose such non-sense for their belief and living faith.

Full faith in Adam, the Talking Snake and Yahveh's Curse is not in these modern days necessary to an abiding faith in the Creator God and in the creature man, though the Catholic Encyclopedia avers that "the first three chapters of Genesis contain facts touching the foundations of the Christian Religion" (Vol. VII, p. 313). That the "Law" was not given by word of mouth of Yahveh, tribal God of Israel, to Moses on Sinai, hinders not to heed the principles of the "Ten Words," valid in every moral Code. To discredit the Virgin-birth by mortal woman of a Son to Yahveh, does not nullify the good in anything the reputed Son may have said of truth and rightcous-ness, nor destroy a manly reverence for woman and motherhood. To throw Hell into the discard does not impair man's ability or will to "do good for good is good to do," spurning "bribe of Heaven and threat of Hell." To relegate angels, devils, witches and miracles to the Limbo of childish fancy along with Santa Claus yet leaves place, freer better place, in the hearts and lives of men for truth, honor and justice, when their minds are freed from that "complete paraly-sis of the intelligence, resulting from irrational surrender to the blight of theological dogma."

As the distinguished Doctor of Divinity quoted in the last line *supra*, earnestly says:

"The work of the Church in bringing Christ to men (*nota bene*—not men to Christ, in the old pulpit cant) is enormously handicapped by associating it with *the imposed belief in the veracity and historicity of what are patently early myths and naïve, childish, primitive folklore.*

"It is of supreme importance to remember that a proper understand-ing of these Jewish stories, *while necessarily working havoc with the ideas of Paul and the elaborate theology that is based on them,* in no wise affects in the slightest manner the Christianity of Christ, the Religion of Jesus, the eternal principles by which he lived and for which he died" (Fagnani, The Beginnings of History According to the Jews, pp. 24–25; 1925).

Again this erudite Doctor of Divinity and Professor of Hebrew Scripture avers Yahveh, God of Israel, to have been *"an imagined, aboriginal, primitive deity,* . . . not the God of the New Testament" (Id., p. 18). But the God is Yahveh in Old and New alike.

While this saving clause yet savors a bit of the original sin of theological dogma, however well diluted, these two frank pregnant utterances destroy alike *in toto* the Bible Fables of Yahveh as true

God, and the false theology of Paul and the Church regarding everything based on these Bible Fables. They leave untouched, except to
mention and to magnify, and instinct with all their pristine worth,
the "eternal principles," all that is good and true and pure and
worthy of all acceptation, in the recorded words and life of him who
is called The Christ, and who gave to all "power to become the sons
of God" (Jno. i, 12)—in the same sense as was the Christ himself.

In the very year of the American Declaration of Independence,
the same year as the American Revolution for political and religious
liberty, a celebrated State Trial was held in England, against a
bookseller for the *crime of Blasphemy*—for selling a copy of the
"Age of Reason," by the immortal American patriot, Thomas Paine.
The distinguished Attorney General of the Kingdom conducted the
prosecution, and made a very remarkable argument to the trial jury.
He expressed in fervent words "the regret and indignation I feel,
that any man in this country should dare to disseminate such pernicious doctrines"; and he declaimed:

"What have we to expect, if those long-established feelings and principles be expelled from the minds and hearts of men? What reliance
have I to receive from you, gentlemen of the jury, an honest verdict on
the evidence which has been laid before you? On what were you sworn
that you would act conscientiously? To what were you referred when
you swore that you would return a true verdict, 'so help you God'? You
swore on that Holy Book. . . .

"What reason have you to believe that the witnesses will speak the
truth, except from the operation of those religious principles which I have
described to you? Are they not sworn on that sacred volume? . . .

"What hold have we on the mind of His Honor, that he will administer
the law with strict justice, uprightness and impartiality? What security
has the defendant himself that pure justice will be rendered to him on
his trial, except the oath of His Honor? . . .

"When any individual assumes a station of trust or power in the
government, the constitution prescribes an oath; . . . that oath is on the
holy Gospels of God. . . .

"I have only, therefore, to remind you, Gentlemen, that this Information was not preferred from any idea that the Christian religion could
be affected in its character or irresistible progress, by this disgusting
and contemptible book; but to prevent its circulation amongst the industrious poor, too much engaged in the support of their families by their
labor, and too uninformed to be secure against artful wickedness. Of all
human beings *they* stand most in need of the consolations of religion, and
the country has the deepest stake in their enjoying it, not only from the
protection which it owes them, but *because no man can be expected to be*

faithful to the authority of man who revolts against the government of
God! Gentlemen, I leave it to you as twelve Christian men, to decide
whether this is not a most blasphemous and impious libel!" (Williams'
Case, 26 Howell's State Trials; 1776).

On this wonderful, specious, fantastic plea of His Majesty's
Attorney General, that Justice could not be administered, nor government maintained, among men, but for the sanction of a superstitious oath on a Book of Fables, the "pure justice" of a verdict of
"guilty" of blasphemy—against the mythologic Yahveh—was returned in a "Christian Court of Justice" against the disseminator
of the truth. Let our English friends remember this eminent English
precedent when disposed to sneer too critically at the "Monkey
Case" in the hill-country of Tennessee!

That sixty percent or more of the people of these United States
are not galled by the yoke of dogmatic theological Religion of any
brand, of itself belies the pretentious casuistry that Justice even
can not or would not be done between State and citizen, between man
and man, but for the sanction of a religious oath with the fear of
Hellfire behind it—as often violated by perjury as observed from an
honest regard for truth; and especially, the unveiled assurance that
it is the *poor*, particularly, who stand in need of the restraints, and
assumed consolations, of this priest-forged rod of Authority, without which they would be quite ungovernable.

Every intelligent person, versed in history, knows that it is
not true that Justice can not be done, or order in government be
maintained, without the Christian threat of hell and damnation to
restrain the false witness or the insubordinate subject or to con-
strain the righteous judgment of the Judge.

Times have changed: not a State of this Union but still retains
the oath "so help me God"; and in this New York the greasy old
tome of Holy Writ must be dragged out and tagged by the witness
as he swears upon it. But such oath is not required; the witness may
in the alternative simply "affirm" that he will speak the truth; or
may break a saucer, or jump over a broomstick, or swear by "the
beard of the Prophet," or whatever other freak of human credulity
he may regard as of most sacred compulsion for him to tell the truth.
It's a piddling performance at best: no oath prevents perjury. A
thousand hands are held to heaven or laid on the musty Book each
day, to speak the truth, "so help me God"; and quite one half of all
the solemnly God-vouched testimony given is lies and perjury. Better to abolish the whole superstitious farce; affirm a man to speak

the truth; and if he lies, jail him for perjury, and perjury will very largely cease to be so much in vogue as means to "justice."

Justice can be done without swearing by Fables. The noblest, most admirable system of Law, the sternest, fairest scheme of human justice, which the world has ever known—under which the whole civilized world lives today—is Pagan Roman Law. It is today the basis of every legal system of Europe, as of Japan; it largely supplements the crudities of the Common Law of England; the whole system of English and American equity is derived from and instinct with the spirit of the stern, impartial justice of Pagan Rome. Many American judges are Jews; others many no doubt quite disbelieve the Christian Faith; American juries are composed in large part of Jews and disbelievers: still justice is rendered between men; yet government, the best on earth, is maintained, protecting men in life, liberty, property, and the pursuit of happiness. It will yet persist; and human happiness be no doubt more perfect when strife and dissentions engendered by religious differences have been relegated to oblivion.

The glory that was Greece, the power that was Rome, they know, have filled the world with Beauty and with Law, ages before the Christian Superstition existed, or the torch of its crude Theology had been applied to the brimstone of hell and its holy fires kindled for the unbelieving soul. Those learned in the Law will recall the immortal Maxims of the jurisprudence of ancient Rome, mistress and lawgiver of the world; maxims gathered by Justinian into the Digest, culled from the olden precepts of the noblest of the old Roman jurisconsults and legal philosophers, and which yet rule the civilized world today. It was Ulpian, Pagan that he was, who described the Roman lawyers as "Priests of Justice, engaged in the pursuit of a philosophy that is truly such and no counterfeit"; and Pagan Ulpian it was who gave the living definition: "Jurisprudence is the knowledge of things human and divine, the science of the just and unjust"— almost a translation of the much more ancient Pagan Greek Stoic concept of "*sophia*." The very first sentence of the Digest thus defines: "The precepts of the Law are these: to live honorably, to injure no one, to render to every one his due." The Pagan Cicero declared: "Law is nothing else than right reason, enlightened by the gods, commanding what is honest and forbidding what is dishonest."

There are today some 243,000 Churches, Temples, Synagogues, and whatnot they may be called, scattered throughout these United States, to minister to some 47,000,000 members of them all. No doubt but they are a force for good in the land: a far greater force they might well be for far greater good, when once they turn from propagating wornout superstitions and strive to further personal and civic righteousness for its own high sake. One little incident may serve for a text for the point sought to be made here. Recently a very well-known "Liberal" Minister in the Metropolis declared through the public press, that his own sons refused to attend Church because, they said, they "did not want to have to listen to a lot of bunk." Nor will or do hundreds of thousands of other men gifted with fair reasonable minds. As this is finally revised, I find the question, so often heard, again seriously put—"whether the Pulpit is any longer useful in modern life"; and this the Dean of St. Paul's, London, thus comments:

"The crumbling of certain parts of the dogmatic structure has undoubtedly increased the difficulty of preaching. There is much uncertainty as to what may be, and should be, said from the pulpit. The people themselves are impatient with dogma. Accordingly, many preachers try to interest their congregations by topical discussions of newspaper controversies, new books, or, worst of all, burning economic problems, in which their ill-informed tirades generate much more heat than light. There seems to be a kind of fatality that the Church always begins to champion a political party at the moment when it is preparing to abuse its power. The Church never goes into politics without coming out badly smirched, and few sermons are more unprofitable than rambling comments or declamations on secular affairs" (The Literary Digest for November 21, 1925, pp. 31-32).

Churches are today largely social gathering places, where the social gradations are as marked and as rigid of observance as at the King's Court, the rich in the best pews, the poor in the rear and side ones, and little recognition or fraternity between them. On Sundays the sacred edifices are solemnly open, and maybe on an evening during the week; all the rest of the time they are mostly closed and dark, and cold as is their spirit when open.

Every "House of God," of whatever God (and there are many) throughout the land should be kept open and habitable and hospitable at all seasonable hours of every day and evening, and should be active centers of spiritual and social and civic interests, and where, most of all, the homeless should find a shelter if not a home. They are in a large and important sense supported by the State, by the public, being freed from all taxation to the extent all told of thousands of millions of dollars yearly; they should be brought to some real return of service of the public, beyond preaching Fables and singing psalms a couple of times a week. The Church houses should be community centers, freely open to every responsible and respectable society and organization, religious, social, civic, political, or open to all such at only the actual expense of service for the occasion.

It is sanctimonious silliness about "sacredness" and "consecration" of Churches, which must not be "desecrated" or "profaned" by honest uses for worthy purposes. All human service and helpfulness is sacred, all human effort that makes for right and for righteousness is holy and is consecrated.

Let the Churches then, if they would attract and hold forcible, intelligent, modern men and women, leave off preaching and teaching the Fables of the Bible as the truthful Word of God, about Adam's talking snake and Balaam's talking ass, and Jonah's marvelous whale, and dead men raised from the dead, and men living in heaven or hell after they are dead—of Devils, and angels, and myths. Let the Ministers quit "skypiloting" for the very dubious Hereafter, and devote themselves to spreading the knowledge of God's real truths of life and nature here on earth; ethical and educational truths, God in his wonders of Nature, the bands of Orion or the bandaging of wounds in first aid to the injured; the cruel hatefulness of War and its ostracism from earth; the beauty and duty of charity to all men, of whatever race or tongue or creed, and the loathsomeness of prejudices of race or color or creed—and speed the abolition of creed. And thousands of things of knowledge and use and beauty, to the true glory of God and benefit of man, may be taught and spread abroad from the Pulpit, with never a hint of Superstition or a whiff of fire and brimstone.

Then may people, in growing numbers, come to hear and remain to benefit and be instructed in things worth while; the vast numbers driven from the Church today by the vacuous Myth-mongering of its preachings, may return with joy to its teachings of wholesome truths, of knowledge in all its scope, of science in popular form, revealing God in his real wonders of nature to men. Then will the influence of the Churches be real and potent and for good to all the people; not restricted as now to Miracle-mongering for a credulous few, and for social display of worldly-wise, but very indifferently believing and behaving Christians.

Make the Churches public Forums, where the public may foregather for every kind of social and civic occasion and innocent diversion, from the instructive scenes on the "silver screen" to the healthful joyful dance: public lectures, political gatherings, social and literary societies—all are quite as socially and spiritually useful and uplifting, and as innocuous and little "desecrating" to the sacred edifices, as Church "rummage sales" and Parish "grab-bag" parties and "raffle" lotteries.

If the Churches will not of good grace make this return of public utility and service for the very valuable public support by tax exemption on their billions of dollars of deadhead property, then tax them the same as rich men's clubs or poor men's cottages, and let them share the common burden of support of government which protects all alike under the Law, and Christians from each other.

Broaden and enforce the laws against "superstitious uses," and make illegal and void the rich legacies, and the painfully scraped pittances of the poor, to the already over-swollen "Treasury of the Lord," obtained by the dubiously honest pretenses of cajoling money as "lending to the Lord," or for praying the souls of the superstitious out of non-existent Purgatory—than both which there is no nearer grand larceny in the annals of priestly avarice. Make it by the Penal Code grand larceny *de jure* as grand larceny it near is *de facto*. Consider for a moment the countless millions filched through the centuries from the credulous through this pious form of confidence game! Justice to a man and to his surviving family comes before superstitious generosity to the Devil to buy surcease of pains of a dead man's soul gone wrong, or tainted only with Adam's Original Sin. Purgatory not only does not exist, for the souls "go down *immediately* into Hell" (Decree "*Unionis,*" *ubi supra*)—but if it did exist, paid prayers are utterly worthless to get the souls out, for it is "revealed" that they writhe there until "the first Resurrection" or until "the last Judgment"—which is exactly when they would get out anyhow, to pass to Heaven or Hell, as the case might be, as noticed in our previous paragraphs on Purgatory.

Once free the mind and soul from the debasing thrall of "imposed belief in the veracity and historicity" of these Bible Fables, and from the "blight of theological dogma," as God's Word necessary to salvation, and what a flood of spiritual light and truth may illumine man's mind and conscience from the Book of God's Work in Nature. True, a writtenly unrevealed and "Unknown God, but still the true Creator God revealed through his wonderous works. Nor need the Bible be altogether disregarded for God's truth. Full as is the Bible, Old and New, of crude, cruel, immoral, revolting fables and concepts of Yahveh as God, it abounds, too, in truly inspired outbursts of the highest fervor of spirit, of the purest morality, of eternal principles of right and wrong, of that righteousness that exalteth men and nations, and denunciations of those sins which are a reproach to any people. Amid the chaff and trash and filth replete in Holy Writ, there are infinite gems of purest ray serene to illumine mind and soul with true godliness whereby to guide in life and light the way unfraid to death. All such gems of ancient devotion are to be cherished as part of the great spiritual treasures of life, to be found in the Bible as in many works of highest worth in many literatures and religions, valid and true wholly apart from the fables and myths of any and all religions. With all the crude gross Bible Fables eliminated and discarded, there yet remains much of truth and beauty; verses which are the gems, and contain the germs, of true religion of the human spirit. This is the religion of clean hands and pure hearts; of fact not of faith; of good deeds, not of credulity. Revolting is the doctrine of theology, that not by the doing of good and by right living, but only by credulous faith, is there profit to man or God—as we have read: "except which a man believe faithfully and firmly he cannot be saved"!—that "Good works done before the grace of Christ are not pleasant to God; but they have the nature of sin"! Better far to so sin and die in such sin, than live in debasing belief in such theological "confidence" stuff!

Micah, Prophet of old Israel, denouncing the credulous beliefs and superstitious practices of his People, struck for once in all the Hebrew Scriptures, the high key-note of inspiration of true religion:

"He hath shewed thee, O Man, what is good: and what doth the Lord (Yahveh) require of thee, but to do justly, and to love mercy, and to walk humbly with thy God" (Micah, vi, 8).

This is not Christian, it was ages before Christ; it is not sectarian, it is catholic, universal; it is not superstitious, but sensible. It is the key-note of the universal religion of the sincere mind and heart, striving after spiritual Godlikeness. Identical is it with the universal, highly religious concept of the very first of the *Praecepta* of the Pagan Institutes of the Law of Nature and of World Law of Rome:

Juris praecepta sunt haec: Honeste vivere, alterum non laedere, suum cuique tribuere: The precepts of the Law are these: To live honorably, to injure no man, to render to everyone his due" (*Institutes*, I, 1, 8).

Under the New Dispensation of Superstition, discounting all the requirements of Faith in its Fables, sounds out, too, one pure note of harmonious unison with the same true religion; uttered by one the own brother after the flesh of the Master of the new Faith of miracles and credulity:

"Pure religion and undefiled before God and the Father is this, To visit the fatherless and widows in their affliction, and to keep himself unspotted from the world" (James, i, 27).

These three golden precepts of religion pure and undefiled by crass superstitions for belief as the only escape from eternal death, the fires of Hell, and the wrath of God abiding on the Unbeliever, are the utterances of three lofty-minded, high-visioned men: an Old Hebrew Prophet crying against the grossly superstitious Creeds and practices of the Chosen People of Yahveh; a noble Pagan prophet and Priest of Justice and Law, human and divine; a Hebrew of the New Dispensation, brother of its Founder, who believed but a modicum of its superstitions, but stressed to its utmost its substance of love and charity and truth, as his beautiful Epistle vouches.

The sum total and golden substance of truth of them all is synthetized by a creedless modern Seer in the living tocsin couplet of The Kasidah:

> "Do good for good is good to do:
> Spurn bribe of Heaven and threat of Hell."

Words these all are which utter the doom of superstition, the apotheosis of godly reason. They are the Golden Rule of highest human righteousness. They spell the noblest terms of religion, of true pure spirituality.

They exclude not God; they embrace the innate sense of God, of walking humbly with thy God, in Micah's golden phrase. God we know not except through his wondrous works of universal creation, save in the unstillable strivings of the human soul for righteousness, for Godlikeness. Whoever, whatever God be, we feel him instinct within us; with the Pagan Poet quoted by Paul on Mar's Hill, we feel that "in him we live, and move, and have our being"; in a very high real sense "we are also his offspring" (Acts xvii, 28). In our souls we feel the impelling stirring of the truth of Festus: "Nothing but God can satisfy the soul that he made great"—the greatest gift of God to his masterpiece Man.

But this God is not the crude tribal Yahveh "revealed" in the figments of Oriental fancy of the Hebreo-Christian Bible. He is not to be worshiped, as I conceive it, by superstitious creeds, but in golden deeds wrought in the heart for the good of the soul and of man.

The Bible is not the inspired infallible "Word of God"; it is the very human record of the human fallible strivings of man's soul after an Unknown but very conscious God-in-Man, urging its realization in men's life, unconcerned in the unknowable of after-death.

That the Bible has been shown to be, *is,* wholly human, fearfully false and cruel in its most part, detracts naught from its immense value to mankind, as a veritable treasury, not of "God's outpourings through Moses," but of man's outpourings, of man's upliftings of spirit, towards righteousness, towards Godliness. That it is over-full of primitive, puerile superstitions; that priests and hierarchies of priests have forged out of its crude Myths a cruel, blighting system of "Theology" for dominating men's minds and souls for the priestly fatal schemes of graft and aggrandizement, of rule and ruin, is unhappily for mankind all too true, as several thousand years of history, and the imperfect, inadequate sketches of this book, prove to demonstration. But when this demonstration is now brought home to the minds and realization of men, why, the damage is done and ended forever. Knowing the truth, men will be free from the dominion of error; the priestly era and occupation will be gone— gone as the ghosts of yesteryear.

But the Bible will endure, to the inestimable benefit of humanity, once it is rated at its true worth. Inestimable evils, far more than from Pandora's Box, have come from this Bible: because misguided, mistaught, Priest-taught men have mistaken it for a Book of inerrant facts of God, instead of, as it is, a Book of wondrous, fallible fables of man, carrying tremendous morals of mighty spiritual truth. Once realize its fables for fables frankly, its inspiration as the genius of man's fervent spirit groping up towards the truths of spiritual life, its gross chaff winnowed away by the discernment of the spirit, then will its "apples of gold in pictures of silver" become more beautiful to the mind's eye, more palatable to the spirit's taste, more vitally nourishing to the soul's salvation from error and superstition.

The most wonderful work of Literature the Bible has ever been. Held as purely a human spiritual literary work; as such cherished, reverently regarded, spiritually and reasonably lived; its superstitions, prolific cause of religious hatreds and intolerance, of wars and woes unnumbered, banished from men's minds and souls; its lofty ideal truths of spirit impressed on men's hearts, not its fatal mystic texts "engraven on their reeking swords," for murderous strifes over its vain Fables and Mythologies; its fine assurance that "of one flesh hath God made all men under the Sun" and that all men are brothers under the universal Fatherhood of God, become effective to eradicate all prejudices of race and color and vanished creeds, reuniting the world in the common bonds of human fellowship—then, then only,

then indeed, will the humanized, revitalized Bible be potent, omnipotent maybe, to perfect the true civilization of mankind; then
triumphantly may be realized the burden of the Angels' storied Song
over the birth of the New Era of the storied Christ:

> "Glory to God in the highest;
> On earth *peace* to men of good will."

11/26/25

ERRATA

PAGE

72–73. To the 350 years indicated, should be added the 94 years
of Levi spent in Egypt, thus making the years of the
"Sojourn" 444 years instead of 350.

184. 4th line from bottom: the words "the son of Solomon"
should be omitted with reference to Jeroboam.

251. Line 6: The words "Sweet Singer of the Ever-verdant Isle,
hot-bed of ever-verdant Faith" are erroneous; the reference is intended to Robert Burns, Scot Poet, and to his
"Cotter's Saturday Night."

279. Line 2: Simon Magnus should read Simon Magus.

INDEX

Abbreviations used: J. C., for Jesus Christ; s, after page-figures, for *et seq.*, or, and following pages

A.

Aaron, death of, contradiction, 129.

Abram. See Abraham.

Abraham: was Pagan Chaldee, 24, 195; heathen origin of, 62; Promise to, 65; sells wife to Pharaoh and Abimelech, 66; dispute about his faith, 375.

Acknowledgement, of "other gods," 210s.

Adam: means "man," not personal name, 49; Christian religion dependent on, 405s.

Adon: means "lord master," use of, 199; Hebrew word shown, 201.

Advent, Second. See Second Coming.

Ahab, "Lying Spirit" sent to, 193. See Lying Spirits.

Alexander VI, Pope, error in partition of America, 266s.

America, discovery of, Seneca's prophecy, 265; error in partition of, 266s.

Anesthetics, banned, and burning for use of, 272.

Ankh-cross, symbol and meaning of, 175.

Anointed: meaning and use, of J. C., xxii–xxiii, 313; contradictions, 334–5.

Antipodes, existence of, denied, 265–6.

Apostles, "unlearned and ignorant," 5, 331; "calling" of, 328s; how chosen, contradictions, 329s; names of, contras, 329; greed and strife of, 331s; Creed, truth of, 262.

Appearances, of J. C. after Resurrection, contradictions, 357s.

Archeology. See Monuments and Inscriptions.

Aristotle, Three Arguments, that earth is round, 265.

Ark, Law put into, 150.

Arms, none in all Israel, 170.

Ascension, of J. C., contradictions regarding, 361s.

Asherah, significance of, 174; falsely translated "grove," 179; in Temple, 180; example in St. Louis, 180.

Asshur, phallic significance of name, 173.

Astronomy, in Chaldea, 64; in Egypt, 65; revelations of Heavens, 424s.

Aten, and Amen, signs, on throne of Tut-ankh-amen, 207.

Attributes of Yahveh, in Bible, 224s.

Augurs, Roman, impostures of, xiii, 450–1.

Author, of Bible, Yahveh as, Doctrine, 365.

Authority: of Scripture, 262–3; of apostles, 199s.; of Church, 262.

B.

Baal: meaning and use, as "lord, master," etc., 198–9; Yahveh as Baal, 198–9, 214–5, 221; Baal-worship of Yhvh, 183s.; David's dance, 158; in Bible-names, 199; Hebrew child-sacrifices to, xiii–xiv; Baal-Peor, significance of name, 188.

Bab-el: Tower of, contradictions, 54; meaning of word, 56; Babylonian Epic of, 64.

Balaam, contradictions regarding, 131.

Banquet, Moses with "the-gods" on Sinai, 140.

Baptism: of Pagan gods, rites, etc., as Christian, 8–9; of J. C. by John, 326s.

Beer, Well of, 97, 130

Bel, meaning of, 198.

Belief: means "do not know," vii; intelligence excluded, xxiii; is childish, viii, 403; is inherited or due to environment, viii, xvii; "*disce primum quod credendum est*," viii, 18; enforced by Inquisition, xviii; of peoples follows that of rulers, 13; as necessary to salvation, contradictions, 370; not necessary, 452.

D.

Printed in the United States
1168400001B/28-33